Other titles in Judaic Traditions in Literature, Music, and Art

American Hebrew Literature: Writing Jewish National Identity in the United States
Michael Weingrad

Classic Yiddish Stories of S. Y. Abramovitsh, Sholem Aleichem, and I. L. Peretz
Ken Frieden, ed.; Ken Frieden, Ted Gorelick, Michael Wek, trans.

Finding the Jewish Shakespeare: The Life and Legacy of Jacob Gordin
Beth Kaplan

From Our Springtime: Literary Memoirs and Portraits of Yiddish New York
Reuben Iceland; Gerald Marcus, trans.

Here and Now: History, Nationalism, and Realism in Modern Hebrew Fiction
Todd Hasak-Lowy

My Friendship with Martin Buber
Maurice Friedman

Place and Ideology in Contemporary Hebrew Literature
Karen Grumberg

Who Will Die Last: Stories of Life in Israel
David Ehrlich; Ken Frieden, ed.

Early Yiddish Epic

Edited and Translated by

Jerold C. Frakes

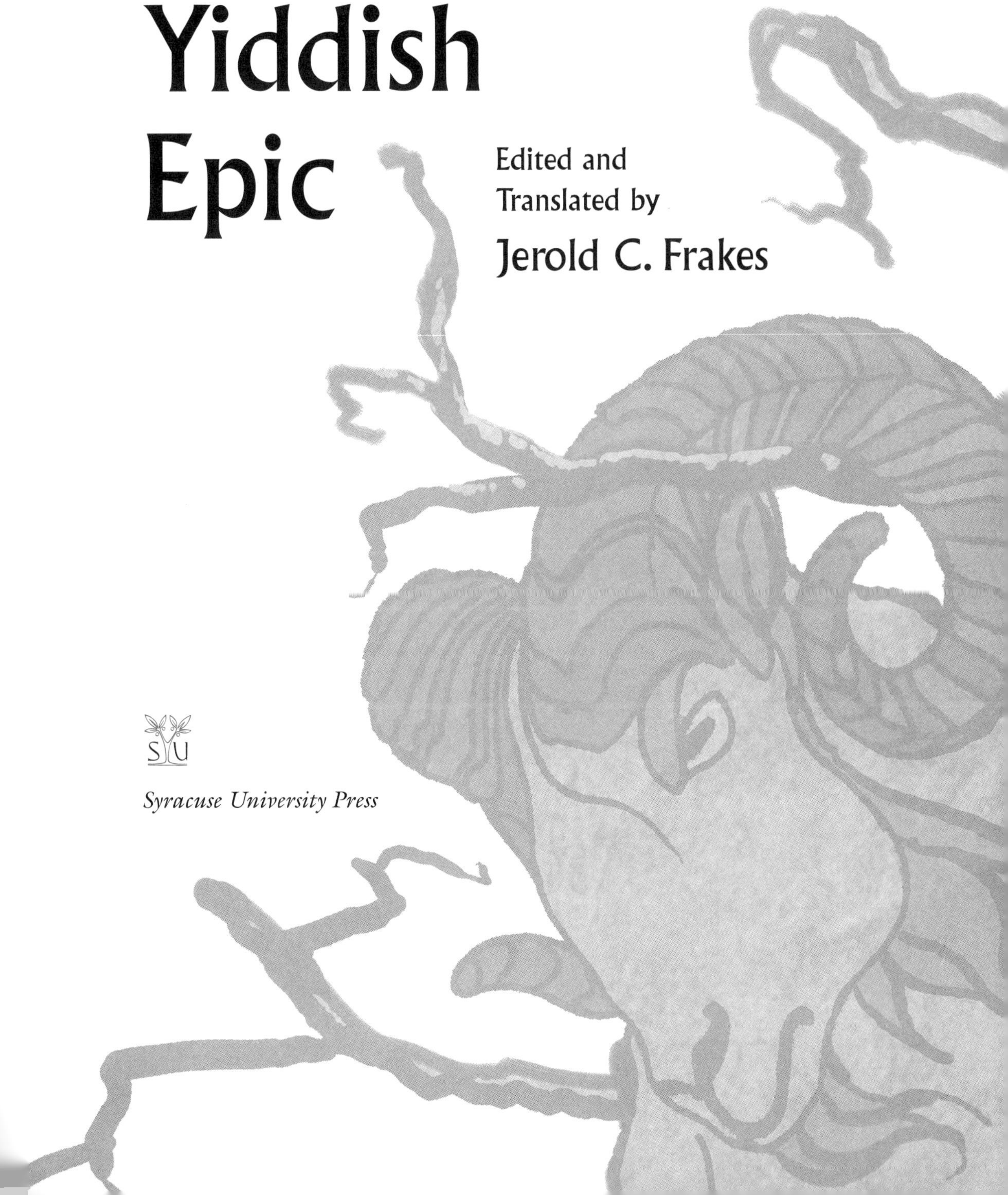

Syracuse University Press

Syracuse, New York 13244-5290

First Edition 2014

14 15 16 17 18 19 6 5 4 3 2 1

∞ The paper used in this publication meets the minimum requirements of the American National Standard for Information Sciences—Permanence of Paper for Printed Library Materials, ANSI Z39.48-1992.

For a listing of books published and distributed by Syracuse University Press, visit www.SyracuseUniversityPress.syr.edu.

ISBN: 978-0-8156-3355-6 (cloth) 978-0-8156-5268-7 (e-book)

Library of Congress Cataloging-in-Publication Data

Early Yiddish epic / translated by Jerold C. Frakes.
pages cm. – (Judaic traditions in literature, music, and art)
Includes bibliographical references.
ISBN 978-0-8156-3355-6 (cloth : alk. paper) – ISBN 978-0-8156-5268-7 (ebook)
1. Epic literature, Yiddish. 2. Epic literature, Yiddish–Translations into English.
I. Frakes, Jerold C.
PJ5128.E27 2014
839'.108001–dc23 2014015851

Manufactured in the United States of America

Contents

Acknowledgments

For granting permission to publish translations of manuscripts in their collections, I express my thanks to the Syndics of Cambridge University Library (T.-S. 10K22), the Hamburg Staats- und Universitätsbibliothek (Cod. hebr. 255 and Cod. hebr. 289), the Bayerische Staatsbibliothek in Munich (Cod. hebr. 100), the Bibliothèque Nationale in Paris (MS hébr. 589 [Sorbonne 158]), and the Master and Fellows of Trinity College in Cambridge (F.12.44).

Introduction

Although it is rather rare in the field of medieval studies to experience "late-breaking news," it does occasionally happen, even in the subdiscipline of Yiddish epic. In 1957 L. Fuks, the librarian of the Rosenthaliana collection at the Universiteit van Amsterdam, published a sumptuous two-volume documentation of a fourteenth-century anthology of eight Yiddish texts (eighty-four pages in its surviving format), five of which belong to the genre of heroic verse/epic. The manuscript was one among the thousands of documents brought by Solomon Schechter in 1896 to Cambridge University Library from the *geniza* of the Ben Ezra synagogue in Fustat (Old Cairo).[1] The publication was a thunderclap in the field of Yiddish studies, spawning scores of text editions, commentaries, linguistic and cultural analyses, book reviews, and conference papers over the course of the ensuing decades, quite transforming the subdiscipline of early Yiddish studies in the process.

Perhaps less dramatically, but in the long term perhaps no less significantly, in 1986 Anna Maria Babbi, a young scholar attempting to reconstruct the complex northern Italian publishing history of *Paris e Viena* (Paris and Viena), an Italian reflex of the Pan-European epic of the Renaissance period, inadvertently discovered a complete copy of the Yiddish adaptation of that narrative, פאריז און' וויענה *Pariz un Viene* (Pariz and Viene),[2] published by Francesco dalle Donne in Verona in 1594, which at that time was otherwise extant and thus known to scholars only in fragments.[3] The anonymous Yiddish text—a magnificent Renaissance epic on an aesthetic par with the works of Boiardo, Tasso, and Ariosto—is still in the process of transforming the conception of the literary landscape of sixteenth-century Yiddish.

And again quite recently (2011) and more quietly still, there was a spectacular find in the realm of early Yiddish epic: a text dated to 1349 (at the latest) was unearthed by an archaeological team excavating a medieval synagogue in the city of Cologne.[4] A somewhat more detailed description of this find and its significance may be in order here, since it is still not widely known. The synagogue on that site had first been destroyed in the wave of anti-Jewish violence coincident with the onset of the First Crusade in 1096, then rebuilt, and again burned in the so-called Plague Pogrom on the night of August 23–24, 1349 (the eve of St. Bartholomew's Day), when most Jewish inhabitants of the city were systematically slaughtered and those individuals who had taken refuge in the synagogue were then burned alive in the arson of the synagogue. Much of the rubble and other remains of the synagogue were then dumped into pits, from which archaeologists have since 2007 recovered thousands of artifacts. Among these artifacts (including book bindings and parchment fragments) recovered from beneath the women's synagogue area are some seventy thousand slate fragments, of which approximately one hundred and fifty are marked with script or designs; the slate fragments probably originated from the upper floor and may date from a period just before the fire.[5] Many of the slate tablets are inscribed with lists of names, a few with Hebrew texts (a biblical verse, two brief halakhic texts), a description of a building (bill of sale, will?), and a game-board design, while several slates bear clear examples of pen (?) trials and the writing practice of beginners; some of the tablets bear more than one layer of inscription.[6] In addition to the Hebrew-alphabet texts, several of the texts are written in the Roman alphabet (German). Much of the writing is indecipherable without diagonal lighting (to highlight the depth of incised letters) and computer magnification.

In January–February 2011, three fragments of a single slate tablet were recovered from the site on which is written a fragment of what Hollender initially calls "eine[] alt-jiddische[] Rittererzählung" (an Old Yiddish knightly tale), but then immediately thereafter designates a Middle High German, that is, apparently *not* an Old Yiddish, text. Timm designates the language "deutsch oder frühestes Jiddisch" (German or earliest Yiddish). When reassembled, the three fragments constitute a single tablet with nineteen lines of texts per side.[7] The tablet is approximately twelve by ten centimeters but has lost approximately 20 percent of its surface, broken away from one (vertical) edge, resulting in substantial loss of text, while further text is lost in broken segments in the center portions; the entire tablet has been severely damaged and discolored (red) by fire. The broken edge perpendicular to the direction of writing has brought about the loss of text at the end of text lines on one side and the beginning of text lines on the other side; since the text is written continuously (that is, not broken into lines of verse), however, it is possible to identify end rhyme sporadically in the text and thus conclude that the text consists of poetry. No words from the Semitic component of Yiddish are present. A sufficient amount of text is decipherable to identify its genre as "secular" epic. The genre is one of late-medieval courtly *Märendichtung* (poetic tale or narrative poetry). Paleographically and linguistically, the text seems consistent with the date of 1349 or somewhat earlier. No extant source of the text nor any text with parallel content is identifiable.

Although the existence of this text is historically of unquestionable importance in documenting the fascination with epic narrative among Yiddish-speaking Ashkenazic Jews yet a generation earlier than had hitherto been known, and at a site perhaps more predictable (in the Rhineland) for Yiddish-speaking Jews than the Cairo find, the *contents* of the text are unfortunately far too fragmentary to alter scholarly conceptions of the tradition of Yiddish epic.

Interestingly, however, the site of the find in each of these three cases of recent "discoveries" is characteristic of essential though distinct aspects of diasporic Jewish life: from the heartland of early Ashkenazic settlement in the Rhineland in the western reaches of late-medieval Jewish habitation in northern Europe to a site of ancient Jewish settlement in the extreme eastern Mediterranean, and then back to the heartland of early "secular" Ashkenazic literature in northern Italy. In Cairo the discovery site in a *geniza* was a deliberate, ritual Jewish depository of textual artifacts, while in Cologne it was a random rubbish dump of the remains of yet another of the recurring acts of bigoted violence perpetrated on Jews by their Christian neighbors over the course of the centuries, and the Verona print made use of the "advanced technology" of the period to transform distribution from a single hand-copied manuscript text to a mass-produced commodity—albeit one that has ironically now survived in a single complete example of the text. Narrowing our focus to the concern of the present volume: in each case, epic poetry, for a Jewish audience, written in the Yiddish language, etched into a slate stone or written on paper manufactured in the eastern Mediterranean region and bound into a Yiddish book comprising predominantly epic narratives, or printed and distributed to a broader reading community in the cities of northern Italy. In any case, epic seems to have been an essential component of Yiddish literature from the very beginning of the literary tradition of that language.

Epic in Old and Middle Yiddish is, however, not restricted to these three exceptional texts, but constitutes a broad and deep literary tradition. It is a tradition of Jewish literature and especially of Yiddish literature that has not yet been adequately studied and documented. Although it would be misleading to maintain that little scholarly work has been done in the field of early Yiddish epic, it is at the same time important to bear in mind what limitations have obtained and in large part still remain. The entire corpus of scholarly books and articles ever published concerning early Yiddish epic hardly exceeds current *annual* scholarly writing on, for instance, Old French epic (romance). Basic and comprehensive studies—philological, historical, literary—of individual texts, of the various subgenres, and of the entire tradition are in general still lacking in the study of Yiddish epic. Take, for instance, the ספר שמואל *Seyfer Shmuel* (Book of Samuel), perhaps the greatest masterpiece of early Yiddish literature and the most famous of the midrashic epics:[8] no modern edition of the text exists, so the would-be twenty-first-century reader has a choice only between reading the 1544 edition (whether in the original edition or a printed or online facsimile of that edition) or the sixteenth-century manuscripts. After reading that text, there is quite frankly very little left to read concerning the *Seyfer Shmuel*: if one were to gather together everything ever published *about* this text in any and all languages, the polyglot reader could read it all in the course of several leisurely days. For the marvelously sophisticated Renaissance epic *Pariz un Viene*, mentioned earlier, there exist a facsimile edition of the earliest extant edition (1594), a modern scholarly edition of the text, a modern Roman-alphabet quasi-Germanized version of the text, a recent monographic study, and a handful of publications scattered through the past century: again, no more than one could work through in a week or two. To return to the example of Old French epic: it might take an ambitious reader a year or more of very selective reading simply to come to terms with the major *trends* in the research in this field over the course of the past century and a half, and it is doubtful that a reader could ever hope to read all scholarship on Old French epic ever published.

Thus, while it would be an exaggeration to pretend that everything still remains to be done in the scholarship on early Yiddish epic, it sometimes almost seems so to an interested reader in the field. The hundreds of narrowly focused or broadly conceived articles, books, editions, and reviews, published over the course of several generations by adherents of the methods of conventional philology, New Criticism/close reading, structuralism, feminism, deconstruction, reception theory, Marxism, hermeneutics, queer theory, literary anthropology, New Historicism, and so on, which make the study of Old French epic a rich and vibrant world, with new text editions and translations continuing to appear, year after year and generation after generation, reinvigorating both scholarly and lay interest in the texts, with film versions and children's versions of, for instance, Arthurian romance that broaden the interest in the texts beyond the academic audience, render the literary world of Old French epic three-dimensionally palpable and accessible to any interested Francophone or indeed Anglophone reader.

In the world of early Yiddish epic, there are precious few modern scholarly editions and translations. While the translators of early Yiddish epic are to be commended for their initiative in a field with few avenues of advanced training, the fruits of their endeavors are generally rather clearly marked as those of "enthusiasts" who lack academic expertise in the field. As one component of his two-volume documentation of the Cairo codex (Cambridge University Library T.-S. 10K22), Fuks included a modern German translation that one might charitably characterize as inadequate.[9] Moyshe Knaphays's modern Yiddish rendering of בבֿא דאנטונא *Bovo d'Antona* (Bovo of Antona) (1962), for the popularizing hundred-volume library of Yiddish literature, *Musterverk fun der yidisher literatur*, renders the poem in eight-line (occasionally rhyming or assonating) stanzas that present not a translation or even paraphrase of the text but rather a retelling of the tale.[10] In 1968 Jerry Christopher Smith completed a doctorate in the field of German studies at Cornell University under the direction of James Marchand with a thesis that comprised a modern English version of *Bovo d'Antona*, which Smith identifies as "a free, though I hope accurate, prose rendering of the original verse romance"; his version often seems less a translation than an ameliorative paraphrase (replete with misunderstandings) that revises the original text whenever it contradicts Smith's conception of aesthetics and ideology, routinely omitting lines, couplets, and even half-stanzas and rearranging the narrative order of events.[11] The prolific commercial translator Joachim Neugröschel has published versions of two of the shorter heroic texts: first, בְּרִיעָה וזִימְרָה *Briyo ve-Zimro* (Briyo and Zimro), which is (with a few exceptions) generally competent, although since he translates not from the original text but from Erika Timm's Germanizing Roman-alphabet transcription, he is misled into distorting some of the characters' names and into some outright misconceptions and mistranslations.[12] The second of Neugröschel's translations is יוסף הצדיק *Yousef ha-tsadik* (Joseph the Righteous),[13] which is rendered as a poetic paraphrase, rather than as actual translation.[14] Finally, although Heidi Graw's rendering of דוכוס הורנט *Dukus Horant* (Duke Horant) aspires to provide an accurate prose translation of the epic, the result is far from adequate for reasons stemming (as she acknowledges in the front matter of the published booklet) from the fact that she has "no particular expertise relating to Germanic literature or languages," which unfortunately makes itself apparent in most stanzas.[15]

Beyond editions and translations, there is only a *single* literary study of any early Yiddish epic that gestures toward an interpretive mode beyond the methodology of nineteenth-century philology (even when that methodology is practiced in the twentieth or twenty-first century).[16] One is thus reminded of the opening remarks of J. R. R. Tolkien's paradigm-changing 1936 essay (still of value today) on the Old English epic *Beowulf*, where he observes that published work on that poem, "while rich in many departments, [is] specially poor in one. It is poor in criticism, criticism that is directed to the understanding of a poem as a poem."[17] The field of early Yiddish studies simply lacks the *five-hundred-volume* fundamental library of scholarship necessary to put it on a par with other scholarly subdisciplines of medieval literature, such as medieval French, German, English, or Latin.

Despite those very real limitations, however, one must recognize what does in fact exist in early Yiddish studies: a tradition of scholarship that began several hundred years ago and has continued by fits and starts up to the present; one must also acknowledge that in the course of the past century, there have been seminal works of scholarship published about early Yiddish epic by such scholars as Max Erik, Israel Zinberg (Yisroel Tsinberg), Max Weinreich, Chone Shmeruk, and Jean Baumgarten, among others. It is nonetheless still the case that in most categories of scholarship in early Yiddish studies, even if one takes into account everything that has ever been published, including the (often outmoded) hundred-year-old publications, there are gaps wherever one looks. The modest goals of the present volume are thus contextualized: if it were a volume of translations of medieval English, French, Italian, Latin, or German epics, it would join literally hundreds of translations of individual texts and scores of other such translation anthology volumes published over the course of the past century and a half. In early Yiddish epic studies, it is, more or less, the first such volume. I do not thus wish to claim any kind of pioneering status for the volume but rather to apologize, as it were, for the embarrassment of publishing it a century too late and with all the inevitable deficient marks of work in a not yet mature field of scholarship.[18]

One of the more difficult problems in early Yiddish literary studies is the lack of pertinent lexical reference books, which is quite easy to illustrate. The language of the sixteenth-century midrashic epic based on the biblical book(s) of Samuel, the *Seyfer Shmuel*, is, for instance, not modern Yiddish—for which there is unfortunately also no comprehensive dictionary: the four folio volumes of the Yiddish-Yiddish *Great Dictionary of the Yiddish Language* cover only the first letter of the alphabet, *alef.* Otherwise, the most useful dictionaries of the *modern* language are the one-volume dictionaries by Alexander Harkavy, Uriel Weinreich, and Yitskhok Niborski (Bernard Vaisbrot), which—competent though they may be (and all three are indeed brilliant)—are in design and scope simply student-level bi- or trilingual dictionaries.[19] One realizes how inadequate they are as comprehensive lexical authorities for an entire language when one recalls, for instance, that the most recent printed edition of the *Oxford English Dictionary* comprises nearly three hundred thousand entries in twenty dense volumes, while the current electronic version of that dictionary includes some six hundred thousand entries, and the Grimms' *Deutsches Wörterbuch* exceeds three hundred thousand entries in thirty-two volumes.[20] But in any case, as noted, Harkavy, Weinreich, and Niborski are dictionaries of *modern* Yiddish, and the *Seyfer Shmuel* is quite clearly not modern Yiddish. One might likewise note that the epic is also not the premodern German that formed *one* of the component source languages on the basis of which the Yiddish language formed. Specifically, the *Seyfer Shmuel* is not, as is often simply assumed by some readers, Middle High German (for which the magnificent multivolume lexicon by Matthias Lexer exists), nor (early) New High German (for which there is Alfred Götze's glossary and indeed the historical breadth of the Grimms' dictionary).[21]

An example may illustrate a typical problem. When, for instance, one encounters the late-Old or early-Middle Yiddish word גידענקט (*gidenkt*) in the *Seyfer Shmuel* (st. 1390,3), how is one to determine its meaning? Because there is no Old or Middle Yiddish dictionary, nor any *comprehensive* dictionary of modern Yiddish that offers aid on this word, one must look elsewhere. Should one then prefer the senses of the word's Middle High German reflex of "think, commemorate, devise" or the senses of its modern German reflex of "commemorate, intend" or the most frequent sense of the modern Yiddish reflex, "remember"? Most readers of the present volume will have an immediate response, dictated by their own conceptions of the text's cultural identity. A mid-sixteenth-century text is most certainly *not* Middle High German and thus not directly explained by Lexer, nor is this late-fifteenth- or early-sixteenth-century Yiddish text to be identified as (early) modern German, which means that Götze and the Grimms may then also be consulted only with great caution; neither then is it modern Yiddish, so the lexica by Harkavy, Weinreich, and Niborski (Vaisbrot) are not directly relevant, and, finally, because the word begins with *gimel*, not *alef*, the *Great Dictionary* (with its often useful information about earlier stages of Yiddish) is unfortunately also of no aid. The "method" here practiced is then a compromise—which, truth be told, is the daily practice of all translators, no matter how well provided with lexica—a constant "triangulation" that attempts, working outward from the context established in the *original* text itself and in similar usages in other relevant texts, to arrive at the word's sense, generally in consultation with the various available lexica. In the passage in question, the word seems clearly to mean "think, consider, reflect on, keep in mind," which is, not surprisingly, not exactly what any one of the identified lexica offers, since, after all, this word is a Middle Yiddish word in a Middle Yiddish text, and its usage is its own.

A further example may put some larger issues of cultural translation in context by considering a word that may seem more familiar to many contemporary speakers of Yiddish and readers of Yiddish literature, especially of the earlier periods: פֿרום *frum*, which we all might immediately tend to understand in the same sense as its modern Yiddish reflex, that is, "pious" or even anachronistically as "orthodox." This misconception of specifically *Old and Middle* Yiddish usage is at the heart of the all but ubiquitous misunderstanding of that widely known cliché of early Yiddish prefaces, by means of which the author or publisher attempts to characterize the putative female readership of early Yiddish books as consisting primarily of פֿרומע ווייבער *frume vayber*. Interestingly, however, it is precisely that adjective which is ubiquitously employed in early Yiddish literature—especially in early Yiddish epic—to designate that specific trait of the martial hero that makes him a hero and that trait of both men and women for which the synonyms "honest, honored, noble, just, notable, principled, respectable, upright, or virtuous" might be used. In early Yiddish epic, *frum* thus most often signals that broad range of traits linked to socially valued behavior in the traditional (non-Jewish) martial culture of European epic from antiquity through the Middle Ages and into the early modern period: courage, nobility, and honor. There is no question that the word may also denote "pious" in early Yiddish (as indeed also is among the connotations of the Middle High German reflex of the word)—and it more than once appears in this sense in the present volume—but in the early periods of Yiddish literature that specific denotation had nonetheless not yet become the *exclusive* sense. While piety was to be sure a widespread concept in the culture, it was generally expressed in early Yiddish by other words, especially by הייליג *heylik* (for example, *Pariz un Viene* 239,2, 241,1, and 242,7). Significantly, in that text, the concepts of piety and honor are employed in a single line to describe the virtues of the narrative's heroine (Viene): זיא וואר גאר הייליקליך אונ' ורומן (she was quite pious and honorable) (st. 399,6), with *heyliklikh* (pious) and *frum* (honorable) denoting the complementary—not synonymous—virtues of piety and honor. Indeed, in the subsequent line *frum* is used in conjunction with, and as a synonym of, the term *ern* (honor). Interestingly, in Elias Levita's די שריפה בון ווענדיג *Di sreyfe fun Veneydik* (The Great Fire of Venice), a variation in the two manuscripts suggests this same synonymity: דז איז איין ערבר מן (that is, an *erber* "honorable" man; Oxford ms.)

versus אז איין ורומר מן (as a *frumer* "honorable" man; Cambridge ms.) (*EYT*, 34, st. 12,2). I realize that my pointing out this complex of semantic usage will likely not correct the ubiquitously popular misunderstanding of the specifically Middle Yiddish phrase *frume vayber* from "pious women" to the more appropriate and more adequate rendering "honorable or respectable women." But in all such instances of semantic drift, words and phrases are better understood from their range of usage in their own cultural contexts than from the narrowly conceived usage of a modern culture still several centuries distant.

The focal texts of the present volume present the reader with yet another cluster of cultural and interpretive problems as well: in terms of cultural history, it is quite interesting that, unlike its temporal and geographical neighbors in various periods and settings, Jewish literature in general is quite sparsely sown with examples of the literary genre of epic, and *ancient* Jewish literature famously lacked the genre altogether, if defined according to its standard literary-historical conception as narrative poetry celebrating the (in general martially, but often simply ethically) superhuman deeds of a traditionally famous, legendary, mortal hero who generally has close (sometimes genetic) connections to the divine. One thinks, for instance, of Gilgamesh, Akhilleus, Hektor, Jason, Odysseus, and Aineias/Aeneas in Sumerian, Assyrian, Greek, and Roman epic. Although both the ancient Jewish poetic tradition and the genre of heroic tales were well developed and well represented in the Hebrew Bible, those narratives were not expressed as independently conceived narratives focused on those characters, and, just as important, those narratives were not expressed in a poetic form specifically dedicated to epic narrative, indeed not expressed in poetic form at all.[22] Thus, despite the astonishing range of literary genres included in the biblical canon, including *heroic tales*, ancient Jewish literature seems not to have included *epic poetry* as such.

Although it may initially seem niggling to criticize individual details in the monumental work of an important scholar such as Frank Moore Cross in the field of ancient Israelite religion, it need be acknowledged that he inadvertently muddied the waters on the subject of Jewish epic by championing the notion that an ancient Israelite "epic cycle" existed. The notion is unfortunately founded on two fundamental errors: not a single such ancient Israelite epic exists (even in fragmentary form), and his ad hoc definition of epic, specifically formulated to accommodate its absence from extant ancient Hebrew genres, is flawed in its assumption that—unlike all other ancient Mediterranean and Near Eastern epic traditions—Israelite *prose* tales (embedded in the Hebrew Bible) must be construed as if epic.[23] While in recent years the use of the term "epic" has, at least in the United States, often been extended to rather nonspecific usage in pop culture, including the achievements of athletes, and while Cross's specific use of the term "epic" is now so well known in the field of biblical studies that it cannot be dismissed with a wave of the hand—and certainly not *my* hand—it seems to me that in literary studies, especially with respect to a culture whose *ancient* literary tradition derived so significantly from the traditions of its geographical neighbors and transformed *every single* epic (that is, *poetic* heroic text) borrowed from those neighbors into *prose* narrative, then the academic use of the analytical genre designation "epic" ought to be defined with some rigor and with some consideration of those specific cultural conditions. Finally, one should note that while it is clear that Cross is operating in good faith and certainly *not* attempting any sleight of hand in his use of the term, that usage is nonetheless imprecise and misleading, as has been pointed out by many scholars over the course of recent decades.[24]

Leaving aside such detours, we might acknowledge that among many others, the tales of the Israelite conquest of the land of Canaan, Samson's lifelong conflicts against the Philistines, and the struggles of Saul and David to establish the Israelite monarchy against the backdrop of continuing conflict with the Philistines (and each other) all but cry out for epic elaboration.[25] Even so, the ancient Hebrew poetic tradition not only did not develop a native form of epic, but did not borrow one from its neighbors. Even in cases such as the tale of the Flood, which appeared in epic form in many ancient Near Eastern cultures, and even traveled so far afield (both geographically and aesthetically) as to appear later in Ovid's *Metamorphoses* (1.253–437)—in the quintessentially epic dactylic hexameters of the ancient Greek literary tradition that had been borrowed whole cloth into Latin—while the Hebrew literary tradition did indeed borrow the narrative from Mesopotamian sources (where it had appeared in traditional epic form in the *Enuma Elish*, eighteenth-twelfth century BCE), the Hebrew narrative took the form of prose myth or fable, not epic poetry, in the book of Genesis.

Even in the postmonarchical period of exile, and later in the period of the composition of the Mishna and the Gemara, when Jews for the first time in recorded history adopted identifiably Gentile languages of empire as their specifically Judaized vernaculars—Aramaic as lingua franca of the Persian Empire and *koine* (Greek) as the lingua franca of most Hellenistic cities throughout the territories of Alexander's conquests—which entailed far greater cultural hybridization than the mere borrowing of a language, no full-scale epic tradition on the model of, for instance, the (non-Jewish) Aramaic epic cycles or the Greek Homeric or Hellenistic epic developed in Jewish literature. Some few individual Jewish epics that participated indirectly in the Hellenistic epic tradition were in fact composed, however, and it is here that the first extant (fragmentary) examples of Jewish epic are to be found. Unfortunately, practically nothing of these Judeo-Greek works has survived: only a fragment of the epic on the rape of Dinah in Homeric style by Theodotus (a Samaritan poet of the second century BCE) is preserved by Alexander Polyhistor, but only as Alexander (whose work is also lost) was cited by Eusebius (*Praeparatio evangelica* 9:22).[26] Of Philo the Elder's (probably early-second-century BCE) epic in fourteen books, *On Jerusalem*, only three fragments totaling twenty-four lines (most of which are unintelligible due to faulty transmission) survive.[27]

It is not until the Middle Ages that Jewish epic is preserved in texts long enough to be appreciated and evaluated, although even there, many of the relevant texts must have been lost, and much of the non-Jewish epic source material was adapted into Hebrew as prose narrative, not epic.[28] The ubiquitously known tales of Alexander the Great's campaigns and adventures in an exoticized and orientalized East, for instance, were translated into Hebrew (prose) in the fourteenth century by Immanuel ben Jacob Bonfils from Leo Presbyter's tenth-century Latin prose text the *Historia de proeliis*.[29] Abraham ibn Ḥasdai of Barcelona (mid-thirteenth century) composed a Hebrew version of the internationally known ethical romance concerning Barlaam and Josaphat (a version of the widespread story of the Buddha) under the title *Ben ha-melekh ve-ha-nazir* (The Prince and the Dervish) in the (nonepic) poetic form of *maqamat*.[30] The earliest example of Arthurian epic as adapted into a Jewish language is a tantalizing *prose* fragment on the subject of Lancelot, dating from 1279, translated into Hebrew.[31] Curt Leviant, the translator of that fragment, somewhat too extravagantly suggests that Hebrew poetry in thirteenth-century Spain and Provence presented "as wide a selection as secular poetry permits," for in fact in his listing not a single epic appears.[32]

It is not until the late Middle Ages and early modern period that a range of Jewish epic appears: the earliest extant Hebrew example is entitled *Iggeret Ya'ar ha-Levanon* (On the Decorations and Vessels of the Temple), written by Moses ben Isaac da Rieti (1388–post-1460), sometimes called the "Hebrew Dante."[33] The *Mikdash Me'at* in two parts (1,050 stanzas) by the same author is a philosophical, rhetorical poem in epic form, the first part of which comprises an examination of Moses ben Maimon (Maimonides), Ibn Rushd (Averroes), Ibn Sīnā (Avicenna), al-Ghazālī, al-Fārābī (Alfarabi), Porphyry, and Aristotle, while the second is a description of the celestial court.[34] In Judeo-Italian literature epic is represented by Mordecai ben Judah Dato's sixteenth-century *Istoria di Ester* (Story of Esther) composed in *ottava rima*.[35] A Portuguese *converso* poet, Miguel de Silveyra (c. 1578–1638), composed a baroque epic in

Castilian, *El Macabeo* (The Maccabean), on Judah Maccabee (twenty books, Naples, 1638).[36]

While these scattered examples of epic—fragmentary or intact—strewn across almost two millennia and the multiple languages of the Jewish diaspora may seem on the verge of establishing a specifically Jewish literary genre whether during the ancient Hellenistic period or the European Renaissance, they in fact do not themselves constitute a *tradition* of epic poetry as such but remain scattered "orphans" of such an elusive genre. In the end it was not in Hebrew, Judeo-Arabic, Ladino, or Judeo-Italian that an actual tradition of the literary genre of epic developed among Jews, but rather in two for the most part unconnected Jewish subcultures: in Judeo-Persian[37] and in early Yiddish, at more or less the same time period. In each case the traditions are relatively broad and deep.

According to Vera Basch Moreen, "Judeo-Persian literature is the product of the confluence of two mighty literary and religious streams, the Jewish biblical and postbiblical heritage and the Persian (Muslim) literary legacy."[38] The influence of the monumental *Shāh-nāmeh* (Book of Kings) of Ferdowsī (Hakīm Abu'l-Qāsim Ferdowsī Tūsī), the "national epic" of Persia, is, not surprisingly, pervasive not just among his Muslim literary successors in Persian, but also among Judeo-Persian epic poets. The earliest major Judeo-Persian epic poet was Maulānā Shāhīn (perhaps of Shīrāz),[39] who flourished during the reign of the Il-khanid Sultan Abū Sa'īd (1316–35) and composed several epics based indirectly on biblical narrative: (1) *Sefer sharḥ-i Shāhīn al-Torah* (Exegesis of the Torah), entitled *Mūsā-nāmeh* (Book of Moses) by some scholars, which deals with the narrative material of the last four books of the Torah, incorporating some materials from Muslim traditions (ten thousand lines, 1327 CE); (2) *Tafsir Megillat Ester* (Interpretation of the Book of Esther), divided into two books and entitled *Ardashīr-nāmeh* (Book of Ardashīr) and *Ezra-nāmeh* (Book of Ezra) by some scholars, which deals with narrative materials from the biblical book of Esther, a love story related to the Shiruyeh (son of Vashti) and a Chinese princess, Mahzād, and a narrative concerning the life of Cyrus the Great, mostly derived from the biblical book of Ezra (six thousand lines, 1333 CE); and (3) *Sharḥ-i Torah, Sefer Bereshit* (Exegesis of the Torah, Book of Genesis), entitled *Bereshit-nāmeh* (Book of Genesis) by some scholars (ten thousand lines, 1359 CE). Shāhīn's works demonstrate a profound knowledge of classical Persian literature and poetic form.

The poet 'Emrānī (1454–post-1536; probably a pen name) of Isfahān composed some twelve poetic works, the most important being the epic *Fatḥ-nāmeh* (Book of the Conquest), an epic paraphrase of the biblical books of

Joshua, 1–2 Samuel, and part of 1 Kings and Ruth (ten thousand couplets, 1474 CE); and the *Ganj-nāmeh* (The Book of the Treasures), a poetic paraphrase and commentary on the Mishnaic tractate Avot (1536 CE).[40] Khājah Bukhārāī composed the *Dāniyāl-nāmeh* (Book of Daniel), based on the biblical book of Daniel and apocryphal and midrashic materials (1606 CE). Aḥaron b. Mashiaḥ composed the *Shofetim-nāmeh* (Book of Judges) (1692 CE) on the first eighteen chapters of the biblical book of Judges. Continuing Aḥaron's work, Mordecai ben David rendered the narrative of Judges 19–21 into epic form under the title of *Ma'ase Pillegesh ba-Giva* (Tale of the Concubine in Gibeah). The seventeenth-century poet Elisha ben Shemuel (pen name Rāghib) composed a version of Abraham ibn Ḥasdai's Hebrew *Ben ha-melekh ve-ha-nazir* under the equivalent Persian title *Shāhzāda va ṣūfi* (The Shah's Son and the Ṣufi) and the *Ḥanukka-nāmeh* (Book of Ḥanukkah), based on the Maccabean traditions.

This lengthy tradition of Judeo-Persian epic narrative is still little known beyond the circle of experts, although Moreen's anthology may well draw scholarly interest that will lead to a rectification of that situation. It is very interesting that this tradition shares so very much with the tradition of early Yiddish epics, the most relevant issues being that in both Yiddish and Judeo-Persian epic, the poets very deliberately avoid the use of Hebraisms (at least in the earlier texts of each tradition). Biblical narrative functions as the frame for many of the epics (virtually all of those in Judeo-Persian), but in fact the actual narratives of the Bible itself are most often of little direct relevance, having been displaced by broader midrashic traditions that provide the actual stories told. The Jewish poets knew the literary traditions *and* their poetic forms of the surrounding majority cultures intimately (Persian for the Judeo-Persian poets, German and Italian for the Yiddish poets) and incorporated that expertise into their own poems. The primary distinction that is immediately apparent is that while the Gentile narrative tradition was well known to Judeo-Persian poets, they never went beyond the biblical or midrashic for epic narrative material. That is, unlike the Yiddish poets, they never developed an entire subgenre of "secular" epic adapted from preexisting Gentile epic texts.[41]

As indicated at the outset of this introduction, beginning at least by the fourteenth century, the Yiddish tradition of epic poetry seems to spring forth fully formed in the Cologne slate fragment and especially in the earliest extant Yiddish codex (from the Cairo *geniza*), both noted earlier. As Jean Baumgarten has brilliantly elaborated, just as Yiddish is a fusion language (as postulated by Max Weinreich), so, too, is early Yiddish literature a fusion literature, "for it incorporated a great many traits characteristic of medieval European literatures as well as characteristics directly borrowed from Hebrew sources." While true in general of early Yiddish literature, this fusion character is even more significant in early Yiddish epic. As Baumgarten notes:

> Yiddish epic literature thus provides a meeting point of traditional Jewish culture and those cultures in contact with which the Jews had lived and whose cultural products Jews had adopted and transformed for a Jewish audience. It represents a clear expression of acculturation which remained one of the constant traits of several of the Jewish diasporic literatures. The study of this literature thus becomes quite important for understanding both the modes of reception and integration of non-Jewish literary forms and the process of the creation of a national literary tradition that complements the central traditions of European literature.[42]

The adoption and adaptation of literary and stylistic models from both German and Italian epic poetry provide yet another type of evidence for the profound cultural contacts between Jews and Christians of the period. This influence is particularly apparent with respect to the narratives translated and adapted from German sources, for one notes much in the way of phraseology, idiom, and even narrative themes integrated directly into the Yiddish texts. Even so, one must also bear in mind that these borrowed components did not themselves constitute the world of early Yiddish literature, for the native Jewish component continued to be dominant: the epic poets—from the earliest texts up through the seventeenth century—were masters of the Jewish textual tradition in Hebrew and Aramaic. There was no capitulation to external influences but rather a creative adaptation and integration of those components that were deemed appropriate.

This fusion character is already quite apparent in the epics from the Cairo codex, which bears witness to yet another aspect of the geographical range of Yiddish language use over the course of several centuries, extending to the eastern Mediterranean and the Ashkenazic settlements particularly in Cairo and Jerusalem in the late medieval and early modern periods. Five of the eight texts of this codex are indeed heroic lays or epics, four of them deriving directly from native Jewish tradition and representing the genre that has come to be known in Yiddish studies as midrashic epic: משה רבנו *Moushe rabeynu* (Moses Our Teacher), גן עדן *Gan eydn* (Paradise), אברהם אבינו *Avrom ovinu* (Abraham Our Father), and יוסף הצדיק *Yousef ha-tsadik* (Joseph the Righteous). They are distinguished by having as their protagonists biblical characters whose narrated deeds derive largely from the *post*biblical traditions of the midrash.

All four of these texts represent the shorter, as opposed to the longer, form of epic in the early Yiddish tradition, which one might liken in some formal aspects to the heroic lay of the Russian *bylina* tradition,[43] most examples of the South Slavic epic tradition,[44] and of the Germanic tradition of "heroic lay" in the earlier Middle Ages, such as the Old English *Battle of Brunanburh*, *Battle of Maldon*, and *Waldere*, the Old High German *Hildebrandslied*, or the Old Norse Eddic lays, such as the *Sigurðarqviða in scamma* or the *Atlaqviða in grœnlenzca*, in that they generally comprise only a few score lines of verse and focus usually on a single moment of crisis, momentous event, or episode.[45] Although it is a virtual certainty that there is no *genetic* link between this heroic short form in early Slavic, Anglo-Saxon, German, or Norse literature and the similar form that developed in early Yiddish, nonetheless in all these traditions there is a very clear distinction—in thematic scope, acuity and intensity of focus, and, naturally, length—between such heroic lays and the full-fledged epic form of, for instance, the Old English *Beowulf* or the Middle High German *Nibelungenlied* in the Christian Germanic tradition and the fifth epic text of this earliest Yiddish literary manuscript, the *Dukus Horant*. In this same context of the distinction between the shorter heroic lay and the longer epic form, one needs to note the distinction specific to the Yiddish midrashic poems: while the shorter lays focus on a single midrashic episode, the longer epics, such as the *Seyfer Shmuel* and *Seyfer Melokhim*, combine extensive midrashic treatment with a (sporadically) much closer attention to rendering into Yiddish the general contents of the biblical book itself.

Unlike the other, shorter, heroic poems of the codex, *Dukus Horant* is adapted from Christian epic tradition and is a representative example of medieval feudal bridal-quest epic (the generally international search for and courting of a princess as bride for a prince or king). It has generally been assumed by scholars that the Yiddish *Horant* was adapted from a Middle High German source text, although no such German source text is extant, and no such narrative is even mentioned in any other medieval text in any language. As scholarship comes to focus more on extant narratives and less on their supposed sources, perhaps *Dukus Horant* may finally become the subject of actual literary critical attention.

Thus, even in this first historical collection of Yiddish epic in the codex Cambridge T.-S. 10K22, the two subgenres that were to define the Ashkenazic genre throughout the late medieval and early modern period—midrashic and "secular"—were already present in fully developed form. Two of the texts in the codex identify the year in which they were copied as קמ"ג = 1382[-3] CE, but because that date may well specify not when this manuscript was copied but rather when *its* source texts were themselves copied, this manuscript may itself actually be somewhat more recent than 1382. The first two of the texts in the water-damaged and worm-eaten codex have deteriorated so much that they are difficult to read as integral texts, as is also the case with the final extant folios of the last text in the manuscript (*Horant*). Only *Abraham Our Father*, *Joseph the Righteous*, and *Duke Horant*—the three most legible of the epics in the codex—are thus translated in the present volume.

In order to characterize early Yiddish epic, it is necessary to differentiate the two primary subgenres, midrashic and "secular."[46] In addition to the poems just named from the Cairo codex, three further midrashic epics are translated in the present volume: the *Seyfer Shmuel* (Augsburg, 1544), עקידת יצחק *Akeydas Yitskhok* (The Binding of Isaac) (1570), and two brief excerpts from the ספר מלכים *Seyfer Melokhim* (The Book of Kings) (Augsburg, 1543). Midrashic adaptations of biblical books (not necessarily epic in conception, although epic in form) are the most numerous of the types of Yiddish epic, other major examples being ספר דניאל *Seyfer Donieyl* (The Book of Daniel) (Basel, 1557),[47] the ספר שופטים *Seyfer Shoftim* (The Book of Judges) (Mantua, 1564), and the ספר יהושע *Seyfer Yehoushua* (The Book of Joshua) (Kraków, 1594),[48] in addition to several others, especially of prophetic books and the five scrolls.

Wulf-Otto Dreeßen first made a case for using the term *Midraschepik* (midrashic epic) to designate the early Yiddish epics that had up to that time simply been called "biblical" epics.[49] He pointed out that the allegorical and (christologically) figural interpretation (for example, prefiguring Christ, Mary, and salvation)—the "intention," as he terms this usage—that necessarily underlay Christian biblical epics is understandably *never* present in Yiddish epic on biblical themes, while the "intention" of the Yiddish epics on biblical themes derives from the radically differing intellectual and religious tradition of midrash.[50] Thus, a Christian epic grounded in the commentaries of Church Fathers such as Augustine and Jerome and a Yiddish epic grounded in the Talmudic and midrashic traditions differ so fundamentally as to be hardly recognizable as narratives deriving from the same biblical foundation. In order to make that distinction terminologically insistent, Dreeßen coined the term "midrashic epic" to designate the particular Yiddish mode of epic based on biblical themes but so profoundly informed by the postbiblical Jewish tradition of midrash that the narratives can be culturally contextualized only through a consideration of the broader midrashic traditions.

Barbara Könnecker has objected to Dreeßen's conception of midrashic epic as a genre identification because, she claims, there is no nonlinear midrashic *method* employed in, for instance, the narrative of the *Seyfer Shmuel*, which, she suggests, narrates the events of the biblical books of Samuel in linear and thus decidedly nonmidrashic order.[51] Her basic conception of midrashic method is, however, quite one-sided, since she altogether overlooks, for instance, the subgenre designated "exegetical midrash" by Galit Hasan-Rokem, "characterized by an anthological structure that follows the order of biblical verses of the book it elaborates," as in *Lamentations Rabbah.*[52] In any case, Könnecker's objection seems irrelevant to the function of Dreeßen's terminological usage, which designates a *source* of narrative content and cultural orientation, not a *method* of analysis. Moreover, in commenting on the mode of extant Qumran scriptural interpretation, Steven D. Fraade has pointed out that there is little in the way of actual citation plus commentary involved, but instead:

> Scriptural verses are paraphrased; that is, they are not explicitly cited at all, but are rather "retold," with varying degrees of expansion, reduction, reordering, and combination with other retold scriptural verses. While one effect of the commentary mode is to differentiate between scriptural text and its interpretation, the mode of scriptural paraphrase (in the absence of explicit scriptural citation) has the effect of blurring, if not effacing, the boundary line between the two. Writings that favor the latter mode have variously been termed "para-biblical" or "rewritten Bible." These sorts of writings are by no means unique to the Dead Sea Scrolls.[53]

His description rather surprisingly and effectively characterizes much of early Yiddish midrashic epic.[54] As will be seen in the translation of the *Seyfer Shmuel* in this volume, that text is only sporadically a "para-biblical" rendering: it is in large part a quite distinctly nonlinear midrash on the biblical text.

The poets of midrashic epic were clearly quite thoroughly educated in the Jewish textual traditions of the Bible, Talmud, midrashic commentary, and rabbinical legend, all of which provide abundant material for their narratives. Moreover, in their mastery of the standard conventions of multiple genres of Christian epic and romance of the High Middle Ages, it is clear that they were also intimately acquainted with those genres—as their audience must also have been, if they were to be appreciative readers and/or aural recipients of the epics. Despite this shared knowledge of extra-Judaic literary traditions, however, there is never any indication in midrashic epic of a movement away from the Jewish tradition—no secularizing or Christianizing tendencies, no retreat from core Jewish traditions, but indeed just the opposite: an appreciation of midrashic epic requires of the reader an intimate knowledge of the sacred textual traditions of Judaism, which enables the texts and the subgenre to function as cultural touchstones by means of which membership in the community was reinforced and cultural knowledge was transmitted to initiates. In this respect, then, midrashic epic functioned precisely as traditional epic functions almost wherever it appears in world cultures: as a storehouse of "insider" cultural mores and values that serves to integrate those values into a complex overlay of networks of cultural knowledge and practice.

The specific nature of midrashic narrative as such should be pointed out in advance, although the attentive reader need not read far into any midrashic epic to realize that the narrative, while not exactly deficient in terms of plot construction, is of quite a different character from other epic narrative conceptions. An example may serve to illustrate the narrative mode and its differentiated use of Jewish textual traditions. The text of *Joseph the Righteous* takes as its narrative prompt the biblical episode of Joseph's rejection of the sexual proposition by the wife of his master, Potiphar (Gen. 39:7–20), but beyond three brief sentences acknowledging that rejection and then quoting it, the poem's seventy-six verses include nothing from the biblical text's cryptic relation of the story, but rather narrate quite a different and (widely known) extrabiblical tale of the proud display of Joseph by his master's wife as her own property, indeed as such spellbindingly beautiful property that her noble female guests are unable to peel apples in his presence without cutting their own fingers to shreds while gazing on his beauty. The poem ends with the implicit moral lesson that illicit lust is both foolish and destructive, while (heroic) chastity explicitly earns the reward of Heaven. No hint of this tale is present in the Bible, and no hint of this tale is anything other than traditional in postbiblical Jewish textual traditions, represented, for instance, in *Midrash Tanhuma*.[55] The components central to one mode of midrashic epic (also present, for instance, in *Abraham Our Father*)—a heroically moral figure, a comically immoral opponent, and a moralizing conclusion (which, however, does not dominate the narrative)—are here apparent.

Just as is the case in other epic traditions, in midrashic epic a high level of cultural literacy is presupposed on the part of its audience. Thus, just as Homer never needed to contextualize Agamemnon's trail of prewar moral compromises that preconditioned his challenged moral authority before the walls of Troy, even as he still exercised political authority over his fellow kings in the Greek camp, the poet of Yiddish midrashic epic never needed to problematize the covenant between Jews and the divine so systematically established in the course of the biblical book of Genesis, nor even to summarize "the story up to this point," as it were: that level of cultural literacy among their audiences is simply assumed by both the ancient Greek and the early modern Yiddish poets. Moreover, the Yiddish midrashic poets can also expect that their audience will be sensitive to subtle modifications of the "midrashicized" narrative vis-à-vis the primary midrashim themselves. Sometimes indeed it seems (particularly in the longer midrashic epics) that that is precisely the point in some brief episodes.

While Robert Alter—taking a page from the theoretical school of *Rezeptionsästhetik*—has made clear that *biblical* narrative often comprises a texture of gaps that must, as it were, be filled in by the reader in order to produce the rich weave of potential meaning embedded in the narrative,[56] early Yiddish midrashic epic seems, if possible, even more essentially gap ridden, for after all it enters a Jewish textual tradition that by the late Middle Ages had through commentary and supercommentary traditions become several layers deeper than the biblical texts on which they depend. For the reasons just noted, contextualizing information is not conceived as vital to an understanding of the plot per se, but the reader is constantly aware that what seems in most ways a richly textured narrative recurringly lacks key information. When, for instance, the mustered Israelite troops are numbered before going out to battle with Amalek in the *Seyfer Shmuel*, it is said that the army comprises "twice a hundred thousand, plus ten thousand" (st. 259). To the uninitiated, it might at first glance seem that this awkward phrasing constitutes an unskilled or at least momentarily inattentive poet's ploy to fill a line of verse or provide a rhyme; or perhaps it might merely be a peculiar and archaic mode of expression. If the Yiddish text were all that was extant, then that explanation might well be the kind with which readers would have to be satisfied. But the biblical text provides ever so slightly more information that makes the puzzling passage clear: there are two hundred thousand foot soldiers and ten thousand additional troops from Judah (1 Sam. 15:4). The "gapped" biblical style, which, as Alter suggests, requires the reader's constant participation and informational supplementation, does not specify that the main body of foot soldiers is from Israel, as opposed to Judah, but rather simply identifies by origin only the ones from Judah, forcing the reader to supply the identification of the main body of troops as Israelite. The Yiddish text, on the other hand, even more cryptically, omits all reference to geographical origin, not, certainly, because it is irrelevant to the sixteenth-century Ashkenazic audience of the *Seyfer Shmuel*, but rather because the epic is *midrashic*, that is, it presupposes a well-schooled audience, many of whose members know the biblical text well enough to be able to recite it from memory. The text then often simply outlines the shape of the (biblical) narrative, adds traditional (post- and extrabiblical) detail or episodes or both—also from texts intimately familiar to the poet's audience—and quite often then leaves the informed reader to complete the narrative as such. In some texts (most notably in some sections of the *Seyfer Melokhim*), it seems almost as if it is not the play script, as it were, before us, but only the director's annotations on the script.

A slightly different example of the specifically midrashic identity of the epic may further clarify its nature: in describing the spatial relationship of the Philistine and Israelite encampments in 1 Samuel 17, the Yiddish poet says: "On two high mountains, they could not be separated" (*Seyfer Shmuel*, st. 303), while in the biblical text that separation is precisely the point: "And the Philistines stood on the mountain on the one side, and Israel stood on the mountain on the other side, with a valley between them" (1 Sam. 17:3). Only after his initial description does the epic poet then acknowledge the obvious: "a valley was between the Jews and the heathens," which complicates and, in its seeming contradiction of the previous sentence, indeed calls attention to the same separation that is essential to the logic of the narrative. The Yiddish epic text thus itself functions as a quasi midrash on the biblical text, a glancing blow, deflecting the thrust of the original text toward another issue or another perspective.

The specific wording, idiom choice, interlingual parallels in phraseology, omissions, modifications, and indeed additions from the midrashic tradition itself are not accidental, nor are they to be plotted simply as a matter of how the Yiddish text differs from the Hebrew text, the vernacular epic from the Hebrew Bible. As already noted, between and surrounding those two texts there existed a complex network of other extrabiblical, midrashic texts, such that the fourteenth- or sixteenth-century "ideal reader/hearer" of Yiddish epic immediately knew on the basis of years or even decades of regular *re*reading precisely whence a given nonbiblical detail in the epic was appropriated by the poet; where else in the textual network another biblical detail omitted from the epic was *also* omitted; how the slight shift in geographical or personal names that often occurs in midrashic epic was to be plotted onto the tradition, that is, following *this* midrashic tradition, not *that* one; how an altered sequence of events was to be understood; and so on.[57] For the modern casual reader of Old and Middle Yiddish epic who has not mastered that sacred textual tradition presupposed by the poets of midrashic epic, much of this complexity is opaque or even invisible, which may often simply make the text seem somehow incomplete. For the sixteenth-century audience, that intertextual modality integrated the narrative into the vast traditional network of sacred texts (even as it remained in another sense marginalized, because of its being a popularizing and vernacular text) and imbued the narrative with an immediate aura of familiarity and its readers with a sense of intellectual belonging and cultural community.

The second subcategory of early Yiddish epic, which, for lack of a better term, one might call "secular"[58]—despite the fact that it is at all moments still imbued with the traditional culture of Ashkenazic Jewry—comprises epics whose mode of composition participates in the medieval Pan-European epic tradition of translation and adaptation from a pool of already existing epics from an earlier period and/or another language (generally originating in Old French), as opposed to the practice in Yiddish midrashic epics, which were clearly not translated or adapted from already existing narratives *in epic form* but rather originally composed in Yiddish as epic poems based on traditional materials in nonepic and generally nonpoetic form. The Old Yiddish *Bovo d'Antona*, for instance, was adapted into Yiddish by the famed scholar, printer, poet, commentator, grammarian, teacher and tutor to Jews and Christian Humanists alike Elye Bokher / Elia Levita. By the time that he composed his *Bovo*, in 1507, that originally thirteenth-century Anglo-Norman epic *Bueve de Hantone* had already marched across Europe and into dozens of languages;[59] Levita most likely based his Yiddish poem on a Tuscan adaptation of the tale, but Levita's narrative differs so radically from the specific Tuscan source proposed by some scholars that it is misleading to deem it a translation at all (see below); it seems far more independent a composition even than many medieval epics that are generally treated as independent compositions, such as, for instance, Hartmann von Aue's Middle High German adaptations of Chrétien de Troye's Old French *Erec* and *Yvain*.

A further consideration of the Yiddish "secular" epics is that their sources are without exception non-Jewish. With one exception, the extant texts had specifically German or Italian sources: as noted earlier, the bridal-quest epic of *Dukus Horant* has no known source text currently extant, but may well have had one at the time of adaptation; the anonymous medieval Arthurian epic ווידוּוילט *Vidvilt* was adapted from Wirnt von Grafenberg's Middle High German *Wigalois*, itself an adaptation and combination of episodes from several earlier Old French epics; as just noted, Elia Levita adapted the medieval epigonic epic *Bovo d'Antona* most likely from a Tuscan source; and the anonymous Renaissance epic *Pariz un Viene* was adapted from a Tuscan prose tale. Each of these epics thus represents a different type or subgenre of epic. In *Pariz un Viene*, Yiddish "secular" epic reaches an aesthetic pinnacle comparable to the achievement in the midrashic *Seyfer Shmuel*, both of which may take their places alongside the most magnificent epic poems of other medieval and early modern European literary traditions.

Not surprisingly, this mode of epic arose in Yiddish at precisely that period when the genre was the dominant narrative mode in both German and Italian literature.[60] Such books were in Yiddish often designated *galkhes bikher* (monkish [or simply Christian] books)[61] by authors of religious books in Yiddish, whose condemnations of such narratives as frivolous or even morally corrupting are all but ubiquitous in the prefaces to early Yiddish books of other genres. In the preface to his Pentateuch translation (Constance, 1544), Michael Adam calls them "worthless" and "nothing but lies and invented things." In the preface to his edition of the Psalms (Venice, 1545), Cornelius Adelkind echoes that commonplace, as does Isaac Sulkes in the preface to his translation of the Song of Songs (Kraków, 1579). That culturally momentous collection of tales איין שוין מעשה-בוך *Eyn sheyn mayse-bukh* (A Fine Book of Tales) (Basel, 1602), generally simply called the *Mayse-bukh*, presents itself as an ethically grounded substitute for such godless tales, which are said to be nothing but שמיץ *shmits* (filth). If nothing else, the ubiquity of such diatribes suggests that such texts were, despite pious disapproval, quite popular among Ashkenazic readers.

Among the "secular" adaptations into Yiddish specifically condemned by the rabbis were *Hertsog Ernst* (Duke Ernst) and *Maynster Hildebrant* (Master Hildebrand),[62] neither of which is extant, and הער דיטרייך Her Ditraykh (Sir Ditraykh) (Kraków, 1597),[63] which has survived and may in fact be the *Ditraykh fun Bern* so frequently identified in the prefaces to early Yiddish texts as a narrative with which readers are counseled *not* to waste their time and imperil their souls. With such texts the Yiddish epic tradition already moves sharply away from the mode of "secular" epic poetry as found in *Dukus Horant* or *Pariz un Viene* and toward what we might almost deem a third subgenre of early Yiddish epic, a chapbook (*Volksbuch*) tradition that is further represented by such minimally adapted works as קייזער אקטאוויאן *Keyser Oktavian* (Emperor Octavian),[64] זיבן וויזן מייסטער *Zibn vayzn mayster* (Seven Wise Masters [of Rome]),[65] טיל אוילנשפיגל *Til Aylenshpigl* (Till Eulenspiegel),[66] שילדבורגער *Shildburger*,[67] שפאנישא היידן אודר ציגיינרש *Spanishe haydn oder tsigayners* (Spanish Heathens or Gypsies),[68] פארטונאטוס *Fortunatus*,[69] and די שינה מגלינה *Di sheyne Magelena* (Beautiful Magelena).[70] Based on their publication histories, these books seem to have been popular, and thus were also easy targets for opprobrium in prefaces to pious Yiddish books. Nonetheless, their literary quality is minimal, and they are for the most part barely adapted from their non-Jewish sources: generally the only adaptations found consist in the excision of specific Christian references and the transcription into a

Hebrew-alphabet text cum minimal translation. For these reasons, no representative of this type of quasi epic is included in the present volume.

Although it may initially seem quite superfluous in a volume such as this one, it is necessary—in order to counter misconceptions developed over the course of several generations—to dip briefly into a consideration of a superseded mode of scholarship on Yiddish epic. In the nineteenth century, German studies developed the conception of a class of medieval Christian *Spielmänner* (minstrels) (singular *Spielmann*) who composed and performed their (Middle High German) compositions at the courts of nobles, as well as in less august settings for the common people, wandering from community to community and receiving food and drink along with remuneration for their performances. This conception was never well founded in documentary or other evidence from the Middle Ages, for which reason it was so modified and reduced in the course of twentieth-century Germanistic scholarship as to play at most a minor role. In the early decades of the twentieth century, however, the scholarly consensus was that much of the medieval German epic repertoire consisted of the compositions of such a class of minstrels. In those same decades, a trio of scholars of early Yiddish literature, Leo Landau, Israel Zinberg, and especially Max Erik, imported this so-called *shpilman* theory of poetic composition into Yiddish scholarship, where it dominated conceptions of Yiddish epic for a half century: they posited a professional class of Jewish "minstrels" parallel in function and practice to the (then) posited Christian class of wandering minstrel poets and performers.[71]

One of the primary types of evidence adduced to support this construction was the recurring apostrophe by the narrator in such poems of a seemingly on-site listening audience, such as "now I need to pause to have a cup of wine," or "now let us leave character X for a while and see what character Y is doing." Such markers seem indeed to suggest a rhetoric of performance and might even suggest its "flavor" to readers, but by the time of the onset of the Yiddish epic tradition, especially as it was adapted from Christian (Middle High German and Italian) epics of the late medieval and early modern periods, such markers had long since become conventional components of the rhetoric of the genre that were embedded in the *written and literary texts* of this epic genre and had no direct connection to actual public performance.[72] Whether the epics were chanted, recited, or read aloud in public or silently in private, such apostrophes to the audience were nothing more than the conventions of the genre, marking the narrative transition from one character, scene, or episode to another, or marking the end of a narrative section or canto (by claiming that the reader/reciter/performer was tired or thirsty and would like to take a break before continuing).

Even if one were to take such statements not as rhetorical tropes but as descriptive of the performer's actual state, however, there is nothing in the statements themselves to suggest that the performer was a *shpilman* as such—that is, an itinerant and (semi-)professional musician and singer—as opposed, for instance, to the community rabbi, cantor, schoolmaster, or indeed bon vivant carpenter or grandmother reading to her family. Although there may well have been medieval and early modern Ashkenazic performers akin to the functions of *klezmorim* (musicians), *badkhonim* (wedding entertainers), and *leytsonim* (jesters) known from *modern* Ashkenazic culture, no explicit evidence of their existence survives from that earlier period. In any case, however, as now seems obvious, such performers as are known from Ashkenazic traditions of any period are quite different indeed from the conception of the *Spielmann* as it developed in German studies.

Max Erik nonetheless adapted Landau's import of the concept and broadened it into a full-scale theory of the genesis of Old Yiddish narrative literature—both "secular" *and* midrashic—even though he, too, lacked all evidence for the existence of specifically Jewish minstrels, and whatever quasi-*badkhonim* and *khazonim* he was able to document were anything but uneducated, vagabond minstrels. He nonetheless posited the *shpilman* origin of several Old Yiddish texts, including *Hertsog Ernst*, *Ditraykh fun Bern*, *Mayster Hildebrant*, and the Arthurian romance *Vidvilt*. In fact, however, there is no extant Yiddish version of *Hertsog Ernst*, although some fifteenth- and sixteenth-century Yiddish texts interestingly identify their form and melody as that of *Hertsog Ernst*.[73] Unfortunately for the *shpilman* theory, however, this seemingly corroborating circumstance brings nothing but trouble for the advocate of the theory, since all of the Jewish texts so identified as *be-nign hertsog ernst* (with the melody/metrics of *Hertsog Ernst*) are in rhymed couplets, whereas the extant Middle High German poem *Herzog Ernst*, which putatively served as the model of the imagined but in fact *nonextant* Yiddish text, comprises thirteen-line stanzas, generally rhymed AABCCBDEDEFFF). Moreover, these particular Yiddish texts that claim the melody of *Hertsog Ernst* are not in any sense *epics*, as is the extant German poem, but are instead overtly Jewish religious poems (especially *zmires*) and are written either in Hebrew or in Hebrew-Yiddish bilingual versions. Most important, most of the authors of these poems on the model of *Herzog Ernst* are in fact identifiable, and they were certainly not vagabond minstrels, but rather well-known rabbis. Indeed, almost all the identifiable "makers" of Yiddish literature of this period—who are frequently identified in colophons of Yiddish texts as *shraybers* (authors or scribes), *sofrim* (scribes), *nakdonim* (punctators), and *melamdim* (schoolmasters)—are members of the midlevel Jewish intelligentsia. Erik's notion that such community positions were filled by men who "moonlighted" as *shpilmener* has been roundly rejected by Chone Shmeruk, who points out that it is unlikely that the shiftless vagabond *shpilman* as conceived by Landau, Erik, and others could possibly have been employed by Jewish communities as Torah scribes or prayer leaders in their synagogues, and those individuals who were so employed would not in any case have needed such secondary "employment" as minstrels.[74]

While the conception of a class of vagabond Jewish minstrels, wandering from town to town with their instruments, may have had (and for some may still have) some romantic charm, there is no concrete evidence that such wandering Jewish minstrels ever existed, nor that there might have been any connection between such hypothetical minstrels and actual extant early Yiddish texts, epic or otherwise. Interestingly, as noted above, the no less romanticized notion of the Christian minstrels, the goliards to whom were attributed both the traditions of medieval Latin love lyric and epic poetry and the Middle High German *Spielmänner* to whom were attributed the genre of *Spielmannsepos* (minstrel epic), was in the course of the twentieth century itself deflated and severely restricted by scholarship in the fields of medieval Latin and medieval German studies.[75] On the basis of new discoveries and reevaluation of manuscript evidence, many of the authors of the Latin poems in question have been identified as high-ranking ecclesiastics and scholars, not vagabond students living a life of carefree drinking, carousing, and the spontaneous eruption of polished, erudite, and ironic songs. Likewise, the romantic conception of the German *Spielmann* evaporated in the face of studies demonstrating the incompatibility of that conception of authorship with the nature of the texts themselves as participants in a broad and deep literary (not primarily oral) tradition. That these poems—Latin, German, and Yiddish—had both authors and audiences was, of course, never questioned, but the definition of both was ultimately reconceived on the basis of better scholarly evidence. In the end, Germanistic scholarship has restricted the corpus of the extant repertoire of the *Spielmann* to only five texts, none of which, significantly, is extant in a Yiddish adaptation.

Shmeruk likewise disassembles Erik's attempt to account for the second primary subgenre of early Yiddish epic, the midrashic epic, as simply another mode of *shpilman* composition. This genre is, as already elaborated above, characterized by the authors' profound knowledge of the learned Jewish textual tradition. During the period in question, such knowledge was attainable only by means of long-term *traditional* methods of study, since, among other considerations, the midrashic tradition was at the time available *only* in Hebrew and Aramaic and *only* in manuscript, not in a print form more easily and inexpensively available to a consumer readership (even in the restricted form that the early period of printed books produced). Thus, it would have been all but impossible for traveling minstrel poets to duplicate this mode of learning,[76] even if they had somehow—before becoming itinerant—managed to gain the linguistic and scholarly training necessary to gain access to the texts themselves: the six thousand folios of the Talmud (thirty-seven volumes in the Vilna edition), for instance, would scarcely fit into a vagabond's traveling satchel.

Shmeruk's conclusion seems directly to the point: "In Yiddish literature we find no evidence for the existence of a *Spielmann*." Looking back on this detour in Yiddish studies, it is sometimes difficult to take it very seriously, especially, for instance, in Max Erik's culminating claim that Elia Levita was "the last *shpilman*."[77] Levita, as author of dozens of erudite scholarly works in the fields of Hebrew grammar, lexicography, and masoretic studies; resident in the Roman palace of and Aramaic tutor to Cardinal Egidio da Viterbo for ten years; correspondent of Erasmus and collaborator with Sebastian Münster, printer, translator, editor, and Hebrew poet, was to be imagined as an itinerant, vagabond poet-musician?! Just as scribes and punctators—and thus members of the Jewish educated intelligentsia—were explicitly identified as the individuals responsible for several of the texts from the Cairo codex, it is difficult to imagine Elia Levita, one of the great Jewish men of learning of the sixteenth century, as one of the band of "wandering magicians, minstrels and clowns, cheats and beggars," and Shmeruk suggests that to do so would be "to dishonor the greatest poetic personality of Old Yiddish literature."[78] The Yiddish *shpilman* is a myth that can safely be laid to rest.

Yet another myth deserves the same treatment in the present context, for it is simply not the case, as commonly imagined, that Yiddish *literature* originated in the Rhineland (or along the upper Danube); eventually moved east into Poland, Lithuania, and the Ukraine; and then via the nineteenth- and twentieth-century extra-European diaspora moved on to North and South America, South Africa, and Australia. However one wishes to construct the other nodes of that trajectory, one must take into account at least one other focal territory: for approximately a century in one of its earliest and most significantly formative periods, Yiddish literature was in a profound sense Italian.

Thus, nonspecialists in early Yiddish literature may be surprised to learn that what they have in their hands in the present volume is in a significant sense a collection of works of Italian literature—not in the sense that the texts were written in the Italian language, of course, but rather that the Yiddish language texts were composed, copied, and/or published either for the first time or very early in their history in northern Italy, more often than not in Venice and the Veneto; a substantial portion (probably not the majority) of the audience of this literature during much of this period was likewise resident in Italy.[79] While one could make the argument that early Yiddish literature in general was *in large part* a product of the Ashkenazic sojourn in northern Italy, it is quite especially the case for early Yiddish epic, which is overwhelmingly a matter of Italian provenance: the primary manuscript of the only Yiddish Arthurian epic, *Vidvilt* (Cambridge, Trinity College ms. F.12.44), is from Italy, probably from Venice. The source manuscript of the midrashic epic *Akeydas Yitskhok*, here translated, was copied in Italy. The intercontinental adventure tale of romance and intrigue *Briyo ve-Zimro* was first printed in Venice in 1597. The *Bovo d'Antona* was adapted from a Tuscan version of an Anglo-Norman epic by Elia Levita while he was living in Padua in 1507 (and later published—albeit in southern Germany—with an Italian-Yiddish glossary). *Pariz un Viene* was also adapted from a Tuscan source text, almost certainly in northern Italy, and published in Verona in 1594. Multiple indicators in both the *Seyfer Shmuel* and the *Seyfer Melokhim* point to northern Italy as the location of their composition.[80] While the earliest of the manuscripts of Yiddish epic, the Cambridge codex recovered from the Cairo *geniza* (Cambridge University Library, T.-S. 10K22), in which *Avrom ovinu*, *Yousef ha-tsadik*, and *Dukus Horant* are included, might initially seem the great exception, even here one might speculate—and it is speculation only—that northern Italian mercantile connections to the eastern Mediterranean may well have played a now occluded role in the presence of the codex in the Yiddish-speaking Ashkenazic community of Cairo, which historically had close familial and economic ties to northern Italy, still documented in other texts from the Cairo *geniza*.[81]

While the connection between the Yiddish and the German literary traditions, as articulated above for the genre of epic, may seem more reasonable based on the long residence of Ashkenazic Jews in German-speaking lands, the Italian connection may initially seem somewhat less clear. For a period of three hundred years, however, beginning in the thirteenth century, several waves of Jewish immigration to Italy radically altered the composition of Jewish communities, particularly in Rome and northern Italian cities.[82] These new immigrants arrived as exiles, including Jews from Provence, Sephardic exiles from Spain (after the persecutions of 1391 and especially in the expulsion of 1492)—both of which groups settled especially in northern Italian cities—and the Levantine Jews who had earlier emigrated from the Iberian Peninsula to points in the eastern Mediterranean and then returned West to the Adriatic coastal cities of Venice, Trieste, and Ancona. It was, however, the Ashkenazim from central Europe that formed the largest group, fleeing outright persecution, serial episodes of banishment and exile, plague, and the economic isolation that restricted their lives. In these polyglot and in some essential sense multicultural immigrant Jewish communities in Italy, there were various literary, musical, culinary, and ritual traditions, which were reflected in a variety of ways, including the fact that books that were intended to reach the entire Jewish community were often published in multilingual editions, which, as Baumgarten points out, was perfectly exemplified in a Passover ceremonial (Haggadah) published in 1599 in Hebrew, of course, but with ritual instructions in Yiddish, Italkian (Judeo-Italian), and Ladino, or Jacob ben Joseph Soresina's trilingual guide to cashering in the סדר הניקור *Seder ha-nikur* (Venice, 1595).[83] While Hebrew naturally remained the most prestigious language of culture in these communities, several vernaculars were commonly used, including Ladino, Italkian, local Italian dialects (especially Venetian in Venice and the Veneto), Turkish, and Arabic. Among them was of course also the Yiddish brought from their northern European residence by the numerically largest group of Jews in northern Italy at the time, the Ashkenazim. In the course of time, this language became an important literary language precisely in the northern Italian cities, in particular Venice, where numerous books in that language were written and published even into the early years of the seventeenth century, by which time the process of linguistic assimilation to the local Italian-speaking Jewish populace seems to have progressed far enough that Yiddish book production no longer had a viable cultural or financial function for Ashkenazic Jews dwelling in northern Italy; it thus ceased there, while continuing especially in Amsterdam and various cities in Germany and Poland.

Significantly, Jean Baumgarten goes so far as to call Italy the "birthplace of Old Yiddish literature," since it was there that the poetic forms first adopted in the German-speaking territories were developed into a new literature that broke with those and other past models.[84] It was thus by means of the expanded contact of Jews with the surrounding culture that Yiddish literature opened to the secular or at least to a conception of literature that extended beyond that which was required for contributions to the sacred textual traditions. This modification came about from multiple causes, including

Jewish contacts with Italian Humanists and Humanism, primarily by means of Jewish scholars tutoring Humanists in Hebrew and Aramaic, among them Egidio da Viterbo, Giovanni Pico della Mirandola, and Marsilio Ficino, who thereby gained at least limited linguistic access to the Hebrew scriptures and Kabbalah.[85] Jewish scholars and scholarship profited from the freedom to pursue their studies that they enjoyed in the more open society of the Italian Renaissance. Even so, one may not speak of cultural assimilation: while some Jews did convert, it was in fact rare, and Jewish culture remained closely tied to traditional values and structures,[86] as is also demonstrated in the Yiddish books printed at the time, which are firmly anchored in Jewish traditions.

According to Victor Brombert, human life itself is by definition (potentially) heroic, since it inevitably deals with questions of death and destiny. The hero, necessarily situated between the divine and the common human and something of a transcendental link still bound by the contingencies of mortality and temporality, exists as a node through whom the divine and the hero's own society articulate, which sharpens the society's definition of its own governing values.[87] As C. M. Bowra comments, the hero differs from other humans in degree, but not in kind: the major heroic attributes are, after all, human qualities.[88] The definition of the activity that constitutes the heroic act is naturally a component in the characterization of the hero. That act must, according to Thomas M. Greene, take place in public and "make a difference in an objective sense to the hero's situation or to society's, in the external, visible world." Only in this way does the hero transcend the level of existence on which the rest of humankind dwells. Taking this social function as fundamental, then, Greene postulates that in the end, "the subject of all epic poetry might thus be said to be politics . . . not limited to society [but] . . . embracing the natural and the fabulous worlds, embracing even the moral or spiritual worlds."[89] In this same way, as Morton Bloomfield notes, literary "heroes frequently reflect class, ideological and historical factors which are dominant in the age which produces such works of art."[90] In the context of Jewish epic, specifically early Yiddish epic, by and large a product of Ashkenazic communities in late medieval and early modern northern Italy, one ought then to consider what kinds of heroes, what modes of heroic action, and what categories of political participation early Yiddish epic heroes embody and champion. There is, for instance, no example in Yiddish epic of perhaps the most dominant narrative mode in world epic that leads to the cataclysmic ends of, for instance, an Akhilleus, Roland, Njál, or Sigurðr/Siegfried, who, Morton Bloomfield astutely observes, are in some demonstrable way responsible for their own destruction: "They are noble and admirable, but we are always left with a niggling and even in some cases a strong sense that they deserved their doom" (31). It is clear from the outset that they are indeed heroes; they are a cut above ordinary men in their physical and generally also moral power engagement, breaking the bonds and testing the limits of what constitutes human limitations and human morality. The epic heroes of early Yiddish literature, on the other hand—Abraham, Isaac, Joseph, Moses, David, Solomon, Bovo, Vidvilt, Pariz—attain their heroic greatness relatively early in life and die at great age and in peace. Theirs is thus perhaps the heroism of the literary "romance," as exemplified by a Gilgamesh or an Odysseus, rather than the tragic heroism of the other figures of non-Jewish epic just mentioned. Norman T. Burns and Christopher J. Reagan insightfully find the modes of medieval and Renaissance Christian adaptation of traditional epic form "to be more suitable vessels for the new wine of a new *ethos*."[91] For obvious reasons, the same could be said with even more emphasis for the Ashkenazic poets in their attempts to transform nonepic midrashic traditions and existing Christian epic source texts into specifically Jewish epic in the Yiddish language. Their heroic figures and in general their conception of heroic action, coupled with the formal poetic models both inherited and adapted from the German and Italian traditions, do indeed yield a newly conceived poetic product: Yiddish epic is like none that preceded it.

Some Remarks on the Translation

It would be pragmatic to justify the decisions that led to the inclusion of the texts here translated and to the exclusion of the many other early Yiddish epics that might have been included. Ultimately, such decisions were based both on notions of literary and historical importance and on breadth of representation of *categories* of early Yiddish epic. The three epics here translated from the Cairo codex (Cambridge University Library T.-S. 10K22) from ca. 1382 are included because they represent the earliest extant state of both midrashic and "secular" epic and both the short heroic lay and the longer narrative epic form. *Bovo d'Antona* is included because, despite what might be acknowledged as its general aesthetic deficiencies, it early became and has remained the most famous of Old Yiddish epics and charms even some modern readers. *Pariz un Viene* and *Seyfer Shmuel* are included as the twin pinnacles of early Yiddish literature, the one a "secular" and the other a midrashic epic, each a masterpiece in its own way. They each demonstrate the best of adaptational techniques: *Pariz* as a quintessentially Ariostan epic in Yiddish, making use of the form of *ottava rima* and canto organization, and even prefacing most of the cantos with a preliminary quasi-reflective culturally critical Ariostan proem. The *Seyfer Shmuel*, on the other hand, took the sprawling, multifocal narrative of the biblical books of Samuel and reconceived their focus on David as central heroic figure in late medieval–Renaissance terms as a quasi-"national" hero. *Vidvilt* earns its place as the only extant Yiddish foray into the vast territory of Arthurian epic, in its myriad Pan-European Christian variations perhaps the most productive epic "matter" in all of medieval and Renaissance Europe; the poet's significant reconception of the epic's finale (in comparison with the German source text) demonstrates a mastery of the form and genre. The *Akeydas Yitskhok* focuses on one of the most deeply significant religious narratives in the Jewish tradition and one that has long been a part of Jewish liturgical practice; in its early modern Yiddish adaptation, it makes abundant use of the midrashic tradition, a healthy dose of the comic (Satan's swallowing the flood), to counter the built-in tragedy (Sarah's death) in circumventing the cataclysmic threat to Abrahamic lineage and the reaffirmation of the divine covenant with Israel.

The inclusion of *Briyo ve-Zimro* requires special justification because, despite its being a swashbuckling adventure tale that includes a Jewish king, a Christian pope, and a Jewish high priest, with a sword in a stone, and an Orpheic attempt on the part of the hero to fetch his beloved from the realm of the dead, with action that crosses the sea from Jerusalem to Rome and back and then beyond the pale of death into the life thereafter, it is in fact not an epic at all—in my own adamantly maintained terms—for the simple reason that it is a prose narrative, and not accidentally so. It is included here, only as an appendix, for several reasons: because it illustrates precisely that development out of a late-medieval aesthetic that appears throughout European national literatures at the end of the sixteenth century, precisely at the moment when epic—then *the* dominant literary genre of narrative—began to transform into the newly developing genres of long *prose* narrative, including, of course, the novel. Not coincidentally, the first volume of Miguel de Cervantes's genre-defining novel *Don Quijote*, that arch-condemnation of the aesthetic and ethos of medieval and early-modern romance epic, appeared in Madrid in 1605, less than a decade after *Briyo ve-Zimro* was first printed in Venice. The early forays into the realm of prose tales in the Yiddish literary tradition are well known through various collections of tales, including the near-contemporary books קויא בוך *Ki-bukh* (The Book of Cows) (1595) and the *Mayse-bukh* (1602). But it might be worthwhile to add a second category to the Yiddish chapbook tradition that was already mentioned above in such texts as *Her Ditraykh* and *Keysar Oktavian*, by expanding it to include other tales both longer than the ones included in the collections of tales and of a different and more adventurous character, including the Yiddish *Ben ha-meylekh ve-ha-nazir* (The Prince and the Dervish) and *Briyo ve-Zimro*, which function as a transitional stage between the mode of lengthy poetic narrative that was epic and the prose form that at least in the beginning was, like *Quijote*, in large part simply an anthology of tales with a recurring frame story to link the whole. *Briyo ve-Zimro* is just such a tale, included in the albeit frameless anthology of similar (in general terms of genre) tales found in the manuscript collection of Munich, Bayerische Staatsbibliothek, Cod. hebr. 100. Thus, the quasi-chapbook *prose* tale of *Briyo ve-Zimro* is here translated instead of, for instance, *Her Ditraykh*, an actual chapbook epic (in verse), primarily owing to issues of literary quality and cultural affiliation: although *Her Ditraykh* was obviously a text read by sixteenth-century Jews, it is, to be blunt, neither good literature nor particularly integral to Jewish and Yiddish literature of the period, whereas *Briyo ve-Zimro* qualifies on both of those counts, as well as embodying the rising and transitional form of prose as the literary vehicle of sustained heroic and postepic narrative. It is thus included here not *as* an epic, but rather as an appendix to a collection of epics.

Finally, breaking with the practice otherwise held in this project of including only full texts, two brief excerpts from the *Seyfer Melokhim* (1543) are included in order to illustrate that second-most famous of Yiddish midrashic epics. Conventionally, it and the *Seyfer Shmuel* are characterized as the matched set of midrashic masterpieces. Whereas that conception of the *Seyfer Shmuel* is quite accurate, the *Seyfer Melokhim*—whether as a result of the rather less promising (for epic) source material of the biblical book(s) of Kings or the lesser poetic talents of the Middle Yiddish poet of the *Seyfer Melokhim*—is certainly not a masterpiece, but in its vast length (2,262 quatrains, the longest poem in early Yiddish literature) is indeed with some frequency readable only with difficulty, owing to its syntactic faults and narrative illogic. Thus, only two illustrative examples of successfully adapted episodes are here included as an appendix to the collection of midrashic epics.

Each text has a headnote that provides a very brief introduction to the text, narrative, and origin and includes information about the current location of the original text witness(es) and the standard scholarly edition of the text and translations, if they exist.

The goal in the various translations included in this volume is to provide the reader with a clear understanding of the narrative content of the work, preserving insofar as possible the integrity of individual stanzas and individual lines; to convey in English prose a clear sense of the stylistic register (*not* the poetic form) of the original Yiddish poetry; and to reflect the specificities of Old and Middle Yiddish poetic and idiomatic usage as adapted to the requirements of contemporary idiomatic English prose. In other words, the translation is always to be readable and potentially enjoyable for a general reader whose interest may not be (or may not always be) in a translation that is a window onto the linguistic specificities of the original text. At the same time, however, I have never strayed into paraphrase of the original, so even the reader who has the original text alongside the translation should always and easily be able to keep track of where he or she is in that text.

In order to maintain the connection between the translation and the original text in yet another way, I have retained the numbering of lines or stanzas (whichever is appropriate to the text).[92] I realize that for some readers such numbering can be an aggravating visual distraction. Knowing where one is in the given poem is, however, quite useful for a range of purposes, not least if the reader is reading the original text alongside the translation or finds a reference to the text in a commentary or study of the text. The stanza numbers are reduced in font size to make them somewhat less intrusive, and, as preliminary readers have reported, one's eye rather quickly learns simply to pass over the stanza numbers without distraction, while they are nonetheless still present when one needs them.

Prose was chosen as the form for these translations not simply because of my own lack of poetic skill, but also because it seemed to me necessary that the first collective volume of translations of early Yiddish epic be in straightforward and idiomatic prose suitable for a broad readership. The goal here is an idiomatic modern English prose that presents the denotation and to the extent possible also the connotation of the source texts, including attention to the stylistic and aesthetic register of the originals. Poetic translations, insofar as they are poetic in the language of translation, inevitably distort the content of the original poem *more* than would a careful prose translation, since the exigencies of poetic form in the source and target languages must necessarily differ radically.

With the single exception of the *Seyfer Melokhim*, only full texts are included here, and—with a single further exception—I have chosen to translate them as integral texts (that is, from a single early manuscript or printed edition of a text)[93] rather than combining various extant versions with a line or stanza from one version followed by a line or stanza from another version, which would enable a version of the narrative that might somehow be imagined "smoother" and thus perhaps more in keeping with modern expectations of what constitutes a more flowing narrative. Although such a practice may—with some texts—produce a somewhat more readable text, it likewise produces a text that exists in none of the extant authentic versions from the period and indeed one that probably never existed. Instead, I have chosen what seems to me the "best" text, which sometimes means the earliest text witness of the existence of a particular narrative, while at other times it is instead the most complete version. In several cases, of course, there is no choice at all, since there is but a single extant text. Thus, to illustrate the principle: although one might be tempted to prefer readings from the extant manuscripts of the *Seyfer Shmuel*, when the Augsburg *editio princeps* (the base text of my translation) presents difficult readings, I have generally avoided that practice, attempting instead to make sense of the narrative as printed there. Sometimes it is clear that simple printing errors or more complicated conceptual errors have garbled the sense, in which case I do not hesitate too long before accepting a reading from the manuscript tradition, but it seems to me important, wherever possible, to translate the narrative as presented by the originator of the printed edition, since this narrative was the one actually read by or to the largest audience of the entire *Seyfer Shmuel* tradition over the course of centuries. Thus, for instance, in stanza 798, the manuscripts read וואל *val* ([shield] wall) as the object into which a military charge is made, as opposed to the שאל *shal* (roar) of the Augsburg edition. The manuscript reading might well be preferable here on logical grounds, but there are other differences in the texts as well: in the manuscripts, it is the Jews who are charging into the "heathens," while in the Augsburg edition it is the opposite. Because שאל may also mean "jubilation" and even "glory," one might imagine that the originator of the Augsburg edition was not fumbling and failing here, but rather expressing a loftier, more abstract, and stylistically more elevated thought—"then the heathens charged into the din/glory/jubilation of the Jews," as opposed to the manuscripts' "then the Jews charged into the [heathens'] shieldwall." Is the editor of the Augsburg text *revising* from the more "original" reading of the extant manuscripts? Or did he have a now lost manuscript that provided his reading? We cannot decide such issues. In any case, his reading does make sense and is here retained: perhaps it is a bit more "epic"—or perhaps only a printer's blunder and attempt at recovery.

There are several peculiarities of style in early Yiddish epic of which the unsuspecting reader should be made aware. Leo Fuks succinctly and ungenerously characterizes some of these stylistic aspects: "This language consists primarily of repetition of certain locutions, in the use of meaningless fill-words or vapid added words for the sake of producing the rhyme, in the listing of habitual epithets for certain figures and things, in the employment of constantly repeated assurances of truth, with which the poet maintains his relationship with the listener or reader."[94] One might note that such peculiarities become bothersome intrusions in some texts, while they are used with restraint in others, but in any case they are not restricted merely to Yiddish epic but are in general characteristic of western European epic of the medieval and early modern periods (and, truth be told, they are integral stylistic features of a broad range of epic traditions, ancient, medieval, and modern). To excise such stylistic characteristics for the sake of the modern reader's "convenience" would be to falsify the texts. The reader will then recognize with some frequency such passages or recurring usages (or both) in some of the texts included here.

A recurring syntactic peculiarity of the style is the *apò koinù* (in common) construction, that is, when a word is syntactically to be construed with both the previous and the subsequent phrase, as in the sentence: הוייט הוט דיר גוט יתברך גיענטוורט דיין ויינד זול דר שלאגן ווערדן (Today God, blessed be He, to you has delivered your enemy ought to be slain) (669, 1): דיין ויינד (your enemy) is the direct object of the verb הוט . . . גיענטוורט (delivered) of the first clause but likewise the subject of the verb זול [דר שלאגן ווערדן] (ought [to be slain]) of the second clause.[95] If paraphrasing, we might supplement the text for the sake of syntactic clarity: "Today God, blessed be He, has delivered to you your enemy, *who* ought to be slain." Such constructions, actually rather common in a broad range of European epic traditions, often make the unsuspecting reader stumble momentarily, but are otherwise rather straightforward.

There is a very clear Rabelaisian element, with a pronounced scatological bent, in several of the early Yiddish epics, which may cause dismay for some readers who may deem such elements vulgar and anything but "epic." As generally in the translation, however, I have attempted also in this regard to reflect the stylistic register of the original text as accurately as possible in contemporary idiomatic English. Several examples may illustrate the issue: in *Seyfer Shmuel*, for instance, "When King Saul had taken a shit in David's house, he wiped his ass and went back outside" (597); or in *Pariz un Viene* the narrator characterizes the loyalty of the nonsiblings Pariz and Odoardo to each other by saying that their love for each other could not have been greater even if they "had been born from the same hole" (265,5); or in *Bovo d'Antona*, when Druzeyne finds Bovo less attentive to her charms than she might have wished, she opens her blouse and exclaims: "'Indeed I have here two fine little tits.' She drew out her two snow-white breasts and said: 'Are these mouthfuls to be refused?'" (135–36). As Jean Baumgarten notes on Levita's bawdiness:

> Influenced by the eroticism and bawdy obscenity of numerous courtly romances of the Italian Renaissance, Levita introduced amorous episodes full of easy humor and references to the body's "lower stratum." This tone was quite a novelty in Old Yiddish literature, which, under the influence of the Italian milieu, freed itself from a certain puritanical morality characteristic of the Jewish literature that had originated in the German cultural sphere. Levita loved to play with this erotic element to give his tale a lighter, more sophisticated and freer tone unencumbered by taboo.[96]

Occasionally, the original text seems too laconic for the reader easily to construct a meaningful conception; in such cases, I have either added a footnote or, if a word or two will do, have simply added them—in square brackets to mark them clearly as editorial additions to the original text. The reader may likewise with some frequency be disappointed by the poets' repetitive diction; in *Seyfer Shmuel*, for instance: "While King David was living in Jerusalem, there was a prophet named Nathan with King David. King David said to Nathan . . ." (1082–83); or with Elia Levita's general carelessness in *Bovo* about the logical order of events, as, for instance, when a ship sails away in one line, but does not raise its sail until the next (st. 273, 1–2);[97] or his very obvious struggle with the exigencies of dealing with stanzaic form and rhyme while attempting to tell a good story, which often leads to quite troubled passages.

Such issues as noted in the previous paragraphs arise with some frequency in the texts. While a morally or stylistically squeamish translator might substitute a euphemism such as "relieved himself" in the first passage concerning King Saul,[98] employ only the term "breasts" for the more vulgar synonym used in the original text in the second, substitute a more conventional "womb" in the third, and exchange a pronoun for two of the occurrences of "King David" in the fourth passage, one might still wish to go beyond mere semantic substitution and actually delete Druzeyne's rather graphic reference to "mouthfuls," and change the order of sailing and raising the sail in the final example. In thus revising both the semantics and the narrative content of the text, however, such a translator would have already crossed the line from translation into revision and thus into that territory known from the cliché about twentieth-century Yiddish translations of world classics, which were sometimes designated on the title page as *fartaytsht un farbesert* (translated and improved).[99] Such operations do indeed falsify the text. I neither advocate nor have practiced anything like literal, word-for-word translation in this volume—which would necessarily also falsify the original by making it unreadable in translation—but insofar as the original is idiomatic for its own audience, then the modern translation must attempt to convey that sense to its own audience in its own appropriate idiom. Obviously, in the case of the repetition of "King David" three times in a sixteen-word passage, it is not a matter of idiomatic or nonidiomatic usage, but rather of the poet's insistent emphasis or the momentary lapse of his poetic abilities.[100] That, too, must be preserved, if the point of the translation is to convey an accurate sense of the original text. With some frequency, therefore, stylistically rather "clunky" turns of phrase and entire sentences are to be found in the translation. I would ask the reader to remember that my intention is there always to reflect the style of the original rather than to smooth, hone, reshape, prettify, and revise the Yiddish original into a new composition, a "new and improved" English version.

There is a peculiarity in the tradition of translation from (early) Yiddish that is *not* followed here. Germanists in particular have gotten into the habit of translating the Yiddish words derived from the Germanic component of Yiddish, but of first transcribing the Yiddish words from the Semitic component into the Roman alphabet and only then translating them, generally in parentheses or in a footnote; for example, "And, so *be-sho'o toyve* (finally, at long last), I will begin with this book . . ." This practice reveals the translator's misconception of the text, its cultural context, and its original audience.[101] The sixteenth-century Askenazic audience construed no linguistic suture in the text between the fused elements of the Germanic and Semitic components of Yiddish: it was all simply Yiddish. Modern translators' insistence on a distinction in component so very important that it must be preserved in their translations can be interpreted in a number of ways: it may be the conventional practice of professional German studies scholars to treat Yiddish as if bastardized German with occasional Semitic vocabulary "intrusions"; the Germanic-component vocabulary is then simply translated, while special attention must apparently be drawn to the "alien" Semitic component via Roman-alphabet transcription *and* translation. Or there may be something else at work with other translators: the Roman-alphabet transcription might be thought to enable speakers of Yiddish (or Ivrit) to take some pleasure in the recognition of familiar Semitic vocabulary. In any case, in order to understand how peculiar this practice is, one might imagine a translator of Chaucer who instead of simply translating the text actually retained (in the translation), italicized, and added footnote glosses on all of Chaucer's French, Italianate, and Latinate vocabulary. At some point, one might maliciously ask: is the goal a *translatio* or a *forma peculiaris* of a *fétiche-glossarium*? In the present volume, the texts are simply translated:[102] such phrases as *mazl tov* are thus simply translated into English along with the rest of the Yiddish text, and not transcribed, italicized, retained in the main text, and translated only in a footnote.

I have tried to present the texts in such a way as to be comprehensible to a broad audience of general readers, translating specifically premodern and cultural (especially Jewish) content that might not be known to that audience in such a way as to make it accessible in the text itself. Notes do nonetheless occasionally provide clarification of issues, especially of underlying ambiguity or complexity for which translation alone cannot account.

Because, as is generally the case in premodern Western epic, the verse line most often constitutes a distinct syntactic unit (such that in a practical sense clauses, and generally sentences, are rather short), the syntax of the translation, too, is in general relatively simple. In terms of stylistic register, I have permitted myself a slight bit of archaizing specifically in order to indicate the stylistic register of the text's original language, which was itself for its original audience generally of an elevated and slightly archaic "epic" register. One finds, for instance, somewhat stilted phrases such as "His father is indeed also present" or "Thus did he also proclaim," which few speakers of English would now utter under any circumstances, but which accurately reflect both the (archaic) style and the semantic content of the original text, and that is, after all, the goal of translation. Despite this slight bow to archaic, quasi-epic style in the translation, I have nonetheless avoided the "thee," "thou," "doth," and "goeth" that characterize some renderings of older literary texts. Style is a special concern in the midrashic texts, with their dual archaic tone of both epic and quasi-biblical style. I have nonetheless avoided simply adopting the phraseology of, for instance, the Elizabethan style of the King James Bible, since in fact Yiddish midrashic epic, while often echoing some aspects of the archaic, stilted, and insistently nonvernacular register of early Yiddish biblical translation, generally rejects the distinctive phraseology directly corresponding to what is found in those biblical translations. The Yiddish epic text goes its own way in rather remarkable fashion, generally following the midrashic tradition, but in fact not always adhering strictly to that tradition, either.

The practice of nomenclature in the current volume is twofold: in early Yiddish "secular" epic, where there is no standard practice of naming for the characters who are generally not already household names for a broad reading public, the names are retained in an approximation of their early Yiddish form rather than attempting any anglicization of them. The name of the female protagonist in *Bovo*, דרוזיינה, could have been pronounced as *Druzeyna* or

Druzeyne (three syllables), or *Druzi-yane* or *Druzi-yana* (four syllables), and there is no clear indication of which to choose. The *Drusiana* of the Tuscan tradition should not, incidentally, mislead us into simple adoption of that form. The same is true of אורײאן as *Ori-yon* or *Ori-yan* or *Orey-on* or *Oray-on* or *Orey-an* or *Oray-an*. There is thus a compromise with my use of Druzeyne and Orayon, rather than, for instance, Drusiana and Orion, thus also indicating that they are, after all, names in a Yiddish narrative. In early Yiddish midrashic epic, on the other hand, where the personal and geographical names from the cognate biblical texts are already well known to English readers, those names are presented in the form common to English translations of the Bible (JPS, RSV): thus, *Solomon* instead of *Shlomo* or *Shloyme* for שלמה. The reader should also note that each syllable of a transcribed name from the Yiddish text should be pronounced: thus, Wate has two syllables (watə), Itene and Viene have three syllables (itenə / vienə), and Isabele four (isabelə).

With respect to geographical nomenclature, the fictive realm of romance presents some obstacles: stalwart heroines, for instance, may actually walk from *Vlandern* [Flanders ?] to *Babiloniya* [Babylon ?] carrying two small children, and ships' passengers may disembark "onto the sand" in Cyprus and apparently *walk* from there to Egypt! Insofar as geographical names can be located and identified, they are presented in the common English form; otherwise, they are preserved as in the original text (with a note). There is no attempt to "localize" geographical names, since their specific objective referents for the original audience are either difficult to identify or objectively improbable. The interpretation of geographical nomenclature is nonetheless occasionally more than simply a matter of finding a suitable equivalent, as is especially apparent in the case of the name באבילונײה *Babiloniya*, which a twenty-first-century reader—especially a reader familiar with biblical and ancient Jewish culture—might automatically interpret as the ancient Mesopotamian city. While in the end that interpretation *could* also be accurate for the term's usage in early Yiddish literature, there are moderately interesting historical and literary complications. In the fourth century CE, the Romans built their own fortress town on the east bank of the Nile just south of the river's delta region, at a site on which other forts had long been maintained by previous conquerors. Already at that time the fortress site seems long to have been designated Βαβυλών (Babylōn) in Greek, as indicated by Strabo and Josephus. The fortress town grew and became a center of Coptic Christian culture and eventually developed into the rapidly expanding Islamic city of Cairo. European military activities in northern Egypt during the Fifth Crusade (1213–21) firmly established for European usage the connection of the long-conventionalized geographical name *Babylon* with the city of Cairo. By the late Middle Ages, then, and despite the Christian knowledge of the biblical tradition of Mesopotamian Babylon, it was extremely rare to find a (Christian) European use of the name *Babylon* (outside a biblical context) to refer to anything other than Cairo: the ancient Mesopotamian city of Babylon had been essentially occluded in Euro-conceived geography (until its archaeological rediscovery in the modern period).[103]

For obvious cultural reasons (quite distinct from Christian traditions), there was no ubiquitous *Jewish* melding of the name of ancient Babylon with the conventionalized designation of Cairo. Babylonia was the destination of the biblical exile of the Kingdom of Judah (beginning in 597 BCE, as narrated in several of the prophetic books of the Hebrew Bible), and important Jewish economic and intellectual communities in several Mesopotamian cities continued to exist through late antiquity, eventually producing the most important postbiblical contribution to the Jewish textual tradition, the Babylonian Talmud. Those communities persisted even into the medieval and early modern periods. While medieval and early modern Jews resident in or knowledgeable concerning Egypt would have, of course, known the usage of the term *Babylon* to designate Cairo, the Jewish term בבל *Bavl/Bovl*, inherited from the Hebrew Bible, would almost certainly have generally continued to designate Mesopotamian Babylon.

In early Yiddish epic, the usage is in this respect quite interesting. In the Middle Yiddish *Pariz un Viene*, the character Dolfin is captured in בָּבל *Bovl* (in the Tuscan source text *Babylonia al Cayro*)[104] while traveling in Egypt and then imprisoned in Alexandria. Pariz becomes aware of Dolfin's situation while he is himself in *Bovl* and travels from there to Alexandria by boat in order to rescue him (st. 540, 591). Thus, in the Yiddish narrative, it seems more than likely that Pariz simply travels down the Nile from Cairo to Alexandria, as it was explicitly also represented in the Tuscan source text.[105] In *Bovo d'Antona*, on the other hand, the identity of Babylon is less clear: it is identified simply as the place where the sultan lives and rules (suggesting Cairo?), one may travel through Brabant and Burgundy to get there (st. 231), and, rather surprisingly, by means of a brief sprint one may also reach the sea from there (st. 271–72). Thus, despite the historical fact that no sultan per se ever lived in Mesopotamian Babylon, no other specific circumstantial evidence in the text makes the reader prefer Cairo over Mesopotamian Babylon or vice versa as the referent of the term (no human could, for instance, *sprint* from either Cairo or Mesopotamian Babylon to any "sea"). Interestingly, however, the author, Elia Levita, is inconsistent in his own terminology: in the text itself he uses the term באבילונייה *Babiloniya* six times (6,3; 231,8; 592,8; 594,6; 612,8; 616,6) and בבֿל *Bovl* twice (313,6; 587,8), and in the Italian-Yiddish glossary appended to the text, he glosses באבילונייה *Babiloniya* predictably as בבֿל *Bovl*, the traditional Hebrew/Aramaic/Yiddish designation of Mesopotamian Babylon, which, one might imagine, ought to clinch the case for the identification of this Babylon as Mesopotamian, but it seems still a possibility that in those cases where he retains the Italianate באבילונייה *Babiloniya* in his Yiddish text, his gloss is chosen to guard against his informed readers' interpreting that name as Cairo. In any case, thus differentiating the variant uses, I have translated every instance of Levita's usage of באבילונייה *Babiloniya* and בבֿל *Bovl* as Babylon and every usage of בבֿל *Bovl* in *Pariz un Viene* as Cairo.

The cultural rite of *ḥalitzah*, which is mentioned with some frequency in the texts, should be explained here, so that its meaning is clear in the various narrative situations in which it occurs. The obligation traditionally enabled exogamous marriage by widows (and thus the possible alienation of property) through public ceremony involving the deceased husband's family: according to the Torah (Deut. 25:5–10), a man whose married brother dies childless is obligated to marry the brother's widow; if he refuses, he must perform the rite of *ḥalitzah*, which requires that he declare in the presence of the community elders, "I have no desire to marry her" (v. 8), after which the widow removes one of his sandals, spits in his face, and declares, "This is what is done to the man who does not build up his brother's house!" (v. 9). Therewith is the obligation abrogated, and the widow may contract another marriage if she so wishes.

In the narratives, the issue arises in a number of situations, such as a potential consequence of a husband's dying in battle, which gives rise to the secondary custom of soldiers' providing their wives with bills of divorce before the army's mobilization (*Seyfer Shmuel*, 323, 1247). Because the rite can be performed only by adults, the obligation would be felt as particularly onerous in the situation described in *Seyfer Melokhim* (316), where the widow's husband dies while his brother is an infant, thus obligating her to remain unmarried for the thirteen years required for him to attain the age of majority, at which time he could either marry her or perform *ḥalitzah* to renounce his obligation to do so. The motif is put to a macabre use when Joab calmly asks Abner to demonstrate the ritual of the sandal's removal, which entails his bending over into a vulnerable body posture, which enables Joab more easily to stab him to death in vengeance for his earlier having killed Joab's brother (*Seyfer Shmuel*, 948).

Two modes of reference to the deity deserve comment. The first is a common trope of pious usage, in which the conventional phrase גוט ית' = גוט יִתבָּרך Yiddish *got yisborekh* (God, blessed be He) occurs as a set phrase practically whenever the deity is designated. Despite the fact that such usage may seem intrusive and repetitive to modern (nonpious) readers, each instance of the usage is of course retained here in the translation because it is very much an integral component of the early Yiddish cultural and literary conception.

The second usage seems restricted in early Yiddish to use in "secular" texts or "secular" moments in texts, or to characters without divine favor (for example, Joab, *Seyfer Shmuel*, 1309, 1638–39): the word בוק *bok* is used in the mild oath בייא בוק *bay bok* (literally, "by goat") presumably instead of בייא גוט *bay got* (by God). While one might immediately tend toward an interpretation of this usage as an early example of Slavic influence on Yiddish (Czech *bůh* / Polish *bóg* / Russian *bog* [god]), one must also note that precisely the same usage appears in contemporaneous German (*bei Bock*), including even the expanded version that appears in *Bovo*: בייא דעם אלטן בוק בֿון שוף הויזן *bay dem altn bok fun shafhouzn* (By the old *bok* of Schaffhausen) (st. 41,7).[106] The usage reflects the traditional Jewish taboo on the divine name and even on the word for God in nonsacred contexts, which historically has led to multiple stages of the tabooization of successive euphemisms (the most important being יהוה>אֱלֹהִים>אֲדֹנָי> הַשֵּׁם), and the widespread substitution of euphemism for divine referents in Christian cultures, as well, such as Chaucer's Host's *for cokkes bones* (by the cock's bones), presumably substituting *cokkes* for *Goddes* (fragment X, "Parson's Prologue," line 29), or the Shakespearean *zounds* for "by his [that is, Christ's] wounds," or the common usage in some English dialects of "by gosh," "by golly," or "by gum" for "by God." It is unlikely that the early modern *German* usage of *Bock* for *Gott* is a result of either Yiddish or Slavic influence (or if it were Slavic influence, then it had been so thoroughly integrated that there would have likely been no "component awareness" on the part of sixteenth-century German speakers). As far as the needs of the present translation are concerned, while "by gosh" might have worked for *bay bok*, that English idiom is not malleable enough to render some of the early Yiddish variations, such as "by gosh's liver" or "by the old gosh of Schaffhausen." So I have rendered the usage via the word "goat," both because of its literal equivalence to the word *bok* in early Yiddish and because it is a near homonym of English *god*, perhaps reproducing some of the playfulness of the original. Admittedly, it is not a perfect solution, but accompanied by this explanation, it should suffice for the reader.

References to coins are treated simply: since it is all but impossible to determine whether a fourteenth- or sixteenth-century author might have attributed some specific "real world" value to a named coin in the fictional world of his epic, and if so what that value might have been, I have simply provided translations of the terms (where possible) without any attempt to calculate the late-medieval or early-modern purchasing power of such fictive "literary" or "mythical" money. The following terms are used:

batsn (German *Batzen*), no English equivalent, rendered here as "silver *batsn*": originally a silver coin minted first in the fifteenth century in Bern, Switzerland, but later debased with other metals.

dukat (Italian *ducato*), translated as "ducat": originally a gold coin, of various weights and values; later also made of silver; at various times a coin of international (European) exchange value.

fenik (German *Pfennig*), translated as "penny": originally a silver coin, but debased in the course of the Middle Ages.

groshn (German *Groschen*), translated as "groats": originally a silver coin (first minted in Tyrol in the thirteenth century), later widely minted in debased form.

guldn (Dutch *Gulden*), translated as "guilder": as the name implies, originally a gold coin, but by the seventeenth century made of silver; in different form and value, the standard unit of currency in the Netherlands until replaced by the euro in 2002.

heler (German *Heller*), translated as "half-penny": originally a silver coin worth half a silver penny (minted in Schwäbisch Hall); debased with copper in the course of the Middle Ages, such that it became synonymous with something of no value.

meyt (Dutch *mite*), translated as "mite": a medieval Flemish copper coin of very low value.

scudo (Italian *scudo*), no English equivalent, rendered here in the plural as "silver *scudi*": large silver coins of various values, depending on the place and time of minting; in Italy minted from the sixteenth through nineteenth centuries.

Square brackets are used in two ways: to indicate illegible or lost letters, words, or sentences in the original text, in which case the brackets enclose three dots, indicating ellipsis—"Thereafter [. . .] went to the [. . .]"; and to indicate editorial insertion of words necessary for the sake of the sense of the passage—"the [gatekeeper] giant" (that is, as opposed to the giant who is lord of the castle). Thus, all words in square brackets in the translations themselves are editorial.

Abbreviations

Baumgarten, *Introduction*	Jean Baumgarten, *Introduction à la littérature yiddish ancienne* (Paris: Cerf, 1993); English translation by Jerold C. Frakes: *Introduction to Old Yiddish Literature* (Oxford: Oxford Univ. Press, 2005).
EJ	*Encyclopaedia Judaica*, 16 vols. (Jerusalem: Keter, 1971); 2nd ed., edited by Michael Berenbaum and Fred Skolnik, 22 vols. (New York: Macmillan, 2006).
Erik, *Geshikhte*	Max Erik, *Di geshikhte fun der yidisher literatur, fun di eltste tsaytn biz der Haskole-tkufe, fertsnter-akhtsnter yorhundert, mit bilder un melodyes* (Warsaw: Kultur-lige, 1928; reprint, New York: Alveltlekher yidisher kultur-kongres, 1979); online facsimile, http://sammlungen.ub.uni-frankfurt.de/jd/content/titleinfo/1806399.
Erik, *Roman*	Max Erik, *Vegn altyidishn roman un novele, fertsnter-zekhtsnter yorhundert* (Warsaw: Der veg tsum visn, 1926); online facsimile, http://archive.org/details/nybc203961.
EYT	*Early Yiddish Texts, 1100–1750, with Introduction and Commentary.* Edited by Jerold C. Frakes (Oxford: Oxford Univ. Press, 2004) [cited by text number].
Fuks, *Documents*	Lajb [Leo] Fuks, ed., *The Oldest Known Literary Documents of Yiddish Literature (ca. 1382)*, 2 vols. (Leiden: Brill, 1957).
Ginzberg, *Legends*	Louis Ginzberg, *Legends of the Jews*, 7 vols. (Philadelphia: Jewish Publication Society, 1938–61).

Grimm	Jacob Grimm and Wilhelm Grimm, eds., *Deutsches Wörterbuch*, 2nd ed. (Leipzig: Hirzel, 1854–1971; reprint, Hildesheim: Olms, 2003–; http://germazope.uni-trier.de/Projects/DWB).
Hakkarainen	Heikki J. Hakkarainen, *Studien zum Cambridger Codex T.-S. 10. K. 22*; 1: *Text.* Turun Yliopiston Julkaisuja/Acta Universitatis Turkuensis, ser. B, vol. 104 (Turku, 1967); 2: *Graphemik und Phonemik.* Acta, ser. B, vol. 174 (Turku, 1971); 3: *Lexikon.* Acta, ser. B., vol. 182 (Turku 1973).
Katz, *Poems*	Eli Katz, ed., "Six Germano-Judaic Poems from the Cairo Genizah" (PhD diss., Univ. of California at Los Angeles, 1963).
Shmeruk, *Prokim*	Chone Shmeruk, *Sifrut yidish: Perakim letoldoteah* (Tel Aviv: Porter Institute, 1978); revised Yiddish translation, *Prokim fun der yidisher literatur-geshikhte* (Tel Aviv: Peretz, 1988).
Verfasserlexikon	*Verfasserlexikon: Die deutsche Literatur des Mittelalter*, 2nd ed., 10 vols., edited by Kurt Ruh et al. (Berlin: de Gruyter, 1978).
Zinberg, *Geshikhte*	Israel Zinberg/Yisroel Tsinberg, *Altyidishe literatur fun di eltste tsaytn biz der Haskole-tkufe*, vol. 6 of *Di geshikhte fun der literatur bay yidn*, 2nd ed. (Vilne: Tomor, 1933; reprint, New York: Shklorsky, 1943; English translation by Bernard Martin, *Old Yiddish Literature from Its Origins to the Haskalah Period*, vol. 7 of *A History of Jewish Literature* (Cincinnati: Hebrew Union College Press, 1975); online facsimile, http://archive.org/stream/nybc200256#page/n0/mode/2up.

Midrashic Epic

1

Abraham Our Father

אברהם אבינו / *Avrom ovinu*

Anonymous, ca. 1382

As is standard in early Yiddish midrashic poems, this heroic lay is based on biblical characters but not directly on biblical narrative itself. It makes particular use of the postbiblical midrashic traditions of Abraham's recognition of the God of the Hebrew tradition and his serial destruction of the idols commercially produced by his father (cf. *Bereshit rabbah* 38, 13, and the Old Yiddish צאינה וראינה *Tsenerene* on Gen. 11:28). The lasting theological import of the narrative is obvious in Abraham's direct recognition of the creator God and that deity's overt intervention in human affairs to save Abraham from harm and thus—in a complete break with the narrative trajectory of biblical narrative—convert all Mesopotamians to belief in the Hebrew God. The Abraham of this heroic lay thus virtually "invents" monotheism while still an innocent child not yet fully initiated into the polytheistic belief system of the Mesopotamian culture in which he lives. Despite its overt theological content, there is more than a hint of humor evoked in the poem, especially in the "tests" to which Abraham puts the sculpted idols. The poem comprises 105 four-line stanzas, rhymed AABB, beginning with a paean of praise to God, a widespread component of early Yiddish poems. On the codex in which the text is transmitted, see the general introduction to this volume.

Source: Cambridge University Library, T.-S. 10K22, folios 6v–17r.

Edition: Fuks, *Documents*, I and II, 25–67 (manuscript facsimile + German translation); Katz, *Poems*, 91–112; *EYT*, 5.

Translation: Fuks, *Documents*, II, 25–67 (German).

Research: Ginzberg, *Legends*, I, 183–308, esp. 213–17, and V, 207–69; Shmeruk, *Prokim* 33–36, 133–39, 182–99; Baumgarten, *Introduction*, 132–36; Walter Röll, "Zu den ersten drei Texten der Cambridger Handschrift von 1382/1383," *Zeitschrift für deutsches Altertum* 104 (1975): 54–68; Walter Röll, "Awroham owinu ('Unser Vater Abraham')," *Verfasserlexikon*, I, coll. 573–74; Wulf-Otto Dreeßen, "Midraschepik und Bibelepik: Biblische Stoffe in der volkssprachlichen Literatur der Juden und Christen des Mittelalters im deutschen Sprachgebiet," *Zeitschrift für deutsche Philologie* 100 (Sonderheft *Jiddisch*, 1981): 78–97.

(1) He who travels the old and well-built streets and avoids and abandons the newer paths will very seldom go wrong. If his faith is in control, it is said that all will go well. (2) If you should [. . .] with new [. . .] too soon, and sing that [. . .], it [. . .] one might find [. . .]. Dear God, I want to turn my mind to another thing. (3) I would like to begin with God, the most exalted, Whose praise no tongue can fully express, Who lets the good sun shine on both good and evil people and purposefully grants His grace in truth. (4) When I can see Heaven's expanse beautifully compassed, then must I avow His mastery and all glory and all the other deeds of His hand that I cannot name: then must I acknowledge His mastery of everything. (5) Whoever then asks, "Where is God?" seems a fool, so that I in turn can ask him: "Where is He not?" He has bespread the whole world with His divinity. Whoever rouses His ire is a fool. (6) Whoever angers Him is dead even as his body still lives: his body must suffer affliction; his soul comes to great distress. Whoever rejoices in His will and earns His grace—his soul will live when his body has died. (7) He is both far and near, as anyone can perceive: He is distant from the evil and is present with the good. He is quite hidden from evil hearts and shines on the good both evening and morning. (8) Whoever has need of His help, let him seek His greeting and entreat Him devoutly: he will find relief from his troubles. He will find complete succor—that I have myself experienced; he will be quite freed of his cares. (9) For bright eyes, He is Himself a radiant light. For the languishing heart, He is a sweet and pure wine, for a bitter disposition even sweeter than figs. I will ever bow to His divinity. (10) His merciful heart is quite rich in virtues. His mercy is unlike human mercy, for His merciful hand is always quite open. He is quite untiring in His generosity. (11) He was the same from the beginning and will ever remain so: mighty King and Lord Host of us all. He well confirms our inheritance, for we are indeed His guests. He was the beginning and is also the end. (12) He created all the wide world with His command: both leaf and grass, mountain and valley, the surge of the savage sea, the heavens and the earth. Thereafter He created a man. (13) He constructed him according to His own shadow-image; He called him Adam. He put him in charge of things both wild and tame. He removed a rib from his body while he was sleeping and crafted it into a woman for him. (14) From those two bodies, we, too, are descended, as we have heard the truth from our

forebears. They lie in the earth; their bodies have died. But their seed is very much alive. (15) If I were to tell everything from the beginning up to now—every birth—it would begin to become too long. I will keep silent about all of them who descend from him and will sing of holy Abraham.

(16) Abraham's father was a maker of images who was never able to write or read a single letter of the alphabet. He could make images of silver and gold and also of wood, according to his desire. (17) The heathens who were there, they had a foolish custom that had long accompanied them up to this point, so that they ever worshipped idols and strayed far from faith in God. (18) They said: "the God in Heaven, who made the heavens and created the seas, is much too exalted for us. He built too high and dwells too far from us. We want someone to whom we can lament for what we suffer. (19) We have to make gods who stay near us. To them we can lament for what we suffer, whom we otherwise wish to praise and serve. And if they do not do so, we will give them a thorough thrashing." (20) They were quite duped by illusory deception; they had strayed very far from God. Each one had an idol to which he lamented his afflictions and told all of his cares.

(21) Abraham's father was at this time praised and honored, his acclaim spread far and wide, for he could make idols expertly, well adorned, so that they could prosper. (22) While they were serving heresy so well, more than I can say or ever wish to sing, there shone a bright star through the dark cloud to comfort the ignorant folk.

(23) A child had been born to that same image-maker, who was to bear little fruit that was true to his father's type. Quite early he began in truth to turn his mind toward the love of merciful God. (24) Good Abraham was three years old, as the Holy Scriptures have truly told us, when he first began to believe in God. He was born at a propitious hour. (25) Now hear a wondrous tale, how that child began to surpass many an older man in his wisdom. He refined and separated the silver from the lead and indeed eradicated heresy.

(26) One day his father said: "Abraham, dear child, take these gods that are ready here. Make your way to market and sell them, every one. If you succeed, we will all be rich." (27) Good Abraham loaded himself up with the gods. He greatly desired that God would know his mind. He went on his way to the market; his burden seemed to him too heavy. O how gladly he would have been done with this. (28) He thought to himself, "If only I knew to whom I could lament, that I, such a little person, have to carry the heavy gods. It would be much more proper if they were to carry me—that I say quite openly. I am going to treat them quite differently." (29) He dumped them on the ground and picked up a large stone. He broke the head of one, broke the leg

of another, smashed the arm of another, and pounded the back of another to bits. He picked them up and carried the pieces home.

(30) Then his father said: "O dear child, how has it happened that these gods have remained unsold?" He said: "Dear father, I was ever unable to sell them: I have never seen gods cause such trouble. (31) As I struggled to carry them to market, they began a great quarrel. Each beat the other; they brawled and punched each other. If you do not believe me, have a look yourself." (32) "Be silent, dear child; your false opinion has indeed deceived you, for how could one small piece of wood thus beat the other?" He dumped them on the ground and let him have a look for himself. He began to tear at himself because of his great sorrow.

(33) He said: "My very dear father, now do not tear at yourself that way. You should be happy that they started such a brawl. For had their great rage been vented on you, you might have suffered great injury." (34) "Be silent, foolish child! Shut your mouth! For how could a piece of wood do me such great injury?" He said: "That same thing has confounded me: that you had not come to that realization. I do not understand what you have in mind with the pieces of wood." (35) Then his father said: "Now put aside your resistance. Sell these gods that are ready here."

With a heavy heart he carefully took them up. He wished that they were lying among the glowing coals. (36) When holy Abraham arrived there at the market, he set all his father's gods before him. He offered them at a very high price to anyone who began to bargain for them. He wished that they were lying in the fire.

(37) Now see where an elderly woman stepped up before him and earnestly requested that he give her a little god so that she could pay for it. As they spoke, a great quarrel arose. (38) "So what is the problem, you foolish woman? You have a childish heart and an old body. That you have acted foolishly for so many years! After all, you are no longer a seven-year-old!" (39) "Tell me, my dear child, what have I done to you? If I have bargained for a little god with you, you should not let that cause you to drive me away, for unfortunately I cannot, after all, pay for a large one." (40) "There is no longer any reason for you to desire either the large ones or the small ones. Indeed if you were to avoid both of them, you could abandon your foolishness for years to come, if from now on you would like to avoid your fraudulent jabbering." (41) "So, what are you talking about, my dear child? It is indeed no fraud, but a little god. If I had it, my sorrows would disappear completely. If I pray to it, I would overcome my sorrows." (42) "So, who has aided you in adversity up to now—provided water and bread for some eighty years? These gods were after all not

yet made before your time. You have been stricken with foolishness." (43) "Tell me, my dear child, who did it? If you identify Him to me, I will gladly give Him his due." He said: "God, Who created you, did it, the one who created the heavens and the earth." (44) "That is true, dear child; you have spoken the truth to me. What I earlier thought causes me sorrow. I will believe in this same God forevermore. He is truly God, a true aid in adversity."

(45) With such words he converted both women and men. He took all of his father's gods away unsold. He carried them carefully on his back. His father's loss was his great fortune. (46) When he entered his father's house thus burdened, how poorly did his father welcome him. He said: "When you go to the market, you do nothing but chatter. You cannot gain any profit for us." (47) He said: "My dearest father, why do you speak thus? If I could have sold them, I would be very happy about it. But they beat me all over my back. That afflicted me—about that you can believe me! (48) If I could have sold them, so that we made a profit, I would never have come home thus burdened. Before I suffer great harm from them, I would burn them on the hearth." (49) "Now be silent, my dear son! How you talk like a child! Of course you know that all these gods are holy and might not be burned in a fire. Now, say no more. Otherwise you will begin to anger me." (50) With those same words the conversation ended, so that the little child rejoiced and was very happy that he had so thoroughly accomplished his will and had not been given a whack.

(51) When this incident had been quite forgotten, his father said: "Up with you and make a journey. If we could sell the gods, we would have done well. I am now quite pinched in my resources." (52) He carefully took them up and departed. He turned his heels toward his father's door, slung the sack over his shoulder, and set out across the fields. He began vehemently to berate the idols. (53) He said: "Cursed idols, cursed may you be! You have ridden my poor back until it is worn out. If the true God sends me His aid, I will quite eradicate your religion." (54) He went on his way to market; the trip seemed too long to him. The burden was too heavy for him; his body was too weak. He came to a broad and powerful river. "In truth," he thought, "here flows forth a great spring." (55) He threw the sack to the ground. He began to grow very weak. He said: "Listen, you gods, I carried you this far. Now, you carry me across. You will ever be honored for that. If you do not do it, I will spread word of your disgrace more and more. (56) If I were to carry you across, I would be acting the fool. Indeed the river has washed away bridges large and small. Now, carry me across; you will surely survive that. If you do not do it, I will let you float away yourselves." (57) No matter what he said to them, they were quiet as a badger. He turned yellow with rage, like a twisted

beeswax candle. He threw the sack to the ground with hatred and ferocity. He dumped them out and let them float away. (58) He said: "Wade across; no need to hurry. You go first and find the ford for me. I will wade right after you. When you get across, wait for me there. If you do not do so, I will spread word of your disgrace." (59) Their heads came to the surface and they floated away downstream. He called after them very loudly, so that it resounded a long way: "Come back, come back! You are not paying attention. You did not quite manage to find the proper ford."

(60) That which he called after them had no effect on them. They floated away and did not turn back toward his words. He turned his back on them, too: he had had enough of them. He arrived at his father's house quite unburdened. (61) When the image-maker saw the empty sack, he was very happy. Now hear what he said: "Well, my dear son, how did the business go? Did we again suffer loss or make a profit?" (62) He said: "Dear father, I cannot hide it: you have to entrust your gods to someone else. They do not obey me: I seem too small to them. When I speak to them, they do not know what I mean. (63) When I had carefully loaded them on my back, I carried them quite directly to the stream of a river. I earnestly requested that they consider carrying me across the river without getting my feet wet. (64) Behold, they gave me no reply and had their fun. Then I also foolishly got involved in a vehement quarrel. I said: 'I would still like to come to another agreement with you: if you wade ahead, I will wade after you.' (65) I dumped them in the river, and they floated downstream. I called after them very loudly, so that it resounded a long way. I imagined that they had floated beyond the right place. But now they have floated off in a different direction."

(66) "Come here, you—now and eternally—foolish child. Well you know that these gods are all wooden, that none of them can either see or hear. Child, your foolishness has beguiled you. (67) The loss has taken place; never has a loss been deflected. A child can be born only with a childish nature. If I had sent a wise man to the market, I would have sold my wares better." (68) He said: "Father, when I carried your gods away, you said that they were respectable, prudent, and noble. Had I known that they were so very depraved, I would certainly never have relied on them."

(69) The image-maker looked at his son in amazement that he spoke so scornfully of his gods. It greatly surprised and astonished him. In his rage he became redder than an ember. (70) He said: "My very dear child, who gave you the advice [. . .] first of all [. . .] my [. . .] steal [. . .] quite from them [. . .] belief." (71) He said: "Dearest father, I will give you this advice: your

gods have to be lifted and carried. How could blows harm me more?[1] My very young heart gives me this advice."

(72) That image-maker fell into a fierce rage. He said: "Most foolish child, which god have you chosen for yourself? Have you seen no other god on earth? Child, you wish to become quite irreligious." (73) "No, dear father. May that never happen to me that you could hear or see my God. He is concealed and hidden from seeing eyes. I believe in Him both evening and morning." (74) "Be silent, most foolish child! Do not say that anymore! You are indeed greatly offending the heathen faith. You need to change your attitude—that is my advice to you now. And spare me your sermons!"

(75) The child kept very quiet so that it was every [. . .]. His father preached to him [. . .] child stood steadfast against him. He said: "You [. . .] that now [. . .] more [. . .] faith well weaken.

(76) [. . .] were; they had a foolish custom. [. . .] up to this point had followed for very many years. [. . .] in every city had a house of prayer, in which they all prayed daily. (77) They all went into the house daily to pray: quite early in the morning and quite late in the evening. Everyone had to stand guard before the gods for a night and protect them from harmful things. (78) Behold, how guard duty had come to the image-maker. He said to his child: "Most beloved Abraham, you are to stand guard in my place; I cannot forgo that." The child said: "Gladly, dear father." (79) When holy Abraham went to the idols, he quietly stepped into the doorway; no one welcomed him. He said: "Who has ever seen such very inconsiderate hosts who could not welcome their guests."

(80) The night was so dark, and cool was the wind. Snow began to fall, and the child began to freeze. He said: "I am freezing! O, how I would like to sit in a warm place! I have never in my life seen such poor hosts." (81) He [. . .] the door. He said: "Now lie there and sleep until I wake you. You will never again be in my father's sack. (82) You have quite completely pounded my [. . .], ridden my back to death from market to market. You have thus far shown little care for me. I have repaid you for that treatment."

(83) Finally he arrived there at his father's house. His father said: "Why do you return so early?" He said: "I have guarded your gods so well. I made a nice fire of them." (84) "Come here, now and forevermore," said his father at once. "I clearly hear by your tone that you have burned them up." He said: "Dear father, now do not shout too much. You will never see your gods again."

(85) When the heathen people were to go to prayer, they found their house of prayer in very bad condition. They saw the smoke surging through the

walls—indeed a Christian priest could have sung there with honor! (86) They all forced their way inside through the door. They saw their gods with great anguish: burnt and quite charred in the hot fire. Scanty were the joy and delight to be found there. (87) Then the heathen people wept and shrieked. Meanwhile they sang a very sad song. They wept and shrieked and wrung their hands. They began to send for the image-maker.

(88) The poor image-maker came very sorrowfully. He had left holy Abraham at home. When he saw his gods smoldering on the hearth, he tore his hair and collapsed onto the ground. (89) They said: "Where is your son? Now, command that he himself come. He will never have any profit from the injury that he has done to us in his burning our gods unjustly. He must suffer the same punishment."

(90) Then holy Abraham came; quite cheerful was his mood. He was not at all afraid; his character was steadfast. His cheeks seemed to burn—they were as red as a bright rose; I say that without any frivolity.

(91) Nimrod, who ruled there, said: "Tell me, most foolish child, who told you to do this—to burn these gods unjustly? For that, child, you must suffer the same punishment." (92) "Indeed they were not gods," said the child at once. "After all, my father made them with his own hands. The gods that my father can make—I pay them little heed. *He* is God Who made my father, (93) the God Who here created the whole, wide world, both leaf and grass, mountain and valley. Faithful to Him will I live and die. I trust completely in Him that He will not let me come to harm." (94) Then Nimrod said: "If the God Whom you have recognized can deliver you from the hand of us all, so that you might survive this hot fire, then I will pay a high price for your faith."

(95) The tiny child was quickly bound. They heated an oven and threw him inside. He lay rolled up like a ball. In the blink of an eye he was discovered. (96) Holy Michael went to stand before our dear Lord. He said: "My most beloved Lord God, now let me go there. I can indeed rescue him and burn those who enrage You every day." (97) Then Holy Gabriel said: "My most beloved Lord, now let me go there. I want to be Your envoy. I can indeed cool down the fiery oven a great deal, so that the one who is being purified in the fire for You will not feel the fire."

(98) Then our dear Lord said: "Indeed he has recognized Me. I will deliver him with My own hand. I will not send a envoy there in My place. I will Myself put an end to his affliction." (99) God's glory appeared to the dear, beloved child.

The inside of the oven glowed the color of red garnet. The fire and the heat began to surge forth from it. The heathenry all had to leap away. (100)

Then our dear Lord said to the precious child: "I have rescued you; you ought to do My bidding. Attend to and rejoice in My will; then I will strengthen you and multiply your seed."

(101) The door of that oven was opened for the child. He got up very quietly and went out. His eyes shone like the morning star. The poor image-maker was very happy to see that. (102) He said: "Fortunate am I, dear child, that I have seen this: that you have experienced this splendor here. I will believe in your God forever more. He is truly God, a true aid in adversity." (103) The heathen people all crowded in there, a great horde of men and women. They made their vows to God and raised up their hands. Behold, heathenry had its end there.

(104) Children, believe altogether in Almighty God. Attend to His will and fulfill His commandments. You ought to do that, you men, along with your wives. If you do that, then you may prosper. (105) Now attend to His will as long as you live. Isaac the scribe gives you this advice. And if you do that, then you cannot be brought low. Thus will you enter the eternal heavenly kingdom.

2

Joseph the Righteous

יוסף הצדיק / *Yousef ha-tsadik*

Anonymous, ca. 1382

Based ultimately on the characters of Joseph and Potiphar's unnamed wife, introduced in the cryptically narrated episode of Joseph's rejection of his slave master's wife's attempt to lure him into sexual transgression in Genesis 39:7–20, this heroic lay's content derives from the widely known postbiblical Jewish traditions, particularly the midrashic sources on the biblical story.[1] The poem's central motif—of the Egyptian women guests of Potiphar's wife being mesmerized by Joseph's beauty and cutting their fingers while peeling apples—originates in the midrash, where it was quite widespread. It was also incorporated into the Qur'ān (12:31) as well as a broad range of other realizations in early Islamic literatures.

The poem is composed of thirty-eight rhymed couplets, with the initial letters of each forming a Hebrew-language acrostic: first a (slightly modified) list of the letters of the Hebrew alphabet, which conventionally would have been followed by the scribe's name, which is not the case here, followed by the word נקדן *nakdan* (punctator). On the codex in which the text is transmitted, see the general introduction to this volume.

Source: Cambridge University Library, T.-S. 10K22, folios 17v–18v.

Edition: Fuks, *Documents*, I and II, 68–72 (manuscript facsimile); Katz, *Poems*, 113–15; Chone Shmeruk, "The Hebrew Acrostic in the *Yosef Hatsadik Poem* of the Cambridge Yiddish Codex," *Michigan Germanic Studies* 3 (1977): 67–81; *EYT*, 6.

Translation: Fuks, *Documents*, II, 68–72 (German); Joachim Neugröschel, *No Star Too Beautiful: Yiddish Stories from 1382 to the Present* (New York: W. W. Norton, 2002), 6–8 (poetic paraphrase).

Research: Ginzberg, *Legends*, II, 3–184, esp. 39–58, and V, 324–77; Shmeruk, *Prokim*, 36–37, 182–99; Baumgarten, *Introduction*, 132–39; Frederic Everett Faverty, "The Story of Joseph and Potiphar's Wife in Mediaeval Literature," *Harvard*

Studies and Notes in Philology and Literature 13 (1931): 81–127; Hans Priebatsch, *Die Josefsgeschichte in der Weltliteratur: Eine legendengeschichtliche Studie* (Breslau: M. & H. Marcus, 1937); Pavel Trost, "Zwei Stücke des Cambridger Kodex T-S 10, K. 22," *Philologica Pragensis* 4 (1961): 17–24; Pavel Trost, "Noch einmal zur Josefslegende des Cambridger Kodex," *Philologica Pragensis* 5 (1962): 3–5; James W. Marchand and Frederic Tubach, "Der Keusche Joseph. Ein mitteldeutsches Gedicht aus dem 13.–14. Jh.: Ein Beitrag zur Erforschung der hebräisch-deutschen Literatur," *Zeitschrift für deutsche Philologie* 81 (1962): 30–52; Peter Ganz, Frederick Norman, and Werner Schwarz, "Zu dem Cambridger Josef," *Zeitschrift für deutsche Philologie* 82 (1963): 86–90; Dov Sadan, "The Midrashic Background of 'The Paradise': Its Implications for the Evaluation of the Cambridge Yiddish Codex (1382)," in *The Field of Yiddish: Studies in Yiddish Language, Folklore, and Literature*, edited by Uriel Weinreich, 2nd collection (The Hague: Mouton, 1965), 153–62; Wulf-Otto Dreeßen, "Midraschepik und Bibelepik: Biblische Stoffe in der volkssprachlichen Literatur der Juden und Christen des Mittelalters im deutschen Sprachgebiet," *Zeitschrift für deutsche Philologie* 100 (Sonderheft *Jiddisch*, 1981): 78–97; James L. Kugel, *In Potiphar's House: The Interpretive Life in Biblical Texts* (Cambridge, MA: Harvard Univ. Press, 1994), 28–65; Shalom Goldman, *The Wiles of Women/The Wiles of Men: Joseph and Potiphar's Wife in Ancient Near Eastern, Jewish, and Islamic Folklore* (Albany: SUNY Press, 1995), 102–6; Chava Turniansky, "Einav ke-khokhavim, se'aro ke-zahav: *Yosef ha-tsadik* be-shir kadum be-yidish," *Tarbiz* 76 (2007): 471–500.

I would like to sing marvels for you—if it were not too tedious for you—how good Joseph tamed his heart in all the situations when his master's wife requested that he lie with her and commit transgressions. Graciously Joseph answered his fair mistress: "How might I bear this transgression for evermore? I would do everything that I could to do your will, except for allowing this transgression to burden my soul."

Then she went away and boldly[2] assembled all the worthy ladies who attended her. How graciously the noble and lovely lady said: "I have the most genial servant whom any lady ever obtained: his eyes are like the stars, his hair like gold, so that my heart loves him beyond all measure. He is like a king in his face, and with his dignities like one who should be the ruler of a land. Virtue and dignity follow him at all times: virtue at the right hand, and dignity at the left. Indeed I entreated him to sleep with me in my herb garden; I wanted to wait for him there. I was quite incapable of bringing it about that I might gaze at his lovely face. Bright and clear are his eyes: brilliant as the morning star and beautiful as the rays of the sun. My heart had been set aflame and [. . .] Thus had the good hero overcome my [. . .]. Now gather around, ladies, and come, all of you, and follow me. I want to let you look at this magnificent warrior." "Keep silent about this matter!" shouted the ladies. "How might a little Jew delight us so?! He simply must be put on display," said the ladies then.

All together they arose and went away with her. She ordered silk pillows and folding chairs well inlaid with gold to be brought in. Demurely the ladies sat, all together. Then the mistress, the noble and lordly one, spoke: "Joseph, my servant," said the lady then, "Come here and stand with courtliness before these beautiful ladies." Quickly he sped to do her bidding. O how courtly did the hero stride forth.

She had beautiful red apples brought out that would give the worthy ladies much delight. "Bring forth the knives—you should choose the finest ones—so that these worthy ladies can peel their apples with them." The servant came quickly with the knives. Each of the ladies took one of the knives. "Peel your apples," said the lady then. They peeled their apples and gazed at Joseph: their hands became carved up and lacerated. Then the worthy, noble and most bold lady said: "Now look, worthy ladies, how you are all so enflamed that you have cut your fingers most exceedingly."

They were quite embarrassed and began to glance around. They themselves did not quite understand how or what had happened to them. "Joseph, my servant," said the lady quickly then, "now serve these ladies drinks with your snow-white hand." He poured them mead and pure wine, which he offered to them there. He was very embarrassed and blushed from shame. He served the ladies drinks with his white hands. The ladies gazed at his eyes; his heart he had sent up to God. He was serving drinks to the ladies at this same moment. They all gazed at Joseph while holding their goblets to their lips. Their bright complexions had gone quite pale, and the golden goblets in their hands sank slowly downward. Because of their great love, they could no longer look at him. They had to tell the whole truth to his mistress. They stood up, all together, and kissed him on the head. They said: "It would be proper for you to rule a noble kingdom."

Now attend to this great marvel, how this hero—only through his heart, which he had mastered—soon thereafter took control over all the lands of Egypt. His virtues were manifold. For God's sake, dear people, take this as your model, that you keep your bodies chaste. Now, if all your bodies be chaste, then you will be granted the holy kingdom of Heaven.

The End.

3

Book of Samuel

[שמואל-בוך] משה עשרים וארבע, ספֿר שמואל / *Seyfer Shmuel*

Moses Esrim Vearba, composed fifteenth century;
earliest ms. 1525; published 1544

The narrative that has long been considered the masterpiece of Old Yiddish midrashic epic, the ספֿר שמואל *Seyfer Shmuel* (Book of Samuel), was also known already in the sixteenth century by the alternate title שמואל-בוך *Shmuel-bukh* (Samuel-book). While the first edition was published in 1544 (Augsburg), there are manuscripts that predate that publication, the earliest now extant dating to the first quarter of the sixteenth century. The date of the epic's composition is unknown and disputed, with some scholars arguing for a date as early as 1300. Most likely it was written in the late fifteenth century, and, based on a variety of evidence, it seems likely that it was written in northern Italy.[1] The epic comprises 1,792 four-line stanzas rhymed AABB, followed by a colophon of twelve rhymed couplets; each line is divided rhythmically into two half-lines of three primary accents each.[2] The poem's melody was also used for the performance of numerous other Yiddish and bilingual Hebrew-Yiddish poems, which were then identified as performed *be-nign shmuel-bukh* (to the tune of the *Shmuel-bukh*). Wulf-Otto Dreeßen argues compellingly that more than merely indicating that a poem is sung to the melody of the *Seyfer Shmuel*, the phrase signifies that the *Seyfer Shmuel* had become a formal model in verse form, stanzaic form, melody, and even genre.[3]

The author's identity, long debated in Yiddish studies, has still not been definitively resolved. At the end of the Paris manuscript, משה עשרים וארבע *Moushe esrim ve-arba* (Moses of the Twenty-Four Books) is named as author. This Moses is now generally identified with an emissary known by that name, who was sent to Turkey from Palestine in 1487 and charged with the duty of collecting money for the poor of Jerusalem. Contrary to Felix Falk's notion that the byname of Moses "of the Twenty-Four Books" indicates his intellectual and educational limitations to nothing more than a reading ability of the Bible, Chone Shmeruk maintains that the epithet identifies someone who had a "great expertise in the Bible," as opposed to, for instance, a specialist in *halakhah* (Jewish law), and is thus not a negative evaluation of the person's knowledge of the Bible and midrash.[4] Max Weinreich, however, rejects all aspects of that identification, dating the composition of the poem perhaps even as early as 1300. The state of the language itself, as well as topical references in the poem, nonetheless point more compellingly to the late fifteenth century as the period of composition, which would match well with the possible attribution to Moses Esrim Vearba.

As Israel Zinberg astutely observes, despite their grounding in texts of the sacred tradition, narratives such as the *Seyfer Shmuel* are not connected even indirectly with the liturgy; they are in that sense, in Zinberg's view, both secular and popular.[5] In keeping with this fundamentally dual nature, he argues that the author not only was intimately acquainted with the Bible and postbiblical Jewish textual traditions (especially concerning the primary heroic characters Samuel, Saul, and David), including rabbinical literature, but was also well versed in medieval Christian epic, especially from the Middle High German epic tradition, for the text is imbued with the conventions of that tradition. While this tonality may be seen in a broad range of indicators, one pertinent example is the Yiddish poet's incorporation of multiple near synonyms for "warrior/hero" that are incorporated from the epic vocabulary of Middle High German literature, including such terms as דעגן *degn* (warrior) (cf. Middle High German *dëgen*) (st. 397,1) and וויגאנט *vigant* (warrior) (cf. Middle High German *wîgant*) (st. 1189,1). Likewise, episodes of combat play a significant role in the *Seyfer Shmuel*, and not surprisingly the weaponry and armor used by David and Saul and the knights of medieval Christian epic—all warrior participants in premechanized warfare—are generally the same: helmet, mail coat, sword, spear, shield.[6] As Jean Baumgarten observes, "The narrative order in combat and jousting scenes follows the classic epic model, characterized by preliminary invective and provocation (flyting), preparation for battle, utilization of tactics and strategems, all culminating in the physical confrontation."[7]

At the same time, however, although there are indeed more than a few phraseological similarities, and while some of the midrashic narratives inserted into the epic (for example, Sir Joab's exploits in Rabbah) also tend in that direction, overall the quasi-chivalric tonality is kept quite moderate: a "flavor" of that literary milieu is given, but there is no real reconception of the narrative in those terms. Thus, the modern popular reputation of the *Seyfer Shmuel* as a recasting of the biblical text as a medieval epic with knights and ladies and swashbuckling heroes must be tempered: the *Seyfer Shmuel* is no biblicized Yiddish Lancelot or Gawain epic. This distinction becomes even clearer when one compares, for instance, the Old Saxon *Heliand*, which has painstakingly (although, most modern readers would agree, in an aesthetic sense not very successfully) reconceived the diatessaron version of the life of Jesus, recasting him as a prechivalric Germanic (quasi-Beowulfian) warrior-chieftain with his *comitatus* of twelve vassals.[8]

Johann Christoph Wolf, Franz Delitzsch, and Nathan Süßkind speak of the *Shmuel-bukh* as a "Davidiad," comparable, in Ashkenazic culture, to the "national epics" of England (*Beowulf*), France (the *Chanson de Roland*), and Germany (the *Nibelungenlied*) in medieval Christian Europe.[9] Certainly, there is no question of the long-term significance of the biblical narrative of David and the tradition consequent thereon—including the *Seyfer Shmuel*—for the Jewish messianic and eschatological conceptions. But unlike, for instance, *Beowulf* (the very existence of which is unattested and unmentioned in the Middle Ages outside that poem's unique tenth-century manuscript), the *Seyfer Shmuel* was actually widely known by its contemporary audience and successive generations. But unlike, for instance, the "national epics" of England, France, or Germany, the *Seyfer Shmuel* was not championed by a broad range of "nationalist" scholars during the romantic period, spawning multiple text editions, translations, popularized and children's versions, and so forth. While the *Seyfer Shmuel* is certainly not a well-guarded secret, no translation of the text has ever been published. Although it may well be deemed a "Davidiad," it has certainly not effectively functioned as a Jewish "national epic" in any period or for any large-scale Jewish populace.

The text is preserved in a complex tradition of manuscripts and printed editions, as is effectively taken into account in the extensive notes to the facsimile edition of the *editio princeps* (Augsburg, 1544) by Felix Falk and L. Fuks, on which the present translation is based.[10]

Source: Augsburg, 1544 (? Paulus Aemilius or Chaim b. David Schwartz [Shaḥor]).

Edition: Felix Falk, ed., *Das Schemuelbuch des Mosche Esrim Wearba: Ein biblisches Epos aus dem 15. Jahrhundert*, Einleitung und textkritischer Apparat von Felix Falk, aus dem Nachlaß herausgegeben von L. Fuks, 2 vols. (Assen: Van Gorcum, 1961) (facsimile of Augsburg 1544]), online facsimile of Augsburg, 1544, http://books.google.com/books?id=N4g6AAAAcAAJ&pg=RA1-PA90#v=onepage&q&f=false.

Research: Zinberg, *History*, 107–18; Erik, *Geshikhte*, 79–82, 112–21, 221–22; Erik, *Roman*, 16–32; Shmeruk, *Prokim*, 182–99; Baumgarten, *Introduction*,

143–52; Felix Falk, "Die Bücher Samuelis in deutschen Nibelungenstrophen des XV. Jahrhunderts," *Mitteilungen zur jüdischen Volkskunde* 11 (1908): 79–85, 97–116, 129–50 (French translation, *Mélanges bibliographiques sur les livres de Samuel en strophes de Nibelungen, précédés d'un exposé général sur la littérature judéo-allemande* [Leipzig: Kaufmann, 1909]); Ginzberg, *Legends*, 4:55–121, 6:245–76; Nathan Süsskind, "Das Šmuel Buch. Eine jüdisch-deutsche Umdichtung der zwei Bücher Samuelis im Stile der mittelhochdeutschen Heldendichtung. Teil I: Untersuchung der Sprache, der Quellen und der Liedtechnik nebst Teilherausgabe des Textes der Pariser Handschrift (Hebreu 92) mit Kommentar, die ersten 350 Strophen umfassend" (PhD diss., New York Univ., 1942); Nathan Süsskind, "Shmuel-bukh-problemen," in *Max Vaynraykh tsu zayn zibetsikstn geboyrn-tog: Shtudyes vegn shprakhn bay yidn, vegn yidisher literatur un gezelshaft* (The Hague: Mouton, 1964), 64–82; Jean Baumgarten, "Une chanson de geste en yidich ancien: Le *Shmuel bukh*," *Revue de la Bibliothèque Nationale* 13 (1984): 24–38; Wulf-Otto Dreeßen, "Goliaths Schwestern und Brüder," in *Röllwagenbüchlein: Festschrift für Walter Röll zum 65. Geburtstag*, edited by Jürgen Jaehrling, Uwe Meves, and Erika Timm (Tübingen: Niemeyer, 2002), 369–89.

Acquire Wisdom[11]

The Book of Samuel

The Book of Samuel in the Yiddish language—[it is] courtly, judicious and also entertaining to read therein. Samuel is the first part of the Book of Kings, for it all belongs together. Previously you had the Book of Kings, and now I have, in addition, printed Samuel as a book. Printed in the imperial city of Augsburg in the year that is counted as 304 [= (5)304 = 1544 CE] in the small count.

(1) He who has turned his mind to our dear Lord with his whole heart—how often has He delivered him; His mercy and His protection have never failed: He succors His servants both night and day. (2) No one—neither woman nor man—can perfect His praise. For that reason, one should be silent, since one cannot make it whole and absolute. He has often given us aid in our affliction and has forgiven us for our sins and our misdeeds. (3) We have often angered Him and opposed Him; so He left us for a while to our enemies. When we again called upon Him and fulfilled His commandments, then He succored us and delivered us from our afflictions. (4) I will keep silent about that—there would be much to sing. I want to tell you, from the Book of Samuel, how God, blessed be He, Who will not abandon us to any affliction in the Exile, has through His benevolence performed great marvels.

(5) In those days when the people of Israel resided in the land of Canaan, there was no king in Israel. There was a high priest whose name was Eli. He was a judge in the land among the whole people of Israel. (6) That same high priest dwelt in the city of Shiloh. In the land of Canaan there was no king. He served our Lord; he wrote and read; in God's service he was proficient; he always did his best; all evil aggrieved him. (7) Now at this same time there dwelt in the city of Ramah a man named Elkanah who fed the poor. This same Elkanah had taken Hannah and Peninnah as his two wives. (8) Hannah was beautiful and comely. Her husband Elkanah could have no child with her then. He was a Levite, an honorable man, as one finds it written. Peninnah had born him ten children. (9) He loved the marvelously beautiful Hannah dearly. He could not get her out of his mind day or night. He had never done anything against his wife Peninnah, although he loved Hannah more than her.

(10) Now the man Elkanah had conceived of a good thing to do, so that he brought his household with him to Shiloh, so that they went to the festival and made sacrifice. Every year they went to the festival there, (11) to the city of Shiloh, where the sanctuary was, with his entire household—he forgot none of them. When he had finished serving God, then he drank wine and always wanted to be festive with his entire household. (12) And the man Elkanah gave portions to his household, to each one separately, both women and children. He took pains not to forget the children, and he always gave Hannah the best. He did that so that (13) she would not be sad about not having a child and so that she always would be cheerful with her co-wife Peninnah.

It aggravated Peninnah that Hannah's gift was good and that she always had the best. She was quite angry. (14) She mocked her co-wife. She said: "Come on, tell me, Hannah, my dear co-wife, what did you buy for your boys, the older one and the younger one. Do tell me! You ought to parade forth the gifts for your children. (15) Do you see how my children are wearing their gifts. You have no joy to speak about: when you die, that will be an end of you; your name will be forgotten and never more remembered." (16) That aggravated Hannah, but she nonetheless remained silent: "I do not wish to tell my husband Elkanah. If I were to tell our dear husband about you, I can assure you, he would not tolerate it from you."

(17) When they again returned to God's service, her co-wife Peninnah was constantly saying many abusive things to her in an angry tone. The very beautiful Hannah could have no peace from her. (18) Therefore she was not happy, but she repressed her own anger. She wept such hot tears that she had no interest in food or drink. Then her husband Elkanah said: "Hannah, I want to tell you: perhaps you are weeping because you cannot get pregnant. (19) I

do love you more than your co-wife Peninnah and always give you the best. So you should be happy."

She was quiet until the meal was finished and went in front of the temple where the high priest was. (20) She raised her eyes and looked at the heavens. "Lord God, help me to bear a child. You have, in Your mercy, so arranged things on earth that people bear children; so let me also do so. (21) For indeed You have in Your heavenly kingdom angels who do not bear children and live eternally. If I am not to bear a child, dear my Lord, then let me live eternally like Your angels. (22) If I am after all to die and be buried, then, dear Lord God, then let me beforehand bear children."

The high priest saw this; he turned toward Hannah; he saw her lips moving but did not hear her words. (23) At this time it was not customary for anyone to pray casually before the temple. He thought to himself: "The woman must be drunk." He said: "Leave here! No wine drinking is allowed here!" (24) She said: "Dear my lord, you have misunderstood. I have had no wine today. You are not a prophet but rather a common man. I am calling on my Creator in my great grief."

(25) Eli, the high priest, looked at the woman. Now you may delight in hearing what he said to her: "God Almighty has commanded me to say to you: 'Go home to your house; you will become pregnant with an infant.'" (26) Then the beautiful woman bowed to the high priest. "You are a proper prophet; now I hear it clearly." She then went home joyously to her tent.

Elkanah and her household went across the fields (27) homeward to Ramah—in truth do I tell you that. The most beautiful Hannah became pregnant with an infant. The child was born and was named Samuel. His name became known throughout Israel. (28) That delighted Elkanah, but he wanted to go the city of Shiloh as he had previously done. This same Elkanah then said to Hannah: "Let us then also return to the city, (29) to Shiloh, to the temple, as we have done in the past." She said: "No, Elkanah, you should leave him here until I have weaned my dear little child. Thus he ought always to be a servant in the temple. (30) Thus I vowed when I prayed to God for him, that he would be a constant servant in the city of Shiloh." "Truly, then," said Elkanah, "let your will be done! Go where you wish with the little child."

(31) She brought her sacrifice there, in addition to two steers, which the child's mother also brought with her. Then the high priest said to a son of a Levite: "Slaughter the sacrificial offering, in order that we carry out the sacrifice properly." (32) Then Samuel, the young rabbi, said: "That is too much! Whatever Jew who there wishes may slaughter the sacrificial offering. There he had spoken against his rabbi and had earned a death sentence, that same little

child. (33) Samuel was arrested; they wanted to execute him. His father and his mother stood there in great misery. Then the little child's mother said: "Eli, dear my lord, it was right here that I prayed for the little child. (34) Now God, blessed be His name, has granted and allotted him to me. Pardon him, dear my lord, then my child will be spared." Then the high priest became filled with prophecy. He said: "I have pardoned Samuel, our dear lad." (35) Eli, the holy man, at once took the child. He said: "I will teach him everything that I can." Then Elkanah rejoiced, as did the comely Hannah.

Then the beautiful Hannah went to stand before the temple. (36) Her heart was filled with such great joy that she became—this one time only—a prophetess. She called out with a clear voice: "God will I praise. You rule on earth. Your kingdom is above. (37) My heart is filled with joy to my Lord. Praised be our Lord forever. I rejoice in the thoughts that God has made known to me, that from my son Samuel are to go forth prophets. (38) From Samuel, my son, will come a man; he and his fourteen will be able to prophesy. And also at this time have I seen right here that great aid will come to Israel, (39) which my dear son Samuel will provide. He will provide great aid against the heathens. Israel, most worthy, will be succored at once and for a long time thereafter against a mighty king (40) who will be named Sennacherib, powerful over all. When he comes against Jerusalem, then he will fail. We will be well avenged on Nebuchadnezzar. Indeed even the Greeks will lose their power. (41) Haman will be hanged and sold for bread. Israel will be given succor in all her afflictions. He will dig a trench in order to capture all of Israel. He and his ten sons will all hang. (42) Lord, You will bestow on me five children. All ten of my co-wife Peninnah's will die. Have mercy, Lord, and let two of them live. I have forgiven her for all that she said to me. (43) You have granted it to me, Lord, and will leave her two. Now I have seven children; I delight in the children. Now I have seven children; all seven are mine, except for the two who are my co-wife's. (44) God, blessed be He, can kill and give life. He makes one descend into Hell and also often gives aid. He makes the rich poor and the poor rich. He brings low those on high and raises the poor most certainly. (45) He raises the poor who lie in the mire. He raises the great lords. His praise is not suppressed. He succors those dear to him and drives His enemies to the abyss of Hell; the flames are blown at them. (46) Holy God will call a tribunal. He will forget not one of the poor or the rich. He will send the Messiah, the high-born king. Thus will our enemies most certainly be lost."

(47) The woman and also her dear husband took their leave. "Now hear," said the high priest, "what I grant to you. God must give you succor and do your will and bestow more such children as Samuel, your son."

(48) They went home to their country and were filled with joy. The very young Samuel stayed there in Shiloh and learned very quickly, so that he was filled with the Torah. Whatever the high priest knew, the child knew just as well.

(49) Now the high priest became gray from great age. He commanded his children to serve God as he had done. One of them was named Hophni, the other Phinehas. They were both very lax in their service to the Lord. (50) When someone brought a sacrifice, they were there quickly and took the meat, still raw, and roasted it. Before the sacrifice was made, they had already digested it. They would not stop it, no matter what was said to them. (51) Against the advice of all Israel, they took the meat from the kettle by force while it was still boiling. They would not wait until the offering had been made to God, blessed by He. Before it had finished boiling, the meat had already been eaten.

(52) The two sinful lads had perpetrated yet more. When after childbirth a woman wanted to make her sacrificial offering, she went to the ritual bath and then wanted to go home, they delayed her sacrifice so that she had to wait a long time. (53) And the noble married women had difficulty getting away from them there—without having to have sex with them—and getting home to their husbands. The high priest was there told much about them. He reprimanded his children and was grieved in his heart. (54) His reprimands were useless and had little effect on them. Our Comforter became angry at all of Israel collectively, and He wished to take vengeance on them for their great transgression. Not very long thereafter many a man came to great adversity.

(55) The very young Samuel was lying in the temple. Candles burned inside there so that it seemed like a sunny day. Most worthy Samuel was lying down asleep. God called from Heaven to young Samuel. (56) The lad Samuel then thought that his rabbi had called him. He arose and quickly ran to his rabbi. He made great haste and ran very hard until he came to Eli, his lord and master. (57) He said: "Dear my lord, tell me what you want of me." "Go back to sleep, dear child. I did not call you. Lie down to sleep again." Then the lad Samuel went back and lay down. (58) When Samuel, the young man, had lain back down, God again called to him from Heaven: "Samuel, Samuel!" When he perceived God's voice for the second time, the lad again went quickly to his rabbi. (59) He said: "Dear master, tell me what you want of me. You called me again, my lord. Whatever you want will be done." Then the high priest realized from the child's words that our Lord was calling to the young lad. (60) He said: "Dear son, go back to sleep. If you should hear the Lord's voice a third time, then say very quickly: 'Dear my Lord, I delight in hearing Your holy word.'"

(61) And when the lad Samuel had lain down, God's voice called again for the third time. "Yes," the boy quickly said, "Dear my Lord. Whatever You ask of me, Lord, will always be done." (62) Then our Lord God said: "I will tell you: Hophni and Phinehas will be struck dead. Thereafter I will avenge myself on all of Israel collectively. It will strike terror into the hearts of both great and small. (63) It will grieve anyone who hears of it. May it truly be said to Eli's household that I have expelled them from the priesthood. They will have to go begging even for a crust of bread. (64) Forever and eternally among Eli's household, the young will die, and no elders will be found."

And then the lad Samuel lay there in great sorrow and then arose in great sorrow, the light of day shone on him. (65) And when the lad Samuel opened the temple gate, the high priest, Eli, awaited him before it. He forcefully ordered him to tell him what God, blessed by He, had said. He dared not refuse him that. (66) And when the high priest had heard the wealth of words, he said: "Our Lord God may do what He wishes." Thereafter Samuel grew and truly became a prophet. All Israel everywhere came to know it.

(67) Not long thereafter, all Israel came to the city of Shiloh and heard Samuel's words. Young Samuel was full of truth: everything that he said, it was all truth. (68) He said: "You dear people, I ought to let you know: great and fundamental sins have been committed in Israel. We are not indeed to battle against our enemies." Nonetheless, the army of the Jews was assembled. (69) All the Jews together drew up their line of battle. The Jewish army was at Ebenezer. Their enemy, who were called Philistines, heard that and came with force to Aphek. (70) All of the heathens together joined with them. The battle was vehement, early one morning. The dead were seen to fall, many a noble man. Many of the mighty heroes came from Israel, (71) struck down quite dead onto the earth. Then all of Israel began to lament quite bitterly: "God, blessed be He, has abandoned us because of what we have done to Him. We most certainly want the ark of God with us. (72) Inside it are the tablets from Mount Sinai. Perhaps God in Heaven will succor us and grant us strength." They sent word to Shiloh: "We want to have the ark, into which God has placed His own Divine Presence. (73) The ark of holiness is to be brought to us here." Then the high priest's lads carried it to them.

When they came to the Jewish army in Ebenezer, they sounded the trumpets and shouted and greatly rejoiced. (74) The Philistines then heard the Jews' great joy. When they became aware of it, it grieved them greatly. All of them together said: "If God has come to them, a great many heathens will lose their lives because of it. (75) We will nonetheless defend ourselves with swords of steel; otherwise we will have to be subject to the Jews. Now do not be alarmed, you good and noble heathens. Strike deeps wounds into them so that their blood then runs forth. (76) Be now dauntless, you bold and mighty heroes!"

There was, however, immediate opposition to the Jews: there one countered spear-point with spear-point and charged through the shield-wall. A great many Jews were seen there falling to the ground. (77) The most spirited and the best were slain. A great many bold Jews stood in great affliction there. Of the Jews thirty thousand men, all of whom drew swords and wore armor, died there. (78) Hophni and Phinehas were slain; the ark was captured; a great lamentation rose up.

When they captured the ark and carried it away, an excellent man quickly sprang forth. (79) He was mighty and bold, spirited and dauntless; his sword sliced powerfully through mail-rings of steel. This very bold warrior was named Saul. He took the holy tablets by force in his hands, (80) and carried them away from there loyally—that will I tell you in truth. Then he had to retreat from there, in order not to be slain. He carried the holy tablets to Shiloh, inside the city gate. He had terror in his heart—that I tell you in truth.[12]

(81) Both weeping and wailing and weeping still more: a great many men and women tore their hair and beat their breasts. Now the high priest sat at the city gate; he was alarmed in his heart—that I tell you in truth – (82) because the ark of holiness had been carried away, he feared in his heart that Israel would be defeated. When he heard the city weeping and wailing so greatly, he cried out pitifully: "What is the matter here?" (83) He could not see; he was practically blind. The high priest was ninety-eight years old.

When he heard the bad news from Saul, he wrung his hands, as was proper for him. (84) And when he now heard that the ark had been taken and had unfortunately come into the hands of the Gentiles, from great sorrow he fell over backwards against the gate. There his neck broke—that I tell you in truth. (85) There he unfortunately had to die when his neck broke. There arose great lamentation among those who witnessed this misery. He was honorable and stalwart—that I tell you in truth. He had judged Israel justly for forty years altogether.

(86) Now, his daughter-in-law, Phinehas's wife, was pregnant with a legitimate child. She lamented bitterly: "Alas, my father-in-law, and my dear husband whom I have lost." Because of her great grief, she went into labor. (87) She bore a handsome son, but she was also to die from it. The women then comforted her, as is sung in the song. They all said: "You should be content: you have a high priest, a very handsome lad." (88) She said: "The child is to be named Ichabod, because Israel unfortunately does not have much honor. The

most worthy and the best have all been slain." Then, while still lamenting, the woman also died.

(89) Israel was defeated and subjugated. They had the heathens and the Philistines as their overlords. Now the Philistines had captured the holy ark. They all said: "It will be advantageous for us." (90) They thought it fitting to place it in their god's house, right beside their Dagon in the city of Ashdod—thus was it named—quite a good city in the heathen land.

(91) In the morning at dawn, when the people were to rise and go to their god in the houses of prayer, Dagon had fallen to the ground before the ark. They stood him up again where he used to be. (92) "You are certainly doing wrong," said the heathens there. "You should not fall down, or we will turn blue." The next morning, when they returned there, they again found their idol lying on the ground. (93) His head and hands had been knocked off and were lying on the threshold. The heathens began to lament. Then the heathens said: "The threshold must be sacred," because their Dagon had suffered torment on it. (94) For that reason, the Philistines thereafter instituted a rule that whoever wishes to step into or enter their god's house may not tread on the threshold; he must step over it. That was done by the Philistines at that time.

(95) Thereafter, the Philistines were grievously stricken by God, blessed be He. They were infected with boils that they also had to suffer, and when they wanted to defecate and empty their bowels, then mice began to enter their orifices. (96) They bit into their bowels and slept inside their asses. They had quite a bad end, squealing like pigs. They all said: "What does the Jewish God want from us? He is mocking us and Dagon."

(97) They sent from Ashdod to their lords. They said: "Dear lords, let us know what we are to do with the Jewish ark. Do what you will with it, only take it away from here." (98) Then the lords said: "Perhaps they were dishonored because we did not take it to Gath, our capital city." Then it was taken to Gath, indeed to the capital city, and as soon as the wagon entered the gate, (99) they were stricken as had happened in Ashdod: a great many men in Gath exposed their orifices: they were afflicted by mice and boils. They fell to the ground and died very quickly. (100) They sent the ark of God to Ekron. There they shouted collectively in the plain: "What is the Jewish God to us? He will strike us dead!"

Then the heathens once more all assembled in counsel. (101) "We would like to send the ark to the Jews, if we knew how to send it so that nothing happened to us." They quickly sent for the bold and sage people. They said: "Dear lords, give us your advice, (102) so that was can just put an end to this catastrophe, and so that the Jews will take back their ark." Then the sages said: "We would indeed like to tell you that you should consider, if God has stricken you: (103) you should make golden mice of red gold and likewise boils and put them in a small chest. You should send that to the Jews as reparation. Then God will spare you and let you live. (104) And send the ark on a new wagon, to which you should harness two cows that have borne calves. Their calves should be tied up behind the house. You should drive out the cows with the wagon.

(105) If they take the correct path away from their offspring, then you will know that God, blessed be He, has done it. If they do not take the correct path but go back and forth, then God was not responsible for this mass slaughter. (106) Thereby you will be able to perceive, recognize, and see the truth. Otherwise, it has just been a misfortune that has happened to us. If they take the correct path into the land of Beth Shemesh, then God has stricken and punished us."

(107) All the lords were well pleased by these words. They sent for the herdsmen to have the cows fetched. The calves were tied behind the house. The cows were driven out with the wagon. (108) The cows immediately took the correct path; they did not have to be shown either path or trail. They loudly praised God with their voices in their language. They went toward Bethlehem, on the right road. (109) When the heathens saw this, they turned around.

Those in Beth Shemesh rejoiced about the ark. They were in the field harvesting grain. When they saw the ark, they rejoiced. (110) They were all barefoot and ran over to it bare-headed. They lifted the two arks right out of the wagon. The two cows were slaughtered and taken as sacrifices. They hewed that new wagon into pieces there. (111) They found in the chest as many golden mice as there were cities and villages in the land of the Philistines. The heathens were healed of their great abscesses, and the people of Beth Shemesh were also not forgotten. (112) Because they had seen the ark thus bare-headed, for that reason great affliction came upon those same people. Many of them died, fallen in the forest, far more than fifty men.

(113) Then all the people said: "We do not want to have it here with us." They sent messengers to Kir'iath-je'arim, in order to tell them: "The ark has come back that the Philistines took from us in battle. (114) Would you keep it, if it seemed proper to you?" Then the people of Kir'iath-je'arim came and took the ark of God to the city of Gibeah into the house of Abin'adab. There they rejoiced in it. (115) Whoever wanted to make a sacrifice had to do it in Gibeah. Shiloh was distressed; of that I can assure you. That lasted a long time; I think some twenty years. Israel was pious—that I tell you in truth.

(116) In this same time Samuel was a judge. With very great piety, the prophet said: "Israel, I wish to teach you all piety. You ought to return to God with all your heart." (117) They served Almighty God with all their hearts. Then the prophet Samuel said: "Now, follow my counsel: gather all Israel into the city of Mizpah. I will pray to God for us." They all rejoiced in that. (118) When they came to Mizpah, all of them together, the people came properly before the pure prophet. Then the heathens began to say in their cities: "Israel has assembled. Let us slaughter them. (119) They have perhaps assembled in order to invade our land." Then all the heathens assembled at once. The heathens then marched on Mizpah from all directions. On both sides arose fear and loud lamentation. (120) The Jew there greatly feared the heathens; they had come against them with a great army. They said: "Dear Samuel, do Israel a favor and pray to God, blessed be He, the Lord, that He succor us."

(121) The prophet Samuel made a sacrifice. Then the Jews went out to meet the heathens. There God, blessed be He, for the sake of Israel, granted the prophet Samuel what he had desired. (122) The heathens who were there all stormed the walls of Mizpah with its pale stones. There God let such a great voice be heard that they were dazed and fled in all directions. (123) When the Jews saw this, they were quickly prepared and ran out before Mizpah; their swords cut the heathens. They slew a great many heathens. The fields were wet with red blood. (124) Then the heathens had to retreat and struggle. That which they had taken from them, they had to return to them, and they dared not enter the Jewish lands. From them they had earned both dishonor and also disgrace. (125) The prophet Samuel had defeated them by force.

And now that the prophet Samuel had become old, so that he could no longer leave the city to judge all Israel, as he had earlier done, (126) then he set up his two sons, Abi'jah and Joel, in the city of Beer-sheba to judge Israel, so that they were to judge and to listen to both the great and the small, the poor and the rich alike.

(127) The two lords then judged the tribe of Israel, and whoever wanted to give them money always received a favorable verdict. All Israel then spoke to the prophet Samuel, and they said: "Dear Samuel, your sons are not like you. (128) They do not have your piety in their hearts, and they are not suited to be judges over Israel. We ask you, trusted sir, now do us a favor and give us a king who will judge us."

(129) These words greatly displeased the prophet Samuel. It seemed very evil to him that they requested a king, for God, blessed be He, on his throne was Israel's king, and they want to have a different king. (130) Then the prophet Samuel prayed modestly to God, blessed be He, that he forgive them for what

they had done. Then our Lord answered Samuel in this matter: "You should yield to them and give them a king. (131) You should, however, first tell them about a king's many rights: that a king always does what he wants." Then the prophet Samuel said: "I will inform them how the rights of kings are exercised: (132) he compels them by force and does what he wants; he will also compel you to do what seems too much to you; whatever well pleases him, he will take all of it. That he will do by force and need not be ashamed of it." (133) They collectively said: "We must have a king. All the peoples of the earth have also done likewise." There the prophet Samuel said: "So, return home. I will seek a king for you who is honorable and noble."

(134) At this same time there was a man named Saul, a warrior honorable and noble, in the land of Benjamin. He was honorable, handsome beyond measure, and well-formed. There was no one among the people of Israel who stood taller than his shoulder. (135) He was a bold warrior. We have already mentioned him before: Saul, of the tribe of Benjamin, from Gibeah. He was honorable and noble and additionally handsome beyond measure. There was no one among the people of Israel who stood taller than his shoulder.

(136) Affliction had come to Kish, the worthy lord. Once he lost his female donkey on the meadow. He then said to the bold warrior: "I will tell you what you ought to do. (137) You are to look for the donkey until you can find it, and take along with you one of the herdman's children." Saul, the hero, then looked for the donkey on the hills of Ephraim; it was elsewhere. (138) They looked for it in Shal'ishah; it was also not there. He looked for it in the land of Sha'alim. His search yielded nothing. He looked for it in the land of Benjamin, as we have heard. He could not discover where it had gone.

(139) When they came to Zuph, to the city of Ramah, the worthy hero Saul went to his companion. He said: "Dear companion, let us go home. My father will think that we, too, are lost. (140) He will have to give up on the donkey and keep his peace and lament the donkey in his heart." His companion answered him: "My lord, I can also say: here in Ramah there is a most holy man. (141) His name is Samuel. He speaks the truth. If you ask him about the donkey, he will give us exact information." Then Saul answered him: "I have nothing to give him. If I were to give him nothing, it would not be proper." (142) His companion then answered him: "I have a small piece of silver. Give that to the pure, holy man, dear my lord." The words well pleased Saul. "On my oath, I will do what you say."

(143) They went then quite quickly to the city of Ramah. When the lord Saul entered the city, he found on the mountain a well of cold water. Beside it were maidens who were comely. (144) They were going to carry water back to

the city of Ramah. The noble hero, Saul, asked the maidens to tell him truly, whether the prophet Samuel was in the city. (145) They were glad to see him there, the high-spirited hero. He was ruddy and white like milk and blood. He was very handsome; they looked at him and long spoke with the worthy man. (146) They said: "My lord, you will find Samuel at once. The noble prophet is right at the gate. He wants to go up on the mountain," said the beautiful maidens. "He has prepared a feast for the city fathers. (147) Now rush on quickly and go to him. The people are waiting for the prophet; they will not eat without him." Saul went quickly into the city. The prophet Samuel welcomed him.

(148) Samuel had waited for Saul at the gate. Then Saul, the hero, also came before the gate. He bowed courteously—that I tell you in truth. The prophet stood up where he had been sitting. (149) He welcomed him with honor. He had waited for him before the gate. There God, blessed be He, said to Samuel: "Now step forward and honor this lord for My sake. He is to be a king over Israel." (150) He welcomed him with honor. He gladly looked at him. Now may you gladly hear how he spoke to him: "May God welcome you, excellent hero of Gibeah. The donkey has been found and is no longer lost. (151) The entire kingdom of Israel is rightly yours. Today you are to eat with me at my request." Saul, the fine warrior, then answered him courteously: "Such authority does not really suit me. (152) Now, I am from Benjamin, quite a small tribe. I am, additionally, the youngest among the splendor of Jacob. Concerning the kingship, my lord, you should be silent. I cannot wear the crown over Israel." (153) Samuel took him by the hand, the fine lad, and led the both of them to the feast in his palace. He seated them both at the head of the table. They ate chicken and fish with Samuel. (154) After they had eaten and were to go to bed, Samuel said to Saul: "You are to get up early. I will tell you right now, God sent me to you. You are to wear the crown over all the land of Israel."

(155) In the morning when the sun rose, Samuel commanded Saul to get up: "Get up, Saul, it is time to go." They walked together to the edge of the city. The prophet Samuel forcefully instructed Saul: (156) "Send the lad ahead and let him go. I want to tell you the message of God Almighty, blessed be He." The lad went on his way home, and when he had left him, the prophet Samuel took a small pitcher of oil. (157) He poured the oil on Saul's head and kissed him with all his heart and wished the best for him. He said: "God, blessed be He, has anointed Saul as my lord. You are to be king over all Israel. (158) When you come to Rachel's grave, you will find ten men who will tell you that your father found the donkey, indeed quite quickly. Now he thinks

that you are lost; he does not know where you are. (159) When you come to the Tabor plain, then you will again find three men—that I tell you in truth. One will carry three small goats, the second wine; the third will carry three loaves of bread. That is all yours. (160) They will give it to you; so take it from their hands. Thus you will come into the holy land of Gibeah. Then a band of prophets will come—that I tell you in truth. Thus will you also be openly revealed as a prophet. (161) When all my predictions have come true, then you ought to acknowledge that you are to be king. And you should, my lord, have royal robes made for yourself. Thus will you indeed become a mighty king in the land. (162) When you rise up to fight at Gilgal, you are to wait for me seven days and let the sacrifice wait. You are not to make the sacrifice until I come to you. Seven whole days are you to wait for me."

(163) King Saul then took his leave and went homeward. Everything that Samuel had said to him happened to him just that way. He also prophesied in the land of prophets. Everyone who had earlier known him was astonished (164) that he was a prophet and sought to prophesy. The people said: "He is quite worthy of it." Abner's uncle said: "Saul, explain to me where you have been. That I want to understand." (165) He said: "I looked for the female donkey, my companion and I. When I could not find it, I went to Samuel." "Tell me on your oath, what did he tell you?" "He told me: 'It has been found.'"

(166) He did not want to tell him about the matter of the kingship. He was so very embarrassed. He acted as though he knew nothing about it. When he had now arrived at home—I will tell you in truth—he made splendid clothes for himself which a king would wear.

(167) Thereafter Samuel very quickly sent out messengers. The people were to come to the land of Mizpah. When they had come to Mizpah, he said: "I will tell you, let us cast lots about who should wear the crown. (168) I want to cast lots among the twelve tribes." The lot fell to the tribe of Benjamin. Among its members the tribe of Benjamin then cast lots. Then the lot fell to Saul who had run there. (169) He had hidden himself; he thought it was a mockery. When he could not be found, they went to ask God. They asked at the ark where he could be found. God said: "In the chamber where the extra clothing is." (170) They quickly ran there and brought the worthy man. He was head and shoulders taller than the rest of the people. No one among the Israelites was taller than his shoulder. Then the prophet Samuel said: "I want to tell you: (171) do you see that God wanted this worthy man; he does not have an equal among the whole people." Then all Israel said: "The king is fitting for us. Noble King Saul, may you live in joy!" (172) Then Samuel told him the

laws of kingship. Thereafter he sent to all the tribes of Israel. Saul, the worthy lord, hurried home. Many people of Israel followed after the king.

(173) They made gifts to the king as tribute, which he gladly received. Now there were many people who did not want the king. They did not want him and were not pleased by him. The king kept silent and did not then want to deal with that.

(174) At that same time there was in Ammon a king and lord named Nahash. He assembled as many as the sands of the sea and marched to Jabesh-Gilead with a great army. (175) In the land of Israel was a small land. He wanted to conquer the land, together with all the cities. Altogether they said: "What have we done to you. If you will let us live, we will take you as our lord." (176) Then King Nahash said: "If you will be my servants, I will let you live; otherwise you will suffer anguish: the men in the land are to have their right eyes gouged out as a dishonor and disgrace. That will I promise to Israel." (177) They said: "Dear sir, grant us seven days. We would like to send messengers to ask whether anyone will come to our aid. If no one will help us, we will indeed serve you and will have to suffer," they then said.

(178) Then they sent their messengers to the city of Gibeah. When the people heard of it, they wept so very loudly. When King Saul came from the field and as he heard the bad news, (179) the king was angry; great was his anger, so that his household was very upset. Then he ran to the oxen, and when he found them he hewed them in half with his own hands. (180) He sent those same pieces along with the messengers who were there. He said: "Go forth and tell them of my anger, so that they thus assemble and come to me here. Anyone who does not come, I will make it difficult for him: (181) I will hew his livestock to pieces; thus he will come to understand."

Then many a mighty man of Israel came there. Then Saul arrived with his army: thrice a hundred thousand men, plus thirty thousand. (182) He said to the messengers: "Now tell your city: 'Tomorrow, when the sun rises, I will make Ammon feeble." The messengers then went there and gave that message. They rejoiced greatly, and all of them were happy. (183) They said to King Nahash: "No one wants to come to our aid. Tomorrow we will come to you, no matter what happens to us as a result. And if you want to scour us with strong lye, then we will cry 'Bloody murder and alas and alack for our right eyes.'"

(184) In the morning when dawn came and the sun rose, the worthy King Saul broke through the whole army. The Jews slew the people of Ammon beyond number; they cast down the worthiest and the best. (185) Noble King

Saul performed best of all. Nowhere were two men together left standing. They had slain them and scattered them. Nahash had fled; that grieved the Jews. (186) The dead could not accurately be counted. There all Israel said: "With all our hearts we wish to elect this worthy man. He can aid us against all our enemies. (187) Someone should point out to us the people who opposed the king. We will kill them because they did not want to have Saul as king. They thought that he could not give them aid, and they did not bring gifts to our lord." (188) "No," said King Saul, "that is not to be done. No Jew is to be killed for my sake. God, blessed be His name, has succored us all. For that reason, I do not wish to have any Jew killed."

(189) Then the prophet Samuel went to stand before Israel. He said: "Let us go to Gilgal rejoicing. Let us elect our king there. They all did it gladly and were all happy. (190) They heartily rejoiced for the king and his army. Then the prophet Samuel said: "I want to tell you more: God is our king, whom you have despised. I tell you in truth: you have done wrong. (191) I will give you a sign, so that you can see that a great wonder will take place. The sun is shining now, and it is very hot. I will call out to God, and thunder and lightning will come." (192) Before the prophet Samuel had finished saying the words, suddenly it was pitch black with thunder and lightning. Then they said to Samuel: "Pray for us, as has always been your custom!" (193) Then the prophet Samuel said: "I will by no means cease to do so. I will pray for you as I have previously done. Serve the Lord God, blessed be He; then He will not abandon you. Whoever does not serve Him, will be as nothing at all."

(194) The noble King Saul had committed no sin. Now King Saul wanted to keep three thousand mighty men with him, but he let all the rest of Israel go home. (195) He let them all go back home to their houses. The king marched out with the three thousand; the king then took two thousand, and gave the other thousand to Jonathan in Gibeah. (196) Now the heathens again wanted to wage war, and they attacked Gibeah. Prince Jonathan and his men began to take up their swords and put on their armor, (197) and hewed to pieces all the Philistines who even entered the city of Gibeah at that time. When the news resounded that the Philistines were defeated, they did not wish to endure it from the Jews.

(198) Then King Saul had a war horn sounded: "Arise, both rich and poor, whoever has sworn an oath to me should immediately come to the land of Gilgal." The Philistines were all attacked. (199) The heathens very quickly marched on Gilgal. They came in force and with a great uproar. With thirty thousand chariots, well clad in steel and six thousand knights, undaunted heroes. (200) There were as many heathens as sand in the sea. They advanced to Michmash

with a great army. Now at this time King Saul was with his people in Gilgal; he was not in Michmash. (201) Israel greatly feared the horde of heathens. Some hid in one place, some in another, until they were quite scattered.

King Saul was, however, still in the land of Gilgal. (202) He was waiting for the prophet Samuel, as he had instructed. On the seventh day the army abandoned the king. It was quite necessary for King Saul to go into battle. It did him no good that the prophet remained away so long. (203) "Am I to wait here until I am all alone? The army is fleeing from here," said the stately king. "Bring me the offering; I will make the sacrifice myself, and then I will give battle to the heathens. (204) Just as the king had made the sacrifice, the prophet Samuel arrived in Gilgal. "Alas," said Samuel, "what have you done?" "In truth," said King Saul, "I will tell you. (205) Since you did not come at the proper time, the army was slipping away from me before the battle with the heathens. Look, dear Samuel, there the heathens are advancing. I prayed to God, blessed be He; now it has turned to grief for me. (206) I have performed that which you commanded. I praised God as I made the sacrifice." Then the prophet Samuel said: "You have acted foolishly. You have disobeyed my orders; your kingship will pass away." (207) Then the prophet Samuel said: "Turn around, King, you and also your small army. Go together into the city of Gibeah." When they arrived there, they were very pleased.

(208) Then King Saul counted the people whom he found, whom he had assembled in all the land of Israel. Only six hundred were remaining there. The others had hidden and were elsewhere. (209) Then the king went to Gibeah to his son Jonathan. They did not know what they should do. The Philistines were all encamped before Michmash with onslaught and strife—that I tell you in truth. (210) The enemy then advanced into King Saul's lands. They robbed and burned everything that they found.

Mighty Jonathan, the son of King Saul, said to his squire: "Hear what I want to do: (211) I know that great boldness is in your heart. Do you want to go into battle secretly with me? Do not tell my father or anyone else about it. Thus we will not endure the iniquity of the heathens." (212) That most bold squire brought him his sword. He said: "Dear my lord, do as you wish. I will gladly cross the stream with you; so let us joyously attack the heathen horde."

(213) They crossed the stream—that I tell you in truth. Then the heathens said: "The Jews are coming forth. Let us ask them where they have been hiding." They said: "Come over here. You need not worry." (214) Then Jonathan said: "In truth, that must be. So fasten on my helmet—my servant and I!" Then Jonathan was well prepared to fight. He and his servant, too, were dauntless. (215) The mountain was so high that they could not keep to their

feet: they had to go up on all fours. Then when they got to the top—those two bold men—young Jonathan vigorously charged the heathens. (216) Jonathan took his sword in both hands and swung it to both sides, so that flames sprang forth from the mail-coats of all the heathens. The heathens whom he slew were beyond counting. (217) His squire had also taken up his shield, in order to follow his lord with great strength. Whoever fell to the ground was slain. Not one of them ever got up again in front of that squire.

(218) Young Jonathan broke through the heathen army. He caused them great discomfort with his good sword. They rushed at the two lads with force. Indeed many of the heathens were slain by them. (219) The huge army was thrown into great confusion. They rushed toward Gibeah, a great army. Quite openly they crossed the stream and advanced with force before the gates of Gibeah.

(220) The guard shouted quite loudly: "King, may I inform you—have the drawbridge raised at once. The Philistines have come with a great force. There are, however, far fewer of them; something has changed. (221) I see in their bands fear and great distress. Many of the heathens are falling and being slain. The sky is full of fiery clouds. The battle is quite tumultuous; that I can now see clearly."

(222) The king shouted loudly at that same moment: "Check immediately and see who among us is missing." The army quickly did as the king wished: Jonathan and his sword-bearer were missing. (223) The king hurried and rushed into battle. All his heroes followed after him. They were all heroes—the best who could be found. They came running vigorously into that army. (224) At that moment he feared for the king's son: the king was at the very forefront of the battle. The heathens had to retreat and fled down into the valley. There they slew many of the heathens, beyond counting.

(225) The heathens could not even determine who was friend or foe; each one of them showed hostility and hatred for the other; with the sword that each of the heathens carried at his side, he himself slew his comrade. (226) All the Jews who had gone into hiding now came running; they no longer needed to be worried. They pursued the heathens. They would have liked to stop to eat. "No," said the king, "I will not have it be done thus. (227) Let us not delay but pursue them. I am eager for us to avenge ourselves on the Philistines. Whoever eats anything today, I swear by God, should be slain. Now fight well, for necessity calls."

(228) The people pursued the mighty heathens very swiftly. They slew many—their swords unsheathed. They pursued them swiftly into the land of the Philistines. Now, hear what the king found while on the way: (229) a great

forest that was quite unusual—the forest was full of honey—that I tell you in truth. The honey flowed from there into the land of the Philistines. Now, no one dared pick up the honey. (230) They dared not eat it; that was a great sorrow for the army. They were very afraid of the king's oath. At that same time Jonathan ate some of the honey; he did not know anything about what the king had sworn. (231) One of them saw that and became very angry. He said: "O hero Jonathan, your father swore an oath that no one should eat anything; he forbade it to our army. We all had to obey, however great our hunger." (232) Jonathan then answered him: "He has done wrong. The honey is quite sweet and pleasurable to eat. It gives me pleasure in swallowing it and does my eyes good. My sight has become clearer, and my stomach is full. (233) My father has done Israel wrong, in not wanting to let them eat of the honey. I wish that all of Israel had eaten its fill. We would have beaten the Philistines all the better."

(234) Night came rushing on. The people ate a great deal. After they had eaten, the king did not forget. He said: "Let us pursue the heathens today. They cannot defend themselves; let us slay them." (235) The high priest said: "Now follow my counsel. I am bearing Urim and Thummim. First God should be consulted." Then King Saul thought, "Why is he saying that? I will obey the priest; he truly knows of something." (236) Then King Saul asked God: "Tell me, Lord God, should I turn back or should I continue to pursue?" God did not then want to answer him. The king well knew that it was due to sin at that time. (237) The king said to the priest: "Put on Urim and Thummim and let us cast lots to determine the man who has here committed this transgression. I tell you in truth that he must suffer grief. (238) By God, blessed be He, who has given us aid, whoever has sinned, I will slay. Even if it were my very dear son Jonathan, he would nonetheless have to die: I would not pardon him."

(239) No one wanted to answer him; everyone was silenced. But the people said: "King, do as you wish." He said: "My son Jonathan and I will be together, and on the other side all of Israel. (240) Let the lots be cast between us and you." The lot fell to Saul and to his son Jonathan. He said: "Now, cast the lots between us two men." Then the lot fell to Jonathan. (241) Saul said to Jonathan: "You must tell me what kind of sin you have committed on this day." He said: "I ate some honey, but not much. Here am I, my father, I will die gladly." (242) Then the king said to him and was greatly alarmed: "By God in Heaven, the Almighty Lord, Jonathan, you must die, as I have sworn." Then the people hid him and did not want to allow him to do it. (243) "Do you want to kill Jonathan, this most worthy man, who has defeated an entire army?" They swore firm oaths that no one should harm him. "We now

repudiate what you have sworn. (244) We want to release you from your oath; you are free and clear." Then Jonathan was freed. They went their own ways. King Saul then went back home to his country, and he again summoned all Israel.

(245) Then King Saul and his spirited troops fought. All Israel travelled over land and over sea. With Moab and Ammon he had great strife, and with the king of Edom he had a very bad time. (246) A people called the Amalekites brought Israel grief, with robbing and burning without any resistance. King Saul slew many of them; in the land of Amalek they soon had enough of him. (247) He had a great war with king of Zobah, and with the Philistines, which was reported both far and wide. God, blessed be He, helped Israel in all its adversity, and among all of Israel's enemies, many were slain. (248) He conquered the lands with such great might that they had to serve him against their will. The Jews and the Philistines could not be separated: they fought constantly, the Jews and the heathens.

(249) Then King Saul said: "If I keep Israel together all the time, then the land will wither away. Both tilled land and vineyards will be devastated in the land. He sent all the people of Israel back home, (250) except for the mighty heroes, whom he did not wish to allow to go anywhere. He had it proclaimed whom he would appoint to positions of power. He often sent out the mighty and bold heroes to fight. The war in the land of the heathens became a very long one.

(251) Then the prophet Samuel entered the city. Noble King Saul welcomed him, for which the honorable prophet courteously thanked him. Then Saul said to him: "Why have you come?" (252) The prophet Samuel then said: "King, give the order for silence! Mighty God in Heaven, blessed be He, commanded me to tell you: 'You know well, King Saul, you were a common man. I made you a king, as I granted it to you. (253) You should remember that and follow My orders. You ought also not to break them.' Thus has God commanded: 'The people of Amalek have caused Me much sorrow and disgrace, when I led Israel out of the land of Egypt. (254) Israel came first to that evil people Amalek, who attacked them and picked them off. They also had an evil custom of magic. They always fought with My people Israel. (255) Then Israel was thrashed and wounded to the point of death. I offered Israel My aid and My comfort. Then I swore on My throne a binding oath and ever after I swear it by My name. (256) I want to be avenged on Amalek until they are all destroyed. Not one of them should be left before My people Israel; none should survive. Thus have I spoken. I have now remembered that oath. (257) Now, listen, King Saul, and attend well my words. You are to fight with them and leave none of

them alive: both people and also livestock are to be slain. Pay close attention to this.' Thus has God spoken."

(258) "Gladly," said the king, "that which God, blessed be He, commands, that will be done." Then the king armed himself in a steel mail-coat. His people were mustered until it seemed sufficient to him. The noble King Saul always wore his armor. (259) He took for himself many of the worthy and bold men: twice a hundred thousand, plus ten thousand men. They advanced with might into the land of Amalek. The cities were conquered and burned with fire. (260) He said to the Kenites who had come from Jethro: "Go away from Amalek. We know that you honor all Israel and Moses our Teacher. Therefore, get away from here, so that we not harm you."

(261) Saul struck Amalek from Hav'ilah up to the city of Shur, as one goes to Egypt. There they slew whatever they came across: the livestock and the children, the women and also the men. (262) Agag, king of Amalek, begged that his life be spared. He said: "I surrender myself to your mercy, King Saul. Lead me away as your prisoner; entrust me to no one else." Saul began to take pity on him. He said: "Let it be done."

(263) Now, the Amalekites had thought up a bewitchment, and some of them turned themselves into fat sheep. They [the Israelites] took the fat sheep well enough, and the lean ones they killed on the spot. (264) "I want to sacrifice the fat sheep in this matter. They seemed too valuable to me to destroy them in this way."[13] Agag lay with a woman that very night. She became a ewe when dawn returned. (265) She ran off toward the forest and betook herself there quickly. She became pregnant with Hammedatha who sired Haman.

Samuel lay that same night in his chamber and slept. God, blessed be He, called angrily to the prophet Samuel. (266) He said: "I made Saul king. He has broken my commandment. His kingship will pass away." That same night, Samuel cried out to God, blessed be He, with his whole heart and with many a prayer. (267) He was struggling in prayer for the sake of King Saul, until God, blessed be He, granted him reprieve for as long as Samuel lived. In the morning at dawn, Samuel came quickly. He found Saul at Mount Carmel. (268) He found him at Carmel and made his sacrifice. When King Saul noticed Samuel, he said to Samuel: "May God welcome you. I, and all Israel, have kept God's commandment." (269) Then the prophet Samuel said: "If you have performed God's commandment, what sheep are here crying 'meh, meh'? Tell me that!" Then King Saul said: "I slew everything except for the fat sheep that I want to sacrifice. (270) Agag, king of Amalek, I captured here. All of that other people have passed away altogether." "In truth," said Samuel, "you have not acted properly. You have broken the commandment of God, blessed be He. Your kingship will pass away." (271) Then Saul said: "Yet I did it with the best intentions. I slew everything except what I have here. If I ought to kill them, too, it will be carried out. I planned to sacrifice all the good sheep here."

(272) Then the prophet Samuel said: "Many of them have slipped away. They can perform magic and bewitch your senses. It is also dearer to God, blessed be He, that His commandment be carried out, rather than that one brings offerings and makes many sacrifices." (273) Then King Saul said: "I have done wrong. I ask the Lord God to forgive my sin. I have broken His commandment, I well understand from you. I want to make a sacrifice. Samuel, go with me." (274) Samuel said to Saul: "You are a sinner. I will not go with you. Your deed is repugnant to me." The prophet Samuel stood up and wanted to leave. Saul grasped him and did not want to let him go. (275) He grasped him by the border of his robe and tore his silk garment. Then Samuel grew angry and said: "That is to be a sign: the one who tears your silk garment will take your kingdom." The king nonetheless said: "I will not let you go like this. (276) Honor me today and go there with me. Here is all Israel, many an honorable man. Do not disgrace me in front of my people Israel." Then the prophet Samuel went with Saul, the son of Kish.

(277) Then Saul said to Samuel: "Dear my lord, I will slay my prisoner, King Agag. Quickly King Agag was led, bound, before Samuel. Then King Agag said: "Alas, the grief of bitter death! (278) Unfortunately, I must die, as I clearly recognize." Then Samuel, that most holy man, answered him: "What sorrow have women ever caused you, that you cut off the fingers that the men had?" (279) Then four rods were pounded deep into the ground; then they were bent towards each other, and the executioner was quickly called. His [Agag's] hands and feet were bound, each to one of the rods. The rods were let go, and Agag was quickly ripped apart.

(280) Then the prophet Samuel went into his house at Ramah. Saul again dwelt in the city of Gibeah. The prophet Samuel surely did not wish to go to Saul any more and grieved all the days of his life for the monarchy.

(281) Then God, blessed be He, said to Samuel: "Stop your grieving over King Saul! I do not want him after all. Go to Bethlehem to Jesse, My servant, and anoint there a king from among his sons." (282) Samuel was very alarmed by that: "How dare I do that? If Saul finds out, I will die." Then God, blessed be He, said to Samuel: "Do not tell anyone. Say that you want to take a sacrifice to Bethlehem."

(283) The prophet Samuel stood up with great lamentation. He went to Bethlehem; the journey caused him great agitation. The people were very alarmed when they saw him. "If only it is something good! What does the

holy man want?" (284) He said: "I want to slaughter a sacrifice to God. Come and eat my meat and bread with me."

He invited Jesse and his sons to eat with him. He came with all his sons, except for one whom he had forgotten (285) who was guarding sheep for his father in the fields. Jesse went with his sons to where Samuel held court. The eldest was named Eli'ab, a very fine warrior. When Samuel saw him, he thought to himself: (286) "He must be a king; he is filled with virility; a brave and mighty hero, that I well see in him." "No," said our Lord God, "I do not want him. He is quick to anger, for which reason, leave him standing there. (287) You can also be mistaken: your powers of prophecy have limits. You cannot know more than I let you know." Then Samuel said to Jesse: "God does not want this one. Let all your sons appear before me."

(288) He let all his sons appear before the prophet. The prophet Samuel then said: "God, blessed be He, does not want any of these. Tell me, have you no other son? It surprises me very much that you do not want to bring forth the right one." (289) Jesse then said to Samuel: "I have one more. He has to spend all his time in the fields with the sheep." The prophet Samuel then said: "These are new tidings. We will not eat until he, too, has come here."

(290) Then the very young lad also came into the house. God, blessed be He, said to Samuel: "Stand up at once! Anoint this young lad at once as king of Israel and of the land and people." (291) The prophet Samuel then took up his horn full of oil and anointed young David. It angered his brothers. Then the prophet Samuel left there in a hurry. He fled from Saul to his house in Ramah.

(292) No one except Jesse and his household knew anything about the fact that David was to be king of the tribes of Israel. Thereafter David, the young man, became a prophet, and the power of prophecy abandoned Saul completely.

(293) Very often a madness came over King Saul. The man raged for two hours or more. His pages then said: "We offer you this advice: look for a man who can play a stringed instrument well. (294) When the madness comes over you, dear lord, then this man, who can play the harp well, should play. In that way, you will again become cheerful; the madness will leave you." King Saul then said: "I want to have one." (295) His pages then quickly and openly answered: "I know an excellent and bold young warrior. He plays organ and harp and all kinds of stringed instruments well." He said to his pages that he should be brought. (296) "Tell me where is he to be found." "He said: "Send to Bethlehem, to Jesse. David, his youngest son, knows much about playing the organ and harp and all manner of stringed instruments."

(297) Now King Saul sent to Jesse: "Send me your youngest son, David, at once!" Jesse then quickly sent his son to Saul and a donkey loaded with freshly baked bread, (298) and he also sent a small cask of wine with him, and he carried a fat young goat in his arms. And when the very young lad came to the king, since he was then in a fit of madness, he then took his harp (299) and played so sweetly. It was good for the king. His madness left him and disappeared every time. Then the king sent messengers to Jesse in his house: "I want to keep David with me in my house at all times. (300) I like him; I am very fond of the boy and would not give him up for his weight in gold. When David plays music for a short time for me, I always get well."

(301) Then there again assembled as many heathens as the sands of the sea, beyond measure or end, a great army between Socoh and Aze'kah. Many heathens came running there. (302) King Saul and his heroes were informed of it. Israel gathered at Elah a great host. The Philistines were encamped on a very high mountain; Saul advanced to another mountain across from them. (303) On two high mountains they could not be separated; a valley was between the Jews and the heathens. They prepared to fight, as is written in the book. Each would have liked to drive away the other.

(304) Let us leave them to their fighting; they wreaked havoc on each other. We want to sing the marvels of a little man. The king said to David: "Go on home, and tell three of your brothers to come to me. (305) And tell three of your brothers to come: the mightiest and the best; the others are to be free [of duty obligations]. Meanwhile you are to stay with your father, until I have driven away the heathens who are here."

(306) Young David was not carefree when he left; he went to his father as the king had commanded him. Jesse sent three of his sons into battle. Then David had to spend some time with the sheep. (307) He diligently pastured the sheep for his father: a most savage bear came running out of the forest; it took one of the good sheep and carried it away. That annoyed high-spirited David. (308) "Monstrous bear, I challenge you! If you intend to rob my father, it will be to your sorrow. My father has other heirs: eight bold men." He took his crooked staff and charged at the bear. (309) With his crooked staff he struck the huge bear such a bold blow in the middle of its back that the staff broke to pieces. Little David was not glad to see that. (310) The bear slung the sheep out of its mouth far away; then it charged at the boy. David picked up three very large stones from the ground. He threw them at the bear with great force. (311) He threw the stone boldly at the bear's head so that the stone broke into little pieces. Little David said to the bear: "Were you not deliberately trying to steal my father's sheep? (312) They are now safe from you. I have

torn you apart. You had bitten my lamb very hard." The lad quite nimbly ran back to the sheep.

Then a huge lion came and carried off one of his sheep, (313) which deeply dismayed that most worthy youth: "Can I then have no peace from these evil beasts!?" He took a huge pole that was thick and long. He swung it at the lion with great force. (314) He gave it such a vehement blow on the back that the huge lion lay stretched out on the ground before him. He thought that he had quite slain the lion, but up the lion sprang and charged at the lad. (315) The lion was enraged and roared in its wrath. They fought with each other, those two exceptional ones. The lion struck boldly at the youth, so that his red blood ran down over his ears. (316) "I think that you want to rage," said the small hero. He chose a very large stone for himself; he threw it with such force at the huge lion, that its red blood flowed down over its ears. (317) The lion was quite enraged and sprang on the man. It again charged him on its hind legs. Then little David said with a raging spirit: "If you want to wrestle with me, that seems alright with me." (318) He attacked the lion, grabbed its mane, and threw it to the ground, which enraged the lion. It sprang back up and bit the youth hard. It gnashed its mighty teeth together. (319) That greatly annoyed the youth; the lion was so strong that it was not going well for the lad. The lad brought the lion to great sorrow: he grasped it by the throat with both hands. (320) The lad had won; the lion was injured. He steeled himself to the lion and quickly slew it. "You most powerful devil; you brought me into great distress. I have now well rewarded you for your misdeeds."

(321) Then David gave himself time to recover until he was well; he was injured for more than thirty days. When he was now fully recovered, then Jesse said to David: "Dear son, (322) I want to send you to your brothers." "Gladly," said David, "my dear father." Jesse then said to David: "Then go quickly and tell your brothers to send (323) their wives bills of divorce, so that they are prepared—if they were to die in battle against the heathens—so that their wives are not obligated to undergo the rite of *ḥalitzah*." "Gladly," said Sir David, "father, it will be done." (324) "Today marks forty days since the battle began. So, go and see how they are doing. Take a measure of barley ears and ten loaves of bread, and ask them if they need anything else. (325) And take ten cheeses to the army, to mighty Jonathan and his men."

David quickly did what his father commanded him to do. He let someone else herd the sheep and the goats, too. (326) David quickly did what his father had said. He took with him a sword that would cut through steel. He said: "On my oath, it will not happen to me again that I go into battle without a sword."

(327) Now, let us leave little David to do as is proper, and let us tell the marvels of a great giant. Israel and the Philistines marched out against each other on two mountains, with a deep valley between them. (328) They cast and shot, but no one wanted to go down into the valley. Then the heathens came rushing with a great noise. There was a great giant named Goliath. He had been brought up in the land of the Philistines. (329) He was mighty and tall—more than nine feet tall. The giant was eager to attack and fight. He wore a great copper helmet on his head, and additionally he wore armor of good steel. (330) Attached to the ring mail were small plates so that sharp arrows could not penetrate. The rings had been well tempered. The heavy armor weighed some five hundred pounds. (331) His shoulder protection was a copper shield. He carried it on his shoulder—in truth I tell you that. What did he carry on his shoulder? A pole that was as thick and long as a ship's mast. (332) At the end of the pole was a point of iron, quite large: the spear point weighed six hundred pounds. He bore at his side a very large sword whose value is beyond estimation.

(333) Goliath called loudly through his great helmet—his strength and great power were beyond measure: "You Jews, you are fools! What are you doing here? Do you want to fight with us, you tiny men? (334) And are you nonetheless the best of King Saul's servants? In all his hardships, you are all he deserves. In all his hardships, you have done your best. Choose one from among all of you who dares to fight me. (335) I am a common Philistine, like any other man. Choose one from among all of you who dares to fight me. If we all come to attack you, then many will die; let us prevent that."

(336) And when the people of Israel looked at the giant and his great strength, how quickly they fled from there. The giant was contemptuous of Saul and his men. He said: "You have warriors whom no one can praise."

(337) The giant had been coming diligently twice a day, at the time of morning and evening prayers, with vituperations and mockery, altogether for forty days—for as long as all Israel had encamped opposite the heathens. (338) King Saul let it be proclaimed: "I will free the one who slays the giant—no matter who it is—he will pay neither tax nor tribute: neither he and nor any of his father's household, for as long as I live. (339) And whatever money he has to pay in duties, he will receive from me. And the king's daughter will be given to him as payment."

Now young David came to the people. The people went to battle, and when he saw that, (340) the very young David cast away everything. He wore at his side a sword that was sharp; the sword was belted on, in a good scabbard. He came to his brothers and asked how they were. (341) The battle was tumultuous; they shouted in the battle. Then came Goliath, may God give him a evil time. He mocked the king and his men a great deal. The people then fled away from there onto the mountain. (342) When he saw the mockery, David began to get angry. The people then told him what the king had said: what was to be given to the man who slew the giant, and also how, because of his strength, he wore huge armor.

(343) Young David heard that and was very pleased by the words. He said to the people who were standing near him there: "What has been offered to the man who slays the giant and does not put up with his wickedness?" (344) The people then answered him: "We have already told you: King Saul's daughter is ready to become his bride, and his father's household is to be freed from tax obligations, and whatever money he has to pay in duties, will be given to him as a reward."

(345) David's eldest brother, Eli'ab, heard that. He began to get angry; he burst with anger when he heard David speak so audaciously. He feared that David would be slain by the giant's strength. (346) "I know well," said Eli'ab, "your wickedness has been revealed: you have come here to try your hand in combat. To whom have you entrusted our sheep in the desert? Get out of my sight. Go home!"

(347) Then Sir David answered him: "What have I done to you, that you, dear brother, will not let me speak?" David went from there to another place. He again asked the people; they told him quickly. (348) They told him what the king had commanded. That well pleased David, the young lad. Word came to the king about what David had said. The king ordered that he be brought, that most valiant lad. (349) How quickly King Saul took David in. When bold David came to the king, he said: "Merciful lord, have armor brought for me. Allow me to fight. I will defeat the giant." (350) The king then burst out laughing, for he was the little one who played the lute. "Little tyke with the fiddle, what do you think you are doing here? You are a little child, while he is a mighty man. (351) He has fought many a battle in his life. Here your organ and your lute will be out of tune. He will tighten your strings so that you will regret it." "No," said David, "King, be not despondent. (352) I have slain bears and lions without a sword. I will not endure the arrogance of the mighty giant." The king then answered him and ceased his mockery: "Then go, young warrior, and may God grant you succor." (353) He said: "You are to wear all my armor." The king took off his armor and armed the little man. A great marvel happened to the little servant there: Saul's huge armor fit the little one well. (354) When the king saw that, it began to annoy him—and that the huge metal armor would encase the little one.

Now, little David was quite a wise man: it seemed to him in his mind that the king was looking at him. (355) "No," said the little one, "King, I want to tell you. I have never in my life worn armor. I do not want to go out to meet him armed this way. I will fight with a sling, as I have done in the past." (356) The youth took off the steel chain-mail. The youth put back on his travelling clothes. He girded his very good sword at his side. He took a sling with him and wanted to fight with stones. (357) That lad took five hard pebbles. In his other hand he took his shepherd's staff. He went toward the huge Philistine while the giant watched him.

"Does this one want to fight me?" he said to himself. (358) He said: "Now, you are a child and have recently suckled. If you wish to fight against me, you will have indeed been betrayed. Do you think that I am a common dog? You come with a stick and want to give me wounds? (359) By my god, Dagon, I would be shamed by fighting you. But no matter how young you are, I will take your life; I will tear away your young life. I will give your carcass to the livestock in the field. (360) The flesh of your body will be eaten by livestock. Your God cannot help you; Dagon has forgotten you."

"No," said the little one, "I have bad news for you. I am going to cut off your head with your own sword. (361) My God has today delivered you into my hand. I will render your sword and your weapons into toys in your hands. I hear by your own words that you are a dead man. You say that I will be eaten by something that can eat no one. (362) You say the livestock in the field are to eat me. The cows and the oxen have made promises to me. You besotted heathen, even today will I take your life. I will give your carcass to the wild animals of the fields. (363) The wolves and the other wild animals and the savage birds—they will rip you apart when I have taken your carcass. You come so well encased in good, steel garments. Nonetheless, God, blessed be He, will deliver you into my hand. (364) I trust in Him with all my heart. He will soon take away your life. You have berated a Lord Whom no one may berate. For that reason He will help me to slay you. (365) You have made God in Heaven, blessed be He, very angry. For that reason all your strength will fail you. My God, blessed be He, will repay you for your mockery. In the name of the Lord God I will strike you dead. (366) You cannot escape me, even though you have long legs. Death will sneak up on you. Your life is impure. When I have slain you, I will put on your armor. God, blessed be He, can indeed give succor to a naked man against a giant. (367) When I have vanquished you, most evil giant, and delivered all Israel from the Philistines, then all the world will see that God can indeed give succor to a naked man against a mighty giant. (368) It is not a matter of your armor or your sword. It is a matter of the Lord God and whom He wishes to aid. Now, prepare for battle, you devilish man. If you do not want to start, then I will. (369) Devil from Hell, I challenge you. You will regret that you were ever born."

The giant was annoyed by the bold speech. Because of his great rage, he growled like bear. (370) "You speak quite boldly, you tiny little dwarf, and even if there were a thousand of you, you would still have to die." "I have heard tell that he who dies from threats is buried to the sound of farts. (371) And whether you were in Heaven or the depths of Hell, I will do you harm with my good sword."

Enraged, the giant attacked the little one. Now, let us sing marvels of how the little one welcomed him. (372) When King Saul saw how they came together, he said to his captain: "Tell me, Abner, you mighty hero, tell me the truth, to whom does the youth who wants to slay the giant belong?" (373) From whom does he come, among the house of Judah, from Perez or from Zerah? Pay attention and tell me accurately." Then the hero Abner said at that time: "I cannot tell you; I do not know the truth."

(374) And when the huge giant went against David, David defended himself and gave him a stern welcome. David quickly took his sling in hand; he wound a large pebble in the sling. (375) He cast the stone with great force at the giant's brow and through all his armor into his brain. He cast it so vehemently at the huge man that he had to fall down on the earth. (376) Then David, the warrior, leapt on the giant. He took the giant's sword in his hand; he knocked off his helmet and took him by the hair. He struck off his head and laid it on a litter. (377) He stripped off his weaponry and took his fine sword. He said: "I will keep it; it is worth a great deal of money." He took the giant's head and carried it away. The king and all his men welcomed him warmly. (378) "Now, may God welcome you, you fine young warrior. When you mature, you will be possessed of a noble spirit. If you grow into manhood, you will be someone to be feared. No one will dare look at you askance. (379) Now, tell me, dear lad, the truth and no lie: do you come from Perez or Zerah?"

Now, David was quite perfected in his wisdom. He also well knew what the king intended toward him. (380) The king slyly considered in his heart whether David was the king who was to succeed him. He said: "Gracious lord, in reply to your question: my father is named Jesse, from the city of Bethlehem. (381) I am still too young and must therefore keep silent. I have never in my life heard tell whether I am of the clan of Perez or Zerah. I do not know, my lord, so do not hold me in contempt."

(382) Quite quickly Jonathan went to David. He took him in both his arms with embraces and kisses: "No one can drive me away from you!" He loved

him as his own life. (383) They swore a firm oath, the excellent heroes, with well-considered intent and no reluctance. They wanted to be sworn comrades in all adversity. No one could separate them—nothing but bitter death itself. (384) Jonathan gave David very fine armor. The two companions armed themselves in steel mail-coats.

When the heathens saw that David, the little man, had slain the giant, they fled from there. (385) They turned tail and fled as fast as they could. The king and his heroes pursued the heathens. The two sworn comrades were seen there dealing mighty strokes: no one whom they overtook could escape. (386) Little David fought a fierce fight. He took a position in a narrow space and soon made some room around himself. And his sworn comrade did not wish to leave his side. The heathens could not but let them have their way. (387) They then pursued the Philistines to the gates of Ekron and to Gath—that I tell you in truth. There they slew many a heathen man. The king and his mighty men rose up then. (388) They stripped the dead whom they had slain, and what they found on them, that they also took home. David bore Goliath's sword and his head into Jerusalem. His armor and his weaponry were to stay in his house. (389) He said: "I would like to sell it, as is proper for me to do: many a guilder and many a penny would have to be given to me."

Saul then appointed David as captain in battle: wherever the king sent him, he struck broad wounds. (390) He captured land and people for the king. He fought with great strength, as the book informs us. He put him in command of the army from that point on. Sir David, the king, and all his men were pleased by this. (391) He did not want to let young David go home. He said: "You have to remain here with me at all times. You are to be in command of all my forces. You fight with great might in your youth."

(392) The king and his heroes went home. They went to Gibeah in the land of Israel. They were heartily welcomed in many a worthy city. Now, hear how they came out of Gibeah to meet David: (393) a great many beautiful and comely ladies stepped splendidly with drums and sackbuts. They greatly praised the king and his men. They sang sweetly and raised up a song: (394) "We all wish to sing—whoever can do so. One hears the chiming of armor on a worthy man. Noble King Saul is full of manly virtues; well can he fight with his sharp sword. (395) The king and his heroes are truly to be praised: one sees the noble lord rampage. With his sword he slew a thousand men. Therefore, we all wish to sing, whoever can do so. (396) Noble King Saul has many a good man. In assault and in battle they are a strong force. These bold and mighty heroes are indeed to be praised. One sees the bold warriors rampaging in battle. (397) One mighty young warrior is named David. He has recently arrived;

we have just come to know him. He is a mighty warrior, the most noble of men whose peer is nowhere to be found. (398) He did not wish to endure anything from the huge and mighty giant. In addition, he slew some ten thousand of the heathens. We can well reckon those whom he slew with his sword. The lad is to be honored; he is quite worthy of honor."

(399) That annoyed the king. He thought the words reflected on himself. He said: "They certainly praise the little one more than me. With their song they mean that he ought to be king and that he will possess my fine kingdom after me. (400) From that time on King Saul hated David. The following morning his madness came over him. Then David took his musical instrument and played very beautifully, but the king's madness would not leave him. (401) The king had a spear in his hand. He threw it at David so that it stuck in the wall. Since he did not hit him, he thought to himself: "I think that God, blessed be He, has put His mark on the lad." (402) He began to hate him and sent him away. He put the young warrior in command of only a thousand men. He had to fight in the vanguard of every battle. He had to suffer anguish before all Israel. (403) The king did that so that he would be slain. Many were the dead who had to be borne away before the lad. All Israel loved David very much. He was always at the vanguard and allowed nothing to happen to anyone.

(404) God, blessed be He, succored David in all his adversities. The king was afraid of him; he secretly wanted to kill him. The king said to David: "Hero, I will tell you: if you fight hard and slay my enemies, (405) then I will give you my eldest daughter's hand; Merab, my beautiful daughter, will be yours." Then David said: "Dear my lord, I am a poor man, that you mock me thus. I am not of the same status as you." (406) "Oh," said the king, "I want to give her to you." He thought to himself that his life was at stake. "I will take care of him and put up with him, but he must be slain by the heathens."

(407) The news spread far and wide that David was to marry Merab, the princess. He did not need to be ashamed of her. But the king did not give her to him: he gave her to Azriel;[14] his hopes were for naught. (408) David regretted it very much concerning the most beautiful maiden, that Azriel was to have the beautiful princess. Since he could not have her, he had to give her up. The king had yet another daughter who was quite beautiful. (409) Her name was Michal the Fair, as she was called. She was also quite beautiful and was dear to the young man. Young David was in her heart. That delighted David, the fine hero, heartily.

(410) A servant of the noble king told him the news, how beautiful Michal would like to marry David. The idea well pleased the king. He said: "I will give him her hand, but it will never profit him. (411) He will have to be slain

by her design." He said to his servants: "Speak with the lad. If he wants the princess, I will give her to him on the spot." They then conveyed the message as the king had commanded. (412) They said: "My dear David, we inform you that the king wishes to have you as a son-in-law. And all the king's servants have desired it. You are to marry Michal; you are quite worthy of the honor." (413) He answered them courteously: "I would like for her to be mine. Does it seem to you a small thing to be the king's son-in-law? In addition, I am poor; my property is not worth much. I know that the king does not want me for a son-in-law." (414) They then told the king what young David had said. Then King Saul said: "I will make it uncomfortable for him. I will give her to him, but he will be slain. Go to David; you are to tell him this: (415) 'If you are not a rich man in terms of property, the king will not hold it against you, if you can take great vengeance on his enemies. Dare to do it then for the sake of his daughter, whom he will then give to you. (416) You should pay close attention to how he wants to have it done. Young warrior, you are to go to the heathens and invade their lands with force. Take your very good sword with you in your hand. (417) A hundred mighty heathens—pay attention to what we mean—you are to strike off the "toes" between their legs. The king wishes to avenge himself on his enemies. Bring them here, to Gibeah, and cast them before the bride. (418) By that means you are to be married to the comely maiden.'"

David the hero leapt up and was a bold man. The young warrior David then armed himself. He and his men advanced into the land of the Philistines. (419) There he found some two hundred heathen men. He slew them all; not a single one escaped him. With his sword he struck off all their "toes," which he then brought to the bride in her father's house. (420) He said: "Dear princess, I want to give you 'toes.' By means of them I want to marry you. I have risked my life. I have taken vengeance on the king's enemies. Your father ordered it; I could not ignore his command." (421) Then King Saul put on a mockery[15] of a wedding and gave him his daughter Michal. It was ordained by God. There the lady took the young man, David, as dear to her as life—as I can tell you. (422) The king was not at all pleased that he loved her. He saw and could recognize that that was from God, blessed be He. He hated his son-in-law with his whole heart. He thought to himself: "He is a proper enemy of mine."

(423) Then the heathens again gathered a great army. David did not long delay: he took all their army. Wherever he went in the land, he was always victorious. His name became more famous than all the mighty men. (424) David the hero was indeed to be praised. The noble warrior was seen rampaging in grim battles. He was now well known in all lands: The hero was called David the Mighty. (425) Noble King Saul, however, consulted with all his counselors

about how he could slay him—that most worthy David. "I must have a subterfuge. It is all over for him: he must die."

(426) Now, the hero Jonathan was also loved by David, as was proper for a dear brother-in-law. Because of his deep love, he could not live without him. If he could not see him, he could not survive. (427) His dear brother-in-law loved him with all his heart. "Gracious my lord king and dear father, while you have lived you have always avoided sin. Why do you want to kill him? After all he has done nothing. (428) If you were to shed the blood of a noble warrior in your kingdom, that would be the deed of a sinner. All Israel knows that he is a noble man, the mightiest and the best who can be found. (429) Now, the young warrior has never committed a sin. Have fear of the Lord God: you ought to let him live! Why blame the young duke, if ladies praise him? Now, your heart also rejoiced when he defeated the giant. (430) He risked life and limb and fought many battles. He took the life of the giant Goliath. Your heart rejoiced when he won. And you want to slay him precisely because of his innocence! (431) Noble and merciful lord and father, think of our God. Let him live, so that he can take care of your daughter."

"You chastise me severely," said the exalted king, "bring your comrade here; I will do nothing more to him." (432) "Gracious my lord and father, I am not taken in by that: how am I to know that nothing will happen to him?" "No," said the king, "you need have no further worries. By Israel's God, blessed be He, I will let him live."

(433) The Jonathan rejoiced and went without any worries to David, his dear brother-in-law, where he had hidden him. He said: "Brother-in-law and comrade, may you live in joy. The king has declared peace and protection for you." (434) Then David went with anxiety to stand before the king and served his father-in-law as he had previously done. Then the heathens again began to cause fear and great adversity; they slew many Jews in the land. (435) They had gathered together—as the sands of the sea—and advanced into the lands of the Jews with a great army. King Saul then said: "David, I say to you: take my mighty ones with you; you are to defeat the heathens."

(436) David and his men then armed themselves diligently. David was at the vanguard; he was the first to fight in all battles. Whoever he could reach lost his life. He waded through blood up above his golden spurs. (437) There were as many heathens as sand in the sea. David and his forces were a small army. They were—every man of them—heroes and were of reckless courage. They slew many a heathen and waded through the blood. (438) Then the heathens with their great army wanted always to defeat the small man. A very great troop of them rushed at David. He then had to make good use of his armor

and his spear. (439) Sweaty blood flowed abundantly through the mail-coats. The heathens had many a strong man. Sir David fought well—great adversity forced him to it. There fell dead many a heathen by his sword. (440) Many of the heathens there attacked the little man. Bolts of savage fire sprang off his helmet. His shield was hacked to pieces. Many a dead heathen had, nonetheless, to be borne away from him.

(441) When the Jews saw David's grim battle, they rushed to him. It seemed to them about time. "If we were to leave our lord, we would be betrayed." They fought their way violently to David. (442) David then rejoiced when he saw his men. From the great battle the vapors burst up into the heavens. There they slew heathens beyond number, and of the king's men a great many also fell.

(443) David feared for his mighty men against the evil heathens. He saw some of his men fall; that deeply grieved him. Noble Duke David did not stay to the rear of the battle line: he played wickedly devilish games with the heathens. (444) He made vigorous use his sword with both hands. He gave the mighty heathens many a stalwart stroke. He cleared a wide circle all around. He made the heathens exude bloody sweat. (445) His worthy men followed David well. Sweaty blood flowed abundantly through the mail-coats. They broke through the great army and their camp and knocked their flags down onto the ground. (446) A mighty cloud of vapor burst up into the heavens, so that a man scarcely could see his neighbor next to him. The Philistines had to flee, forced by their great afflictions. No one was able to count their dead left lying there. (447) They fled from there into the land; David pursued them. Many a heathen was then very eager to escape. Thereafter David and his men rushed homeward with such great joy that no one can describe.

(448) Saul was sorry that David had not been slain. He began to lament for it secretly in his heart. The next morning his madness came upon him. Then David played sweetly and beautifully on his musical instrument. (449) Saul vigorously took his spear in his hand. He wanted to nail young David to the wall. But David—that honorable man—dodged the lance. The spear stuck in the wall; David escaped from there.

(450) David escaped home to his own house and to his dear wife who was looking out the window. She saw the king's servants come running behind him. She slammed the doors closed when she recognized the envoys. (451) They surrounded David's house: "Indeed he cannot escape us. And when day comes, he will have to die." Then young David realized that he would have to suffer pain. He had thought that he would be without any worries in his own house. (452) Then the princess went before her husband. "David, my dear husband, my most comely beloved, you must flee from here. You are in

serious trouble. If you do not escape from here, you will be dead tomorrow. (453) Where have you left your light cuirass, your very good sword and steel mail-coat?" He said: "My dear, beloved lady, I fled; I was in trouble. Your father, the king, wanted to slay me. (454) I quickly fled from there, so that I might survive. No one could give me my sword and armor. My dear, beloved lady, now give me your counsel; help me get away from here tonight so that they do not slay me." (455) She said: "I love you; I will do what I can to help you. Let me not suffer for it hereafter, my beloved husband. If I help you get away from here, as seems good to me, I will get in frightful trouble with my father. (456) I will have to risk it, you high-spirited hero. Remember me, my lord, when your condition improves. If you should leave me, you undaunted hero, I could have no greater sorrow in my life." (457) "Now listen, dear lady, you can rest assured: if God in Heaven, blessed be He, grants me aid, I will not forget you." She let him down from a window on a rope. She said: "Dear my lord, may God, blessed be He, grant you good fortune and safety."

(458) When he came to the ground, he made haste to flee. He fled from there to the city of Ramah. When he came to Ramah to the prophet Samuel, he lamented to the honorable prophet about why he was there. (459) He lamented to him about what Saul had done to him.

Now let us leave Sir David to lament to the prophet, and sing of his lady and what she did and what she told the king's men. (460) She said to the servants: "Why have you come here? What does my father want? Or what is his desire?" "Noble lady, princess, we would like to inform you that the king has great need of David. (461) Tell your lord that he should go to the king. He is not to disobey his command on pain of death." The noble princess then said: "That cannot be; my dear lord has fallen ill."

(462) The messengers went quickly to the king to tell him the news. Then the princess ordered that a large image be brought to her. First she bound a goatskin to its head, then she laid it on the bed and covered it well with a blanket. (463) They went to the king and told him the news, how David was sick at home. He said: "Tell my daughter that you want to go to him, and bring him—with the bed. He must die."

(464) Then the messengers went and wanted to see him. "We want to see his illness," they said to the lady. They wanted to carry him away from there, but he was not inside. They found a large idol lying in the bed. (465) They then told the king the news, how a large idol was lying in the bed. Then King Saul sent for his noble daughter. He said: "You have helped David, my enemy, to escape me. (466) In addition, you have deceived me with a large image. For that I give you my solemn promise that I will repay your disloyalty." She said:

"My dear father, I was forced to do it: if I had refused to help him, he would have killed me. (467) I had to defend my life against him in my own house. He would have slain me, so I let him escape."

Now let us leave Saul and his daughter to deal with it, and sing further about what was happening with Sir David. (468) David quickly lamented his misery to Samuel. The prophet Samuel then said: "Then stay with me for a while." Samuel then taught David so much Torah that it became the lad's desire and his heart's delight. (469) This news was soon announced to Saul, how Sir David had been seen in Ramah with Samuel. He said: "He has then most assuredly lost his life. I would not give a fig for him and for Samuel. (470) No one can help him. I am going to slay him." The king sent his messengers: "Go there and bring him quickly." When the messengers then came to Ramah, they saw Samuel and the other prophets. (471) Now, hear how a marvel occurred there. And when the king's messengers looked at the prophets, they also became prophets and prophesied with them. The king's message never even occurred to them.

(472) Saul was told the news about how a marvel had occurred: "We saw all your messengers prophesying." Then the king sent other messengers there. They also became prophets and prophesied in the group. (473) Enraged, he again sent messengers: "And do not you dare become prophets! Beware lest you do it!" When they saw the prophets openly prophesying, then the prophecy of God, blessed be He, indeed also came over them. (474) They prophesied before Samuel as other legitimate prophets.

"Not with me!" said the king. "If this continues, I will soon have no men left. What I want done, I will have to do myself!" He had his armor and sword brought to him. (475) The king himself rode to the city of Ramah. That same ruler of the land asked the people: "Where are Samuel and David? Tell me that!" They said: "You will find both of the lords in study." (476) The warrior Saul then dismounted onto the ground. He went to where they were studying and found David there. When he also looked at the prophet Saul, he again became weak from his madness. (477) He then raged in the house: he threw himself onto the ground and gave himself injuries. He took off his clothes and ran away from there naked. The man was deranged all night and all day. (478) Then the prophet Samuel said: "David, my dear son, I will tell you what you are to do. Great are the envy and the hatred that the king has. If you were to stay with me any longer, he would have you slain. (479) For as long as the kingdom is granted to you by God, blessed be He, you will have to save your life by haste alone; your fear and distress are just beginning. You have to flee from him as from death itself. (480) Flee then in the name of God Who can well aid you." They were both weeping much, the two honorable men. "Then grant me leave, my lord" said David to Samuel. Their eyes were misted with tears.

(481) Sir David took his leave and left there and came to Gibeah to Jonathan. He said: "Brother-in-law and sworn companion: help me, I am in need. Your father, the king, again wants to slay me." (482) "No," said Jonathan, "indeed that cannot be. My dear father does nothing without my knowledge. How could he hide from me such deeply felt pain? For that reason, it is a lie," said Jonathan to David. (483) "Alas, it is true, my dear brother-in-law. I am scarcely one step away from being stabbed to death." He lamented all his hardships to Jonathan: "By God in Heaven, blessed be He, he wants to slay me. (484) Your father certainly knows of our great love. For that reason he has now not informed you. So, counsel me my dear brother-in-law, you worthy man." He said: "I want to help you as best I can."

(485) Jonathan said: "Hear my counsel: tomorrow is the first of the month, when one goes to dine with the king. All the king's servants must be at the table. I know that the king will indeed remember you. (486) I will say that you have already gone to Bethlehem and that I have given you leave to go there: all your brothers have prepared a fine feast and have also invited David to it. (487) If the king is silent and lets it pass by, then he will do nothing to you. That is what my sense tells me. If he gets angry at me because I let you go, then I will understand my father's intentions. (488) If he wants to bring you under his control and if he wants to kill you quickly, then I will not bring you to my father. You need have no worries, my brother-in-law and comrade. (489) Why would I want to deliver you over to my father? Or why would I have you killed?"

David said to him: "You most worthy man, if your father wants to kill me, then help me get away from here. (490) But who is to tell me, my dear brother-in-law, how your dear father answers you?" Jonathan then said to him: "That I can tell you. Come, let us go for a walk: you will understand my words exactly."

(491) They went out together onto a broad field. There Jonathan said to David: "Conceal yourself; it is time. You are to hide in this cavern until I come out again with my squire. (492) I will shoot three sharp arrows at this stone. If I say to my squire, 'Bring them here, and hurry!' and then: 'The arrows are closer,' then bring them to me yourself, you need have no worries. (493) If, however, I shoot the arrows far beyond the target, then I will say to my squire: 'The arrows are much farther,' then flee quickly from here, my dear companion. Pay close attention to my words; that is to be your sign."

(494) The love was great between the two of them. They swore an oath to each other and renewed their old oath. David stepped into the cavern with great anxiety. Jonathan returned to the city of Gibeah. (495) All the king's

servants came to the table to eat with the king; they took their food. All his servants and many a bold man came there. David's place was empty; no one sat there. (496) The king was silent on that day. He thought to himself: "Perhaps he cannot come; perhaps he has to go to the ritual bath tonight; perhaps he is unclean. Tomorrow he will come: so my thoughts tell me."

(497) On the next morning, when it was again time to eat, David's place was empty; no one sat there. The king said to Jonathan: "Tell me the truth. Why does the son of Jesse not come, neither yesterday nor today?" (498) Jonathan then answered him with fine courtliness: "I gave him leave to go to Bethlehem. All his brothers and his clan are having a great feast and celebration. (499) He entreated me so firmly that I immediately gave him leave. He said that his elder brother had sent for him." The king was angry; his rage burned in him. "You take after your mother, Jonathan, you villain! (500) The mother who bore you is malicious; there is much to say about her wickedness and contumaciousness. She is constantly leaving the house and even took me along. There is no escapade that is beyond her. (501) You act in every way like your mother. You constantly wish to rescue my own proper enemy from me. As long as David is alive, you cannot be my heir, and you need not think of gaining the kingship. (502) Tell me immediately where you have hidden him. Summon him, he deserves to be slain." "My father and my lord, let the people know why he must die. Indeed what has he done? (503) If you are a proper judge, my dear father, then, for the sake of God, blessed be He, let your noble son-in-law live."

Then the king was so filled with rage that he could at that time not say a word. (504) Because of his great wrath he took his huge spear and threw it at Jonathan with a vehement heave. Shame entered Jonathan's heart, who lamented miserably for his dear brother-in-law. (505) From sorrow and rage he rose from the upper table. His father had shamefully denigrated his mother. He wanted never again to eat or drink with the king. He grieved deeply for him and for his comrade.

(506) In the morning when it became day and the sun came up, he went with his squire to the cavern, where he had hidden his dear comrade. He had lain there with his worries until the fourth day. (507) Jonathan carried a copper bow and vigorously cocked the crossbow with his foot. He quickly shot three arrows, as I wish to say, toward the cavern, far beyond the target. (508) He said to the squire: "Go and fetch the arrows. They are far beyond the target. Go and be quick!" He ran and brought the arrows as his lord had commanded. From that David clearly understood that he again had to flee. (509) Jonathan gave the squire the bow and the arrows. He said: "Carry them home; go,

and be quick!" He ran so quickly that the sweat ran off of him. Jonathan and David wept hot tears. (510) They kissed and embraced each other, the two worthy men. They wept so pitiably that David began to sob. It was a great sorrow to them that they had to part. Their cheeks were then streaked with tears. (511) Jonathan said to David: "My dear comrade: go and save your life. May God, blessed be He, be with you, since I cannot help you, my sworn comrade. I have never had a more sorrowful day in all my life." (512) They parted from one another. Jonathan returned home.

David fled from there unarmed and alone. He fled to a city called Nob, where there were priests whom David knew well. (513) They bore Urim and Thummim. That is the reason why he went there. He thought: "I will ask God; perhaps I will find out what I should undertake and what I should do, and where I should go—bewildered man that I am." (514) He ran across a very broad heath covered with many wild herbs. He walked over one herb, called *bulimus*, whose effect I will explain to you. (515) Whoever steps on it becomes ill. He must eat bread with his mouth immediately; if he delays a while, he will die. From the effect of this herb David came to distress. (516) He said to the high priest, who was named Ahim'elech: "Give me bread to eat; I am weak from hunger." The honorable high priest then became quite alarmed. He said: "Now tell me sir, why are you alone. (517) Where are all your men, most excellent Duke? And your good armor and your knightly spurs? Tell me why you are alone." He said: "I am on a pressing mission from the king (518) to a secret place; I cannot tell anyone. The king sent me; I must keep silent. Do not keep me waiting for a long time. Give me some bread to eat. I am almost dead from the effect of *bulimus*." (519) Then the priest answered him: "I have no common bread, but only show bread that has been in the temple." "Give it to me; I may indeed eat it in order to save my life." He then gave him five loaves; he ate a great deal of it.

(520) One of King Saul's servants was also there, a bold and mighty warrior, which displeased many a man. Doeg the Edomite was the servant's name. He saw the high priest having a great banquet. (521) When David had then eaten what he wanted, he said to the priest: "Do you not have a sword somewhere? I left my sword and weaponry at home. I had to leave the king in a great hurry." (522) The high priest then said: "There is no sword here, except Goliath's sword, whom you killed in the valley of Elah. If you want it, I have kept it well." "That and no other do I want," said the good warrior. (523) He consulted Urim and Thummim for him and brought him Goliath's sword. Sir David was delighted. He said: "It is most valuable." He took both courage and joy there.

He then turned to the Philistines and went to Gath. (524) He thought that he could be quite without worries in the land of the Philistines: "They will hide me from my lord." Now the Philistines had again come to a consensus and made one of their number king. (525) The king's name was Achish, and Gath was his capital city. David entered Gath without any worries. When the king's men saw him, they clearly recognized him. They said to the king: "He should be killed." (526) They said: "That is David from the land of the Jews. He has caused great harm to many a mighty heathen. He would be suitable as a ruler; he has conquered us. He is the David about whom the women sang the little song: (527) 'Noble King Saul has slain a thousand men, and David some ten thousand.' We cannot endure it from him." Then King Achish said: "Then bring him to me as a prisoner." Then poor David thought: "It is all over for me!" (528) He constantly called on God Almighty, for which reason He did not abandon him in any adversity. They brought him as a prisoner before the king. Then poor David again had to suffer.

(529) Now this same king had a daughter—that is the truth. She had been insane for many years. David had been captured and wanted to delay no longer. Before the king he played the role of the court fool. (530) He knew well how to act the fool—the man played the fool—with a great deal of foolishness, as I can well tell you. He became the court fool and spared no folly there. He let his spittle run down over his beard (531) and took it in his hands and played with it and patted it in his hands and on all the walls. King Achish then said: "He is a fool. Do not bring him to me; drive him far away from here. (532) Do I, alas, have too few lunatics in my house. You remind me of all my sorrows. Just get him out of here."

They drove the fool out, and away he ran. Sir David was delighted by this beyond measure. (533) He ran to a cavern in the land of Judah. He wished to dwell there; he thought that no one knew. His father and mother then came to him in distress. They had fled from Saul who wanted to slay them. (534) Everyone whom Saul oppressed fled to David, and those who had great debts did not long delay, and whoever for love of adventure wanted to experience knighthood, they came to David in the cave of Adullam. (535) He was glad to have them all—anyone who wanted to be with him. No matter where they came from, he gladly took them in. Several hundred very mighty men swore him their service. King David then again took courage from that.

(536) David left there and went to the land of the king of Moab. He said: "Gracious my lord, tell me whether you will help me. Allow my father and my mother to stay here with you until I have a secure place for my servants. (537) I bring them to your honor and entrust them to you to give them shelter

from King Saul for me." The king of Moab then said: "David, that will be done. I will keep them safe from King Saul." (538) Then they stayed with the king of Moab for many a day, until it was reported to King Saul. Then, however, King Saul sent an order: "Slay all of David's household! (539) If you do not do it immediately, I am prepared, and consider yourself, king of Moab, already challenged to combat." And the king of Moab was then afraid of King Saul's order. He had David's father and mother slain, (540) in addition to all their household whom he found there. David's brother fled to the land of the Ammonites to King Nahash who held him by force until David's affairs became more promising.

(541) David and his men had a stronghold from which they often made sorties in order to get provisions. Then the prophet Gad came to David. He said: "Get away from here; do not stay here! (542) Saul will soon be searching for you here. So get away and go to the land of Judah." David and his men went to the land of Judah. Saul grieved sorely that he did not find David there.

(543) Saul was dwelling in Gibeah, in his best city. The prophet made a point of constantly praying for him. He would otherwise have been most ignominiously stabbed to death by his men. He said to his servants: "You have betrayed me. (544) I know that the son of Jesse will make lords of you all. If I cannot find him, you can indeed laugh up your sleeves. You concealed from me that Jonathan made a pact with him. That indeed kindles my wrath against you. (545) You have given my servant great power, so that he raises his hopes concerning me and plots against my life. That will still come to cause great sorrow among you all that Jonathan made a pact with the son of Jesse." (546) Then Doeg the Edomite answered him: "I saw the son of Jesse when he was not here—with the high priest in the city of Nob. He fed David until he had eaten his fill. (547) He consulted Urim and Thummim for him, gave him Goliath's sword, and did everything that the son of Jesse desired." King Saul then sent his messenger with an order to the high priest in the city of Nob (548) He said: "Tell the high priest that he and his father's household are to come to me. Order that most holy man to come to me." And all his father's household went there with him.

(549) When they had then come before the king, the king said to Ahimelech: "Understand my words!" The most holy man then answered him in great fear: "Whatever you desire, my lord, it will be done." (550) He said: "You have betrayed me and acted against me, and you have yielded to all the desires of the son of Jesse. "And in truth," said the priest, "there is nothing unusual in that: I consulted Urim and Thummim for him, when he came to me there. (551) Now, it has always been the custom of the hero David that he comes to see

me during every conflict. How am I to avoid it? Many times have I informed him of the words of God. (552) My lord, I should remind you that he was not with you, and indeed none of your men is as truthful as he is. And in addition, he is your son-in-law, an excellent hero. That he is your enemy—I would have denied under oath. (553) I knew nothing of this tale, and none of my father's household knew anything about it." "No, priest," said the king, "I will tell you straight: you must die—you and all your clan.

(554) The king called the armed soldier who sat beside him: "Now, slay the priests of God. They knew well that David was on the run from me, and in addition they helped him, so that he could get away." (555) None of the king's servants would perform this task. Not one of them wanted to slay the very holy men. "What is the king to us, that he would have us sin?" None of them would draw his sword against them. (556) The king said to Doeg the Edomite: "You told me about it. So avenge me on the priests who have caused me grief!" Then Doeg slew the priests who were standing there. Unfortunately they had to die; he struck them deep wounds. (557) Doeg ran quickly into the city of Nob. With his sharp sword he entered the streets. There he slew whatever came toward him: the livestock, as well as children; women, as well as men. (558) All the livestock was slain. He did not spare the infants in their cribs. Regrettably, he slew eighty-five men. They were all priests who bore Urim and Thummim.

(559) Quickly the priest Abiathar, the son of Ahimelech, escaped from there and fled to David. He then told him the news of what had happened to him and how he would never again see his people. (560) Then the warrior David lamented most pitiably: "Now may God, blessed be He, have mercy that I came to this land and that many a man is dead because of me. Oh, mighty God in Heaven, I am innocent in this. (561) When I saw Doeg the Edomite present at Nob, I was deeply alarmed: he has, alas, brought all this about. Abiathar, dear friend, you must stay with me. Anyone who threatens your life also threatens mine."

(562) When Abiathar had now come to David, he brought Urim and Thummim with him. David the warrior rejoiced for it. Abiathar had to stay with him, wherever he was in the country.

(563) At that same time, the heathens again invaded. They took a great deal of the grain stores of the people of Keilah. They robbed their wheat and grain from the barns. That annoyed David and incurred his wrath. (564) David said to Abiathar: "Consult Urim and Thummim and ask whether I may come to the aid of Keilah." Then our Lord God, blessed be He, granted that the Urim said to him: "Go and help Keilah; defeat the Philistines!"

(565) Then all of his men said: "David, do not do it. We are not even sure what to do with Judah. Are we then to start a war with the Philistines? If Saul finds out, he will make it hard on us." (566) Then David again consulted the holy word: "Should I hide here, or should I fight there?" "You should help Keilah," said our Lord. "You will defeat the Philistines just as you wish."

(567) David and his men at that time began a fierce battle with the Philistines. They drove the heathens from the battlefield; they were forced to abandon their provisions and livestock. (568) The Philistines had to withdraw from the wide field. David and his men plundered their camp. David, along with their people, at once took up residence at Keilah. They had won handily and thought themselves mighty. (569) Saul was told that David was at Keilah. "Now I know where to find him! How good that is! He has moved his dwelling place into the cities. Arise, my men, let us get the rogue!"

(570) He sent his messengers throughout his lands; he quickly brought together many bold heroes. He said: "We must march: we must be in Keilah. So, let us send the messengers inside over the walls." (571) Duke David was then soon informed that the king marched on him with a great troop. David again consulted Urim and Thummim about whether King Saul would come to the city. (572) God then answered him: "He will indeed come, with strife and assault, against the city of Keilah." "Tell me, dear Lord God, can Keilah hold out? Or will Keilah deliver me to my lord?" (573) "They will hand you over to Saul during the battle." "Now, arise, my men; it is time to flee!"

David fled from there, he and all his men. There were some six hundred of them who wore armor. (574) When Saul heard this, he was not pleased by the information that David had fled the city of Keilah. He halted his march and broke off his expedition. David and his men went into the forest. (575) They made a stronghold for themselves in the wilderness of Maon, from which they made many a sortie to get provisions. Saul then searched for David for many a day. Nowhere could he find him—that I tell you in truth.

(576) Jonathan, the son of Saul, was told the news about how David and his men were in the wilderness of Maon. Jonathan then arose and went to David. With what great joy did David welcome him! (577) Jonathan said to him: "Have no fear. He will not find you. My father will have to give up his search for you." They again swore firm oaths of friendship. Jonathan arose and returned on his way.

(578) Now there were men who knew how to make pitch, which they made quite viscous from the resin of trees. They became aware of David and his men, who were living in that same place. (579) They went then to Saul and told him the news about how David and his men were hidden in the forest. Saul

heartily thanked the pitch-makers. "Go and pay close attention and bring me news! (580) Note all the places where the rogue hides, and if I can find him, then woe to him! He is not to be found: he is a clever man! Where one sees him today, he is gone by tomorrow! (581) If you can keep an eye on him, I will reward you well." They went to the king that same time; they showed him the wilderness on that same path. They showed the king and his stalwarts the trail. (582) The stronghold of David and his men was very high up. When they saw the king, they were eager to escape. "Into the wilderness of Maon onto a crag—there he will not be able to find me—so I think to myself."

(583) The charcoal-makers told him where David had fled. Saul did not long delay and pursued him. While he moved up on this side of a crag, David fled to the other side. (584) King Saul's men quickly surrounded the mountain. David cried out in his heart: "Help me, God, blessed be He. I am in need. My lord has surrounded and quite entrapped me. I fear that I must die. Samuel lied. (585) Oh, mighty God of Heaven, I have committed no sin. So, since You want to abandon me, grant aid to my men. Since I have to die—suffer torment in my innocence—then grant, dear Lord God, that I give my soul into Your keeping."

(586) God, blessed be He, sent an angel to Saul in the forest, in form altogether like a man. He said: "King Saul, go home! The heathens have done great harm in your land. (587) They are not far from here with a great army. They are plundering and burning. King, come quickly and fight!" His men counseled him to defend his land. "David and his men cannot escape us. (588) Capture David and his army another time. If the land is lost, you will never regain it." Saul quickly went from there to the heathens. David raised his hands to Heaven with great joy. (589) David again fled even farther, into the wilderness of En-gedi. He hid his men on a high mountain.

King Saul drove the heathens far away into their land. To En-gedi the king then turned. (590) He took with him three thousand of the mightiest men, the most worthy and the best to be found. They searched for Sir David on a high crag—ibexes were at home there. The king pursued David. (591) Now, in the wilderness there was a mountain with a cave, which David and his men filled up: they dwelt there in great anxiety. They were all hidden in the mountain cave. (592) Now, there was a great spider web stretched at the entrance. "Obviously no one is in the cave," said the king. The king wanted to relieve himself, so he went into the cave. He wanted to take care of his need in private, without his men.

(593) Then one of David's men reported to him quickly: "He is in your hands; now slay him quickly!" David rose quickly and crept slowly over there. He cut something off the king's garment without his realizing it. (594) He

removed a large piece of the hem. David returned to his men. They wanted to slay Saul. He held them back with his words. He said: "Keep still! (595) If we slay our lord, we will commit a sin. If God, blessed be He, has anointed him king, who would not want to have him. If a person then opposes God, misfortune will then befall him. Moreover, the whole world will mock him. (596) I will not lay my hands on my lord. He is to be unharmed by me or my men. I regret that I cut his hem. I ruined the garment, which now grieves me."

(597) His men had nonetheless ever wished to slay him. David wanted to prevent them with his sugared words. When King Saul had taken a shit in David's house, he wiped his ass and went back outside. (598) When King Saul had gone a good distance from there, David took the piece of the garment in hand. He took a position on a mountain that was very high. The king and his army were passing beneath the mountain.

(599) David called out loudly so that it resounded at a great distance, both on the mountain top above and in the valley down below. He said: "My lord king, why do you believe the people who spread slander—as I would explain it to you. (600) They say that David desires the king's death. Now, look, dear my lord: who has cut your garment. In the cave you were in my hands. You barely survived my men's intention. (601) They wanted to slay you, as I can tell you. I was barely able to save you from my men. At the same time, you ought to consider that I have never done anything to you. My lord, you always want me dead. (602) It is a disgrace to you that you are pursuing me, and you want to slay me despite my loyalty. Dear my lord, I have never done anything to harm you. Ever will God in Heaven have to vindicate me. (603) Whom does the king of Israel pursue? Against whom does he come forth? Against a dead dog he comes forth out of his house, against a commoner, worth no more than a flea. He it is whom the king pursues with an entire army!? (604) May God be a witness of my misery and judge between the two of us and avenge on you what you have done to me. You were in my grasp, and I let you go. (605) I would not lay my hands on my lord. It is for that reason that you have retained your noble life."

"Is it you, David, my son?" the king then said. Then the king wept and wept loudly. (606) He said: "David, my son, come back. I will not harm you anymore. I swear that on my honor. You could well have taken my life, while I was relieving myself in the cave. (607) You are more honorable than I, that I admit to you. If I had found you in there, I would have slain you. Only now do I realize that you will be king and will possess my good kingdom after me. (608) You tore my hem; now I can clearly see that. Once in anger the prophet Samuel told me that after my death you would do no harm to my children.

Swear that to me with a binding oath. (609) Then you will be safe from me." "Gladly, dear my lord" said Sir David. David then swore a binding oath to Saul that he would not harm his children after his death.

(610) Saul then went home and was not slow about it. David and his men went back to their stronghold. At that same time, great lamentation began: the people were saying that the prophet Samuel had died. (611) All Israel wished to lament the death of the prophet Samuel. They lamented the prophet; he certainly was worthy of it. He was buried at Ramah with great honors. Yet all Israel had to suffer the loss.

(612) Now, there was a man in Maon named Nabal. He had great wealth in the land of Carmel. He was quite free from care because of his sheep and cattle. He always had three times as much of everything as he needed. (613) Now, his servants were grazing their sheep near David. David and his men helped them at all times. They also let no one do them any harm. Willingly they left Sir David alone.

(614) It was a custom at that time that when one sheared his sheep, he held a banquet. Whoever want to eat came running. Nabal was now shearing his sheep in Carmel. David and his men found out about it. (615) Now the man Nabal had a very beautiful wife. She was graced with all virtues. She was noble and good and could do all things well. Now her husband, Nabal, was full of every kind of wickedness.

(616) Now it was two or three days before the celebration of the new year that David was told that Nabal had decided to shear his sheep. David and his men did not have much to eat. (617) David sent his messengers to Nabal in Carmel: "Give us something to eat from your sheep, and well may you prosper. Keep in mind that we have treated you well. We have never let your shepherds in the fields lack for anything, (618) day or night. In that you can believe me. Ask your shepherds; they will tell you. We have little to eat for the holiday. You have shorn your sheep. You ought not forget us. (619) You ought to consider our poor people and give us, dear Nabal, some of your food." David commanded his servants: "When you get there, for my sake give him my greetings and offer him kind words."

(620) David's messengers came to Nabal. No one wished to welcome them. The miserable lads were left standing there. A great deal of food and drink was being carried around the house. It would have been enough for a king. (621) Then the messengers went before Nabal. They said: "Duke David sends his greetings." They delivered the message as David had said it. Nabal then answered: "I will give him nothing but heartache." (622) He became truculent to his lord, for which reason he had to endure hostile comments his whole

life long. "If I gave every runaway lad enough to eat, I would not even have a turnip left to show for my own hard work. (623) The son of Jesse is a villain; I recognize him well. His whole lineage descends from Ruth the Moabite." Then the messengers said to him: "Do you not wish to give him something better. We will tell our lord; it is not proper for you." (624) "Now, all of his men have run away to this place. Do you really think that I dare not say who the son of Jesse is?" The messengers then went away; they had become red with shame, and they at once told the king of Nabal's response.

(625) David and his men then consulted together. They all said: "He deserves to die." Four hundred mighty heroes put on their armor, and only two hundred men remained in their refuge. (626) David said angrily: "All the good things that we have done for him are for nothing; that makes me very angry. Let us slay whatever we come across: the livestock and also the children, the women and also the men. (627) I swear on my life—or let it be all over for me—that tomorrow when the sun rises so that one can see, I will turn his house with its foundation into a disgrace for him. Not even enough will remain to him that a dog can piss on a wall."

(628) One of Nabal's servants went to Nabal's wife. He said: "Dear lady, now you must do something to help yourself. Duke David sent messengers here, to the honor of our lord, who has in return insulted him. (629) What he said greatly dishonored the hero David. I fear that Duke David will not leave it unavenged. In the wilderness they let us suffer no deprivation. Whatever we asked of him, they did it all. (630) Now, our lord Nabal ordered a great many shameful and dishonorable things said to David. He will not endure it from him. I fear that he will slay us all. We dare not say anything. Now you must take care of yourself."

(631) Abigail then hurried and took two hundred loaves of bread, and she quickly loaded two kegs of wine, and five roasted sheep stuffed full of eggs, and at the same time she took five measures of barley ears, (632) a hundred green grapes and two hundred green figs. She said: "I will give him this as a gift; perhaps he will keep his peace." She said to her servants: "Now, load the donkeys right away. Ride quickly; I will follow immediately after." (633) She said to her servants: "Keep silent, so that no one finds out about it, and do not tell Nabal." Then they rode quickly up the mountain. David and his men met them there. (634) Then Nabal's servants said: "Our lord sends you this." It was abhorrent to David and his men. He said: "They must die. Not even a toe will be left of them. They spoke dishonorably to us. The shame causes us pain."

(635) When Abigail then saw David coming, she fell from the donkey because of grief and discomfort. She bowed to the earth before the very

worthy man. She fell before his feet. He paid her no attention. (636) David and his men were armed with good swords and had shields in their hands—he and all his men. Then Abigail said: "The guilt is all my own for what happened there to your worthy messengers." (637) She said that so that he would listen to her: "Would Duke David not first exercise mercy?" She said: "Dear my lord, do you want to slay the innocent? Now listen, and let me tell you, the guilt is indeed mine. (638) My lord, do you want to shed innocent blood? David is so noble that he does no such thing." Then the duke stood still, so that she could tell him why she deserved to be slain, (639) and whether her husband Nabal had already done things that earned him a death sentence. David then thought to himself: "I want to hear this quickly. I do not want to shed the blood of any honorable man as long as I live and can bring it about." (640) She said: "Noble my lord, do not let what the villain Nabal does to you and your people affect you. His name is Nabal, and so is he also:[16] he does every kind of wickedness; no sin is too great for him. (641) I tell you, dear my lord, David, God, blessed be He, has told me that Nabal will soon die; he has committed many sins. Let him die on his own, my lord. Shed no blood! When you have become king, it will be advantageous for you. (642) In my house there are many noble men, children, and also women who have no guilt in this. Let him die on his own; do not shed any blood, so that it will not cause trouble for you in your kingship. (643) God, blessed be He, will abandon you in none of your deeds, and all those who have harmed you will have to die. You and your children will be kings. At that time then, my lord, do not forget me. (644) Now take these gifts from my hand, dear my lord." Worthy David turned to the woman. She said: "Dear my lord, the dishonor would not have taken place had I been there and seen the messengers." (645) David said to Abigail: "Now I will praise God who has sent me to meet you today. Praised be God in Heaven Who has blessed me. May God in Heaven, blessed be He, give you your just reward (646) for coming here to meet me. May God, blessed be He, reward you for your words and all your deeds. If you had not come to meet me at once, not even a dog would have been left to piss on the wall there. (647) Now behold, for your sake, I will let it go." She said: "May God in Heaven preserve you." Then he took the gifts directly from her hand. He then thanked the woman. David sent her home again.

(648) Abigail and her servants then rode home again. In her wisdom she did all things properly. Nabal and his men had sufficient pleasure in eating and drinking as much as was humanly possible. (649) The lady kept her peace and told Nabal nothing. He was besotted and drunk, Nabal the villain. In the morning when dawn came and the sun rose, she told him what had happened.

He grieved in his heart. (650) He was horrified that she had given David gifts, and that he had almost lost his life. And because his heart almost broke from sorrow, soon after the new year's celebration he became weak from illness. (651) When the Day of Atonement came, Nabal the villain died. When David heard it, he courted Abigail; he soon sent his messenger to Abigail: "If you will take David, he will gladly have you." (652) Abigail bowed. Now listen to what she said: "Now, I am not worthy to be his maidservant." She hurried and rode away from there and soon answered: "Yes." She rode there to David with five maidens. (653) David then took her as a wife. He said: "I want to have yet another wife: a maiden from Jezreel named Ahinoam." She was noble and beautiful. David also married her.

(654) When King Saul heard that, he said: "My daughter Michal should not have to endure it from him. I will give her to someone else, since he has married two others. If I could only find him, it would not go well for him. (655) I will kill that villain, David, and take his life. I will give him his two wives with my sword, so that he feels it all the way down to his toes—him and all his men, if I could only find them." (656) At once he had Palti, the son of Laish summoned. He said: "I will tell you what you have to do. You have to take my beautiful daughter Michal as your wife. I tell you, you young warrior, you need not be ashamed of her." (657) Saul gave Michal to Palti, the son of Laish. He said: "I will give her to you, but you are to do nothing to her. I am doing it only to grieve the villain. If you take her as your wife, he will leave her." (658) Palti, the son of Laish, then had to do what the king desired. He laid a naked sword between himself and Michal. Thereafter Merab died, and he took her child and raised her five children and Palti's household.

(659) Then the pitch-makers again came to Saul. They said to King Saul: "If you want to have David, he is hidden with us in the wilderness of Havilah,[17] on top of a mountain in a high forest." (660) The king armed himself and was hostile toward David. He took three thousand mighty heroes with him. He went with his army to the fields of Ziph. The night was very dark when they set up their camp. (661) From a very high crag David had seen that a very great army was entering the wilderness. He then sent his messengers at once to see whether it was Saul, the mighty king. (662) The messengers returned and told him the news about how it was King Saul and his people. David then went alone and secretly observed where the king and his men lay down to sleep. (663) Where they all slept, of that he took precise note. He went back to his own people there. Saul lay in the middle—that I tell you in truth. The army was on all sides around the king. (664) Now, next to the king lay the mightiest man of all, whose peer was found nowhere in the army. King Saul had made him a

commander over his army—a bold warrior, and the name of that mighty one was Abner.

(665) There were two mighty men with David, too, such as one could scarcely find among his men. The one was a Hittite and was named Ahimelech; the other was named Abishai. They were both courageous. (666) Abishai, the son of Zeruiah, was very well known—he and his mighty brother who was named Joab. David said to Ahimelech and Abishai: "Which of you wants to come with me into grave dangers? (667) I want to go in among King Saul's army." The hero Abishai leapt up: "My lord, I want to go with you." Together they went in among Saul's army. They were all asleep and slept deeply and soundly. (668) They went through the army until they came to the king. His spear was stuck into the ground at his head, and additionally, a glass jug of water stood there. The hero Abishai then said: "David, my lord, (669) God, blessed be He, has today delivered to you your enemy is to be slain. I will put my spear through him, deep into the ground." "No," said his lord, David, "Do not do that. He is God's anointed. Let us not do anything to him." (670) But Abishai did not want to obey David. "No," said Sir David, "by God, blessed be He, my Lord: nothing will be done to him by me or my men. The time will indeed come when he will be seen dead. (671) Either God in Heaven, blessed be He, will strike him dead, or he will suffer adversity in battle. Take his spear and also his glass water jug from him, and let us go quickly from here, so that no one notices us."

(672) Abishai, the wondrously mighty man let himself be persuaded. He took it and carried it away, as David had commanded him. Abishai stepped over Abner and wanted to wait for David. David was too small to step over Abner. (673) Abner had drawn in his foot. David lay bent down and wanted to slip through under Abner's leg—that was his intention. It chanced that Abner stretched his leg out again toward David. (674) David dared not move underneath Abner's leg; otherwise he would have awakened and killed him. In his heart David called to God in Heaven, blessed be He. A stinging wasp came flying. (675) It stung Abner in his leg so that it itched. Abner drew his leg back toward himself. David was nimble and slipped under the leg. He and Abishai again went all alone (676) quite far away from there, onto a high mountain. David was small but had great strength. David called to Abner: "I have something to say to you. How long must I call you. Abner, answer me!"

(677) Abner then answered him: "Who ever can you be, that you will not let my dear lord sleep?" David said to Abner: "Listen, and I will tell you. The king ought by rights to have you put to death. (678) Go on and tell me, Abner, you villain, who is your equal in strength and daring throughout the kingdom? You are supposed to protect the king; that would be proper for you.

But you slept through it—you and all your men— (679) so that one of my men got to the king. I could barely come to his aid and save his life. Where is the king's spear that was standing at his head, and his glass water jug. Look and see whether he still has it. (680) By God in Heaven, you and all your men have earned a death sentence—he could legitimately put you to death. Ought you to allow sleep to be so dear to you that you not guard my dear lord?"

(681) The king recognized David by his voice. He said: "Is that your voice, David, my dear son?" David said: "Dear my lord, it is indeed my voice. Saul, dear my lord, listen and pay close attention to my words. (682) I have never done you any harm, dear my lord. You fall into my hands, and I always let you go. If it is God's will that you must pursue me, then may he accept offerings and spare me. (683) If it is the people who are doing it who spread slander and constantly drive me out of the land of Israel, then may God curse them for my sake. Here on this earth may they be cursed. (684) They drive me out of the land of Israel so that I have to wander. It is as if they were to say: 'Go and serve a different God.' Now, I have never opposed you, dear my lord. At the same time, you should observe that I have here your spear. (685) How great is your sin against me, dear my lord! Now, I have in my entire life never done anything to harm you. Whom does King Saul pursue? A weak flea. You treat me as does the cuckoo on a high mountain. (686) It searches on the mountain for other birds' fledglings and whether it might also find its own young. You search for me, dear my lord, throughout the mountains as if my men and I were nothing but savage dwarves."

(687) King Saul then said: "I have done wrong. Come back home. I will leave you alone from now on." David said: "Do take note of your spear. Send one of your servants; I will return it to you. (688) Your life is worthy in my eyes, just as my life must also be in God's eyes." The king then answered him: "Truly, you are right. You could have stabbed me; I acknowledge it to you openly." (689) Then King Saul went back home to his land.

David and Abishai returned to their men. David began to chat with his men thus: "King Saul would like once to get me in his claws. (690) Nothing is better for us than that we are left alone. Let us go to the heathens in their land." David sent to Achish: "You need not be embarrassed to take six hundred mighty heroes into your employ. (691) David, the marvelously mighty one wishes to be your servant. Do you want to take him in with six hundred mighty heroes?" "Gladly," said King Achish, "if you will be loyal, I will pay you well, so that you do not regret it."

(692) David and his men entered the Philistines' land and went to King Achish in Gath, the capital city—he and all his men with their wives and

children, and with all their property and all their households. (693) When King Saul heard that David had gone there—into the land of the heathens—he thought no more of him. He gave up searching for him; he stayed at home.

Now, listen to what David did in the land of the heathens, (694) he and all his men, their wives, and their property. In Gath, the capital city, they were well sheltered. David said to Achish: "Gracious my lord, why must I stay in Gath, in your capital city?" (695) David pled with King Achish: "Give me some city in your land, so that we do not become too great a burden for you in Gath." Thus did Duke David say to Achish, the son of Maon. (696) He did that so that Achish would not know whether he had robbed his people of anything. King Achish gave him Ziklag; that was to be David's. David and his men took over Ziklag. (697) David was delighted by that: "Let us win property and conceal it here inside our city." David and his men did not want to delay any longer: "Let us fight the heathens, without Achish's knowledge." (698) They went far from there in the land of the heathens until no one recognized the worthy warriors any longer. They marched against the Geshurites and the Girizites and also against the powerful people of the land of the Amalekites. (699) David and his men angrily slew friend and foe alike, whoever was there. They did not want to leave any people alive so that no one could say: "David did it." (700) They quickly devastated that very fine land. They slew them even into the land of Egypt. They took a great many sheep and cattle and camels and all of their jewelry, as I can tell you, (701) and whatever garments of gold and silver that they could carry. David and his men loaded many a wagon—the plunder was so great that no one can describe it.

They went back to Achish, David and his men. (702) King Achish then said: "You have come with riches and additionally with full wagons. From whom have you taken it?" Sir David then answered him: "My lord, I will tell you. I struck on the southern side of Judah, (703) the south of the Jerahmeelites and the south of the Kenites. I took the property that I have here from them. I slew everyone whom I encountered, so that no one will come to complain to you, neither woman nor man, (704) so that no one may say, my lord: 'That the property is mine. Your servant David took it from us.' We would like to give you whatever you would like to have. No one will come to complain to you. We will go to Ziklag." (705) Achish praised David in everything that he said. Now, hear how Achish spoke to his people: "David has acted in strong defiance of the king [that is, Saul]; now he will have to stay with me as servant forever." (706) Thus it was that Sir David did, while he dwelt at Ziklag: when he robbed the heathens, he said that it was the Jews. King Achish believed him and came to love him. He gave David and his men rich payment.

(707) Now, King Achish had many a bold man; he also gained many mercenaries. The bold and mighty heathens were dauntless; they were well equipped with hard steel mail-coats.

(708) At that same time, it was reported to King Saul that Israel had many sorceresses in its cities. They occupied themselves with necromancy and soothsaying. They served them as if a god. That enraged the king. (709) Noble King Saul sent for his mighty men: "Go from city to city through my entire land. Kill whoever serves necromancy, or whoever has the power of soothsaying." (710) Those stalwarts then did as King Saul had ordered them: they slew men and women in many worthy cities.

At this same time King Achish sent and gathered all his forces through his entire land. (711) He had the bold and noble warriors picked out. There were so many of them that they could not be counted. He gathered a very great host of the heathens. There were as many as the sands of the sea. (712) Achish then said to David: "Bold and noble Duke, you and your stalwarts are also to do your best. King Saul has done me great harm. I lay that case before you, my dear David, you undaunted warrior. (713) Now avenge me, bold warrior, on that enemy of mine, you most worthy warrior, you and your stalwarts." Sir David then answered him: "My lord, since I have no official appointment in your land, you ought to excuse me from it." (714) "I will not excuse you from it, you excellent warrior. You are to stand guard at my head when I sleep. In my land you are ever to have that appointment." "Gladly, my lord" said Sir David, "let it be so."

(715) David and his men went with the host, in the rear by the king—they were to protect him. They marched up forcefully before the city of Shunem. Saul and his men came up on the mountain at Gilboa. (716) When Saul saw the heathens, his heart quailed: they were all equipped with steel mail-coats. Even from the high mountain he could not see the entire army. "Oh, mighty God in Heaven, blessed be He, what is to become of me?" (717) He consulted Urim and Thummim, but they gave him no answer. He said: "Mighty God in Heaven, blessed be He, I beg for Your mercy. If I have ever sinned and acted against You, do not make my people Israel suffer for it. (718) Dear Lord God, blessed be He, You should avenge it on me alone and not reckon my sin to the account of my people Israel. You ought to be a just judge in Your Heaven. If, my Lord, I have sinned, then the sin is mine. (719) Send a prophet to me, my dear Lord God, blessed be He, in my army, or answer me in dreams, Lord God, blessed be He, I beseech You."

The worthy man's prayer was so fervent that both Heaven and Earth began to shake. (720) The sun in the sky ceased to shine. Nevertheless, God, blessed be He, did not wish to accept his prayer. God in Heaven, blessed be He, said to his angels: "My people have sinned and earned grief and adversity." (721) God, blessed be He, paid no heed to the king's prayer. King Saul then said to all his men: "Do you not know of a woman anywhere who knows how to practice necromancy? I want to consult her about my people Israel." (722) Perhaps it is no sin that I consult via necromancy for the sake of all Israel. For that reason I do not shirk. And it is better to do so with a woman than with a man. Perhaps God, blessed be He, will not acknowledge her sin."

(723) Then Israel answered him: "King, it is true: a woman who knows magic dwells in Endor." King Saul then took off his royal robes; he dressed in other clothing, so that no one might recognize him. (724) He went to Endor with two of his men and arrived there still before nightfall. King Saul then said to that woman: "Conjure with necromancy; I wish to see your magic. (725) Bring to me the dead person, whom I order you to bring." The woman said: "I will not do it, for all Israel knows that King Saul has sorcerers slain. You have come for that purpose, because you want to report it to the king." (726) "No," said Saul, "by the living God. You will come to no harm on my account." Then the woman said to him: "Whom do you want to have?" He said: "The prophet Samuel; command him to arise for me. (727) Bring that dead man out of his grave. He is to tell me whatever I want to ask him."

Then she conjured with necromancy so that Samuel arose. He asked Moses and Aaron to come with him. (728) He thought to himself that, since he had to arise, it must be the Last Judgment. He did not know about the conjuring. Whoever conjures with necromancy brings about three things. Now, let us sing of what those three things are: (729) The one who performs the magic sees the dead person arise, but does not hear what the dead people say; the one who has them conjured up hears what they say. He can see nothing. The other people are quiet: (730) everyone who is present is like nothing at all—they neither see nor hear anything at all of the magic.

When she saw Samuel and Moses and Aaron arise, the woman knew for certain that he was the king. (731) They walked upright on their feet, with the hair of their head to the sky (otherwise when one was conjured up, he was upside down); they did that in honor of King Saul. They walked on their feet and bowed deeply. (732) "Alas and alack!" said the woman. "How you have deceived me. You are yourself King Saul. Why did you lie?" He said: "You need not be afraid. Tell me whom you see there." She said: "Two angels of God and a man who is gray." (733) "What is the man's appearance? Describe him for me!" She said to him quickly: "He is wearing a splendid robe." The king then bowed and understood that the old man was the prophet Samuel.

(734) Samuel then said to Saul: "Why have you had me awakened and startled out of my grave?" Saul said to Samuel: "My lord, I have sorrows. My enemies, the heathens, have marched on me. (735) Now, Almighty God, blessed be He, has abandoned me and will no longer give me any information by means of prophecy, nor does he any longer let me know anything by means of Urim and Thummim. For that reason, dear Samuel, I had you conjured up, (736) so that you might tell me what I am to do: whether I can conquer the mighty heathens." "Indeed," said Samuel, "why do you wake me tonight, since God, blessed be He, has become your enemy? (737) If God, blessed be He, has abandoned you, since I am his servant, what then am I to tell you? Mighty King Saul, in truth I will tell you: you and your sons will be slain. (738) Tomorrow you will die, you and three of your sons at the same time, and you will come to me in the kingdom of Heaven. Everything that I have said with happen to you. The kingdom has been prepared for your comrade, David. (739) I dare to mention his name to you; I do not fear you. Tomorrow you will come to me where I am. You have brought it all about through sin and opposing God, blessed be He. You ought not to have left anything of Amalek alive."

(740) Then the king hurried and fell down on his face. His limbs failed him because of fear and misery. His strength had left him, who had been so highly favored. He had had nothing to eat or drink all day and all night. (741) The sorcery came to an end—that I tell you in truth. The woman saw that the king had had quite a shock. She said: "Dear my lord, I have done your will and had to conjure up for you the one whom you wanted. (742) Now, O excellent king, do in turn my will: you should eat something; then your fury will also pass." "No," said the king, "Now I will eat no more." Then both his servants and the woman pled with him. (743) He got up from the ground and sat down on a bed. His strength had left him because of hunger and emptiness. Then the king thought: "If I am to be slain, then I will beforehand take vengeance and will not endure it from them." (744) Now, the woman had a fatted calf in her house. She hurried and had it slaughtered. She thought it would be the best. She took fine flour and quickly baked cakes. She gave the king and his men meat and bread.

(745) The king and his two men arose. He hurried away in the night, and when King Saul came to his army and when day came, the heathens began: (746) they advanced to battle before their fine king. The heathens then said: "What are these Jews among us?" King Achish then said: "It is my dear servant, David of the Jews; the duke serves me properly. (747) As long as Duke David has been with me, he has allowed few of my enemies to survive." Then it enraged the heathens: "You may regret it, if you entrust life and property to

a Jew. (748) Send him to the city that you have given him, so that he does nothing improper to us during the battle. How better could Duke David arrange it: if he were to attack us from behind, Saul would laugh about him. (749) We do not want the bold and mighty warrior with us. Do you not remember what the ladies sang on that field? 'My lord Saul has slain a thousand; and David ten thousand.' He ought not be with us." (750) Achish said to David: "You should go home. The heathens do not want you with them." David said: "Dear my lord, that would disgrace me. The people could say that I am not loyal. (751) What have I done to you, dear my lord, that you will not let me conquer my enemies." "You most worthy warrior. In truth I say this to you: you are like an angel of God in my eyes. (752) Only my noblemen, the heathens, do not want you with them."

Sir David took his leave and left the field. He and all his men came to Ziklag. They found all the gates standing open. (753) The city had been thoroughly burned by fire. All joy left David and his men. Not one of their wives or children was there. Their livestock and their property had been taken away. (754) There was neither human nor animal in the city any longer. David and his men all wept bitterly. His men wanted to stone him because of their great grief. They all wept with great lamentation and wretchedness. (755) David, however, cried out to God in his prayer. God in Heaven, blessed be He, then helped him out of his great misery. He said to Abiathar: "Bring Urim and Thummim here." The priest did as David wished. (756) He had the question posed to God: "Should I pursue the people who have laid waste my city, and should I slay them?" Then our Lord God said: "You should pursue them. You should destroy those who have done it to you."

(757) David and his men quickly searched for their wives and children and all their households. They came then to a brook named Besor. Two hundred of his men remained there without crossing it. (758) They wanted to search no more; their property was elsewhere. David left the baggage there with the two hundred. David and his men then turned away from there; only four hundred men followed him then. (759) They then found an Egyptian who was half dead. They revived him both with water and with bread. They brought him to David, and when he came to him, they gave him half of a fig from which he gained strength. (760) And they gave him two of the dried grapes. He had eaten nothing for three days.

Now, when his strength had returned, Sir David then said to him: "Tell me, whose man are you?" (761) He said: "I am an Egyptian, the servant of an Amalekite. I became quite ill; I am still sick. I thought that I would die and not survive. A great host of Amalekites was here, (762) because the heathens had moved out of here, and the Jews were also not in their houses. So we advanced into the territory of the Jews and also of the heathens, on the southern border. (763) No one resisted us, no matter where we went. We took as much as we could carry, and we also caused trouble for the hero David: we took everything that he had. (764) We then took captive women and children. In Ziklag we found a king's treasury. We took it all and immediately carried away and burned down Ziklag."

(765) "Comrade, will you show me where I can find the army?" "Gladly," said the Egyptian, "if you will also swear to me that you will free me and grant me my life and not put me into the hands of my lord." (766) The noble Duke David promised him all of that. Then the Egyptian showed him where the Amalekites were. They were close by in that territory and incautious; they were dividing their plunder and rejoicing in it.

(767) It was evening when David arrived there. David and his bold men bound their helmets tightly. The army of Amalek was also ready to fight. Then they charged each other and were dauntless. (768) Now, the Amalekites had so many soldiers that the field was full; they charged at their targets. David and his men numbered only four hundred. They charged at the great host of Amalekites. (769) Now, the Amalekites had heroes who were aggressive: they struck hard at Sir David's liegemen. The Jews defended themselves well with the points of their swords. Out of the hard, steel rings was not a word to be heard. (770) And when Duke David saw the strength of the Amalekites, he wanted to be at the forefront of his men; most quickly did he rush forward. He began to grasp his shield, that most worthy man. He drew his good sword—the one that he had won from Goliath.

(771) He said to his people: "Stand behind me." Then he struck powerfully through steel-ringed mail-coats. There the servants of Amalek were also dauntless. They struck at Sir David so that it grieved the Jews. (772) Now, David's heroes were indeed to be praised: they attacked the Amalekites and clove their helmets. In that battle the Amalekites lost half their men. The Amalekites scattered out, which angered Sir David, (773) and since he could not stand at the front of all his troops—they had spread out widely on the Amalekite field—he and all his men were in great adversity. A great many Amalekites fell there and were slain. (774) The battle spread to fill the entire field. The swords of David and his men far resounded. David wielded wrathfully in both hands his very good sword. He slashed through Amalek. (775) There he hacked everything to pieces that he encountered. They slashed out around themselves so that flames sprang forth. Sir David fought well with a courageous hand. A great many bold heroes they struck down to the ground. (776) Great and

mighty deeds were performed by him and his men. The Amalekites lay before them on the ground. They had surrounded Amalek on all sides. Amalek could not flee, but had to fight with them. (777) David and his men had enclosed the mighty host of Amalek, both the least and the greatest. There were nothing but heroes there who had ample strength. The Amalekites fought well until they were slain.

(778) Wherever one of David's men stood in dire need, when Sir David saw him, he quickly rushed to him. He cut broad avenues; close quarters brought him no harm. They all suffered his vengeance and bore the burden of his sword. (779) In the middle David struck at Amalek. His army around him had battle enough. David slung his shield onto his back and struck on both sides with his keen blade.

(780) The battle lasted all night and all the next day; not until it became dark did the battle abate. Great heaps of corpses lay before the Jews, and broad streams of blood flowed red. (781) The battle was fought on all sides of the Amalekites, until they were driven together in the middle. Then the people of Amalek were slain everywhere. They unfastened their helmets. Gone was the clamor.

(782) The couriers of the Amalekites were small. The couriers commonly rode on camels. When they saw that they had lost the battle, they fled from there. That made Sir David angry. (783) He could not catch them; they galloped away from the field. God, blessed be He, let them survive and have the benefit of what their parents had done: when Esau had gone to Jacob and wanted to slay him, four hundred of his men quickly escaped from Esau. (784) Now, the four hundred couriers were descended from those four hundred men, and they had now received their reward, in that Duke David could do nothing to them there. Each son there enjoyed the fruits of his father's courage. (785) At that time David and his men found all their wives and children and property. All that the Amalekites had stolen, they found there. The plunder had been so great; Sir David was now delighted. (786) The livestock was beyond count—that I tell you in truth. They drove it before the noble Duke David. They told all the people: "That is the plunder of David: not a thing from all our property has gone missing." (787) Sir David did not know what to do with it—there was so much in the way of property that they now found. David then said: "I also want to give something to my friends; it is also proper for my tribe of Judah."

(788) When they then came to the brook of Besor, the two hundred men had still remained on the other side. David's men then said: "We do not want to give them anything—we risked life and limb for it— (789) except for their wives and children. They should go away from here with their households."

"No," said Sir David, "that would not be proper. Whoever has guarded the baggage here should also have a share. (790) They also have to risk life and limb. They do not want to give our property to anyone else." Then they left there with their great property. They were in good spirits in their city of Ziklag. (791) David sent to the elders of Judah whom he knew: "A gift you are to have from Sir David's hand. He has won it from his enemies who have robbed and plundered you."

(792) Now let us sing about the ones to whom Sir David sent gifts: to the elders and the lords in the land of Bethel, and those of Ramoth of the Negeb, and those of Jattir, and those of Aroer he also sent at once. (793) Now let us leave Sir David at Ziklag, and let us sing of what Saul had done, when he returned to his men that same night. In the morning when dawn came, the battle began.[18] (794) Nor does he let those of Siphmoth and those of Eshtuon[19] and those of Racal be spurned, nor in the cities where the Jerahmeelites dwell and in the cities where the Kenites dwell, (795) and those of Khorman and those of Ashon,[20] and those of Athach, and those of Hebron, and all the cities to which they had gone, where he and his men had been welcomed.

(796) Now let us leave Sir David dwelling at Ziklag, and let us again sing of what Saul had done, when he returned to his men that same night. In the morning when dawn came, the battle began. (797) King Saul then wanted to be at the forefront of the battle. "No," said his men, "it is not yet time. Who ever saw a king in the vanguard." He ever wanted to force his way ahead; they did not want to let him do so. (798) The heathens there charged into the turmoil of the Jews. There the heathens struck down many of the Jews. King Saul raised his noble eyes: "Mighty God in Heaven, blessed be He, my dear Lord, (799) I want to confess the sins that I have committed. Do not make all Israel here pay for it. When I made the sacrifice—when I should have waited for Samuel—I did it with the best intentions. You well know that, Lord God. (800) When I let some of the people of Amalek survive, I did so with the best intentions. Thus did I sin. I had the priests of Nob slain. Therein did I sin. They gave bread to David. (801) I sinned against my servant David. I did indeed want to slay him and nowhere left him in peace." He bound on his helmet with his crown. "Now, dear Lord God, blessed be He, I commend my soul to you."

(802) Then King Saul himself charged into battle. He struck the heathens broad and lethal wounds. Many of the heathens fell before him in the forest. Many a bold man came against the king. (803) When his stalwarts saw that he was in distress, they struck down dead a great many of the heathens. A mighty cloud of vapors burst up into the heavens, so that a man could hardly see the man next to him. (804) It greatly grieved the king that they forced their way to

him. He called quite wretchedly to his mighty men: "No one should suffer adversity for my sake. The time has unfortunately come for me to die."

(805) "No," said his men. Many a man lay before him. "Not one of us desires to live a day longer than you. And if you, dear my lord, are slain, then our corpses will have to be carried away from here. (806) If we must die, then we will take our revenge in advance. Many a heathen will first have to be laid on a bier." There hero leapt at hero, many a mighty man. They struck each other blows so that flames sprang forth. (807) On both sides were seen how swords clove helmets and how their shields flew in bits and pieces. Many of the mighty heathens fell in death. Saul and his men, too, were in great adversity. (808) Each struck down the other; they fell on both sides in the forest. They slew many heathens there, and the heathens also slew the Jews; they could not be distinguished from each other. (809) On both sides rose up fear and great misery. The worthiest and the best were slain. Now, on both sides many were slain. Saul and the heathens began to lament bitterly. (810) Saul could not protect his beloved men. They rushed powerfully in front of their lord. If Saul, the king, forced his way in front of them, many a bold hero leapt in front of the king.

(811) So many of the mighty heathens were slain there that they could not be counted; they would lament that bitterly. The heathens nonetheless fought on in their misery; many of the noble king's men were slain. (812) There were unfortunately still too many of the mighty heathens. King Saul's men slew them beyond numbering. The great host did not wish to suffer anything from the Jews there. All of King Saul's heroes were there slain, (813) and King Saul himself was in great distress, and many a mighty heathen also lay dead before him. Now, when Jonathan perceived his father's death, he slew many a heathen until he got to his father. (814) He and his two brothers forced their way through them all. They struck down many a mighty heathen. One of them was named Abinadab—a fine young warrior—the other, Malchishua; they waded in the blood. (815) Now, when the three brothers got to their father, they took the lives of many a mighty heathen. He then lamented loudly when he saw his children. He said to himself: "Now may God have mercy. (816) That I was ever born—of that I complain to God, blessed be He—that my children are to be slain because of my sin." The two princes were in great danger: their steel mail-coats were red with blood.

(817) King Saul was there seen to lament miserably. "That my children are to be slain because of my sin!" The king also slew a great many mighty heathens. A great throng of them pressed forward; there were still plenty of them. (818) Among them the two princes were slain. Saul and Jonathan lamented

bitterly. Up slashed Jonathan with his sword; there he avenged his brothers. He pierced many a mighty heathen. (819) The bold and noble warrior was greatly to be praised. His sword was seen to rampage among the mighty heathens. The heathens vehemently pressed upon the man. He began to lose his footing under their mighty strokes. (820) Noble King Saul leapt toward his son. His sword resounded loudly on the heathens. The bold and noble lords were both in dire distress. Mighty Jonathan's mail-coat ran red. (821) The mighty one fought with a valiant hand. He clove through helmet and shield. Now may God, blessed be He, have mercy on you in your great distress. Mighty Jonathan was slain. (822) The lamentation of the noble king was most great. He gave the heathens many a keen thrust. He struck them fiercely—so many mighty men. Many of the heathens there fell before Saul in the forest.

(823) Then the heathens again advanced, as did the archers who then shot with their bows. They shot intensely at the worthy man, until the red blood flowed from the king. (824) The sharp and pointed arrows penetrated his armor. The noble king was then weakened by the projectiles. When he felt them, his strength left him. The king turned to his squire. (825) He said to his squire, who followed him and carried his sword: "Listen, my dear son, to what I wish from you. I am so grievously wounded that I will very soon die. May God, blessed be He, defend me from my enemy's hand, (826) so that they—my enemies, the heathens—not capture me. If I were otherwise to lose my life, it would not grieve me much. You have ever been true to me, your whole life long. I am so grievously wounded that I cannot survive. (827) Now, I beseech you: draw your sword and give me my death blow. Do as I wish." "No, on my oath. May God, blessed be He, help you, my lord. You will not be stabbed by my hand."

(828) The king himself took his sword in hand. He turned the pommel to the earth. He fell upon the sword-point—vigorously did he do it. There did he, alas, have to die; he did not survive the wound. (829) Since he did not want to fall into the hands of his enemies, he stabbed himself, so that he fell down dead upon the ground. The squire who followed him and carried his sword witnessed what happened to the noble king. (830) The squire then at once also drew his own sword; the squire also turned the pommel to the earth. He fell at once—for great sorrow—on his sword. He died with his lord; both were, alas, dead.

(831) Then all the Jews fled the land. A great many of the heathens then pursued them at a run. The cities that were nearby suffered greatly. The Jews abandoned them, and the heathens occupied them. (832) The heathens returned the following morning. The heathens stripped the dead and took

their clothing. They saw King Saul lying on his sword. They rejoiced greatly; their hearts desired nothing more. (833) They took off the king's battle gear and at once cut off his head. They sent it into their country to the temples of their idols, in order to convey the good news to all the heathens. (834) They took his head to Ashdod; his body they hung on the wall of Beth-shan, and three of his sons they also hung there.

The people of Jabesh-Gilead heard about it that same day. (835) They said to each other: "Now, King Saul helped us against King Nahash; let us do something good for him." Then the men of Jabesh-Gilead walked the whole night until they came to the king's body on the wall. (836) They then took the king and all three of his sons and carried them home, these bold and noble heroes. They buried the king: he lay at Jabesh-Gilead. They mourned and wept and fasted for seven days. (837) When King Saul then lay dead, David was in Ziklag and did not know of this misery. He received no message for two whole days, and on the third day a runner reached him. (838) His clothes were torn to tatters from his lamentation and his mourning. When he arrived he had soil upon his head. He bowed to the earth when he went before David. Sir David thanked him and requested that he speak.

(839) He said: "My dear comrade, what does your so grievous lamentation mean?" He said: "I have run here from Israel." "So tell me, on your honor, what has happened in the battle." "Woe and great misery I saw in the battle. (840) Many of the people of Israel have been slain—and also the king and Jonathan, of that I can assure you. And all the king's mighty warriors have been slain. There are hills and valleys of nothing but red blood. (841) The king is slain, as are three of his children: mighty Jonathan and the king's household." "How do you know that they are, alas, dead? Oh, mighty God in Heaven, blessed be He, the wretched misery of it! (842) Where did you see it, or how do you know to tell it that the king and Jonathan have, alas, been slain?" He said: "I was in the battle on Mount Gilboa when that great misfortune, alas, took place. (843) Noble King Saul was in great distress, and many of the heathens also lay dead before him. The charioteers and knights were fighting well. The king had been wounded by arrows so that his blood was flowing from him. (844) The worthy man was leaning on his spear. The king turned around and saw me. He said: 'Dear comrade, whose man might you be?' I said: 'My father was an Amalekite convert.' (845) He said: 'Now make haste and stab me to death quickly, so that my enemies do not capture me and cause me misery. My sins have overtaken me; I must lose my life. The obdurate heathens are not to do as they wish with me.' (846) When I saw that the king was indeed going to suffer great misery, I arose and gave him his death blow. His crown and his

prayer phylacteries are sufficient tokens—I have brought them here for you, my lord, David."

(847) Duke David and all his men were horrified. They rent their clothes and began to weep. They lamented sincerely the misery and the woe. Until the evening none of them ate any bread. (848) For King Saul, and for all his men, and for the people of God, and for Jonathan, and for the house of Israel that there lay on their swords—David and his men, each one of them, desired to weep. (849) King David then said to the messenger: "Tell me, who is your father? Where do you come from?" He said: "My father was an Amalekite convert. Believe me, my lord—that I tell you in truth." (850) Duke David then said: "I will not endure it from you. How dare you slay the anointed one of God! Did you have no fear of sin? How dare you be so bold!" "No, I, my Lord, I lied to you. (851) I saw him lying dead on his sword. That is why I lied: I wanted a messenger's reward." "May your guilt be on your head; you have earned a death sentence. I will have your proper messenger's reward given to you." (852) He called one of his servants: "Now, put him to death at once. You are to give him his messenger's reward with your sharp sword." He then struck him dead, as his lord had commanded. Then the Amalekite convert lay dead before David's servants.

(853) Noble Duke David's heart was overcome by emotion. He was overwrought; he was aggrieved in his heart. A lament for Saul and for Jonathan now began. No one could comfort him, neither man nor woman. (854) "Alas for the noble lord whom we have lost. Now, alas, we will have to submit to the domination of the heathens. Great lamentation and misery rose up in the land. Judah had to battle bitterly, just as Moses our Teacher has written. (855) If you wish to pursue your enemies until they flee before you, then you must at once draw your sword, your bow and your arrows, until your enemies incline their necks to you in submission. The mighty ones of Judah must defend themselves with determination. (856) The leadership of Israel is, alas, dead. One sees the red blood on the hills and in the valleys. Oh, mighty God of Israel, the wretched misery, that the bold and mighty heroes have been slain. (857) You bold and noble warriors, what has become of you! In all battles always only the best could be said of you. How the mighty have fallen and lie in the blood. Now, you have indeed carried good swords and worn good armor. (858) I wish that it be said to no one in Gath. Alas, for the evil news in the streets of Ashkelon! Alas, in the cities of the Philistines, how the heathens rejoice in their cities! Alas, for the great misery! (859) That you should rejoice—alas, the great wretchedness! The leadership of Israel is, alas, dead. O mountain of Gilboa—the blame was prepared for you: upon you did that great heartbreak

occur. (860) May God, blessed be He, for that reason give you your recompense: no dew from Heaven are you ever to have, nor any rain from the clouds are you to have. Alas, King Saul, you excellent warrior! (861) No fruit is to grow upon you, neither on trees nor in the fields. No one is to bless you; you deserve to be cursed. Saul and his stalwarts had good shields; they could not help them; they are lying in the blood. (862) They were well hardened—fine, cured leather. They did not help them; they are lying on the field. They were well oiled, more lustrous than a mirror; no arrow could cling to them. O, God, blessed be He, how did it happen (863) that the sharp arrows clung? Through shields and through mail-coats went the evil arrows. O, mighty God in Heaven, blessed be He, the wretched misery! No longer is any shield of the mighty oiled. (864) They have cast away their oil and their luster. Alas, King Saul, your shield has no luxuriance, as if it had in its time never been oiled. It bristles with all the arrows of the heathens. (865) Before they were to encounter any distress, many a mighty one should have lain dead before King Saul, and also before Jonathan. O, my sworn comrade, Jonathan, never in all your days did you draw your sword or your bow in vain. (866) Saul, you noble king, you bore a good sword. You strove in all battles for chivalry. You never in your life left a battle in which your sword did not do its part.

(867) "Alas, Saul and Jonathan, what is to become of me? Am I never again to see you both. My dear friends, I would much prefer to have died before you. You had the people's favor; God honored you. (868) Strengthened by great honor and piety while you lived, now you have presented your lives as an offering to God, blessed be He. At all times you served God, blessed be He, until body and soul had to part. (869) You were swifter than an eagle in your service to God, blessed be He, and as strong as a lion in your ceaseless service to God. O, mighty God in Heaven, what is to become of me? Brother-in-law and sworn comrade, you can never again see me. (870) Now, God, blessed be He, must have mercy, since I was not with you. I would like to die of grief; I bear hatred toward myself. Daughters of Israel, weep for the exalted king. He will never more present you with jewels taken from his enemies. (871) When King Saul took plunder from his enemies, the daughters of Israel came at a run. He gave them fine scarlet woolens and wished to sate them therewith; with gold and with silver he sated them according to his wishes. (872) Lament pitiably for Saul, the exalted king! You will have jewels from him no more. Alas, mighty heroes, how they lie in the blood. Alas, my comrade, Jonathan, my heart burns in a fervent blaze. (873) On the high mountain you gave up your life, and if I cannot avenge you, then I do not wish to live. I am aggrieved for you, my friend, Jonathan. Alas, for our friendship; alas, you precious man. (874) Now,

God, blessed be He, must have mercy that I ever gained your acquaintance. No one, neither man nor woman, can believe our love. There is no woman on earth for whom I have such love as for my comrade whom I must leave lying there. (875) Woe is me for my dear comrade who has been slain. My heart will ever grieve for you, Jonathan. Your manliness, which was great, cannot help you, nor can your well-forged armor. O, how you have been defeated! (876) May the battle be cursed that did it to you! Alas for the dear comrade whom I have lost. Alas for my good comrade who has been slain! I will mourn for you all the days of my life. (877) O, how the mighty are fallen! How gaping are their wounds! And all their battle gear is lost."

The lament of the worthy man came to an end. He said to the priest: "Consult Urim and Thummim." (878) He asked our Lord God, blessed be He: "Tell me, should I go to the cities of Judah?" Our Lord God answered him: "Yes, go to them." Sir David then asked him again: "To which city or to what place?" (879) Then our Lord God, blessed be He, said: "Go to Hebron." Sir David arose and said: "It will be done." Duke David and all his good heroes marched out with their wives and children. They were in an exalted state of mind. (880) They then took their wives and children to Hebron, and everything that they had: their households and all their personal belongings. There in Hebron Sir David dwelt freely. His men dwelt in the neighboring cities.

(881) When the tribes of Judah became aware of David, all the tribes of Judah came to him in Hebron. All the tribes of Judah then anointed Duke David. "Formerly you were a duke; now be a proper king. (882) You are to be a king over all of Judah." King David then took control over the whole of the land of Judah. Then there were some who told King David that the men of Jabesh-Gilead had buried Saul. (883) They carried the lord from the walls of Beth-shan and buried him and mourned him honorably. King David then sent his messenger to them: "I have been informed about the good deed you that did for Saul. (884) God, blessed be He, will bless you and reward you for showing mercy to your lord. I will be all the fonder of you for as long as I live, because you have buried my father-in-law, Saul. (885) Whoever has done a good deed to him or his men, I will surely always let him live and prosper. And be bold heroes and take good counsel, for Saul can no longer help; he is, alas, dead. (886) Now the tribe of Judah has decided on me and have with confidence made me king, and if you were also to swear allegiance to me, I have committed myself in all ways." The people of Jabesh and Gilead did not then reply to David's messenger.

(887) Now, King Saul had left one son. He was forty years old and of large stature. In the battle against the heathens, a mighty hero had survived: it

was the mighty Abner, a commander in Saul's army. (888) King Saul's son was named Ishbosheth. The commander Abner took him to the land of Mahanaim. The young King Ishbosheth took over all of Israel except for the tribe of Judah that wanted to stay with David. (889) Abner gave vigorous aid to King Saul's son.

Then King David put a bold hero, whom he knew well, in command over his army: the commander was the mighty Duke Joab. (890) Duke Joab then advanced with King David's men before the city of Gibeah;[21] he did not intend to fight. Abner and his men and all of Ishbosheth's men also came to Gibeah on the other side. (891) They were sitting by the water, these on one side, the others on the other side. By no means did they wish to fight. Then the hero Abner said to Joab: "As God may succor me, think of me what you will, I have no love for you. (892) Choose twelve of your men, and I will choose twelve of mine. Let us see who the best among them is; thus we will see who can win the fight." "Gladly," said Duke Joab, "only a whore's son would pass it up." (893) Twelve of Abner's men from the tribe of Benjamin then went across. Joab also sent twelve, none of whom had any benefit from it. Then they sprang on each other, man to man. Each attacked the other's head. (894) Each took the other by the hair and stabbed him in the side; indeed they all fell down. They—all of them together—fell down dead. There arose there on both sides fear and great distress. (895) None of them wished to leave the other unavenged. One saw there how spearpoint was vigorously borne against spearpoint. It lasted the entire day with fear and great distress. They were all heroes who there fell down dead. (896) Marvelously mighty Joab, a murderously fierce man, with exceedingly great strength won the field. Abner and all his heroes were forced to flee. Joab and his men rushed after them.

(897) Now the hero Joab had two brothers there, the one named Asahel, and Abishai, son of Zeruiah. Now, Asahel was fleet of foot, swifter than a doe in the field. (898) Asahel ran nimbly on his feet; with his sharp sword he ran in among Abner's army. Now Asahel, the hero, was of unbounded courage. The hero Abner was likewise a fine warrior. (899) Abner turned around and looked at Asahel. "Is it you, Asahel, you most worthy man?" "Yes, it is I. On my oath, you ought to give yourself up to me. Abner, if you otherwise wish to live longer, surrender and be taken captive." (900) "Back away from me," said Abner to Asahel. "Get away from me; otherwise I will send you to Hell. Go to the right side or to the left side. Strike whomever you wish and take his garments." (901) "Now, the poorest of men enjoys living as much as the richest of men. Now, Abner, come on! Give yourself up, hero, and be my prisoner, if you would otherwise like to retain your noble life." (902) "Asahel, get away from

here and turn away from me at once. I am stronger than you; that I will prove to you. If I strike you down dead, then you will realize it. How will I be able to answer for that to your brother, Joab? (903) Now, get away from me here; I will send you to Hell." "Abner, give yourself up," said Asahel. Fiercely Asahel ran toward Abner. With his sword Abner pierced Asahel deeply, (904) indeed with great strength, through his steel mail-coat, through all his armor at the fifth rib. He stabbed the bold and mighty hero vehemently, so that the point of the blade burst forth from his back. (905) Asahel, the hero, then lay dead at Abner's feet. Abner fled from there; he was desperate to escape.

Both Joab and his brother Abishai were in haste—for the sake of their dear brother, they were pursuing Abner. (906) All the men of Benjamin charged into the battle. Abner and his men went up on a high mountain. The sun had set. Abner at once said to Joab: "Joab, how long will you slay Jews? (907) In the end it will turn out badly for you—by God's will. You have won the battle; what more do you want? Order your men to turn away from us and let them go away from us. You have won the battle; what more do you want?" (908) Then Sir Joab answered him: "The guilt is certainly yours. If you had not provoked me, I would have let it go. If you had given yourself up and said so long ago, I would have stopped fighting, on my honor." (909) Then Joab's war horn was sounded. He had lost nineteen men in the battle, and his dear brother, who had been a mighty hero. He counted for as much as the other nineteen. (910) From the tribe of Benjamin, three hundred and sixty of King Ishbosheth's servants lay dead there. Then Abner and his men escaped home to their lands.

The noble Duke Joab went to his brother. (911) He mourned him piteously when he found him lying there. He took him to Bethlehem and buried him there at once, where the father of all of them was buried. Then they went to Hebron—that I tell you in truth.

(912) In the morning when the dawn came, David heard the news. When the sun rose, Joab went to him. At once he complained to him piteously about his brother. The king was at that time encamped in the lands of the Jews. (913) David and his men grew much stronger, and all the following of Israel grew much weaker. The strength of King David then grew greatly and King Ishbosheth never won a battle. (914) Now King David had adorned his life: he had with him in Hebron six lawful wives. Each one of them bore King David a child, as I can tell you. (915) The first was named Amnon; his mother was named Ahinoam. The second was named Chileab, as one found it written; Abigail, the wife of Nabal, gave birth to him there with King David; the king was delighted by that. (916) The third was named Absalom, the most handsome man whom one can find anywhere in the world; his mother was

named Maacah, a beautiful queen. Her father was named Talmai; in Geshur he wore the crown. (917) Adonijah, the son of Haggith, was the fourth in the sequence. The fifth was named Shephatiah; his mother was named Abital. The sixth, Ithream, as one finds it written; his mother was named Michal,[22] King Saul's child. (918) Now, let us leave them to grow—all of the children together.

Thereafter David possessed the entire kingdom. Now, I want to sing to you what happened thereafter. The noble Duke Abner took a lady as his wife. (919) She had been King Saul's concubine, as we have read it here in the book. She was named Rizpah, the little daughter of Aiah. Abner began secretly to love her. (920) Ishbosheth became aware of it and was filled with rage. He thought to himself: "He has lost his life." Ishbosheth said to Abner: "I would like to be able to say to you that you dishonor my father in his grave. (921) You are lying with his concubine, and why are you doing that? You are a simple commoner; my father was a king." The words enraged Abner, the warrior. He said: "By the Lord God, that is most painful. (922) If I were the least officer in David's army, he would not have refused me. I want to make that clear to you. I will certainly deliver your kingdom to Sir David. I will help him in that, if God grant me life. (923) Now, I brought you to the kingship, and you slander me because of a woman. Am I to serve a person who does not understand whether one serves him loyally and whether one does good to him. (924) I will leave King David the monarchy. How could I prevent it, since God wants to have him. God, blessed be He, has promised the kingdom to David. I will help him in that, even if it enrages you."

(925) Then King Ishbosheth was quite horrified. He could not even answer him, so great was his fear. Abner immediately sent out messengers to King David in the land of Hebron: (926) "If, my lord, you will guarantee me on oath my safety, then I will swear to you, my lord, a counter-oath: I will give up the entire kingdom of Israel to you." "Gladly, comrade," said Sir David, "that suits me perfectly, (927) if one thing only I may say to you: you gave Michal, Saul's daughter, to another man. If the noble princess is not retrieved from him, then not a single one of you should even come into my sight. (928) She helped me to escape from her father when I was in danger. For that reason, Abner, you ought not come into my sight, unless you bring Michal to me, the dear and beloved one who was loyal to me—that I tell you in truth.

(929) Then King David himself sent out messengers to King Ishbosheth in his house: "Send me my wife, Michal; take care that you do not ignore this. By means of the foreskins of a hundred Philistines did I marry her." (930) King Ishbosheth then sent to Palti, the son of Laish: "Send me David's wife;

take care and do it quickly." The messengers then went to Palti at once; he then sent her home to Sir David in his land. (931) Sir Palti had had her quite a number of years. He went along with her and wept—that I tell you in truth. Then the hero Abner said: "Palti go back home!" Sir Palti took his leave and left her to him alone.

(932) Then the hero Abner spoke to all Israel there and to the tribe of Benjamin. They were all pleased. "When King Saul was still alive David fought at the forefront in all battles. (933) In King Saul's times he always performed the best; the mighty warrior was always seen to fight valiantly, and God, blessed be He, promised him, as I can assure you, that he would vanquish all his foes. (934) Let us at once take him as our king, that mighty warrior. Thus will God, blessed be He, help us out of all our distress." All of them together said: "We would like to have him." Duke Abner informed David of the news. (935) He went to him in Hebron with twenty of his servants. He said: "Noble King David, the matter is quite simple." The guest was well treated in terms of food and drink: they had to go to the table in King David's house. (936) King David there made for Abner and his servants a good meal with food and wine. Duke Abner then said: "Long live the king! Dear and gracious my lord, grant me leave. (937) I wish to bring to you many a worthy man from all Israel, all of whom I can muster, so that all of them will swear allegiance to you, dear my lord, as legitimate king and lord of the land."

(938) Abner and all his servants took their leave from King David. The matter was quite simple. Now Duke Joab had not been at home, neither he nor any of his heroes, as we have read. (939) They had been in a battle with many a mighty man far away from there. Abner and his servants had not yet gone far, when Duke Joab arrived with his great army. (940) They brought along goods, as much as one could wish for. The plunder was most great—of silver and of gold. Joab was told the news: 'Abner has been with the mighty king." That seemed quite curious to Joab. (941) He was told how the king had treated him with great honor, and with great honor the king had granted him leave to depart. That began greatly to displease the warrior Joab. At once Joab went to see King David: (942) "Noble King David, you think yourself wise and are beshitting yourself in your wisdom. I do not praise you for that. If Abner, son of Ner, has been with you here, by rights you could have slain him. But you let him live?! (943) Do you believe the lies that that false knight tells you? It may well cause grief for you and yours. If you trust Duke Abner, I know that he will make a fool of you. He wants to spy out the city and know what you are doing. (944) You think that Abner of Benjamin is on your side? I know that Abner will capture the city." "No," said the king, "I know Abner well.

He swore an oath to me. He is full of honor. (945) Well do I know, dear Joab, whom I should trust. I can assure you, I will not regret it."

Then Duke Joab left the king. He thought in his heart: "I have a plan for this." (946) Joab sent out messengers with great deception, as if it were King David's own sincere intent. The messengers then came running to Abner: "The noble King David has sent us after you. (947) You are immediately to come here to the king. He has more to say to you in the matter." Duke Abner then made haste to the king—that is true—and when he came to the gate at Hebron, (948) he then met Joab on the Hebron bridge. He began to draw his good sword from under his cloak. He said: "Peace be to you, Abner, tell me, how does a woman unfasten her shoe when she has to perform the ceremony of *ḥalitzah*? (949) Sir Abner then answered him: "Joab, I will demonstrate it to you." Sir Abner bent over in order to untie his shoe. Duke Joab then presented him with the point of his sword and vigorously thrust it into him at the fifth rib. (950) "You slew my brother Asahel. For that reason you must bear my sword by its point." Abner—the worthy man—alas, had to die from that.

The king then said: "I am innocent of it, (951) if Abner has died and was slain. Abner, you worthy warrior, how am I to mourn you adequately? You have been quite ignominiously vanquished, for which Duke Joab will be afflicted by plagues: (952) on this earth Joab and his people will for their sins be plagued by an issue of blood and leprosy; they will never be free of gout in their legs, and in addition they will be slain in arduous battles. (953) And they will also always have to beg for bread because they have so ignominiously slain Abner."

When they now bore Duke Abner to his grave, the noble Duke David himself accompanied him. (954) King David then said to Joab alone and thereafter to all the people, both great and small: "Now, tear your garments and put on sackcloth and mourn piteously for Abner, the worthy man." (955) Then Duke Abner was buried with great honors. The king then began to weep and to wail. King David there wept miserably, and all of his men wept with him. (956) David raised his eyes and looked to Heaven: "Now I mourn to God, blessed be He, for this worthy man. Abner, you were, alas, slain like a scoundrel who deserved it (957) and who should by rights be slain with a sword. You did not deserve it. For that reason I must mourn you. You most worthy warrior, your hands did I recognized well—they were never bound by any human hand. (958) From your earliest youth until the graying of your locks, you were never held captive in irons or in the stocks. You have, alas, fallen, you proud and noble warrior, just as one cuts down a murderer in the woods."

(959) There was even more weeping there by the king and his men, and when the king then returned home, they wanted to refresh him and give him

something to eat. "No," said King David, "as I truly live, (960) I will neither eat nor drink this day. I wish to mourn the valiant one in grief and in sorrow." Thereby did all Israel recognize, and it was made clear to them, that the king's grief was sincere.

(961) Ishbosheth was very alarmed when he was told that Abner had been slain at Hebron. All Israel was quite disheartened, and it grieved King Ishbosheth sincerely.

(962) Now there were two officers who had remained at Gath. King Saul had exiled them long ago. Now when they heard the news in Gath, they went to Mahanaim; the trip was not difficult for them. (963) They came running to King Ishbosheth's house with two sacks, as if they wanted to buy wheat. King Ishbosheth lay on his bed and slept quite peacefully in the middle of the day. (964) They cut off his head; he was then, alas, dead. They fled from there; they were compelled to flee. The one was named Rechab, the other Baanah. They went as far as Hebron and were both pleased. (965) They came running to King David. Rechab carried King Ishbosheth's head in his hand. They said: "Noble and most mighty King, God has just aided you against your foes; (966) against Saul and his people you have now gained vengeance. Right here is the head of Ishbosheth; he can do nothing more to you."

King David then became an angry man and was deeply disturbed, as I can tell you. (967) He said: "By God in Heaven, blessed be He, who has help me against all my enemies and in all my distress, when I was still in Ziklag, a messenger came there and told me similar news of Saul. (968) He said that he had just slain Saul. He thought he would become rich from the messenger's reward. I had the proper messenger's reward given to him. In my city of Ziklag, I had him slain. (969) Am I to put up with such a murder by two scoundrels who slay an honorable lord in his bed?"

The king called to the executioner: "Slay them at once." Their hands and feet were cut off—the king commanded it. (970) At once their hands and feet were hung above the waters, so that people would be reminded of the ignominious forfeiture and that King David was grieved in his heart. King Ishbosheth's head was then buried in Abner's grave.

(971) All Israel then came to the king in Hebron. Noble King David now wore the crown of the land. All Israel alike swore allegiance to him. Not before this time did King David become a proper and mighty king. (972) Then King David did not wish to remain any longer in Hebron. He went about through all Israel and won over all the cities. Then the distinguished King David came to Jerusalem. The city's lord was a Jebusite. His wrath arose (973) because King David wanted to take the city. He said: "The city was all mine

since the days of Abraham. Now, Isaac and Jacob swore to my ancestors that the city would always be safe from David. (974) For that reason there are two images affixed to the battlements as memorials, images of Isaac and Jacob, which still contain the oath. On them is written how they still retain the oath. King David ought to leave the city undisturbed."

(975) King David then asked the scholars and the elders whether the Jebusites had kept the oath. They then told the king that the oath had been broken: they had plundered, struck and stabbed Israel. (976) King David then said: "Why am I so abhorrent to them that they have said: 'David will not come here'? Why does my heart despise the images so? I wish that they were burned tonight in a fire. (977) I will keep the promise; I will not touch the images. Now come on, all you men of mine, whoever can mount an attack. I may not be anywhere near the door and gate; so, dear comrades, help me get inside over the wall, (978) since the images bar me from the door—whoever rips these images from the door for me—since they have forbidden me, the city is not mine. So, dear comrades, help me get inside over the wall. (979) I want to see the attack; I will not be far away. Whoever captures the city and begins the battle is to become a commander of my heroes. Now, get to the walls and raise up the ladders."

(980) Joab, the marvelously mighty, strode up to the gate, as the king and all his servants bid. With his very great strength he exerted himself on the gate. He soon captured the city—that I tell you in truth. (981) Joab found a tree by the wall that was very tall. Joab hurried to the tree. He bent it over the wall; he called to his king: "Noble King David, leap over the wall to the inside. (982) Now grasp the tree by the branches and, O noble king, hold tightly to the branches." The noble king did as Joab requested of him. David let himself be hurled up over the city. (983) Then David said: "I have God, blessed be He, in my thoughts. Now, look, dear people, how I am flying over the wall."

And when King David then came into the city, he took Jerusalem, the good city, as his capital city. (984) Then King David built a castle and stronghold on Mount Zion, quite a wondrous work. He intended, with his worthy warriors—they had exalted spirits—to be secure inside it from his enemies. (985) David dwelt in his fortress and called it the City of David. They there presented many a mighty heathen with check and mate. God, blessed be He, provided King David aid wherever he turned. He was famous far away in foreign lands. (986) Wherever King David heard of a mighty man, he at once sent his messenger to him and gave his warrior very good pay so that he would have the stalwarts in his battles.

(987) Now, I want to name some of the excellent heroes who were in all the battles with King David. They were bold heroes, the most worthy of men whose peers can nowhere be found in all the lands. (988) The first was Adino the Eznite, a good and noble knight. He bore a good sword and had great courage. Eight hundred mighty warriors were nothing but a puff of wind to him. He prevailed over many a mother's son with his sword. (989) When the mighty warrior was to go into battle, he could terrify those who were to fight against him. Now, the bold warrior was also able to perform in matters of religious devotion, with some of his other comrades, in Torah study and in writing. (990) Eleazar, the son of Dodo, was one of the worthiest of knights. He certainly took none of the mighty ones prisoner: very many of the mighty heathens lay dead before him. I think that no one in the world was his equal. (991) Shammah, the son of Agee, was also one of the mightiest on whom the sun ever shone. He struck many a heathen dead. Whoever wanted to test out his sword fighting soon had enough. (992) Abishai, Joab's brother, was quite a untamed youth. He killed three hundred mighty heathens as if nothing but a puff of wind.

Now, in that same time, there was a valiant man whose name was Jehoiada, as I can tell you. (993) He had with his wife a very dear child, a youth mighty and bold, as one finds it written. Benaiah the Mighty was the name of the good warrior. He rejoiced when he heard the news (994) that King David was looking for mighty heroes. He said to his father: "Give me my sword at once. I want to ride to David. I cannot do otherwise." He had to let him ride away but did not do so willingly. (995) He then found on the road a troop that was battle-ready, led by two counts of Moab, as the book tells us here. The counts first wanted to rob Benaiah. "By my faith," said Benaiah, "you must let me ride on. (996) My hard strokes from the good sword that I hold in my hand are unknown to you." The counts then said: "Do not let him go anywhere. We want his sword and good mail-coat for ourselves." (997) When Benaiah heard that, how he did rage. He leapt from his war-horse and ran onto the grass. He drew his very good sword from its sheath. With undaunted courage he charged at the great host. (998) They thought to capture him against his will. With his sharp sword he conquered them. They charged him vigorously and thought that they had him. They carried away many a corpse killed by that same lad. (999) For the Moabites, the battle lasted a long time. Many a corpse was carried away, killed by that small child, until the bold warrior had quite won the battle. Benaiah the Mighty charged at the counts. (1000) He slew them both, sparing neither. The army fled from there. The lad was left alone there.

Benaiah stripped off from his body his steel mail-coat. He wanted to rest for a while and lay down on the ground.

(1001) It began to snow heavily; that angered the lad. He wished to ride away from there; he put on his spurs. Then the young warrior heard such a great clamor that it troubled the youth deeply. (1002) "Truly," said Benaiah, "before I ride away from here, I will indeed have to find out what devilish thing cries out thus." He turned toward a pit in order to follow the clamor. There he found a mighty Egyptian underway. (1003) He held a great spear in his hand. The hero Benaiah had left his sword lying on the ground beside where his horse had gone. He picked up a great pole—that I tell you in truth. (1004) He advanced toward the Egyptian with that pole, so that he took his spear away from him by force. He stabbed him to death with his own spear. He also left that dead Egyptian lying there. (1005) He hurried toward the pit from which the clamor came. There he found a mighty lion that roared from hunger. The Moabite counts had put it in there for the sake of entertainment. "Truly," said Benaiah, "Sir Lion, I must have you." (1006) He hurried to fetch his sword and put it on while up above, and he leapt into the pit, that marvelously bold man. He thought that he could carry off the lion. The lion then roared with rage and attacked the man. (1007) The lion roared with rage in that heavy snow. Clawing and biting, it caused the youth great pain. The youth nonetheless defended himself in his deadly peril, until he had also slain the mighty lion. (1008) The lad then rode from there until he came to David. Noble King David heartily welcomed him. He gave the mighty warrior a good assignment, which instilled the youth with high spirits in times of adversity.

(1009) Asahel, the brother of Joab, was indeed very mighty. He could, however, not survive his confrontation with Abner. Elhanan, the son of Dodo, a very mighty man, joined King David in Bethlehem. (1010) Shammah, the Harodite, was seen to rampage in battle. Elika, the Harodite, must also be praised. Helez, the Paltite, was a very mighty man. Ira, the son of Ikkesh, was likely his equal. (1011) Abiezer, the son of Anethoth, was an excellent warrior. Zalmon the Adohite[23] can legitimately be reckoned alongside him. Maharai from Netophath was an undaunted warrior. Heleb, the son of Baanah, rode out of Netophath. (1012) Ittai, the son of Arbi, was from the land of Benjamin. Benaiah the Tirathite, he was no trifle. Hirai from Gaash was possessed of high spirits: the warrior was good in assault and battle. (1013) Abi-albon from Archot was a most valiant hero. Armaveth from Parhayim was a good warrior. Eliahba from the Euphrates was indeed a mighty man. Jonathan, the son of Jashen, was likely his equal. (1014) Shammah the Arudite had seen many a battle. Of Ahiram the Ardite, one ought to say honorable things. Eliphelet the

Hosni never failed. Ahithophel was a hero from Giloni. (1015) Hezrai the Carmelite wished to have the prize. Paarai the Arbite was seen to act with valor. Igal, the son of Nathan, was an excellent hero. Mighty Bani was by origin a Gadite. (1016) Zelek the Ammonite was a very mighty hero. Naharai the Beerothite can legitimately be reckoned alongside him.

These bold heroes had to yield to Joab, the bold hero—who would dare challenge him? (1017) For marvelously great strength his name was known far and wide. Joab, the wondrously mighty, was a hero in all battles. King David had chosen him as a commander. Many a man met his end at his hands. (1018) Ira the Ithrite and Gareb the Ithrite—those two bold heroes were never seen to fall. Uriah the Hittite, he was good in adversity. He was valiant and noble, for which his spirit rejoiced. (1019) They were bold heroes and all of them mighty men. There were many other stalwarts, not all of whom I can name.

David dwelt with his men at Jerusalem in the stronghold of Zion—that I tell you in truth. (1020) There was a king in Rome[24] who was named Hiram. He knew noble King David by reputation. Hiram sent messengers to David saying in front of all that they should build a house for King David. (1021) He sent him fine wood and as many builders, carpenters, and stone masons as one would want. They built him a house according to his wishes. King David and his men dwelt therein. (1022) Noble King David dwelt in Jerusalem. He married even more wives—that I tell you in truth. Now, let us name the excellent children who were born to King David in Jerusalem. (1023) Shammua, and Shobab, and Nathan, and Solomon, Ibhar and Elisha; he delighted in Nephesh. Japhnia and Elishama and Eliada and Eliphalet—those were the children there.[25]

(1024) It was immediately reported to the mighty Philistines that King David had assumed control over the land of the Jews and that all Israel wanted to have him as king. The heathens then assembled and wanted to prevent it. (1025) When King David in Jerusalem found out that the mighty heathens wanted to come there, King David made haste into his stronghold. Then the heathens came and a battle ensued. (1026) "I regret it so much, and I cannot cease mourning him—my dear comrade Jonathan, whom they killed." Then King David sent Eleazar, the son of Dodo: "Go and assemble all Israel and then return here."

(1027) Mighty Eleazar certainly did not shirk: he assembled all Israel as the king had commanded. The heathens then marched toward him in the field, and they did not want to let all Israel join the king. (1028) Eleazar, the son of Dodo, then said: "Be valiant, Jews! They will have to clear the field for us, even if it pains them. You are all to wait right here, and I will go out to them. Let us see," said Eleazar, "if one might defeat them." (1029) The hero armed himself in his steel mail-coat. He confronted the heathens with his good sword. He gave the heathens quite discourteous strokes. The heathens fell there as if they were seeds being sown. (1030) He slashed many a vehement stroke on each side. Many a mighty heathen there lay on his side. All Israel had quite enough travail there in carrying out the corpses of those whom the hero slew. (1031) The Philistines had to flee, with injury and with shame. His good sword adhered to Eleazar's [bloodied] hands, and he could in no wise detach it except when hot water loosened it. (1032) Then the hero Eleazar rode and told Sir David the news, what had happened with the heathens.

King David then sent Shammah, the son of Agee. He said: "Go to the Jews and stay with them a while. (1033) Perhaps the mighty heathens will again attack. Report it to me; it will do them no good." The wondrously strong Shammah was delighted with the mission. He went to the Jews and there attended the Jews. (1034) The heathens then returned with many mighty heroes. In assaults and in battles they excelled. They attacked the Jewish troops with vehemence. The Jews had to retreat. Shammah made a stand there. (1035) There was a field planted with lentils in the Jews' land. The heathens wanted to grieve them by ruining it. The warrior Shammah there made his stand in the planted field. He struck many a heathen to the ground. (1036) He denied the mighty heathens the field. Swords were heard to resound outside the gates of Zion. Many a mighty heathen was there seen to fall dead. The hero Shammah was also in great adversity there.

(1037) King David and his mighty men were informed that the mighty heathens had returned. They were then very quickly prepared to fight. He and his heroes were dauntless. (1038) David was at the vanguard, the man at the very front; he vehemently charged at the bold and mighty heathens. All his stalwarts rushed after him. King David was eager to get to Sir Shammah. (1039) Anyone who wanted to get at them had to make a wide detour around him. They drove a devilish battle into the middle of them. Many a mighty heathen did he slash and slay, until he got to Sir Shammah. Then, for the time being, he had given them enough. (1040) "Shammah, loyal servant, stand at my back. I will be your sworn companion in this adversity." "Thank you, my gracious and noble king," Sir Shammah replied, "I trust my sword; I am causing them some trouble."

(1041) Now, all Israel wanted to get to the king. "No," said the king, "you are to wait on the field. The heathens have so many mighty men. They belong to my mighty warriors, whom I can send to attack them. (1042) Just be prepared and let no one escape, so that not a single heathen gets away from us." Then King David called to his dauntless heroes: "I lament to you my great and heavy heartache. (1043) They slew my sworn companion. I want to avenge Jonathan myself, even if it brings about my own death." The heathens then answered him: "You can count on the same thing: we will give you the same strokes as we did Jonathan."

(1044) Then many saw how hero leapt at hero. Noble King David slew many of the heathens with his sword, and the king's stalwarts fought a grim battle. They gave the heathens many gaping wounds, (1045) until the mighty heathens fled from the battlefield. David and his men did not want to let them escape. They struck at the heathens there so that the blood spurted from them; the blood flowed from them like a great brook. (1046) The heathens fled from there and left their idols there. King David said: "I will treat their idols without respect." He made a great fire on the ground. In a short while he had burned them all.

(1047) David and his men went into the assembly hall. Then the heathens said: "The battle is not yet over." The heathens again gathered together a very great host, as the stars in the sky and the sands of the sea. (1048) They marched violently into the king's lands. Many a warrior marched into the valley of Rephaim. David and his men were in Jerusalem. The helmets of the heathens gleamed like the radiance of the day. (1049) Then the heathens marched up to the gate of Bethlehem. They encamped outside it, attacking and assaulting. David and his men marched to Adullam. The distinguished warrior was eager to fight.

(1050) Three of his mighty warriors were not with him there—Adino the Eznite, and Eleazar and Shammah—for which reason the Jews were sorrowful and unhappy. Then all three of them arrived there. (1051) When the three heroes then heard the news that the mighty heathens had come against Israel, the three heroes came running to the army. Israel—those who knew the warriors—was delighted by that.

(1052) The king and his stalwarts were in his stronghold. King David then said: "You mighty and distinguished heroes: the heathens are encamped with great violence outside the gate of Bethlehem. There is a cold well there. (1053) If anyone could bring me a drink of that water, I think it could extend my life by a year." The three stalwarts heard that and took counsel with each other: "We will bring him the water, even if we die in the attempt." (1054) The three bold men armed themselves; they dressed in steel mail-coats. They began to grip their shields, those three warriors did, and their very good swords they took in hand.

(1055) They came to Bethlehem, where many a heathen was encamped. There they received many a heavy blow. The three bold knights carried good swords. They waded up to their knees in the blood of the heathens. (1056) They vehemently forced their way through the vast army. Many a heathen there was never again seen alive. The three mighty knights came before the gate. The gates were there unbolted for them; not for long were they left outside. (1057) They then drew water from the cold well and set out on their way. Their strength was manifold. The heathens then charged at the three comrades. There one saw many of the heathens fall from their horses.

(1058) The three bold men slung their shields on their backs and charged with vigor at the heathens. Each carried the water in his left hand and a sword in his right, until the army was parted. (1059) Many hard blows rained down on the backs of that vast army encamped before Bethlehem before they finally broke through the great host. They returned to King David and brought him the water. (1060) They brought him the water, of which he knew nothing. "Noble King David, now, sate your desire: it is from the cold well in Bethlehem. In front of it, many a heathen has lost his life." (1061) Then King David, the worthy man, answered him: "Were I to drink the water, I would not be acting properly. You have risked life and limb in adverse conditions. God forbid that I should drink the water. (1062) If I had known of the affair, I would have stopped you. You distinguished heroes; you have won honor herewith." He took all that water from their hands; he poured it on the altar and burned it as a sacrifice.

(1063) Then the heathens again conceived of a trick and dug a great many pits in the field which King David was to cross to get to them: "If they fall into the pits, then we will catch a bear!"

(1064) King David then commanded that Urim and Thummim be brought forth. He said: "My dear Lord God, again tell me: should I again go into danger against my enemies? Then many of the heathens will die at the hand of my stalwarts." (1065) Then God, blessed be He, said: "Let them stand. Do not let yourself be seen by the mighty heathens. Surround their army, behind them on the field; then set up camp there with your men. (1066) Wait for me at the willow trees. I will myself be with you in this battle. Thus you will hear treading upon the trees that are there. So, make haste with your warriors. God will go before you."

(1067) Noble King David truly did not shirk: with his men he did as God, blessed be He, had commanded. He went to the trees; they were very tall. He heard the angels treading; he was at once eager for action. (1068) Then many a heathen man was slain. The king and his men were not in danger. That was a great heartache for the mighty heathens. God, blessed be He, himself fought for the Jews. (1069) Many of the heathens there were quite eager to flee. David and his men pursued them relentlessly. From Geba to Gezer he pursued them. He killed many a mighty heathen with his sword.

(1070) Then the king allowed Israel to return home. He said: "The dead heathens may well not get up again. If the heathens again invade our land, then we will play with them, bouncing their heads off the wall."

(1071) At that time King David dwelt in Jerusalem, and the holy ark was still in Gibeah, where King Saul had always had it with him. Now King David wanted to have it brought from there. (1072) He had the holy ark brought from there. With him were some thirty thousand men, with dancing and leaping and great rejoicing, with organs and with harps and with all types of stringed instruments. (1073) A priest named Uzzah grasped the ark; that priest then died. David fled from there. "I want to the leave the ark here; it will certainly cause me trouble. I could also fall into sin. I am afraid of death." (1074) He left the ark in the house of Obed. Then God, blessed be He, gave aid to Obed in all his affairs. Only then did David consider what he had done: he should have let the holy ark be brought. (1075) Then King David had the ark brought home, with such great rejoicing that there would be much to tell. He made many sacrifices during that journey. He thought to honor the Lord God, blessed be He. (1076) King David was not wearing much clothing: the worthy man was dancing in a linen girdle. The lord of the land made many a fine leap before the holy ark in honor of God, blessed be He. (1077) When King David then arrived in Jerusalem, Michal, the daughter of Saul observed the king. When Queen Michal saw him dancing, she thought to herself: "You may well be a dissolute youth."

(1078) The holy ark was then carried into Jerusalem below the gate of the tabernacle. David made a great many sacrifices there. He made presents to all Israel and had them go home. Then the noble king went into his house. (1079) He was not well received by Queen Michal. She said: "King David, you may well be a dissolute youth: for dancing and leaping you clothe your body as any other dissolute youth courting wicked women." (1080) "No," said the king, "it is not like that. God, blessed be He, has chosen me. For that reason I rejoice thus. He never wanted to have Saul, your father. For that reason I am rejoicing; for that reason did I do it. (1081) Now, I did not court any wicked women. All women honor me, because I have dedicated my body wholly to the service of God, blessed be He. I want to serve my God, blessed be He, as long as I live." (1082) Michal had sinned against her dear husband, so that she bore no child in her entire life.

While King David was living in Jerusalem, there was a prophet named Nathan with King David. (1083) King David said to Nathan: "Now give me your advice: I think I would like to build a temple to God." The prophet said to the king: "Do as you wish. Our Lord will always give you aid." (1084) That same night the prophet lay asleep, until the voice of God, blessed be He, called him from Heaven: "Nathan the Prophet, truly I tell you—Go to King David and tell My beloved servant: (1085) 'You have in your heart to build a house for Me. Abandon your plan; just let it go. You have slain many a man with your hands. For that reason I do not want a temple from your hands. (1086) David, my beloved servant, I tell you, you bold knight: you considered it in your mind and in doing so you did right, for you will be buried right here with great honor. After your death your son will have your kingdom forever. (1087) He will possess your kingdom with great honor, with wealth and power and with great wisdom. That same one is to build Me a temple right away. Your son will be famous everywhere beneath the heavens."

(1088) The prophet Nathan told the news to the king. He rejoiced in his heart because of it; his grief disappeared. He thanked God, blessed be He, with great praise, with harps and songs and all kinds of stringed instruments, (1089) that after his death his kingdom would endure and remain under his children and never disappear. King David rejoiced greatly in his heart because of that and thanked our Lord with great joy.

(1090) Thereafter King David dwelt in Jerusalem in very great honor—that I tell you in truth. He conquered with great strength a great many lands. King David then became famous far and wide.

(1091) During that same time, as I can tell you, the Philistines had a very large man, an enormous giant, a dauntless warrior. He was Goliath's own brother, as the book tells us. (1092) He was also named Goliath and wore good armor. This enormous man was raised in Gath. He clothed himself in a steel mail-coat and bore a pole in his hand. Then the heathens again invaded the land of the Jews. (1093) King David and his men march out against them. The mighty giant rushed toward Sir David. "Mighty King David, herewith are you properly challenged. Today I wish to avenge on you my great heartache. (1094) In the valley of Elah you slew my brother, which I lament. My pole will certainly bring about the end of you." "Do not beshit yourself," said King David. "Oh my, how frightened I am! If I slew your brother, then perhaps I will slay you, too. (1095) Beware of my sword—there where the blade bites you. I will hack your pole to pieces like a rotten willow twig." "What, can you do nothing but babble!?" shouted the huge giant. "Now, I will squash you like any other flea."

(1096) They stopped their waiting; it seemed to them that it was time. Then they fought quite a fierce battle. The giant was clumsy; David was agile. The enormous Goliath also came to a bad end there. (1097) David struck him dead; many other heathens were slain with him. The heathens fled when they saw him carried away.

Some time later the heathens again returned with many a mighty heathen. The king was made aware of it. (1098) David and his men again bound on their helmets. That same hour they made haste toward the heathens. Now, Goliath had yet another brother, a young warrior, a mighty and enormous giant named Ishbi. (1099) He had never in his life fought in a battle. Only now did he wish to begin; it seemed to him that it was time. David marched at the vanguard of all his heroes. He gave a great many mighty heathens a discourteous welcome.

(1100) The battle lasted for a long time—that I can tell you. A great many mighty heathens were slain by David. He struck with his sharp sword through steel mail-coats. There fell many of the heathens at King David's hand, (1101) until King David began to grow weary. David, that worthy man, wanted to rest a while. Young Ishbi, the huge Philistine giant, noticed that. He bore in his hands a spear of immeasurable size. (1102) The iron spear head weighed three hundred pounds. The young giant also had sufficient strength for that. He charged at King David with great force. "I will not let you rest," said he to the worthy man. (1103) "I have never in my life seen a battle in my country. If I slay you, it will be shameful to the Jews. You put my two brothers in the ground. For that I want to earn my spurs against you today." (1104) Sir David then replied to him: "You would earn great shame thereby, if you were to strike down an exhausted warrior on the battlefield. Let me rest for a short while. Then, mighty giant, I will willingly fight you." (1105) "Are you then so exhausted? That I gladly hear. You must atone to me for my two brothers whom you slew. Today I will avenge on you many noble men." "No," said Sir David, "you are wrong about that. (1106) If you need red gold, I will give you enough. For just a little while, let me take some rest." [The giant said:] "You would carry on until tomorrow! Now, quickly, defend yourself!" [David said:] "Your frothing is what I will fend off. Your life is at an end! (1107) Thus will I defend myself, exhausted as I am, as best I can, and if my stalwarts see it, you will not live a day. You ought to back off from me and let me take some rest."

The giant struck forcefully at the exhausted warrior—(1108) a stroke with his spear onto his helmet so that the fiery sparks glowed brightly. His steel mail-coat there shielded him from death, before King David fell down indeed onto the ground. (1109) This stroke resounded so far that Abishai observed King David's fall. "O, mighty God in Heaven, blessed be He, safeguard my lord." He slung his shield over his shoulder and charged toward him. (1110)

He reached him at just the right moment—the time had seemed long to him. Noble Abishai sprang in front of his lord. Now, the hero Abishai was a murderously fierce man. He charged at the giant with the greatest of strength.

(1111) His outward expression was of misery and sorrow: King David lay there exhausted on the ground. He [Abishai] screamed most miserably: "Alas, such great adversity! You have slain my dear lord! (1112) If you then strike down an exhausted warrior onto the ground, then strike me down dead, too, you great demon! Joab, my dear brother, will avenge us both. So I will first attempt whether I can crush you to pieces—(1113) your neck with your armor and with your life! Alas, noble King David, dear my lord!" The warrior David was recovering from the blow: for sorrow and for exhaustion he sat down on the ground.

(1114) The fact that he was alive grieved the giant. Now, hear what the king said to the giant: "If you will let me rest right here for a little while, then none of my stalwarts will fight against you. (1115) I am confident that I will slaughter you and your men before the day is out." [The giant said:] "It astonishes me greatly that you have come back to life." Abishai then rejoiced when he saw Sir David. He said: "Noble King David, now make yourself comfortable. (1116) Against his will, he will have to let you rest." The wondrously strong Abishai leapt toward the giant. They both performed great feats of strength before one of them struck the other down to the ground. (1117) Abishai grasped his sword wrathfully in both hands and charged at the giant. He then slashed apart the rings of his chain mail so that they flew into the air. And his good helmet was also cleft open. (1118) The giant wanted to withdraw; Abishai did not want to let him. One saw how the knight fought wrathfully. He attacked the giant with most discourteous blows. He struck him many a deep wound at that time. (1119) The giant had to fall; he was forced to it by adversity. Abishai was enraged and slew the giant. Now, when young Ishbi had been slain, the heathens began both to weep and to mourn. (1120) They fled toward Gath, for which they had good reason.

Then all the stalwarts among King David's servants swore: "King David is no longer to go with us, when we battle the mighty heathens. (1121) He always wants to be at the forefront and the first to fight. At some point someone may come along who will take his life. If he were at some point to be slain—may God, blessed be He, guard against it—then all Israel would be without joy. (1122) King David should no longer go along with us. We wish to leave him at home in the stronghold." All the stalwarts swore a binding oath to that effect. That was a matter of profound grief for King David. (1123) King David then said: "What could be worse for me than to know that my beloved servants are in distress!"

Not long thereafter the heathens again returned. They took Saph, the mighty giant, with them. (1124) He was also Goliath's brother and was named Saph. Noble King David sent all his own stalwarts, as well as many mighty men from Israel. Sibbechai, the Hushathite, charged at the giant. (1125) They then fought a long battle. Sibbechai struck the giant broad mortal wounds until the giant grappled with bitter death. Then the people said: "Sibbechai, you have our eternal gratitude." (1126) Then the heathens had to retreat and take the disgraceful way homeward. The heathens then sent word far into the lands; many a warrior came out there to help them.

(1127) The heathens had forgotten yet another enormous giant at home. If one wished to know his size, one would have to measure him. He had six toes on his feet and six fingers on his hands. He was also Goliath's brother from the land of the heathens. (1128) He was mighty in his feet and also his hands. He was a bold and agile warrior in all battles. Sir David's stalwarts then came: it was a small band. They called the enormous and most mighty giant to come to them there: (1129) "Today we will get compensation from David for all our sorrow: he has put nothing but fools in command over you, if he thinks he can fight a battle with so few troops. For the Philistines are like the sands of the sea!" (1130) That was heard by Jonathan, David's nephew: "You will soon repent for your scolding and chiding." He quickly went out in front of the mighty giant. The battle was fierce, before he felled the giant. (1131) The heathens had to retreat; they were forced by great distress. The battlefield was in general red with blood.

When the king's stalwarts arrived in Jerusalem and glimpsed Zion, the king heartily welcomed them—he and all his men. (1132) Then King David said: "I want to offer some advice for us: are we to be troubled by the heathens forever? Then let us ravage their lands, put their people to death with the sword, take away their gods and destroy their cities. (1133) Let us advance into the heathen lands with a great host and capture the capital city. With that we will have won it all. Then King David summoned many a noble man until he had brought together a great army from Israel. (1134) It aggravated the king that he was not allowed to go along to accompany his men in battle. Then he thought to himself: "I must find a ploy by means of which I may again go out [to battle]: how long am I to molder here in my house!" (1135) Then all Israel—the mighty heroes, his beloved servants—had to release him from his oath. They then advanced into the homeland of the heathens; their cities were captured and their houses burned down. (1136) Gath, the fine capital city, was quickly captured. They demolished the walls and slew the people. He settled nothing but Jews in the city of Gath. The noble King David enfeebled the heathens.

(1137) The heathens assembled a very great army—as the stars of the heavens and the sands of the seas. King David also assembled all Israel there. With many a noble Jew did King David come out. (1138) Their great strength helped the heathens very little. The swords of David and his men bit grimly: they caused discomfort through steel and through iron. The vapors burst vehemently up into the heavens. (1139) The heathens were forced to flee because of mortal danger. Heathens beyond counting were slain there. The heathens fled from there; they hurried toward Gath. David and all Israel marched up before the capital city of Gath. (1140) There they encamped for a long time—as I can tell you—attacking and assaulting until he captured the city. He slew the people and took the city. King David settled nothing but Jews there. (1141) David and his men campaigned throughout the heathens' land. He slew everything that he encountered. The heathens were slain and quite annihilated, so that they never again invaded the land of Israel. (1142) Anyone who had survived was slain. They were forced to bear tribute and taxes into the land of the Jews.

Thereafter, King David rode into the land of Moab. David declared war on the king of Moab. (1143) "Remember, king of Moab, what you have done to me! I wanted to leave my father and my mother with you until I freed myself from my afflictions with King Saul. You slew my father and my mother. (1144) Moreover, I want to avenge my brother on you, on all your necks. I will destroy your cities." King David then also conquered the land of Moab. King David took vengeance with his own hand. (1145) He took a great rope and bound it full of people [in a line]: he slew two and let the third live. Thus did King David do in general: to men and women, old and young. (1146) The people of Moab were forced to be subject to David. He wanted great tribute and taxes from them.

At this time there was a mighty king whose name was Hadarezer[26]—that I tell you in truth. (1147) He was a powerful king in the land of Aram-Zobah. He invaded the land of the Jews—he did not yet know their strength. Indeed did he capture the cities by the brook Euphrates. King David and his men learned of it. (1148) Sir David and all his men armed themselves: they put on the hard steel rings of their mail-coats. King David then advanced to the brook Euphrates, where King Hadarezer and his men were. (1149) [Hadarezer said:] "Tell me what you want, you greenhorn!" King David then said: "Where do you come from?" A challenge was quickly issued to the mighty heroes there. David and his men were ready at once.

(1150) They fought with the Jews, as one finds written. The Jews there smote many a mother's child. Hadarezer was forced into flight; thus did the battle end. Sir David captured seventeen hundred noble knights (1151) and twenty thousand foot soldiers—the best of his [Hadarezer's] servants—they were all taken captive. David captured them. He had the horses' hamstrings cut; he retained only a hundred of them for himself to ride. (1152) "God, blessed be He, commanded it; for that reason have I done it. No king subject to Israel is to have a lot of horses." Hadarezer had to serve David; he at once forced him to do it. With his troops, David occupied all of Hadarezer's land. (1153) From Betah and Berothai—both cities of Aram—King David then took copper without measure and many of the golden shields—one cannot even say how many—that Hadarezer's army had carried in battle.

(1154) That which King David took from all the other peoples, all of it together was taken into the tabernacle. King David had it retained and securely locked up, in order to build the temple therewith. (1155) Toi, king of Hamath, heard the news that King David had defeated Hadarezer. King Toi rejoiced at that, according to his custom, for he had fought with Hadarezer his whole life. (1156) King Toi then sent his son, Joram, to David and conveyed his deep gratitude to David and honored him greatly. The king's child brought him good silver and jewels. Sir David thanked him for that, as one finds it written. (1157) That was also deposited in the tabernacle. Above all, King David did not want to give up that which he had taken from all his enemies in all lands. He did everything that he could to make sure that that was done well. (1158) He had dedicated himself with his whole heart; the king wanted to live fully in the fear of God, blessed be He. He did not put too great a burden on his people, except that he held strictly to the service of God, blessed be He.

(1159) Now, Duke Joab had caused Edom much pain. He had had eighteen thousand of their men slain. King David then commanded that all the dead be buried. All the people then said: "King David must be thanked. (1160) King David is so honorable and so stalwart: when he slays them, he in turn has them buried; when he has slain them, he has them buried right away." Then all the people said: "Thanks be to Sir David!"

(1161) King David appointed the hero Benaiah over the archers, the slingers, and the camp.

Now, as King David was dwelling in Jerusalem, then with great honor King David said: (1162) "If there is a man or woman of King Saul's kin alive, I would like to give him the best treatment for the sake of Jonathan. King David could not then find out the truth. Then King David had Ziba summoned. (1163) Ziba had been King Saul's servant. David said: "Ziba, pay attention and tell me the truth: is any woman or man of King Saul's kin still alive? I would like to give him the best treatment for the sake of Jonathan. (1164) Ziba then answered him: "There is one man to be found. He is King Saul's grandchild, the child of mighty Jonathan. He can, dear my lord, neither walk nor ride with you: he limps so severely on both sides. (1165) When Saul and his children were slain, his nurse carried the young lad away. She dropped the child hard: because of her great alarm, she let him fall. For that reason, he has had to limp his whole life long. (1166) The boy is named Mephibosheth, dear my lord." Sir David then said to him: "Where can the lad be?" "He is in Machir's house in Lo-debar." King David quickly sent his messenger there (1167) and had him, King Mephibosheth, Jonathan's son, brought quickly. Mephibosheth was then very much afraid that David would do something to him. He came to the king and was very frightened. He bowed to the ground before the exalted king.

(1168) King David then said: "Mephibosheth, are you here?" Mephibosheth fell down on his knees. "Yes, I am, lord and king, O gracious lord of the land." King David then noticed that he was very frightened. (1169) The king said to Mephibosheth: "You need not worry. As long as I live, nothing bad will happen to you. I will give you the best treatment for the sake of your father. You are ever to be in Jerusalem with me. (1170) You are to eat at my table as one of my children. Throughout all of my kingdom—hear what I intend—from that which had previously been King Saul's patrimony, you are to have the grain of those fields and the harvest of those vineyards. (1171) All your father's patrimony is to become yours. Ziba, Saul's servant, will see to it for you. His sons and also his servants will take care of it for you—the fields and the meadows and the vineyards." (1172) Mephibosheth then became a most cheerful man. He profusely thanked the king, as indeed was proper for him to do. Mephibosheth then remained with the king for many years. He gave him the best treatment—that I tell you in truth. (1173) The king treated him as one of his children. And he was quite lame in both legs.

Mighty King David dwelt in Jerusalem. He was now safe from all his enemies. (1174) He had conquered the lands, as we have heard. All warriors were firmly compelled into subjection to him. At that time King Nahash died, and his son Hanun took over the kingship. (1175) King David then said: I must show honor to Ammon. I am deeply saddened about the lord of the land. When the king of Moab slew my father, my dear brother fled to the king of Ammon. (1176) Nahash, king of Ammon, vigorously maintained him until my own situation improved." David sent his messengers to convey to Hanun his greetings and favor and to mourn his father. (1177) Then they mourned the king in Rabbah, the city of the sons of Ammon. The noble messengers were shown great honor there. The king of Ammon showed them great honor. Then the servants and the advisors of the king said to him: (1178) "Do you think that King David honors your father, if he is already sending his messengers here to Rabbah? He wants to spy out the city—that is what he has in mind. He wants to conquer the city. Now, follow our counsel: (1179) send his messengers home in disgrace; then it will never happen again that he sends his spies to the lord of a land." King Hanun then said: "You are certainly right. I would not give even a little hair for these spies."

(1180) It was at that time indeed a great disgrace, when it became known that one's beard had been shorn. King Nahash then said to David's envoys: "Let me tell you something curious: I am going to have half your beards shaved off!" (1181) He also had all their garments cut off, behind above the ass and in front above the genitals. Anyone who wanted to blow [an enema] into the asses of these messengers would have to raise up neither cloak nor hose. (1182) Because of their shame, they did not know what to do or where they should go in order to get away from there. They could cover themselves neither behind nor in front. On could see their asses from behind; their clothes did not suffice. (1183) They were sent away in disgrace. David found out about it. King David sent other clothes to them there. He said: "Stay at Jericho until your beards grow back. I will avenge you on him, if it is the last thing I do. (1184) Fare you well, my dear servants. There will be vengeance on King Hanun—that I tell you, my dear servants, certainly in truth. More people will have to die than the number of hairs that he sheared from you." (1185) The envoys remained in the city of Jericho until their thick, long beards grew back.

War was declared on King Hanun, as he deserved. King David made many people suffer. (1186) Those in Ammon sent a great deal of silver and gold and hired many mighty warriors and paid them a great deal. They hired Aram Beth-rehob and Aram Zoba—twenty thousand mighty heroes who were delighted in their pay—(1187) and King Maacah, a mighty man indeed, with a thousand mighty warriors in armor, and Ish-tob, a prince famed far and wide. He brought twelve thousand mighty heroes into the land.

(1188) The news was told to King David in Jerusalem, how so many foreign guests had arrived. King David then sent many men against them, all in armor and bearing swords. (1189) King David then sent the warrior Joab, and he sent with him all the king's stalwarts. Duke Joab there advanced onto a broad plain before the city of Rabbah, as we have heard. (1190) Now they were encamped before Rabbah on the broad plain; with their good steel mail-coats they were undaunted. Their armor shone like the radiance of the sun. Joab and his men formed a battle wedge. (1191) Meanwhile the king of

Ammon had mustered troops from his entire land, who also came charging out of the city of Rabbah. Ammon had assembled as the sands of the sea. All Israel advanced there in a great host. (1192) Israel there aligned itself against the foreign mercenaries. Ammon advanced on Israel from behind; that was grievous for the Jews.

When Joab was told, the hero's wrath arose: "Do my enemies now wish to overwhelm me like a blizzard from the front and the back?" (1193) He chose from Israel the best whom he could find. He formed a wedge there, directed toward Ammon. He put the rest of the host of Israel under the command of his brother, Abishai: "Now, listen to what I tell you, Abishai, my dear brother. (1194) We must quickly form two battle lines against them. So you must fight and defeat Ammon with your men. I and all my stalwarts will pound the lice out of the foreigners. Now, my dear brother, do not let yourself be terrified of Ammon. (1195) If I see that Ammon is going to be too strong for you, then I will, on my oath, give you aid in time. If the foreigners are too strong for me in the battle, then come also to my aid, when the time seems right to you."

(1196) Ammon charge at them from behind with great speed. Abishai and his men turned their battle wedge toward them. The battle was so vehement that Joab was displeased. His strength and his might were great beyond measure. (1197) The hero Joab came charging into the army. There many rings were split by his hands. He slashed wide around himself and cut a large circle. He caused many to break out in a bloody sweat. (1198) No one could make a stand before his good sword. He struck down the mighty heroes on the battlefield. Now the mighty and distinguished ones were in distress. A great many of their mighty knights were lost. (1199) The battle in which hero was attacking hero lasted a long time. He welcomed a great many with discourteous blows. No one in the world had ever seen a greater battle than when King David's warrior broke through that great army. (1200) The enemy forced a path to King David's servants. One observed among those stalwarts the fighting of the evil Devil himself. Their equal was to be found nowhere in any land. Many a helmet was split by their sharp swords. (1201) The Jews struck down to the ground many a foreign man. The blood then flowed far on the field. Whoever was unable to flee had to die. Their bright steel rings turned red with blood. (1202) The foreigners had to flee—it seemed to them that it was time. Abishai fought a very fierce battle with Ammon. Now, when all the foreigners had fled before Joab, they also fled before Abishai and soon marched away.

(1203) They escaped into the city of Rabbah. The Jews had to remain outside. Joab and his men came to Jerusalem. King David and all his men welcomed him. (1204) They told King David how they had scarcely survived and how there were so many of the mighty enemy. "If I had known that," said the exalted king, "I would have been with you. It will never happen again."

(1205) Then Hadarezer said: "Now, I have miscalculated. King David will eat me alive. All my men have been slain outside the city of Rabbah. I cannot put up with it any longer from him and his men." (1206) Then Hadarezer mustered troops throughout his land: whoever could even carry shields and swords in their hands. Like the stars in the sky and the sands of the sea, King Hadarezer came with a great host. (1207) He sent for Aram that was on the other side of the brook. He left neither the mighty nor the feeble at home: all of them came to Hadarezer, like the sands of the sea and the stars beyond count. (1208) Then King Hadarezer advanced with his great host, and the king made Shobach commander of the host.

At once the news was brought to King David: "The army that is advancing into the land cannot be numbered." (1209) King David quickly had his messengers sent forth. He mustered troops from all Israel—he had to have a great host. All Israel came to him; they were dauntless. The king and his men were at the forefront of the battle. (1210) He said: "I do not wish to wait for them to come here. We will go out to meet them. Let us see who will fight us!" David and his men crossed over the Jordan, with their steel mail-coats, with their swords and bows. (1211) There he found Hadarezer with nothing but mighty men. Hadarezer and his men began the battle; they fought a very fierce battle with the Jews. David said to his men: "Now it is time, (1212) you noble and stalwart warriors—now show your strength." No one could hear a word, because of the striking of their swords: sparks of wildfire burst up into the heavens. The dust and the smoke looked like clouds.

(1213) "I want to show them that I can also fight." Noble King David himself charged them. With his men he struck them. Many a man fell: no one in the land could count them all. (1214) Noble King David there proved his might. Sparks of wildfire flashed from the armor. Many charioteers charged at the king: he struck down seven hundred charioteers with his own hand. (1215) King David had by that point advanced far beyond his own men. Between him and his troops were some thousand men. That both grieved and angered the men of Israel. They all thought that they had lost their lord. (1216) Then his stalwarts slew many men: they went seeking their lord in misery and adversity. They were all lost—he had forced his way from them. They sought their lord until they found him.

(1217) He constantly served Almighty God, for which reason He never abandoned him in need. David the hero defended himself well. He felled forty thousand knights with his own hand. (1218) He was standing in the midst of them, David the worthy man. His men rejoiced when they saw him. On the third morning—that I tell you in truth—Aram fled; Hadarezer scarcely survived. (1219) Shobach, the commander, was slain, and many men died with him. The bold and mighty heroes trampled Aram's banner into the muck; their might was manifold. They struck down everyone, young and old. (1220) Aram fled from there—whoever could flee. They were beyond number—the dead and the wounded. King David and his men returned home. Hadarezer fled thence in great disgrace. (1221) The kings who were subject to Hadarezer were frightened, so that they no longer wanted to support him when he went to war with David. Thereafter Hadarezer lost all of his supporters who remained at home and ventured forth no more. (1222) King David went home, he and all his men, with such great honors, that no one can tell.

When summer came, and the wind became calm, so that hay and oats and all types of food could be found, (1223) King David sent Joab and all his stalwarts forth, and with them all Israel, before the city of Rabbah. "I want to have that city by assault and by attack." "Gladly, my lord," said Duke Joab, "it will be done. (1224) Neither wall nor moat will help them. And even if it kills me, I will have that city." They then advanced on Ammon and devastated all its territories—Joab and all Israel there before the walls of Rabbah. (1225) They advanced there onto the broad plain before Rabbah. They encamped in front of the city with many a campaign tent. Now, the city of Rabbah was well defended from assault and was secure at all times and against all adversity. (1226) Now, they besieged Rabbah for an entire year with assault and with attack—that I tell you in truth. And while Duke Joab encamped before the fine city, King David again focused his mind (1227) on the practice of all piety and derision of all sin. No man had ever been born who praised God as much as did King David: with organs and with harps and with all kinds of stringed instruments. (1228) Noble King David took his instrument; he praised the Lord God, blessed be He, so that it resounded up to the clouds. And otherwise the king's desire was for nothing but piety.

Once King David said: "Test me, my dear Lord. (1229) I know that Abraham does not measure up to me. I serve You, my dear Lord, by night as well as by day. Now, hallow Your name still more through me. Measure me against Abraham, who was the father of us all." (1230) Our Lord God, blessed be He, then answered David, the lawful king: "David, you cannot measure up to My servant Abraham. I tested him in ten ways, however I wished. He was steadfast in My will, for which reason he is dear to Me." (1231) "Test me, test me, Almighty Lord! Test me and test me! I want to be tested! If I were not like Abraham, it would grieve me forever. I have prepared myself in my heart and in all piety. (1232) Now, in all my life I have never committed a sin. O, mighty God in Heaven, blessed be He, what do You want from me!? My thoughts are pure; You know my heart. And measure me against Abraham in earnest and in jest." (1233) "Leave off your pleading," said our Lord. "You cannot measure up to My servant Abraham. If I were to test you, you would not pass." "No," said King David, "that will not happen! (1234) If I were to break Your commandment, then I would be a villain! Test me and test me! I will not break Your commandment!" God, blessed be He, then said: "David, you will see. Today I will test you with a beautiful lady."

(1235) King David locked himself into a chamber. For the sake of his favor he ordered all his men: "Today, no one is to open the door for me." The king so commanded them: whoever wants to let me out is to be slain. (1236) God, blessed be He, would you like to bet me, if that can be done: I will keep Your commandment today, the entire day." The king was locked up, a prisoner in the chamber. He was not accustomed to it, for which reason he had desires: (1237) he stepped up to a small window, for the sake of entertainment. The Devil turned himself into the form of a raven and constantly flew back and forth in front of his window. King David then said: "What is the point of this? (1238) Now I cannot see anything because of this bird." He drew his crossbow, stout and thick. "If you wish to make a fool of me today in front of the window, then I will just see if I can shoot you."

(1239) He shot and struck the bird. So it seemed to him, as he saw it and as the bird fell onto a roof. He said: I must fetch you here into my house." Noble King David climbed out the window. (1240) He walked along the roof to look for the bird. There he saw, in a courtyard, a most beautiful lady. King David then said: "I have to tell the truth: I have in all my life never seen a more beautiful lady." (1241) She sat in a brook and wished to take the ritual bath. King David then said: "I must have this lady! If she is not mine soon, then I will die of grief. So I will indeed try whether I can obtain her."

(1242) He climbed in again and ran to the door. He quickly summoned his servants and his doorkeeper: "Who lives in that courtyard; tell me the truth." They said: "The wife of Uriah the Hittite, your loyal servant." (1243) David sent his messengers most quickly: "Go and ask who the lady is who is going to the ritual bath tonight. And, when she has returned home, bring her to me in here." "Gladly, my lord, we have understood."

(1244) The messengers then went before Bathsheba: "Beautiful lady, you are to go to before the king." The beautiful lady then went into the chamber. All those who accompanied her had to wait outside. (1245) King David then said: "Now, tell me, lady fair, do you have a husband or not." She said: "Gracious my lord, I have a valiant husband: the most worthy warrior to be found. (1246) He is now encamped before the city of Rabbah with other heroes: Uriah the Hittite, in Sir Joab's army. He has given me a bill of divorce, so that in case he is slain in a great battle, (1247) I am free of his brothers, so that I am not obligated to undergo the *ḥalitzah* ceremony, my noble lord." "So, dear my lady, tell me the real truth: you went to the ritual bath; for whom were you preparing yourself?"

(1248) "So that—gracious and noble my lord—since my ritual impurity has passed, if my husband Uriah were suddenly to arrive, I would be prepared for the honorable man. For that reason I went to the ritual bath. Now, I have told you." (1249) King David then said: "Since you have accepted a bill of divorce, I have taken you as my wife from the moment that you entered here. You have gone to the ritual bath, which I well understand." He took her as his wife and then let her leave.

(1250) Our Lord God, blessed be He, then said: "Tell me, David, have you passed the test, according to Abraham's manner?" Sir David then answered him: "Lord God, blessed be He, now stop it: I did this for the sake of Your honor. (1251) You created by Your words the heavens and the earth; and all things in general You brought into being. You said so overtly that I would not pass the test—I did it for the sake of Your words! (1252) It had to be just as You said it. For that reason, dear my Lord, I transgressed. If I had passed the test, people would have legitimately said: 'the Lord lost, and the servant won!' (1253) Before it happens that Your holy word does not come to pass, may I never again be seen alive in the world. If, Lord, You had said—'David, you will pass the test'—I would not have transgressed (a thousand amens!). (1254) But I will not say, my dear Lord God, blessed be He: 'Test me, test me.' From that will I desist."

Thereafter Bathsheba sent and let it be said to the king: "Alas, for my honor: I am pregnant. (1255) My joy has come to an end; the secret will burst forth about what I was doing so late in King David's house. I sense in my body that I carry a little child. Now, I have heard said, noble my lord, (1256) the old proverbs—none of them fails—more things have indeed taken place than what is happening to me right now: never was anything so finely spun that it did not finally come into the light of the sun."

(1257) King David at once sent a messenger to Joab: "Send Sir Uriah to me," he commanded him in earnest. Joab sent Sir Uriah, the dauntless hero. The king then questioned him about the entire state of affairs: (1258) about Duke Joab and indeed about the army, and how everything was going in the army of the Jews. Uriah, the hero, told him everything. The questioning came to an end, and the king said to him: (1259) "Tonight you are to be in your own house in all comfort and take your ease with your lady until you receive my detailed response [to your report]."

Sir Uriah took his leave to depart from the king. (1260) Noble King David sent gifts along after him. He said: "That is to be given to Uriah, the warrior." Mighty Uriah did not want to go home: he slept on the floor with David's men, (1261) with other comrades in the king's house. Then King David said: "Get out, Uriah! I ordered you to go home; so why are you staying here? Tell me that!" (1262) "Noble King David, God, blessed be He, forbid that I should take my ease with my lady, since all Israel is encamped on the broad fields, and Duke Joab and his men are living in tents, (1263) and they also have the ark of holiness with them in their assaults and attacks before Rabbah, the city of the sons of Ammon. How could I give account for it before God, if I were to take my ease, while they are all in adversity?"

(1264) Then King David said: "So stay here with me tonight! Tomorrow I will indeed send you into battle." And when evening came, and food was served, the king commanded him to drink a great deal of the good wine. (1265) He made him very drunk and ordered him to go home. Uriah stayed in the king's house and slept on the floor.

Now, at that time it was the custom everywhere that whatever the king said, one dared not disobey. (1266) The undaunted hero had there earned a death sentence. David wanted to honor him. Now, listen to what he said: "He is a bold warrior, for which reason he will be spared. I will not have him executed. He will, nonetheless, be shot dead."

(1267) David wrote a letter and sent it with Uriah. "Give this letter to Joab himself—directly with your own hand!"—"Pay attention in the battle that Uriah be slain. You are not to kill him yourself. Listen and obey what I am telling you! (1268) You are to place Uriah at the very forefront of the battle. Forbid the noble warrior to retreat very far! When you see the heroes come out to fight him, then you are to draw away from him and leave him there alone."

(1269) Uriah, the Hittite, carried the letter himself. It then grieved Duke Joab sorely. But even so, Duke Joab placed him at the forefront of the battle, when it seemed the right time to him. (1270) Then Ammon charged at the Jews—that is true. Then they forced the Jews toward the gates of Rabbah. The archers then shot vigorously from the walls. Joab withdrew from the walls with his many liegemen. (1271) Uriah indeed dared not retreat before Sir Joab. The hero was shot outside the gates at Rabbah. The news was presented and told to King David that Uriah had been slain. He acted as if he were grieved.

(1272) Bathsheba mourned him for a full seven days. The mourning came to an end. King David had the message delivered to her: "You are to give your body to King David. He wants to take you, beautiful lady, as his wife." (1273) King David then took that most comely lady. He loved her deeply; she was so beautiful.

King David had then committed so many sins. He [God] wanted to avenge them on him and did not want to let him get away with them. (1274) It then at once displeased God, blessed be He, profoundly. God, blessed be He, sent the prophet Nathan to David. Then the prophet Nathan went to David: "Noble King David, I cannot desist: (1275) I must tell you of the marvel that has taken place here. I cannot desist; I must tell it to you. There are in your land two good fellows: one is poor; the other is rich and of good spirit. (1276) He had a great deal of silver and gold, as well as many sheep and cattle, while his companion, the poor man, had none of those things. He had, nonetheless, nurtured a single lamb. (1277) He loved it dearly and let it eat with him, because he had raised it from infancy, and it slept in his bed, just as his most dear wife and children do. (1278) Then a guest came to visit the rich man, and the rich man came sneaking and there took the poor man's beloved lamb, which he had lovingly nurtured, and slaughtered it at that time for his guest. (1279) The rich man thought it too dear to take one of his own and secretly climbed over onto his neighbor's property and took his beloved lamb, which he had lovingly nurtured. You are to render judgment. My description of the case is not a lie."

(1280) King David grew wrathful; his wrath was great. The villainy of the rich man irritated him very much. He said to the prophet Nathan: "I must have this man. I swear by the Lord God, blessed be He, he must lose his life. (1281) In addition he must pay full and proper compensation to the poor man: he must give four of his best sheep to the poor man. How could he be so pitiless in his heart that he could not let his fellow keep his lamb!"

(1282) The prophet Nathan then said: "Be silent, king! God, blessed be He, the Lord of us all, commanded me to say to you: You are, King David, that same man who took the beloved lamb from his neighbor! (1283) You have, King David, so many wives for the sake of all your desires and all the delight of your heart. You should have let your neighbor keep his wife that he had so beautifully nurtured with love and tenderness. (1284) You are held accountable before God, blessed be He. Your rendering of the accounts does not add up. It is a matter of King David attempting a cover-up: when she became pregnant, you wanted to hide your shame. You feared the people more than you did God, blessed be He. Your rendering of the accounts does not add up.

(1285) In addition to taking the pious man's beloved wife, you also took the mighty one's life and additionally have married his beloved wife. Almighty God, blessed be He, has commanded me to say still more to you: (1286) She has conceived by you a fine lad. Almighty God, blessed be He, has commanded me to say to you: in your youth you did nothing but pasture sheep. He made of you a king, by which He delighted you. (1287) He has always aided you in all adversity: your lord, King Saul, never managed to find you, and He also gave the king's wives to you, as well as the entire kingdom of Israel and everything else that you have. (1288) Now you have angered God, blessed be He, your Lord. This great sin has now been registered to you: Uriah the Hittite have you slain, and you have taken his wife. That is very much in opposition to God. (1289) Thus has God, blessed be He, said: one of your clan will seek your life and wage war against you. He will avenge on you the wrath of our Lord God, blessed be He, so that you will lament that you were ever born. (1290) You secretly took the wife of the mighty warrior. The one who will avenge it on you will come openly, publicly in front of the entire house of Israel. He will love your wives—that I tell you in truth— (1291) in the light of day, and not secretly as you have done. And your household will suffer misfortune—that I tell you in addition. Often will they be slain in grim battle. Uriah will be avenged! Thus you have the message! (1292) The sword will never again leave your household in peace. That is your proper recompense for Uriah the Hittite."

"Alas," said King David, "for this evil message. I have sinned so greatly, Almighty God!"

(1293) David did not cease to praise him well, until our Lord God, blessed be He, commanded to be said to him: "King David, you have yourself pronounced the judgment: there must be vengeance on the life of the rich man. (1294) Our Lord God, blessed be He, does not wish to remember that with respect to you—He will grant you your life. He makes of that judgment a gift to you. You said that he ought to pay four sheep for the lamb that ran freely in the poor man's house. (1295) So, you must pay with four of your children. Your son with Bathsheba will die quickly."

Noble King David did great penance. He served God, blessed be He, both early and late.

(1296) Now, when the prophet Nathan left King David, the child was about to die; its illness had begun. King David then at once had misery enough. He beat himself with both hands. (1297) From the depths of his heart he beseeched his Lord God, blessed be He, with fasting and with weeping for the infant. He lay on the ground for six full days; his tongue was never still in his mouth.

(1298) The Torah scholars went to the king. They heard his great lamentation and his prayers. They wanted to raise him up from the ground. He did not want to get up from his lamentations and prayers. (1299) Nor did he wish to eat anything. "Lord God, blessed be He, by your mercy attend to my cry!"

On the seventh day the child, alas, died. His servants there feared his negative reaction to the news, (1300) so that they did not dare tell the king. They were afraid that the king would beat himself in his grief. His servants were speaking quietly, but he heard them and was saddened: "Is the child dead. Tell me the truth!" (1301) They said: "It is, alas, dead. May God, blessed be He, compensate you for it." He arose from the ground and had his stool placed there for himself. He bathed and anointed himself and put on fine clothes. He turned to the ark of holiness. (1302) He returned home and commanded that food be brought for himself.

That astonished all his servants so much that they were obsessed by it. They said: "My lord, tell us, without rancor: earlier you lamented pitiably, and why now do you do thus? (1303) No one has ever seen a king lament as you did while the child was alive. But now that it is dead, you no longer mourn. We would like to know the truth of it, O noble and exalted king!" (1304) He said: "While the child was still alive, I prayed to God, blessed be He, that He restore its health, if the King of all the world were to be mindful of His mercifulness and would show mercy to David, His servant. (1305) Now the child is, alas, dead. I desire no more lamentation. Even if I were to mourn, I could not bring it back. I cannot bring it back to this earth. I will myself have to go to him in the next world."

(1306) The king comforted Bathsheba, and she now let herself be comforted. She conceived another son for King David. The child was born and was named Solomon. Among all the sons, he became well known. (1307) The prophet Nathan took the infant; he called it beloved of God; it had to remain with him.

Now, all Israel was encamped before the good city of Rabbah. It was well defended against assaults and attacks. (1308) All Israel at once said to Joab: "Noble Duke Joab, our land is being devastated. The fields and vineyards are not being cultivated. The city is so strong that they are dauntless. (1309) We want to withdraw into our own land." "No," said Duke Joab, "by Goat, that will not happen! It would be a great disgrace for King David, the warrior, among all nations where he is known. (1310) If we were thus to withdraw from here in disgrace, then, first of all, the nations that now flee us would attack us. Before I would accept such disgrace for my lord, I would rather that I myself die before the wall." (1311) "The city is so strong and well defended against assault. It is excellent beyond measure on all sides. If we wish to starve them out—they have a good supply of food." "Well, come on, then," said Duke Joab, "listen to what I advise you: (1312) bind me into a catapult and hurl me over the wall to the inside. My armor and my sword are to be with me at all times. Bind me into a featherbed and hurl me into the city. If I survive that, I will give them all the battle they want! (1313) If I survive the fall, wait for me outside for four weeks. I will make the blood run out here in front of the gate. If you then see that no blood runs out at the gate, then you will know for certain that, alas, I am dead."

(1314) Joab was at once bound into a catapult; many a good featherbed was wrapped around him and his very good sword and steel mail-coat. The hero was hurled over the wall to the inside. (1315) He fell into a widow's house. Many a man saw it. He fell so hard that his sword broke. The people then said: "Whose man might you be?" He said: "The Jews captured me and hurled me in here." (1316) "Are you one of the Jews who are exhausting us?" He said: "What are you doing, asking me that?! Of course I am indeed no/a Jew![27] I have been hurled so hard that I cannot do anything. What are you doing, asking me that?! I—a Jew!? You whoreson!

(1317) Duke Joab lay in bed in that same widow's house. For four whole weeks he was well cared for, until the bold warrior again regained his strength. He thought to himself: "It is time to get started." (1318) He took off his armor. "I want to look around the city. Now, lend me other clothes," he said to the lady. She lent him ladies' clothes, for she found no others. Then Duke Joab put on his landlady's garments. (1319) He went out into the city, looking here and there. He found a sword maker—that was what he wanted: "Blacksmith, my fine fellow, make me a good sword. I will pay you well for it, more than it is worth." (1320) He made him a good sword—it seemed good to the sword maker. He said: "With this sword you are well defended." Joab took the sword; he wanted to try it out. He cracked the sword like a rotten turnip. (1321) The smith was terrified when he saw his might. He made seven swords for him, all of which he broke. The eighth time, the exalted warrior himself made a very good sword; he was well pleased with it. (1322) That sword that was so good passed all the tests. It exalted the spirit of the bold hero in times of adversity. He said: "Smith, my dear fellow, tell me the truth. Whom would you most like to see slain with the sword?" (1323) "In the whole world, there is no one to whom I would more like to see it done than Joab, the commander of the Jewish army." "What lies under the ashes; tell me that!" The smith turned around and wanted to tell him. (1324) Then the warrior Joab hewed him into pieces: the smith fell into two pieces on the ground.

Before the gates, Israel did not see red blood. They mourned Duke Joab: "Alas, he is now dead." (1325) There was among the Israelites both weeping and lamentation. "He has fallen to his death or has been slain." They checked carefully at all the gates, whether the blood so red came flowing out.

(1326) Duke Joab then said: "I want to try out my sword." He went before the king's court. His desire was to fight. He was wearing his landlady's clothing. He found four hundred men, all of whom he slew. (1327) "A good sword is being borne by someone wearing only lady's clothing." All the people then said: "The Devil slew them!" Then the warrior Joab went into his lodgings. He quickly bound on his armor and his helmet. (1328) Then he ran through the city. He said: "I want to tell you, I am Duke Joab. I will slay you all." The people were terrified by the good warrior. Then he made the red blood to flow from them. (1329) Then the people gathered together against the single man. He then slew everyone whom he encountered, until the red blood flowed out at the gates. All Israel then became cheerful and again filled with courage.

(1330) Then—because of the blood—his very good sword was sticking to his hand and hindering him in battle—that warrior who was worth so many. He then ran into the widow's house and found her daughter there: "Quickly warm some water for me and free up my hand." (1331) "Nothing but the Devil will I warm for you! Him may you carry with you! Now, you have slain all my people with this sword." He then plunged the sword and his hand into her belly. That lady was pregnant with a child. (1332) He then rubbed his hand until it came free and then washed it quite well. Sir Joab then returned to the stronghold. He slew everything that he found.

(1333) Then all Israel assaulted the walls and the gates. No one could ward them off; they let no one come out. Then the city by the water was captured. King Hanun then fled into the castle and stronghold. (1334) Joab sent his messengers: "Tell King David: 'I have fought quite effectively against Ammon. I have taken the city by the water. Now, King David, you ought to come here yourself (1335) and take the castle. And do not fail to do this, so that no one may say that Joab did it. If that were said about you, it would not be an honor.'" King David then assembled quite a fine army. (1336) Joab and his men let King David into the city. King David commanded his men to attack. The castle was also captured, in addition to the city. Ammon was subjugated; David enfeebled them.

(1337) King David found a treasure there that was enormous: the bare and sundered head of their idol, a beautiful crown of a hundred-weight of gold and in addition as beautifully ornamented as could be. (1338) And there were many jewels on it. King David placed it on his head. He also took a great deal of gold from them in the city—so much that it cannot be told. Many a loaded wagon was driven up to Jerusalem. (1339) David at once had the people of the city and of the land of Ammon sawn and dismembered. He had them chopped up like dust in the sun, ground up into clay and ashes.

(1340) Noble King David and all his men returned to Jerusalem with very great honor. They had won a great deal of property—he and his heroes—everything that had been Ammon's was now taken over by the Jews.

(1341) King David then dwelt in Jerusalem undaunted. His enemies had been subjugated; none fought against him anymore. King David had a son at this time: he had no equal in all Israel. (1342) He was handsome beyond measure; his name was Absalom. He had a beautiful sister such as could not otherwise be found. She was his proper sister—of the same mother—and was named Tamar, a noble princess. (1343) David had taken the daughter of Talmai in battle. She was pregnant with that same Tamar, as we have read, at the time when King David took her as his wife. Handsome Absalom, however, was her child with David.

(1344) Amnon, David's eldest son, loved Tamar. His heart within him wished to die for his great love of her. He could not, however, possess the chaste and well-mannered maiden. Her brother could not get her out of his heart, neither by day nor by night. (1345) Amnon had a companion, the child of David's brother: Jonadab, the most clever whom one could find in villainy. He said to Amnon: "What is wrong with you, that your bright cheeks have grown so pale?" (1346) "Jonadab, my dear companion, my joy has quite left me. Tamar, my step-sister, fills my thoughts." Jonadab said to him: "So, take my advice." Often one person gives another one advice when he himself has none. (1347) "I know precisely what kind of advice you need: now, at once, act as if you were ill. People will say: 'He is exceedingly ill. He has grown so pale, that he will die very soon.' (1348) Then your father will come to see your illness. Then say that you would indeed eat if Tamar were to bake for you. 'If I were to see her baking little cakes for me before my eyes, I would indeed eat them, if she were to make them for me.'"

(1349) Amnon then did as Jonadab commanded. He lay down and pretended to be ill. He allowed no one to visit him. Then David, the splendid king, came to visit him. "Amnon, do you want to eat?" "No," said Amnon. (1350) "Amnon, you have to eat; without food, no one can be strong. And if you will not eat, then the light in your eyes will die." Amnon then said: "If I see my sister Tamar bake little cakes in my presence, if she would do it for me. . . ."

(1351) King David then summoned Tamar thus: "Go to Amnon, your brother, and bake him some little cakes." The beautiful maiden then went, as the king had ordered her. Young prince Amnon gladly let her in. (1352) She kneaded and made little cakes while he watched. She baked them in a pan there where all this took place. "Now eat them, dear brother. They are so fresh and so fine." "No, it was something else that I have seen." (1353) Amnon did not want to eat them thus in front of other people. He said: "I cannot eat unless no one is here. Bring them to me in the chamber. I promise: I will eat the little cakes, when no one can see it." (1354) They all went out, as Amnon wished. He said: "Tamar, dear sister, bring the little cakes here, into the chamber, and do it quickly. I want to eat the little cakes from your snow-white hand." (1355) The servants said to each other: "Whatever this may be about—unless my senses betray me—it is going to cause a blizzard." The others answered: "What a laugh! They are going to bake little cakes without a fire!"

(1356) Tamar took the little cakes into the chamber. He grabbed her by the hem: "Lay with me, my sister." She said: "No, dear brother, do not commit this villainy, so that you are not called 'Amnon, the villain' (1357) throughout all Israel, wherever your name is spoken. In addition, I would also be disgraced all my life. If you do not wish to leave me alone, dear brother, then you ought first to go to the king, for honor's sake. (1358) Ask the king; then he will give me to you. Before I allowed myself thus to be raped, I would rather die." Amnon did not wish to listen to his sister's words. He hurried very quickly to the bed with her. (1359) She then long defended herself against her brother's haste. He was stronger than she. But she nonetheless fought back for a while. He took there the honor of the most beautiful maiden, as people do beyond the seas.

(1360) When it had then been done, he said: "Now, be on your way." He began to hate her deeply; his hatred was great. He hated her more than he had loved her beforehand. She then said: "Dear brother, why are you doing this? (1361) Let me stay here in your house as your concubine. Do you wish to rape poor me and then also to drive me out?" He did not want to listen to her—that I tell you in truth. He ordered two of his servants to drag her outside the gate. (1362) "When she is outside, you are to lock the door."

Then they dragged Tamar out of Amnon's house. She wore a fine silk robe around her body. She ripped it in her grief and her misery and her pain. (1363) She grasped at the earth and filled her hands with mire and smeared it on her head, in her misery and her distress. She wrung her white hands over her own head. She trudged on and screamed: "Alas, my heartbreak!" (1364) She went to her brother, Absalom. "Alas, dear brother, Amnon has done it to me." He said: "Dear sister, be silent. You are to tell no one of the disgrace of yourself and your brother. (1365) You are to stay in my house and have no worries." She obeyed her brother. His proposal was agreeable to her. She grieved secretly and alone for her distress. Absalom began to hate Amnon. He spoke no word to him. (1366) He said neither good nor bad to him. But his sister's grief caused him pain. That lasted for a long time, some two full years.

Absalom was publicly shearing his sheep in Hazor.[28] (1367) It was customary at that time that when one sheared his sheep, he had a feast for his relatives. Absalom there prepared a great feast for all his brothers and all his father's household. (1368) Absalom went to the king. "My father and also my lord, I invite you and all your servants to eat with me. I have shorn my sheep and slaughtered many of them." (1369) "No," said the king, "my dear son. If I were to be your guest tonight with my servants, we would at once consume all your food. We would very quickly burn up all of your seasoned wood." (1370) Absalom begged him: "Go with me, my father." David said: "Dear son, it is not to be." The king blessed him and did not wished to go with him. Then he said: "Let all my brothers go with me, (1371) since I cannot have you, dear father." King David then said: "My son, that will be done." King David sent with him all of his sons to the plain of Hazor. None of them stayed at home.

(1372) When they had almost finished eating, Absalom had still not forgotten the villainy that his brother Amnon had committed against Tamar. He said to his servants: "Now, give Amnon his wages. (1373) When he has finished eating and grows merry with wine, be bold men—strike him down dead!" His men did as Absalom commanded. One struck him dead—he thrust a sword through him. (1374) Then the children sprang vigorously away from the table. They ran hard to get away from there; their tongues were soon wagging. It was told to King David in Jerusalem: "Absalom has slain all of his brothers." (1375) The king ripped his clothes and grieved. He sank to the earth. He became weak with sorrow. And all the king's servants there ripped their clothes. They mourned with the king, and all of them were sad. (1376) Then Jonadab, David's brother's child, said: "If that rumor is not a lie, then strike off my head. I know that Absalom has slain only Amnon: he could not endure the villainy that he committed against Tamar. (1377) Otherwise indeed nothing has happened to the children of the king. Therefore, stop your mourning; you will see the truth." The watchman on the gate-tower cried out loudly: "I see a lot of people running this way; they are making haste to flee." (1378) Jonadab then said: "David, dear my lord, your children have come; my words were all true." Absalom fled to Talmai in great haste. He was with his grandfather; he kept him for a while.

(1379) Then the king's children all arrived at a run. Noble King David turned to his children. The king and all his children wept very loudly; for

Amnon, their brother, they were eager to weep. (1380) The king wept a great deal; but then the pain subsided. He had in mind that he wanted to capture Absalom. Absalom had fled—that I tell you in truth—to his grandfather, who kept him two full years.

(1381) Noble King David wanted to go out after Absalom. Now, Duke Joab loved the lad very dearly. Joab took a wise woman and sent her to Tekoah. He commanded her to take a message to the king. (1382) She said: "Help me, dear my lord and royal crown!" "Then tell me, my dear lady, who has caused you trouble." "Gracious lord of the land, I must lament my sorrows to you: my husband died and left me with two lads. (1383) They were in the field, both the one and the other son, and fought with one another, as children often do. No one else was with the children. They fought so fiercely that one of them barely survived, (1384) while the other one died there in the field. My husband's brothers were gladdened by that death. They said, all of them together: 'Let us also slay the other one. He has murdered his brother; he should not be allowed to get away with it.' (1385) They are doing that, dear my lord, only because I have so much wealth; my husband was very rich. They intend to slay the lad, so that they may inherit their brother's property. (1386) They want to slay a man's son, so that they can carry home the wealth. Now, there are no witnesses that he did it. Who tried to prevent him with 'Now, leave your brother alone'?"

(1387) David said to the lady: "Go home to your house. I will write to the people so that they leave him alone." The lady then said: "Pardon me, my lord, if I have overrreached with respect to my son. (1388) For then the most noble and mighty king would be indebted to me. Do not withhold your comfort and aid from me." "Then, dear lady, tell the people who have taken him captive to come to me, (1389) and I will command them to let him go free." "Merciful and noble lord, crown of virtues, how might I assemble the relatives all together? One could perhaps come and slay my lad. (1390) Ought my son to flee into a city of refuge? The way is too long for him; the lad is still too young. Think, my lord, on Almighty God, so that my only child will not be slain." (1391) "You need have no worries," said the king to her. "By the Lord God, blessed be He, no harm will come to your child." "Gracious lord of the land, I wish to bring my words to a conclusion. Grant me permission to speak further, and do not let it irritate you." (1392) "Say on," said the king, "what do you lack now?"

She said: "Gracious my lord, may Israel not do such a thing, that they slay a man for the sake of wealth. No one saw it who can give evidence. (1393) I have presented you with a analogy, dear my lord. I have devised it on the basis of the case of Absalom, the son of Maacah. Grant clemency to the child whom she bore you. If you wish to kill Absalom, then her heir is dead. (1394) Then it would be as if the noble princess had never been born. Most excellent king, grant justice for her child—grant that that which would be just for someone else also be just for her and let her beloved child be returned to your favor. (1395) Whether Absalom's servants killed Amnon, or whether Absalom ordered it done—who can say for sure? Perhaps it grieved Absalom that Amnon was slain. If Absalom's servants have sinned, what can Absalom do? (1396) King, you are a judge: even if he gave the order to his servants, Absalom has not for that reason earned a death sentence. Even if he gave them the order—now, cast it out of your mind—only evil sinners would then carry out such an order. (1397) Lord of the land, you ought not to renounce your own verdict. Do not contradict your honor and piety. You swore to me, my lord. Now, hold to that, my lord. Take back your son, Absalom! (1398) Why would the king wish to exile his own child? It is said that we are all here only for a short while, just as the waters that flow down in the valley. Thus is it also with people who rush toward death. (1399) The waters that flow away—they are never again to be seen. So it is also with people when they unfortunately pass away: we can see them no more. All of us must pass away. We will have to wait a long time for the dead to arise again. (1400) Keep your children with you in your house! They are after all your children. Drive none of them away! You are a fine king with all honors. You are like an angel of God on His heavenly throne."

(1401) "Now, tell me, dear lady—and do not lie to me about it—what I want to ask you," said the wise man. The lady then answered him: "Say on, my lord." "You will be judged by me on nothing but the truth. (1402) So tell me, on your oath, did you conceive this speech? Or did Joab make you say it to me?" "Wise King David, you have perceived accurately: Joab, your servant, commanded me to make this speech. (1403) Who is your peer in matters of wisdom? You are like an angel of God on his heavenly throne." "Then, go home, dear lady, to his house. Tell Joab that my wrath has passed."

(1404) The king said to Joab: "Did you do that? Then go and tell Absalom to come home." Duke Joab then bowed indeed to the king: "Now I know better than I did earlier (1405) that I was serving you according to your will and that by my will you would give up your anger." Then Duke Joab rode very quickly to Geshur and gave Absalom a good message (1406) that the wrath of King David had passed, and he wanted to have his son Absalom at home again. Duke Joab then led him out of Geshur and took him home to King David's house. (1407) The king said to Joab: "Take him back to his house. I cannot look at him; tell him to go back outside. He is to live in his own house, as you now have now heard. He is never again to come into my sight." (1408) Absalom went home to his own fine house and dared never again go into the sight of King David.

Now the hero, Absalom, was the most handsome of all men, whose peer no lady in our day ever obtained. (1409) From head to toe, his beauty was manifold. He had no deficiency and had a fine form. The hair on his head was like small golden rings. Nothing in the world could be more beautiful. (1410) Once a year he had to cut it because of its great weight: he could not endure it, because of its great weight. Each time the hair weighed precisely two hundred pounds according to the royal standard of Sir David, the mighty king. (1411) Absalom had two very fine sons with his wife; the third child was a maiden, whose equal had never been born. There was no more beautiful maiden on earth. Absalom's little daughter was named Tamar.

(1412) Now, the hero, Absalom, dared not go to his father. It was well into the third year, as we have heard. That irritated Absalom. He sent out messengers to Duke Joab so that he would come to him in his house. (1413) "Go to my father for me, my dear Joab; you are to deliver a message which I will explain to you." Joab said to the messengers: "Tell him that I cannot always be dealing with his foolishness." (1414) Absalom sent his messengers a second time: "Joab, come. I do indeed need you now." Joab did not want to go when Absalom asked him. Absalom led his servants out of the city. (1415) He said to his servants: "Go to the barley field that is next to my barley, and burn Joab's barley completely." Then Absalom's men went to Joab's barley field. (1416) They burned his barley right down to the ground. Joab then came to Absalom in that same hour. He said: "What have I ever done to harm your servants. They have burned my barley. I want compensation for it." (1417) "Well," said Absalom, "money I can produce! The fact that you have to come to me—that diminution makes me laugh. I wanted to force you to go to the king, but you were too grand for me and refused to come to see me. (1418) I was able to play a trick that made you come after all. Do you have regrets about the barley? Look, it is still burning!" "You are indeed a wanton child," said Sir Joab. "What do you want, Absalom? May you have an unprosperous year!" (1419) "Joab, you are to tell my dear father that if I am to remain forever in disfavor, I would have much preferred to stay in Geshur, to which my dear father had initially driven me in exile. (1420) I want to come into the sight of my father. If I have earned a death sentence, then he should have me slain." Joab then told the king Absalom's desire. King David then said: "So, tell him to come here." (1421) Then the hero, Absalom, came quickly to the king and gave an accounting of Amnon's death, as the lady had told him: "Why did he not allow my sister to remain a maiden?" (1422) Absalom then bowed to David quite to the ground: he fell before the feet of the noble King David. The king then commanded him to arise again. The king then kissed him and commanded him to go in peace. (1423) Absalom took his leave from the exalted king.

Not too long thereafter, he began other escapades: he made for himself a chariot, wore fine courtly clothing, and young Absalom also rode fine courtly horses. (1424) He had to have fifty fine servants to run ahead of him on the ground. He and his servants observed at all the gates who was involved in disputes and came there for legal judgment. (1425) He said: "Tell me what you need." Then he told Absalom and his squires about his dispute. Absalom then always said: "You are in the right. I well understand your situation. The king will not be able to render a verdict for you. (1426) He has so much to do that he cannot also listen to you. He has appointed me to judge both women and men." He did that for all Israel: whoever came there to him received judgment. Neither the king nor any of his men knew anything about that.

(1427) When anyone bowed and came to Absalom, he embraced him and kissed him and took him in his arms. In this way Absalom at once stole the heart of Israel. They all thought that the noble king had commanded him to do it (1428) and appointed Absalom to be in charge over all Israel so that he was to judge great and small. Not too long thereafter, Absalom went to his father. Oh, how very genially the king welcomed him. (1429) He thanked the high-born king honorably. He said: "Gracious my lord, I swore an oath when I was in your disfavor, dear father, and was living with King Talmai in Geshur, (1430) that if God, blessed be He, returned me here to Jerusalem, I would make sacrifices, if my wish were granted. That is indeed to be done in Hebron, since I have seen you here again, my father and lord. (1431) Now God, blessed be He, has granted that I am here again. I wish to keep my oath; I have never broken a vow. I wish to keep my vow in Hebron indeed." King David then said: "Well, go there then, my dear." (1432) "My father and also my lord, value my words: give me a letter and seal so that to whomever I show them, he will come with me to the city of Hebron." King David did that, as Absalom requested. (1433) He thought to himself that he did not want to ride alone: twenty or thirty ought to accompany him. In Jerusalem he showed the letter to some two hundred men. They went with Absalom; he had gained a great host. (1434) He sent word throughout the land of Israel: "The people are at once to assemble in Hebron. When one sounds a very fine horn, then say: 'Absalom has become king in Hebron.' (1435) See the king's letter; I have not tricked you. The king has ordered it, and it is his earnest concern." The people assembled in the city of Hebron. A great many bold warriors followed Absalom.

(1436) King David had a counselor whose wisdom no one in all Israel could match. The counsel that he received from him was as good as from Urim and Thummim, when one consulted them. (1437) The wise counselor was named Ahithophel. His counsel was the best in all the land. Ahithophel was very closely allied with Absalom. No one knew more of his fractiousness (1438) than Ahithophel and Absalom. Many people from all the cities came to Absalom. That was told to King David in detail, how all Israel wanted to have Absalom as their king (1439) and had chosen him as their lawful king; all the lords of Israel had sworn oaths to him. Now King David had all his stalwarts elsewhere. They were in the cities: one here, the other there.

(1440) The king was very alarmed; his heart was full: "Now, come on, my men, all of you who support me. I must flee from here, from deadly peril. If savage Absalom finds me, he might well strike me dead. (1441) If he comes here at this time with all Israel, then the city here will not be well defended. I have to flee from here out to the fields. If it is then rumored that the king has left his house, (1442) then my stalwarts—and whoever else is loyal to me—will hear of it, and they will come quickly when it comes time to fight. Then my men will hear that I have begun to go in terror of my son Absalom who wants to pound the lice out of all of us."

(1443) The king took the best of all treasures with him and left ten concubines to keep the stronghold. His wives and also his children, he took far away with him. "Let us go, all my people, it is time to flee!" (1444) Then all of his men said: "Noble my lord, whether you stay or flee, we will remain with you." King David then said: "It is time to flee. I do not have my stalwarts with me here so that I might fight with him." (1445) King David fled Jerusalem with lamentation and sorrow. The men who were there went with the king, and all the king's servants who were with him there: the archers and the slingers—the king was glad of that. (1446) The king and his people went away on foot. Their intention was to flee, empty-handed and barefoot. Then Ittai came to him with six hundred men, and his stalwarts also fled with the king there. (1447) The king said to Ittai: "Go on home!" He said: "My lord, by the Lord God, I will remain with you. I will not leave your side, David, my lord. I will be with you in life or in death." (1448) Then Ittai and six hundred men crossed over, as did all whom the king had earlier gained in his adversity. In the land there were lamentation and mourning aplenty: lamentation and sorrow and other iniquities. (1449) Whoever was loyal in his heart to King David, he mourned and wept. He did not forget his lament. Once there was a king who was most powerful; his name was King Landless. King David was like him.

(1450) Zadok, the priest, and all the Levites brought the ark of holiness to David, the splendid king. The king said to Zadok and Abiathar: "You two priests, carry the ark there (1451) into the city of Jerusalem which is prepared for it. If God, blessed be He, lets me return and rejoices in me, then I will serve God, blessed be He, and will make sacrifices. Above all else, take it back home. (1452) If God, blessed be He, does not want me to return, I will accept his punishment, whatever happens to me. Zadok and Abiathar, you were ever loyal to me. I must flee from here in mourning and in contrition. (1453) Just remain in Jerusalem for my sake. Act as if you willingly accept Absalom, as if you wished to break with me. Let him understand it thus. You are constantly to send me messengers and keep me informed (1454) about what savage Absalom wishes to undertake against me. I was once a king! Alas, poor me! I am fleeing into the wilderness. There I will await you—until you send me a message. Only do it in good time! (1455) Now, send me all things with the two sons: Ahimaaz, the son of the priest Zadok, and with Jonathan, the son of Abiathar, so that I can make adjustments according to what savage Absalom is undertaking."

(1456) David commanded Abiathar to make sacrifices. Abiathar laid the sacrifice on the altar. God, blessed be He, did not want to accept it in his spirit as long as the people of Israel were crossing the water. (1457) David said to Zadok: "Try your luck, too, whether God, blessed be He, will answer or whether the fault is mine." As soon as the priest Zadok went toward the altar, God, blessed be He, willingly accepted the sacrifice from him. (1458) God, blessed be He, did not want to accept it from Abiathar. The time had now come that they should no longer be priests. "You and all the house of Eli!" David loved Abiathar. He said: "I say to you rightly: (1459) you and Zadok, too, are righteous priests. The priesthood must depart from the house of Eli, as our Lord God informed the prophet Samuel. For the sake of your father, I do not want to let you go. (1460) Zadok and his sons are to be the priests." Then the two priests carried the ark back into the city of Jerusalem, the two holy men.

David and his men fled away from there. (1461) They quickly went up on the Mount of Olives. Barefooted and bareheaded, their heads all befouled with filth. They went up and wept—he and all his men. Many of his men there joined King David. (1462) Many of his mighty men joined to the king. They then told the king what the news was: "Ahithophel is in Absalom's council." Then poor David said: "Help me, O one and only God! (1463) If you do not help me quickly, I will be building on an icy foundation. Make Ahithophel foolish; do not let him be wise. I know his counsel well; it is always good. Lord God of all the world, give him a fool's disposition." (1464) David then went and climbed up to the top of the mountain. The king bowed toward the temple. Then Hushai the Archite came to him—that I tell you in truth—who was in complete support of David. (1465) David said to Hushai: "My dear companion, unfortunately I can no longer take care of your needs. If you indeed wish to serve me, my dear and loyal servant, then go this year to Jerusalem and—pay close attention to me— (1466) consistently act as if you support Absalom. Then Absalom will let you into his confidence. My dear Hushai, you must employ wit and intelligence: whatever Ahithophel counsels concerning me, you must undo. (1467) If you can block the counsel of wise Ahithophel, then you will have done much good for me in my distress. Whatever is decided in the council, tell it to Zadok and Abiathar. You will find them with him there."

(1468) Hushai the Archite went into Jerusalem. Absalom and his men had arrived there earlier. He was now king in Jerusalem. "Peace be to you, Hushai, tell me, what do you want? (1469) What, have you broken with you companion, that you are not going with him and you are coming back here to me?" "King and also my lord, may you live in joy! He whom Israel takes [as king] is also proper for me. (1470) I wish with all my heart to be subject to the one whom God, blessed be He, and all Israel want as king. I will serve you, King, as I did your father." "Gladly," said Absalom, "I will accept you."

(1471) When King David came from the high mountain, Ziba, the servant of Mephibosheth, came to him and brought to King David and his men food and bread and good wine. (1472) David said to Ziba: "Where might Mephibosheth be that he does not ride with me? You ought to be taking care of him." "Noble King David, he is a proper villain: he is in Jerusalem; now listen to what he says: (1473) 'David has indeed fled from here, after all. Israel will publicly make me king. My father's kingdom will indeed come to me!' He is speaking thus to all the people in Jerusalem." (1474) David said to Ziba: "I treated him well. Of everything that I gave to him, you are to have half." At once Ziba bowed to the king. Ziba had lied. He turned toward Jerusalem.

(1475) Then King David fled into the wilderness, he and his men, with a great shout. And when King David came to Bahurim, Shimei, the son of Gera, from the house of Saul, heard David's complaint. (1476) He threw great stones at him and at all his men, and at all the stalwarts who going with David. "Are you now fleeing in disgrace, you spiller of blood! You betrayed your lord, you false murderer! (1477) You scoundrel and bastard and murderer and oppressor and abomination! You are now fleeing in disgrace. I rejoice in your misfortune! God, blessed be He, will avenge Saul and his kin on you. You will have to lose your life to Absalom, your child. (1478) You will die in your villainy. The judgment of God, blessed be He, is falling on you. You have spilled so much innocent blood." Then the hero, Abishai, said: "David, my lord, let me go over there. It will be the end of him! (1479) Let me go over there, David, dear my lord. I will strike off his head. Then he will berate you no more. Why should that dead dog curse a king? I will test out my sharp blade on his neck." (1480) "No," said King Landless, "do not start any confusion. He is a Torah scholar, a very honorable man. I think that it was God, blessed be He, Who commanded him: 'Go and curse David thusly!' (1481) How otherwise would he get that into his mind. I think that God, blessed be He, Himself is doing it to me. Thus I will willingly accept it all gladly. Perhaps God will have mercy on poor me. (1482) I think that God in Heaven commanded him to do it, since my own child is seeking my life. Shimei the Benjaminite is right to berate me. God commanded him: 'Berate David, my servant.' (1483) If God then commanded him, who would wish to interrupt him? Perhaps God will have mercy on me and will see my suffering."

David went along the right path on the mountain. On the other side, Shimei confronted him with stones. (1484) He threw great stones and stirred up a great deal of dust with ashes over the noble King David and his host of stalwarts. He went along berating the king and his men, until King David came to the Jordan River. (1485) They could not go any further because of fatigue. King David wanted to stay there for a while, until he might receive a message from his people, whom he had sent into Jerusalem.

(1486) Now, Absalom was living there in Jerusalem; young Absalom was in his father's house. Absalom said to Ahithophel: "Now, counsel me, you wise man, how we want to attack old David." (1487) Ahithophel then answered him: "Truly I will tell you: all Israel will again abandon you. They will consider: 'if we continue to support Absalom, he will reconcile with his father, and it will go badly for us. (1488) The father and son will reconcile; Absalom will leave us in the lurch; then we will be without purpose. The king and son will always be reconciled. Then we—all Jewry—will all become good for nothing but sacrificial victims.' (1489) Whoever forces himself between a rock and a hard place—so the old folks say—will soon be stuck fast. If, however, you want to hold onto the monarchy for the rest of your life, then follow my counsel and listen to what I tell you. (1490) Your father left ten concubines here. You need to grasp all of them far above the knee: you should sleep with them so that all Israel sees it. Then the people will say that the conflict cannot be reconciled. (1491) Then they will aid you and support you." "And truly," said Absalom, "this advice makes good sense to me."

He had a bed made high on a rooftop. He lay with all his ten concubines, so that all Israel saw it. (1492) Absalom did not want to come down from the rooftop, until he had had carnal knowledge of all the concubines. "What do you advise now, Ahithophel? That thing has now been accomplished. All Israel has watched me." (1493) "I will counsel you properly: you need not be ashamed of it. You are to take the mightiest from all Israel who are here in Jerusalem: twelve thousand mighty heroes who are indeed to be found here. (1494) Tonight you are to pursue him until you overtake him there. His men are tired and quite frightened. They do not know that they need to protect themselves because we are pursuing them tonight. So, let us charge into their crowd suddenly. (1495) They will be terrified—that is our intention. One will flee in one direction; the other one in another direction. Thus we will find the king, and only him will we slay. Otherwise not one of the king's servants will be slain. (1496) When King David has been slain, then you may honorably wear the crown of your father." Absalom then answered him: "This counsel well pleases me. And all Israel will say: 'He is to be obeyed.'"

(1497) Absalom then said to him: "Here is yet another wise man who likely can give advice concerning old David. Hushai the Archite would likely advise us well. He knows King David's mind and all his affairs." (1498) Absalom said to Hushai: "I would like to hear how we can come to master old David. Thus has Ahithophel now advised me. Both I and all Israel are quite pleased by the advice." (1499) Hushai then answered him: "I do not believe it, dear my lord, that you and all Israel are so foolish, that you are thinking of following this advice of Ahithophel's. A one-year-old child would understand this. (1500) Even if Ahithophel has previously striven for wisdom, then this time he has indeed beshit himself with his wisdom. Noble Sir Absalom, since you have asked for my advice: what Ahithophel has advised is not worth a dungheap. (1501) If you want to do battle against your father with your twelve thousand men, then there is no reason for us here in Jerusalem to await your return. Now, all Israel after all knows his might, which is indeed great: mighty King David has never yet been defeated; (1502) nor have all the stalwarts who are with him. You and all Israel are blind even with seeing eyes, if you think tonight to pursue with twelve thousand men. Then all Israel would have laughed for the last time. (1503) David is certainly full of all wisdom: he does not stay with his men but conceals himself well. They are indeed so valiant that we might go in dread of them. If we advance with only twelve thousand men, they will pound the lice out of us. (1504) If, Absalom, you lose the very first battle, the people in the entire land will abandon you. Whoever serves you and is subject to you—if you lose the first battle—then they will leave you. (1505) Even if they were all heroes and had the courage of lions, if you lose the first battle, to whom would it seem good? Now, all Israel knows your father's might and what all his stalwarts have accomplished. (1506) My king and my lord, my advice and my instruction is: gather all Israel, as the sands of the sea and the stars of the heavens, that no one can number. Then we will march in strength against him and his men. (1507) Then their manliness and their strength will not help them. You will have so many stalwarts that his host will be able to do nothing. We will march on them with numbers like dust in the sun. We will slay them; not one will escape. (1508) My advice is the best, as I can understand it. I do not wish to advance against him with twelve thousand men. If Ahithophel was ever wise, he has misread the letters this time."

(1509) All Israel and his servants said: "Hushai the Archite certainly speaks rightly. It could not help us, if we were already filled with remorse: it is best to sleep with a whole hide. (1510) Let us follow Hushai; his advise suits us. Wise Ahithophel ought to be shown a German fig."[29] Hushai quickly went to Zadok and Abiathar: "Quickly send your two sons to David, (1511) so that he moves out of the plain of the wilderness deftly and swiftly." Hushai the Archite told them his and Ahithophel's counsel: "Run and quickly tell it to David, so that the lord of the land is not overtaken."

(1512) Now, their two sons were Ahimaaz and Jonathan. They had not gone to Jerusalem at that time. They were in En-rogel in the same group when the two priests heard the message. (1513) The high priests sent a maiden there, in order that she tell their sons in Rogel. Now when the two priests heard the news, they did not long delay but ran there to David (1514)—there, to Bahurim; they did not go to Jerusalem. They were afraid that the villain, Absalom, would notice. One of Absalom's servants had seen them going there. They ran very quickly. He then understood clearly (1515) that they wanted to run quickly to King David. The fact that he could not stop them caused him such grief that he wanted to do himself harm. He went to Absalom and told him: "I saw the two young priests going very quickly (1516) and running very fast to the old rogue." Absalom then answered him: "Then woe to their people!" Absalom sent his servant out to capture them, and the two priests were then pursued at great speed. (1517) The two priests saw and perceived that someone was hurrying after them there and wanted to capture them. They quickly fled into a lady's house. Her husband was encamped at Bahurim and was a trusted ally there. (1518) The man had dug a well in his courtyard. The two noble lads climbed down into the well. The lady saw it; her husband was not at home. She ran quickly and brought out a large bed sheet. (1519) She spread it over the well, so that no one knew what the story was or that there was a fine well underneath the bed sheet. She spread wheat on the bed sheet to dry there in the forest. The lady took her distaff and sat down there to spin. (1520)

Absalom's servants then came into the house at a run. "Where are the two priests? Surrender them at once!" "They came in," said the lady, "that is true, but they ran out at the other gate. (1521) They crossed the water deftly and swiftly. Had I known, I would have cried out. I would have shouted loudly that they were to be held. They have crossed the water. You have to let God, blessed be He, be in control of it." (1522) They crossed the water and pursued them. They could not find them, no matter how they hastened. They rode home again when they could not catch them.

Then the two noble lads climbed out of the well. (1523) They went to Sir David, that most worthy man. He then rejoiced in his heart when he saw them. They told him the news about all the things that had happened, and how Absalom had almost captured them, (1524) and what Ahithophel had there so rightly advised, and how Hushai, his beloved servant, had subverted it. King David and all his men arose; they crossed the water and set out (1525) for the city Mahanaim which was good in times of need: it was well defended from assaults and attacks. "Come to me, all Israel! The competition [for supporters] will provide clear signs: if I have to fight with him, then I will not do it willingly. (1526) Willingly or unwillingly, unfortunately it is all the same. Now, help me, God in Heaven, blessed be He. I was a mighty king: my son, my own child, wants to pursue me. Forgive me and my men, if I have to fight and defeat Israel."

(1527) The advice of Hushai the Archite was heeded—Ahithophel clearly noted that. Now, previously Ahithophel had always been heeded: whatever he had advised, it had been done. Now Hushai the Archite was obeyed—that he could well see. (1528) He had to let him be obeyed; he could no longer prevent it. He might well fail—that he could well see. In great sorrow, he left Jerusalem. He mounted a donkey and rode home to his house. (1529) When he came home to his city of Gilon, he asked forgiveness from his household and everyone else. Then Ahithophel made a will for his household—what they were to do after his death. (1530) He wrapped a long towel around his neck; he tied a slip-knot around it so that it quickly tightened; he climbed on a bench there behind the door; he fastened the towel to a high timber beam. (1531) He had there made for himself a hasty gallows. He overturned the bench. He twitched there for a while. Between heaven and earth he had made for himself a tomb—he had not thought it through properly. (1532) When it was told to Sir David in Mahanaim, he praised the Lord God; how greatly did he rejoice: "He has received his wages; he will do nothing more to me beyond baring his teeth at me in a menacing snarl. (1533) If there were a still more ignominious death in the world, then the Lord God would have let him do it. The towel is around his jaw. Praised be God in Heaven. Oh, what a shameful death!"

(1534) Thereafter, Absalom gathered his great army, as the stars in the heavens and as the sands of the seas. He won many a bold knight there. Then he crossed the Jordan, he and all his men. (1535) Then wild Absalom appointed a commander over his army: a bold knight who was mightier than anyone knew among the troops anywhere. The steel rings of his mighty armor gleamed. (1536) He was named Amasa the Mighty, as one finds it written. Amasa and Duke Joab were cousins: the sons of two sisters. Absalom chose Amasa as commander. Then a host beyond number advanced into the land of Gilead.

(1537) While King David was then encamped at Mahanaim, the city was not well provisioned. He had nothing to eat. Now there were three men who brought provisions for the king there: for him and all his men. That pleased the king. (1538) The one was named Shobi, the son of Nahash—he was from Rabbah, the city of the sons of Ammon; and Machir, the son of Ammiel, born in Lo-debar; and Barzillai, the Gileadite—he had come there from Rogelim. (1539) They brought the king the food supplies that he needed and the things that were needed in the adversity of battle. They brought the king beds and bedding, and pots and bowls, and all kinds of food at once: (1540) barley and flour and barley ears, and beans and lentils and peas, you are also to receive; honey and butter, and cheese of both sheep and cow's milk, as we have read in this book.

(1541) All Israel then advanced quickly to Mahanaim. The bad news was given to King David. The King David arranged his stalwarts and his men. He said: "We will attack them with three companies. (1542) If there are all the fewer of the Israelites slain, if they flee away from us, then you are not to pursue them. If God, blessed be He, grants us the good fortune that they are wounded, then, dear comrades, spare whomever you can spare. (1543) Their host is so great, while we have a small army. But on three sides we are well defended." Then King David counted the soldiers of his army: there were twenty thousand—nothing but mighty men. (1544) David made three companies in the land of Mahanaim. He put one of them under the command of Joab; the second he gave to Abishai, his brother; the third he gave to Ittai. See, there you have it!

(1545) Sorrowfully, David armed himself in his steel mail-coat. He said: "I want to be with my people in adversity." They bound on their helmets and their bright steel garments. David's army and his servants then at once said: (1546) "David, my lord, you ought to stay home. This battle is against Jews—it is not proper for you. You might perhaps even do us harm in this battle. You ought to stay home; it seems to us the right time for that. (1547) You want to spare the Jews, lord and splendid king. Now, all their thoughts are only focused on you alone. One hears it said of them: 'You would much prefer to slay him alone than ten thousand of us.' (1548) Therefore, follow our counsel and stay here at home. We will have to fight fiercely: we will have to fight for our lives. Now, all their thoughts are to strike you dead. Therefore, remain at home and pray to God for us. (1549) It is much more advantageous for us that you pray for us than that you go into battle with us. Then, when we have to fight, we can fight merrily." "That which you desire," said King David, "will be done."

(1550) King David positioned himself at the gate in Mahanaim. Then all his men formed up before the noble king, well and diligently fastened into their steel garments. Many a bold knight turned toward the king. (1551) They bowed to their lord as they were about to march forth. Then King David said: "May God protect you!" King David then ordered the warrior Joab, and at once also ordered Abishai and Ittai, (1552) and all the commanders who were in the army: "If my son Absalom falls into your hands, then do not engage him in fierce combat; take him captive and do not slay him." Thus did the king earnestly order all his men.

(1553) All the king's troops advanced into battle. "O, mighty God in Heaven, may You protect my people!" Quickly did the heroes advance on the army of Israel. They found the army of Israel there in the forest of Ephraim. (1554) Then the servants of King David bound on their helmets. Absalom and Israel began to fight. Absalom could not wear a helmet. That is the truth. He wore on his head a great shock of hair. (1555) There were many mighty men to be found in the army of Israel. Joab and his men charged at that enormous army. Abishai and Ittai rushed out onto the battlefield. There it was seen how King David's servants fought most chivalrously. (1556) The battle was scattered through the broad forest. King David's servants fought a fierce battle. Great feats of manliness were there performed by the heroes: they struck down the foremost of Israel on the battlefield. (1557) They had slain twenty thousand heroes; each one had to carry away his own men dead. Israel had to retreat before David's undaunted stalwarts. Absalom was aggrieved by the slaughter. (1558) Nonetheless, they had to retreat and flee from the forest. The beasts and wild animals felled a great many of them. God, blessed be He, sent the wicked animals to rip them to pieces. The beasts bit more than twenty thousand to death. (1559) Joab and his men pursued them all; Absalom and Israel fled quickly from them. Joab's servants followed Absalom swiftly. Absalom fled from there. Oh, how fast did he run! (1560) He ran under a linden tree there with his great mass of hair. His hair became entangled in a limb—that I tell you in truth. The mule swiftly ran out from under him: the mule went on its way, while Absalom remained hanging there (1561) between Heaven and earth on a tree branch. He could not free himself; he was indeed firmly entangled. He tried to cut himself down with his sword. He then saw Hell yawning beneath him.

(1562) One of Joab's men said to Joab: "I saw Absalom hanging in a high linden tree." "Ah," said Duke Joab, "if you had slain him, you would have worn a belt with a buckle as a gift from me, (1563) and I would have given you ten pieces of silver. Go to the linden tree and quickly take his life." "Not I, on my oath! I will not follow your counsel. I would not take a thousand guilders to slay him. (1564) Now, we all heard—as many of us as there are—that David, my lord, ordered us—all captains of Ittai and Abishai—that nothing was to be done to endanger the life of Absalom. (1565) If I were to kill Absalom, my lord, the king, would certainly not endure it from me. If I were to say that you ordered me to do it, you would repeatedly deny it, and you can act like the old man from Vienna." (1566) "I do not wish to give you a firm order," Joab said to him. Joab himself rode to the linden tree. Joab quickly made three pointed stakes for himself and thrust them into his [Absalom's] heart, so that he was, alas, dead. (1567) Ten of Joab's mighty men followed up with their swords: they hacked him down from the linden tree. Israel fled from there.

During the battle, Joab blew on his war horn. He had not lost a single man in the battle. (1568) When they heard the signal, and when he drew out his horn, they let Israel go: they did not pursue them. Then Joab and all his men assembled there. They found a great pit there in the field. (1569) They then cast Absalom down into the pit. They cast a great heap of stones on top of him. Then all Israel went home again. Absalom had died—they were not delighted by that.

(1570) While Absalom had still dwelt in Jerusalem, all of his children had died—not one of them survived. He had built a courtly building there in the king's valley, which was called the City of Absalom. He conceived that himself, (1571) so that thereafter his name would be remembered, if he were to be killed in the battle.

Now that young Absalom had been slain, Ahimaaz, the son of Zadok, said to Joab: "Let me tell Sir David, (1572) 'David—good news for our lord! We won the battle. Absalom is dead.'" "No," said Duke Joab, "you ought not go to him. Absalom is dead: he will not give you any reward. (1573) Ahimaaz, you deserve to deliver a good message. You will not receive any messenger's reward for reporting that Absalom has been slain." Joab said to the Cushite: "Run there; it is time. Tell King David everything about the battle." (1574) The Cushite bowed. Ahimaaz was still standing there. The Cushite ran away swiftly; he made haste to Mahanaim. Ahimaaz said to Joab: "Even if I do not receive a messenger's reward, how I would like run there, if it could be done with your favor." (1575) "Then run there," said Duke Joab, "while there is still time. I have cut King David's son too deeply." Then Ahimaaz ran off along a winding path. He came to a winding path before the Cushite.

(1576) The gate-keeper cried out loudly: "King, I wish to tell you: I see someone running swiftly in this direction, rushing to us." The king at once said: "If it is a single runner, then Duke Joab has sent me a messenger." (1577) "I see that yet another is swiftly following him. Since he is also alone, then he, too, has a message, as far as I understand it, David, my lord. Ahimaaz, the son of Zadok, is bounding swiftly along toward us." (1578) "That is good," said the king, "if he runs here himself. I think that he must be bringing good news."

Ahimaaz said to David: "Dear my lord, we have won the battle; Israel has fled." (1579) Ahimaaz was ordered to step back for a time, while the Cushite also quickly arrived: "Gracious and noble my lord: we have won the battle. We have thrashed your enemies like dust in the sunlight." (1580) "Is my son Absalom alive or dead?" [Ahimaaz said:] "I do not know, dear lord. I had to run, when Duke Joab sent me here to you. I do not know where Absalom is in the midst of the battlefield." (1581) "So, tell me, my dear Cushite, how Absalom fares. Is my son Absalom alive, or is he dead?" "May all your enemies—and all who evilly struggle against Israel—live just as Absalom now lives! (1582) May all those who make evil decrees against the Jews and make property seizures so live, just as Absalom now lives, my lord."

Then the king was stricken and ran to the tower. He wept piteously and cried out wretchedly. (1583) "Alas, my son, Absalom! Absalom, my beloved son! If only I had died before you! Alas, my son, my son! My sins have caused your death. Your life is lost. Alas for my dear son, that I was ever born! (1584) Oh, that I have ever laughed—the miserable grief! Oh, mighty God in Heaven, take my life, too!" Then the king threw himself on the ground in his great grief. He clasped his hands above his head. (1585) He raised up his voice to express his lamentation: "Alas, my dear son, whom I have lost! O, mighty God in Heaven, what good is my life to me now! Alas, my dear child! Alas my dear son!"

(1586) Then Duke Joab went in to David. "By God in Heaven, blessed be He, you may be certain that if you, King David, do not come out to your army, I will bring a misfortune on you that you will never more overcome.

(1587) All your servants who were ever good to you see that if they had all been slain, you would rejoice, if only your son Absalom were still alive. Thus would you have gladly risked all Israel. (1588) If you do not go out and comfort your servants, then we will in the course of this night no longer be with you. We will indeed find a king," said Joab to David. "We will do worse to you than has ever happened to you."

(1589) Then King David had to stop his lamentation and had to go down from the tower to his people. He dared no longer grieve in front of Sir Joab. The king then sat cheerfully at the gate of Mahanaim. (1590) Then all his stalwarts came before the king. Israel sent to him: "We would like to have you. We thought that you had chosen Absalom as king. We would have denied on oath that he was lying to us. (1591) We all thought at first that it was your doing. Thus did Absalom trick us all. Now, you have helped us against every one of our enemies. Come back home, again, to your land, noble and mighty king." (1592) David said to Zadok and Abiathar: "Go in. Speak with all of Judah about why they are the last ones to bring back the king. That is shameful for us. All Israel has now already long ago sent for me. (1593) Now, you are after all my brothers, my blood, and also my flesh. And tell Amasa that it is the king's command: because of what Duke Joab has done to him, he no longer wants to have Duke Joab as his commander. (1594) He [Amasa] is ever to be commander of Israel. Just as Joab was, now the king takes you in." Judah then answered him: "David is right and proper for us. Come home again, you and all your servants."

(1595) Then King David came—he and all his men—to the Jordan, where they saw him. All the clans of Judah came to the king there; they came out to meet him, when they became aware of him. (1596) They wanted thus to honor King David, the mighty king. At once they brought him to this side of the water. Shimei, who had so malignantly berated David, hurried there; he came quickly to King David with a thousand men of Benjamin, (1597) and Ziba, Saul's man, with ten of his children and twenty of his servants, in order to find King David. They then quickly divided the Jordan with their shields. They did that in honor of David, the mighty king.

(1598) Then Shimei, the son of Gera fell before the king's feet: "Noble King David, I want to atone for my sin. I have acted against you, dear my lord. For that reason, I am the first to come before you on the ground. (1599) I am worthy of death. Forgive me for it, my lord! The first am I to come to you. Please overlook my sin." The hero, Abishai, then said: "I say quite earnestly: he has cursed God's anointed; he has earned a death sentence." (1600) "No," said King David, "I will do nothing to Shimei. He need have no fear that harm will come to him. If I were to kill all those who had broken with me, then I would have to leave none alive in Israel. (1601) If I were to kill Shimei tonight or tomorrow, then all Israel would have great fear of me. If I mercifully allow Shimei to go home, then all Israel will themselves stand fast. (1602) No one broke with me so fiercely as he did. If I leave it unavenged and let him go free, then all Israel will be without fear of me. I want to be their king. Therefore I will spare him. (1603) "I will not kill you," said David to Shimei. "Gracious lord of the land, then swear me an oath." Then King David swore an oath and convinced him that he would not avenge anything that he had done to him.

(1604) Then Mephibosheth, the son of mighty Jonathan, came. He also now wanted to welcome King David. He had never been shorn and had no joy of any kind and had grieved very sorely for the unblemished king. (1605) He wore black clothing and had laundered no shirts and had not washed his hair. Lice had all but eaten him alive. He had grieved so sorely from that day on, when he had fled from Jerusalem. (1606) David said to Mephibosheth: "Now, I have to ask you: why did you stay at home? That greatly surprised me." "Gracious lord of the land, my servant Ziba deceived me and has additionally maligned me to you. (1607) I am lame on both sides, so that I cannot walk well. I ordered my donkey saddled and wanted to ride to join you. He took my donkey from me, and whatever else that I had prepared. He himself rode to you; I do not know what he said." (1608) Then King David said: "Now, cease talking. I have given him half of what is yours." "Gladly," said Mephibosheth, "since you have now come, I willingly give up all that I have." (1609) A voice came from Heaven: "David, you are too hasty. You are not to believe any slander or any calumny. With Mephibosheth you have unjustly divided that which was equal. For that reason your kingdom will also be divided."

(1610) Barzillai the Gileadite also came to the king. He accompanied the king and all his men. He had given King David food in Mahanaim. "Come with me, Barzillai, you are also fitting for me. (1611) I will also feed you for all the days of your life." Barzillai then answered him: "Lord, that is not fitting for me. I have now become old. I can no longer hear the singing in any king's house, and neither dance nor leap. (1612) I want to die at home in my father's house. I am no longer any good for carrying on close relations with the king. I have a son named Chimham; may he be commended to you." "Gladly," said the king, "let him ride in with me. (1613) Whatever you want from me in Jerusalem, it will all be done, for your father's sake." The army and the exalted king then crossed over. The king blessed Barzillai and kissed him fervently. (1614) Barzillai the Gileadite turned homeward. King David then at once took in Chimham.

All the tribe of Judah was there, while half of Israel was elsewhere. (1615) They all openly aided the king. Then all Israel came there—their shame angered them. They said to the king: "Judah has spurned us. We will not overlook the disgrace. They have acted unjustly. (1616) They have ignominiously and secretly stolen away so that they could fetch you across, dear my lord. If they had offered to us and told us, then we would also have come and rejoiced." (1617) Then the tribe of Judah said: "Put aside your anger. Noble King David is my kinsman. For that reason we went to fetch him and his servants. If you had given us gifts, then you would have again acted properly. (1618) That you have ever been so easily angered! Now, we have not taken a bite out of the king." Israel then answered them: "You are wrong about that. Now, all Judah is only a single tribe. (1619) For we are ten tribes, and indeed also the eleventh. We have ten times as much claim on the king as you. You should have called upon us to welcome the king and should have waited until the evil hour had passed. (1620) Now, from the beginning we have given the king full authority: we want the proper lord of the land. Now, you have so disgracefully kept us away that it makes us more than slightly angry at you."

(1621) Then Judah at once answered them angrily: "Thus may all Israel pass away at the wall: you want to ram your heads against it. We will be happy to see that. No matter that it bothers you a great deal, it has already happened. (1622) You ought to trim the claws on your paws so that you do not scratch holes in your asses. Who ought to let their anger boil over as all Israel has now done against us?"

(1623) They had with them a scoundrel named Sheba, the son of Bichri, of the tribe of Benjamin. He said: "Let us get out of here." He sounded a horn, and Israel followed him. They all broke with David at that time. (1624) Sheba, the son of Bichri, was so full of anger. He said: "We did not, after all, swear a marriage oath to David. We do not wish to get involved with the son of Jesse so quickly." All Israel then followed Sheba, the son of Bichri. (1625) Then all Israel said: "Sheba is suited to us. For the son of Jesse we do not give a fig—an Italian fig[30]—if that will not make you angry. You have lost all Israel once again!" (1626) The tribe of Judah remained with Sir David, and otherwise all Israel broke fully with him.

King David then came home to his house. He expelled every one of the ten concubines. (1627) He drove them out of his house and no longer wanted to have them. "Gracious lord of the land—what they have done to us when your son Absalom grappled with us on the roof—there we were forced against our will! (1628) Therefore, O lord, you need not separate from us. He did it with us against our will: it was forced pleasure." "No," said King David, "it is not true: you did it willingly. Now, I wish you an unprosperous year! (1629) You screamed so loudly up there in the hall; you screamed as loudly as a thief in the stable. All Israel certainly saw it clearly. It all happened to you willingly and cordially." (1630) King David put the ten concubines in a house and provided them food for the rest of their lives, but he did not let them out. King David did not indeed have relations with them any more, as is in fact forbidden in the Torah. (1631) They were forced to live out their lives as if widows. King David was not permitted to have further relations with them. Now, let us leave the women to stay in their cloister and instead entertain ourselves with King David.

(1632) David spoke with Israel; his flattery had no effect. He could not subdue them; they had no interest in him. Sheba, the son of Bichri, had them in his power. David then said to Amasa: "Now, go there quickly (1633) and assemble Judah and then return at once. I will not give over my kingdom to the villain, Sheba. I have conquered the lands. None of the Gentiles does anything to me. Now, all Israel wants to break with me. (1634) I have conquered the lands and defeated Israel's enemies. I will not put up with the wickedness of the villain, Sheba. You and all Judah are to be with me again, according to my will, within three days. (1635) Then I will send you after Sheba to fight indeed." Then the hero Amasa assembled all the tribe of Judah. Then he stayed away too long, far beyond the time limit. Then King David said: "The battle is delayed too long." (1636) The king said to Abishai: "I am eager to pursue Sheba. Take my stalwarts with you and pursue the villain, before he captures all the fortified cities, for then he would be safe from all of us."

(1637) Abishai, Joab's brother, certainly did not shirk. He took his stalwarts with him, as the king commanded. He and all his stalwarts who came there with him, they pursued Sir Sheba, wherever they heard that he was. (1638) The archers and mighty slingers were all eager. Joab and his stalwarts followed after Abishai. It bothered Sir Joab that he was not in command. He said: "By Goat's lung, liver, and lice! (1639) I cannot put up with it in the long term, Abishai, my brother. I want—by Goat's liver—to be a commander again."

When they came to Gibeah to the very high stone, and all Judah came marching there, (1640) Joab girded on his sword with the point upward and the pommel toward the ground. No one noticed. When his sword shot out and fell on the ground, Duke Joab at once thrust it back in. (1641) He continued with that until he came to Amasa: Joab took up his good sword from the earth. "Greetings to you, Amasa, my dear friend. Where have you been so long? What happened to you?" (1642) He grasped him by the beard, as if he wanted to kiss him. Amasa had no fear there of his good sword. Then he thrust the sword into him at the fifth rib. Then the hero, Amasa, had to give up his life. (1643) One of the servants of Joab called out to the people: "Whoever wishes King David and us well today, let him quickly follow Duke Joab and leave the hero Amasa lying in his blood." (1644) The people were standing and saying to one another: "O mighty God in Heaven, who has slain him?" Then Joab's men dragged him out of the way and covered him with a cloth. (1645) Then all the people at once followed Duke Joab. Amasa had been slain and lay in the mire.

All Israel assembled to follow Duke Joab. They said: "We would gladly have King David. (1646) We will never break with him again. We have all sworn an oath to him. Judah has held us in contempt; that has angered us all." Then they all followed Duke Joab. Sheba fled before them to Abel of Beth-maachah. (1647) They advanced up to Abel—that I tell you in truth. They built a ramp in front of the city walls. Their bombarded the walls with their lead projectiles. The wall shattered into pieces; the large ones became small. (1648) The wall had to fall down; the stones were shattered. They had built up a great mound in front of the wall. The catapults shot into the city, so that the houses split. The wall was broken down; the stones were pulverized. (1649) They had thrown that first wall into the forest. Joab and his men assaulted the second wall. They wanted to capture the city by force. The people who were inside could do nothing to help themselves there.

(1650) Then a wise lady came up on the wall. She called out to the mighty heroes who were standing outside on the ground: "Now, call Duke Joab for me, and do not let it seem too much trouble for you. I have something to discuss with him, here on the wall. (1651) When Duke Joab approached the wall, that same lady called to him. How earnestly she implored him: "Are you Duke Joab, the commander of the army?" "Yes, I am, on my oath, what do you want to say to me?" (1652) That same lady then said: "Will you listen to me?" "Yes, I will, on my oath. Say on. What do you want?" She said: "My name is Serach, daughter of Asher. I told Jacob our Father that Joseph was still alive. (1653) Then Jacob answered me: 'So may you live and prosper!' Now, look, dear my lord Joab. That is why I am still alive: I showed Moses our Teacher where Joseph's coffin was and where it was sunk beneath the water. (1654) My children have never broken with you. They praised God joyously that David had returned. If you had asked us who had our support, we would have said my lord David. (1655) Now, you want to destroy my dear children, the city and also the people who in truth are with you." "No," said Joab, "understand me rightly: Sheba, the son of Bichri, has done wrong. (1656) He has broken with King David. That will have to be avenged on his neck, even if for his sake I have to have every one of you slain. Now, in all my life I have indeed never committed such a sin. (1657) Now, I have been an honorable fellow all my life. Give me Sheba, the son of Bichri, and all of you will be spared." The lady then answered him: "My lord, you will see it clearly: we will throw his head over the wall to you."

(1658) That same lady then went to her people. She said to her people: "It is better that one man lies dead rather than all of us. Slay Sheba, the son of Bichri and follow my counsel. (1659) If the city is captured, then we will be slain, and Sheba will also have to die. I can assure you of that. He already has one foot in the grave. Even with all his wit, he cannot escape from here." (1660) They cut off Sheba's head—that I tell you in truth—and gave it to Duke Joab in front of the gate. Duke Joab blew on his war horn. The distinguished heroes then withdrew from the walls.

(1661) The people returned home and served David consistently. Only now did poor David become a mighty king with wealth and honor as he had been previously. He had now survived all his enemies.

(1662) Joab and all his stalwarts returned then: "Noble King David, we have indeed brought it about that Israel will serve you as they previously did. Let me continue to be a commander. See, I have returned. (1663) I brought it about that the hero Amasa had his fill of leadership. It will not happen again so quickly that someone will take my place. Let us see," said Sir Joab, "who will force me out. I will give him mighty blows with my sharp blade."

(1664) David had done penance for his sin as best he could. He had been firmly in God's service both before that and thereafter. He had burdened himself with no sin in all his life, except for Uriah the Hittite, whom he had arranged to have slain. (1665) God had forgiven David, the mighty king, for that. He had done penance for all that. The accounts were now settled. King David was then again an exalted king. The people had to serve him on land and on the sea.

(1666) Now, Duke Joab was commander of the army. No one in all Israel again displaced him. Benaiah, the son of Jehoiada, a bold warrior, was commander of the archers and the slingers in the king's land. (1667) Adonirim[31] was the master of the annual payments who collected the tribute. Jehoshaphat, the son of Ahilud, was the master of records, who publicly and efficiently arranged to receive the information first. (1668) Azariah[32] was the king's scribe. The priests Zadok and Abiathar made the sacrifices. Ira, the Jairite, was one of David's nobles. David dwelt in Jerusalem with great honor.

(1669) In the land of Israel lamentation and great distress arose. There was famine for three years; no one found any bread. King David asked God to tell him: "Through what sins have we earned this—what have we done?" (1670) Our Lord God then said: "David, I want to tell you: when King Saul was slain, then not all Israel lamented the king. He well deserved to be mourned—that is why this is happening to you. (1671) And when the priests were slain in Nob, they were bearing Urim and Thummim. And seven Gibeonites were in the city of Nob, when Doeg the Edomite entered Nob. (1672) Now, all Israel had sworn a lawful oath to safeguard the Gibeonites. Thus they said: 'The oath has been broken'—that I can tell you in truth. King Saul had them slain."

(1673) That most splendid hero, King David, then sent word that the Gibeonites were all to come to Jerusalem. The Gibeonites—a great band of them—then came there to King David in the city of Jerusalem. (1674) They then bowed to the king—he was indeed worthy of honor. "What do you want, lord of the land, that you summoned us?" He said: "I want to ask you to forgive Saul for slaying the Gibeonites—as many of you as were in Nob. (1675) Thus God will preserve our lives and deliver us from the great famine." "Noble King David, grant us leave to be on our way. We will not forgive King Saul for it. He wretchedly slew our poor people." (1676) King David then said: "But then you immediately prove that you are not born of Israel. You refuse to have mercy on any of us. Your hearts are unmerciful, much harder than a stone." (1677) Then King David said: "Tell me, what do you want in exchange for praying to God, blessed be He, on his heavenly throne, for Israel?" They said: "We will not even look at silver or gold; nor do we want to kill any man of Israel." (1678) "Tell me then what you want," said the king. "Whatever you dare desire from me, I will give that to you in payment." They said: "Lord of the land, we will tell you that: we would like to slay the heirs of King Saul. (1679) Give us seven surviving men who are his descendents. We will hang them on a high gallows outside of Gibeah." King David then said: "I will give them to you, so that we do not lose our lives in the famine." (1680) King David had mercy on Mephibosheth, the son of Jonathan: for Jonathan's sake he did not wish to do anything to him. Lady Rizpah, the daughter of Aiah, had borne two sons to King Saul—that I tell you in truth. (1681) The one was named Mephibosheth, the other Admoni.[33] King David ordered that they be brought before them, and the five children that Michal had raised for Merab, her sister—it is true and not a lie. (1682) The Gibeonites were there given seven men. They hanged them at Gibeah on a high gallows. They died together; not one of them survived. Now, may God have mercy on you for the misery that was there.

(1683) Rizpah, the daughter of Aiah, put on sackcloth. She stayed by the gallows both early and late. She did not let any bird land on the corpses by day and stood watch at night so that they not be taken. (1684) The beautiful lady guarded against wild animals, mourning and weeping for around half a year. It was told to King David in Jerusalem: "Lady Rizpah guards the corpses, mourning and weeping." (1685) The king was moved to pity in his heart for the lady, King Saul's concubine and Lady Aiah's daughter. Noble King David rode to Jabesh-gilead, he and all his stalwarts—they were dauntless heroes. (1686) King David had Saul dug up, and also the remains of Jonathan, where they were buried. They had stolen them from the wall at Beth-shan and buried them secretly in the ground. (1687) Then Sir David—the pure and noble king—had the remains of the noble dead borne into the city of Gibeah. Indeed he also took down the corpses from the gallows. They were also buried at Gibeah—what I say is true. (1688) They were buried in the tomb of Kish, Saul's father. David commanded Israel to mourn for Saul. All Israel then immediately mourned King Saul. The famine came to an end in the land of the Jews.

(1689) Then King David dwelt in joy and in justice in the city of Jerusalem—he and all his servants. No one in the world any longer opposed him. He praised the Lord God; his grief had passed. (1690) The world had to serve David, the splendid king. He had no enemy beneath Heaven. Almighty God had delivered him from all adversity. He diligently praised Almighty God.

The Song of David:[34] (1691) "I praise you God in joy, my grief has passed. My enemies have departed. Your mercy has gladdened me. You did not leave me to my lord Saul; You aided me against all my enemies so that they had to wither away. (1692) Sole and unique God of Israel, who can praise You comprehensively? Your enemies go to Hell; You aid Your friends at once. You aided me marvelously on a high crag: an angel that came to me, You sent to me especially. (1693) I was soon free. I praise You, my Lord. You aided me in the forest, when Saul advanced there. Your castle and Your fortress and Your very great aid—You are God in the highest, on which I can rely. (1694) My protector and the one who aids and strengthens me. You aid me and give me good strength. I desire Your aid. I praise with a loud voice God, my Lord. I let my throat resound; let it be obedient to You. (1695) You aid in all adversity David, Your servant. You can well kill Your enemy. You always ruin his affairs. When they have encompassed me and threaten my life, You can provide me Your aid—they fall to the ground. (1696) I call out in my grief: 'My Lord God!' In His holiness, He hears me; He accepts my prayer. God is justly praised, both night and day. He aids his servants; His aid never yet ceased. (1697) It has never yet failed: He aids His servants. Let my throat resound: God, let it be obedient to You. He has given us great signs. He aids us both early and late. His power cannot wither. (1698) He performed great wonders for us against

Pharoah. The earth quaked as if it wished to perish. The Heavens wished to
wither before God's great wrath. God, blessed be He, aided His children until
they were delivered. (1699) He divided the sea and led us across with dry feet.
He gave evil comfort to Egypt: smoke from Heaven went there: His wrath
burned in a great fire of coals. (1700) He leads us powerfully with His great
might—mighty God in Heaven from Mount Sinai. Egypt had to sink and pass
away in the water. Who can even remember all the good that He has done
for us. (1701) The Heavens were let down, and that caused us distress. A cloud
had closed over us—no one could see God. He came with the Holy Throne,
with cherubim and wheels.[35] Israel became very joyful; they praised God with
their voices. (1702) Dark clouds were around Him; no one could see God. With
streams manifold and all the Heavenly hosts, from the great light that shone
on Him, hail and coals burst forth, but the fire was not extinguished. (1703) He
stormed from Heaven with His holy voice. Egypt's soul slipped out into the
water's stream. He shot with fiery arrows far into the lands. He confounded
them at once with thunder and lightning. (1704) All the bodies of water in the
world were divided: God directed His great wrath at them. God called to the
waters that they were to split apart. Then they split apart, so that we went
through forcefully.

(1705) "God sent Moses and Aaron into the land of Egypt. He sent an angel
of Heaven to Saul. He aided me against my lord, just as He did my parents.
My God, blessed be He, will I honor, both early and late. (1706) God, blessed
be He, leads us through the waters with His holy radiance. God aided me ever
against my enemies. Egypt forcefully subjugated us, but God delivered us. My
Lord God also aids me in all adversity. (1707) God, blessed be He, allowed us
to survive when we came into the wilderness. We put our trust in Him—we
took no food with us. God, blessed be He, also wishes to remind me of many
of my acts of devotion. He can well aggrieve my enemy; He lets great strength
flow into me. (1708) I carried out very precisely all of God's commandments to
Israel. I was not lax in Your service; my sins have been forgiven me. All the
tribe of Israel keeps the commandments of God, blessed be He. I am also
mindful of the Torah. I observe and keep it properly.

(1709) "In general all of Israel cried out to God. He aided both great and
small out of their adversities. My heart and mind steadfastly cleave to God.
All injustice grieves me. The Torah is good. (1710) God, blessed be He, can
well avenge me, whoever my enemy may be. No one who lives here on earth
can comprehensively speak His praise, and likewise there can be no one in the
turning gyre of the Heavens who can complete Your praise. I praise You, O
my Lord.

(1711) "Whoever serves our Lord—his service is never lost. His deity will
ever find him well; his reward is excellent. Abraham was noble; his piety was
just. In return He did good to him in return—to him and all his people. (1712)
Right here You gave him his reward quite forcefully. You retained his soul at
the heavenly throne. With his piety Jacob strengthened himself in Your justice.
His reward was well prepared—for Your servant, Jacob. (1713) You can reward
Your unblemished Isaac richly. Your deity appeared to him; You are full of
mercy. Esau was contentious; You gave him his reward: that he was to have
no portion in Heaven. (1714) And also contentious Pharoah, who permitted
nothing to be said to himself. He held Israel captive—he was grimly defeated.
Thereby I notice, Lord God, that You aid me yet again. You strengthen the
weak and You bring low those on high. (1715) God, blessed be He, makes my
lamp at once to shine, so that He delights me in my kingdom. He has prepared
it for me. I have obtained great wealth. He will also grant it to me there in the
world to come. (1716) God, blessed be He, can well protect me; my God aids me
at all times. I charged at great armies; my enemies did I slay. When I first took
Jerusalem, I was not supposed to climb over the wall that I came over. (1717) I
sprang over the wall, holding elegantly onto a tree. It did not go sour for me:
the tree swung me inside. God loves courage: He gives appropriate aid to His
servant. I have made ready my heart for God for as long as I live.

(1718) "Ever does He perform that which He promises to His servants. We
justly praise God; His mercy does us good. No god is more than God Himself, blessed be He. My unique Creator—that is the One Whom I mean. (1719)
Our God of Israel, unique and holy God: He protects us, both body and soul,
which He has given to us. He strengthens us with power; He grants me great
might. He makes my sword bite, so that it performs well. (1720) He makes me
to run swiftly like the does in the fields. I raze my enemies. He uplifts me to
the heights as a hero. He teaches me combat; I am an expert in defense. How
could I delay any longer: I must praise my God.

(1721) "He hangs on my bar a great copper crossbow. When my enemies
approached me, my strength greatly distressed them. No man can cock the
crossbow in the house—so said the men. He wants to terrify us. He cannot
cock it either (1722) except when we fight with Him. For that reason He has
done it. I could delay no longer. I had to let them see it. I cocked it with a
mighty draw and ripped it apart with my arms. (1723) You give, dear Lord God,
Your aid and great might. You protect me from all adversity. Your humility
cleaves to me. You make me to take long strides so that I stand fast. My enemies must wait a long time: they will never again bring me low. (1724) I pursue
my enemies—You well know what I mean—until I have slain them. I leave

none of them alive. I slay them faithfully; they topple before my feet. I do not regret their wounds. I will soon punish them. (1725) You quickly grant me great might in great battles. I strike broad wounds into my enemies so that they fall to the ground. They turn their backs on me—they are eager to flee. Then I hack them to pieces and pursue them from behind. (1726) I compel them by force—they squeal like pigs. I leave none of them alive: they have to be stabbed. They cry out to their idols—they never help them! I have to mock their foolishness. I am mightier than they. (1727) Their god cannot match my great might. For if he calls on mighty God, blessed be He, he nonetheless does not do so successfully. Thus I say: 'If you had called on my Lord at first, He could have saved you and I would have had to let you live. (1728) So quickly do you call on your god who cannot help you; then you run after my God.' I will ravage my enemies like dust on the ground, like mortar on the street that is ground up.

(1729) "Ever did You aid me—against Doeg the Edomite and in the death of Saul. You confused the counsel of Ahithophel; neither did the slander help the wicked charcoal-makers. Saul never found me with his sharp blade. (1730) You have preserved my soul, so that it will be well with it hereafter. The Messiah ought vigorously to help Your people. God, blessed be He, made David name in the light of the sun, which people—I do not know—but nonetheless wish to rule as king. (1731) If I do not judge them justly—so that nothing happens to me—I will settle things with You. I will do nothing to Israel. I will not spare the peoples; I will openly subjugate them so that, because of their great sorrows, they will tell me lies. (1732) I will soon put my enemy—who would otherwise soon escape me—in irons and in stocks and in deep prisons. I cannot afford to slumber when they come into my house. They will ever have to limp when they depart.

(1733) "God gave us the Torah on Mount Sinai—with signs and wonders and with great might. Living God, my Creator and my Eternal Aid, sole and unique God, holy and mighty King. (1734) God avenged me on my enemies. My enemies were broken and had to become my servants. Whoever, among all of my enemies, ever caused me distress, they always had to fall; God, blessed be He, has succored me. (1735) Their wickedness has never been of aid to any scoundrels on earth. These false villains had to become sacrificial victims. God can well deliver me; I rightly praise God. He aids His servant David against all evil. (1736) I want to praise You openly before all peoples. I praise You, God, with my voice, up above in Your Heaven. He aids His servant David with His might. He will attach peace to me; all my sorrow has departed. (1737) I have not earned His great mercy. In addition, He will not abandon my children in any adversity. How could I ever praise Him in full for what He has done for us? You are above in the highest on Your heavenly throne. (1738) It is good to be silent—no one can bring Your praise to completion. I will bow to You; I will hold my tongue. Grant me leave, dear Lord, that I depart. May You teach my heart to serve You."

(1739) Now, when King David had spoken his praise, then a prophecy of God came to him, the dauntless one. "Now, I must speak more," said the worthy man. The son of Jesse, who could not keep silent, spoke. (1740) That same man, who is here raised up, said: "He, who is above in the Heaven, made me a king. My God, the God of Jacob, had me anointed. I made many sweet songs of Israel. (1741) The songs of praise to God, blessed be He, that I have made and have collected are to be sung in praise of God, blessed be He, in the temple. Thus has God, blessed be He—the Lord of us all—said. Listen to me, Israel, I want to tell you more: (1742) from my mouth comes forth the pure prophecy of God. It is nothing but prophecy that I have sung. The God of Israel said that I was to be king. God wants to aid Israel for my sake. (1743) In addition, God told me that I am a pious man. He sanctifies His name; prophecy came to me. My kingdom will be strengthened and will grow as does the grass, as some of the grass became wet from the rain, (1744) and as the sun grows ever stronger before mid-day. So will my kingdom also grow ever stronger, and hereafter it should go well for my children. Almighty God has now told me that. (1745) As long as my children hold to the Torah, Almighty God has granted me great mercy. I have received from God, blessed be He, all my desire. God will never be more merciful to any king (1746) as He ever is to me when I call on Him; my God will always grant it to me when I pray to Him. But the evil sinners are like a thorn that pricks people and irritates them. (1747) Whoever wishes to have contact with them, pricks himself so that it bleeds. The thorns must be burned—they are good for nothing more. Thus are the villains worth nothing in the world, until they are burned up in Hell. (1748) Now, listen, my people Israel, for that reason should you be honorable. My Lord God, blessed be He, commanded me to say that."

Noble King David dwelt in Jerusalem in great honor. Nothing honorable did he neglect: (1749) a king and a prophet and indeed an honorable and wise man. God aided King David in whatever he undertook to do. And now that King David had become old, he said to Duke Joab: "Now, go quickly (1750) into the land of Israel into the cities and elsewhere, and count for me all Israel—that I now wish to have and know: how many stalwarts there are among my people Israel, and bring me the written number here in Jerusalem. (1751) And take with you my lords and count Israel accurately." Joab said: "My lord, have mercy on your servant Joab. Why does the king wish to start a disturbance and to count a great people that no one can count? (1752) May God, blessed be He, bless them and increase them to that number again, and that much again, and a hundred times as much, so that my lord the king must see it with joy. Do not have the people counted; I fear that something will happen to him. (1753) As we have heard in the past from our parents: counted sheep like to go missing—that I tell you in truth!" King David, however, made a jest of it: "Go on and count Israel. My God aids me ever."

(1754) Duke Joab and all the lords of Israel went forth and counted all Israel. They did it unwillingly. They went into the cities, large and small, and counted all Israel in common. (1755) They went around the country from city to city and recorded the number in writing after they had been counted. It took nine hundred and twenty days before they could report the facts to King David. (1756) They came before King David—that I tell you in truth. They gave him the numbers that had been recorded. Of undaunted stalwarts in Israel there were three times a hundred thousand scattered through the land. (1757) Nothing but heroes were they, who bore good swords. They all knew how to fight and had the courage of lions. And when King David heard the great number, a prophecy of God issued forth from the king.

(1758) The king well knew that he had done wrong in having all Israel counted. He said: "My dear Lord God, sole and unique Lord, I have sinned so greatly. Forgive me for it, my dear Lord. (1759) I have acted foolishly in my sin. Forgive me for it, my dear Lord God on your heavenly throne." The king was standing there before dawn: he did not neglect to praise the Lord God, as was his custom.

(1760) The prophet Gad came to King David: "My lord and king, God has told you: the Lord God has sent me to you. You are to choose one of three things [to happen] in your land. (1761) One of the three things will certainly happen." [David said:] "If only it could be good!" [Gad said:] "I am afraid, my lord." Then the prophet Gad said: "I know nothing good to say. We have to have one of the three things. (1762) Choose for yourself at once the best of the three: do you want to have seven years of famine in your land; or do you want to flee from your enemies for three months, so that they pursue and follow after you; (1763) or do you want three days of pestilence in the land. Whichever you want to have will come at once. Israel will be diminished: God has decided that. My lord king, you are not to know their number again.

(1764) King David was so stupefied that he could not say a word. The prophet Gad looked at the king piteously. "Now, tell me, dear my lord, king of the land: what is your answer to the Lord, who sent me?" (1765) The king said to the prophet: "I am most aggrieved: among the three things is none that suits me. But I do not want to fall into the hands of any man; and I do not want any famine in my land. (1766) I will deliver myself, body and soul, to God's mercy. His mercy is so great. Perhaps He will allow us to live. May God grant us clemency in His great mercy." David lamented greatly. Gad wished to be on his way.

(1767) The king said to the prophet: "We will take the pestilence. It will be the same for the rich and poor. If I had chosen famine, I would have won the game: I cannot run out of bread; I have a great deal of food. (1768) What would the poor have had in my land. Are seven years of famine to be in our cities? Had I chosen to flee from my enemies, perhaps I would not have been slain, if they had pursued me. (1769) I would have long made a stand against them with my sword. My stalwarts would have supported me, whoever would have come with me. What would all Israel then have done in my kingdom? Many of them would have been slain. That, too, would have been disproportionate. (1770) Let us choose the pestilence. It will strike the rich and poor, the strong and weak alike. Lord God, have mercy on all Your people in Your great clemency and in Your glorious name.

(1771) As soon as the prophet Gad turned from the king, God sent the pestilence throughout the land of Israel. From that morning until the next morning, seventy thousand among the whole tribe of Israel died. (1772) The angel of death entered the land of Moriah. There was a great barn on the mountain there. The angel of death bore his naked sword in his hand and slew all Israel; he turned toward Jerusalem. (1773) King David saw how the angel of death slew the people. He was deeply horrified and aggrieved. He cried out from his heart to Almighty God: "O, mighty God in Heaven, slay me in their place! (1774) May You be the judge in Your Heaven proper. Lord God, I am an intercessor for all the people of Israel. Let Your poor lambs live! You ought to avenge Yourself on me—I committed the sin!"

(1775) And when King David desired God's judgment, God said to the angel of death: "Sheath your sword! My servant David desires a verdict from me." David called to God on his heavenly throne: (1776) "God, You are a judge; that I now well know. Even if Israel had been worthy of death, You are full of mercy; if all Israel had been worthy of death, You would have been merciful, Lord, when You saw their distress. (1777) Have mercy on them, Lord, since the guilt is mine. Let it be avenged on me and my family. Now, Your poor lambs have not earned it through sin. Be merciful, Lord! O, how Your servants are falling." (1778) Then God, blessed be He, at once forgave him for all his sins.

God said to the angel of death: "Slay no more! I will do the will of King David. I have forgiven the people for what they did."

(1779) Then the prophet Gad came running to the king: "King, hurry and buy the barn, and build at once an altar in the barn. The dying will cease: thus has God spoken. (1780) God has designated the barn as a sanctuary. Isaac was to be sacrificed at the same place. God wishes to have a proper sanctuary there." King David and all his servants quickly ran there. (1781) Now, that barn belonged to Araunah the Jebusite, and he had hidden in it from the angel of death. When Araunah the Jebusite saw Sir David coming with all his servants, now hear how he spoke. (1782) He bowed and said: "King, why are you coming here? What does my lord the king want? This is indeed something strange, that you yourselves are all coming here to your servant. Noble King David—if only it can be of benefit to us!" (1783) David said to Araunah: "I have run here so that I might buy with money your large barn. I want to build an altar in it to our God. Thus will Israel be delivered from death. (1784) I want to make a sacrifice; that must take place in this barn." Araunah the Jebusite began to say to David: "Noble King David, let the barn be yours: the wood and the cattle and all my livestock. (1785) I want to give it all to you, noble my lord and king. May God give you authority and answer your prayer." Then King David said: "I will not do that. In this matter I do not want to accept any gift. (1786) I want to pay you with pure silver. Thereafter I want to make the sacrifice to God there." Araunah said to David: "Since you do not want to do otherwise, then you are to have the barn for fifty *marks* of silver." (1787) David at once bought the barn for fifty *marks* of silver. The noble and mighty king then made his sacrifice. God then at once granted the king's request for Israel. The pestilence was stopped in the land of the Jews.

(1788) David held the kingship with great honor. He was compensated for all the grief that he had suffered. Not long thereafter, the noble king died. His most beloved son, Solomon, acquired the kingdom. (1789) He held his father's kingdom with great honor. All the nations at once served the noble King Solomon. He was a mighty king, master of all. He collected possessions beyond number and beyond measure. (1790) The noble and pure king had a temple built of nothing but gold and silver and fine jewels. No more praiseworthy work had ever been accomplished under the sun. He had conceived it to praise and honor God. (1791) And whoever wants to know everything about how it was built, let him read the Book of Kings, if he does not trust me. There it is written—that I tell you in truth—with all its construction, up and down, so that not the least thing is omitted.

(1792) Therewith I will end it: the book has come to its conclusion. May God send us the Messiah—ever do I pray to God for that—and lead us quickly to the Holy Land, so that we all experience it. Say amen at once!

Praised be God, who has given me energy and strength to begin and to end this work: God of Abraham, Isaac, and Jacob, Who helped David in all his adversity, Who will also send me His aid, so that in His work I have success in printing other holy books, even more than I have thus far. The melody of the Book of Samuel is known to all Israel. It is the same as for the Book of Kings. I doubt that there is anyone anywhere who does not already know the melody. So he can save himself the tuition fee for learning it. So the price of the Book of Samuel is also not very high. If anyone wants to have it, I will—with one word—give it to him for four silver *batsn* or for a quarter guilder. I have to say that for the sake of the rhyme,[36] which would otherwise not have suited me. But making sure that it rhymes is after all not that important to me.[37] So give me the money, take the merchandise, have a look, and fare you well.

4

The Binding of Isaac

עקידת יצחק / *Akeydas Yitskhok*

Anonymous, composed fifteenth century; earliest ms. 1579

The reaffirmation of the divine covenant with Abraham, his son Isaac, and their future descendants is the primary function of this core narrative of the Jewish tradition, as it is also articulated in the sixteenth-century Yiddish version of the traditional story of the averted sacrifice of Isaac from Genesis 22. The renewal of the covenant that had already been established is consequent on the positive outcome of the test by the Hebrew God of Abraham's faith, whom he had already recognized while a child in Mesopotamia, as represented in the midrash and the Old Yiddish heroic lay on that midrash, "Abraham Our Father." The episode of Abraham's testing by God early became part of Hebrew cultural sacred history and of a later Jewish tradition of Hebrew *piyyutim* or *akedah-sliḥot* that were recited as part of the paraliturgical tradition during the Days of Awe.[1] As Jean Baumgarten points out, the theme of Isaac's sacrifice took on great significance during the Middle Ages as an allegory of the divine plan (including divine protection) as it was worked out in the Jewish exile and the recurring martyrdom of the Jewish people during periods of persecution.[2]

Here, as elsewhere in the early Yiddish treatment of biblical episodes, that source material was significantly modified by the developing corpus of legend that also entered the midrashic tradition. The narrative of the Yiddish poem is thus defined in large part by postbiblical motivic supplements from the Talmud and midrash. The text consists of eighty quatrains (rhymed AAAA, BBBB, and so on, according to a stanzaic model derived from Hebrew poetry [*piyyut*]). The very complex early textual tradition is witnessed by three variant manuscripts that ultimately obstruct the construction of a critical edition. The most complete of those texts, the Paris manuscript of 1579, is here taken as the source for the translation. Although it is impossible to be certain, it seems likely that the text was originally composed a century before that manuscript was copied.[3]

Source: Paris, Bibliothèque Nationale, MS hébr. 589 [Sorbonne 158], folios 125v–130r.
Edition: Percy Matenko and Samuel Sloan, "The Aqedath Jishaq: A Sixteenth Century Epic, with Introduction and Notes," in *Two Studies in Yiddish Culture*, edited by Percy Matenko and Samuel Sloan (Leiden: Brill, 1968), 1–70 (with manuscript facsimile); Wulf-Otto Dreeßen, *Akêdass Jizḥak; Ein altjiddisches Gedicht über die Opferung Isaaks; mit Einleitung und Kommentar kritisch herausgegeben* (Hamburg: Leibniz, 1971); *EYT*, 60.
Research: Erik, *Geshikhte*, 124–26; Zinberg, *History*, 104–7; Ginzberg, *Legends*, I, 271–86, and V, 248–55; Shmeruk, *Prokim*, 181–99.

(1) Jewish tribe of the worthy kind that was born of our father Abraham and of Sarah, our dear mother, neither of whom stinted in their service to God. (2) And when they had now reached their old age—ninety and a hundred years—there was born to them a distinguished son, Isaac by name.

(3) Now, the Holy One, blessed be He, wanted to test whether he would willingly go serve Him. He said to him: "Take Isaac, your only son. I wish to have him as a sacrifice." (4) In the morning, Abraham got up early, in order to go serve God willingly. He did not object or ask any further questions. He took his servant Eliezer and his two sons, Isaac and Ishmael. (5) Thus did they depart from their tents. And when they had now come into the fields, Isaac wished to say to Abraham: "Beloved father, where have you left your good sense?" (6) Abraham began to say to Isaac: "My dear son, that you will indeed see. God, blessed be He, has commanded me to make a sacrifice. His holy will ought always to be done." (7) Isaac said to his father: "Indeed I do not understand the matter: you are neither a priest nor even a Levite." Abraham again said to Isaac: (8) "I also said that to the Holy One, blessed be He, and He gave me the answer: when we come to the place and when the altar is prepared, then He will make us both priests." (9) They both began to walk on further.

Then Satan came and turned himself into an old man. He said to Abraham: "Where are you going?" He then answered him: "I want to go pray." (10) "Never in my life have I seen it that when someone prays to God, blessed be He, that he takes along wood and fire and a slaughtering knife. That is not the custom in any land. (11) It also makes me quite angry at you, that you let yourself be made a fool. Satan has perhaps talked your ears full, that you are to slaughter your only child." (12) "I will pay no attention to you, you Devil's whelp. For it was the Holy One, blessed be He, who yesterday commanded me to do it, and no other, nor any of the Devil's clan. It is my God Whom I wish to serve properly."

(13) When he saw that he could accomplish nothing with Abraham, he thought: "I will go and take advantage of his son, and I will quickly make a monkey out of him." He said: "My dear son, Isaac, whither are you running?" (14) For he could make no progress with Abraham; so he conceived of another deception and turned himself into a boy, a little imp, and joined up with the young Isaac. (15) He said to Isaac: "Where do you think you are going? Or, what does your father want to do with you?" Isaac then gave him a fine answer: "My father wants to let me study Torah." (16) "Are you then going to study Torah after you are dead? You know nothing of what is about to happen to you. Your father is planning to sacrifice you. I would like to give you some advice." (17) Isaac at once answered Satan: "I immediately recognized exactly what was going on, and even if my end were to come today, I have given myself, body and soul, to the Holy One, blessed be He." (18) "I am telling you: you are going to your death today. Your youthful blood is going to be spilled and spoiled. Turn back and do not cause your mother—who bore you in pain in her old age—grief for the sake of her heir." (19) Isaac did not wish to pay him any attention, no matter how many tales he told. For all his desire was to honor the Lord God.

(20) Since he could not persuade the young lad—because he had no trust in the words of the Devil—both father and son refused his advice, then he went trotting off to his mother, Sarah. (21) He said: "Dear Sarah, where is your only child, whom I do not find here with you?" Sarah then answered him quite quickly: "He has gone to study Torah, like other honorable children." (22) "Certainly, dear Sarah, of course: let me tell you: your husband has carried him off to be sacrificed." She was so overwhelmed that the power of sight left her eyes, and she was stricken in all her limbs. (23) And when she again regained consciousness, she raised her eyes to Heaven: "Almighty God, named Lord in all the world, may Your holy will be done ever and at once."

(24) Now that all his assaults had been unsuccessful, he returned to Abraham and came up with a very nasty trick: he turned himself into a great stream without a bridge. (25) He intended to fend off Abraham therewith, so that he would turn back, for he would be oppressed by the depth. But Abraham had great trust in his Lord God, blessed be He.

(26) Abraham said to Isaac: "My dear son, I will test whether the waters are deep." Then, when he stepped in, it barely reached up to his leg. (27) He said: "O Isaac, my dear son, come here; let us pass through the waters." They thought that they would pass through there. Then Satan did not want to let

them. (28) They stood in water up to their necks. Abraham raised his eyes to Heaven. One tear after another was falling. He cried out to the Holy One, blessed be He, and said: (29) "O Almighty God on Your heavenly throne, You Yourself commanded me to go and make a fine sacrifice of my son Isaac. Now, I have had no evil thoughts and do not wish to renege. (30) Lord God You also told me 'A multitude of descendants are to come from you.' And when we both drown quickly, then who is to carry out the desire of Your name?" (31) From Heaven came the voice of God: "Abraham, you need have no fear and especially no horror because of this. Through you My name will be allied with joy and glory."

(32) God, blessed be He, screamed at Satan with a terrifying roar that he had to drink all the water. He drank so that his belly swelled up—his belly was round and full. (33) He was quite distressed by that, as well as by the fact that he could accomplish nothing more with his deceptions. He ran around, back and forth, because of his discomfort, and roared like a bear in his great wrath.

(34) Now, let us leave Satan there and sing more of Abraham and Isaac. When they then began to go further, Eliezer and Ishmael—both of them—began to quarrel. (35) They had a great and bitter quarrel about which one was to take over the position and inheritance of the first-born son—they were expecting that Isaac was to be sacrificed and Abraham was to die—which was to take the position of the first-born and become the heir of the great inheritance. (36) How great was the quarrel between them? So great that the Holy One, blessed be He, shouted down from Heaven: "You are not going to inherit much here: Isaac has not died!"

(37) Now, when Abraham and Isaac arrived at the proper place, the altar was quickly built, the wood stacked, the fire lit. Just as quickly great misery descended on Isaac. (38) His young heart was greatly troubled that he saw that no sacrificial victim had been brought along. He said: "Dear father, what is going on? I see no sacrificial victim. That is difficult for me." (39) When he noticed this state of affairs, both Abraham's heart and his face fell. Isaac quickly said to Abraham: "Dear father, do not let that confound you. (40) Even if the Holy One, blessed be He, wants me as a sacrifice, I will yield both body and soul to Him in order to honor His holy name. I do it willingly with all my heart."

(41) Both father and son comforted each other in their mutual distress and great sorrow. Isaac himself stacked the wood on the altar, like a bridegroom who rejoices at his wedding canopy. (42) "Roll up your sleeves and tie my hands and feet tightly, so that I will not so easily twitch when I see the knife with which I am to be slaughtered and made a sacrifice. (43) And when you have

burned me to ashes, keep my ashes well and take them to my mother and leave them to her as a memorial."

(44) Isaac's face was covered with hot tears: "Dear father, what are you going to say to my mother, when she does not see me returning with you?" "Dear son, I well know what will happen to us both. (45) After your death, your dear mother, Sarah, and I will not long remain on earth, for who could comfort me in my misery and your mother in her grief and pain." (46) Isaac again said to Abraham: "He who comforted you both before I was born and was here on earth will have to comfort both of you in your grief and pain."

(47) And at once when the words had passed away, the altar was built, and the fire burned. He bound his four limbs together and rolled up his sleeves and took the slaughtering knife in his hand. (48) Father and son were of the same mind—to slaughter and pour out blood. They praised His name and kept His commandment. That well pleased the Holy One, blessed be He, and it seemed very good to Him. (49) The weeping of both of them was great: Abraham shed many tears over Isaac, so that it seemed that a stream was washing over him. They praised His name beyond measure and beyond counting.

(50) Abraham said to Isaac, his son: "How could the Holy One, blessed be He, give us greater joy—since you have already forgiven me for [spilling] your blood—and now send us a little lamb for the sacrifice." (51) At that, Isaac raised his eyes to Heaven: "I will not become despondent in God, blessed be He." He said: "I lift up my eyes to the hills." That means: "I will wait for God's aid and be silent."

(52) At once he took the slaughtering knife in his hand. Isaac turned his eyes to Abraham. He said: "Who will tell my mother: 'Your only child, Isaac by name, has been slaughtered?'" (53) And when he saw the slaughtering knife, Isaac again said to Abraham: "Dear father, say the blessing loudly, so that I may also say 'amen' to it. (54) Alas for my mother's great sorrow!" As soon as he mentioned his mother, Sarah, both Heaven and earth quaked, just as if they were about to sink and perish from horror.

(55) The Holy One, blessed be He, said to His worthy angels: "See there how Abraham praises and honors My name. He perverts absolutely nothing in My commandment. If I had listened to you, I would not have created human beings on earth." (56) The entire heavenly host all began to weep piteously, now that they saw and perceived: they thought that he was indeed to be slaughtered. (57) They all wept abundantly; the tears fell there onto the slaughtering knife with which he was to be slaughtered, so that it did not cut and [the slaughter] could not be performed with it. Then the Holy One, blessed be He, called the angel Raphael, his beloved servant: (58) "Go to Abraham and

say to him that he is to let his only son live and do no injury to his body." The angel Raphael went there quickly and called "Abraham, Abraham"—twice, with loving tenderness—(59) "Do not turn your hand against your child." Abraham then quickly answered the angel: "Even if you are the angel Raphael, it nonetheless does not seem proper to me (60) that I should act according to your commandment: the Holy One, blessed be He, Himself commanded me to do it. When a rabbi and a Torah student are together, it is proper that the rabbi's command be followed." (61) The angel there again called to Abraham: "Abraham, this I say to you in truth: no angel may command anything, unless the Holy One, blessed be He, has already ordered him to do so."

(62) With both hands, courageous and bold, the angel Raphael blocked his knife. And thus did he say to venerable Abraham: "Lift up the knife and put it behind you." (63) He laid down the slaughtering knife, and Abraham again unbound his son, put him down on the ground, and at once said the blessing: "Blessed is the One Who resurrects the dead."

(64) The Holy One, blessed be He, Himself said to his servant Abraham: "Since I find you to be righteous in all things, for you and for all your lineage, I will consider and remember the binding of Isaac as if you had sacrificed him. (65) Your descendants after you will ever prosper because you have kept My commandment and did not spare your son Isaac. I will therefore help your descendants out of all their suffering." (66) God, blessed be He, showed Abraham a ram that was caught in the thorns and underbrush: "Take it as your sacrifice and bind it instead of Isaac, your dear and wise son."

(67) How can we at all times praise the Holy One, blessed be He, that through the Binding he made a bequest to us. Let us first of all indeed honor His holy and exalted name in this deep exile in which we rant and rage (68) and in which we are mired all the way to the bottom. Therefore let us indeed praise God, blessed be He, with our mouths and think of it hour by hour, whether rich or poor, in good health and bad.

(69) Let us indeed bless Abraham and Isaac, the noble men. Blessed be the knife. Blessed be the ram. Blessed be He both before and thereafter. Blessed be He in all song and in all parts. (70) Blessed be the mountain and the thorn. Blessed be the ram that stood fast. Blessed be its hide and its flesh and its horn: when we blow it, the Holy One, blessed be He, lays aside His wrath. (71) When we blow it, Satan must quickly go into hiding and flee hence with all his henchmen, and not let himself be seen that same morning, and he has to crawl underneath the mountains in disgrace. (72) For Satan boasted to the Lord God, how he would obstruct the Binding, how he knew for certain that Abraham would not willingly do it, and that he would prove it as the truth.

(73) Now, you have heard how he tried all his clever tricks: he turned to Sarah, who sat benumbed. He showed her the Binding above in the clouds. Thus did her soul depart from her with weeping and sighs.

(74) It is also written in our holy books that when we blow the three traditional tones on the ram's horn,[4] then many of the gates of mercy open and all evil decrees and evil vows are torn apart. (75) And yet more is written in our Torah: that on that day the evil impulse has no power over us. We have all that benefit from Abraham, Isaac, and Sarah, if only we become pious and enlightened. (76) And no one will be able to harm us, and the Holy One, blessed be He, will always be merciful to us. And we will soon be delivered from the exile. And he will send us the Messiah even as far as Cremona and Venice.

(77) Nonetheless, no one should hold me to that. If you want to know the truth, I do not think much of people. I swear to you as a true Jew: they are only so pious that they indeed need another Binding just about every day. (78) Now, be that as it may, I cannot change it. I will ask His Name, blessed be He, that He hasten and end it and soon send us the Redeemer. And with that I will right away conclude and make an end. (79) And let us ask the Holy One, blessed be He, that He not consider our sins and not let us any longer chase around like dogs, and have mercy on our poor fellows and send the Messiah to deliver Israel, his first-born child. (80) And remember us at all times in the exile by virtue of the good deeds of Abraham and Isaac and Jacob, for the sake of the love that he showed You. And let us for once experience great joy, and send us the Messiah for whom we have long waited.

The End—The End—The End.
Tuesday, 3 February 1579

"Secular" Epic

5

Duke Horant

דוכוס הורנט / *Dukus Horant*

Anonymous, ca. 1382

Since the initial publication of דוכוס הורנט *Dukus Horant* (Duke Horant),[1] which was until the recent discovery of the epic fragment of 1349 on the Cologne slate reckoned as the earliest Old Yiddish "secular" epic, a vast sea of scholarly publications—especially in the field of German studies—has spread. Most of those publications have taken as their thesis (acknowledged or not) that *Dukus Horant* either is not Yiddish at all or is interesting only for the opportunity it offers philologists to speculate about the lost text(s) that functioned as its source material. That initial edition of the text spawned a surprising number of reviews, further editions, and commentary from Yiddishists and Germanists alike, almost none of whom (of either discipline) had any training in the field of *early* Yiddish language and literature, for the simple reason that such advanced training was at that time all but nonexistent in the universities of the world. That almost ubiquitous lack of expertise in the specific language of the text and the culture that produced the text seemed, however, to deter few from entering the fray.[2]

The narrative itself is an example of the widespread subgenre of bridal-quest epic. Perhaps the most characteristic epic of that tradition is the Middle High German *König Rother*, which in fact displays some striking similarities to the general plot of *Dukus Horant*, although the two narratives share no common characters. The general scholarly tendency has been to view the narrative content of the Old Yiddish *Dukus Horant* as ultimately belonging to a cycle of heroic narratives whose central figures were Kudrun, Hagen, Hilde, and Horant. Even in the absence of an extant Middle High German "Hilde-saga"—so desperately desired by source-reconstructing Germanists—there are nonetheless several extant medieval literary and artistic representations of the general narrative of the character of Princess Hilde. Most important are *aventiuren* (chapters) 4–8 of the Middle High German *Kudrun* epic, which may be summarized here for those readers interested in comparing that narrative to *Horant.*[3] As a prelude to the heroicized bridal-quest epic of Kudrun herself, these early chapters of *Kudrun* narrate the quasi-parallel bridal quest of her mother, Hilde, which is presented as a bridal-quest embassy of the Danish King Hetel (whose analogous character is Itene in the Old Yiddish *Dukus Horant*), led by Wate and including in the entourage the supernaturally talented singer Horant, who journey to Ireland (that is, the wild, wild West, as opposed to Hagene the Savage's home in the exotic East in *Dukus Horant*) to fetch home Hilde as bride for the king. In both texts the task force tactically poses as "noble merchants" (an oxymoron and nonexistent social category of the period) exiled by their king, the would-be groom. While the fragment of *Dukus Horant* breaks off during Horant's proxy courtship of Hilde by means of his singing, in *Kudrun* that courtship is successful in convincing Hilde to leave with the bridal embassy without her father's permission: as the bridal-quest task force takes leave of King Hagen and his court at the harbor, with Hilde still on board, apparently innocently inspecting their trade goods, the sailors cast off and sail away with her. Her duped father, Hagen, then follows them to Denmark with his army, where a bloody battle takes place on the shore, during which an abrupt reconciliation takes place, after which Hilde becomes queen of Denmark and bears Hetel a daughter, Kudrun. Thereafter follows that epic's primary narrative. Thus, up to the point where the text of *Dukus Horant* breaks off, it seems to treat essentially the same plot motifs as the ones found in the section of *Kudrun* that narrates Hilde's bridal quest, with a more or less common cast of characters, albeit with some stark exceptions. At the same time, however, it is obvious even to a casual reader that the Yiddish *Horant* is not a translation or even a paraphrase of this section of *Kudrun*: even with all their similarities, they tell distinctly different tales.

Intriguingly, the general tale of Princess Hilde seems to have been quite broadly known not just in the Yiddish *Horant* and the Middle High German *Kudrun* but indeed throughout Germania as early as the sixth or seventh century (in widely diverging forms and with variant content), as witnessed by a carved figure stone from Stenkyrka in Gotland, one scene of which seems to depict Hilde attempting to reconcile the warring parties fighting for her possession.[4] The Old English canon likewise knows the tale well: the poem "Widsið" mentions the central characters—Heoden, Hagena, and Wada (that is, the Itene, Hagene, and Wate of *Horant*)—while the poem "Deor" mentions "Hoerrenda . . . leoðcræftig monn" (Horant, the man skilled in song).[5] In the thirteenth century, the Icelandic politician and antiquarian author Snorri

Sturluson summarizes the tale in the *Skáldskaparmál* section of his *Edda*,[6] and additionally cites as an addendum to his work the "Ragnarsdrápa" by the skaldic poet Bragi, in which Hild plays a significant role.[7] The Danish ecclesiastical historian Saxo Grammaticus mentions the tale in chapter 5 of his *Gesta Danorum*.[8] There also exist several ballads in Spanish, Franco-Catalan, German, and Norse from the late Middle Ages that seem to preserve some plot fragments of the tale.[9]

Despite the breadth of this tradition, there is little actual evidence of the *epic* treatment of this narrative material beyond the Middle High German *Kudrun* and the Old Yiddish *Dukus Horant*. Otherwise, there are only *very* brief summaries or mere mentions of the names of characters. There is thus precious little evidence of an epic cycle per se. Scholarly speculation concerning various nonextant epics—such as a "Hildelied," a "Herbortlied," or a "Rotherlied"[10]—in order to flesh out speculative theories concerning such a cycle, bears witness to the late intellectual offspring of typical nineteenth-century philological imaginative excesses that still occasionally surface in twentieth- and twenty-first-century scholarship among those individuals who find the invention and description of nonexisting medieval texts more interesting than the study of actually extant texts. Perhaps rather than allowing our bewilderment or irritation to grow too strong, however, it might be better to view such scholarship as simply quaint and then move on.

Although there is no evidence to support the widespread scholarly assumption that *Dukus Horant* is merely a Hebrew-alphabet transcription of an originally Middle High German source, the unlikelihood that a Jewish poet would have simply created the Old Yiddish poem without any antecedents should also be acknowledged: not because of any supposed deficiencies in Yiddish-language literary culture at that time (the quality of which is attested by the range of other epic texts in the same codex in which *Horant* is transmitted) or of any presumed superiority in German literature of the period, but rather because newly composed fourteenth-century European epics in English, French, German, Italian, and, indeed, also in Yiddish were almost never made up out of whole cloth. English, German, and Italian epic poets generally translated and adapted French texts into their own languages, while the poets of those French texts generally either adapted or claimed to have adapted the texts or at least characters and motifs of earlier Celtic or Latin narrative traditions. The invention of the modern conceptions of originality (and plagiarism) by the thinkers of the European romantic period was still some centuries in the future.

One must moreover keep in mind that such Pan-European "adaptation and translation" include both some texts that are slavish reproductions of the source in the new language and others—such as the Old Yiddish *Vidvilt*—that drastically abbreviate their sources, reconceive significant components (for example, the representation of Muslims), and substitute innovative endings, or, as in the case of the Middle Yiddish *Pariz un Viene*, which turns its brief prose source into a grandiose Humanistic epic, take the source as a starting point for a radically new composition. Thus, even if one acknowledges that *Dukus Horant* could well have had a German-language source and could have been adapted in the conventional mode of the late medieval period, at least a century and a half before the adaptation of *Pariz un Viene* in the quite distinct Renaissance mode of adaptation, there is no reason to treat *Dukus Horant* as an ill-executed example of cross-cultural plagiarism, as has generally been the case in much scholarship on the text.

It seems to me that in this situation, there is little benefit in inventing presumed lost sources instead of the rather less audacious scholarly act of granting the poet the possibility of having written a poem adapted from ideas and characters and plot motifs found in the (then) extant traditions of epic poetry: that is, loosely based on some basic plot structures of the genre of bridal-quest epics (in particular *König Rother*), on the general scope of characters of the *Kudrun* epic, and especially on the basic plot of the preliminary episode of that epic (summarized above), which runs directly parallel to the plot of *Dukus Horant* in the fragment extant.

In any case, *Duke Horant* is a unique epic, that is, it exists in a single manuscript and only in Old Yiddish, and no amount of Germanistic speculation about its alleged Middle High German sources will change that fact. The text still awaits its first literary or cultural study from the perspective of twentieth- and twenty-first-century postphilological, literary scholarship.[11]

At the same time, however, it ought also to be acknowledged what readers of this volume will recognize as they proceed: in terms of literary quality, *Dukus Horant* does not compare to the epic masterpieces of the Pan-European medieval period. As a late-fourteenth-century bridal-quest epic, however, it is on a par with its peers in that particular (and peculiar) subgenre, and within that smaller context and as the first extant epic in Yiddish to be of greater length than the brief heroic lays of the midrashic tradition (from the same codex), one might well recognize it as something of a triumph.

As already noted, the plot of *Duke Horant* is indeed in most respects a typical example of the widespread medieval subgenre of epic generated by the narrative motif of bridal quest or "wiving," which represents the conventional international (literary) process of providing a ruler with a wife, ultimately for the strictly utilitarian (in feudal society) purpose of producing an heir to the throne. As indicated in the comments above on the relevant narratives beyond the Old Yiddish text, the character Horant is generally a minor figure and is traditionally known as an almost supernaturally gifted singer; in *Horant* he appears as a vassal of King Itene and functions as the king's emissary and agent in the royal bridal quest. The exaggerated qualities of the material culture represented in *Dukus Horant*—the phenomenal amount of wealth requested by Horant from Itene for the bridal-quest embassy, the ostentatious silver adornments of the ship's fittings, and so forth—seem so extreme that they might prompt readers of the Yiddish text to imagine that they were introduced by the Jewish author-adapter in order to parody Christian feudal literature. It is then, on the one hand, sobering to realize that precisely these components of the Hilde tale are also very specifically present even, for instance, in the analogous episode of the Middle High German *Kudrun* epic: such motifs are simply routine in this epic subgenre. One must nonetheless acknowledge that the presence of such motifs in the Christian tradition and in a *Yiddish* adaptation of that tradition does not preclude the possibility that the text-specific function of the motifs in the Yiddish text might still be parodic: agency and audience are always components in signification.

The poem is composed in a four-line stanzaic form that resembles the so-called *Rabenschlacht*-stanza in Middle High German literature, rhymed AABB. In the surviving fragment of the poem, there are some 270 identifiable stanzas (many of them severely damaged), which on the manuscript's last extant pages become only sporadically legible before the manuscript breaks off altogether. Despite that illegibility and thus the impossibility of providing a comprehensibly *connected* translation of these damaged passages, the fragments themselves have—to the extent feasible—been retained in the translation here, since the reader might occasionally reconstruct some approximate sense of the general content of the damaged passages even from the scattered words preserved. In any case, the poem's original length and the complete plot's ultimate shape can no longer be determined.

The text is here translated primarily from the manuscript itself, the edition in *EYT* (st. 1–65), and the full edition by Eli Katz. On the codex in which the text is transmitted, see the general introduction to this volume. The bracketed ellipsis [. . .] signals illegible words or passages in the manuscript.[12]

Source: Cambridge University Library, T.-S. 10K22, folios 21r–42v.

Edition: Fuks, *Documents*, I and II, 81–169 (manuscript facsimile); Katz, *Poems*, 120–63; Peter Ganz, Frederick Norman, and Werner Schwarz, eds., *Dukus Horant*, Altdeutsche Textbibliothek, Ergänzungsreihe 2 (Tübingen: Niemeyer,

1964) (Roman-alphabet transliteration with Germanizing Roman-alphabet transcription); *EYT*, 9.

Translation: Fuks, *Documents*, II, 81–169 (German); Heidi Graw, *Dukus Haurant* (n.p.: Lulu Press, 2009).

Research: Shmeruk, *Prokim*, 33–36, 97–120; Baumgarten, *Introduction*, 132–35, 142; Max Weinreich, "Old Yiddish Poetry in Linguistic-Literary Research," *Word* 16 (1960): 100–118; Hans Neumann, "Sprache und Reim in den judendeutschen Gedichten der Cambridger Codex T.S.10.K.22," in *Indogermanica, Festschrift Wolfgang Krause* (Heidelberg: Winter, 1960), 145–65; Dov Sadan, "The Midrashic Background of 'The Paradise': Its Implications for the Evaluation of the Cambridge Yiddish Codex (1382)," in *The Field of Yiddish: Studies in Yiddish Language, Folklore, and Literature*, edited by Uriel Weinreich, 2nd collection (The Hague: Mouton, 1965), 153–62; Manfred Caliebe, *Dukus Horant: Studien zu seiner literarischen Tradition* (Berlin: Schmidt, 1973); Jerold C. Frakes, *The Politics of Interpretation: Alterity and Ideology in Old Yiddish Studies* (Albany: SUNY Press, 1989); Gabriele Strauch, *Dukus Horant: Wanderer zwischen zwei Welten* (Amsterdam: Rodopi, 1990); Wulf-Otto Dreeßen, "Horant als *Schadchen*?," *Jiddistik-Mitteilungen*, no. 23 (Apr. 2000): 1–9.

(1) In the German lands there was a widely famed king, a very bold warrior: Itene was his name. He was generous and handsome; he wore the crown of honor. (2) All German lands served him mightily: Lombardy and Apulia were in his hands; Sicily and Tuscany had no choice but to be subject to him. (3) Denmark, where he wore the crown, was quite in his control. All Spanish lands also had to serve him well. The King of Hungary was subject to him and wore the crown by his grace. (4) The lords of the land were all subject to him.

Three dreadful giants from the forest served him. One of them was named Witolt; he was a bold warrior. (5) He carried a steel staff that was twelve fathoms in length, with which he had vanquished all the German lands for noble King Itene. He had a brother named Asprion; he had performed a great many marvels. (6) And Wate of the Greeks, the marvelously bold warrior—many a hero lay dead at his hands. They served Itene, the noble ruler, as his bondsmen.

(7) When King Itene turned sixteen years old, he was stalwart and strong, and bold in all battles. He was the most generous of men who ever won the name of king. (8) He also had a comrade whose name was Horant. He was a mighty duke, born in Denmark. He was the most prudent[13] of all men who ever won the name of ruler.

(9) They had great pleasure with each other and many kinds of joy and much grand entertainment. Sometimes they went hunting with dogs in the forest. (10) Horant said to the king: "Dear my lord, an exalted queen would

befit you as wife." Youthful Itene laughed at that. He there began to blush greatly. (11) He said: "My very dear Sir, send forth your men. We will have a grand festivity this Pentecost. Thus will we then confer about a lovely lady."

(12) By Horant's counsel, envoys were sent out through all the German kingdoms. Right away twelve quite splendid kings came to him, each of whom [wore] a golden crown. (13) Three dreadful giants came to him from the forest: Witolt with the Staff, his brother Asprion, and Wate the mighty lord. Quite laudably did they come there. (14) They were well received by mighty King Itene. They were given rich gifts: magnificent clothing, war-horses, saddle-horses, silver and gold. The gentlemen were therefore all staunchly loyal to him.

(15) Then the king ordered that a festival be organized and fine seating that stretched far and wide. They had joy and entertainment. Many fine gifts were given there. (16) The festivities lasted until the twelfth day, so that the noble king took part in it with great honor. When it was time for the festivities to come to an end, the king went to stand before the lords. (17) He said: "Now, confer all together, both kin and vassals, about a beautiful lady whom I can marry with honor and who is fit and proper for all of you. I would gladly take that one as my wife. (18) All of them were silent. Then an elderly duke said: "I have been in France. The king there has raised such a delightful maiden that her peer cannot be found anywhere in the world. (19) May she be yours, dear my lord. The exalted queen would be a proper wife for you, and the crown would be proper for her. She is wise and beautiful."

(20) Then King Itene said: "You should drop the matter at once: she is not suitable to be my bride. Her father is a lawful vassal of mine. No one is to speak of it to me. I could be disgraced by it." (21) The duke quite held his peace. An elderly pilgrim stepped into the ring; he was a courtly man. He was quite gray—hair, beard and his eyebrows—due to his age. (22) He had performed a great many marvels in his youth. As penance for his sins, he had wandered through many a land; he had been a pilgrim for thirty years or more. He had crossed the savage sea twelve times. (23) He said: "Noble King Itene, now give the order for silence. Of a beautiful maiden I can tell you many a marvel. In the land of the Greeks did I see her. She is called Hilde the Fair. (24) She is more beautiful than Isolde, the daughter of the king of Ireland, or than the queen of Troy—Ilion was her name. Troy was destroyed because of her, as we have heard in the song. (25) Because of a woman's desires, many a hero was lost. It was an evil hour in which she was ever born. Menelaus was her lawful husband whose life Paris took.[14]

(26) "Her [Hilde's] father is named Hagene the Savage, the most dauntless man who was ever born in this world. Twelve very noble kings serve him as

bondsmen. (27) He has twelve marvelously strong warriors [. . .]. [. . .] stalwart, who his daughter [. . .]. He would take my life [. . .] give to no one as a bride. (28) May she be yours, dear my lord. This exalted maiden would be quite suitable for you as a wife. All the German lands would be fitting for her. She has no peer alive anywhere."

(29) And when King Itene had well heard these words, he gave rich gifts to that same pilgrim. He said: "I will possess this beautiful maiden, or I must lose my life." (30) There King Itene saw the duke from Denmark standing before him. He embraced young Horant in courtly manner. He said: "If you, Sir, would be my envoy, the beautiful maiden would be mine. (31) I honor you well, dear Sir. You are such a courtly man. If you were to bring me home the maiden by means of your sweet singing, I would give you such rich gifts that you would live joyously ever after. (32) You are appointed as a duke in Denmark: if you bring me the beautiful maiden, then you will wear the crown over all of Denmark's lands: Denmark will be your own property."

(33) Then gracious Horant answered him in courtly manner: "Lord, even if I were thereby to gain all the German lands, I would turn down all of them, before I would dare undertake this journey. (34) I know Hagene well. He is indeed an evil man. If I were to lose my life for the sake of the maiden, too bitter would be for me the beautiful maiden. You should let the matter drop."

(35) Noble King Itene fell on his knees before him. He said: "By no means, dear Horant! Either I will lie here forever, or you will do my will and go fetch the beautiful maiden."[15] (36) "Now, get up, dear my lord. Either I will put my young life at risk, or I will bring you the marvelously beautiful lady from Greece. And if I am to go to the Greeks, I will not stint with your property. (37) Order, my lord, that two hundred of your men be put under my command. They should be young knights and fine lords; and Morunk, my dear brother, is to be with me on the journey, (38) and Wate of the Greeks, that marvelously bold man, and Witolt with the Staff and his brother Asprion. They are to be with me on the journey. Thus will I win you the maiden. (39) And order, my lord, a most magnificent ship built for me, and order it spread for me with rich velvet. The sail is to be white silk, the rudders all worked with silver, (40) the mast sheathed with gold, the anchor of silver, the cables and lines are all to be of white silk, and a magnificent barque, spread with rich silk cloth. (41) I want to have thirty thousand marks of gold along with me, and order, my lord, fine saddle-horses to be supplied to me whose trappings are all studded with gold, which the horses are to wear in Greece. (42) Thus will I travel to Greece—either to put my life at risk, or I will bring the marvelously beautiful

lady to you from Greece. I will attempt all that I can, or I will bring the beautiful maiden back here."

(43) Noble King Itene embraced him immediately. With great joy he kissed him on his red mouth. He said: "May God give you long life with honor. You have given me good comfort." (44) "Now order all things brought to me that I desire: war-horses, saddle-horses, armor, knights, shields, and lances." "I will give you not one but two of every thing that you desire."

(45) They sent to the forest for the giants, for Witolt with the Staff and his brother Asprion, and Wate, the marvelously bold man. They came and stood before the king. (46) He told them the tale of that most delightful maiden. He courteously asked Wate, the noble lord, and Witolt and Asprion to undertake the journey. (47) Then bold Wate answered him in courtly manner: "By your will I shall gladly undertake the journey. I will bring you the beautiful maiden, or I will lose my life." (48) Witolt with the Staff said: "Dear my lord, I will not do much begging for the beautiful maiden. He will have to give you the young lady, or I will take his life there." (49) Bold Asprion strode before the king. He said: "Dear my lord, I am delighted about the journey. You must have the beautiful maiden, or I will slay all the Greeks."

(50) Then the king ordered a most marvelous ship built. He ordered it spread with rich velvet; the sail was white silk, the rudders all worked with silver. (51) The ship was equipped according to Horant's counsel; the knights and squires were most properly outfitted. Then he ordered carried into the ship that which they would need for the journey: (52) a great deal of fine silk cloth and much fine velvet, all worked with gold and with jewels, and also fine ermine, of which there could never be better. (53) He also ordered to be brought for them enough of everything: war-horses, saddle-horses, and armor. Their food that they needed for the journey was taken on board the ship. (54) The ship was worked with silver and gold, such that the sailors could only say: "It cannot take any more."

Then they at once boarded the ship—Horant and all of his men. (55) The noble King Itene went with them down to the sea. A great multitude of ladies and men followed him. When they came to the sea stream, the giants went to stand before the king. (56) All together they took their leave from noble King Itene. Each of them individually bowed to him splendidly. Then King Itene, the young warrior, said: "May God keep you today and forever." (57) After they had taken leave of him, the warriors were led in, and when the great giants had all come to the ship, Horant took his brother Morunk and went before the worthy king. (58) He said: "Grant us leave, dear my lord; let us depart with your grace. May noble God in Heaven protect your life." The king then embraced Horant. He kissed him on his red mouth. (59) He pressed him to his heart and began to weep a great deal, so that the ladies and gentlemen all began to have pity. Then he said: "Cease your grieving: we will survive the Greeks."

(60) Itene, that same bold warrior, granted him leave to depart. "May God in Heaven attend both of you—you and the young man, your brother." Then Horant went aboard the ship. (61) Then they raised their sail and sailed out to sea, Horant and his comrades, a great and mighty host. Horant and all his men, they sailed away on the sea. (62) They sailed directly out onto the savage sea, Horant and his comrades, a great and mighty host. Horant began to sing, so that it resounded up through the clouds. (63) He sang so loud: "Now, on this day, today, may He Who delivered the Jews on the sea come to comfort us. In God's name do we fare; His mercy do we desire."[16] (64) Then he began to sing so loudly and so sweetly that the mer-men began to rush toward the ship, and the fish in the depths all swam to the surface. (65) They traveled with great joy on the streams of the sea. God in Heaven then sent them delightful weather, so that they arrived in twenty-eight days, as we hear it said in the song.

(66) And when the gentlemen had all come to land, in courtly manner Horant went before the dreadful giants. He said: "I do not wish to wait any longer. I want to ride into the city (67) and take lodgings where we may dwell with honor. Now follow my instruction, my very dear comrades. First we will proceed prudently and guard our own honor." (68) Then bold Wate answered him in courtly manner: "What you command us to do, my lord, that will be quickly done. Ride off then through the city to find pleasant lodgings." (69) He clothed himself handsomely in pure velvet. He was marvelously resplendent from the gold. They brought him a wonderful saddle-horse, on which the bridle and harness were studded with rich gold.

(70) They led him out onto the shore. When he stepped onto the shore, he leapt most splendidly onto the most praiseworthy horse and rode off through the city. Both ladies and men looked at him. (71) He rode straight until he saw a splendidly dressed townsman standing there before him. He was a courtly man. When saw Horant coming toward him, now may you hear what he said: (72) "Welcome, my dear lord, from me and from God in Heaven. I see clearly from your deportment that you are a worthy lord. If you need anything at all that I have, your wish will be quickly fulfilled." (73) Horant then bowed in courtly manner to him all the way to the ground. He said: "Now may God reward you, townsman, for your worthy greeting. Can you point out to me a man who could take me in as a guest? (74) And show me a hostel where I

could lodge with honor, along with two hundred of my comrades; that I ask of you, on your honor. For we have been exiled here from German lands; we have retained very little property." (75) He said: "Dear my lord, do you see this courtyard that stands before you? There you and your comrades will find comfortable accommodations. My house is so delightful, it would be fitting even for a noble and mighty king."

(76) He said: "May God in Heaven reward you, dear my lord. If you would provide us with credit, we would gladly be your guests." "Yes," said the courtly merchant, "I can indeed give credit. (77) I will lend you two thousand marks of gold on international collateral. If that [. . .] I will lend you still more." Then bold Horant said: "That will not suffice for us. (78) If you could lend us thirty thousand marks of gold or more, we would return them to you when we have crossed the savage sea. Two thousand marks would be of no help to us. We would use them up in a single day. (79) We are exiles; for that reason we cannot stint. I can assure you, we want to lead a genteel life." Then the courtly merchant said: "Then I do not dare provide you with lodgings. (80) But, dear my lord, I can well direct you to lodgings—where you can stay with honor—with a wealthy merchant who can easily lend you money. (81) You will find much good in his house. You will find in his lodgings entertainment and pleasure. He is the most courtly man who ever won the name of townsman. (82) Now see that gate before you, dear my lord: there the noble merchant lives with his household. Ride in there, dear my lord. There you will find what you desire." (83) He showed him a [. . .] from there through the city.

The courtly merchant stood, splendidly dressed, at the side of the courtyard, for he was wealthy beyond measure. (84) And when the townsman heard Horant's words, he waited no longer, toward [. . .]. He welcomed him quite splendidly, Horant [. . .] lord [. . .]. (85) Horant dismounted onto the ground. He went toward the townsman. So very splendidly did he embrace him. He said: "God's greetings to you, noble merchant. I have heard much about you. (86) I was sent to you. My comrades and I would very much like to be your guests. We have been exiled here from German lands; we have retained very little property. (87) I lead two hundred comrades, noble and stalwart knights. They have crossed the sea and suffered great adversity. If you would provide us with lodgings, you would suffer no loss on our account. (88) And if you could lend us thirty thousand marks of gold or more, we would return them to you when we have crossed the savage sea. For even in poor times we have to lead a genteel life. We cannot stint in spending."

(89) Then the townsman there answered him in courtly manner: "Indeed I would be happy to have you as guests. If you choose my inn, you will be

lords there (90) and in my house you will be in charge of everything that I have, except for my wife alone, whom I would like to retain for myself. You [. . .] lend [. . .] you therefore need not [. . .] (91) [. . .] in my house all that you desire. [. . .] a hundred thousand marks of gold will be granted to you. [. . .] with me for ten years, it will not make any difference to me. (92) I have so much property and am a very wealthy man. Whatever you need, you will have not one but four of them. That you will see for yourselves. That you will have to say is the truth."

(93) "I would like to see it myself. I would like to have a look at your house. If I like the lodgings, then we will very likely close the deal." The innkeeper then began to get angry. He said: "Indeed you are an untrusting man. (94) In my house you will find both the goose and the hen. And, if you would only believe it, I would like to take the very best care of you." Horant then said: "Do not be angry, and ride with me to fetch my comrades. (95) I would be happy to believe everything that you have told me." They led forth for the townsman a beautifully caparisoned saddle-horse on which the bridle and harness were splendid, worked with gold and fine jewels.

(96) He mounted up with his retinue and rode with him to the sea. There they led ashore a great and mighty host. When the townsman saw the huge giants, how happy you would be to hear what he said: (97) "I will always regret having taken you in. They are the spawn of the vile Devil. They have all come from Hell! Lord God protect me from that one who is standing there with the steel staff."

(98) Thereafter [. . .] went to the [. . .]. Hey, how he went before the great [. . .] we will [. . .] to Wate [. . .]. (99) They were led [. . .] so finely covered [. . .] many pack-animals [. . .] there heavily loaded [. . .] (100) The townsman rode in front; Horant rode behind him. Thereafter rode the dreadful giants. They hurried to their lodgings. Women and men who caught sight of them fled. (101) When they came before the inn, the gates were opened for them. The noble townswoman came out with her maidens all dressed so splendidly [. . .]. (102) [. . .] in a fine silk. When she saw the warriors, she gave them a very fine greeting. Now, hear how she spoke: "Now, I never saw exiles wear such noble clothes. (103) He was a mighty king who exiled you. He could [. . .] ruined you, if you had remained with him. You subjugated all German kingdoms to his possession." (104) Horant said: "Dear lady, it came about because of our own responsibility. The king of German lands [. . .] us [. . .]. We did not want to be [. . .] him. For that reason we had [. . .] this [. . .]." (105) She took him by the hand and led him into the courtyard. There bold Horant [. . .] a beautiful linden tree [. . .] marvelously. Its branches

were of rich gold. (106) At the top of the linden tree small birds sang. They sang so beautifully; their feathers were resplendent. Whoever heard the birds' sweet song, he had to give up his grief. (107) Underneath was a magnificent chair of radiant crystal and of rich gold. There had never been such a noble man that he might honorably sit there.

(108) The landlady then led him into a beautiful hall that was everywhere ornamented with gold and lapis lazuli and sheathed in marble of various colors. (109) The hall had three hundred windows that were all of crystal, so beautifully made; they gave radiant light. [. . .] as if there had been a mirror there; the light was just like the sun. (110) The stone floor was made of marble, greener than grass, as clear as the glass of a mirror in which fish seemed to swim, as if they were alive. (111) That hall was fashioned with such wondrous cleverness. It was everywhere vaulted on marble columns. I [. . .] never entered such a praiseworthy hall.

(112) [. . .] in the house a [. . .] fountain sprang forth, piped into a rich golden pillar and running through golden pipes that could never be more beautiful. (113) The fountain was constructed with such wonderful art. The fountain was never simply drained: as the water flowed out of the house, it was caught by another pipe. (114) As the water left the house, another pipe caught it, so that that same fountain flowed into the kitchen, and ran very quickly into the townsman's chamber, (115) and out of the chamber into a very splendid orchard, piped into four marble pillars, richly worked with gold. They were full at all times.

(116) Then the townsman said: "Horant, my dear lord, here you and your comrades are to be lodged with great honor. Whatever you need or wish to have, you should just let me know." (117) Bold Horant then said: "We lack nothing. Command the very poor people to come to us. I want to give them rich gifts. Then they can also live joyously." (118) Then it was ordered that it be proclaimed throughout the city: "whoever, for the sake of God or honor, [. . .] goods, should go to the exiles. A bold warrior has come; he wishes to take care of the poor."

(119) Now hear of the great splendor of bold Horant. He ordered all his saddle-horses to be shod with golden horseshoes and fastened with a single nail, so that they would quickly fall off, (120) so that the poor people and travelling folk could gather them up. Horant and his comrades thus left their lodgings. They let the giants lead the way. That was cleverly done. (121) Then the townsman said to bold Horant: "If you are exiles, you should abandon your sadness. It would befit you, noble warrior, for all German lands to serve you."

(122) The praiseworthy heroes lodged in the inn for twenty-eight days until Pentecost eve arrived. Then Hagene the Savage sent out a summons; a great many noble warriors came to him (123) from afar in Greece to his festival. He also ordered [. . .] fine seating set up far and wide. He wanted to put his sovereignty on display for both men and women. (124) He also wanted to put on display his praiseworthy daughter, who had no peer anywhere in the world. He wanted to display her to the people, so that they would have to admit the truth. (125) To that very place in Greece came many a [. . .]. Hagene the Savage welcomed them with very fine praise. Twelve fine kings came to him with golden crowns. (126) He wanted to show them his worthy daughter, whose peer was not to be found anywhere in the world.

Now when Pentecost had come, and the queen was to go to prayers,[17] (127) the streets were spread with many a rich silk cloth, worked so beautifully with praiseworthy gold. Both men and women packed the street, when the king was to go to church. (128) Loud music was heard from many minstrels. One could hear the music for more than a mile. The wide streets became crowded with such great throngs. (129) The queen was dressed in rich velvet. It was green in color, with gold and worthy jewels. The very beautiful queen wore a golden crown. (130) Then the townsman said: "Horant, dear my lord, do you not wish to see the noble queen. You will never see a maiden so marvelous. She is like the radiant sun." (131) "Yes, I would very much like to see the beautiful maiden."

Horant and all his knights dressed quickly. Horant [. . .]; he was resplendent with gold, like the sun. (132) And his brother Morunk also was [. . .]. [. . .] such young lords were alike. And Wate of the Greeks donned a cuirass that was very splendid. (133) It was of red gold; his helmet was the same. At the top of his helmet was a marvelous serpent. It was well studded with gold. He could wear it with honor. (134) Witolt with the Staff armed himself immediately. He very quickly equipped himself with his steel garment. [His] brother Asprion did likewise—they all armed themselves. (135) Witolt the Ogre took his steel staff; with a great leap he landed in front of Horant. He said: "My brother Asprion and I want to go out in the streets today (136) and want to have a contest that you, my lord, should venture to allow: I want to slay a great many of the Greeks with my staff, so that many a one will curse the day that ever he laid eyes on me." (137) Then bold Horant laughed heartily. "By no means, warrior Witolt! You are to leave off your fighting, and stand in courtly manner before the noble queen." (138) Horant and his brother were ordered to lead the way, thereafter Wate of the Greeks, and Witolt and Asprion, thereafter two hundred splendid knights, altogether and alike.

(139) And when the [. . .] came [. . .] the streets [. . .] there stood many a man [. . .] they saw the lords [. . .]. They said: "He strides so splendidly. He may well be a noble lord." (140) Then a duke and his men also pressed forward. He was a young lord and also wore rich clothing. He led a fine company who must also have been his men. (141) Witolt the Ogre began to get very angry: "Because, Sir Horant, you order me to be remain calm—not at all am I able to be at peace before this great company." (142) The bold duke very forcefully made his way in front of Horant. Witolt the Ogre gave him a great swat: he flung him over ten thousand men before he ever came back to earth. (143) His comrades at court crowded in forcefully, without [. . .] a splendid company. They wanted to defeat the mighty giant. In that regard, things could only turn out quite badly for them. (144) Witolt the Ogre took his steel staff: he wanted to lay into them with a great blow. Then the bold warrior, Horant, said: "No, Witolt, we want to remain peaceable." (145) An elderly count stood there; he was a wise man. He said: "We have to let these lads do as they wish. They are the comrades of the evil Devil from Hell!"

(146) Meanwhile now [. . .] began [. . .] him/them [. . .] the noble queen [. . .] heard a fine assembly. Three hundred lovely maidens walked ahead of the lovely, praiseworthy queen. (147) Beside the queen stood two noble kings. They were richly attired in matching clothing. Each wore baldachin[18] than which there could never be any better. (148) Each carried in his hand a staff of red gold on which perched two peacocks that shone radiantly. They had fanned their tails and held them over the maiden. (149) They shaded her while she was walking. They stood just as if they were alive above the lovely queen. After the beautiful maiden, Hilde, came her father, Hagene the Savage. (150) After Hagene the Savage marched ten noble kings who were richly attired in matching clothing. It was all of baldachin than which there could never be any more beautiful.

(151) When Hagene the Savage saw the three giants, Hagene the Savage said to the queen: "[. . .] dreadful men who could well defeat an entire army." (152) When the young queen came quite close to Horant, she looked him in the face and gave him a friendly glance. She bowed in courtly manner to Horant, the noble lord. (153) She thought to herself: "My God, who is this man? He strides so properly and is so handsome and has such a splendid bearing, he may well be a noble lord."

(154) Then she went to church. When the service had finished, the young queen was seen going to her lodgings. Horant stood there with his men. The queen again looked at him. (155) She greeted him with her eyes and gave him

a friendly glance. She bowed in a courtly manner to young Horant. She then went to her lodgings.

Horant was pleased with the greeting. (156) Bold Horant then went to stand under the linden tree. He addressed Lord Wate, Witolt, and his brother in a courtly manner: "How do you like the young queen?" (157) Bold Wate then said: "[. . .] certainly have [. . .], or I will [. . .] slay them all." [. . .] his brother. "I never saw such a beautiful maiden. (158) Before I leave behind that marvelously beautiful lady, I would lose my life to the Greeks. May my steel staff break—if that would win us the maiden." (159) Bold Horant then said: "You are to leave off your fighting. I can win the lovely maiden much better: with my sweet voice I will bring the maiden to us."

(160) He began to sing in such a clear voice that it resounded up through the clouds and halted little birds in their flight— (161) they all began to rush to the linden tree, so eagerly did they listen to bold Horant sing—and the wild boars had to give up their rooting around in the ground.

(162) Now the young queen had gone up to the battlement. She listened so happily to the song; it seemed so lovely to her. She quietly listened for a long time to the sweet song. (163) And when the song so sweetly before [. . .] had ended, then the queen said to the worthy daughter of a duke: "Now, I have never heard better singing, nor a voice sound so sweet. (164) You are to go for my sake to the linden tree and tell the lord for me [. . .] has sung there the sweet song, I would very much like to see him, if it could be done with propriety. (165) [. . .] the bold warrior [. . .] thousand marks of red gold would [. . .] beautiful maiden who would be his bed companion."

(166) The maiden [. . .] beautiful very quickly won. She came and stood in courtly manner before the lords. She greeted them quite handsomely, the noble and lovely maiden. (167) She said in courtly manner: "Who will show me the man who so marvelously sang the sweet song? My lady, the maiden, would like to see him, if it could be done with propriety." (168) Then Duke Morunk said in courtly manner: "Now behold, [. . .] maiden, this young lord, who sang so beautifully." Thus spoke the noble lord. (169) [. . .] bold warrior, if you should want to go to the chamber of my lady, you would have ten thousand marks of red gold as a reward. You would also have a beautiful maiden tonight who would be your bed companion."

(170) Then Horant answered her in courtly manner: "Most [. . .] I would not go a single step for the sake of her gold, for if your lady wishes to hear singing, she must take a walk and come to the linden tree. (171) You say that you were sent by a beautiful maiden whom I am to have as a bed companion tonight. When [. . .] I gladly here [. . .] myself a beautiful lady whom [. . .]

as my own life." (172) [. . .] said the lovely maiden: " [. . .] queen here to the linden tree [. . .] what I good [. . .] through the [. . .]."

(173) The very beautiful maiden very quickly [. . .]. She came in courtly manner before the young queen [. . .] said: "Noble queen, you must [. . .] the words [. . .]. (174) The very handsome lord who sang so marvelously would not go a single step for the sake of your gold. He is the most splendidly courtly man who has ever won the name of lord. (175) I also offered him a beautiful maiden as reward, who would certainly be his bed companion. He said that he himself has a beautiful lady who is as dear to him as his own life. (176) If you wish to hear singing, noble and lovely maiden, then you will yourself surely have to go to the linden tree. There you will find the young knight who sang so well."

(177) "Before I do without his song," said the lovely maiden, "I would surely rather go to [. . .]. She [. . .] a maiden by the hand [. . .] linden tree that she there [. . .]. (178) [. . .] he came to [. . .] he said [. . .] a [. . .] (179) [. . .] "Morunk, my dear brother, [. . .] not [. . .] the young queen." Then the marvelously bold man said: "There [. . .] should we already go." (180) He embraced [. . .] the beautiful maiden. "May God welcome you, very noble queen of the Greeks. Tell me, lovely maiden, why you have come here." (181) She said: "[. . .] song so sweet, which I heard clearly. I came here to the linden tree for the sake of entertainment." He said: "Noble queen, my song is to be [. . .] for you."

(182) He seated the queen beside the linden's trunk; he knelt down in courtly manner before the praiseworthy maiden. He began to sing beautifully, a [. . .] voice that sounded so sweet. (183) Then the wild birds flew to the linden. Their marvelous plumage made praiseworthy shade, and the wild boars had to stop their rooting around in the ground, (184) and they all began to rush to the linden [. . .] animals came from the forest and listened to the singing. The queen [. . .] so that the animal there [. . .] (185) [. . .] surely [. . .] noble [. . .] lord was. (186) "I would like the [. . .] quickly done [. . .] I would [. . .] that [. . .] the young [. . .]."

(187) "Now may God in Heaven reward you, most noble [. . .] I have no need of your property, most noble queen. I myself have so much property [. . .] I wish to redeem you." (188) Then [. . .] hands a gold ring [" . . .] bold, that is to be your own. I will tell you marvels of the stone's power. You [. . .] thus gladly wear. (189) [. . .] to/from his hand my [. . .] by no weapon [. . .] lord, you must from me [. . .] be done."

(190) "Now may [. . .] reward you, beautiful maiden. Now you are [. . .] may it be concealed [. . .] you were firmly [. . .] (191) [. . .] I was [. . .]

sent. A noble king did that, whom all German lands serve. He is the most handsome of men who ever won the name of king. (192) While I may have sung well, most noble queen, that cannot equal my dear lord. He sings much better than I did and is [. . .] a generous man. (193) If you wish [. . .] to leave here, most noble queen, you will be crowned in all the German lands. There you will wear the imperial crown over twelve very fine kings."

(194) Then the beautiful maiden said: "Dear my lord, I would like to be [. . .] to you yourself. That I would do [. . .] right away. With you I would abandon my father's land." (195) He said in courtly manner: "Most noble queen, I am not a proper husband for you. Indeed I could be your bondsman. Moreover, I have the most beautiful lady, whom I love as my own life. (196) And if you take my lord [. . .] I [. . .] your servant [. . .] then I will [. . .] at all times at your [. . .] go, and I will sing for you, lady [. . .]." (197) [. . .] queen: "I will very happily do all that you wish. I will grant your requests; I cannot do without your sweet singing." (198) Then the lovely maiden in courtly manner said: "All [. . .] my father's time [. . .]. Then I will leave here with you, may God protect you! (199) Now grant me leave [. . .] dear lord. Now I must leave you. I certainly will do what I have promised: either I will come back here to you, or death will lay me down."

(200) He took her, the lovely queen, in his arms and embraced her. Then she went in courtly manner back to her chamber. Horant was very pleased that his time had been successful. (201) They went to the assemblage. There was a great deal of noise: tabors and pipes were heard everywhere, as were fiddles and many trombones. The music played by many hands was to be heard there.

(202) The bold warrior Horant went to stand before the great giants. He said: "We must surely go to the king's festival. There well [. . .] noble maidens." (203) [. . .] Horant and his men. He [. . .] a golden crown on his head [. . .] and Morunk, his dear brother. Their clothing was resplendent in the light. (204) In his bright cuirass, Wate of the Greeks was also quite ready. That was a stately hero. He was marvelously adorned; his surcoat was noble. (205) A deep green velvet was his surcoat, the best that one could find in the kingdom of Morocco. There were golden lions on it. He seemed an angel and not a man. (206) Witolt with the Staff armed himself right away. He readied himself worthily in a [. . .] garment. Thus also did his brother Asprion, in a praiseworthy cuirass. (207) [. . .] then, very quickly [. . .] the very marvelous saddle-horses. They were bespread with many a rich silk covering; their trappings were gold, than which there could be none better.

(208) Now hear of the great splendor of bold Horant. He ordered all the saddle-horses to be shod with golden horseshoes, fastened with a single nail,

so that they would quickly fall off, (209) so that the poor people and travelling folk could gather them up. Horant and his warriors departed from the inn. They let the giants lead the way [. . .]. One [. . .]. (210) They [. . .] the streets [. . .] before the [. . .] before the dreadful giants. (211) Thereafter rode Horant and his brother Morunk, then came the young knights, a fine company. They rode off through the city; they led many a fine man.

(212) Witolt with the Staff walked there, holding his steel staff in both hands. He thrust it into the earth twelve fathoms deep. In addition, with what great leaps he there vaulted! (213) He drew it out of the earth and tossed it high in the air and caught it in one hand as it came back down. He swung it around his head as if it were a small stick. (214) His brother Asprion saw two [. . .] stones standing in front of him which he took up with both hands. He ground [. . .] them together, [. . .] the bold man, so that a strong flame spurted forth.

(215) Then both men and women fled the streets. They thought they were going to lose their lives to the giants. Horant the excellent man [. . .] ordered them [. . .] (216) They came [. . .] assemblage; there was a [. . .]. There were welcomed with great honor [. . .] stewards came forth [. . .] good well [. . .]. (217) There sat [. . .] down [. . .] the stewards [. . .] they brought [. . .] silk, than which there could be none better. (218) [. . .] Horant [. . .] when the [. . .] became [. . .] very [. . .] still higher [. . .] must. (219) Witolt and his brother and the noble Lord Wate sat down among the assemblage [. . .] a [. . .] secretly [. . .]. not to go before her. They thought the dear [. . .] (220) Food was served to them [. . .] meat of both wild game and domestic stock. One [. . .]. They were served very good wine. His [. . .] was all of red gold.

(221) [. . .] a dreadful lion, which, for the sake of entertainment, he let [. . .] go through the assemblage. It went before the table of the giants and took a loaf of bread from the table. (222) Witolt began to get angry. He gave the lion a blow on the head with his fist, so that the lion lay dead before him, and then he tossed the lion into the assemblage. Ladies and gentlemen fled. (223) Its master came to where he saw the lion was dead. He wept pitifully. Now hear what he said: "Can anyone tell me, who killed the lion?" (224) All of them alike said: "Now leave off your [. . .]. The giant with the staff killed it." He began [. . .] dear before [. . .] (225) [. . .] stand before Witolt. He said: "Dear my lord, what did the lion do to you?" He said: "It caused me great distress. The lion took my bread from me here." (226) The master began to upbraid him: "You killed it ignominiously. The Devil from Hell brought you here." Witolt said: "Stop your babbling, or the same will happen to you!"

(227) He quickly fled from him and feared his anger. He thought his life [. . .] immediately [. . .] He fled swiftly to the most noble king. (228) When King Hagene caught sight of him in front of him, he immediately began to ask: "What has happened to you?" "My lord, I can tell you a marvel: the lion has been killed! (229) The giant with the staff struck him dead. The Devil from Hell brought him here. If I had not myself come here so quickly, he would also have taken my life." (230) The bold Hagene said: "We must let them do as they wish. They are of the Devil's household. I know that without [. . .]. The Devil brought them here. The damage [. . .]."

(231) [. . .] they there had [. . .] everywhere [. . .] and all kinds of string music [. . .] (232) [. . .] saw [. . .] One could see someone toss a stone very far [. . .] his [. . .] These ran; those leapt; these danced; those sang. (233) Many a knight and many a noble youth armed themselves. Whoever wished to joust came to the ring. There, in front of the noble maidens, one could see marvels.

(234) When bold Horant was watching the knightly deeds, the noble lord said to his brother Morunk: "I do not wish to wait any longer. I will [. . .]." (235) He mounted very quickly and [. . .] He rode swiftly to the inn. He armed himself meticulously in a white cuirass. (236) He fastened a helmet of red gold on his head, set with both sapphires and jacinth-stones. It was well ornamented and finely constructed. (237) On top of the helmet was an eagle of red gold that spread its wings and was resplendent in the light. Horant fastened it on his head, [. . .] the hand.

(238) [. . .] the assemblage [. . .] before the maiden [. . .] in courtly manner [. . .] maiden [. . .] (239) [. . .] there [. . .] lord [. . .] he [. . .] youth. He came riding to the ring. (240) He was [. . .] prepared; his weaponry was most noble. Weaponry [. . .] they were both equal [. . .]. from gold it quite glowed. A [. . .] so [. . .] (241) He led on his [. . .] warrior. He rode [. . .]. "[. . .] you should my [. . .] a joust before the noble queen."

(242–50)[19] [. . .] dear lord [. . .] very gladly I [. . .] defended [. . .] must to me [. . .] that a heart [. . .] I will [. . .] defeat you in [. . .] lovely [. . .] a fine war-horse [. . .] so very marvelously [. . .] there [. . .] that [. . .] would [. . .] that was a [. . .] who mine [. . .] that [. . .] in the [. . .] who [. . .] there [. . .] very many a noble [. . .] man. He rides before the [. . .] what [. . .] the [. . .] he over a very [. . .] hero go and [. . .] allowed [. . .] under [. . .] a [. . .] such [. . .] mighty [. . .] said to [. . .] with his [. . .] he [. . .] so that the lord [. . .] self [. . .] many [. . .] there

(251) [. . .] quickly to a poor minstrel. He said: "Take the war-horse and the trappings of red gold, for the sake of the young queen." (252) The poor minstrel then began to rejoice greatly. He said: "Now, may God reward you,

dear my lord. You have treated me well [. . .]. As far as I know, I have no peer anywhere else: I was poor before, but now I am rich." (253) He sat his war-horse so handsomely; he joyfully rode before the young queen and many a merry lady. He thanked them all alike for the most rich gift.

(254) Then he rode most handsomely before Hagene, the noble king. He said: "My very dear lord, these praiseworthy gifts were given to me by a noble hero. May God grant him long life with honor." (255) The king began to look at the most marvelous war-horse, and also the fine caparison and the trappings of noble gold. He said: "Now, I would very much like to see this man who can give such noble gifts. (256) Now, ride, for my sake, to the generous man and ask him for the sake of his chivalrous courtesy that he might come to me. I certainly wish to thank him for these most lavish gifts."

(257) The minstrel rode very quickly to the good hero. He said in courtly manner: "Noble-hearted warrior, you are to go to the [. . .] king. He very much wants to give you a fine welcome. (258) He also wishes to thank you for the noble gifts. [. . .] my lords. He [. . .] could never be better."

(259) He pulled an ermine [. . .] cloak around himself. He took all his knights [. . .] he went in stately manner before the king. He went through the assemblage; many a noble man followed him. (260) He went before the mighty king and his fine company. He received him most courteously and welcomed him. He said: "Welcome Horant of Denmark; you have a most generous hand. (261) May mighty God in Heaven grant you, sir, a long life. You can give such generous and noble gifts. It would be fitting, noble warrior, for all German lands to serve you. (262) If you need anything of my property or anything that I have, that will all certainly be done. [. . .] share all my kingdom with you." (263) [. . .] generous Horant bowed in courtly manner to him. He said: "Noble and mighty king, we have come to your land and have been driven out of German lands and have retained little of our property." (264) He said: "Noble and exalted King, I have heard much about you. I have come to the Greeks because of you, and my comrades and I would gladly become your vassals."

(265) Hagene, the noble king, embraced him cordially. "You offer me your service, worthy warrior. If you wish to remain in my lands, you are to be [. . .] lords." (266) The lords [. . .] one [. . .] in [. . .]

(267) "I do indeed wonder, who might the lord be, who would drive you and your comrades into exile." Horant answered him about that: "He is named King Itene. Where I lead one warrior, he leads a thousand men and twelve great giants. No one can triumph over him. He is himself the most stalwart of men who ever won the name of lord." Then Hagene the Savage

said: "Dear my lord, you and your comrades are to become my courtiers for as long as you desire it and seek out my court here."

(268) Horant and his men bowed in courtly manner to him. "Now, may God in Heaven reward you! You have treated us well. May mighty God keep you! We must go to the inn. (269) We will come back here tomorrow to your festival. We wish at all times to be your courtiers."

He took leave of the king; then he walked across the courtyard. (270) He went to his lodgings under the marvelous linden tree. There he dwelt in great joy until Pentecost eve arrived. The warrior went to the hall; it was furnished everywhere (271) [. . .] with candles all [. . .] the [. . .] marvelously [. . .]. The stone floor [. . .] with many a rich silk cloth, and [. . .] than which there could never be better.

(272–end)[20] The innkeeper's wife was [. . .] she bore [. . .] body. When she [. . .] him [. . .] my lord [. . .] queen [. . .] who [. . .] who [. . .] over [. . .] her [. . .] the [. . .] he [. . .] lord [. . .] marvelously beautiful [. . .] many [. . .] we have [. . .] -ly [. . .] that [. . .].

6

Vidvilt

ווידווילט / *Vidvilt*

Anonymous, fifteenth to sixteenth century

One of the most enduringly popular of the "secular" Yiddish epics (alongside *Bovo d'Antona*) was the single Arthurian romance adapted into Yiddish by an anonymous poet in the fifteenth or sixteenth century from Wirnt von Gravenberg's early-thirteenth-century Middle High German epic *Wigalois.*[1] Versions of the Yiddish epic—variously entitled *Vidvilt* or *Kinig Artis houf*—are extant in numerous manuscripts, printed editions (with variously revised reprints), in rhymed couplets, *ottava rima* stanzas, and prose, over the course of three and a half centuries. While there were many narratives in which Sir Gawain played a major role in the various traditions of medieval Arthurian romance, in Wirnt's poem and the Yiddish adaptation it is Gawain's son Gwigalois[2] / Vidvilt who assumes the primary role.

The earliest extant version of the Yiddish epic comprises more than forty-two hundred lines in rhymed couplets (not organized into stanzas or the quasi-stanza-like groups of couplets, as in Joseph Witzenhausen's later version), which reduces by almost two-thirds the twelve thousand verses of *Wigalois.* Irving Linn comments that the Yiddish poet displays "consummate skill in the manner in which he knew how to eliminate elaborate descriptions, long speeches and tiresome episodes, and to reduce the whole romance to a compact story full of lively incidents and uninterrupted progress."[3]

In addition to his drastic abbreviation of the narrative, the Yiddish poet undertook other major changes. As was the conventional practice, the Yiddish poet de-Christianizes the narrative to a great extent, especially with respect to the divine role in mundane affairs. In *Wigalois*, for instance, the hero immediately frees himself—by means of prayer—from a split tree trunk into which he has been wedged by a giantess; Vidvilt, on the other hand, needs three days to get free, which he accomplishes by heroic means without prayer. Later

Gwigalois prays when confronted with the sword-wheel bridge, resulting in the freezing of the water that turned the wheel, enabling him to jam the wheel and cross. Wirnt's narrator then claims that nothing is too great for God's power (6714–6919). In *Vidvilt* there is no prayer or authorial comment on divine power. Instead, the giantess is so frightened by the screech of Vidvilt's horse (which she mistakes for the dragon) that she flees at high speed across the bridge, destroying the mechanism in the process, so that Vidvilt is thereafter able simply to ride his horse rather anticlimactically across the bridge.

The *Vidvilt* poet also drastically reduces the violence of the narrative. It is only in the direst of situations that the hero kills his foes; otherwise, he defeats them and sends them as prisoners to Arthur's court (a characteristically Arthurian knightly mode of action, incidentally, the import of which the Yiddish poet obviously learned from a broader knowledge of the Arthurian repertoire).[4] Finally, the *Vidvilt* poet quite effectively eliminated the anti-Muslim bigotry ubiquitous in *Wigalois* that likewise formed a widespread characteristic of medieval and early modern Christian epic: in *Wigalois* King Lar has been driven off his land by the Muslim Roaz, who is, characteristically for Christian epic, a monstrous giant in league with Satan, to whom Roaz has surrendered his soul in a pact that gives him superhuman strength. In *Vidvilt* the giant is not a Muslim, and Satan plays no role whatsoever. The king and his land have been ravaged because he refused to grant his daughter in marriage to the giant. In this manner the *Vidvilt* poet systematically excises the entire bigoted plot motive and substitutes for it an alternative motivation for the romance's plot that indicates an extensive knowledge of Arthurian narratology.

There are three closely related sixteenth-century manuscript versions of this earliest recension of the text, all probably of northern Italian provenance;[5] Leo Landau and Linn suggest that while the Hamburg cod. hebr. 289 dates to the sixteenth century, its language may be as much as a century older.[6] These three manuscripts rather closely follow Wirnt's plot through most of the narrative (abridging the action and in general eliminating explicit Christian references), but offer a very different conclusion to the tale. Typically for the specific stylistic register developed in early Yiddish epic, the poet avoids Yiddish vocabulary from the Semitic component. The scribe identifies himself at the end of the Cambridge manuscript as "Sheftl by name, from the city of Goteyn" (Kojetein in Moravia) (fol. 84r). While all major characters are named by Wirnt (including the dragon), the *Vidvilt* poet names only Arthur, Gawain, Vidvilt, Broktin, and Lorel; all others are identified only by relationship or state of being: giant, giant's mother, king, king's daughter, and so on.

The well-known Hebrew printer Joseph b. Alexander Witzenhausen was responsible for the first printed version of the *Vidvilt* epic: איין שין מעשה פון קיניג ארטיש הוף *Eyn sheyn mayse fun Kinig Artis houf* (A Fine Tale of King Arthur's Court) (Amsterdam, 1671), which was reprinted at least a half-dozen times during the century thereafter. His text is approximately a thousand lines longer than *Vidvilt*, and the language is noticeably modernized, with much added vocabulary from the Semitic component of Yiddish. It was Witzenhausen's version that Johann Christoph Wagenseil republished in his massive and influential *Belehrung der Jüdisch-Teutschen Red- und Schreibart* (Königsberg, 1699). In the late seventeeth century, an *ottava rima* (ABABABCC) version of the *Vidvilt* epic in 580 stanzas, entitled קינג ארטש הוף / *Kinig Artis houf* (King Arthur's Court), was published in Prague by Israel ben Judah Katz (Prague, 1671 and 1679). This stanzaic form clearly links the poem with the northern Italian tradition of Yiddish epic in Elia Levita's *Bovo d'Antona* (1507, published Isny, 1542) and the anonymous *Pariz un Viene* (Verona, 1594), and in fact the stanzaic *Kinig Artis houf* was itself also probably composed in Italy. At the end of the eighteenth century, a prose version of the narrative was printed in Frankfurt an der Oder, in which Greenland, Russia, and London are mentioned, and Gawain himself journeys as far as China.

The text has not yet been provided with an adequate scholarly edition. Wagenseil merely reprinted a late version. As laudable as Landau's publication was in its time, its imprecise and inaccurate Germanizing transcriptions (without the Hebrew originals) distort the texts as much as present them. Linn's edition of the Hebrew-alphabet text, which constituted his doctoral thesis, is an admirable attempt to deal with a complex and frustrating textual tradition, but, as his introduction acknowledges, his lack of training in the field of Jewish studies severely compromised his edition, which still leaves much to be desired. Robert Warnock dedicated many years of his career to an edition of the broad tradition of the texts, but did not live to complete and publish it. More recently, Michael Wenthe has worked on editing the texts, but has apparently now left the professional field.

The earliest version of the Yiddish epic is here translated, with the Cambridge manuscript taken as the base text and the Hamburg manuscripts substituted for the pages of the Cambridge manuscript that have suffered from the probably well-intentioned but ultimately devastating attempts by nineteenth-century librarians to improve the legibility of the text by means of the application of chemical reagents (which caused the ink to eat through the parchment) and by twentieth-century librarians to prevent further deterioration of those damaged pages by means of the application of glued-on page reinforcements, which have covered some twenty pages of the text and rendered them inaccessible for as long as those appliqués remain in place.[7]

Source: Cambridge, Trinity College, F.12.44; Hamburg Staats- und Universitätsbibliothek, Cod. hebr. 255 and Cod. hebr. 289.

Edition: Irving Linn, "Widwilt, Son of Gawain" (PhD diss., New York Univ., 1942) (edition of the Cambridge manuscript: Hebrew-alphabet text, with accompanying Germanizing, Roman-alphabet transcription); Leo Landau, *Arthurian Legends; or, The Hebrew-German Rhymed Version of the Legend of King Arthur*, Teutonia, 21 (Leipzig: Avenarius, 1912) (edition of the Hamburg manuscripts in Germanizing, Roman-alphabet transcription).

Research: Zinberg, *Geshikhte*, 53–66; Erik, *Roman*, 91–142; Wulf-Otto Dreeßen, "Zur Rezeption deutscher epischer Literatur im altjiddischen: Das Beispiel 'Wigalois'-Artushof," in *Deutsche Literatur des späten Mittelalters: Hamburger Colloquium, 1973*, edited by W. Harms and L. P. Johnson (Berlin: Erich Schmidt, 1973), 116–28; Wulf-Otto Dreeßen, "Widuwilt," in *Verfasserlexikon*, col. 1006–8; Wulf-Otto Dreeßen, "Wigalois—Widuwilt. Wandlungen des Artusromans im Jiddischen," in *Westjiddisch: Mündlichkeit und Schriftlichkeit/Le Yiddish occidental: Actes du Colloque de Mulhouse*, edited by Astrid Starck (Aarau: Sauerländer, 1994), 84–98; Wulf-Otto Dreeßen, "Lilith und der Artusritter," *Jiddistik Mitteilungen* 29 (Apr. 2003): 1–9; Christoph Cormeau, "Die jiddische Tradition von Wirnts *Wigalois*," *Zeitschrift für Literaturwissenschaft und Linguistik* 8, no. 32 (1978): 28–44; Robert G. Warnock, "Wirkungsabsicht und Bearbeitungstechnik im altjiddischen 'Artushof,'" *Zeitschrift für deutsche Philologie* (Sonderheft *Jiddisch*, 1981): 98–109; Robert G. Warnock, "Frühneuzeitliche Fassungen des altjiddischen 'Artushofs,'" in *Kontroversen, alte und neue: Akten des VII, Internationalen Germanisten-Kongresses Göttingen 1985*, edited by Albrecht Schöne, vol. 5, *Auseinandersetzungen um jiddische Sprache und Literatur, Jüdische Komponenten in der deutschen Literatur—die Assimilationskontroverse*, edited by Walter Röll and Hans-Peter Bayerdorfer (Tübingen: Niemeyer, 1986), 13–19; Robert G. Warnock, "The Arthurian Tradition in Hebrew and Yiddish," in *King Arthur through the Ages*, edited by Valerie M. Lagorio and Mildred Leake Day (New York: Garland, 1990), 1:189–208; Robert G. Warnock, "Widwilt," in *The New Arthurian Encyclopedia*, edited by Norris J. Lacy et al. (Chicago and London: St. James Press, 1991), 512–13; Achim Jaeger, *Ein jüdischer Artusritter* (Tübingen: Niemeyer, 2000).

One properly praises the noble kings and princes and lords, as they expand their sovereignty. It is, however, nothing but a phantasm, for without God's aid they cannot bring it about.

Now I would like to tell you of a noble king whose peer is not to be found in the world. He was named King Arthur; he ruled over thirty-four countries. That king had great authority and a mighty company of knights, and an exceptionally beautiful wife, whose body was adorned with noble virtues. There would be much to say of her beauty, but I would like for the present to pass that over and tell you more about the king and his great might and honor. He had at his court many a noble knight and count, and a great many abbots, bishops, and prelates, and in addition a great many knights and foot-soldiers, and otherwise some four hundred or more other noble knights who at all times guarded the king's honor.

Now, such was the king's custom, when someone came riding in, that no matter what his desire, it was granted him at once. Additionally, he had nine very powerful kings subordinate to him who owed him their feudal allegiance, and when the period of radiant Pentecost came around, the nine kings all had to ride to court, each one with his troops and, in addition, with his ladies and noble knights, in honor of King Arthur, their lord. He showed them great honor with food and drink. All sadness was put aside. In truth will I tell you: the assembly at court lasted eight full days every year. On a fine, broad meadow many a splendid tent was pitched. On those grounds there were great delights: music of all kinds of stringed instruments, of drums, shawms, pipes and trumpets, cornetts, sackbuts, and other rarities. And when the eight days had passed, the king gave them leave and let them return home.

It was also a law at the court, that no one, whether knight or count—and even the king himself and the noble queen— and anyone else, whoever it might be who was at court, dared—that I tell you in truth—drink or eat until, every day, new tidings had been told. And if anyone broke this precept, he had to lose his life, no matter if he had all the property in the world to pay [in compensation]. So great then were the comings and the goings here on all sides, every day and at all times. They never delayed any longer: they heard many new tidings even before dawn.

The great authority endured for many a year. That which I tell you is true: that one day it happened that no new tidings were either heard or seen, as the day dragged on—the household was very eager to eat. That had never before happened, and no one has ever seen it since. When mid-day arrived, the people of the court were at the point of growling. The king and queen could not have been more sorrowful; the warriors were all sad. They said that they would have broken their oaths. And when evening came—that I tell you in truth—and no new tidings had been heard or seen, there was great suffering and discomfort at court, for they all had to go to bed without having eaten. No one dared to speak up against it.

When the dawn appeared, the queen delayed no longer. She went to stand on the battlements with her lovely maidens, to see if they might have the good fortune to hear or see something new. They looked far out into the land: someone was galloping toward them in courtly manner: a knight was riding very swiftly. He was the very boldest of men who had ever won the name of knight. He was well equipped with armor, as a knight properly should be. The fine jewels inlaid in his cuirass gave off a bright radiance. His steed was also well equipped with a golden caparison. The warrior bore in his hand a fine lance. He had borne it up to this point in many an assault and battle throughout the wide lands, as the book informs us. The king and all his lands could hardly have paid for the jewel that this unblemished warrior bore.

He came riding to the castle; she awaited him. When he saw the queen standing on the battlements in her noble crown, he called up to her and said: "Is it the queen standing there?" The court tutor answered him thus: "It is our gracious lady, the queen, who is here." At once he slid chivalrously from his horse and bowed nobly to the queen. "Gracious lady, my queen, may it meet with your favor, I would like to make a request, which you might grant to me for the sake of the honor of all ladies, for I have come here for your sake. Before I came to you, I had heard much of your virtue, your praise, and honor. You should therefore now permit me to make this request of you, now at this time. It will adversely affect neither your nor the exalted king's honor, life, or property. Your souls will remain uncompromised. I give you my word in pledge that what I want to give you is better than a whole country."

He drew a small belt from his body and passed it to the wondrously beautiful lady on the tip of his lance. "Wear this belt for my sake, as dear to you as all knightly virtues may be. I will wait for you right here until tomorrow morning at this time and await your answer here by this garden."

The queen there took the belt. Her heart was delighted. She said: "I will say in truth that I have never seen its like." She said: "Dear my lord, ride in to us, inside the castle, and let us commence with the gaiety before you depart from here." He said: "Distinguished lady, I have decided that I will take no rest under a roof before God grants me what I have taken into my head and before I have again returned home. I will await your answer here until tomorrow. Do not let it upset you. If you do not wish to wear the belt for my sake, I will not therefore be more hostile toward you."

The people were everywhere delighted that new tidings had come to the hall. The order was given to serve at table. Their stomachs were delighted by that! Now, when they were seated and had eaten and drunk, the queen said to the king: "My lord, go to your chamber and take along your council." How quickly did he do that. When all those who had sworn loyalty to the king had come there, then she told him the tale, about how a foreign knight had come and had requested that she wear the belt. She asked whether she should refuse or accept.

The king said: "Decide, dear my lords, whether it may be done with honor. Now begin at the beginning. I want you to understand me: my lady wants to accept the belt and need not be shamed by it. It must indeed be a magnificent lord who wants to honor my lady therewith. Why should she spurn him? On my oath, I would like to say that I have never seen a more beautiful belt." He investigated all sides of the issue, both the straightforward ones and the more complicated ones. The verdict was thus: that she was to wear it. The king was pleased by that. When the question came to the very last man, it was a worthy knight; it was one of the finest of all the warriors on whom the sun had ever shone. He was both wise and famous. His name was Sir Gawain.

The king said: "Sir Gawain, tell me, what is your counsel?" Then the highly praised man said: "Since you want my counsel, I will tell you, on the oath that I have sworn to you—and I will say it quite openly: all my senses tell me that my lady may not by any means wear the belt. As I will now tell you, it seems to me that it would be more proper for Your Grace to give gifts and not receive them. For you are thus named in all lands 'King Arthur, warrior king!' Thus would I say, furthermore: if anyone speaks better, then by all means follow his advice." The king then spoke thus: "I am pleased by your counsel and will follow your advice, abandoning it for no one's sake."

In the morning, when dawn came, the queen was told to go again and stand on the battlements, where she had left the knight, and return the belt to the knight. "That is what my king wishes." The queen again went up to the battlements with her maidens. The knight was waiting in front of them. She said: "My dear, worthy knight, take your belt, you honest man." "Yes, my gracious lady, your servant would ever be willing. Please give me your counsel, so that I may comply with it." She said: "Receive my answer—although it is not to my liking—I may not wear the belt. It disturbs me greatly in my spirit. If you have need of silver or gold, or if you would like rich payment, you will be given that in abundance. According to our law and lives, we are to give gifts and not receive them. That practice is indeed fitting and appropriate for us. As for myself, however, I would have liked to wear the lovely belt for your sake. That was prevented by a single man, as I can now tell you."

The dauntless knight then said: "In advance then do I challenge that same man who has prevented it. I say it quite in earnest and to all your knights: I am going to awaken them all. I will fight them, one after the other, for as long as I live. I will wait here. Command them to ride out at once. If they do not come out immediately—in truth you should believe me—I will carry out such things at King Arthur's court that people will still be talking about me in a hundred years."

The queen was then greatly alarmed by his words. She said: "You did not speak thus to me yesterday. You said that you would not be more hostile toward me, if I were not to take the little belt, and that it was also to be without rancor—you said that yesterday morning." The fine knight then answered her: "Toward you I will not be more hostile. It has come about through no fault of yours. That I have now clearly understood. Likewise there will now be no rancor. Nevertheless, I will fight the fine knight who gave the counsel, even if it were to cost me my life."

The queen tarried no longer; to the king she then strode and told him the news—how angry the knight was. "Another time one follows a single man and leaves aside all the others." The king sent for all his warriors. He said: "I admonish and exhort you on your loyal hands that you preserve my honor in this situation. It cannot be delayed any longer. I clearly understand from the knight's tale that he has come here in order to dishonor us all. Now, quickly fend that off. Then I will share with you that which I have, as I have done in the past."

Then all the warriors answered him with a great shout: "My lord, if you had followed our counsel, you would not have had this trouble. We cannot get out of the castle without a fight. Whoever has taken refuge inside is now turned out."

Sir Gawain then said: "My dear and gracious lord, I understand these words well: it is all done because of me. For God's sake I wish to fend it off, even if I were to suffer death. I wish at all times to give you my best counsel according to my understanding and wish to serve you steadfastly at all times and also to preserve your honor, and will spare no pains. Order my spurs and my sword given to me, and order my good horse saddled."

The young man then armed himself; he put on his good armor. Without using the stirrups, he sprang into the saddle. The king then expressed his gratitude to him and said: "Now, may God stand by you, you bold man, so that you defeat the knight. I will share with you, you dauntless warrior, all that I have. That is a promise." "My lord, I will preserve your honor today, which all the people ought to see. Quickly will I defeat him, even if he is four times my size."

Sir Gawain galloped out of the castle. Then all the people at once went to stand everywhere on all the battlements and watched what was to happen. Many a sweet blessing was said for him there by many a beautiful maiden and by the people everywhere and by the people who stayed in the hall.

Sir Gawain came riding out of the castle. The other one was waiting for him, and when Sir Gawain looked at him, you may now hear what he said to him: "May God welcome you, O knight from foreign lands. Who summoned you that you wish to dishonor my lord and all of his warriors, as well? In truth your great arrogance will never do you any good. I will take vengeance on you for my lord and all his men, even if it should endanger my life. You have arrogantly ridden into his lands in quite an aggressive manner."

The knight from foreign lands said: "My strokes are unknown to you. If you were to know my manly courage, you would be better off to avoid battle with me. I have never experienced greater disgrace than has happened to me here. On that I swear a firm oath. Now I will fight you; I issue the challenge to you!"

Sir Gawain took his lance in hand. He quickly bound on his helmet on which there was a golden wheel. The foreign knight charged toward him, and they came together like two blazing falcons. They struck each other with their lances so hard that they could not last any longer: they at once shattered right up to the grips, so that the pieces lay all over the ground. They did not then hesitate but reached to their sides and drew their sharp swords and spurred their horses. The two murderously grim men charged at one another. Then they struck each other many deep wounds. One could hear their strokes resound more than a mile away. Their strokes were so mighty that the king grew alarmed. No need to waste words: the foreign knight did great injury to Sir Gawain—that I tell you in truth. He struck him down onto the grass. He had to surrender to him, or it would have cost him his life. He said: "Wait here for me. I will ride to the king and queen and take my leave of them. Then we will ride away together." He rode to the king. Now, hear what he said to him: "King Arthur, I have defeated you and have taken captive the worthiest of all the men who were at your court. Indeed he may not survive, because of the disgrace to which I was subjected. Farewell, good king and queen. I am taking Sir [Gawain] away."

The king and the queen began to weep hot tears; and all the warriors were weeping. "Alas, dear knight, let him live. I will give you half of my kingdom."

He said: "What is your kingdom to me? I have more land than four such as you. I have decided that he must go away with me."

The knight was eager to ride. Sir Gawain rode after him. They rode through many huge fields, where no street ever led. Neither of them ever took shelter in any city, nor did either rest under any roof. The two heroes then rode on quickly for four entire weeks. During the fifth week—in truth I tell you that—they came to one of the most beautiful cities on which the sun had ever shone. They began to ride through it. They found many fine cities and castles near one another. Sir Gawain then said in a courtly manner: "Now, I have ridden through many a land. I want to say, on my oath, that I have never seen a more beautiful land. If it is a kingdom, then nowhere is to be found the peer of the one who rules this land." Then at that same time he saw there before them the most beautiful city that could be found anywhere in the world. Rising above it was the most splendid building which any person had ever entered. The roof on the castle was made of the finest gold; the bosses were all of red garnet. Never was the night so dark but that one could see their radiance from thirty miles away. They began to make haste toward the castle. Beside the castle the bold heroes relaxed on a green lawn.

The knight said to Sir Gawain: "Look around in the beautiful chamber that is here before us." "Tell me now, at this time, who might be the lord of the castle?" "I am, dear my lord"—so said that same bold man. [Gawain said:] "I have never seen a more beautiful land."

"Sir Gawain, do not despair, I will tell you the honest truth: the lands that you have seen, and additionally the many beautiful cities, they are all my own alone. I will show you still more beautiful lands, which are all my patrimony. Now, I will tell you something else, O noble knight, I declare you free from your imprisonment. But first I would like now to discuss something with you. Now I will tell you, you bold man, that I have, unfortunately, no heir, except for a daughter, who is a beautiful maiden—may that be said to you in truth— the most beautiful who has been born here. She is sixteen years old. I know that you are a bold man. When you see her, you will grow pale, and your strength will increase—because of her great beauty, which God has granted her. For she is with respect to appearance as beautiful as the radiant sun. Since it is not God's will that I have a son, then I will indeed be a loyal father to my dear daughter and will give her in marriage to a man who is a worthy warrior and a mighty hero and a distinguished warrior. Much has been said to me of your manliness, although I did not expect much of it until I arrived at King Arthur's court and saw you there. Then I vowed to the Lord God that I would not return home unless I also brought that lord home with me. Now I will tell you more: you have not seen the half of my lands, for I have many a fine city. I want to show you my daughter, whom I will give you for your own. I will make my kingdom and that which I have subject to you because of your great manliness. And I will not like you the less, if my daughter does not well please you—you may be without any obligation to her. You are to be released from your oath. I will accompany you back to your lord."

Sir Gawain said: "Dear my lord, what is the point of this jest? You will find another husband for your daughter, as I can well understand. Since you are such a lord here that your peer is not to be found in any land far and wide, and since your daughter—so worthy of love—is such a beautiful maiden, as you have told me, who might then be her equal in all the German kingdoms?" The bold man then answered him: "You courageous man, you should believe me that I am not jesting with you, and if it is God's will that you are to take my daughter, then I will certainly be true to you, for the sake of your great manliness. So, come on and get ready!"

Then they rode at once to the castle. The guard announced to the people that their lord was coming. The lords made great haste and rode out to meet him with rejoicing, all the princes and the lords, and welcomed them with great honor—the guest and their dear lord. When they came to the castle, they received the lords well and at once took off their armor and clothed them in silk robes. And when that had all been done, he said: "Now, come, you must see my daughter." Thus spoke the noble lord. He led him courteously by the hand into a small chamber in which the princess sat with her mother. There had scarcely ever been such delight on earth—of the gold and jewels that were in that small chamber I do not wish to say anything more.

The guest and the lord, too, went into the small chamber, where they were both quite well received. The princess delayed no longer: she embraced her father and pressed him to her breast and embraced him and kissed him, too. The comely queen also gave Sir Gawain a fine welcome. As soon as he looked at her, he was so stupefied that he could not speak to her. He went completely pale because of the maiden so worthy of love. The lord called to him: "Are you not a bold man? What has happened to you that you cannot speak? And you have grown so pale? She is indeed lovely. Why have you grown pale before such a distinguished maiden?" Then he came to himself and said: "I've never seen anything more beautiful! Everything that you said—it is certainly all true!"

The king did not wish to delay any longer. He seated him next to his daughter. No man had ever had it better: he forgot all of his suffering.

They served him enough of everything that the world had ever borne. Then the mighty king said to his very courtly guest: "You dauntless hero, it is now all up to you. Tell me whether my daughter well pleases you and whether you desire her, O undaunted warrior." Sir Gawain then said: "Dear and gracious my lord, I well see that it was no jest, although I have—for God's sake—not deserved it, and since you want me, how could I renounce the beautiful maiden?" The king said to Sir Gawain immediately after the handshake: "Now I will make subject to you lands and people and all that I have."

Then he sent envoys everywhere and had proclaimed with great rejoicing: "The king wishes to give his daughter in marriage to a man. Whoever wants food and drink and high living—it is to last for four full weeks." Quickly everyone from all the lands came there. The book tells us that there was much entertainment there—more than I want to say—of sword-fighting and jousting, dancing and chivalric entertainment. There was no one on the field who had done better than Sir Gawain, the warrior, to whom the prize was given.

And when the wedding festivities had come to an end, the king summoned before him all his knights and his servants. He said: "Listen to what I will tell you—that you are all to vow and swear allegiance to my son-in-law, the young lord, so that after my death he is to be lord of all my lands, and everything that I have I also make subject to him. I swear it here on my sword that he is well worthy of the honor." Then they answered all together with a great shout: "My dear and gracious lord: that which you wish, that will be done. Since he is honorable and dauntless and pleases you so well, then we would gladly have this stately man as our king." All of them swore to that effect. He was then delighted; he had then become king there.

How could he have had it better than when he dwelt with the queen? And when he had been with her for half a year— that I tell you in truth—and cultivated great honor with her, he was lying with her once, and his thoughts went back and forth about how it was not right for him not to be able to know what his lords—who dwelt so far away from him—were doing and not to be able to tell them the tale of what had happened to him. He made a firm decision: "Where I stay one night I will not stay a second night until I come to King Arthur's land and I can myself tell him of my jolly life." He there swore a firm oath.

In the morning, when dawn came, he then told the young queen. The noble queen then said: "No, dear and gracious my lord, do not imagine that you could get there, for it is too far—that I tell you in truth—so that even if you were to ride for ten entire years in a row in that direction, you could still not get there. That I learned from my father." Her husband said: "It cannot be otherwise." She said: "Dear my lord, do not ride there. Wait and hear my plea. That which I will ask of you will be of great aid to you. I am telling you, dear my lord, that I am carrying your child. It is a son—that you should not doubt. You must tell me what his name is to be." He said: "Call him whatever-you-want [*vi-du-vilt*]." The amiable queen took precise note of that.

In the morning, when dawn came, he rode away and told no one. And thereafter he came to regret that he did not wait for her counsel and that he did not go to her and hear her plea. When she learned that he had gone away, her eyes became wet with misery. She suffered so much misery that it was beyond measure and without an end.

Now let us leave that to be as it may and tell what was happening to Sir Gawain. He rode through many a kingdom and through many a noble city. He could find no one who had heard of King Arthur. When seven years had passed, then he came indeed to King Arthur's land. When he arrived at the castle, and the watchman saw him, he at once shouted into the castle and announced to the people. He said: "Let me give you new tidings: Sir Gawain is riding this way. I recognize him from the golden wheel on his helmet. God must grant him welcome." The king said: "Is it true? I will indeed give you a good messenger's reward." Then the lords all got ready and rode out to meet him with great rejoicing and welcomed that same lord, doing everything with great honor.

Then he told them the tale of what had happened to him. They were then all delighted that he had become a king there, and they treated that same lord with great honor. And when he had been there for four weeks—that I tell you in truth—he went before the king in knightly manner and graciously asked for leave to depart. He said: "I have been away too long. My wife does not know whether I am dead or alive. My lord, I tell you in truth, I have been away from her for some ten years." He said: "Sir Gawain, it might be to your advantage. If you were to stay with us longer, we would first want to have some entertainment. Since your wife has waited so long, then you should first ride back home."

He took his leave from the king and queen and rode away. He rode through many a land, as the book informs us. And when he had ridden for an entire year and had fought with many a dwarf, he again came to King Arthur's land. He had seen and heard nothing of his own land. He turned around and rode many a straight and many a winding path, and when he had ridden a great distance—that I tell you in truth—he again came to King

Arthur's court. Then he thought to himself: "I will stay right here and amuse myself until a traveler comes here and tells me the news."

If you would be quiet, then I will tell you more. Meanwhile, his wife had borne a son—that I tell you in truth. He was handsome in appearance and was now in his twelfth year. He was strong and tall. His manliness was beyond measure. On a holiday the young man was to go with his retinue to relax.[8] Many a stately warrior who attended to his well-being went with him. He was well clothed in gold, as a king properly should be. When the people first saw him, they immediately said: "A more handsome man was never born. He excels all men in strength and beauty. God has granted him much." A wise man then replied: "He does not compare with his father, whom our lord brought here from a foreign land. He is a famous lord; he is a distinguished lord. His peer has never been born."

The youth heard those words very clearly. He said: "If God grants me life, I will delay no longer. I will find out the true story." When he came from his relaxation, he took his mother aside: "Tell me, my dear little mother—God bless you—whether I still have a father. Tell me who he is or where he is. Tell me right now!" Tears ran down over the bright cheeks of the beautiful maiden. She wept abundantly and said: "You remind me of my sorrow. Do not speak of it, dear child, or you will make me blind to all joys." He said: "O, my dear little mother, stop your crying and tell me what I asked you while I am standing here with you, for I wish to know. Otherwise I will do something drastic."

She said: "Since you indeed want to know, I will tell you much of your father. He is the boldest of men who ever won the name of knight. My father brought him from the land of King Arthur. His name is Sir Gawain. He rode away from me—that is true—it has been some thirteen years. If he had heeded my plea, he would have returned here long ago. Since he has, alas, not done that, then I must have lost him. I do not know if he is living or dead or otherwise in adversity." He said: "My dear mother—may God ever bless you—if you have told me the truth, then I will certainly prepare myself and will delay no longer, but will ride away. Where I am one night, I will not stay the second night until I find my dear father." His mother wept and said: "Alas, my misery and sorrow! Will you ride away from me? You know neither track nor trail, and the lands will be inconvenient for you, and therefore, if you should dare it, I fear that you will never return here, just as happened to your father, the bold lord. I would never cease lamenting for the two of you. That I will say to you in truth." He said: "Your words help not at all. I want to ride away—that I tell you in truth. It cannot be otherwise. I want to seek my dear father. I want to take the risk, even if it should cost me my life. And I would take neither silver nor gold to give up my plan. Whoever counsels me against it, I will no longer hold in my favor."

The mother delayed no longer. She strode away to her father. She said: "My dear father, let me lament my sorrow to you! I am blind to joy. My dear child wants to leave me. I cannot prevent him. He wants to seek his father and my dear lord." The king spoke thus: "These words certainly delight me: that he has such an intention— for that reason he certainly has my favor." He made a decision and ordered him to come before him. He said: "I want to inform him—at this time I want to tell him, how he is to conduct himself." He came to his grandfather and mother in a small chamber. He said: "Dear father, what do you want from me?" He said: "Dear child, Vidvilt, my dear son, what have you decided to do?" He said: "Dear father, I wish to tell you that I have heard that I have a father who is one of the boldest men on whom the sun has ever shone. Thus do I hear it said. But I have never seen him. Now I have decided that I will ride very far away. Where I am one night, I will not stay a second night until I find my dearest father."

He said: "You young warrior, may God ever protect you! I am pleased by your words that you have thus decided to seek your father. For that reason I love you dearly. You have such strength and might. Now pay attention to what I want to say to you: neither flee nor retreat from anyone, and you will by no means have any equals, for I have taught you to fight so well that you can indeed defeat a hundred warriors. Because of your great strength and courage, I am not saddened by your riding forth. I will give you my good armor—in it you will have knightly courage—and in addition a good lance and sword and one of the best horses. For I am now an old man; no longer do I think of fighting. If you wish to find your father, then you must find your way: you must ride to King Arthur's land. If he is still alive—your dear father—then you will recognize him easily: he has a golden wheel on his helmet. You will recognize him by that—and where you hear "Sir Gawain" named." He said: "My dear father, that which you command will be done."

His mother took him by the hand and led him to the end of the hall: "So, look at this little belt and gird it around your naked body. Do not take it off, whether a maiden or a lad lies beside you, and keep a shirt on over it. You must swear this to me by your troth. This belt will ever give you the strength of twelve men. You will therewith never lose courage. I will tell you more of it: in whatever city you have in mind that you would like to be, even if it were ten thousand miles away, you need not hurry there. You will get there in four weeks. On that you can truly believe me. If your father had taken it from me, he would have long ago returned here. He rode away from me secretly, for which reason I have great heartache."

He said farewell to everyone who was there and gave his horse the spurs. He was also not at all lax in his riding. No knight had ever ridden forth more splendidly. The gold and the jewels worn there by the noble warrior could not have been paid for with an entire kingdom. His horse moved forward only by bounding. The golden bells [of his horse's harness] could be heard far away, indeed at a distance of a hundred miles. He headed toward King Arthur's court. When the four weeks had come to an end, then he had arrived in King Arthur's land. When he saw King Arthur's castle, that young man was delighted.

On a great plain stood a stone of marble, as we have heard. If you would be quiet, I would tell you many wonders about this throne. No one could get closer to the throne than four ells, as we have heard, unless he had committed no sin and was a pure lad and a mighty man. There was also no man on earth who might become a king unless he had first sat on the throne. Thus was its law and its ordeal. That the throne had such great power—it was all done by means of magic.

When young Vidvilt came close enough that he could look at it, he sent his horse off to graze. He sat down there on the throne, and that was his heart's delight, for the throne pleased him quite well. When the gatekeeper saw him sitting there on the throne, now you may like to hear what he said: "I will tell you new tidings: an angel has come here, for indeed it cannot be human. He has such an inner radiance. He has sat down upon the throne. His countenance fills me with joy." When the lords all heard that, they rejoiced with a great shout. The king rode out in great honor and with many a bold lord.

The bold man sat on the throne. When he caught sight of the lords, he delayed no longer. He strode to his horse and at once bound on his helmet. He charged at the lords quite courageously and wanted to fight them all. The king at once commanded a knight to ride against him and commanded him to give him the news that they were all friends. And when the king approached him so closely that they could see each other's eyes: "May God grant you welcome, O warrior from foreign lands. Who sent you here? I say, by my crown, that I have never seen your peer. You could be a lord throughout the world. Now tell me, who are your relations."

Then Vidvilt, the mighty warrior, took up the word quite courteously: "Dear and gracious my lord, my relations are too far away from you for you to know them, even if I were to name them. I have heard much concerning your court, for which reason I have come here; and I have wanted to see your court, whatever might happened to me as a result."[9] The king said: "You noble lad, I would be delighted to have you with me and will take care of you as well as if you were my only son."

They rode into the castle. The noble queen came and welcomed the young lord with very great honor. Sir Vidvilt was at court; he forgot all his sorrow. The king sent for Sir Gawain so that he would come at once. The bold man then came and stood before the king, who spoke to him thus: "Sir Gawain, are you here? Let this young lord be given into your care— that I say to you on my oath—and instruct him in the best things, and teach him everything that you know: sword-fighting, attacking, fencing, jousting and riding." Sir Gawain said quite quickly: "Gracious my lord, that which you command me to do, I will carry out willingly—that I say to you on my oath."

He heard his father named; he recognized him by the name, so that he looked at him closely. In his heart he said: "Praise be to God Who has granted me such a father. I see clearly that it is all true what was said to me at home." Sir Gawain was a dedicated teacher, and his son was glad to have him as his master. But he told him nothing about being his son or anything else. He lay beside him every night—that I tell you in truth—and he held to what his mother had commanded him: that he never take off the belt. Day and night he wore a shirt over it. When he was learning sword-fighting, fencing and jousting, he could do it all better than four others together. Whether it was fencing or fighting, learning to write or to ride, he could do it all better than the warriors and all the lords who were at King Arthur's court, because his grandfather had taught him many years before.

Sir Gawain said to the king: "My lord, I have never seen such a person as young Vidvilt, whom I am supposed to teach. He can fence very well, as I can tell you. God has granted strength and great courage to him. He could defeat the warriors who are at court all by himself. Against him they would be like a puff of wind." The king answered him thus: "I am certainly delighted by this. I will hold this young lord in great honor." Sir Vidvilt remained there. He performed great wonders there in fencing and in combat.

Know this, that the feast of Pentecost then approached, so that the nine kings came there, each with his retinue, for that was a custom, as I said earlier. They had a great many entertainments, as I will now tell you. There was a great plain—as I have now heard—on which the entertainments took place, where they had the feasting and drinking, after which they watched the sword-fighting and jousting, and there was dancing and chivalric entertainment. The festival at court lasted a full four weeks—that I tell you at once.

And while the court was at the celebration, the king sat and feasted, and Vidvilt, the noble warrior, sat right beside him, and only thereafter came the nine kings with their great sovereignty, each according to his seniority and nobility. There was a great deal of piping and singing to be heard there, joy without measure on the grounds. Many a fine tent stood there on the field.

A maiden was there seen riding toward them from afar across the field in a bold manner on a fine palfrey, and a dwarf stood behind that beautiful maiden on her palfrey, to serve her at all times. His hand lay on her shoulder. That beautiful maiden came riding quickly. She said with her plucky spirit: "Who can direct me to the good king?" The lords answered her at once: "It is not permitted that just anyone appears before the king." She said: "I will seek him—the worthy king—myself." She galloped through the whole crowd and gave no heed to their shouts. When she came before the pavilion in which the king was sitting, how quickly did she rush inside, against the will of the people. She saw the king sitting there splendidly and with his noble crown. The beautiful maiden then said: "Dear and gracious my lord, a queen from foreign lands far, far away, has sent me here to you. She had heard much of your courtliness and might, and your great authority was made known to her: how you have many warriors and mighty men beyond counting at court, who at all times venture into combat for the sake of honor. Now she has me plead with you courteously that you lend her a man who can fight for her."

The king said: "You beautiful maiden, who may this queen be? What is her situation? Tell me!" She said: "Command the people to be quiet. Then I will tell you of great misery and the greatest slaughter of which any man has every heard, which has happened to my lady. That you will hear from my mouth. My king, who was well known and whose wife has sent me here, was one of the noblest men on whom the sun has ever shone. He was my dearest lord. May God ever have mercy on him. He has a great many lands and people and knights and servants beyond counting; he has authority over them all. Now he is, alas, dead. His entire land is burning like a lime kiln. That I tell you in truth. Cities and castles, and everything that he had, are burning—that is the result of sorcery. All his nobles and commoners— now hear what I tell you—young and old in all his land, they are all cursed and burned. My lady alone has survived, with nine others, in a single castle, named Wachsenstein. Nothing else has been left to her."

The king said: "These are strange tidings! Who is the sorcerer who could cause such a slaughter? And [what are his] powers, and what is his name?" "I should think that he is unknown to you, for his homeland is very far away from here, and his mother is a proper she-demon who has done the injury to my lord. I will tell you why she did it. My lord has a daughter—that I tell you without any jest—her peer can nowhere be found, and no man has ever seen her equal. She is in appearance purer than the sun's radiance. No painter has ever been so artful that he could paint her equal. In addition, she is wise and courteous in her proper nobility. She is famous in all lands. Her name is Lorel the Fair.

"The mighty giant became aware of her beauty; he soon sent his envoys to my dearest lord, so that he would give him the maiden in marriage. He said: 'Before I would even consider it, I would drown her, instead of giving her to a devilish man whom no son of man ever sired. She will find enough royal suitors that I will not give her to him.' That is the reason for the slaughter. His mother said: 'I will not pardon him for this!' And she cursed all his lands and burned them with sorcery, as I mentioned earlier. Gracious my lord, take pity and lend my lady a man who can defeat the mighty giant in combat, for the sorcery is in force as long as he remains alive. If he were then to be slain— that I will tell you in truth—then my lord would be delivered from his affliction, and his people, who have been burned and slain—they would all return and be healed, as if no harm had ever befallen them.

"But I offer you yet more: the lord who will take on the battle and defeat that same man and take the life of the mighty giant— my lady will give him her dearest daughter with her noble body as a lawful wife; and she will make her entire kingdom subject to him. Give me your answer."

The king said: "Beautiful maiden, dismount and drink some pure wine. I will send to my warriors and will tell them your story from beginning to end. Whoever wishes to ride with you— I will let you know that in a short while." She said: "Do that, dear my lord. I will remain on my palfrey, for God well knows that I will drink no wine and eat no meat until I return home and bring a man who will take on the task."

The king sent for a duke. He said: "Go at once through that field into the warriors' tents and tell them the whole tale for the sake of which the maiden has come here. And whoever wishes to ride with her—tell him to delay no longer, but command him to come at once to me here." The duke did not delay but strode to the warriors. He told them the whole story about why the maiden was there. The warriors all answered him with one great voice: they did not want to ride with her and fight with the devil. Since he had dealt thus with an entire kingdom, how might a single man defeat him? The duke took precise note of their words; he returned to the king. He told him all the warriors' intent. The king said: "Well do you hear, O beautiful maiden: if he were an actual human, my aid to you would be undaunted."

She said: "Now, in order to have aid, I will have to take along servant boys! It is certainly nothing but lies that are sung and told about King Arthur—none of it is true! Fie on you, King Arthur and all your warriors! All of them together would not frighten a mouse! I will spread the tale of your shame and disgrace wherever I ride in your land." The king could not speak for shame. The disgrace of which she spoke caused him pain. The maiden waited there no longer but rode away at once. No one wished to accompany her.

That vexed Vidvilt, the fine warrior. He was both grieved and angered. He said: "Nobly born king, gracious my lord, I will today preserve your honor, or I will lie dead. That I say without any jest. Is she to say of you that you have cowardice at your court? I will defeat the great giant by myself, even if I am only as tall as his legs." The king said: "Be silent, you foolish child. Against him your sword-play is nothing but a puff of wind. You have never been in combat in your entire life. Just look at the warriors: not one of them will take up the challenge. What do you wish to do, young man? I will not let you leave me, no matter what happens to me as a result."

He said: "Command my armor and my horse, my lance and my good sword be brought to me at once. I will ride after the maiden and will tarry no longer, and will pursue the maiden. No one is to stop me." In his rage he growled like a bear. He shouted: "Hand me my armor here!" The king recognized that he did not want to remain. He said: "If you are successful, I will give you rich payment." But in truth he regretted it. He felt pity for the bold young warrior.

They brought him his good armor and his spirited and frisky steed. He donned his armor at once. He was eager to follow the maiden. He said: "God in Heaven well knows that I would defeat my peer if only I had a helmet that fit me. Then I would indeed be a joyous youth." Then Sir Gawain, his dear mentor, said: "I will let you enjoy your great courage and will give you my good helmet. Wearing it, you will have exalted courage." He said: "My dear father, hand me your radiant helmet. Whether night or day, I would be honored to possess your helmet. For you are my actual father. That I tell you at this time." Sir Gawain said: "If God wishes that I be worthy of that honor, that you might be my son. . . . But it cannot be." He said: "What I say to you is true. It is almost sixteen years since you rode away from my mother. And because you did not wait to speak with her, for that reason you cannot return to that land. But she lives without any disgrace." At that time he gave him a great many signs that it was he. Sir Gawain embraced him and said: "My dear son!" At once he kissed him on the mouth. Vidvilt said: "Dear father, cease your embraces and bind your helmet on my head and let me ride after the maiden at once. For I am eager to be out of the land. I fear that she is riding away from me so quickly that I will not be able to catch up with her."

Sir Gawain then said: "My dear son, I say to you on my oath, where do you want to ride with the maiden, when you know neither track nor trail? No warrior wants to take it on. What do you wish to do, young man?" Vidvilt said: "Do not advise me against it, and let God be in control, for it cannot be otherwise: I will risk my life for the king's honor." His father pled with him there, as did everyone else who was standing at that place. He said: "It cannot be otherwise: I will live or die." Sir Gawain then said: "Wait here, my dear son, until I am prepared, so that I can be of help to you. I will ride with you and will help you fight, and I will give up my life alongside you. God will stand by us both." He said: "That is not to be. Father, I do not need your help." Sir Gawain said: "I will not let you ride alone, no matter what happens to me as a result." Vidvilt said: "By my troth, I will not let you. I will allow no one to accompany me." And king and queen and many a noble lord and many a beautiful maiden said many sweet blessings for him, so that God would protect his health and his life. He sprang into the saddle without using the stirrups, for which they expressed their thanks.

He was eager to pursue the maiden; he galloped swiftly after her. He was not able to overtake her for a long time, for she did not wish to tarry any longer. When he had caught up with her, he said to the maiden, who did not wish to wait: "O noble maiden, I wish to ride with you and fight against the mighty giant. I will rescue your friends from their affliction, even if I should lose my life." She glanced at him over her shoulder. You may now like to hear what she said to him: "I know of no one here for whom I should wait, and if you are out for a courtly ride or anything similar, I have no need of it: my intent is, regrettably, not for courtly amusements, nor for jesting or for taking a leisurely ride." He said: "O beautiful maiden, I wish to be your escort and want to attack and assault, whether against giants or dragons. I did not come here for the sake of courtly amusements. In addition, unsuitable things are abhorrent to me." She again glanced at him over her shoulder. As she looked at that young man, she said: "If I had wanted to choose such a one, I need not have been at King Arthur's court. I could have found many of them in every land. I do indeed wish to vituperate King Arthur's court. I want to spread and increase its disgrace, since he did not show me any honor. I intended that he lend me a man who was well experienced in combat. But instead he sends along behind me a babbler, a child, who—even with seeing eyes—is blind."

He said: "O maiden, I am young, that is true: I am only sixteen years old. But I hope to hold my own as well as anyone on earth could do." She, however, snapped at him bitterly. The young man was quite alarmed. He looked at her amiably. She did not wish to show him any mercy. She said: "If a person has something to do, then he should do it and not bother me with his glances!" He said: "My dear maiden, let me be your escort. I will stand by you loyally as long as I live."

She did not wish to do anything that he said, until the dwarf, who stood behind her on the palfrey, advised her: "My dear maiden, let him be our escort. He is one of the courtliest of people on whom the sun has ever shone. Who knows what he is capable of doing. He is a young and noble man." She said: "I will pay him no attention, no matter whether God has him ride here or there." His heart rejoiced that she was at least this satisfied. He rode there against her will.

They rode in great haste a distance of thirty miles without taking a rest and without entering any shelter. She spoke not a single kind word to him that he heard, and they made very great haste until they came before a great forest. She rode in front; he rode behind. They were eager to get out of the forest. They rode for eight full days. They found no path that would lead them out of the forest.

A small snow-white dog ran toward them, whose equal might not be found on earth. It had a golden collar around its neck that was worth more than an entire land. The little dog barked steadfastly at them. Vidvilt again dismounted onto the ground. He began to approach it. He wanted to catch the little dog; he wanted to give it to the maiden, so that she would cease her petulance. He thought that he would win his case if she were to accept it from him. He picked it up and handed it to her. It was abhorrent to her. He said: "O beautiful maiden, accept the little dog from me." She said: "I would like to be left in peace," and gave the little dog a shove in its haunch. "And do not again give me things that belong to other people, for it may well be avenged quickly and indeed may endanger one's life." He said: "My dear maiden, do not be concerned about that. Accept the little dog from me." She did not want to accept it before the dwarf advised it. She accepted it over her shoulder, as if it were abhorrent to her. She put it inside her cloak. Vidvilt's joy was thereby aroused.

When they had thereafter ridden a short while, scarcely a half mile, they encountered in the savage forest a great giant. He was larger than a tower. He was quite prepared to attack and fight. He bore in his hand a steel pole. The maiden began to plead. She said: "If I had been left unburdened [by someone else's property], the giant would not have encountered us on the trail. I knew well that the little dog was his. And because I followed your counsel, you evil little dwarf, we must lose our lives. Why did we not leave it behind?" Vidvilt then said to her at that time: "My dear maiden, calm yourself. Compared with him I am not so small. By myself I could defeat ten like him."

He began to charge ahead of her, so that the golden bells jingled. He rode against the giant. The giant tarried no longer. He shouted: "Stop at once, all three of you, or I will rob you of all joy." Vidvilt answered him quickly: "How do you mean that? Tell me that." He said: "How dare you be so bold, that you steal my little dog from me, which was left to me by king and emperor. Indeed the theft will be much too burdensome for you, so that even if all the world were on your side, you would have to lose your lives in recompense."

Vidvilt answered him quite courteously: "Why are you so very petulant that you wish to destroy the health of a knight and a maiden for the sake of a disgraceful dog?" The giant said: "I wish indeed to use force on you. On your guard, if you want to fight, or I will quickly let you know how my steel pole tastes." He said: "That which you desire of me, will be readily granted you. On my oath, you are properly challenged to fight for the dog and your heart's affliction."

The giant had placed his pole on the ground; he vehemently took it in hand and struck vigorously at him. And had Vidvilt not dodged the blow, well, he would not have survived. If his horse had not been extremely quick, he would have had to suffer distress: the giant would have struck him dead. The giant laid hands upon the youth; he thrust his pole two fathoms into the earth. Vidvilt began to grasp his lance in a knightly manner, and the very chivalrous man charged at him. He there stabbed the giant so that he could neither see nor hear. He nonetheless quickly came to himself. He said: "That wound will never give you an advantage over me; I did not attribute such strength to you, because I know that God has forgotten you." He raised his pole quite vigorously, and had Vidvilt not succeeded in dodging him, he would have been in serious trouble: the giant would have slain him. He struck the pole deep into the earth. Vidvilt charged at him from the other side and struck him such a blow that the blood burst forth from his chest.

Then the maiden and the dwarf, who were then suffering great agony, rejoiced. They were staying behind a tree not far away and watched as that was happening there. The giant did not delay and raised up his pole. He swung it around his head—his wound caused him pain. He said "Now your life is in danger." Meanwhile, before he again raised the pole and again struck at the young man, he [Vidvilt] had stabbed him numerous times; and he again struck at the young man. At the same time, he gave him many deep stab wounds, so that the blood flowed from him like a stream, so that the giant could neither hear nor see, and so that he began to stagger. Even so, the young man did not leave it at that and struck him a vigorous blow, so that he lay on the ground before him. He leapt from his horse right onto the ground. He said: "I will—against your will—cut off your head. You need not ask for your little dog anymore. Likewise, you will no longer harm anyone with your pole, with which you have caused distress to many whom you have slain." "No, O young and mighty man. Let me keep my life a while longer. I will surrender to you as your bondsman and will behave to you in a friendly manner: when you are in trouble, then I will help protect you from death." He said: "Your chatter does not interest me."

Then the maiden took pity on him. She said to the dwarf: "Run to the forest and plead intently with the young man to spare his life, and plead with him to do it specifically for my sake." The dwarf did not shirk but did what the maiden commanded. He ran into the forest and pled intently with the young man to spare his life. "Gladly," said the fine warrior. Vidvilt then said: "Swear that you will go to King Arthur's court and tell the tale about how I have dealt with you. And be King Arthur's prisoner there until I return to the land." He swore his loyalty to him by his hand. Then the giant rejoiced in his heart. He said to the warrior: "I will serve you loyally and honestly." He swore that to him in a full oath.

He went to King Arthur's court. Now, hear how he welcomed him: when the gatekeeper saw him striding up, he said: "These are strange tidings that have come into the land. You worthy warriors, prepare yourselves at once. I think that we have newly arrived guests, from whom we will have no profit." The warriors quickly donned their armor. Many a bold man armed himself. They rushed out of the castle and wanted to find out whose man it was who was approaching so [stealthily] that they almost did not notice him.

He said: "O my noble warriors, cease all your fighting against me, for I am a prisoner. I can tell you that in truth: Vidvilt, the young warrior, almost took my life." He told them the whole story, how he was King Arthur's prisoner and how he had been defeated. That delighted the knights and the warriors, the king and Sir Gawain, his dear father. They could not have been more delighted that Vidvilt, the young warrior, had defeated the giant. The king let the giant return to the forest, but he arranged it thus, that he know where he was, and when he had need of him, that he had to come. Now, let us leave the giant and tell what was happening to Vidvilt.

While he was receiving the oath of the giant, and when the dwarf had returned to the maiden, they rode away and did not wait for him. He sprang onto his steed, boldly and unscathed, for he was not at all wounded. He hurried after them into the forest, more than a half-mile behind them. When he had overtaken her, he said: "Maiden, did you see how I dealt with the giant and how I took him prisoner? I have indeed dealt justly with him. Do you still not want to have me with you?" She then again snapped at him, the young man, bitterly over her shoulder. She said: "If a person must fight, then God grant that he fight, whether he deals justly or not, and just leave me to take care of my own business and leave me, miserable maiden, in peace." That grieved him in his heart. He thought: "I will nonetheless protect her. Although she does not wish to tarry any longer, I will nonetheless ride with her."

Then they rode on together, and she spoke not a word with him. They made great haste until they came to a forest. They rode over many great mountains through which there was no road, and past many cities and castles and villages. They entered none of them. They came to a broad field on which there were many fine pavilions. They had not ridden far from there when they heard new tidings. They looked far across the field and saw the most beautiful maiden riding along. Her horse galloped fiercely, and she urged it on with whip and voice as best she could—that I tell you in truth—her hair was like pure gold; she was tearing it out in rage and shouting with a loud voice. No more beautiful maiden had ever been born. She shouted: "Alas, what I have lost!"

When Vidvilt saw it, now hear how he spoke to the maiden: "O fine and dear maiden, let us ride to that maiden and let us find out what troubles her and whether I can make it right for her." She said: "None of it concerns me: he who has much to make right ought to get up early." He said: "Then wait a little while for me, and let me see what troubles the beautiful maiden." She said: "I know no one for whom I would wait; I will continue on my way." He said: "I will nonetheless not let the beautiful maiden die of grief. I will find out who has caused her grief. Perhaps I will again find your path."

He rode to her at once: "O beautiful maiden, now tell me who it is who has caused you grief. Who can it be?" She said: "My dear knight, may you be forever blessed. You can unfortunately not avenge me—not with blows and not with thrusts, for you are, alas, yourself too weak for the man who caused me this grief." He said: "Tell me all your sorrow and conceal nothing from me. Who knows how weak I may be. I will help you—on that you have my word." She said: "You are as courtly a young man as I have ever seen. Therefore, I will tell you my sorrows and will make my miserable lament to you: there is a kingdom right here, and I will now tell you about how it is the custom of this place that it has many courtly maidens, and the most beautiful of them is given three gifts: a fine and handsome horse that is indeed worth a thousand gold coins, and also a bird, like which there is no other—it can also speak well (which is unusual), and a noble bird house, as well, made of pure gold. These are the things that one gives to the most courtly. Therewith did God thus honor me, and he granted me the great favor, for I was myself [judged] the most beautiful. But little good did it do me: when I was given the three gifts, and I wanted to return homely freely, a knight—a villain—came, who did me the deed of taking all three gifts from me, for which reason I am bereft of joy. For he has a daughter, a beautiful maiden, whom he thinks should be the most beautiful. When she was not [so judged], it enraged him. For that reason I have unfortunately lost what was mine. He took it from me by force. My father scarcely escaped with his army. He would, moreover, have slain him [my father], if only he could have caught him. My father is a poor knight, a noble man. That one is too powerful for him. For that reason I had to lose that which was mine. For that reason I want to kill myself for sorrow, here on this meadow." He said: "Tell me at once when that took place." She said: "It was scarcely two hours ago. The villain is indeed not far away; he is with his army hardly a half-mile from here." He said: "Then let us at once make haste. He will have to return to you that which is yours, or he will have to take my life." Then they made great haste until they could see the army.

He rode into the army with vehemence. He said: "Now tell me quickly, who is the leader among you." One of them then said: "I think he is insane: he is a young and noble man. What could our lord have done to him?" The wicked man was pointed out to him. The youth bowed courteously. The lord gave the guest a fine welcome. "Now, tell me what you want, you courtly youth." He said: "It has been said to me how a great transgression against morality has been perpetrated—how you robbed a maiden. I would indeed not have believed it, had I not seen the stolen goods with you. You cannot but acknowledge it yourself." He said: "Now, tell me, O youth, what concern is it of yours?" He said: "I am a young knight, and I have made the decision that when I see knighthood disgraced, then I will right that wrong, if I can. If you are a knight and knight's companions, then you should by rights have left her property to her, for it is not fitting for a knight to rob a maiden. Therefore, return to the beautiful maiden her three gifts whose loss she laments and which God has destined for her."

The knight laughed and jested. He said: "You young fool, I tell you in truth, whence do you come, galloping up here, or who sent for you, that you speak so foolishly to me? If I were not so forgiving of your youth, it would not turn out well for you." Vidvilt answered him very quickly: "I will take this task on myself, until you have returned to the maiden that which is hers, even if it were to cost me my life. I would not ride away and leave you in peace, even if I were to have to fight with you for that reason, you wicked thief and defiler of women!" The knight began to grow angry. He said to the young man: "Although I would have gladly spared you because of your youth, you have spoken abusively to me. I will never pardon you for that— that I tell you in truth." Vidvilt said: "I will fight you and all your army; or give the maiden that which is hers and let her go." The knight said: "It will not happen that my retinue would give me aid. Indeed I think that I would like to give you a caning and give you a whipping on your behind." Vidvilt said: "I should tell you and make quite clear to you that I have outgrown whippings. Know that I will waste no more time. Prepare yourself, if you wish to fight me." He said: "That will be quickly done."

At once he bound on his helmet. He ordered his entire retinue to withdraw well back behind him. The two bold men there charged at each other in knightly manner and at that time struck each other many deep wounds. The knight was also a very mighty man, but he could not defeat Vidvilt. He gave him a mighty blow, so that he lay on the ground and fell from his horse. His retinue was quite perturbed, but they were not allowed to come to his aid, since he had forbidden it before he began to fight with him.

Then young Vidvilt sprang from his horse onto the ground. He raised his sword and would have taken his life. He said: "Spare me! I surrender to you as your bondsman, and I make everything that I possess subject to you." Vidvilt said: "Your property is abhorrent to me. Swear to me at once that you and your four hundred men will ride at once from here to King Arthur's land and make him aware of these deeds—of how I dealt with you, and remain a prisoner there until I return to you. Remain there as my prisoner. Moreover, first of all, return to the maiden that which is hers, if you otherwise wish to keep your life." He said: "You young hero, it is all up to you. I will do it in all truth." Then he swore a lawful oath to him. Then the knight had to ride to King Arthur's court and was not allowed to delay any longer. When he arrived with his four hundred men, he received quite a fine welcome. Then he told the king the tale about how he was his prisoner.

Vidvilt took his bird and the cage and the horse— that was well worth an entire country—and wanted to return it to the beautiful maiden. She said: "God forbid! How might it be fitting for me to take that for which you have risked your life? I very much want to give it to you, for I grant it to you with all my heart, you noble young man." He said: "That would not be proper for me, if I myself were to take it all. Since you desire it of me, then take the birdcage and the horse, and I will take only the bird." The maiden responded: "No! Take the birdcage, as well. And do not be embarrassed by it. Grant me that." Sir Vidvilt responded: "Gladly." The maiden said: "Now, let us first ride away from here and not delay any long, and may it be God's will that I be worthy of it, that you would desire to have me as a wife. My father is a distinguished knight and also of the most noble and high-born. He is of a ducal lineage, even though he does not have much property, and since you would not value that highly—you young and noble man—I would then wish to give you my noble body and self as a wife."

Vidvilt said: "You beautiful maiden, you might well—in all honor—be the wife of a king: you have as noble a body as any woman has ever had. Should I spurn you because of property? I will tell you the proper truth: I have previously made a vow to a beautiful maiden. That I tell you in truth. I have come here for her sake, and I have undertaken a great task. Otherwise, I would gladly take your noble self as my wife." She said: "Then ride home with me; we will have entertainment. I will give you great honors and will have your wounds healed." He said: "No. I have tarried too long. I should have long ago ridden away from you. I have a companion who does not wish to wait for anyone. I am concerned that I will not be able to overtake him [!] for a long time. I am also not seriously wounded. In two days I will be hale and hearty." She pled with him firmly and long, and when she saw that he did not wish to pay any attention to it, then the beautiful maiden fell on the youth's neck and kissed him on the mouth more than a hundred times. She said: "O unblemished warrior, may God protect you."

He took his birdcage and bird in hand. How quickly did he say farewell to her and gallop away. In no less than two miles he was able at great speed to overtake the maiden. When he had then again caught up with her, he said: "O maiden, did you see how I dealt with the knight and took him and his four hundred men prisoner, and sent him to King Arthur's court? There he is to remain as a prisoner until I return to the land." He showed her the bird. He said: "Take this as your own. The maiden gave it to me for risking my life." She turned her mule away and said to him: "Go your own way. It is all of no concern to me!" Then the young man thought: "O God, put it into her mind that she give up her petulant life! I would have thought that she should have accepted me, but she now does so even less than she did before." She did not then wish to accept the bird until the dwarf again asked her to do so.

Then they rode many miles, for the maiden began to make haste. They then rode night and day. They arrived at a place where a fine castle stood before them. The maiden rode toward it with the dwarf. The fine warrior followed them. Now when they entered the castle, their host welcomed the guests warmly and gave them great honor. The handsome man then also came—he was a knight, a noble warrior. He said: "Tend well to the guests." He was the host there; he was quite pleased with the guests. They were given quite enough of everything that was brought to them there. When they had been seated and had finished eating and drinking, the knight said to Vidvilt: "I have never seen a more courtly young knight. What were you thinking that you have come here?"

Vidvilt said: "Dear my lord, I am following the beautiful maiden. She told her grief to my lord, King Arthur and lamented her sorrows to him. He commanded me, my lord, to ride with her and fight and battle for her, at the will of the beautiful maiden. She told my lord much of her sorrows. I then wish to rescue her from her adversities, even if it were to cost me my life." The host said: "I have heard many things said of your lord, King Arthur: how he has great honor at his court, and a great many mighty knights, and bold men beyond counting. And if that were indeed true, then he would have lent another man to the beautiful maiden who would have been more suitable for combat than you, little laddie. You would have been better off to stay at home. Ride home again; that is my counsel. You are still too young to suffer adversity." Vidvilt said: "I will not follow your counsel, no matter what happens to me as a result, for God has destined me for attacking and assaulting. For that reason I wish to ride with the maiden." The host said: "Indeed do you want to go with maiden to that place. Now I will tell you my intent: before you came here, I had decided that I would ride with the maiden and would fight for Lorel the Fair. Now she has no need of two men. For that reason, let us fight each other. Whichever one defeats the other—that one will ride with the maiden, and the other will be his prisoner." "Gladly, dear my lord," said Vidvilt, the young warrior: "I have to risk the battle. But he has treated me so well that I am not so eager to oppose him. I may not at any time refuse battle to anyone."

They went to a broad hall; all the people then went there and wanted to watch them and see whom fortune would favor and who would defeat the other. The two bold men approached one another with dagger, sword, shield, and lance. The host immediately grasped his dagger and threw it at young Vidvilt, at his good shield, so that it resounded through the castle. Had he not intercepted that throw, it would have pierced him through and through. Vidvilt said: "If you can do that, then you can do more. I thought that there was no longer anyone on earth who knew this throw besides me and my grandfather. Wait, I will be on my guard against you! Now, protect yourself as you wish, I will throw right through your shield, so that my dagger will pierce your body. And if you can stand up to the throw, then I will count you as a mighty man." He began to fight with his dagger and threw it through the host's golden shield, and the dagger went into his right arm so that it stuck there. The host was very shocked by the throw. He said: "I considered you a child. I may well have been blind. You have made a mighty throw at me. It might well have taken my life." Then young Vidvilt said: "Now wait, I will deal with you in a different way." He took his shield in his left hand and with his sword made the host aware of the fact that he was no child. Nor did the host forget his own courage and charged him in knightly manner. Then young Vidvilt had to give ground. They drove one another from one wall to the other. Neither gained much of an advantage. The clanging of their swords could be heard more than a mile away. At this time they struck each other deep wounds so that the rage burned in Vidvilt. He began to grasp his sword in both hands and charged furiously at the host so that he had to retreat before the young man. He drove him around the hall like a whirling top. He gave him many a hard blow to the head. He also caused the warrior such pain that he could hold out no longer. He could no longer hold his shield in his hand; he had to let it fall to the ground. Then he gave him a stroke so that he lay on the ground before him. He said: "How your fighting is like a puff of wind—that you have fallen before a child!" He said: "I must acknowledge the prize as yours. I have never seen your equal." Then he also had to swear to him that he would ride to King Arthur's court and be his prisoner, until he returned to the land. He gave him his pledge, by his troth, to do that.

The maiden had stood at a small window that looked down on the hall from a chamber and had watched the two fight. Then she wished to tarry no longer. She then took her leave of everyone who was in the house. She took her leave of the host and she rode out of the castle. Nor did Vidvilt tarry longer; he rode after her at once. When they had ridden scarcely a half-mile, the maiden dismounted from her palfrey, as did the little dwarf, as well. Vidvilt also dismounted there. Then she fell to the ground at the feet of the worthy warrior. She said: "Dear my lord, bold man, I have discourteously opposed you. Now I ask you, for the sake of unblemished God, that you forgive me the wrong that I have done you, or I will lie here with arms outstretched until my soul departs from me." The words delighted the fine knight. He said: "Arise, you beautiful maiden. My devotion to you is undiminished. You have done nothing to me. Why then should I allow you to lie there?" She said: "I have consistently snapped at you, but I have done it for your sake, for I have feared for your young life, which God has given you. I was glad to see that you returned. Now I recognize clearly that God has granted you great strength. Therefore, forgive me, you undaunted knight, for I recognize clearly that you can give aid to the noble maiden." He said: "Arise, and sit down here next to me. All is forgiven you. Only tell me quickly, how far away from the land are we still?"

She arose and sat down next to the young lad. She said: "Dear my lord, when we are on that mountain over there, then we will have some ten miles to go. Then you will see the great sorrows of my lady." He said: "Now, let us be prepared so that we both get there and so that I see the land precisely." And so she always spoke amiably with him, and she gave him precise information about everything.

Now, when they arrived at the top of the great mountain, the young lady wrung her hands and wept quite miserably. She had great pity for the noble warrior. They could see more than a thousand cities and villages, all of which were suffering very great sorrow: they were burning so that the flames rose up to the heavens. Then the youth again said: "I will give you aid in your distress, even if it brings about my death." The young lady then again said to the lad: "I will tell you how far we still have to go to reach the castle. We ought to make haste. We are still fifteen miles away from there. O young and noble man, we will be in sight of it by tomorrow morning." Then the young man again said: "How can it be that there is such a radiance around it?" She said: "That is the house from which I rode out, where my lady has remained. Moreover, she has retained nothing else besides that house alone, which is named Wachsenstein. The roof is of pure gold. The bosses are jewels whose value is that of a great deal of money—they are pure red garnet: no matter how dark the night, one can see their radiance for more than thirty miles."

They began to make great haste to get there. Vidvilt looked at it intently. He said: "I thought it would never happen, that I would see the equal of my own castle. Now I must stand by the truth: this one may well be comparable to my castle. It is as delightful. I well see by the castle, as I should say, that he was a mighty lord. I reckon that I, too, must live or die for its sake." She said: "On the outside it is nothing but child's play. Inside you will see many wonders in many magnificent constructions of gold and precious gems."

They rode toward the castle. When the gatekeeper caught sight of them, he shouted into the castle: "My dear and gracious lady, may you be well, and know that dear guests are coming for you. It is your maiden and the dwarf. One is riding with them who is resplendent with gold and fine jewels. He is quite as well armed from his head down to his feet as a knight properly should be. On his horse he has a caparison that is a splendid gold coverlet. His armor is of gold and rich gemstones. He rides like an angel." The two queens went to stand at a window and saw the young lady and the young man coming, as did everyone in the castle.

I tell you, there were not very many more people in the castle than ten in all. I will tell you the number: there were the two queens, and the fine maiden, and the gatekeeper, and a cook, and in addition the dwarf, and two young dukes who were the king's nephews, and a man-servant and a maid-servant who had nothing noble about them. They were all in the castle.

When they now came into the castle, the guest was warmly welcomed. First of all they stabled the guest's horse, as was proper to do. Then the maiden came and took his hand and led him into a chamber in which the two queens both were. Now they entered there; they welcomed him and the little dwarf, as well. All three of them went in, and they welcomed the noble warrior. At once his armor was removed, and he was clothed in a fine silk garment. When the elder queen first saw him, she said: "You dear, young lad, how can you have it in your heart to wish to risk your life, and do you want to give up your young life so easily, since you can give us very little aid?" Then his companion, the unblemished maiden, said: "My gracious lady, let it in truth be said to you, that he indeed has the strength and courage in him to give you aid indeed. In truth do I tell you that. If you had seen so many manly deeds from him [as have I], you would yourself have to affirm it."

He was seated—against his will—on a bench next to Lorel the Fair. This I tell you in truth—that no person had ever pleased him as much as Lorel, the beautiful maiden. The undaunted warrior rejoiced. He thought: "You have to become my wife, or I will lose my life." He was served quite enough of everything that the world had ever borne—of fine food and drink. Now when they had finished eating and drinking, and they had also sat there for a while, the maiden told them the tale of what had happened to them: how the knight from King Arthur's court had ridden with her, and how he had fought the giant and the knight. Then she gave to Lorel, the beautiful maiden, the little dog and the bird, which the undaunted warrior had given to her. She said: "The young warrior won this with his sword." Then she began at once to speak with the splendid little bird. She spoke with it about this and that. The little bird was so wise, that it told them everything. Lorel saw that the bird spoke well. She set it on her lovely white hand. She would not have given it up for an entire country.

Then the elder queen said: "Tell me, you fine young warrior—you have come here for our sake. That I have clearly understood from my maiden, that you are ever undaunted by battle and are well able to give us aid. If you will now undertake the task, you noble young man—and may God, who can aid us in our adversities, help you— then Lorel, the beautiful maiden, will not be denied to you as wife. If it is the case that you want her, then you will have still more: all my people and all my land. Here is my hand and my oath on it. Now tell me, you dear child, who your relations and family are, or whether you are of noble birth. God did not spare his art on you, and even if you are not equal to my daughter in terms of lineage, I will give you my daughter, you young lad. For that reason do not conceal from me your relations, your nobility, your family and your knighthood."

He answered her in courtly manner. He said: "Gracious lady, so worthy of love, I have come here for your sake. In my heart do I desire your daughter. I have never seen her—or also my dear mother's—equal, she who wears the crown over all other ladies. She is a queen over the land of Lorraine, and she is named Broktin the Fair. Except for her, I have never seen Lorel's equal—that I must affirm as the truth. I want to have her as my wife, or I will lose my life. I will tell you my noble lineage, if you can recognize it: my father is a widely known king. All of Lotagn[10] is subject to him. His mother was from England, a queen by her lineage. I will identify his father to you precisely: he was the brother of the king of France. His equal was not to be found anywhere. I will tell you at this time what my mother's lineage is. If you would understand me properly, you would not need to be ashamed of her nobility: her father is a king of the Frisian land; his name is widely known. He is one of the mightiest men on whom the sun has ever shone. Her mother was from Milan. My ancestors have I now identified for you." She said: "Praised be God, who has destined you for my daughter. As far as I am concerned, you are quite sufficiently well born."

Then she did not want to delay any longer. Lorel, the beautiful maiden, then had to vow marriage to the dauntless warrior, so that if he were to slay the mighty giant, and she were to emerge from her distress, then he would be a lord and king of the entire kingdom and of the maiden. When the handshake had sealed the pact, then Vidvilt began to say: "You ought to tell everything about how I should begin this undertaking, or whither I should ride, or where I am to find my opponent." She said: "We cannot tell you that, except that when midday approaches, then one of the most beautiful of stags on whom the sun has ever shone, approaches. It comes up to the castle—then one can see the tears running down its cheeks—and it knocks on the gate three times with its antlers. That is the only information that we can tell you about it. If there were a young man who would not despair and who would pursue the stag—he would find out everything from it." He said: "Those are strange tidings. I will not despair of God, and will pursue the stag tomorrow."

The young man was well cared for during the night. When day came, Vidvilt delayed no longer and donned his good armor, in which he had exalted spirits. Nor did they forget to give him food and drink. And while he was eating and drinking, Lorel sat by his side. She loved him with all her heart. Her heart was in great pain: she feared for his young life. She said: "May God grant you favor so that you return hale and hearty and that you set right our heavy hearts. Then you are to be lord of my noble body, you fine, young warrior."

When midday began to approach, the young warrior began to make haste. He sat his horse in chivalric manner. His body yearned for combat, and the dauntless warrior took his leave of the elder queen and Lorel, the beautiful maiden and, additionally, everyone else who was in the castle—they began to be miserably disconcerted. And his companion who had come with him—her eyes became wet from weeping. They said many sweet blessings for him, so that God would protect his life.

When it was midday, the stag then came walking up and knocked three times on the gate, as it had previously done, so that it resounded loudly. It turned downhill away from the castle. One could see the tears flowing from its eyes. Then, however, the fine warrior galloped after it. Then they all ran up to stand on the battlements and watched the young man until they could no longer see him. The young lord pursued him on his horse; the stag ran along many winding paths. Then it turned about on the warrior and acted as if it wanted to butt him. That young lad then took his lance in hand in knightly manner. He did not turn away from the stag. That same noble warrior did not wish to withdraw from it so much as a hair's breadth. When the stag saw that, it turned and ran farther. When it had run a while longer, then it turned again to the warrior. It did that three or four times. The young lord did not wish to retreat from it. Then they came to a broad meadow. Vidvilt quickly rode after the stag until they came to a spring that was long and broad. The stag leapt into the spring, and young Vidvilt came to a lurching halt at the spring: "O, dear God, how am I to succeed? If I leap in after the stag, then I will indeed be undone: I will drown and be dead."

As he was thus speaking for a while—he was sad and without joy—there came a man climbing out of the spring who was lordly and tall. He was quite naked. He had a forked beard that hung down over his shoulders. He welcomed the youth warmly: "May God grant you welcome, noble youth. What do you seek here on this savage field?" He said: "The one whom I seek is that one who, only a moment ago, disappeared before my very eyes. Tell me, my dear fellow, what kind of person might you be? Are you a normal human being? Tell me that right now." The man said: "I will tell you the truth and will not lie to you in the least: I was, years ago, a normal human being. Now, alas, I am bereft of all joy—that is said to you in truth. I am the stag that you pursued. I am the king of the kingdom, except that, alas, now it is not going well for me. Lorel, the beautiful maiden, is my daughter. I suffer great grief for her sake, as do also my people and my land that is all cursed and burned. Now, I know well, you fine warrior, that you have made the decision that either you will die, or you will win my daughter and redeem me and my land. In truth I wish to make known to you that you cannot accomplish it. For that reason you should put it out of your mind. Therefore, ride home again and preserve your young life. That is my good advice. I can no longer stay here, for I am thus cursed that I must run through this broad land as a beast. Now I am permitted every day a period in which I may take human form. That time will now quickly be over, so that I can no longer remain here with you, until tomorrow again, after midday."

Then Vidvilt, the fine warrior, said: "With your permission, dear my lord, I have most firmly decided it—and I have to that purpose come from King Arthur's court—that I wish to win your daughter by combat, even if I am to die for her sake. So do not advise me against it anymore, and tell me, dear my lord, how I am to begin the undertaking, and where I am to find the one whom I am to defeat. I want to redeem you from your adversity, even if I should suffer death because of it." "O young and noble warrior, may God ever care for you and reveal his aid to you. Here you have with my hand, my pledge: if you defeat the great giant, you will have my daughter as your wife. You are no coward—that I well know—for I tested you three times. If you had had any cowardice in you, you would have shied away from me. I have found your equal nowhere. You did not wish to withdraw from me. For that reason, I will show you whither you must ride. If you then otherwise wish to fight with the mighty giant, you must first ride through all my lands, which are cursed and burned. There you will see many cities and villages that suffer great sorrow. There you will see how the people run and rampage and fight. You should be well on your guard against them, young warrior, so that you touch none of them; otherwise it will cost you your life. It will seem to you because of how they dance and pursue courtly amusements, and how they engage in sword fighting and jousting, and how they eat and drink, that even God has forgotten them, so that underneath their clothing they are nothing other than pure fire. For that reason, you must be on your guard that you not touch them. Otherwise, O youth, their Hellfire will also take you. Then you cannot help us; then your aid to us would be as a puff of wind. Avoid them altogether, and ride your own way, and touch no one. Then they can also do nothing to you. They will call and beckon to you to eat and drink with them and share their spirit. Pay no attention to that, you fine warrior. Only after you had left them would you become aware that you could not help us— that your courage had disappeared." Before the king had finished saying that, Vidvilt could no longer see him: he had disappeared from before his eyes, indeed quite suddenly. He thought: "Why should I wait here any longer; I will ride back to the castle. Tomorrow I will come back to him here; then he will tell me the rest of the tale." At once he turned his horse; he galloped back to the castle.

When the gatekeeper saw him, now hear how he spoke to the queen: "My dear and gracious lady, the fine youth is returning." Then they all went to stand on the battlements and saw the young man coming, and the gate was at once opened for him. The two queens came forth with their noble crowns, and they welcomed him warmly, and he told them the tale of how he had returned. He did not want to tell them anything of the matter, except that he thus told them how the stag had run away. He wanted to wait until the next morning and then pursue him again. They attended to him as well as one should do with such a man. In the morning when it was time, he again prepared himself for the ride: he took leave of everyone who was in the castle. They all began to become miserably disconcerted.

When the stag returned, he again gave his horse the spurs and rode out the gate and rode after the stag as he had previously done. The stag did not test him any more to see if he would fight him, for he had now recognized him. When they again came running up to the spring, the stag again leapt in. Vidvilt waited there for him until he again climbed out in human form. Vidvilt bowed chivalrously to him. He said: "Dear my lord, you are suffering wretched pain that I can no longer endure. I will certainly come to your aid, you miserable man. Your misery causes me pain. I can no longer endure it. Therefore, tell me at once where I should ride, or where I find the one with whom I am to fight." He said: "Yesterday I had to leave you too quickly—whether I wished to do so or not.

"Now I will tell you more: when you have gone through my entire land and before all my people, who are burned there, then you will come, O noble warrior, into a very great forest, out of which you cannot come. Your life will be taken from you in there—even if all the world were on your side—that I swear to you on my oath, for a great dragon roams there. When he senses your presence—he can smell people from more than thirty miles away—then he will begin to make haste. You cannot defeat him. Believe me, amiable warrior. The forest is broad and fifty miles in length—let that be said to you in truth. If you have been blessed by God so that the dragon does not sense your presence, then, bold warrior, you will have to give up your life for the dragon's sake, for four hundred women run through the forest. If they see you— I will make this known to you—then you will be burned by them, for they are proper she-demons. They will make you quite bereft of all joy; they will cause the death of your body. They are the subjects of the giant's mother, and they have to go around in the forest and have to stand guard and keep a lookout and reconnoiter quite carefully. If anyone enters that land, then they inform their lady. Then she comes with her demonic army. For she greatly fears that someone might slay her son.

Now, I will tell you in truth: if God indeed grants you His favor so that you retain your life against him, then, O youth, you cannot defeat the mother of the mighty giant. If she becomes aware of your presence, then it is indeed all over for you, for she is both huge and monstrous. She will rob you of all joy, even if all the world were on your side. She will take you by one leg and smash you against the wall. Against her your sword-fighting is like a puff of wind. She will not let you survive. She is well aware that you are going around here and that you intend to slay her son. I will tell you in truth: you can barely see up to her head. She has caused all my pain. Let that be said to you in truth. And if God wishes to be so merciful to you that you overcome that she-devil and emerge from the forest, then you will at once come to a huge and long body of water, where you will be disgraced against your will, for it is so deep and huge [. . .][11] O unblemished warrior, if you have taken on this battle, if you wish to fight the giant, then you will have to cross it. The bridge is constructed with sorcery, and it is so marvelously conceived as I will now tell you—except that now the time has come that I can again no longer remain with you, until tomorrow again after midday."

Before he had finished speaking the word, Vidvilt again could not see him. Then he again rode to the castle, as previously. There the gate was opened for him, and they again cared well for the young man. He again told the queen that the stag had run away from him. He again wanted to wait until the next day and wanted to ride after the stag again, to see if he might have the good fortune to find out or say where the stag went. The next day he again decided that he wanted to ride after the stag. When the stag approached, he made haste and took leave of everyone who was in the castle. They all began to be miserably disconcerted. When the stag again came to the spring, he again leapt into the spring and again climbed out in the form of a man. Vidvilt again bowed chivalrously to him. He said: "Tell me the rest, dear my lord. Your great grief causes me pain." He said: "My dear son, let it cause you pain. Two great wheels extend out of the bridge that I mentioned to you yesterday and rotate. No one can survive them. Each one of them has four hundred strong, steel shearing blades, and they are of hardened iron, and wherever the shearing blade gives you so much as a scratch— that I tell you in truth—then you must die and perish in misery, for they are quite poisonous. Moreover, do not think to smash or pound them, for they are very strong and very great in size, and they are bewitched, and they turn both day and night.

"If you were, however, to get across—which cannot happen— then in half a day you would come to the house where the mighty giant is. Your life will then be in danger from a giant who stands before the house and who will first of all deliver you to death. And if God gives you aid, young man, so that you defeat the giant, and you enter the house, then you will first of all be quite uncordially welcomed by the great she-devil, for she will at once become aware of your presence. And if you had everything in the world to give her, she would not let you live, for she will understand that you want to slay her son, O dauntless warrior. If, however, you have the good fortune that she does not become aware of you, and you get to the mighty giant, I hope that you will at once give him what he deserves. He is monstrous and huge, but he is without skill in battle: he fights with a huge, long club. Whoever is hit with it has to die, like it or not. If you can only leap and evade his boorish blows, then, noble warrior, you will slay him.

"Now I have told you everything, and I am certainly sorry for your sake that you will give up your noble life for a woman." He said: "May God bless you, dear my lord. Where I stay one night I will not stay a second night until I have delivered you from your troubles, even if I should lose my life for it."

Then the good warrior took his leave and rode from him with undaunted courage until he came to one of the burning cities. There he saw the people all running. It seemed to him that they were joyful and singing, dancing, and leaping, and that they were engaging in sword-play and courtly amusements.

And as they danced and jousted, they all shouted to him: "Dismount and drink with us, you courtly young lad." He did not wish to pay any attention, and he rode ever on his way. Then someone rode toward him on a jet-black horse; he took his lance under his arm; he wished to joust with him. Then the noble warrior thought: "My grandfather commanded me: 'You are not to retreat from anyone.' I will obey his command, even if I should lose my life for it." He at once took his lance under his arm. How quickly it began to burn. The bold warrior then cast it from his hand onto the green earth. There it burned to powder. Vidvilt was glad that the fire had not touched him. He said: "Wait, I will protect myself better from now on and will not get entangled with you, and will obey my dear father-in-law."

Then the good warrior, miserable in spirit, thought: "How am I to accomplish such a great battle when I do not have a lance? I cannot fight with anyone or accomplish the task without a lance." Vidvilt tarried no longer; he rode back to the spring and waited until the stag came bounding from the castle. When he came, he did not long wait; he leapt at once into the spring and at once climbed out in human form. Vidvilt again bowed to him courteously. Then he said to the young warrior: "Tell me, how did it turn out so that you have returned so quickly. Tell me that." He said: "Gracious my lord, may you ever be blessed. I did not follow your counsel, for which reason I almost came into adversity. I could not leave it: I had to joust with one of your men and wanted to break lances for the sake of glory. I had scarcely touched my lance, when it began to burn from the inside. If I had not immediately cast it from my hand, I myself would also have burned. Now tell me, dear my lord, with what am I to fight. Can I defeat all those with whom I must fight, or where can I find another weapons-maker in the land who could make me another, as my first one was made. For I am worth nothing in combat if I have no lance but only a sword."

Then he said to the young man: "I will instruct you justly; I will show you a lance. You will have to praise it yourself. It is better than any three of your lances. And follow my counsel better, and do not touch any more of my people. You are to ride at once over that mountain into the forest. Underneath there, O bold warrior, is a lance. I myself bore it in many an assault and attack and killed many a giant, dwarf, and dragon with it." Then he again took leave of him in courtly manner and bowed to him courteously. Then the warrior rode until he came under the linden-tree. He took the lance in hand. It pleased him exceedingly well, and he said: "I will go do what I have to do." The unblemished warrior took it in his hand and charged many times at the stones. The lance passed the test and would not break. He said: "First I will avenge the people who are suffering such great pain there. Now may God grant me aid."

He tarried there no longer; he rode from there until he came through the land of the people who were there all burned. When he had then gone through that land, then he rode farther, until he came to the forest. The noble warrior rode into it and rode on until the ninth day, without taking any rest. He did not want to ride out of the forest; he first wanted to fight with the dragon. While he was riding on that ninth day—in truth I tell you that—the noble warrior heard quite a miserable cry and heard her miserably lamenting her distress. Alas, the death of her dear husband and son. Then he made haste; he rode in the direction of the cry until he got there.

There he found lying on the earth the most beautiful of ladies whose body a man had ever won. She lay there face-down—that I tell you in truth. No man could have paid for the clothes that she wore—worked with gold and precious stones. The unblemished warrior said to her: "Why are you suffering such great pain? Tell me all your troubles. I will give you aid, if only I can." She said: "No, you can give me little aid. I will weep until my soul leaves me." He said: "Often one may give counsel who has none for himself. Tell me all your bitter grief; you will not regret it." She did not wish to pay him any attention. Then the young lord dismounted and helped her up on her horse, against her will. "Now, dear lady, tell me your distress."

When she looked at him, she thought: "I will tell him about it, since he pleases me so well. He is a mighty young hero. If God were to give him aid, perhaps he could help me out of my affliction." She said to the young man: "I will tell you of my grief. I was indeed until recently a noble queen. Now, alas, I have been robbed of all my joys, for I have, alas, lost my dearest lord and also a son. That will I also lament to you. We came to the forest to hunt, for the sake of pleasure—that will I lament to God in Heaven— then a dragon came along that has caused me great grief. He took my two dear kinsmen from me in that brief moment: my husband in its mouth, my son on its tail—for that reason is my lament thus profuse—and carried them away altogether—that will I lament to God in Heaven."

He said: "Tell me where this occurred." She said: "It has just happened." He said: "Might I still ride after the dragon?" She said: "Dear my lord, it is pure fire: wherever it has passed, the earth is scorched. Ride along that same path, you worthy warrior; you will come directly to it. But I counsel you to spare your young life and stay here, for you cannot banish my grief. For it is better that it has eaten only my two dear kinsmen, than that you also should become its fodder." He said: "I will delay no longer and will ride after the dragon, and will bring it about that your kinsmen retain their lives for longer than an hour. Despair not, therefore, if God stands by me: it will cost the dragon its life."

Then he galloped away from the lady and picked up the dragon's trail, which was scorched. Nor did the lady tarry longer; she rode after the young man. She wanted to see if he could vanquish the dragon, and if she might find her husband and her son still alive.

Vidvilt hurried after the dragon. He pursued the great uproar until he came within sight of it and saw it bearing the two men: the younger with its tail, the elder in its mouth. Then he saw at the same time that they were still alive and were moving. The young man was quite gladdened by that. Now I will tell you in truth: the dragon wanted to take them into a den. Vidvilt thought to himself: "If he takes them into his cavern, I cannot be of any aid. Just wait; I will deal with you in another way."

He quickly ran before the cavern's entrance. He took his lance in hand in knightly manner and charged the dragon there. His thrust injured him not so much as a hair, for his skin was of horn—in truth I tell you that. The young man gave him many a thrust, and the dragon saw that he did not want to let it enter the cavern. Then it let the king fall from its mouth and spewed fire at the fine warrior, and he was almost burned, but he extinguished himself at once. And after it had spewed the fire, it again caught the man with its mouth. That did the man no good, for it almost took his life there, for it gave him great blows beyond measure. It greatly perturbed Vidvilt. He was battling the dragon stoutly: he gave it many a firm stroke with his sword, and he did not thereby hesitate. The warrior then at once thought: "If I should continue this against the dragon for very long, then it will kill the one man with the hard blows that it is giving him."

Then the young man first gave it some thought and cast his lance onto the ground and took his sword in both hands and ran on foot—quite in knightly manner—at the dragon. And the dragon would have been quite unwilling to yield ground to him. Then he gave the dragon a blow that was so great, that it quite vexed the dragon. He again let the man fall from his mouth. At the same time he again spewed fire at Vidvilt, so that he was almost burned.

Not until then did he grow quite angry and, enraged, charged the dragon and, with his good sword, struck it in the middle and through its horny skin into two pieces. It gave a bitter cry. The front part suffered such pain that it could no longer hold on to the man. Its hind parts—its wings—were injured, completely damaged. Then it began to stretch its tail in front of it and then grasped young Vidvilt and quickly pressed him to itself and crushed him quite severely, so that it would have cost him his life—on that I will give you my oath. It again began to stretch its tail and flung young Vidvilt. The tail was huge and so mighty that it quickly flung Vidvilt more than seven miles, so that he lay in a great body of water and did not know whether it was night or day. He could only lie there unconscious.

Now I will tell you how the lady rejoiced when she found her husband and son alive and rescued there by the noble young son of a knight, for she had followed Vidvilt and had seen the battle. They were both quite without strength; the blood spurted from their mouths and noses, and covered their beards, as if they were dead. Then the lady took an abundance of good herbs, all of which she was carrying with her and revived them and placed them in their mouths, until they began to move and to stand up. Then the king asked her what had happened to them, and where the man was who had given them that aid. She said: "I do not know what became of him. I fear that the dragon has slain him. His horse is running here, and there lie his lance and his sword." Then they both said: "Never have we suffered such sorrow as now that I cannot see the noble man. In that I have suffered great sorrow."

When they had recovered, they took Vidvilt's horse with its golden caparison, his lance, and his sword—which was worth an entire land. They all three mounted the horse—for it was large and strong and noble—so that it could carry all three of them. Then they rode a short while until they came out of the forest; then they immediately made great haste until they came to their land. Their servants well saw them coming, and they welcomed their lady and their lords, and they were taken home with great honor, and they rejoiced greatly—more than I wish to tell you. For they had given up on them and otherwise did not know anything of them, except that they were all three in dire straits and were perhaps lying dead, slain by the dragon. The king said: "It is to be proclaimed throughout my land that no one, whether by hand or by foot, is to play any stringed instrument, or joust, dance, or practice any courtly amusement." That prohibition was to remain in force for an entire year, because he had lost young Vidvilt, who had provided him that great aid.

When night had then fallen, the queen delayed her course no longer and went with her maidens to the battlements. She wished to remain standing there all night, in case it might be granted her that she hear or see something of the warrior. A great canal flowed just outside the castle wall. That water flowed very swiftly. Vidvilt was still lying unconscious that whole day. A boatman lived down below the castle who was the king's bonded fisherman. He was going downstream in his boat with his fishing net, and he had his wife with him, for he wanted to make a good catch of fish, which he was able to do, since his wife knew how to help him.

When the queen saw him, she called to that boatman, for she knew him well, so that she denied no one her greeting. She said: "Where are you going, my dear fisherman? Do you not wish to stay at home today?" He said: "Dear, gracious, and comely my lady, I am your servant. I must go at once, and I must catch good fish for my dear lord, for I have heard, how he is sorely wounded. For that reason, I will now catch for his sake those that will heal his wounds." She said: "Go then in God's name."

The fisherman went downstream until he came to where the young lad lay. Then the man saw the radiance of Vidvilt, the fine young man, in the water. His wife saw him first. Now, hear how she spoke to him: "Look, my dear husband, what is that shining there so brightly?" He said: "What is it that you see? Do not deceive me." They went to the other side. Soon the fisherman saw it. He said: "There lies an angel that has come from Heaven. For indeed it cannot be a human. It gives off such a sweet radiance." She said: "Let us go over there. Then we can see clearly what is in the water." They quickly went over there. The boatman climbed out onto the bank to him. He saw the young man lying there. Look here! God has here provided for us, so that we will become rich from this dead man. He is wearing such good armor that one could not pay for it with an entire land." They at once took off his armor, his helmet, all his knightly garments, and his golden belt that his dear mother had given him. And the fisherman saw that he was still warm. Then he said to his wife: "We will both lose our lives, for he is not completely dead. If he revives, then he will see that we have despoiled him. Then our lives will be in danger. Hand me the pick from under the pot in the boat. I will prevent his blabbering. I will make it so that we are safe from him. I will pronounce sentence on him first." She handed the pick to her husband.

She then looked at him for the first time: she had never seen a more handsome person. Then she immediately said to her husband: "O, how can it be in your heart that you wish to murder this young man? I have never seen his equal on earth. You are not going to do him any harm here!" He said: "Your chatter is of no interest to me. I will arrange for his silence." He raised the pick and wanted to strike him in the head. The woman grabbed him around the neck and said: "Keep still, my dear husband, and let me tell you something! He is so deeply unconsciousness; if he survives, he will not know who despoiled him. Why do you wish to burden yourself with this great sin?" He said: "Get away from me, or I will strike you so that you are laid out flat on your back." She said: "If you do not wish to listen to me and wish to murder the young lord, then I will tell you right now that I will no longer lie at your side, for I do not want to have a murderer as my husband."

Then the fisherman looked at her and was considering it carefully: "If I do not do what she says, then she will indeed get me killed." He said: "I will do what you say." The woman was then glad. They sailed away from the bank, and they left Vidvilt naked and despoiled, so that he was quite befuddled, so that he did not know what was what. They had almost crossed the water; they had covered the armor with a good fishing net. And the fisherman again went beneath the castle, but the queen saw him, for she had been standing there the entire time. She then spoke to the fisherman. She said: "My dear fisherman, why are you returning so quickly?" He said: "Dear my lady, it is because of my good equipment that I have caught fish so quickly, and it turned out quite well for me. And if the moon had not shone so brightly, I would not have returned so quickly."

He took his leave from the queen. As soon as he got home, he put the armor in a sack, and he took the fish to the castle. Thus one says: "Never is anything so finely spun that it does not finally come into the light of the sun." Thus it happened to the fisherman there; I will tell you how. When the fisherman was sailing away from the queen and had the armor covered with his fishing net, and the moon was shining so brightly, then the armor was seen by one of the young ladies who was there[12] and who was standing near the queen. She then went to the queen. She said: "My gracious lady, if it could be done with your favor, I would tell you strange tidings." The queen said: "Tell me what it is." The maiden said as follows: "Did you see there what the fisherman was carrying in his boat? It was certainly pure red gold and fine jewels. The moon shone so brightly on them, how could you not have seen it?" The queen then immediately said: "Is that true, what you have said?" The maiden said: "It is certainly true. I am not lying to you at all."

The queen then did not shirk: at once she secretly let herself out with her two maidens. They wanted to have a look at what the maiden had perceived and what the fisherman had transported. Scarcely did she have to wait before they arrived at the fisherman's house—which she recognized— and stood before the fisherman's door and looked inside through a crack. The fisherman was sitting by the fire, and there was great joy there. The fisherman said: "Bring me the good wine, and let us rejoice. Yesterday we were poor, and today we are rich. Our equals are to be found nowhere among all fisher-folk. Tomorrow I will go to the market and sell the armor. It is worth a thousand pounds; that will be good for our well-being. And that little belt will be for our son. He is to wear it on holidays."

The queen understood that the armor belonged to young Vidvilt. She knocked firmly on the door. The fisherman came forth. He said: "Who is knocking here?" The queen then spoke thusly: "Open up, my dear fisherman, it is your lady, the queen." He opened the door at once and fell to his knees. In all his life he had never been so terrified. "May God grant you welcome, gracious my lady. What is your grace doing at my house? I have never seen you here before—that I will say on my oath." The queen clearly saw that he was quite terrified. She said: "Have no fear, my dear fisherman, and tell me very precisely what you were transporting in your boat. We perceived and saw it." He said: "My gracious lady, nothing other than fisherman's tackle." Then she said: "I will give you my pledge, if you tell me the truth, your life will be in no danger, nor will be that of your wife. If you do not do it, it will cost you your lives." He said: "Grant us our lives, gracious my lady, and I will undertake to show it to you." She said: "Have no worries for life and property." Then he went where he had hidden the armor and brought it—and the fine belt—before the queen.

When the queen saw the armor, she recognized it at once and said: "My dear fisherman, how or where did you get that?" The fisherman then said: "Yesterday we went to catch good fish. When I had gone perhaps a half mile, I found the courtliest of lads who lay as if dead by the moat. I took off the good armor and left him lying naked under a willow." The queen said: "For God's sake, tell me if he is still alive or is he dead?" He said: "He was not yet quite dead; he was still warm and had good color." She said: "Make haste to your boat, and take me and my maidens there." She said to the fisherman: "For the time being, keep the armor and the belt for me." The fisherman did not shirk; he did as his lady commanded and took her downstream at once. She made haste at once to that lad.

If you will keep quiet, then I will tell you how young Vidvilt fared. When he got some air, then he regained consciousness. He sat up and looked at himself and saw that he was not wearing his armor. He said: "Am I not the man who is to fight with the mighty giant? On what am I to ride? Where is my armor, and where is my horse? Where is my lance? Where is my sword? Naked, I certainly cannot defeat him." As he was sitting there with those thoughts, he became aware of the ladies who were approaching. He was ashamed and went away. The boatman saw him; the queen also caught sight of him. The fisherman said: "He is ashamed; he wants to go away." The queen said: "Tell him to stop." She called to him herself: "Stay here, young man; we are harmless. Have no fear and stay here." He said: "I am never afraid of a lady. I am ashamed, for I am naked and unclothed. If I were to appear thus before ladies, it would be a great dishonor." The queen took off her ermine fur-piece from her neck, for she made great haste for his sake. At once the queen spoke to the fisherman. She said: "Take him the cloak, and tell him to come here at once."

The fisherman did not shirk but did as his lady commanded. He put on the fur; the young man went to the lady. When he came to the queen, she fell on his neck and embraced and kissed his mouth more than a thousand times. "God be praised, that it has been granted to me that I see you alive." He said: "Tell me, dear my lady, who you might be, that you are so friendly to me. I am without all property. I will tell you on my oath that I am not aware that I have ever seen you before in my life." She began to laugh heartily. She said: "Be silent; I will soon make you rich. Do you not know me, O noble warrior? I am the lady whom you found in the forest. I am loyal to you with all my heart. I will give you a rich reward. Why should I not be loyal to you? You kept my dearest kinsmen alive, and if not for you, they would not have survived against the dragon." He said: "I do not know what happened to me. I myself saw nothing more. I do not know if I dreamt it: it seems to me that I slew a dragon that bore a man in its mouth and another in its tail. Now my fortune is exposed to the elements. Where is my armor? Where is my horse? Where is my lance? Where is my sword?" She said: "Be assured that it will be fine, young man, and let us leave here at once. Have courage. Everything will be restored to you, O fine warrior."

The boatman pushed off from the bank. She then immediately told the warrior everything that had happened to the two of them. She told him the whole story. They continued until they arrived at the castle. The guards saw them clearly and shouted, asking who they were and who was coming there so late. They said: "Open up and let us in, it is your lady, the queen." The gate was opened for her at once. How quickly she went in and led him into a splendid hall. Then the people were awakened everywhere, including the king and his son. They were so delighted that they did not know what to do. They embraced him, and they welcomed him a thousand times and gave very great honor to the young lord, and gave him his armor, sword, lance, and his good horse—and also his courtly belt, which delighted the fine warrior. The king sent at once throughout his land for doctors. They came immediately and healed him of his wounds. And when he was again quite well, he wanted to ride away.

The king said: "You must stay longer. You must remain here. I give you my daughter in marriage. She is so worthy of love; her peer is not to be found in an entire country. I will not ask concerning your nobility. You are to have my loyalty; take my pledge here with my hand, and I give to my daughter in addition half my land (my son is to inherit the other part). You, after all, obtain your full share as a dauntless knight." Vidvilt said quite courteously: "Dear and gracious my lord, this is something that cannot be, for I have a wife, as I wish to tell you." Then he told him the tale about how he had come there: "I would not otherwise spurn your daughter— I wish to tell you that in truth." The king said: "What will you now undertake, young man? You cannot fight with anyone or accomplish the task. So remain here and spare your young life, and take my daughter as your wife. Your vow to Lorel is that if you slay the mighty giant, then it [the marriage to her] will take place. Now, lad, if you do not do it, then the engagement is broken." Then he said: "I have decided that I will first ride there and rescue the king from his distress, even if I were to die a hundred deaths."

Then he had to promise the king that if, with God's aid, he were to defeat the mighty giant—or whatever else might happen to him—he would not abandon him, and that above all he would return there. That was to bring them good tidings. When he had been there some thirty days, which he whiled away with great honor, then he wished to delay no longer. He wanted to ride away.

He [took his leave] of everyone who was in the castle and rode away in a cheerful mood, until the good warrior returned to the forest where he had slain the dragon. He arrived there in about two days outside the cavern in which there were huge, young dragons. He dismounted and took off his golden spurs and crawled into the cavern and slew the youngsters that were inside. There were nine or more of them. He thought: "If they were grown, they would have destroyed an entire army. I have to slay you, so that the world will have peace from you."

When that had been done, he at once mounted his horse and rode around in the forest for days, sometimes by a straight path, sometimes by a winding one, during which he neither heard nor saw anyone, which made him quite uneasy, for he would very much have liked to fight. When he had ridden even up to the seventh day, he came to a great fire in the forest around which sat four hundred monstrous women. They were exceedingly black; they were the Devil's companions. They were the maidens of the mighty giant's mother. They caused Vidvilt a great deal of sorrow. When they became aware of him—that he had come there—all of them together leapt up with a great shout. Each of them had in her hand an earthenware pot with fire inside, with which they almost burned Vidvilt. They carried searing fire inside there. Moreover, they were huge and monstrous. Each one of them took the fire in hand, and they threw the fire at him in a rage and almost burned him. But he at once extinguished the fire on him.

Then the young man said: "If you do not stopping your throwing, then I will have to take your lives, if I wish to save myself. However much I am displeased by fighting against women, you are yourselves acting even more boldly toward me than I can endure. Indeed I have to fight with you." That which I tell you is true: they paid no attention whatsoever to him. They said: "We know well that you have come here because you want to kill our lord. Wait, we want to tell our lady." They continued unceasingly to throw fire at the hero. He slung his shield in front of himself, and he drew his sword from its sheath, with which he caused the she-demons a great deal of grief. Whomever he encountered, she lay on the ground in front of him after the first stroke. They cursed and all went to their lady with a great shout and told her the tale of what had happened to them and how the man had come there.

His mother said: "I will certainly take his life, even if he has all the world in property to offer me." She quickly ran out of the castle; she wanted to kill him. She raged and rampaged like a proper she-devil. She then wanted to burn the young lad. So Vidvilt rode around in the forest, and she sought the noble warrior everywhere in the forest. She was eager to find him. She was mighty and huge and so tall that she butted against many trees that were there, huge beyond reckoning, because she was in such a hurry to find the young lord. Then the young man heard a great uproar in the forest: in her haste, she crashed into and shattered the trees.

When she found him, listen to what she said: "Now, tell me, you young villain, how can you consider me such a nothing that you dare to ride here so very boldly and wish to fight with my son and have additionally fought with my maidens? Most assuredly I will not endure it from you!" He did not know what kind of reply he ought to make to her, for his whole life was in danger, for she was so huge and monstrous—as the tale tell us—that he could scarcely see her head. For that reason, he was so terrified that he could not speak. Then she took the fine, young warrior by his head and slung him over her shoulder, quite against his will. Quickly he took courage, took his sword in hand, and gave the monstrous woman a hard stroke on her head and body. She crushed him to herself so stoutly that he could not fight with the sword. He scarcely felt the great blow. She carried him to a tree and began to split it open. She thrust the young man inside with his feet and hands, so that he could not turn or move. There the noble warrior sat quite miserably. Then she took his own sword. She said: "I will make it so that you will never again ride a horse." She wanted to strike off his head—that I wish to tell you in truth. Now, hear how his great fortune aided him in this affair: as she was preparing to strike him, she heard Vidvilt's horse shriek from the place where the dragon was accustomed to pass by. Then she ran away from the knight who was caught there, and she dropped the sword.

Then Vidvilt was saved by great good fortune, for she did not know that the dragon had been slain. That I tell you in truth—she feared nothing on earth more, for she still had great fear of the dragon, so that she made haste and fled and sought neither track nor trail and shattered all the trees that she encountered until she got out of the forest, as fast as she could run, until she came to the deep stream. She made great haste to the bridge and thus she herself shattered the great wheels on the bridge—that I tell you without falsehood—when she crossed the bridge, and she ran happily into her castle with all her maidens.

Vidvilt will just have to remain captive until you give me good wine to drink. Then I will give him good aid, if you will bestow a full glass on me!

Vidvilt lay in his prison until the third day, so that even with all his abilities he could not free his hands or feet. Nonetheless, he had so much strength—as I can tell you—that he broke out of the tree with his great might. No man had ever experienced such joy as he, when he stretched open the tree and was at once free. His horse ran to him in the forest. He quickly mounted it. Then he thought: "I will never give up; I will find the mighty giant. And even if I were to know for certain that his mother would catch me by the hair, I will not ride around like a coward—until I have slain the mighty giant."

Then the young man rode until he came out of the savage forest. He rode until he came to the deep stream. He spurred his horse so that it galloped. He rode up along the stream until he found the bridge, which he rode across at once. He saw that the wheels were broken and the shearing blades had been lost, which his father-in-law had earlier described to him. The dauntless warrior then rode over a high mountain. There he saw before him a great castle. He had never seen a larger fortress. He thought: "I will find the mighty giant right here in this building. I can recognize that no human man lives in it." He left his horse to graze in the grass, for he wanted to fight the mighty giant on foot.

He went toward the castle at once. He found a huge giant in front of the castle. And when the giant noticed him, he at once charged him there with his great steel pole. He shouted: "Surrender or I will strike you dead! Tell me who commanded you to come into my lord's land!" He said: "That I will answer with fighting. May it otherwise be granted to me to see him[13] with my own eyes. And if you had a pole that were twice as big, I would not surrender to you." The giant said: "If you want to fight my lord, then you must fight me first."

The giant raised his pole up quite high. Now Vidvilt did not flee from him: he then struck the giant many deep wounds. Their combat was indeed mighty. Blood spurted from the mouth of the giant. Vidvilt gave him such a stroke that he lay on the ground in front of him. He was about to strike off his head. The giant said: "No, you young and noble lad! Let me live! I will surrender to you as your bondsman and will be loyal to you, if only you let me live. Then I will tell you how you will be able to defeat the mighty giant. I am of more use to you alive than dead." Vidvilt offered the giant his hand: "So swear it at once."

O how delighted the giant was. He swore to him and led him into his chamber. The giant explained to the youth and told him the tale about how foolish it was of him that he had undertaken the task since he could not accomplish it: "For when his mother notices that you have come, she will take your life, even if you had all the world's goods to offer. But if you have the good fortune first to see him, you might defeat him in battle. But it cannot be: she protects too well against it, that evil mother of his, and she has arranged things too well. It is because of that that no one has slain her. For that reason you should give it up and go away." He said: "Indeed I will not do that, no matter what happens to me as a result." He took his leave of him and went away from there. The giant said: "May God protect you, young man, and remember, noble youth, and above all do not neglect first to come back to me here. That is the counsel that I give you, for I know the roads and paths. You cannot get away, for that monstrous woman who will take your life—I have been her prisoner for almost sixteen years, so that I have had to be her gatekeeper."

The fine warrior left him; into the great monster's house he then went. There was no one who welcomed him. He went back and forth in the house: he wanted to find the great giant. He came to a great hall; there was no one anywhere in it. It was wider, longer, and higher than any ever seen before or since. He had never seen a larger hall. He immediately thought: "If I can bring about the death of no one here, and if I should leave here without combat, I will have never suffered greater grief. That I swear by my firm oath."

Before he had finished saying those words, he then saw a she-demon who ran into the room there. When she noticed him, she turned around at once and ran to where her lady was. "Dear and gracious my lady, a guest has entered our house who has acted very arrogantly toward us. Let us at once try to take him prisoner. He caused us much grief in the forest. Hear how arrogant he is!" The monstrous woman said: "Certainly I will take his life. He wants to slay my son, for which he must certainly suffer distress." Then a great many women—beyond counting—came running into the hall. Each one stood on a bench. Vidvilt did not find it entertaining. Then the she-devil was seen striding into the hall. She picked him up against his will and smashed him against the wall. The unblemished warrior would have gladly defended himself, but his defense was of little aid to him. She said: "You want to take my son's life. Now I will give you your proper reward. O, how bold and noble you are! You must have become acquainted with me in the forest, and despite that you have entered my house. Therefore, this must be your end right here." She then began to abuse the man. She took his lance out of his hand and thrust it through his shoulder. She broke it in two in the middle and left one piece of it inside his body. She said: "Let that be a gift for Lorel, your bride, for whose sake you have come here. Now I will tell you exactly what I am going to do to you. I will let you enjoy your great courage, granted to you by God, and I will let you live. But you must give me your vow that you will not speak or say a word until you have been healed and Lorel bids you three times. And where you are wounded, you are to allow no one to remove the piece of the lance—whoever it might be—except Lorel, the beautiful maiden."

He swore that to her with a proper oath. Then the poor mute went out miserably from the monstrous house. He could not get to the mighty giant. His heart wanted to stop beating from grief. For his [the giant's] mother kept a close eye on him: she was concerned that he [her giant son] would steal out after Vidvilt and pursue him by force. Then he [her son] might lose his life.

When Vidvilt again came out to the [gatekeeper] giant, the giant readily noticed him. He asked him the news about how it had gone for him. He gave him no answer at all: it had after all been forbidden to him. The giant looked at him steadily; he did not know what had happened to him. He saw clearly that he was seriously wounded.

In that moment the mighty giant [the lord of the castle] became aware that someone was there and had undertaken the task of fighting and defeating him. Then he wanted to delay no longer: he slipped out, unbeknownst to his mother, in order to try to get to Vidvilt. He bore a great club on his shoulder. It was of sufficient length and size. He ran quickly past the [gatekeeper] giant's house. The giant noticed him there. He said to the young warrior: "Come on, and may God protect you. Now avenge your great pain and liberate the people who were suffering pain there. Did you not see your enemy run away there?"

Vidvilt was glad, but was not permitted to say anything. He made haste and pursued him. The giant said: "You ought to wait and not fight with him until he has quite crossed that mountain, so that no one [here] becomes aware of it. Then I will follow you slowly. If you should come into distress, then I will fight alongside you." He did not run off at once; he did as the giant told him. But he was eager to pursue him. He stole along behind him until he had crossed the mountain, so that he could no longer be seen from the castle. Then Vidvilt ran up to him.

When the mighty giant noticed him, he said: "Are you the base scoundrel? It is going to cost you your head!" He raised his club up very high. Vidvilt did not flee from him. The worthy warrior evaded the blow; it would otherwise have knocked him down. Then Vidvilt, that worthy warrior, drew his sword, with one leap he charged at him chivalrously and gave him a powerful stroke—did that same unblemished warrior— he reached only up to his leg. In a short while he gave him many deep wounds. Before the mighty giant again raised his club and again swung it at Vidvilt, he had given him such mortal wounds in his legs that it would have to cost him his life. The blood flowed from him like a brook. The [gatekeeper] giant observed surreptitiously.

Vidvilt thought of the poor people who were then suffering great pain. "Now God knows in this matter lies all his fortune. God save us! I will take the risk!" He immediately grasped his sword in both hands and charged with force at the monstrous man and hewed off one of his legs with a single stroke, so that he fell down like a sack. He hewed off his head. Then the people who had suffered such great pain were liberated. I tell you in truth—they were as if they had suffered no injury.

Then the [gatekeeper] giant came running to him: "Come on, you bold man, and let us get away from here at once, if we can outrun the she-devil." Then he went out onto a broad meadow. There stood his white steed. Then he led him through an abundance of great forests, through which no road or path led. The lance caused him pain in his body, and he was also no longer permitted to speak. They made great haste until they came out of the forest and until they came to a castle and a city which belonged to the king whom he had rescued from the dragon. Then the giant said: "Dear my lord, may it meet with your favor that I take my leave of you, and let me go to my kin. I have been away from them for some sixteen years. They do not know whether I am dead or alive. They must think that they have lost me. And if you sound the horn here in this great forest, then I will come to you at once and will be at your service." Then he swore a proper oath to him. They parted there; the giant was delighted by that.

Vidvilt rode at once to the castle, where he found the king whom he had rescued from the dragon. When the gatekeeper saw him, he shouted into the castle: "Attention! Dear my lords, prepare yourselves well, for a dear guest is arriving here—Vidvilt, the young man, who has stopped there in the meadow." There was a great uproar. The king with all his servants, and the queen, as well, with her beautiful little daughter—they all rode out with very great rejoicing. As they got close to him, they began to welcome him warmly. He was quite courteous to them in gesture, but the noble warrior said nothing.

The king asked him the tale of what had happened to him—what I tell you is the truth. He answered not a word. The king did not know what had happened to him that he would not speak or talk. They led him into the castle at once and clothed him in silk robes. When the king saw that he was wounded, he at once sent for doctors—four good physicians. They came there very quickly. They wanted to draw the lance out of him, but he did not wish to let them near him and pushed them away from himself quite discourteously, for he had sworn—the noble warrior—that no one was to draw it out except Lorel to whom he was true.

The lance caused him such pain that he could neither sit nor walk and had to lie in bed from the pain that he had from it. When the king saw that, he said to his daughter: "My dear little daughter, now help the fine warrior. If you do not help him out of his distress, then he will surely die." "Father mine, father dear, give me your counsel about how I am to help him. May God grant that I am able to do it well." He said: "Go to him quite late and play a board-game with him. Then cool wine will be brought to the two of you in a golden cup. When he puts it to his lips, then at that moment you should be ready and draw the lance out of him at that moment. You need not flee from him; he will do you no harm at all, for he ever treats ladies with great courtesy."

The princess did not shirk but immediately did as her father had commanded. She at once drew the lance out of him. He then sank back against the wall and fell unconscious there. The king was glad. He sent at once for good doctors who healed his wounds. Now that he was hale and hearty, and had remained there some six weeks, he wished to ride away. The king then said: "You must remain here, young man. I will give you my daughter in marriage." He gave him a sign for "No." The king said: "You unblemished warrior, you must take her in marriage whether you like it or not, although I hope that it is not very abhorrent to you. I do not know anyone up and down the German lands to whom I would rather give her, for I hold you in great favor." The king at once sent out messengers everywhere in all lands: whoever would like to eat, drink, and live well for four weeks should come—he was giving his daughter to a man in marriage. Vidvilt thought: "Let him go ahead and prepare for it— indeed I will not go through with it!"

King Arthur was made aware of the matter. He then also wished to be of service to the king who had long been his good friend. He brought with him a great host of warriors and many bold knights.

Then Lorel's father also wished to strive and be of service to him and also wanted to go there. He wanted to banish all discomfort there. Lorel said to her father: "I would also like to come along; perhaps I can find out something about my dear husband." Her father said: "Let it be done. I hope that we can find out whether he has survived. That giant was quite perfected in its great might."

Vidvilt's mother was also told of this great wedding. She went before her father, who had now become an old man. She said: "My dear father, may you ever be blessed; let us delay no longer, and let us ride to the wedding, and let us be of service to this king, and perhaps we might find out something about my dear husband and my dear son." The king said: "I will do that gladly, since a great company will assemble there. I hope that we will learn of them. I am now quite an old man and have performed great wonders in my day. Since it has been years since anyone has sought my service, now I would like to lay club on shield." Then he led a great host, some eight thousand or more, whom he clothed in matching livery of the best cloth that he could find.

Now when they arrived there, and Vidvilt saw them all, he recognized all his kin, but the same was not true of the fine warrior—what I tell you is true—they did not recognize the resplendent hero. There was great joy at court from music of many kinds of stringed instruments, from singing and courtly amusements, sword-fighting and jousting. There was no one there to whom it seemed that the bridegroom had a peer in strength, great beauty, and manifold worthiness—except that the people all regretted that the young lord was mute.

I will abbreviate the tale for you: Lorel also went there with many a beautiful maiden and wished to see the bridegroom. The beautiful maiden who had also ridden to King Arthur's court for young Vidvilt also went with her. As soon as she caught sight of him, she clearly recognized him and her heart then filled with joy. Then she went quite quickly and led Lorel into a chamber. She said: "Dear and gracious my lady, may it meet your favor that I would tell you welcome news. May God be praised that you have come here." She said: "Do you not recognize the bold man who is to be the bridegroom? It is Vidvilt, my dear lord." Lorel said: "Be silent. You remind me of all my grief. I fear he is, alas, dead or otherwise in great adversity." The maiden again said to her: "It is he, on my firm oath." Lorel said: "How might that be?— He was, after all, not mute." She said: "Mute or not, it is he and no other!"

Indeed Lorel was not lax and had herself taken to her father and there told him of the matter. He was then quite delighted. He sent for all his counselors and asked them all, on their honor, how he might proceed in the matter. They said: "My lord, be not lax. Go to King Arthur, tell him of the matter, and ask his counsel." The king quickly did that. When he came to King Arthur, he took him by the hand. He said: "Dear and gracious my lord, give me honorable counsel." King Arthur said: "Dear my lord, what can this mean?" He said: "The lands and peoples know well that my land and I have suffered great torment from a devilish woman who cursed my land and people and my own body, so that only a single castle remained to me that is still called Wachsenstein. My wife sent out a beautiful maiden who rode to you at your court and she brought back with her a man who was to fight the mighty giant. Vidvilt is his name. He came riding with her into my land. When he saw my troubles, he had great mercy on my discomfort. He said: 'I will deliver you from your adversity, even if I have to die for it.' Then my wife promised him, on her oath, my daughter Lorel, the beautiful maiden. If he were to deliver us from our suffering, then my daughter was to become his wife. Now he has delivered us, scarcely ten weeks ago. I have had a search conducted for him in all lands. I could find him nowhere. Now I have found the young man right here. It is he who is to be the bridegroom. I hope that he is to take my dear daughter."

King Arthur thus said: "I am certainly delighted by these words and know well that it is true. His father is indeed also here." He was quite quickly summoned; then the noble knight came at once. They then told him the tale and what the situation was. Then a great uproar arose among the people everywhere concerning who was to be whose bridegroom. The tale resounded far and wide.

When his mother heard it, her suffering was then overturned. Then she and her father at once went where they found King Arthur and told him that she was Vidvilt's mother. He said: "Now I am certainly delighted by that, since you have found your husband right here, whom you had lost for many years. That is certainly true." Then they sent for Sir Gawain, who came to his lords. When the worthy knight drew near to his lord, King Arthur, then King Arthur thus spoke to him: "Sir Gawain, are you here? Do you not know this beautiful lady and this elderly man?" He said: "I cannot deny that I have seen them both. That I declare on my oath." The fine lady then began to weep pitiably and fell on his neck and pressed him to her breast and embraced and kissed him. She said: "Fortunate am I that in this dear hour I have found you here, dear my lord." He was certainly also delighted.

He then said to his wife: "Let us not remain here any longer, but let us go to our dear son." Then they went at once to where they found Vidvilt—many ladies and men went with them—and when they caught sight of him, they fell on his neck; they embraced and kissed the fine youth. His mother said: "Dear son, what has happened to you that you do not wish to speak or talk. You were indeed not born mute." Then he turned away and acted as if he were not there. She said: "Alas, the sorrowful tale! Why will you not name yourself and not identify yourself to us. You are, after all, our child. Speak to us, or you will make blind our joy." They pled with him and wept pitiably. He paid them no attention, that young lord. All the ladies and the men who stood there on the ground pled with him to name himself and identify himself. He paid them no attention.

Thereafter the beautiful Lorel also came with her maidens: there one could see a courtly company! As soon as she saw him, now you might well wish to hear what she said: "May God grant you welcome, dear my lord, who have delivered from great pain my father and all his land. They would have burned forever. Now do not let me be dishonored—did you not fight for them?!—and speak to me and remember that we have made vows to each other." No matter what plea she made or what she did, he indeed steadfastly kept his oath to keep silent until she had given him the command three days in a row. She embraced him and kissed him and wept pitiably. Then he laughed, the young man. The maiden who also requested that he [. . .].[14]

The night grew dark so that she had to leave him. The next day she began to return to him and took with her the parrot, the beautiful little bird that he had given the beautiful maiden. The bold man had won it with his sword. As soon as the parrot caught sight of him, it flew around his head: "Welcome, dear my lord!" For it had been taught to speak. The people were delighted to hear that. Lorel again pled with him as plaintively as she had done before. She said: "If you wish to leave me in this distress forever, then tomorrow I will kill myself before your very eyes." He did not speak, but smiled at her.

On the third day when she began to plead, he gave her his hand. "It is I, Vidvilt, your beloved husband." They were all delighted. Then Lorel's father thus said: "Come then, my dear son-in-law, Lorel—and all that I have—is to be your own. I make it all subject to you." Then the other king said: "No!

God forbid! He is to have my daughter as his wife. She kept him alive; he would certainly have died." Then Lorel's father again spoke there: "I hope that no one may take him from me, since it is obvious that he first made a vow to my daughter. He is rightfully mine, without any jest. Now, let us have a legal verdict rendered—king and duke, knight and squire—which of the two of us has the legal right. Let them render a verdict at once."

Nor did that other king oppose this. A court was convened. Everyone there rendered the verdict that in all respects—since he had first made a vow to Lorel—he was to keep that vow at once. The verdict remained thus. Lorel was quite delighted by it. He was led home with great rejoicing. And all the lords and ladies who had come to the court all went with him, along with his father and mother, King Arthur and all his council, and his grandfather with his great host.

Why prolong the tale any further: they had a splendid wedding, than which none more splendid has ever been said to have occurred either before or since. Now, let us refrain from further words: Vidvilt became a mighty lord and won very great honor. After his father-in-law died, he obtained his entire kingdom. His father and his mother went home to their land, as did his grandfather, the bold warrior, who also soon died, as did, long thereafter, his father, the bold warrior. Vidvilt was the sole heir of all of them and continued to live at Wachsenstein and sought honor all his life, that same young lord. Thereafter he accomplished a great many grand things in combat: he slew many giants and dwarves.

The tale of Vidvilt herewith has an end. May God send us his aid and soon lead us to the Holy Land, according to our heart's desire. Thus does the scribe—who here gladly serves all honorable ladies—entreat and desire.

7

Bovo of Antona

בבֿא דאנטונא / *Bovo d'Antona*

Elijah b. Asher Halevi Ashkenazi [Elia Levita / Elye Bokher], 1507; published 1541

The author of בבֿא דאנטונא *Bovo d'Antona*, Elia(s) Levita / Elye Bokher / Elyahu Baḥur / 1549–1469) אליה בחור), is one of the most interesting men of letters of the period of European Humanism. It often seems that his biography could itself function as a (slightly skewed) cultural history of the late fifteenth and early sixteenth centuries in central Europe and northern Italy. Born in Ipsheim near Neustadt an der Aisch (near Nuremberg), Levita worked as a teacher, publisher, printer, and author of scholarly texts as well as popular romance and biting satirical diatribes in both Germany and Italy. He was mentor, friend, and colleague of the great men of church and synagogue, university, and the arts and toiled tirelessly for most of his adult life in the fledgling printing industry, as lector, editor, translator, scholar, and poet. He worked with Paulus Fagius, Johannes de Kampen, Sebastian Münster, and Cardinal Egidio da Viterbo, among others, and counted other famous Humanists in Padua, Venice, and Rome as his students in Hebrew and Aramaic, from whom he seems himself to have learned some Latin and Greek. By means of his grammars and lexica of Hebrew and Aramaic, *Sefer ha-baḥur* (Rome, 1518), *Meturgeman* (Isny, 1541), and *Shemous devorim* (Isny, 1542; *EYT*, 44), he opened Jewish literary and cultural traditions to a broader range of Jewish readers, but also served the needs of the newly developing Christian scholarship on Jewish textual traditions, in particular the Bible, Talmud, Targum, and Kabbalah. While his Yiddish translation of the Psalms into Yiddish (Venice, 1545; *EYT*, 49) was neither the first such translation of the book nor a particularly innovative one, it did nonetheless broaden the effort to make this important text of the Jewish tradition accessible to Jews unable to read Hebrew. His pioneering research into the origin and development of the masoretic tradition *Massoret ha-Massoret* (Venice, 1538) made a long-term contribution to the development of textual criticism in biblical studies.

In addition to his historical poem די שריפה בון וונידיג *Di sreyfe fun venedig* (The Great Fire of Venice) (1514; *EYT*, 34) and his biting Venetian satire, הַמַבְדִיל בֵין קוֹדֶש לְחוֹל *Ha-mavdil ben koudesh le-khoul* (Ha-mavdil Song) (1514; *EYT*, 35),[1] Levita's *Bovo d'Antona* was one of the most enduring tales of early Yiddish literature. As he notes in his preface, his source was a Tuscan text,[2] which was itself the descendant of a long tradition of translations and adaptations of the originally thirteenth-century Anglo-Norman romance *Bueve de Hantone.*[3] Although not published until 1541, the preface notes that the text was composed thirty-four years earlier. Two manuscripts seem to record the earlier version of the text.[4]

While, as noted, Elia Levita was one of the great intellectual lights of his age, not just in the Jewish sphere, and while his *Bovo d'Antona* was immensely popular over the course of centuries, and while it has even today remained one of the most widely known *titles* of a literary work from the early Yiddish period, this early-sixteenth-century example of a late medieval epigonic romance is, it must be acknowledged, interesting primarily because it is in Yiddish. As any knowledgeable reader of late medieval and Renaissance European literature perceives in reading *Bovo*, whether browsing stanzas here and there or reading the whole, neither the larger plot as conceived by Levita nor its specific poetic execution is aesthetically remarkable: the poet seems trapped by the strictures of the rhyme scheme, which causes the missequencing of events; the monotonous overuse of line-filling auxiliary verbs ("he began to . . ."); the beginning of line after line with a filler דא "here, there, when, then, that . . . ," which stretches the bounds of the idiomatic in order to fill out a line, a compositional pattern that often seems only very slightly removed from doggerel; and so on. Zinberg seems also willing to acknowledge some narrative problems in the text, suggesting that *Bovo* has a confused plot (68 and 72), while still maintaining that Levita is a master of the verse form, whose "verses are rich, resonant, and often overwhelm one with the unexpected assonances" (75). One might also note the remark by Jerry Smith: "The hero is static and two-dimensional and evidences little growth or maturation in the course of the tale; the action is extremely episodic and there is little overall structure or plot development. . . . [T]here are no underlying themes or broader implications."[5]

Very often it is simply a momentary slip that undoes Levita's verse. A couple of examples will illustrate the recurring imprecision. When Bovo inherits his father-in-law's land at the latter's death (st. 647), the text notes: און אלי שטרייט נאם ער עס איין (without any battle he gained control of / captured it), a formulation that already verges on imprecision. In the previous sentence, however, the reader is told that ער דורפֿט עש ניט ויל גיווינן (He did not have to win / conquer it very much). Were the text to read that he did not have to fight much for it, then it would have been an example of the typically epic use of *litotes*, but as it stands the statement borders on nonsense, since conquering is an absolute—land is either conquered or not, and if a man now possesses it, then he either conquered it or he gained it without conquest. But it is logically not possible to conquer "more" or "less" or "much" or "slightly." Likewise imprecise, in stanza 475, a lion rears up not on its hind legs, but rather on its הינטרשטי (hind-most) legs—again, as with the conquest image, almost right, but then in fact so very wrong that it seems almost comical in a genre in which this particular type of wordplay is all but absent. In stanza 533 Alborigo leads the troops—and his brother Dodon—into battle; a few lines later, however, without any further information about where they are in relation to each other or their troops, suddenly Dodon is said to be at the front of the troops. Earlier, instead of there being "many people" in a hall or its being "full of people" or "full everywhere," Levita writes, "It was everywhere full of many people" (511,5); such a combination of several possible and more or less equivalent idioms into a single nonidiomatic phrase skews the entire expression.

Levita thus, again and again, almost finds the proper expression, but only occasionally does the poet rise above the mundane with an astute observation or a memorable line. In general, *Bovo* is a very ordinary example of what had by 1507 become a very ordinary genre, predictable in poetic form and narrative content.[6] As noted above, its only legitimate interest is that it is in Yiddish, not English, French, Italian, or German, where it would have joined scores of other equally colorless make-work romances from the same period and of the same ilk, instead of being one of only a handful of such works in its own language tradition. Its mere existence in Yiddish makes it interesting in terms of cultural history, while in literary terms it is, regrettably, quite forgettable.

This last remark should not be misunderstood, however: the very fact that *Bovo* is in Yiddish and the further fact that the story continued to be reprinted and adapted over the course of centuries are indeed of great *literary-historical* importance. That such a work drew such long-term interest from Jewish audiences should not be understood as a criticism of them any more than a parallel statement acknowledging the fact that audiences of other vernacular literatures of the period enjoyed similarly intellectually undemanding and uninspired texts should be so understood, especially since all those literatures (including Yiddish) also offered a broad range of other very accomplished literary texts.

It seems to me that scholars have made rather too much of the idea that the light, quasi-comic tone of *Bovo* can be read as a Jewish satire of the Christian world of chivalry.[7] In the time and place in which the Yiddish narrative was composed, the mode of knightly chivalry represented was not an actual mode of life in Christian society, nor obviously was it so in Jewish society. Moreover, one might acknowledge, chivalric romance of, for instance, King Arthur's court and his knights' battles with giants and dragons had never been a remotely *realistic* portrayal of any society for any audience, and for the nonaristocratic sixteenth-century Christian audience of such romances (as opposed to the strictly aristocratic audience of chivalric romance during the period of its inception in the late twelfth century, whose values were refracted in the ones of the knightly society depicted), the world of Orlando or Ruggiero or Buovo was as alien as it was for the Jewish audience of *Bovo*. It might be worth noting that even for that aristocratic twelfth- and thirteenth-century "ideal" audience, the literary world of Arthurian chivalry was an alien fantasyland with little connection to the lived daily reality of life—even of actual knights at an actual royal court.[8]

Thus, although there may well be an ironic tone in the Yiddish text, it is not because the Jewish audience—more so than the sixteenth-century, urban, merchant-class Christian audience of the Tuscan source text—was more "alienated" from the values and mores of the protagonists. It might be salutary to remember that this period was the age of Ariosto's highly stylized and ironic Renaissance perspective on romance and that *Bovo*'s publication date is only slightly more than a half century removed from the savage satire of the obsolete world of chivalry in Cervantes's *Don Quijote*. It is thus troubling to assume that a specifically Jewish adaptation of romance would somehow necessarily or "naturally" ironize the world of chivalry more than its Tuscan source or any other (near) contemporary postchivalric knightly romance.

One final item must be noted: at several points in the course of the tale, Levita hints at or simply assumes that the protagonists are Jewish, as, for instance, when Druzeyne mentions to her father that she has forgotten to have her infant sons circumcised (st. 498), or when the noblewoman Troyen exclaims, "as surely as I am a Jew" (387). It is impossible to reconstruct how the sixteenth-century Jewish audience would have reacted to such an identification of some members of the ostensibly aristocratic feudal classes as "suddenly" or "momentarily" Jewish. While Erika Timm claims that it was clear to the Jewish audience that such characters, with such names, could not *actually* (!) be Jewish,[9] the poet—by means of recurring and overt narrative markers—in fact sporadically claims that they are. Perhaps I should note on

Timm's remark that just as I am unsure what she might mean by the "actual" as opposed to the fictional ethnic identity of fictional characters in an at least slightly ironic work of fiction published a half millennium ago, I am likewise disinclined to doubt the author simply because his claims present modern readers with interpretive problems, especially in a narrative set in a fantasy world in which a single mother can walk from Flanders to Babylon carrying twin toddlers or a talking creature who is half-human and half-canine despoils a monastery for the benefit of its human allies. It is the world of late-medieval romance, and it entertained Yiddish-language audiences for centuries, perhaps in part because Levita teased them with sporadic hints that some of his characters were Jewish.

Over the course of the centuries, this tale of the heroic adventures of the noble Bovo indeed proved to be one of the most beloved tales in the early Yiddish literary tradition, with numerous reprintings (with and without adaptation) even into the twentieth century. The plot is that of quite a conventional adventure romance of the later Middle Ages: the hero is exiled from his homeland by the machinations of his murderous mother, wanders through the world (eventually as far as Babylon), along the way growing to love the princess Druzeyne, from whom he is then long separated before ultimately celebrating a triumphant return home and finally reuniting with Druzeyne and their twin sons. The entire romance comprises 5,262 lines, divided into 650 stanzas, in addition to the prologue and epilogue in rhymed couplets, followed by a glossary of Italicisms in the Yiddish text. The *ottava rima* verse form (ABABABCC), borrowed probably from the Italian poetic tradition (instead of the then new Italian-based Hebrew use of that form), entered Yiddish in *Bovo* significantly before it was adapted into other European traditions. The author himself published the *editio princeps* of the text (Isny, 1541) while working for Paulus Fagius in his Hebrew print shop in Isny (Allgäu). The text includes numerous terms peculiar to the Yiddish of Ashkenazim resident in Italy, which prompted the author to add a two-page Italian-Yiddish glossary to the end of the text, most likely in order to increase the book's potential audience by making this specialized vocabulary accessible to Ashkenazim outside Italy. The text here presented is translated from the 1541 edition, with only occasional use of the manuscripts (when they clarify an issue).

Source: Isny, 1541; extant: Zurich, Zentralbibliothek.

Edition: Judah A. Joffe, ed., *Elye Bokher, poetishe shafungen in yidish, ershter band: Bovo d'Antona* (New York: Judah A. Joffe, 1949) (facsimile of Isny 1541 edition); online facsimile of Isny, 1541, http://archive.org/details/nybc207004.

Translation: Moyshe Knaphays, trans., *Elye Bokher, Bovo-bukh* (Buenos Aires: Yoysef Lifshits Fond baym Kultur-Kongres, 1962); Jerry Christopher Smith, trans., *Elia Levita Bachur's Bovo-Buch* (Tucson: Fenestra Books, 2003).

Research: Zinberg, *Geshikhte*, 82–112, 406–9; Erik, *Geshikhte*, 179–95; Erik, *Roman*, 33–90; Max Weinreich, *Bilder fun der yidisher literatur-geshikhte* (Vilne: Tomor, 1928), 149–71; Shmeruk, *Prokim*, 97–120, 141–56; Baumgarten, *Introduction*, 166–89; N. B. Minkoff, *Elye Bokher un zayn Bovo-bukh* (New York: Vakser, 1950); G. E. Weil, *Elia Lévita, humaniste et massorète, 1469–1549* (Leiden: E. J. Brill, 1963); Benjamin Hrushovski (Harshav), "The Creation of Accentual Iambs in European Poetry and Their First Employment in a Yiddish Romance in Italy (1508–09)," in *For Max Weinreich on His Seventieth Birthday* (The Hague: Mouton, 1964), 108–46; Erika Timm, "Wie Elia Levita sein Bovobuch für den Druck überarbeitete. Ein Kapitel aus der italo-jiddischen Literatur der Renaissancezeit," *Germanisch-Romanische Monatsschrift* 72 [NF 41] (1991): 61–81; Claudia Rosenzweig, "La letteratura yiddish in Italia: L'esempio del *Bovo de-Antona* di Elye Bocher," *Acme: Annali della Facoltà di Lettere e Filosofia dell'Università degli Studi di Milano* 50, no. 3 (1997): 159–89; Claudia Rosenzweig, "Il poema yiddish in versi 'Bovo d'Antona' in una versione manoscritta del XVI secolo," *Medievo Romanzo* 26, no. 1 (ser. 3, no. 7) (2002): 49–68; Claudia Rosenzweig, "The Jewish Knight, the Jewish Princess, and the Sceptical Reader," in *Early Modern Yiddish Poetry*, edited by Shlomo Berger (Amsterdam: Menasseh be Israel Institute, n.d.), 7–25; H. D. Vos, "Elia Levita's *Bovo d'Antona* Commentary" (typescript, 2012), 82 pages.

Bovo d'Antona is the title of this book, a courtly piece of work. Elye Bokher's work is well known. It was printed in the city of Isny, and 302 equals the small count [of the year of publication].[10]

Preface:

I, Elye Levi, the author, honorable and courtly servant of all honorable women, am troubled, as you well know, that some ladies take it amiss that I have not also published some of my Yiddish books for them, so that they might enjoy them and read from them on Sabbaths and holidays. Well, let me tell you the truth: it also seemed right and proper to me—since I have written eight or nine books on the Holy Scriptures[11] and sent them out into the world in print—that I now undertake—since I am now drawing near to the end of my days, and if, today or tomorrow, I should be laid out with my toes turned up, then all my books and my poems would be forgotten and lost—and for that reason, lest any of them slip away from me, I will publish them all, one after the other. Even if there were twice as many, I would not shy away from reaching the goal. So I will begin—may it go well—with this book that is called *Bovo.* And it is quite true that I made it out of an Italian book thirty-four years ago, but I additionally invented a great deal of it. Whoever reads from it will understand it, but there are several Italian words in it; whoever does not understand them should look at the very last pages of the book, where I will explain them thoroughly in alphabetical order. I cannot, however, convey to you the melody that fits the book, unless one were able to read music or knew solfège: then I could indeed help him. But I sing it to an Italian melody. If anyone can come up with a better melody, he will have my thanks.

(1) God be forever praised and His wonders proclaimed, for He is honored and exalted on the lips of the pious. He is mighty above and below. His praise is infinite; none can fully comprehend it, for it has neither conclusion nor end. (2) May His Holy Name give me strength so that I not fail to complete this task of rendering this Italian book into Yiddish, and that I pay attention and not be deficient in any way such that people would laugh at me. But enough, it is time for deeds!

(3) It is said that in Lombardy there dwelt long ago a duke, of great chivalry, without peer far and wide. Duke Guidon was the dear man's name, a mighty warrior in all battles. He wore the crown with great honor in a city named Antona. (4) It was there that he had passed his time, now a man of sixty years. It is written in the book how this most nobly born duke had remained without a wife and without any entanglements with ladies his entire life. And when he reached old age, the better he was covered and tucked in bed, the colder he got. (5) No matter how warm it was, it was not enough for him; he acted as if he were freezing to death. His wise warriors said to him: "Gracious my lord, follow our counsel: send out and search high and low and everywhere for a spirited young maiden to warm and take care of you." It would have been better for him had he lain alone even longer!

(6) The daughter of the Duke of Burgundy was given to him in marriage. Her peer could not be found this side of Babylon. He liked her well, and she was a suitable match for him. She was called Brandonia the Fair. She led a splendid life with him: her every desire was fulfilled. She had fine days and evil nights. (7) She kept him warm by effective means—I cannot tell you more, lest scandal burst forth. Brandonia the Fair became pregnant and, by God's grace, bore a son. No one had ever seen a more beautiful child, whose looks and bearing were altogether fitting. He called him by the name of Bovo.

(8) You might well imagine how great was his father's joy. He had a burgrave whom he asked to foster the lad for him and be his guardian and mentor. This earl, whose name was Sinibald, did as he [the duke] wished. His forest castle was called San Simon. (9) No mightier castle had ever been seen. The duke safeguarded his own property in that castle, which was some ten miles from Antona and built on a steep peak. The duke began to speak to Sinibald: "Take my son and have your wife suckle him and order him to be cared for in all things. And if he cries, then have someone sing to him."

(10) Sinibald took the young lord and brought him to his wife at San Simon. She very happily suckled him. She [soon] did not know what to do with him: it was clear when he began to grow up that he had become a man in body. When he was a ten-year-old boy he constantly carried with him two training foils in his hair.[12] (11) And Sinibald taught him fencing—thrust and parry—and also jousting. He wanted to slay and slaughter everyone, such wild ideas coursed through his brain.

Sometimes he went out riding with four or five squires to visit his mother, but she was not in the habit of showing him any affection: she hated him because of his father, (12) whom she no longer wished to see or hear; he gave her little pleasure. One day she began to say to herself: "Alas for the great sorrow in my heart! My father and mother did this to me. May God give them both diarrhea. How could they have had such evil hearts as to give this old fart to me. (13) I will come up with a plan, even if costs me my life. I have no desire to stay with him and wither away, grow moldy and corroded. I will track down a fine youth who will sport with me as I wish."

Now she had a courtier named Ritsard who was savvy in the ways of evil. (14) One day she called him to the chambers that the duke had had built for her. She said: "If you will not betray me, I will entrust an important matter to you and will give you a thousand ducats. If you refuse to do it, you will regret it: I will scream that you are trying to rape me and have you killed on the spot." (15) Ritsard said: "Gracious my lady, why do you need to make such a grand request. There is nothing under the sun that I would not do, if you asked." Nonetheless he was almost overcome by a bout of the shits, and the tremors came over him as though he had a fever. He thought: "If I escape your clutches this time, you will never catch me again."

(16) Brandonia said: "You must undertake a journey to France, where there lives a noble young warrior named Duke Dodon of Mainz. My husband once thrust a dagger into his dear father's belly. Because of that you should say to him that I wish to help him avenge his father. (17) And you should take this

letter to him, so that he might come here to Lombardy. He is to kill my husband: the game preserve is in *that* forest. I will send him there to hunt. Tell him to wait there with his vassals. There will not be much of a skirmish or battle. Only tell him to take care of this scum there. (18) Then he is to come here helter-skelter and before all else take control of the city. Then I will weep and wail—if only I can, while holding back my laughter. I will soon join up with him, and right away we will have the wedding. Then I will cling to him day and night: I want to catch up on what I have been missing."

(19) Ritsard took his leave of her, took the letter, and set out on his way. He nonetheless thought of his worthy lord and struggled with his own great sorrow; he often had the inclination to turn back, but the Devil would not let him. The situation had to play out. He went his way and arrived in Mainz. (20) He rode to the palace and tied up his steed. He went up and entered the hall and told Dodon what she had commanded and gave him the letter as she had requested. Dodon read the letter two or three times. Thereafter he showed it to his wise counselors and said with great rage to his summoners: "Quick, take your cudgels and beat him. (21) Seize him and throw him in prison. This traitor must hang. I will not trust the treacherous whore. She plans to trap me there with the same treachery with which they betrayed my father. They think they can lure me by this means."

Ritsard was terror-stricken and began to say: "Gracious my lord, you dare not make this mistake. (22) Send and get information for yourself. I promise you, if you find out that I have lied, then you should flay me alive." Dodon thought: "I should risk it. Perhaps he is telling the truth; I will find out. There is after all one thing plausible here, for a young wife does not want to have an old husband." (23) He said to Ritsard: "Go quickly and tell her to prepare herself well for it. Say that I will help her out of her distress; I pledge myself to it for her sake." Thus did Ritsard bring her his reply.

Now listen to what she was able to devise. When the time seemed right to her to get started, she began to feign illness. (24) On a Sunday at three o'clock in the morning—may the Creator demolish and destroy her—she began to groan and shriek; no one could quiet her. She was sick to death and vomited up her insides. She said: "I now belong to Death. Alas, I must die. My uterus is trying to expel my heart." (25) The duke went to her side. "My darling, what has happened?" He handed her a specimen glass and said: "Sweetheart, give us a urine sample, and tell me what you desire. You will lack for nothing. Tell me what you would like to have, and if it exists in the world, you shall have it." (26) Brandonia said: "If I dared trouble you, I would like to ask you a little favor: that you rise early tomorrow morning and ride out hunting for wild game. I would like to eat it in a broth, or make a hot roast. And, my lord, if you could accomplish that for me, I think it would revive me."

(27) He lay down with her, and they talked until dawn approached. Then he leapt out of bed and ordered his armor to be brought. He said: "Sound the trumpets!" He wanted to go out hunting with all his vassals. When Brandonia began to see that, she said: "My lord, let it not be done thus. (28) I tell you in truth, dear my lord, your armor will make you too warm. Since you need not fight with anyone, I would astutely advise you to ride out with only two men, leaving the others at home. Those two will provide you with enough company." The dear fool let himself be persuaded.

(29) The noble and honorable duke rode out that same morning with his two squires and without a care; on his hand a sparrow hawk. Now Duke Dodon, ruination of kingdoms, had taken cover in the forest and lay in wait with four hundred men in armor not far away. (30) Duke Guidon had been hunting with his dogs only a short while when Dodon thought the time was right and suddenly came forth and quickly gave Guidon deep wounds, while his men shot him with arrows that remained in his body. He died, alas, on the spot.

(31) After that had taken place they hurried into the city and began to shout "Dodon! Dodon!" and to murder and to burn. As soon as Brandonia saw him, she recognized him from afar and quickly ran to meet him and led him home: he had to lie with her.

(32) Therefore, dear sirs, you can see what catastrophe comes from evil women: how they have their husbands hacked to pieces so that they can carry on their debauchery. All misfortune comes from women. Look at what King Solomon's books record, how he sought a virtuous lady and never found one his entire life.

(33) Now the city was filled with howls of distress and the hot tears of many townspeople and gentry, both rich and poor, merchants and shopkeepers. A stone would have been moved to pity. There was much screaming and shrieking: "Alas, alas, our dear lord!" (34) Many there were who wished to resist and avenge their dear lord. They took up sword and lance and wanted to stab the murderers. Brandonia immediately sent for them and began to speak to them with good words: "Why do you want to oppose the two of us. What is done is done. You should make the best of it. (35) And although the old Duke Guidon long proved trustworthy, now look at my dear husband Dodon, this young, mighty, noble giant. You will all have gifts from him, such as vineyards, fields, and meadows, and this year not one of you need pay tolls, or fees, or taxes. (36) You should, therefore, follow my advice and view it now as

square and even, and you should swear your loyalty to him, so that you will virtuously pay homage to him." They, too, thought: "Why should we fight this so vehemently? Let us just let it slide." And they all swore loyalty to him, albeit unwillingly and with great sorrow.

(37) Now Bovo had heard the clamor and hidden in fear. Sinibald, his honorable guardian, was very worried about the youth, not knowing where he had gone. He looked for him the whole morning all over the house, behind every cask and every sack. (38) Then he look for him more than once in all the nooks and crannies of the stables. Now Bovo had lain down in a great hayloft, and when he heard his worthy guardian, he came out immediately, embraced him with both arms, and said: "Dear guardian, what has happened?"

(39) Sinibald then told him the whole situation, including the distressing tale concerning his father. Then Sinibald quickly went out to assemble the old lords who he knew had always been loyal to Guidon and told them that they should be on their guard and that they should withdraw with him to flee with Bovo to San Simon. (40) Thus, in a heavy rainstorm at three o'clock in the morning or even later, they secretly left that place with great sorrow and gnashing of teeth. There were perhaps sixty men altogether. Among them was Ritsard, the traitor who had taken the letter to Dodon, but none of them knew anything about that. (41) They trusted him in all things, thinking that he was the same as in times past. The traitor wanted to better his position. He thought: "There is no need to wait any longer. How can I improve my position with Dodon. Secretly I will turn around and ride the other way, blow the whistle on them all, and enable him to capture them."

(42) He quickly returned to the city and betrayed them all to Dodon, identifying them to him one-by-one—those who were taking Bovo to his foster-mother. Dodon immediately flew into a rage. He said: "By the old Goat of Schaffhausen, if I get my hands on them, I will beat the lice out of them quite thoroughly with clubs. (43) I will awaken their lice for them not otherwise than with great whacks." He immediately said to his mighty warriors: "Go, see if you can catch them. Urge your horses onward and let them feel your spurs in their flanks." They replied: "Gladly, my lord." And they ran off as though they had lost their senses.

(44) After Ritsard had betrayed them, he began to ride back to them and said to them: "Dear companions, I would advise you to ride a bit slower with the lad. Why hurry so? We need fear no one; we are now safe from everyone, and need not give a hoot about anyone." (45) So they began to ride slower, and after only a short while they saw from afar, a half mile behind them, a large hostile force hurrying after them directly across the fields. Sinibald said:

"They are after us. If we do not flee, they will capture us." (46) Ritsard said: "I will go see where they are going and who they are." No sooner said than done. He rode like an arrow shot from a bowstring and began to speak to them: "Ho, give your horses their heads, for they have seen you now. If you do not ride fast, they will get away from you." (47) And he quickly turned and again cleverly took up his traitor's role.

Now, Sinibald had a much admired son, called Teyrets the Mighty. He could defend himself well against ten men. He rode in front on point and saw Ritsard riding back and forth. He could clearly recognize that it was a matter of treachery. (48) He began to say to his father: "Do you not see what is going on? Ritsard is obviously betraying us. I see how he is working his treachery. By Goat, I am going to go skewer him." He charged him with great force and thrust his lance into his belly, so that he fell there and turned up his toes. (49) His neck was broken. Before he could utter either "Woe" or "Alas," his treachery was already avenged. May all traitors suffer the same fate!

Now that Teyrets had slain him, he turned around and began to say: "Whoever wants to sleep tonight in one piece, let him trust his safety to his speed."[13] (50) While they turned to flee—they were eager to reach San Simon—the others chased after them at speed. But they could not keep Bovo with them; he was riding a very large horse, which did not turn out well for him: when he spurred it, then it reared and bucked. (51) He had to jump off the horse and fell on his back. The enemy galloped over quite easily; how quickly they snatched him up. The others rushed to San Simon and quickly drew up the drawbridge. When they saw that Bovo had remained outside, there arose a great lament.

(52) Bovo would have liked to jump on the horse, but he could not get away from them. They took the poor lad along with them back to Antona. They rushed into the city and barred all the gates and with great delight took Bovo to Dodon and Brandonia. (53) They looked at him askance and wasted few words on him. Let us leave them for the moment and speak further of those at San Simon.

They did not want to wait in the castle any longer. They rode out the gates to burn and rob and steal, and they took whatever they could get their hands on. (54) They did just as the wise would do; otherwise they would have been lost. They stocked the castle well with provisions for many a year: with stock animals, wood, iron, wine, oil, and grain. There were four hundred holed up inside. The Devil himself could not have taken the castle.

(55) That enraged Duke Dodon, who said: "I will not put up with this. All the land that has now become mine—I will use it all up to wage this war."

Now he had a noble brother whose name was Alborigo the Mighty. He then sent all the way to France, and he came riding with a thousand knights. (56) He sent him with all his knights to scale San Simon. They surrounded the castle, and the ones inside gave them all the finger and bared their buttocks to them. Thereafter they had to keep their peace, for the siege went on for many a day, as you will later hear.

(57) And when the war had lasted almost three years, Dodon himself set out from Antona and made himself comfortable on a meadow with all his lords and barons. He had his tent pitched nearby. One night as they all lay under the pavilion and everyone had already fallen asleep, Dodon suddenly began to scream bloody murder. (58) Everyone was awakened and greatly alarmed by this. His brother asked him what the matter was, and why he set up such a howl. Dodon said: "I myself have to laugh, for I was lying here dreaming how Bovo rode over to me here and slit my gullet." (59) Alborigo spoke: "Follow my advice; I tell you, dreams are not all lies. I swear to you on my honor, brother, that this lad will still cause you trouble. For that reason, you will want to defend yourself against him. At once put aside any further questions and order his mother to have her son secretly killed." (60) Dodon said: "Go quickly and tell my wife the dream. I am sure when she hears it, she will drive her son out or even have him killed—so much does she love me—so that the dream will not come true." Alborigo said: "Gladly will I do it."

(61) He then went into the city and told Brandonia what had happened. She was then quite alarmed but had no desire to underestimate it [the dream's importance]. She said: "Tell him not to worry. I will take care of the matter for him: he can let me see to Bovo, and then he will have nothing to confess to a priest." (62) Alborigo went back out and wanted to tell Dodon her response. Now Brandonia made a plan—may the evil plague strike her—how she could put her son to death, so that it would not come to light. And when she had hatched out a plan, she immediately sent for Bovo. (63) Bovo came to her and said: "Dear mother, what is your wish?" She said: "I was longing for you. Come, let us go for a walk." She took his hand and led him through some four chambers, locking him in the one in the very back. The poor lad yowled and shrieked! (64) Now, she wanted to make quite sure that no one could hear his screaming; so she closed the doors of the rooms leading to the chamber where he was, and put two props against each door.

This jest began to annoy Bovo; he wondered: "When is this going to end? Alas, my mother has forgotten me here. Damn, am I hungry!" (65) He began to scream and screamed very loudly for three whole days and nights. Now the evil crone Brandonia was afraid that someone close by would hear the screams and thought: "I will give him an herb secretly mixed in some food. It will kill him as soon as he eats it. What profit is there in torturing him further?" (66) She roasted a chicken for him and had it rubbed with the herb. Then she called her maid, a very old chambermaid and said: "I have, on my honor, left Bovo, my son, my dear one, my beloved child, my great delight, down there all alone in a chamber. (67) He has sat there the whole day. Bring him the chicken and tell him to eat it and be revived. I unfortunately forgot him. Tell him not to be angry with me."

The chambermaid took the food and immediately took it to the lad. She unlocked the door and found him sitting down, so weak that he could hardly speak. (68) He crawled along the wall to her. He had all but breathed out his soul. He attacked the chicken with both hands. He was about to shove a bite into his mouth when the maid quickly prevented him (for she loved him for his father's sake) and said: "Dear son, listen very closely to me, and on your life, do not eat a bite. (69) Your mother is trying to cause a catastrophe: she wants to kill you. She has poisoned the chicken. If you eat it, it will disagree with you mightily."

Now the story tells us that a puppy ran into the chamber with her as soon as it had been opened. (70) The lady was weeping for the boy and spoke to him as follows: "If you do not want to believe it, I will give you proof of it." She cut a bit from the chicken and tossed it to the puppy. Before it could even swallow the bite, its throat swelled closed so that it suffocated.

(71) As soon as Bovo had seen that, he began to beat his breast and tear his hair. "Alas and alack, what is to become of me? I would give up everything to get away from here. If I try to escape, someone will see me." He nonetheless set out running as fast as he could, and quickly ran through the whole city, right through the filth and mire. (72) No one told him the way or the route. He aimed directly for the city gate and ran right through crowds of people. Additionally, his appearance was so miserable that no one recognized him: his hair was shaggy and unkempt, and his fine color had turned quite pale.

When he passed through the city gate, (73) then he struck out right across the fields—he had no path. No horse could have kept pace with him; it would have been as much as a giant could do. Then his strength began to fail; he sat down in a meadow. After he had rested for a little while, then he again began to hurry away from there (74) and ran a bit further until he came to the sea, where he rested again. He was so hungry that he ate some grass. His limbs were completely exhausted, and after he had sat for a while, he lay down to sleep and remained lying there by the sea, asleep for the whole night. No one needed to rock him to sleep!

(75) In the same place where he was lying, it was not far from Illyria. When he had slept a good three hours beyond sunrise, a courtly galley came sailing by—it is all true, what I tell you—it had come from Barbary. One was keeping watch, in truth, and saw him lying there on the ground. (76) He began to say to the merchants: "I see there, not far away, a man who has been killed, unless all my senses deceive me." One of them said: "Let us bring him aboard. Whoever he is, we will easily find out."

Four of them jumped into the ship's boat and brought the poor boy to the galley. (77) He looked like someone who ought to be buried. He moved not a hair: he was unconscious. They had to revive him with sugar and pearl powder and by rubbing the lad—all his limbs, the upper ones and the lower ones—with vinegar and then with Madeira,[14] a whole cask, until he began to show signs of life. (78) And when they had revived him and he had regained consciousness, he was very surprised and began to look around. He wondered: "Did I go lame? Or have I not been beaten? How then did I get onto this galley? Did the Devil bring me here?"

(79) They told him where he had been and how they had brought him to the galley. Bovo had now completely recovered, and his great beauty was indescribable. They made a great fuss over him and showed him their great affection. Whenever and whatever they commanded, he did immediately. (80) Before they could say it, he had already jumped to it, serving all the merchants with joy, with constant singing, cheering, whooping, and rejoicing.

Now each one wanted the boy for himself, which led to a great conflict among them. One said: "I was the very first to see him." "But I revived him," said another. (81) A third one spoke up: "But I carried him on my back." A fourth said: "I would sooner let myself be stabbed than let any of you drive me away." They wanted to bash in each others' heads. They began to draw their weapons and shouted and had a huge bluster. Bovo quickly picked up an oar (82) and launched into the crowd whacking them with delight and bending the oar in doing so; thus did he separate them. They all had to drop their weapons. He said: "I swear on my oath, by no means may you fight about me. Let us discuss it, worthy fellows. Step back a bit, everyone, (83) and if you will follow my advice, step over here a bit, and you will lose nothing by it, I promise you. Listen to me for a couple of words: I promise I will serve you all until we come to the next port. Then sell me as a servant, and you can all divide the money as you wish. (84) So they all let Bovo settle the dispute. The pact was acceptable to everyone. They were all reconciled with each other. Bovo made them shake hands. And thereafter everything settled down.

They were sailing on the sea, sometimes with wind, sometimes becalmed, and they chatted for a long time with Bovo. (85) He told them a lot of new tales, and afterwards they began to ask him who his father and mother were and whether he had close family or kinsmen. Bovo said: "The Lord God has afflicted my parents; they are poor and maintained at public expense. They both live in Nuremberg in the almshouse. (86) My father is Hungarian, and my mother is French. She would have let me starve to death; she is a stingy and evil person. I was a wicked boy: I would have shit in her lap[15] before I would have put up with her any longer. For that reason I left the whole country behind." (87) The merchants laughed a good while and hid their giggling behind their hands.

They sailed another two or three miles when a violent storm arose. They hurried toward land. They were all trembling with fear. They wanted to sail as far as the port of Ancona. Then a great sea storm began. (88) There was great wind and rain and horrible thunder and lightning. Their lives all hung in the balance. They threw their property into the sea and began to say their best prayers, each his own separate one. They covered a great distance in a short time, while water rushed into the ship from all sides. (89) The sail was ripped to shreds, and the rudder broken to bits. They thrashed around in water up to the middle of their backs. They were like bath-house attendants.

But God granted them the good fortune to find an island in the middle of the sea, and they moored the galley there right away. (90) They tied it up so that it could not move, sparing no effort in bailing out the ship. The wind began to abate. They recognized that they were in Flanders. A fine city was across the water from them, and they began to sail over to it. That city was named Armonia. They sailed to it in the galley. (91) There was quite a powerful king in the city who was named Arminio. The galley was seen from the city, in which arquebuses were heard to fire. The king went up to the battlements with his nobles; they saw the galley sailing toward them. They sailed into the port and dropped anchor there.

(92) And after that had taken place, the king and his nobles went for an excursion there and began to have a look at the galley. The king was chatting with the merchants. The merchants said: "Gracious king, would you like to buy a boy? We will sell you one who lacks any defect." They told him the whole story of Bovo: (93) everything about how he came to be with them. Then they showed him the lad. He was white and ruddy and had a fine head of hair. No one could find a fault of any kind in him. He looked him over, front and back, and had him trot back and forth; just as with a saddle-horse that one wishes to sell, he had him run back and forth.

(94) Therefore, my dear sirs, consider this, how a duke's son came to this pass. Thus indeed no one should ever rely on possessions and money, for he can never know what will happen when misfortune suddenly strikes him. For the world is like a ladder: one goes up, the other comes creeping down. (95) As then also happened to our Bovo. Consider to what straits great misery had driven him.

When the king had looked him over, he asked them their price. The merchants began to say: "Not a penny less than a hundred ducats." The king said: "If you will not take less, then take the money and give me the lad." (96) Now the king had a master of the royal stables, and it was to him that he handed over the dear boy, and said: "Since I am entrusting this servant into your keeping, have him tend the horses. If he refuses, then beat him to pieces; rip his hair out of his scalp. For I see in his eyes that a beating will not be wasted on him."

(97) The stable-master took him to the stables. He worked there for two years. He had to tend all the horses, muck out their stalls, and spread straw for them. He found favor in the eyes of all. He was a delight to whoever saw him, for he became finer by the day. The stable-master was pleased with him. (98) He was well-fed and had grown well-proportioned, and his hair was like hammered gold; on his cheeks there seemed to burn two roses; and he had a fine pair of dark eyes. When he rode forth, wearing his doublet and hose, the whole city had something to talk about.

Now the noble king had a courtly daughter of eighteen years. (99) No lady or gentleman had ever had a more courtly form or more beautiful body. She had two eyes in her head like two orbs of radiant garnet. Her beauty was quite indescribable. She was called Druzeyne the Fair. Once she saw from afar as Bovo rode across the square. (100) She noticed how well he sat the horse, and urged it on with his spurs to jump a foot-and-a-half into the air. The whole city was watching him. When the noble young maiden saw him, she said to her ladies-in-waiting: "If I have ever in my life seen such a courtly lad, then let me fall from this window."

(101) Thereafter she began to think to herself: "Oh God, that is the best looking lad! What money and property I would give to have a husband like that. His good looks have made me weak; if he were here with me, he would have to revive me. If I do not see him again soon, I do not know what will happen to me."

(102) One Sunday morning it happened that Bovo and also some of his comrades went out for a ride. Druzeyne the Fair was to one side of him. She looked at him with loving eyes and began to court him. Her heart burned for

the youth. She would gladly have jumped down to him. (103) Bovo rode on his way; her smiles and waves were to no avail. She heaved another great sigh for him and almost fell into a faint. So great was her longing for him that she could neither eat nor drink. That same night she went to bed without having eaten. All night long she tossed and turned. (104) She yearned deeply for Bovo. She could hardly wait for dawn to come.

Straightaway she went to her father's chamber. His head projected out of the bed covers. He received her quite congenially, saying: "My dear daughter, you are my comfort in all my sorrows. What do you want so early in the morning?"

(105) She said: "Dear father, merciful lord, I will tell you my desire. You should grant me a request today: you need to let me set up a kitchen, for I would like to have a great banquet for my ladies-in-waiting at mid-day, and you should also give me some servants to wait at table, those whom I like and who are suitable for me."

(106) "By all means, my dear daughter, I grant it to you gladly. Take whatever you wish and whichever servants you would like to have." Druzeyne said: "It would seem best to me, if I took Bovo, the young lad, him and his close companions." The king said: "Well, go and give the orders."

(107) As soon as Druzeyne summoned him, the excellent warrior came. How pleasantly she gazed at him; she inspected him back and front. It seemed to her that she was fully revitalized. Then she whispered in his ear: "You beloved form, you radiant star, attend to me and wait on me." (108) Bovo began to say: "That will be done."

The guests then took their seats at the tables. They began to serve delicious dishes: braised and roasted chicken and fish. Druzeyne never took her eye off Bovo and did not eat a bite of the meal. Her desire grew ever stronger. She would have liked to have a different 'appetizer.' (109) Her desire grew so strong, that everyone who was present in the room began to notice. The people began to say to one another: "Oh, how she is carrying on indecently over that runaway stable boy."

Now she wished better to satisfy her desire, so she deliberately let her knife fall under the table. (110) Bovo immediately took care of it; he told the maidens to move out of the way, and got down on his hands and knees in order to retrieve the knife. Now Druzeyne was also adroit and bent down under the table. She said: "Oh, may you go blind, if you do not find the knife first!" (111) And, as if she were reaching for the knife, she kissed him under the table. Then she tossed in another remark: "Oh, how poorly the knife has been sharpened!"

Bovo leapt up and wiped his cheek. It was as if a goose had honked at him. He quickly lowered his eyes and blushed redder than a ember. (112) He feared that the people who were sitting alongside her had seen what had occurred.

And after that had happened, they got up from the table; the meal was over. All began to express their great thanks. Bovo, too, wanted not to forget that. He went to Druzeyne and wished to take his leave and could hardly speak because of his great embarrassment. (113) He said: "God bless you, noble my lady." He spoke without dissembling: "Pardon me for not staying longer with you, but I have to go and muck out the horse stables." She said: "Go along, dear heart. May God preserve you. You have served me; may God reward you for it. But take care and do not stay away so long the next time." (114) He barely raised his eyes because of his embarrassment. He had to hurry to the stables. Druzeyne yearned greatly for him.

Thus it remained for a good while. Then one day a noble warrior came riding in from a foreign land; he lived a hundred miles from Armonia and was named Makabrun, a distinguished warrior. His father was a noble king. (115) This same worthy king had no other heir. Makabrun had no equal on earth. He was dying for love of Druzeyne. He came riding with a thousand knights. He intended to win her. He had expended a great deal of money to that purpose. The king showed him great honor. (116) He had a great hall prepared for him, which he decorated with golden tapestries. There was much feasting and drinking in there, and occasionally they also went out riding. Later the king organized a tournament for him in Armonia in the square and had a wide jousting arena set off by constructed barriers, as well as grandstands with many benches.

(117) When the time had come for the day of the tournament, a huge procession of many knights and great lords was seen riding in. Many people came from far and wide and from many a distant city, many of them fine and splendid jousters. Everyone ran to their windows and up onto their roofs to see them.

(118) Druzeyne the Fair also came out; for she also wanted to see the jousting. She made a stately entrance with many noble and courtly maidens. She took a seat in a row up high, carved from marble. Next to her stood a page in doublet and hose who could sound the horn quite well. (119) He had been directed to blow the horn when Druzeyne so ordered. Then everyone was to stop jousting. If anyone were to disobey that order, he would forfeit his life. They began to bind on their helmets and to charge swiftly at one another.

(120) Now, Bovo had ridden out of the city to cut grass for the horses. After he had cut it, he wove a crown for himself out of willow twigs, with fine flowers on the inside. Oh, how fine it looked on him! He tied two bundles of

grass onto the horse. The worthy hero sat down on top of them. (121) He hung his scythe by his side and rode back into the city without a care in the world. From far away he heard aggressive whooping and shouting coming from the square. He began to ride straight there and watched a few jousts. He saw how Makabrun, the mighty warrior, was superior to all other competitors. (122) With his iron-like strength he struck them all down: all because he wished to show Druzeyne how strong were all his limbs. Up to this point, he held the prize and would have liked to continue jousting. None of the others wanted to fight him anymore. When Bovo saw that, he began to laugh (123) and said to one of his comrades: "I would also like to joust, if you could only arrange for me to have a shield and lance. Oh, how I would bring Makabrun down, even if he were twice as noble."[16] His comrade said: "Oh, you dear fool, you will be crushed in the turmoil."

(124) Bovo galloped away from the square in order to stow the grass. A lad came riding toward him carrying a shield. Bovo snatched it by force right out of his hand. The lad dared not make a fuss. He [Bovo] would have liked to take a lance from someone, too, but could not find one anywhere. (125) He galloped straight to the stables and took the grass inside. He looked in every corner to see if he could find a lance. He found there a pole that had fallen down and was lying behind the door. It was a long, thick, heavy bar, twisted and bent and rough as a hedgehog. (126) As soon as he saw it, he went for it. He thought that he had never been so rich and said: "Now you are just what I was after. If only you were a bit straighter. Oh, how I will give Makabrun a tickle. If he is wise, he will back off."

Quickly he took the horse between his spurs, and in the blink of an eye he was back at the tournament again. (127) "Make way, make way," he began to shout. "Makabrun will have to defend himself against me. I will avenge everyone on him today." He went at him with his pole. Makabrun immediately charged at him to joust, but Bovo withstood the charge quite honorably. He gave Makabrun such a jab with his pole that his soul all but left him. (128) He could not but fall from his horse to his full length on the ground, so that he again bounced right up. There was no way for him to avoid it. All his pages came running to him. They set him on his horse again. Everyone started smirking and hooting and laughing and whistling and hissing. (129) He was so ashamed that he would have liked to crawl away. He scarcely dared raise his eyes. His arm was all but broken, which he dared not tell anyone because of his shame. His servants would have liked to take revenge, and they began beating him [Bovo]. Druzeyne saw it, which enraged her, and she immediately had the horn sounded.

(130) When the horn had sounded, no one dared move anymore. The tournament was now stopped dead. Druzeyne had herself taken home; everyone went where they belonged. Bovo put his pole back behind the door, and he returned the shield to the lad. And he thereafter lay down to sleep for a while. (131) He was so tired that he scarcely moved, so mightily had he raged and rampaged. He lay down on a bundle of grass and wanted to sleep until evening. People talked about him in all parts of the city, everyone praising his great courage. They all said that if the boy survived, he would turn the world upside down.

(132) Druzeyne, however, now desired him even more. She could think of nothing but him. And since no one was on the street now—the people had gone to eat—she went down to him on his bundle of grass and would have sat near him for a while. There he lay and slept on his back, and his cheeks seemed to glow—red as two roses. (133) She saw how he slept so sweetly with his four limbs all stretched out. She took him by the feet and tugged until she had awakened him. She greeted him quite amicably. She asked him why he enjoyed sleep so much. "Get up; you have been lying down long enough. Come, sit next to me, you splendid warrior."

(134) Bovo said: "These are strange people. What do you want, noble maiden?" She said: "If I had not been there today, they would have hacked you to pieces. How often have I waved and signalled to you, but you never wanted to look at me." Bovo would have loved to run away, but she kept a tight grip on him and did not let go. (135) She said: "You are my heart's desire. Why then do you turn your back on me. If you knew how well I love you, you would snuggle up closer to me. Why are you being so annoying? You are breaking my heart completely to pieces. I am not really all that loathsome. Indeed I have here two fine little tits." (136) She drew out her two snow-white breasts and said: "Are these mouthfuls to be refused?" She shook with laughter. She said: "How can you reject them?" Bovo did not pay any attention; he lowered his eyes. He was so embarrassed that he did not want to look at her—but not a chance that it would have turned out that way with Elye Bokher!

(137) Druzeyne was quite distraught and heartsick. Her heart became quite weak. She said: "Now farewell to you; give me something by which I can remember you, now before I leave you. You ought to give me something. My dear, foolish little rogue, give me your rose-crown for a bit." (138) Bovo tossed the little crown over to her, so that it fell on the ground in front of her. Druzeyne was now even more unhappy and said: "What bad manners you have! Pick it up and put in on me, or you will regret it." He put it on her and

scratched his head. She kissed him on the mouth so that it made a smack (139) and said: "How genuinely fine you taste, you splendid and distinguished warrior, and so exquisite that I must say that it immediately enlivened me. And dear friend come on and tell me your lineage. Tell me the names of your father and mother, and tell me where they dwell and who they are."

(140) Bovo said: "Because you entreat me so, I will tell you. I left them on the other side of the sea; they threw me out of their house. I have little honor from them: they wander up and down the country and go from one poorhouse to another." (141) Druzeyne said: "I do not believe it. You are surely lying through your teeth. Judging from your physique, you do not look like you have eaten a lot of oatmeal porridge. You are surely no beggar's son: your mother endured the violation of a neighboring student or priest and kept it secret." (142) She made many good jests about nothing but peculiar topics. She was entertaining herself well and often made Bovo laugh.

Now, listen to another tale that misfortune brought about. While they were there together, a great misfortune took place. (143) For meanwhile the sultan and his son had come riding up and brought ten thousand stalwart men with them. The tower watchman sounded the alarm and it became known in the city.

The king became very alarmed; he ran up onto the wall with all of his warriors (144) and asked the sultan what he wanted or what otherwise might be his pleasure. He said: "My son is worthy of your daughter. I want you to give her to him. Or I will take her by the sword, which will cost you all your lives. You promised her to him. You must keep your promise. So give her to him amicably, and God's will be done."

(145) Now, this same sultan's son was the most hideous man who had ever been born. He looked just like a dragon and had huge eyes and huge ears. Whoever but caught sight of him ran away. He was blacker than the Moors and had a beard like a goat. And his name was Lutsifer. (146) He looked quite like the Devil and was not at all like a human being. He was huge and tall and, in addition, old. He would not back down even from a whole army. And with his great strength he had subdued many a kingdom, for he was one of the mightiest men who had ever walked on two legs.

(147) As soon as the king saw him, he said: "You repugnant heathen, I say to you and also to your father, get away from here. I never promised you my daughter. I shit on oaths like that. So you should not presume to claim her. My daughter would not let you kiss her ass. (148) Am I to give my daughter to a devil!? I would rather butcher her with my own hands." Lutsifer said: "Now listen very carefully to me: you are truly going to have to fight me. And it will

cost all of you your lives. Just come on out with all your servants." The king said: "If that is what you want, I will give it to you. That you can believe."

(149) He quickly said to his warriors: "Now quickly fetch your best weapons. We do not want to let ourselves be frightened off. Moreover we should not be caught off guard. The clamor was great throughout the city. Makabrun and his men also came running. He said to the king: "Do not be terrified. I believe that I can thrash the lice out of Lutsifer (150) in much less than one brief hour."

They all gathered in one place. Twelve thousand of them came together. The king sent them out through the gate. Then he and Makabrun bound on their helmets and took sharp lances in hand, and with swords and bows and arrows they hastened out through the gate. (151) They found their people in a murderous battle, fighting against the heathens. Many on both sides fell; they could not be separated. The king and Makabrun rode up and joyfully entered the battle, each into a different horde and charged into them with a great crash. (152) It would have been a delight to watch Makabrun and the noble king: many a heathen they struck down there. It was a matter of life and death. There was never a greater battle before or since. That I will swear on my oath.

Lutsifer was fighting in a different place. He was the bitter death of many. (153) He rode on a huge elephant. No one dared take a stand against him. He wielded a steel pole, long and broad. Makabrun charged him. Makabrun said: "Now wait, now wait. I will put an end to your lasciviousness," and charged the one with the pole, and said: "You villain, now surrender."

(154) Now Lutsifer was not idle either and had no intention of being intimidated. He feared nothing that he could see. He charged him with great strength and thrust Makabrun from his horse, so that he lay there on the street. Lutsifer ordered that he be led away and bound so that he could not move. (155) Thereafter he again charged ahead and knocked many to the ground, so that they lay dead on the grass. He did not wish to spare anyone. He came to the place where the king was, whom he recognized by his crown, and said: "You are by rights the guilty party. Just wait, I will make you suffer." (156) Before the king knew what was happening, he was lying on the ground beneath his horse. He himself did not know how it had happened. He shouted: "I want a truce!" Lutsifer again told his men to go away from there with him and lead him, too, to the other one. "Both of them will have to go home with us."

(157) When his [the king's] people saw this, they immediately began to retreat; they took to their heels one and all; they succeeded in reaching the city. Some of them wanted to rescue their lord; they would have died before

fleeing. They slashed into the heathens as if into a pack of dogs, each side striking deep wounds.

(158) Now let us leave them to fight each other like fighting cocks, and speak a bit about Bovo. He was still in the stables with his Druzeyne. Now a great lamentation rose up from the city. Everyone began to scream and weep. Druzeyne heard that uproar, and said: "What can that noise be?" (159) Bovo said: "Gracious maiden, I have been hearing it for a while already. Let me run and see what that shouting and roaring is." She said: "I fear that you might flee and not return. Swear to me that you will come back." Bovo swore that otherwise he would be baptized.[17] Then she kissed him on the mouth and let him go.

(160) He snatched up a vineyard stake and immediately ran out of the stables. There he found many armored men who were all weeping and shouting. He asked one of them what was going on. He said: "Alas, how we have been defeated. The sultan gave us a poor reception. The king and Makabrun have both been taken prisoner."

(161) That saddened Bovo; he felt sorry for his dear lord. He ran right back into the stables (he had not been far from there). Druzeyne was still standing there, waiting for him. He told her the miserable news. "You have lost your dear father. He and Makabrun have been taken prisoner." (162) Druzeyne almost broke down in tears, but she had to control herself, for she feared that she would be dishonored, if she were found in the stables. Bovo said: "Weep no more! I will undertake the task of rescuing your father, though I know that they will crucify me." (163) Druzeyne said: "If you want to go and dare something marvelous, then I will arm you to the teeth with the choicest armor and with a fine, sharp lance. That all belonged to my dear, departed brother. He was killed in Moorish territory, so that truly the Creator must avenge his blood. (164) In this armor, you can dare courageous deeds, and you should wear it for my sake. But one thing I would like to ask you first, and you may not refuse me. You have often lied to me before. Now you must tell me the truth. It would cheer me up a bit. Tell me who your parents are."

(165) Bovo said: "Since you want to have it, then I will let you know the truth. My father's name was Duke Guidon, ruler of Antona. He was treacherously murdered by Dodon. My mother watched it happen not very unwillingly. She married him and flipped me the finger. There would be much there that is better left unsaid."

(166) As soon as Druzeyne heard that, she joyously sprang up and ran to get the armor that was to be his. And she herself helped him put it on and picked up the helmet from the ground and set it on his head with her own two hands,

and gave him a sword named Pomele, and gave him a horse named Rondele.[18] (167) One could have shorn hair and split a thread with the sword; it was the greatest sword of all; it reached down to his calves. And a spell had been put on the horse, so that no weapon could harm it. It had been joined with the Devil, which enabled it to fight against a hundred men.

(168) Now that Bovo was fully equipped, he leapt agilely onto the horse. Druzeyne wept and said to him: "Go forth, you dear, worthy warrior. May Almighty God, who created the heavens and the earth, go with you. Bend down toward me a bit." She kissed him on the mouth; he kissed her back.

(169) While she was standing there with him, with her arms around him and kissing his red mouth, someone came in. He was then carrying the king's banner on a staff. His name was Count Uglin, the king's cousin. And he had seen everything. (170) And he said: "What are you thinking, Druzeyne! You are indeed engaging in immoral behavior. It would be appropriate for a whore. I fear you may become one. I will not let you forget your lasciviousness. You will wish that you had never been born. Your father is captive; they want to let him rot, and you are standing here cavorting with a servant boy! (171) Are you not the least bit horrified!? You are not even lowering your steely glare. You would do better to see that you go home. May the plague strike you down!"

He let fly with many angry words. Bovo did not want to put up with it from him. He said: "You are sure full of reproach!" And he hit him on top of the head with his fist (172) so that he fell down in front of him and bounced off the ground. That blow reverberated through all his limbs. He ran off and dropped the banner. Druzeyne immediately picked it up again. Bovo galloped out of the stables. Druzeyne watched him for a good while and recited her best blessings for him.

(173) On the way he found a lot of people retreating, who were being chased by the heathens. Bovo pled with them vehemently: "Dear my lords, let us not give up hope. Come, let us fight them. Have you never heard the proverb: 'He who flees is pursued, and he who fights not is beaten.'" (174) Now there were very many there who had a change of heart and turned back with Bovo, and began to come to themselves. He brought it about with his good words that they all gained new courage. All along the way they saw misery in the great slaughter that had taken place there. (175) It would have caused a hard stone to shed tears. They lay there dead but still warm; the blood of many men had been spilled. One had lost a leg, another an arm; and that one had been shot with an arquebus; this one's blue intestines were hanging out. Some were fleeing with bandaged heads; others were fighting back as best they could.

(176) Bovo, the bold warrior, charged forward and gave Rondele its head, riding in among the heathens. They thought he had lost his mind. Rondele snorted and whinnied and snarled, and bit and kicked with both front and back hooves. No one dared come close to him. In just a moment he cleared a space around himself. (177) With his sharp lance, Bovo troubled many a man. No shield remained whole under his attack. He smashed them all to bits. He led the dance, and the others steadily followed him. One might wish to watch it for a while, as long as it did not catch up to him. (178) How Bovo fought like a raging storm! And how he embodied the hostility of a furious dragon! It would have sufficed in such dimension and in such form, that no heathen could escape death in the face of his continuous striking, and thrusting, and charging.

Then he saw Lutsifer fighting in the distance. (179) He saw how he struck down his people with the steel pole that he carried, so that they all lost their lives there. He spilled the blood of many. It made Bovo angry and sad and quite sick at heart. He turned Rondele and galloped toward him. When he saw him, he recognized him well enough. (180) He said: "Now, tell me, comrade: are you the one I have heard spoken of? Are you the Devil from Hell, who wishes to strike everyone down dead? I will fell you with my lance; I will not stand for your wickedness." Lutsifer looked him in the face to see whether he was serious or only jesting. (181) And said: "You poor child, what is it that you want? You look like you would be better at courtly entertainments. Come along to my father's house. You ought to serve him at his table and become a heathen and an apostate. Why do you want to lose your life?" Bovo said: "I shit on you and your faith. Defend yourself, if you want something from me!"

(182) Bewildered, Lutsifer glanced at him, and had no interest in him. He did not make of him a close friend. He did not assume much of a battle position. He did not look for such strength in him. Bovo charged him vigorously and struck him right through his shield, leaving the lance stuck in his body. (183) He was unable to stay in the saddle. His soul at once wanted to slip away. The lance lodged more than a foot deep in his body. How the heathens lamented cannot be recounted or told. They all screamed bloody murder, when they saw him fall from the elephant.

(184) Nor did Bovo's people wish to lag behind: all of them together followed him. They pursued the heathens in such a way that they struck flames from them with their strong blows. And they hewed deep wounds with their swords. And they slashed into all the heathens whom they could find as if they were dogs.

(185) The sultan was not himself on the battlefield; he had not ridden into battle. He guarded the prisoners in camp. He did not leave them even by so much as a single step. There was a whole world of prisoners there: the king sat in the center. They were bound and could not move. The sultan sat right at the gate. (186) He saw someone galloping toward him; he had turned his back on the army and galloped like an arrow shot from the bowstring. One arm had been hacked off. He was unidentifiable because of all the blood. He had a great wound in his cheek. He immediately dismounted and sank to the earth before the sultan. (187) The sultan got no more from him than: "Your son has been slain." Before he had managed to get the word out, he turned up his toes and died. The sultan swore by Muḥammad: "I will I not put up with this from them!" and began speaking to the king: "I will take vengeance for my son on you. (188) I will give you your reward. You have to go home with me. It will truly cost you your life, even if you were to give me all of Flanders."

Meanwhile he saw someone else rushing toward him on foot. He came to the sultan and said: "Gracious my lord, alas and alack, I have very bad news. (189) You have lost your dear son. He lies dead on the ground. An eighteen-year-old youngster did it. He is killing your people beyond all counting. He is on his way here in great rage. He is not far behind me. His men are trailing him, coming as fast as they can. I know of no better course of action than to flee."

(190) The sultan wept and wailed: "Alas and alack, my dear child! Alas, where is all my glory now? Never will I be able to overcome this. Now I want only to flee quickly overseas." He ordered the prisoners immediately to be tied up; he wanted to take them all with him. Then he saw the great army approaching. (191) He said: "They are going to roll right over me; they are coming with a great force. It is of no more use to delay. I do not want to fight with them." He immediately left everything where it was and ran away with ten of his servants to the sea, which was two miles away. Bovo and his people quickly pursued him. (192) With a great hue and cry they rushed toward the sultan. He had no other choice but to leap into the ship, push off from land, and sail away. They quickly raised the sail. Bovo shouted after him: "You are not off the hook yet. I am going to come after you and attack you there."

(193) Bovo rode quickly back to the camp, where they found many prisoners. He found the king lying there, bound hand and foot. Bovo leapt from his horse, untied him, and said: "Blessed is the hour in which I again set eyes on my dear, merciful lord!" (194) The king said: "I no longer expected it to happen," and began embracing Bovo, weeping for great joy. There was great happiness and rejoicing there. Makabrun also reconciled with him, as

did all the others. Anyone who could not shake hands with Bovo thought he could live no longer. (195) Bovo began speaking to them: "Up and away, dear comrades, let us slay the surviving heathens." He had a horse brought for everyone, and they set out in pursuit of the heathens. They killed every one whom they found.

The king saw Bovo raging and storming, and said: "You are a praiseworthy warrior. (196) For that which you have done for me on this day, I will remember you for the rest of my life. You will no longer attend to the horses nor rinse out bowls. You will be the highest ranked of my barons. Whatever you want, I will give to you." Bovo said: "So let us call it even between us with the hundred guilders that you paid for me." (197) They thus spoke together the whole time, Bovo riding at his side. After they had slain all the heathens, they rode back into the city to the sound of shawms, pipes and trumpets. The great clamor could be heard far and wide, and they were received with great joy. Druzeyne the Fair also came out. (198) Now, I do not need to describe the joy that they had from one another or how congenial they were to one another, or how they kissed each other and rubbed cheeks.

Night had fallen, and everyone went home. Bovo and Druzeyne stayed with the king. She sat down on the bench next to her father and said: "Dear father, you have me to thank (199) that this worthy warrior rescued you from the heathens. I armed him head to toe and additionally gave him Rondele. But I promised and swore to him that he would be fitting for me as a husband, and I would be his wedded wife, if he rescued you. (200) Now he has done it, so I must also do it. I have to take him as my husband. He is incidentally the son of a duke. I need not be ashamed of him. His father's name was Duke Guidon. So let him thus also be titled. I want him and none other. He is worthy of being a duke in Flanders."

(201) The king began and said to her: "Dear daughter, if you indeed want him, then what you wish, so do I. I freely give you my permission." Then she stood up, while her father watched, and sat down next to the handsome lad. And when they had sat together for a good while, the two of them were called to come to the meal. (202) Druzeyne talked with Bovo for the entire meal; the king himself had to reprimand her. Now when Bovo had finished eating, the king commanded that he be taken to sleep in a splendid chamber and splendid bed, and many servants running around him. He slept in the chamber without any cares until the next morning arrived.

(203) The next morning arrived. It became known in the city how Bovo had become the king's son-in-law and how Druzeyne had taken him as a husband. They all said that that was good news. "It will bring us great benefit. Now

we can live in great joy. We need have no worries about the heathens." (204) As soon as the king arose from bed, he ordered that a splendid golden chain and a black velvet mantel be chosen for Bovo. Thus he went out and also had many servants with him. Everyone doffed their hats to him and shook his hand and congratulated him, except the villain, Count Uglin. (205) As soon as he became aware of the matter, said to himself: "May diarrhea strike me, if this marriage ever takes place. He struck me yesterday; I had to run away. I will not forgive him for that today." And he came rushing up to see the king, with his head bandaged and his arm in a sling. (206) He entered the king's chamber, and he welcomed the king [back] and said: "Praised be he, who frees those who were captive. Now tell me, my dear cousin, what is this about a wedding? I cannot honestly congratulate you, for you have contracted a marriage with a very bad bridegroom. (207) Who has ever in his life heard of greater disgrace and scandal: that a king should marry his daughter to a runaway boy from who knows where!" The king said: "Listen very closely to me: your words enrage me. Do not be so concerned with this matter; it is not really any of your business. (208) I have been looking for someone with good character, and I found it, and for that reason it is done. Why should I care anything about the ignorant son of the neighboring king. Our sages have also said that one should value a good character, for what good is the status of father and mother, if he is himself not a good person? (209) For that reason, I say to you, Cousin Uglin, you should take care in what you say."

Uglin left the king, having been chastised. He was very annoyed by the king's words. He said: "I must be losing my mind! This villain must die!" He quickly sent for all his comrades and told them how he wanted to kill Bovo. (210) And he told them the whole story: how Bovo had treated him, and how the king had rebuked him, and the shame that he had experienced. He said: "I have set a trap for how I want to catch the villain, so that we can slay him. And I will now tell you how and when. (211) I have had a copy made for myself of the key to the chamber where he will be sleeping. For that reason we will all stay awake tonight, arm ourselves with our best weapons, and slit his throat, and punish him by death." They swore an oath to him, and he to them.

Now it was night, and Bovo went to bed. (212) When it seemed to Uglin that he was asleep, and people were out of the way, he quickly called his comrades, unlocked the chamber, and he led them in. There lay Bovo, deep in his bed and had pulled the covers up over his head. And there was a candle burning brightly by the bed. And under his pillow he had Pomele. (213) There were perhaps twenty of them, all with their swords drawn. Uglin said: "Easy now, get on with it, and attack him with your swords." First each one of them looked at his fellows, but none of them dared to risk it. They feared that if they failed to get him, he would cut all their throats.

(214) Now, among them was a very old villain, who said: "Settle down and listen carefully to me; pay attention to my idea; I will give you some good advice, for in this business there is no profit for us: we could well all lose our lives. If he wakes up, we will all be slain. Come outside, and I will explain it to you." (215) They went out, and he spoke with them, and said: "When dawn approaches, I will lie down in bed and begin to moan and groan vehemently, as if I had the ague. And I will have a bandage wound round my eyes. And thereafter you will send for Bovo and give him to understand that I am the king. (216) For I have a beard just like his, and I can pretend to be him. And when he comes, then woe to him, I will ably bring him down. I will send him on a mission to the sultan, and write to him: 'Here you have the youth who killed your son with his lance. If you so wish it, your son is avenged.'"

(217) This advice seemed good to all of them, and they had a bed set up. And just as one does for sick people, he ordered all kinds of things brought to him. One of them quite reluctantly went to fetch Bovo and said: "Sir Bovo, I am to tell you that the king has become ill, for which reason he summons you." (218) Bovo took fright, quickly got dressed, and hurried to the place where that one was lying in bed pretending to be sick and motioning to him with his hands, and said: "I can trust no one; I must send you to the sultan. And you must carry this letter to him. And you must tell no one of this. (219) And do not tell Druzeyne anything about it either, as you value your life. And as soon as you return, I will give you her hand in marriage." Bovo said: "I will gladly do whatever pleases you and is, moreover, proper. Gracious King, you need not worry, I will leave this very morning. (220) God give you His blessing, dear and noble my lord." And he gave him a big kiss.

Now, he would have liked to have his armor and Rondele to ride on his journey, but that could not happen without Druzeyne's knowledge, so he had to forego that. He went into the stable among all the horses and took the one that he liked the best. (221) And swiftly that fine warrior rode away. No one had ever seen anyone ride faster, right past many cities without ever entering them. He let nothing hinder him. It would have taken any of us much longer. As one says to children in stories: that is really true, on my oath.

He rode until he came to a large open meadowland. (222) The sun made him sweat so much that he almost died of the great heat; and from great thirst he could barely speak; and he almost died from hunger. Then he found a German beggar sitting there with a large beggar's basket. He was drinking good wine out of his bottle and eating cheese and bread out of his bag. (223)

Bovo said the blessing for his meal and wished him health. He thanked the boy kindly. Then Bovo asked him if he did not have something to sell, so that he could be revived. The beggar said: "I will share with you; you will have as much as I." Bovo sat down beside him on the ground and held his horse by the bridle. (224) He ate a piece of bread, and there was so much mold in it that he wanted no more. He almost broke his teeth on the cheese without managing to get a bite of it. He left all that for the sake of the bottle, as long as a drop remained in it. The beggar thought: "If you want all of the drink, then I will make you pay dearly for the wine."

(225) Now, he had a little glass bottle hanging on his left side, in which there was a good sleeping potion. He gave it all to Bovo to drink. And as soon as he had drunk it, he sank down into sleep. The beggar did not delay for long and took the ring from his thumb. (226) Thereafter he came upon his money purse, which he ripped from his side, and then he took from him his good sword, with which he was accustomed to fight; then he took the horse by the bridle and began quickly to ride away, leaving him lying there on his back next to the basket of leftovers.

(227) He lay there for twenty-four hours, just like a dead man in all respects. And when the next day came, he began to wake up, but he could still not get his eyes open, so strongly were they stuck closed. He wetted them for a long time with his spittle until he softened them. (228) He looked around for the horse; he did not know where it had gone. Then he reached for his sword, which had also been taken from him. He also wanted his purse, but found no sign of it. Then he looked at his thumb: someone had removed his ring. (229) He saw the beggar's basket lying next to him, and he began to realize how the beggar had paid him his wages when he drank from the bottle, for as soon as he had taken a drink, he sank down asleep. He said: "That beggar really shat on me! It would have been better if I had eaten not a bite. (230) Now I have been confounded. What am I to do? I have not a cent. What should I do? How will I escape my hunger? I will see what is in the basket." He found quite a few pieces of bread in it. He said: "They are good enough to keep me alive. He picked out the best pieces and put them inside his shirt. (231) The rest he left there. And quickly began to hurry away.

He had not planned to walk so much. But misfortune had taught him to cope. Misfortune could no longer harm him, for he had nothing left to lose. He passed through Brabant and Burgundy until he came to Babylon. (232) There he asked where the sultan lived. They directed him to a palace in the distance. He found many men there, and the sultan with all his lords. The sultan looked at him for a long time. He began to grow suspicious. It seemed to him that he had seen him before. Bovo bowed and began to speak: (233) "King Arminio, the worthy king, has sent you this letter." As soon as he looked at the letter, he almost collapsed. And when he had revived a bit, he again began to read it and began shouting and saying: "Alas, he killed my son! (234) Alas, my poor, dear son! Alas, may Muḥammad have mercy. Oh, seize the murderer and lead him away. And string him up at once."

His knights willingly began to do so and seized him by both arms. Bovo tried to free himself from them by force. He had no weapon; he had to scratch and bite. (235) He put many a heathen in danger with his blows and punches. No one had ever seen anyone defend himself so well, but many hounds are the death of the hare. He could not escape capture; they brought him down by force and tied both hands behind his back (236) and led him out of the city. The executioner had him on a chain.

Now the sultan had a daughter who was not at home. Her name was Margarete the Fair. She had ridden out with her serving men and hunted all day long. Now it was evening. She wanted to ride home, when she saw a great crowd from a distance. (237) She began to ride over to them and saw the handsome man brought out. She looked at him and was astonished and said: "It would be a pity to hang him. I will go see what I can do, whether I can save his life." She hurried into the city, much more swiftly than an arrow flies from a bowstring. (238) She dismounted and ran up the stairs to her father and fell to the floor, bowing before him. Her father said: "Stand up at once. Whatever you want, it will be granted you." Margarete said: "What is your purpose in having such a worthy youth killed?" The sultan said: "Why should I not tell you? That is the person, who, alas, slew your brother." (239) "Well, if he slew my brother, then he must indeed be a mighty warrior. Who knows what my brother did to him. He most likely had to defend himself and was victorious. Therefore, dear father, follow my counsel just a bit: let it go for now, and I promise you that I will bring my sense and wits to bear. I will bring it about that he will become an apostate." (240) The sultan said: "If he wishes to do that, then I will yield to you this time."

Margarete was happy and hurried away. She very much wanted to save his life. And when she went out of the city, she there saw from afar how the executioner had him up on the gallows and was about to throw him off and hang him right away. (241) She shouted: "Wait until I get there." She began to shout "Mercy, mercy!" The executioner turned around when she shouted a couple of times and said to Bovo: "You noble warrior, be of good cheer; you have been set free. I see the sultan's daughter hurrying this way. I can see that she has had you pardoned."

(242) Margarete almost rode her horse lame, she was so afraid that they would hang him. And when she got to the gallows, she ordered them to lead him down. His face was quite bloodless; it was as if he were dead; he could hardly move. Margarete said: "If you will only do as I say, you need not give up hope. (243) If you will believe in our Muḥammad and if you will betray your faith, then my father promised me and said that he will grant you your life and additionally will give you a golden chain around your neck and make you a great lord, and you will become his commander-in-chief in charge of all his armies." (244) Bovo answered her not a word, and he was paler than the earth. Margarete did not want to waste time there. She ordered him quickly to mount a horse. She rode next to him off to one side to see if she might get an answer from him. But he spoke as much as a mute until he had again come to the sultan.

(245) And when he came before the sultan, he fell on his knees. The sultan looked at him for a good while and said: "Have you come back? Now tell me quickly, you noble man, do you wish to become a worthy heathen? If so, then I will grant you your life this time, and I will forgive you for what you have done to me." (246) Then he answered as follows: "You need not ever again imagine that I will ever abandon my faith, even if you were to give me your entire country. I believe in a God who is honorable and great. I will not waver from His commandments. His Holy Name will I acknowledge. For His sake I will let myself be hanged and burned. (247) He is my Creator, praised be He. He has never in my life abandoned me and has aided me up to now. I will not lose hope in His Holy Name. Therefore, just give up your desire; you need not mention it in my presence again. Do not advise me to abandon Him. I will not exchange a living God for a dead one."

(248) The sultan began to grow enraged and in a fury began to say: "Take this villain away again, and let me never see him again!" Margarete said: "Do not do it! I will not let it happen! He cannot escape you in this matter. Just put him in prison for a while." (249) The sultan said: "For your sake I will extend his period of reprieve a while, and see if you can speak with him enough that you can bring him into the great congregation.[19] And if he does not wish to do that, then I will hang him right away on a high gallows."

His mighty knights all quickly came forward and led him away and threw him into prison. (250) The prison was some ten fathoms underground. There he was grievously imprisoned. There were many evil crawling creatures in the prison: lizards, adders, and snakes. He squashed all that he could catch: he smashed them with his feet. Now, Margarete did not wish to forget him and brought him food and drink herself. (251) She went to visit him—up above at the port-hole—and shouted down and called loudly: "Hey, are you dead, or are you still alive? Have you been able to defend yourself against the snakes? Please tell me that you want to become a heathen. I will bring it about that you are greatly honored. Why do you want to allow yourself to rot away like this?" She began to howl with grief. (252) Bovo said: "Spare your words, O noble, high-born maiden. That makes nothing but more misery, and your words are all in vain. Before doing that, I would prefer to suffer a bitter death here."

The words enraged Margarete. And after she had sat there for a while, she let down the food in a basket, (253) but it made her scornful that he repeatedly refused her, despite the fact that she brought him food and drink, morning and evening, day in and day out. The sultan no longer gave him any thought: that, too, she had brought about, that he spared his great manhood and gave her a grace period of twelve months.

(254) His imprisonment was indeed difficult. When he had been there for about seven months, and Margarete had been visiting him every day and trying to force him by kindness to convert to her religion, and he was steadfast in his refusal, and when he did not want to yield to kindness, she began to lose her temper and rage at him. (255) And said: "I swear an oath to you, that I will not give you any more to eat." Bovo said: "I am sorry about that, but you have to do what you think is right." Margarete, the fair maiden, went away, thinking: "I want to see how he manages to live. I will still bring him around to my way of thinking. He will have to do without food and drink for a while."

(256) She left him without food for a whole day, thinking that she could win him over that way. And when she then saw and was certain that he would sooner starve to death, she ordered her most trusted servant not to let him die. She said: "You are to take him food, and you are not to tell him that I ordered it." (257) The servant took him food every day and did not let him lack anything. And since he was so grievously imprisoned, he began to think to himself: "Let me see what I am able to accomplish, whether I can dig or break out of this cursed prison at all." He searched whether he could find anything with which he could break out or dig. (258) He found a great pile of dirt, in which he began to search and sift. He found an old, rusty sword there, which made him rejoice greatly. He said: "You are worth as much as gold to me. I will defend myself against the heathens with you." He laid it down in a corner and covered it with straw.

(259) And when the twelve months had passed that Margarete had delayed, she was in her father's house one day. He began to ask her about Bovo. He said: "Has he not yet become an apostate? Why have you lied to me?" He ordered his servants to bring him and hang him at once. (260) And when he had given

them leave to depart, twenty of them ran off quickly, and nine of them let themselves down into the prison cell in order to tie him up. Bovo was a dauntless lad. He quickly found his rusty sword and began joyfully to slash among them, sometimes with the blade, sometimes with the tip.

(261) A great racket arose there in their whacking and jabbing each other. Bovo raged and rampaged and made the blood flow from many of them. Those who had remained up above heard the uproar; they lowered nine more of them, but before they reached the bottom, he had already killed all of the first group. (262) He looked at the new ones and laughed at them and said: "I will not be bound by you!" He went at them with the sword and stabbed very deep wounds into them all and hacked into them so that at once there was a great uproar. And in much less than an hour he had hacked them to bits.

And then he stripped one stark naked. (263) And he put on those same heathen clothes, so that he looked just like a heathen. And then he took a turban from one, which he wound around his head perhaps a hundred times. There were still two strong men up above—the king's best servants. They were waiting while the others tied up Bovo. They were to pull them up, one at a time. (264) They called down and shouted loudly: "Hey, have you not yet tied him up? Hey, get on with it! How much longer? Have you not yet overcome him?" Now Bovo had learned the heathen language and shouted up: "Now the time has come. Start pulling him up. We have tied him up; he cannot escape."

(265) Thus the two of them alone pulled him up, and when he got up to the sill, he quickly stabbed the sword into one and knocked the other fellow down, and at once took to his heels as if a demon from Hell were chasing him. He quickly ran out through the gate. Neither the gatekeeper nor anyone else recognized him.

(266) That one whom he had knocked down immediately got up again and went to the sultan and said: "We have come up empty. Alas, the murderer is no longer here. We could not prevent his escape. He slew all my comrades and gave me such a blow that it laid me out."

(267) The sultan was greatly annoyed. But Margarete was glad to hear it. The sultan ordered two hundred men to see whether he could get him back. One was called Abrian the Mighty, who had a brother who was a mighty lord. They set out with the troop in pursuit of Bovo, who had a two-mile head start. (268) Abrian was eager to catch Bovo; he was off and galloping ahead of the others. There he saw someone fleeing, and he could well see that it was Bovo. He began to gallop after him more swiftly than an arrow flies from a bowstring. And he was stabbing at him with his lance, saying "You villain,

you have to die." (269) Bovo dodged his lance and quickly turned around to him and leapt right to him and took his sword in both hands and plunged it into the horse's paunch, so that it fell right down. Abrian wanted to jump out of the saddle, but he could not get his feet out of the stirrups. (270) Bovo struck him a blow with his sword and split his head open down to the mouth, so that he spun round like a top. He was already dead. Then the poor fool had to start running. He saw the others coming after him. He said: "If I want to stay alive, then this time I will have to turn tail and run."

(271) He ran right across the fields, whether plowed or sown. He did not have too far to go to reach the sea. He began quickly to rush in that direction. That great troop thereafter came galloping up and found that son of Haman slain there. They recognized that it was surely Bovo who had slain him. His brother began to weep and mourn. (272) They delayed only a short while and did not stint in pursuing him.

Bovo was at the sea and found there a fine little ship sailing by. He called to them, and they came to the port. There were only heathens in the ship. And as soon as they had taken him on board, they saw the great army approaching. (273) They immediately sailed away on the ship. They had raised the sail. Abrian's brother quickly ran to the sea with a great, loud cry: "Set the murderer ashore, for he has escaped from the sultan. If you do not give him up, you will regret it. The sultan will build a gallows for you."

(274) The sailor turned the helm; he wanted to bring him ashore. Bovo begged him not to do it but to continue to sail straight ahead. The sailor said: "Now stop it. I will not be hanged for your sake." Bovo said: "If you will not treat me in good faith, then I will in truth have to fend for myself." (275) The merchants began to get very angry. They did not want to endure it from him. They all ran at him with their weapons. They wanted to drive him away from the helm. Bovo threw one of them into the sea and beat another to death. He beat them with great joy. The whole time the heathens were watching from the shore.

(276) Bovo brought it about that none of the sailors even dared to move a muscle in his presence. They said to him: "Noble lord, you should choose your course, and tell us where you want to go, and we will gladly take you there." Bovo asked them where they were from and then said that they should at once sail there.

(277) How quickly they then turned the ship around, and the heathens loudly shouted after them. But they paid them no attention and did not want to do so. All their twisting and turning did not help them at all. And now that they saw that they had quite sailed away, they had to return home with great

shame and tell the sultan how the ones in the ship had taken him aboard. It was an affliction for the sultan and a delight for Margarete.

(278) Now let us leave Bovo to travel many a mile and go a very long way, and I want to sing to you what had meanwhile happened to dear Druzeyne. When Bovo had left in great haste and imagined that he would receive great thanks, no one knew about it except those who wanted to kill him: Uglin and some of his comrades. (279) That same morning when they sat down at the table, Bovo had not yet gotten out of bed. Druzeyne let go a sob, anticipating the misfortune. She said: "Perhaps he is not awake." They told her that he was gone. Her father said: "I want to tell you, I imagine that he has ridden out hunting."

(280) Thus that day passed without Bovo coming to eat. It troubled Druzeyne's heart greatly. She went around the house growling. She asked everyone with a great lament whether they had found out anything. No one knew anything to tell her. She could scarcely wait for dawn. (281) She went to stand before her father and said: "Dear father, please help me. Something must have gone wrong with Bovo. I am afraid someone has slain him. So do not keep silent any longer, dear father. You should not ignore this. You should have a proclamation made with trumpets [to determine] whether people have seen him anywhere." (282) The king said: "I am quite afraid that someone somewhere has taken his life. I will have neither rest nor respite; I will find out what has become of him. It is a burden on my heart, for I lament for such a valiant warrior. Therefore, dear daughter, you have my permission: go have a proclamation made just as you wish."

(283) Druzeyne went swiftly and quickly and had a proclamation made right away: if there were anyone who was guilty by deed or counsel in bringing about Bovo's death, if he should now betray his comrades, it would be forgiven him, and the king would forever hold him in favor and moreover grant him a thousand guilders. (284) She had the proclamation made some eight times in the squares and in all the streets.

Now Uglin had a disloyal man. He heard the proclamation. He thought: "I am entitled to that money. I do not wish to give it up. I will go tell Druzeyne everything. A thousand guilders are not to be passed up." (285) He quickly ran to the king's court, went to Druzeyne, and told her the whole tale from beginning to end: what they had undertaken with Bovo, and how it was Count Uglin who had done it all, and gave her a long slip of paper on which were written the names of all those who had participated with Uglin in the betrayal.

(286) As soon as Druzeyne heard this, she ran to her worthy father and did, alas, as was appropriate: she fell to the ground before him. The king raised

her up again and said: "What is the meaning of this behavior?" She quickly told him everything and gave him the slip of paper to read. (287) The king was deeply distressed and solemnly swore that he wanted to kill them. And quickly he told all his warriors that they should arm themselves and take up positions in all the streets and be fully prepared to do his will and catch Uglin with all his comrades. And Uglin was to be drawn and quartered, and the others hanged with hempen ropes.

(288) They caught them quite easily; not one of them could steal away. They led them out before the city gate and hung them up by the neck. Uglin said: "It is quite true; the old proverbs are rarely wrong: 'never is anything so finely spun that it does not finally come into the light of the sun.'" (289) None of his entreaties helped him at all: the traitor had to die. The king took all his possessions; he let his [Uglin's disloyal] servant inherit it.

Thereafter Druzeyne did nothing but weep and bitterly lament. She often sent forth to see if she could find out whether he [Bovo] were still alive or anything had befallen him. (290) She could not find out any reliable information about what had happened to him. Some said that he never got there; others said that he had been taken prisoner; still others said that he had died altogether, that the sultan had long since hanged him.

After many a day had passed, her father began to say to her: (291) "Dear daughter, what do you wish to do? Do you want to waste your life? I am telling you, no cock crows for Bovo. You need no longer have any hopes for him. Therefore I would like to give you another husband. No backtalk! And I know of no one who is as well-suited to you as Makabrun. I will give him to you." (292) Druzeyne first began to weep, and then she began to say to him: "Alas, I fear that unfortunately you are right. I will never see Bovo again. But I beg you to wait a year. Who knows what might then happen. And if he does not return to Flanders in that time, then I will take Makabrun as soon as any other. (293) So then, my dear and most noble father, if I must now become engaged to him, then I want him to wait for the wedding. And it is to be postponed an entire year."

Thus the king sent for handsome Makabrun. When he came, he had him sit on the dais and said: "You have long wooed Druzeyne. I wish to give her to you; she has become available to you via [her betrothed's] death. (294) But you will not have the wedding for a year. We must endure it with love and joy." Now you will want to know how Makabrun reacted: Druzeyne had to give him her hand. He then began to embrace and kiss her, as if his lips were stuck to her. It seemed to him that he had never tasted anything so good, but to Druzeyne it seemed like cheap wine.

(295) Makabrun lived it up that year. But one rarely saw Druzeyne laugh. And when the year had completely passed, he wanted to have his wedding. He took Druzeyne home to his house and had all things prepared in a courtly manner, and a great many people went home with him. People knew of the wedding far and wide.

(296) Now, Bovo had sailed far in the ship, sometimes with wind and rain, and with great storms and destructive tides. They were at sea an entire month and came to where they could see from afar a beautiful city facing them. In the distance they saw the beautiful towers. Bovo ordered that he be taken there quickly.

(297) They quickly began to go there, and they did not stint in rowing. They came to where there was a fisherman who was fishing with his net. As soon Bovo noticed him, he called to him, and he came over. Bovo ordered that he be put aboard his [the fisherman's] boat. He sent those in the ship on their way.

(298) Bovo said to the fisherman: "Now, tell me: whose city is that in the distance?" The fisherman said: "I can tell you that it belongs to a splendid lord; Makabrun is the name of the noble man. His wedding is about to take place, and in the city a splendid life is now led. King Arminio has given him his daughter in marriage. (299) Druzeyne is the name of that beautiful maiden. It is said that her peer has never been born, and to Bovo—that high-born warrior of noble character—to that same one she had betrothed herself. She waited for him for an entire year, but he remained lost. And because he was unable to become hers, she is taking Makabrun, but quite reluctantly."

(300) When he heard this speech, Bovo was glad at heart. He thought: "There is no time for delaying. I will go right to the blessing of the wedding guests. Oh, how Makabrun is going to turn blue [with rage]; how I will make him grumble and growl. And my dear Druzeyne's grief will I turn to joy." Quickly he ordered the fisherman to put him ashore. (301) The fisherman took him to a level place, there where people disembark. Then Bovo thanked the fisherman well. The fisherman bowed to him. He would have liked to have a penny as payment. But Bovo had nothing of his own.

He immediately rushed to the city. There he met a pilgrim who came from Rome. (302) He came toward him on the track with his beggar's gear making a racket: he was carrying many bags and baskets that were banging around on him. Bovo said: "Honorable man, let us make an exchange. Your torn cloak suits my needs, and I will give you my good coat for it." (303) The pilgrim said: "I will not do it. I do not want to wear a good coat, for if I wear it, I cannot not get any alms. Everyone would drive me away. But when I beg for alms dressed as I am, they cannot refuse me." Somehow Bovo raised up the beggar's cloak; there he saw how a sword was sticking out. (304) He looked a bit more closely at the sword; he then recognized it by its sheath. That was the sword Pomele that Druzeyne, the fair maiden, had given him. Then he realized that that was the beggar who had taken it from him on the meadow. He said: "Where did you get it? You treacherous thief; you took it from me. (305) Do you think that I do not know that you put me to sleep there on the meadow? Here you will have to suffer a bitter death. I will give you a mortal punishment."

The beggar could answer him not a word. He immediately gave him his weapon. Bovo said: "You need not imagine that I am going to make you a present of the remaining gear. (306) But tell me quickly and simply—or I will knock you down on the ground—where have you put my golden ring? And what did you do with my horse?" The beggar said: "I will confess everything to you, O brave and worthy warrior! I lost the horse in a dice game. The ring I gave to a man who pimped a Gentile woman to me. (307) O, dear my lord, now forgive me for it. I will never do it again as long as I live. Nothing good comes from gambling. Have you never heard that said?" Then it was Bovo who said: "Whoreson! Whoreson! I will indeed not pardon you for this." And he quickly drew back to strike him and chased him around the field.

(308) The beggar began a great cry and a murderous shriek: "For God's sake, kill me not, O gracious and noble my lord. I will teach you two things from which you can become rich." Bovo said: "If I have not yet paid you enough, I will surely improve upon it, if you lie to me." (309) The beggar did not delay long. And he had two flasks hanging at his side. In one of them was the sleeping potion that he had given him to drink. And in the other there was a different trick. That suited Bovo fine. It was a powder that, when someone rubbed it on himself, he took on a different color in the face. (310) He became green and yellow in the face. And when the beggar handed them to him, Bovo was quite sly with respect to it: he wanted to make sure that [the pilgrim] did not cheat him. He smeared his hands and face and neck. He immediately lost all color as a result. He had a face that made the beggar laugh at him. Then he taught him how to make it. (311) Thereafter he took his broad-brimmed hat pinned all around with [pilgrim's] lead medallions. Thereafter he took his cloak, which was not a good one. It had about a thousand patches. And a rosary that was worn around the neck. And took in his hand the pilgrim's staff, and on top he knotted a kerchief and went on his way looking like a Spaniard.[20] (312) He gave the beggar his good coat. He had received many a blow for it.

Thereafter he ran helter-skelter until he arrived in the city. There he heard many bells ringing, and the whole city was buzzing with joy. In one place he saw dancing; in another he saw leaping. In one place he heard piping; in another he heard singing. (313) On the square he came to a place where he saw a great crowd. He found a great many townspeople sitting there who were playing chess with each other. He said: "Listen to me for a moment. I come here from Babylon. I beg you, I am a poor pilgrim. For the sake of Bovo's soul give me a half-penny." (314) They said to him: "What are you saying there? Makabrun will not give it to you, for he has had a proclamation made such that whoever says Bovo's name is to be drowned, for the queen becomes sad for a day if she but hears Bovo mentioned." Bovo said: "If you will not give me anything, then show me the way to the palace, and long life to you."

(315) He came to the palace and shouted quite loudly: "Give me something to eat. Do not leave me in need. Give me some soup for the bride's sake. Do you not have some soup on the fire. Give it to me for the sake of noble Bovo, so that it will be of aid to his soul." Shouting like this, he entered the kitchen. The cook said: "I will do your mother one for you! (316) You villain, get out of here right now, if you wish to preserve your honor." He struck him on the head with a burning piece of wood. Bovo did not wish to put up with that and quickly raised his pilgrim's staff and defended himself against the cook. They fought each other, but I will abbreviate it for you: Bovo caused the cook to tumble into the fire. (317) The cook's assistant said: "What is going on? And what is this all about? Did the Devil bring you here? Can no one survive in your presence? Truly you will not get away with this. He drew the stick handle out of a broom. He wanted to drive him away with the stick. Bovo struck him dead on the spot. (318) Then a servant came in who was carrying the staffs in his hand. Bovo told him what they had done to him and how they had not wanted to give him anything to eat. He said: "You have given them their just reward," for he, too, feared for his life. He said: "I will give you some rich soup. I well see that you are a savage lord." (319) Bovo said: "Now listen to me for a moment. I will make it worth your while. Go and drag the bodies aside and pay attention that no one notices. Then I will go to the dance over there, to see if I could earn a penny." The servant said: "You need not worry. The matter will remain hidden."

(320) Bovo went out into the great hall and watched the dancing for a good while. He was looking for Druzeyne everywhere. Then he saw her swaying back and forth. She was wearing gold and countless pearls and a gown entirely of gold. Bovo said to her: "Give me alms. For the sake of Bovo's soul, with whom you learned to skirmish. (321) Druzeyne was stunned and looked at

him closely, and she began to grow pale in the face, and suddenly she left the dance and went into a chamber as if she wished to relieve herself. She said: "Summon that poor man to come to me here. I wish to give him alms." Thus he was summoned. He went to her. Druzeyne received him amiably (322) and said: "Tell me, honorable man, what do you know of Bovo?" Bovo said: "I know that he and I were captives of the sultan. That same prison was too difficult for him. His noble body could not endure it. Thus he became so ill that, God have mercy: he lay in my arms as his soul left him. (323) Thereafter God granted me the good fortune to break out of those hard stone walls." Druzeyne turned away and, weeping, went to a window. Bovo said: "Come on and give me a piece of the left-over bones." Druzeyne wiped her eyes and ordered food brought to the beggar. (324) Then he was brought a plate with fish, fine fat pieces from the belly. Druzeyne seated herself right next to him at the table and watched him wolf down the food. She sighed many a deep sigh that was heard by everyone, and she repeatedly began to speak of Bovo.

Makabrun came into the chamber with the two of them (325) and said to Druzeyne: "What are you doing here? What is your business with the pilgrim?" Druzeyne answered him and spoke thusly: "For the sake of God, I had a plate brought to him. But he told me something that made me sad, for which I would like to give him three half-pennies. He said that he was recently with my father who was very ill and had not yet recovered." (326) Makabrun said: "Now, do not be sad. You should not believe everything that everyone says. Someone would have written me something about it. Come, say farewell to the pilgrim."

While he was standing next to her, three or four serving boys came running up to them and said: "My lady, you should know that Rondele has broken free (327) and is running around loose in the stable. We can say that in truth: whoever goes near it, it strikes him dead; it has driven everyone away." Makabrun went pale, ran down there quickly, and wanted to see whom it had killed. Bovo said: "What is this creature in whose presence no person can survive?" (328) Druzeyne said: "It is a horse that I gave to the late Bovo. And since the worthy warrior has gone away, no one has been able to come near it. I take care of it and do what it wants, and its needs are met by me. And if it even hears Bovo mentioned, then no one near it is safe."

(329) Bovo said: "It would have to be very wild, for me not to tame it. So lead me down there, O vision of beauty. It will be as child's play for me." Druzeyne said: "Do not be so generous. The horse will put an end to your laughter. It will beat in your skull with its iron horseshoes. Come along with me, however; I will show it to you."

(330) She went with him up to the stable. They found many people standing there. It had kicked one so that bile oozed out of him; it had struck deep wounds into another. Makabrun stood there with all his men. They would have liked to tie it up again. Not one of his servants dared enter the stable. They were holding the gate closed with great force. (331) Bovo went up to the gate and easily knocked it open. As soon as Rondele saw the noble man, he came bounding out to him. A great turmoil then ensued; they were all pushing to get up the stairs. Fortunate was he who could flee ahead of the others. Makabrun ran into a room and locked himself inside. (332) The horse drove everyone from the courtyard. They fled from there as if they had wings. Only Druzeyne remained there with Bovo. She held a club in her hand. Rondele ran to Bovo and rubbed against him. Bovo took it by the reins and led it into its separate stall. Druzeyne saw this and was quite astonished. (333) Rondele walked along right by his side and laid its throat on Bovo's head.

Bovo said: "Now, now, look here. How can you act like you know me better than your mistress. Even I have to laugh at that." He unintentionally raised his cloak; then she saw that a sword was sticking out. (334) Then she ran up to him very quickly. She recognized that it was Pomele. She said: "That was Bovo's. Tell me where you got it. Tell me quickly. I also clearly heard what you said. How does Rondele know you so well. I think you intend to make me think that you are Bovo. It might well cost you your life. (335) That your nasty form should resemble the noble and fine lord's! Ha! The difference between his dear face and yours is like the difference between the Holy Sabbath and the common weekdays."

Now a barrel full of water was standing there. He plunged his hands into it and washed his face with the water. Then he had the form that he had had many a day in the past. (336) As soon as Druzeyne had seen that, then she began to hug and kiss him. She clung to him like a burr. She let him know that he was welcome. She said: "O lover dear, father dear, if I were to satisfy my desire with you here, alas, how could I maintain myself against Makabrun? Today we are to be laid in bed together." (337) Bovo said: "Follow my counsel, and you need not worry. And quickly come down to me today, and make sure that it stays secret. We will swiftly ride away on Rondele—many a mile—before morning comes." She said: "How am I supposed to get out of the room without Makabrun's noticing?'

(338) Bovo said: "I will tell you a trick, and listen to me very closely. Here I will give you a flask with a potion. You are to give him some of it to drink. Then he will fall down onto a chair or just as likely somewhere next to one. And he will sleep like a sow there. Then come downstairs to me and bring me

my weaponry. (339) Druzeyne said: "That is a good plan. He will have nothing to confess to any priest. I will make him drink according to all my desire. I will fill his head with my blabbering. Just give me the flask and then let me go to work with it. And I will take care to get your armor for you. I will arrange everything for the best." (340) She took the flask and went away. But beforehand they kissed for a while.

Now you can see what her intent was: She hurried to Makabrun. She said: "Should I not tell you about the pilgrim? He has no peer for many a mile. He says that in three days he will make Rondele stop biting and kicking." (341) Makabrun said: "That is very good. Order food to be brought to him, and order the horse to be given water. And if he does that, I will gladly give him something." Druzeyne said: "He desires no payment, but only that it be remembered to take him food, and also at night he wants to sleep down there. I want to have a little bed made for him under the stairs." (342) Now Druzeyne thought of a plan and quickly went into her chamber and there took a large mattress and tied Bovo's armor inside it and thus said to a servant boy: "You will find a beggar down there in the stable. You are to give this mattress to him. And tell him to lie on it where he pleases."

(343) The servant boy did as she said and carried it down to him in the stable and said: "Druzeyne sends this bed for you. You are to lie down wherever you wish." When the servant boy had given it to him, then he untied the bundle and wanted to lie down on it and sleep for a while. He found his good weaponry inside.

(344) Now, Druzeyne had gone to the dance, as if she had forgotten everything. And when the night had become quite dark, everyone was called to the table, and when they had then filled their bellies full and had sat there a while and had sufficiently serenaded the bride and groom, they ran along with them and forced their way into their chamber. (345) Makabrun drove everyone out and locked the door from the inside with a bolt and immediately began to get undressed. He feared that the time would get away from him. Druzeyne drew forth her flask that contained the sleeping potion and began to speak to Makabrun: "Let us first drink for a while. (346) First have a drink of this fine Madeira. It will quite refresh you. And after you have had a drink, give it to me, and I will drink the rest. Makabrun immediately drank it up. Then he began to feel very strange. He began to feel the drink in his head, and it was roiling in his heart. (347) He sank down there on a chest; his eyes rolled back in his head. He could not hear or see or speak. He was intoxicated by the sleeping potion. Druzeyne did not fool around. When she thought that he was quite asleep, she slipped out of the chamber and locked

it properly. (348) She took the key and delayed no longer, and ran down the stairs very quickly and went into the stable. There Bovo stood and saddled Rondele and was armed to the teeth, and at his side he carried Pomele, and as soon as she had come into the stable, he jumped into the saddle and took her up behind him (349) and galloped away like an arrow, the whole night without a pause and for a good while into the next day. When they came into a large forest, they had ridden seventy miles. There they found an extraordinarily beautiful spring. Then they got down there by the spring and rested there in the sun (350) and ate what they had there by the spring and fully refreshed themselves. Not until then did all their joy begin. Bovo did what he had to do. Druzeyne screamed like a thief in the stable. Oh, he did not need to peck at her crest, for she was indeed not trying to evade him. What they got out of it you can imagine for yourselves.

(351) Now let us leave them sitting there having their entertainment with each other and write a while about our dear Sir Makabrun. There was no one who took vengeance for the night when Druzeyne ran away and left him sleeping until the morning when everyone got up. (352) Not until three hours into the day did everyone grow astonished about why he was lying with Druzeyne so long, and neither she nor he came out of the chamber. Makabrun's father said: "May the plague strike them! Both of them should be ashamed! In their own company, I think that they have quite forgotten themselves. Now everyone must go without breakfast for their sake."

(353) Suddenly he wanted to wait no longer. He began to bang on the door; he remained standing there a good while. He heard nothing moving inside. He said: "There is something wrong. They must be doing something strange in there." He immediately ordered that hammer and tongs be brought, and he broke open the chamber by force. (354) Then many a good warrior ran inside and immediately went up the steps to the bed. They saw that the bed was still made and untouched. They were so astonished that they immediately fell silent. They saw Makabrun lying face down there in a corner, tangled up in his trousers, as if someone were to blow [an enema] into his ass. (355) They were horrified, and they all ran over there and began to shake him hard. It was as if he were altogether dead, as if someone had beaten him with cudgels. They carried him to where a great fire was burning and began to rub and shake him and poured Madeira down his throat, until he began to wake up.

(356) Then they asked him what was going on there and what had happened to him. Then he asked where Druzeyne was, but none of them had seen her. Then he shouted so that it could be heard from afar. "Alas and alack," he began to say. "Alas, I drank a sleeping potion. Alas, I fear she has run away.

(357) I cannot just now make any sense of it, nor do I expect any good to come of it. I fear that the pilgrim from yesterday was the villain Bovo. Therefore, run quickly down to the stable for me and find out the full story for me." His servants ran there very fast. They found neither the pilgrim nor Rondele. (358) Then he realized and knew for certain that she had ridden away with Bovo. He let out a great shout. All joy had left him; he tore out his hair for grief. He would have liked to slit his throat. He wept and lamented quite vehemently. He repeatedly said "Druzeyne, Druzeyne, (359) Druzeyne, I would never have imagined that you would leave me. I did not reckon with this calamity. Alas, my heartfelt sorrow! That means—a wedding without the bride. Alas, how little joy!" And at once he said to all his men that they should hurry after him with all their forces.

(360) Makabrun's father began thus and said: "Dear son, give it up, for I can assure you that they cannot overtake them. Therefore let all your men remain at home and do not be so crudely swindled. And if you do want to have him pursued, then listen to what I will tell you."

(361) Now the book tells us how Makabrun held a captive who was half man and half dog. No one had seen anything like him for a long time. He ran many a mile in an hour. He had stalked many people. He ripped up whole trees with one hand. And his name was Pelukan the Mighty. (362) He was grievously imprisoned in the dungeon, and he was to be hanged any day now. His father said: "If I were you, I would send him to bring them back and would promise him—just as he wishes—to spare his life." Makabrun said: "I cannot imagine a better plan." He immediately ordered him released from the dungeon. (363) Pelukan came swiftly and nimbly and knelt before Makabrun. Makabrun told him everything and said: "Pelukan, you very brave hero, see to it only that you are successful this time and bring both of them back to me here. Then I will grant you a reprieve from prison, and you will have no cares for the rest of your days."

(364) Pelukan said: "Gracious my lord, so fine, I promise you that you need not worry. You will have both of them back before this time tomorrow. Only give me my bow and arrows and my armor that you hid from me, and rest assured that I will hunt them down." Makabrun had his gear brought to him. (365) Pelukan got down on all fours and stretched himself out fully and ran away helter-skelter, raising his tail up high. He looked in all hedges, large and small, and just like a dog he sniffed everywhere. He snarled and howled and trotted on ahead; the great noise he made was heard from afar.

(366) Now Bovo lay by the spring and slept. He had his head in Druzeyne's lap. Druzeyne heard how someone was running vigorously. The noise was

growing ever louder. She called quickly and woke Bovo from his slumber. She said: "I fear that you must defend yourself. Do you not hear the noise, you worthy warrior?" Bovo was startled and at once leapt onto his horse. (367) He had on his good armor, and he took his sword in both hands. He said: "I see a lone man running; he is running this way very swiftly." Druzeyne said: "If only it is not Pelukan, for he would slaughter us both." Bovo said: "He is running this way on four legs." Druzeyne began to weep piteously. (368) Her color and her red mouth grew pale. Bovo said: "O my dear delight and joy, do not worry; I will give him a good pasting. I would never fear a hundred dogs; should I now not defend myself from half a one?"

Meanwhile Pelukan rushed up and said: "Turn around and go back with your whore." (369) Bovo said: "Now stop that for the moment. I will teach you a lesson. I am not afraid of your arrows, nor of their sharp iron." Then Pelukan quickly leapt backwards, a praiseworthy leap, and quickly, one after the other, drew forth [his arrows] and shot at Bovo with his bow. (370) Bovo took Rondele by the bridle and dodged the arrows. Pelukan immediately took another arrow and shot another shot in a different way. Bovo at once went galloping toward him, striking at his head. Undeterred, Pelukan continued to shoot at him until he had shot all his arrows. (371) And since he now had no more arrows, then he drew his sword from its sheath. Then they raced at one another and struck each other with joy. Before one of them could save his life from the other, the sweat of battle poured from both of them. Pelukan fought with great might, and Bovo twisted and turned like a dragon. (372) Rondele helped Bovo with great favor. It put great pressure on Pelukan. They made a great cloud of vapor like the steam rising from a lime kiln. Bovo's skill began to fail him; he had never been so afraid in his life. Pelukan stifled his merry valor. With great blows he made him fall from his horse.

(373) As soon as Rondele noticed that Bovo had fallen off, then it began and sprang immediately at Pelukan and struck at him mightily with all four hooves; it struck him often, so that he was knocked to the ground so hard that he bounced right off of it. Pelukan immediately twisted backwards and jumped onto Rondele's back. (374) Rondele was wild and quite untamed; it did not want to put up with having Pelukan on its back; it ran with him through thorns and trees, ripping his face. Pelukan thought: "If only I were back home, I would leave Bovo to his own troubles." Meanwhile he could barely endure so much, so that he jumped down onto the ground. (375) Now that he was on the ground, he had then lost his sword. He had dropped it in the grass; thorns had torn it from his hand. As soon as Bovo had seen that, then he thought Pelukan was doomed. Then he ripped up a tree by the roots and hit Bovo in

the head, so that he tumbled. (376) He staggered well into the forest; he fell right in front of Druzeyne and rose up again like a new man and began once again to take courage and ran back to Pelukan, and again they went at each other like fighting cocks. Around and around Druzeyne, together they ran, while Druzeyne screamed bloody murder.

(377) "Oh, Pelukan, spare me at least from this. What calamity are you trying bring about here? Remember the loyalty that I showed you while you were sorely imprisoned. How often I pled your case with Makabrun; he would have otherwise long since hanged you. I beg you, for God's sake, let me mediate between the two of you and reconcile you and Bovo. (378) And let us leave here together. You two, such brave, young warriors—you will conquer the whole world. Who is the man who could overcome the two of you? Pelukan, if you return to Makabrun, he will kill you. Do you really want to trust that villain; truly you cannot depend on his word."

(379) Pelukan ran over to her at once and said: "I wish to follow your counsel; only tell Bovo also to obey you, and order him not to fight anymore. I will forgive him, if he forgives me. Let us swear brotherhood to each other. Wherever he wants to go, I will go with him. We will escape from Makabrun." (380) Druzeyne was very pleased with these words, and Bovo ran over to her, and she said: "Pelukan says as follows: you should lay down your sword; then he will stay here with us and will no longer oppose you, and he will always travel with us until we reach my father in Flanders."

(381) Bovo threw his sword on the ground and at once went over to Pelukan. Each extended his hand to the other and they embraced. They sat down in the sand by the spring, and afterward they went to catch Rondele again. Pelukan again found his sword and arrows, and thereafter they began to hurry away. (382) Druzeyne sat behind Bovo on the horse. Pelukan had handed her up behind him, and he ran on the ground beside them. He was loping along vigorously beside them on foot; the worthy warrior followed Rondele; he leapt over very wide ditches. Many a mountain they climbed with each other. Then they saw a fine castle before them.

(383) At that moment Pelukan said: "Bovo, my brother, should I not tell you that I know that castle well? I was inside it in the past. It is occupied by a count who is full of virtues. He fought against Makabrun and almost killed him with his lance, and Makabrun has not yet avenged himself on him, (384) for he has never been able to get at him. He would have long since hanged him. This same count is named Orayon. He will receive us cordially." Druzeyne said: "He is an honorable man. I, too, knew him long ago. He will take care of us, my dear Bovo. Troyen, his wife, is my close kinswoman."

(385) In this way they rode up to the castle. There they had securely locked up on the inside. The warden of the gate announced them with his trumpet. The count went up to the battlements. As soon as he saw Pelukan there, he thought to himself: "Makabrun has sent him here to kill me." (386) Thereafter he saw Bovo and the woman and heard them talking and laughing. He observed them very closely and carefully and marvelled greatly at the matter. He called his wife and said: "Look, now, can you recognize who these people are?" She said: "It is, by the Creator of the universe, my kinswoman Druzeyne. I will go and greet her. (387) And, as surely as I am a Jew, she has the handsome lad, Bovo, with her. I suspect that she has hoodwinked Makabrun. How otherwise is the matter to be understood?"

Then she shouted down to her from the battlements: "Is it you Druzeyne? Is it to be believed!" Druzeyne said: "Yes, my dear kinswoman. Come and open up for us and let us in." (388) The count said to his wife: "Shout down to her thusly, that if she drives away Pelukan, then I will let her and Bovo inside. For I fear that he will kill me with his great might." The countess did as her courageous husband ordered her. Druzeyne shouted up and replied: (389) "Without Pelukan I will not come in there, even if you gave me a whole wagon of gold, for now he is my servant. He is my Bovo's sworn brother. Therefore tell your husband not to worry, for we are not laying a trap for him." When the count heard these words, then he went down and opened the gates. (390) Then they rode inside and into the courtyard.

There they were received quite cordially. Orayon, the noble count, then asked them what else they desired. Then they told him from beginning to end all the things that had happened to them. Then he had a beautiful room prepared for them. He had many tapestries and many carpets spread inside. (391) Pelukan placed quite a nice bed for himself outside the door—so that if anything should happen to Druzeyne and Bovo, he could save their lives. And food and drink were served them; they had all their hearts' desire inside there.

They were in the castle many a day, about which Makabrun knew nothing. (392) Since Pelukan had not returned, he thought that he had run away altogether and had never pursued Bovo at all and had gone a different direction. He sent out many a band of his men and promised them a great treasure. They were to look for him in all lands and capture him wherever they found him. (393) Thus it was that many days had passed that Makabrun was unable to find out that they had been at Count Orayon's the entire time.

They were well entertained there. Once they rode out hunting with Pelukan in the forest where the castle was. In the distance a peasant was cutting wood. He saw Bovo and Pelukan riding one behind the other. (394) The peasant thought to himself: "This should yield a profit for me. I will go to Makabrun and give him this message, and I will see to it that I earn enough to buy a horse and wagon." He ran off along the winding path and ran day and night so that he could arrive quickly. (395) And when he arrived in the city, he ran right to the palace. He immediately ran into Makabrun's chamber, for he found the door wide open.

Makabrun said: "What do you want from me that you sashay right in here?" The peasant said: "If you would give me something, I would tell you something that is of interest to you." (396) Makabrun said: "Go ahead and tell me. I will pay you for what you say." The peasant said: "I have seen Pelukan hunting with Bovo in a forest near the castle that Orayon holds. I think that they have taken up with him." Makabrun said: "I am happy to hear that. Now they cannot get away from me; I will get them!" (397) Thereafter he said to his servant: "Go and see if there is anything for the peasant to eat and give him in addition four ells of grey homespun so that he can make himself a funeral coat. Thereafter I wish no rest or repose until I have blasted down the walls of that castle, and all three must endure a bitter death, and I myself will cut out Druzeyne's genitals." (398) He at once ordered all his men to set out with him, everyone who could so much as shoot an arquebus or draw a crossbow. Thus they marched right up to the castle. He had twelve thousand men with him. They surrounded the castle on all sides. Many a fine pitched tent was seen there.

(399) He besieged the castle for a long time. They shot away many of the battlements. And if he had camped there his whole life, he could not have captured it. He said: "Because I cannot do it any other way, I will starve them out—those who are inside. But his plot failed completely, for they had supplies for an eternity. (400) After he had camped there for some eight months and saw that he could not capture it, one night he took a servant and cantered up to the castle and called up: "Go and ask Orayon whether he will permit me to speak a word or two with him off to the side where no one can hear the two of us." (401) One ran and told him the tale. Orayon came quite quickly and called down: "Who is it, who has had me summoned?" Makabrun said: "I would like to speak with you in a place where no one can hear us." Orayon drove away all his men. (402) Makabrun called up: "If you understand me, it will bring you great benefit. I say to you, it is I, Makabrun in the flesh, and I will tell you why I have come. You know that you have opposed me in taking these people in. Give them up, and I will not hold it against you, and I will give you an entire city." (403) Orayon answered him right away and said: "Makabrun, listen closely to me. Even if you gave me all your land, I would

not hand them over to you, for it would bring eternal sin and shame, were I to cause their deaths. So get away from here right now, or I will have you shot from the battlements." (404) Makabrun immediately turned tail and ran. He was afraid of their arrows. He galloped back to his tent in great haste. He hardly felt safe anywhere.

The situation did not change for quite a while. One day Pelukan began to say: "Let us go out and fight them." (405) Bovo answered Pelukan and said: "Yes, indeed, you bold warrior." Orayon said: "It is my business, too. I heard what you said." His men could all be seen there arming themselves. A thousand men wanted to come with him. Thus they charged out of the gates, Pelukan leading the way. (406) He had his sword at his side and in his hands his bow and arrows. Bovo rode not far behind him. Orayon also came thereafter with his troops, who were prepared to fight. They all wanted to risk their lives. When they were not too far from the castle, there they found great bands of enemies. (407) Pelukan began to shoot his sharp arrows among them. He shot many of them in a short while, so that all of them lost their lives. Bovo galloped quickly after him; he bound his helmet tightly, and he took his lance under his arm and made the blue intestines of many of them gush forth. (408) And before the enemy had charged, many of them had lost their lives. Bovo stabbed them in the chest, like an outstanding warrior. He charged right into their midst, and Rondele struck both backward and forward. There was a great deal of shouting and roaring. Orayon and his men had also arrived.

(409) There was a huge and fierce tumult that was heard on all sides, so that Makabrun immediately recoiled: thus did the uproar terrify him. He was quickly armed and mounted his horse with his men. They galloped fast toward the noise. There they saw how they were slaughtering each other. (410) Makabrun saw Pelukan there—how he hacked many people to pieces—and rushed toward him with all his men. Pelukan turned his back on them. Then they immediately found Count Orayon, for whom it did not turn out well. They ran at him in a great crowd. Makabrun stabbed him over and over. (411) He fell from his horse right into the mire. He shouted: "I surrender." Makabrun said: "Take him away. The villain must be hanged." Then only did a great slaughter begin. It swept through Orayon's troops. Pelukan and Bovo defended themselves for a while. Thereafter they made haste to the castle. (412) They were very eager to get inside the castle. Thus they came bounding inside. Part of their troops followed them, in order to save their own lives. Makabrun shouted loudly with hostility: "Quickly, let us right away force our way after them." But those inside raised the drawbridge, and those who remained outside were hacked to pieces. (413) In the castle there now began a

great lamentation and great mourning. They did not know but that Orayon had also been killed. The countess grieved mightily for her husband. The great lamentation cannot be described.

Now Makabrun had now reached his camp and had Count Orayon brought before him (414) and said: "Traitor, are you here? How do you think that I can allow you to live?" Orayon began and said thusly: "Noble my lord, listen to me carefully, and if you do not kill me, I will certainly deliver all your enemies into your hands. Let me live; you will not regret it." Makabrun said: "I do not wish to trust you." (415) Orayon said: "Gracious lord of the land, if you do not wish to believe me, I will give you as a pledge my two dear sons, the handsome lads. You will hold them until you get the others." Makabrun was pleased by these words and said: "Yes, that is the way that I will play it."

(416) Then Orayon wrote a letter to his wife, and he had a servant take it there, and he wrote to her: "God bless you, my dear one. Tomorrow I will be beheaded or hanged. Now I beg you, do what I write to you, so that God might lengthen your days: send out to me my two dear heirs, so that I may thereafter die more easily. (417) Let me see them before my death, my dear, sweet precious ones; before that let them put their dear hands in mine; before that let me embrace and kiss them. Makabrun has promised me—you should know this—that they will be sent back to you at once." The servant took the letter went on his way. He was granted an audience with her.

(418) As soon as she had merely glanced at the letter, then she began tear her hair out and strike herself and called Bovo and Druzeyne, too, and she lamented her sorrow to them. Bovo began and said to her: "Gracious my lady, how could you refuse him? I think that since Makabrun has given him his word, then he will not put their lives in danger." (419) The countess was greatly distressed; her heart was almost broken. She lay two baskets across the back of a war horse; she set her two handsome boys in them. Everyone who was in the castle there wept, but the boys laughed and sang. They thought they were about to have a great adventure. The servant went away with the children. (420) He drove them before him as if they were a mule's freight, until he had brought them to their bold father.

Orayon took them both in his arms. He kissed them; they kissed him back. And as soon as night came on, so that everyone lay down, he also lay down with his two sons directly on God's earth just as soldiers do. (421) In the morning, the fine count got up, and he let his two children sleep and ran to his castle and began to scream bloody murder: "Open up immediately and let me in. For I have escaped from Makabrun." How quickly they opened the gate for him. His dear wife came to meet him. (422) They embraced and kissed each other as is appropriate in such situations. She said: "Where are my children, since I do not see them." Orayon began to laugh: "I would rather the children's lives be at stake than my own: I can make more for you. If, however, my head had been cut off, I would have sired no others."

(423) Then Bovo and Druzeyne, the beautiful maiden, came in and were pleased by what had happened and received him with great joy, for they imagined no evildoing. But Orayon—may God grant him heartbreak—he began to carry out his treachery. He summoned into a chamber many a good comrade and told them how he wanted to bring about their fall, (424) and told them what the situation was, and what had happened to him, and how he had promised and advised Makabrun, how he wanted to hand them over to him as prisoners, or wanted to kill them in their beds, or his two sons would be hanged. "Therefore, dear comrades, let it remain secret. We will get plenty of property and money out of it. (425) Therefore, take care that you are prepared and take your best weapons today and do not stand too far apart, and when it seems to you that they are asleep, then force your way inside all at once and punish them with death—but Druzeyne is to be spared; we want to give her to Makabrun alive."

(426) They said: "We understand. We will obey you as an honorable man, for we do not wish to be eternally held captive here. For what are we to do: we have almost no more bread and wine. We will lose our lives. If Makabrun gets inside, we will all have to die. Is it not better that we earn his favor?" (427) And now that they had made their pact, they all separated, each to give attention to his weapons and armor, because they wanted to execute the brave lords.

And when it was deep in the night, so that everyone had lain down to sleep, Bovo also lay down with his Druzeyne, but Pelukan began to suspect a calamity. (428) For he was quite extraordinarily wise. He could have ruled an entire country. He could hear very quiet sounds with his ears, and he could track like a dog. It seemed to him that treachery was in the offing. He went and listened at Orayon's door; he stood with his ear to the door. Orayon was enraged at his wife there. (429) He heard how she let out a great scream and said: "This murder is not to take place! For Druzeyne's sake, I will not allow it!" Thus she repeatedly shouted and spoke. Orayon said: "Oh, be quiet, or, by Goat, I will not forgive you for it." She said: "I would rather let myself be chopped to bits." He raised his hand and slapped her in the face (430) so that the chamber at once echoed from it, such a blow did he give her.

Pelukan quickly leapt through the hall, and quickly he rushed to Bovo and said: "Quickly, waste no time at all, or we will all die. Orayon wants to have us all slain. He has arranged a grand betrayal." (431) It caused Bovo a great deal of anger and pain. The noble lord quickly armed himself. Pelukan carried his sword with him. He took up a position at a distance before Orayon's door. There he heard how Orayon was still beating his wife and made her squeal like a sow. Naturally, she wanted to come out and warn Druzeyne. Pelukan quickly began to gather his courage (432) and ran with his head against the door and broke it down with great force, and quickly he drew his sword and split his [Orayon's] skull. He said: "Next time it would not be inappropriate to remain loyal to a comrade." He murdered him in bed beside his wife, but he did her beautiful body no harm.

(433) Thereafter he spoke few words. He let his wife scream and howl. He found Bovo and told him of the murder. And both of them went away from there. Then they heard there in a chamber some two hundred men together. They heard how they were milling around, and they were all putting on their best weaponry. (434) Both of them leapt into the chamber with a great shout and roar. Bovo said: "On my oath, we have come at just the right moment." They struck them with great joy. Many lost their lives there before they could arm themselves and get prepared. They slew many of them. (435) One ran this way, another that way. Lucky was the one who could escape.

Bovo found an old soldier who had been there for fifty years. He said: "Have mercy on me, noble my lord; I will make you aware of something, so that you can successfully escape from Makabrun, and he will not be able to pursue you." (436) Bovo said: "Go ahead and tell me, if you do not otherwise wish to be slain." He said: "I will show you a hole, a cave that goes underground. It is ten miles long or even longer. A person can walk through it and even ride a horse." Bovo said: "Come, you have to show it to me." Then he showed him a door made of iron. (437) Bovo said: "Thank you, thank you," and right away left him, and ran back up like a dauntless lad and wanted to begin murdering again.

There they were all jumping off the [castle] walls; many had broken their limbs. Makabrum waited there with his army for Orayon to open the gates for him. (438) These men [who had leapt from the wall] told him the tale and everything that had happened to them, and how Orayon had already been slain. It was disturbing and worrisome to Makabrun. Now Bovo's heart was heavy. He very much wanted to get away. He was afraid that Makabrun would give him his last rites. He told Pelukan about the cave. (439) He said: "We can get away from here, so that no one knows of it, and before Makabrun finds out, we will be far away from here." Pelukan said: "Let us do it. No need to think about it any longer." Bovo and Druzeyne mounted Rondele, and they began to ride into the cave. (440) They dashed through the cave in a very short time. Then day began to break. Druzeyne could not ride so fast, for she was nine months pregnant. And when they had ridden forty miles, then she began to complain a lot, so that they had to ride a bit more slowly.

There they saw a beautiful forest in the distance. (441) They rode until they entered the forest, where they dismounted from their horses [!]. Pelukan quickly cut branches; he built them a little hut on the ground. Druzeyne had a great many labor pains. They began to become longer and stronger. She wept hot tears and began to say: "Alas, what is to become of me without a midwife? (442) Alas, how am I to birth a child by myself? And with what am I to revive and cleanse myself? I have not a blessed thing that a woman in childbirth should have." Pelukan said: "Do not cry, dear child. You have me and Bovo, the handsome lad. He will hold you by the back, and I will pull the child out of you."

(443) Meanwhile she then began to give birth. A beautiful child came forth. Pelukan had to act as a midwife: he had to receive the child. There she gave birth to a beautiful, fine son, a large, excellent, long one. She shouted: "Alas, I am going to give birth to another one. It seems to me that there is another one still inside me." (444) Before she had finished saying those words, she gave birth to another beautiful lad. And now that she had given birth to them, she had nothing with which to revive and cleanse herself. They laid her on the ground, for she had no bed. And they could have no fire. Pelukan said: "I will run off and take care of everything and will moreover not buy it." (445) Bovo said: "Wait no longer and make sure that you are back promptly."

Pelukan began to go away from there. He strode quickly through the forest. From far away he saw there in the distance a fine monastery. He thought: "Then I will not delay any longer. I will completely clean out that monastery." (446) He quickly ran up to it, right up to the house and knocked with a stick. A small monk looked out the window and fell right over backwards for fright, and with fear and horror he ran away from the window and told the abbot, shouting and weeping: "Someone is outside the door who walks on all fours. (447) He knocked and wants in. I have never seen a more horrible man." The abbot said: "Who can it be?" He began to speak to the other monks: "Go quickly and have a look, and do not let him in." About ten of them ran over to the window and saw him knocking. They broke out in a sweat for fear. (448) An old monk yelled down: "What is that knocking and banging about? Believe me, you are not getting in. So be on your way quickly. The abbot will not allow us to let you or anyone else inside."

Pelukan said: "I will make it sour for you, and he climbed over the wall on all fours (449) and jumped down like a goat. The monks all fled before him; they ran, helter-skelter, to the abbot with a great, loud shout. The abbot ordered the alarm bell rung, and as soon as they had pulled the bell cord, then all the monks came running with large clubs and staffs (450) and said to him: "Get out! You are not to remain in the monastery. What is a dog to do here among us? Do you want to study, or do you want to write?" There were now about twenty of them. They wanted to drive him out by force. They began to hitch up their cassocks like aprons. One of them threw a wooden shoe at him and knocked him down, (451) and he got up again very angry and began to fight with the monk. He took his naked sword in hand, and he was splitting their hides for them. He whacked on them so that their blood flowed. He made three of them turn up their toes, for he had struck them on their tonsured pates so that they sang vespers out their asses.

(452) As soon as the abbot saw that, how quickly he ran away. Pelukan would have otherwise caught him, too, if he had not hidden. He trotted into his chamber, but he did not leave the door open. He locked it with about three bolts and leaned on the window and began to shout: (453) "Tell me why you have come here. Why do you want to take our lives?" Pelukan said: "It is my desire that you give me food and drink." When the abbot heard that, how happy he was. He said: "Just tell me what you think would be appropriate. I will have a meal prepared for the two of us, only promise me that you will do nothing to me." (454) Pelukan said: "Have no fear. I guarantee your safe passage." The abbot began to come out, and quickly said to all his servants that they should by no means delay any longer: "You are to slaughter many chickens and geese, and some of them are to be roasted and some braised, for I wish to make peace with this noble man."

(455) The servants did as he had said, and quite quickly they began to cook. Many chickens and geese were prepared there. They slaughtered a fatted calf. All the monks who had scattered here and there, all of them came creeping out. They sat down at the table and ate and drank. The abbot and Pelukan sat at the head of the table. (456) Pelukan ate until his belly was full, for he had not eaten for two days. Thereafter the abbot said to Pelukan: "You should tell me what else you desire." Pelukan said: "You noble man, you must allow me to carry away from here food and drink, so that I can feed my other comrades, or I will show them the way here." (457) When the abbot heard that, he was terrified. He feared that the others would also become aware of it and said: "Take as befits your honor, everything that you can imagine. You need not worry that I will resist you in anything, even if you take away everything that is here." Pelukan said: "That is what I will do, for you will not believe in a saint who does not make signs and wonders."

(458) Thereafter he went into a small room there, where he found many chickens in a coop. He said: "I want to take all the chickens. The priests will have to keep quiet." Thereafter he found rice and farro and raisins and currants and figs in a chest, and he filled an entire bag full of herbs and spices. Next in line then was the kitchen; in he went. (459) There he took a large pot of rendered fat and a bag stuffed with bread. And thereafter he took a small bag of salt and a great deal of smoked tongue out of the chimney and a small cask of aged boiled wine; the hoops were about to burst off of it. He said: "We can manage to drink wine out of that." He laid all the supplies in a pile. (460) Thereafter he took all kinds of tableware, bowls, spoons, and plates, and a kettle and a small pot or two (which one can buy for three half-pennies), and a small pan in which one can coddle an egg. And thereafter he went down to the cellar and drew off two large bottles of wine for himself, and he took a tub in which to wash diapers.

(461) And when he had taken that, then he went into a chamber next door. There he found a well-made bed. He said: "That will be just right for me." No monk had said a single cross word, for they feared for their lives. They had to gather together all the supplies. He said: "Now it is time that I wander on my way." (462) He had taken everything up to and including a tinderbox, and much that I cannot say, for I am concerned that I not lie. Therefore I will here break off. He said: "Now, may God be my witness that I do not want to carry all these supplies. For why would I wish to burden myself. They will have to lend me a horse in addition." (463) He went into the stable and was not idle. Many horses stood there in front him. He picked out a fine saddle horse. He began to put the pack saddle on it. In fact it was not a horse; it was a mule. He drove it out with great blows. In addition to all their losses, the monks had to carry the supplies down and help load them. (464) Thereafter he got down on all fours and drove the mule before him. Then he saw there the feet of a monk protruding from behind a stone. It was one of those same monks whom he had slain. Then he quickly stripped off his monk's garment, to make woolen diapers from it for the shitty little lads. (465) The abbot saw that he took it and had to let him carry it away. He took it and threw it over the mule's pack and went on his way and continued until he came to the hut. There night was just falling. Bovo came out to meet him and received him warmly.

(466) Pelukan told him what had happened. And when they had unloaded the equipment, they lit a large fire and warmed water to wash the children. Bovo, the noble man, became a cook. He made good pastries and pancakes and almond rice and dumplings and good dishes: apple sauce and small cakes and hot roasts.

(467) Rondele grazed around the hut near them on the path. And Pelukan and Bovo went out for days gathering wood, berries, and chanterelle mushrooms, and occasionally they began a hunt and took deer and rabbits and ate and drank only the best, and they fattened themselves up like sows.

(468) They carried on this way for about thirty days, and Druzeyne had now recovered. Bovo said: "This is no good. We have to start doing something else. I will go and see what I can see and whether I can choose a path for us. I will ride as far as the sea and look whether I can see a ship from afar. (469) Then we could all cross the sea and together go to Lombardy. Thus I would return to great honor; I know that many people wait for my return. Therefore, dear Pelukan, I beg you: take care of my dear children and also care for my wife. I will not be gone for more than a day or two." (470) He went inside the hut to Druzeyne. He asked that his two children be handed to him. He kissed both fine young ones, holding one in each arm. He said: "Take care of my children. And do not yearn for me: you have Pelukan; you need not worry. I will be back tonight or tomorrow."

(471) The fine warrior rode away, out of the woods and on his way. He had left Druzeyne well protected: he had left Pelukan with her. He did not leave her for the whole day; they sat together in the hut. And when night came, he made her bed for her and stood guard outside the hut all night. (472) And when it was three hours into the next day, Pelukan lay down behind the hut and slept in the sun like a dog. He let nothing disturb him. Druzeyne now began to wake up and offered her children her breasts.

Then two lions came up, chasing a doe and wishing to catch it. (473) The doe ran away quickly, just as does are accustomed to run. The lions now saw the hut; they quickly ran inside. Druzeyne began to scream. They sniffed her and the children and began to wag their tails, for a lion will do nothing to a person of noble blood. (474) Pelukan was unaware of everything. He was lying down there, sleeping on the ground. Druzeyne woke him with her screaming. He began to raise his head. He then saw the two wild animals. The two lions stood in the hut. He nimbly leapt up from the ground and took his sword in both hands. (475) As soon as the one lion saw him, it leapt out of the hut. Pelukan gave him a stroke—not a small one—on the head with his blade. The lion stood up on its hindmost legs. He wanted to grapple with Pelukan. Pelukan turned toward him with his sword and defended himself from the lion. (476) The lion was in great need; it beshat itself from fright. Thereafter it ripped a large piece of flesh out of his cheek with its paw, so that he was immediately red with blood. He began to hack at the lion and then thrust the sword into its belly, so that it fell with all four limbs outstretched.

(477) Now when the other lion saw this, it came rushing out of the hut and sniffed the dead lion with its nose and began to howl and snarl. Pelukan was tired and sat down on the grass. The lion got on top of him, roaring, and swatted him with its tail. Pelukan very much wanted to chase him away. (478) The lion was so lively and spirited and was vigorously pounding and biting; it ripped off his [Pelukan's] mouth and nose. Thereafter it pulled him down and dragged him by force through the mire and sat down on him and stripped off his flesh and poked a paw through the middle of his back and ripped his windpipe and gullet to pieces. (479) It gulped down the forequarters; it left not a bite. Now that it had eaten its fill, it ran off and went its way.

When Druzeyne had seen this, she began a great lament. She feared that Bovo was also lost and torn apart by the lions. (480) She said: "If I wait here any longer, I will also lose my life. The lion will follow up its meal. I fear that it will come back. But I will let it go for today and will wait for the brave warrior. If he does not return today, then I will go away from here and go back to my daddy and mommy." (481) All by herself she lamented and carried on miserably. She lay on the ground inside the hut with the children all day. Thus it happened that Bovo, the worthy warrior, did not return that day, for he had ridden through a savage forest and fought with dragons.

(482) She did not get any sleep that entire night, and in the morning she got up quite quickly and ran around in the hut like a crazy woman. She bundled up the children's things. She slurped out two fresh eggs and then suckled the children and bound one to her back and one to her arm and said: "May God have mercy! (483) Why did I not obey my honorable and worthy father and mother! How happy I then might have been, if only I had listened! Alas, the great sorrow and pain! Alas, what has become of me! I may now well say the proverb: 'Necking has now gone for my throat.'"

(484) She ran away quite quickly with the children, helter-skelter, until she passed through the forest, the children ever screaming and crying. Their sorrow was great and manifold, and she, too, did nothing but weep. She ran directly across the fields like one who is lost. Then she saw from afar a shepherd. (485) She was then glad and went to him both nimbly and quickly. She said to the shepherd: "Tell me where I can find the nearest city." The shepherd said: "Sit down and rest awhile with your children. Thereafter I will guide you on those paths, and I will show you a fine city." (486) She sat down with him at a brook. He began to smile at her with affection, and thereafter he demanded of her 'thus and so': he wanted to make a pass at her. She said: "Oh, may your name and memory be blotted out! How dare you expect such a thing from

me!" The shepherd said: "Do not hold it against me: a man may demand it, and a woman may refuse it."

(487) Druzeyne did not wish to wait any longer. She suckled the children quite quickly and began to go away quite quickly. The shepherd showed her the right path. She said goodbye and left him standing there. The shepherd bowed to her. He would have liked to look at her forever. He had never been sadder in his whole life.

(488) She continued until she saw the city there and went there in a short time. The sea abutted the city on one side. There were always many merchants to be found there. She went right up to the port. There she saw many ships tied up. Then she saw a galley there from afar. It had her father's standard on the side. (489) She saw how they were rushing to make ready and wanting to sail away from there. They raised the anchor out of the water. They raised the sail tautly. Druzeyne called to that crew. Four men jumped into the ship's boat. They clearly saw that she was a pretty wench. They went to her and offered their services. (490) Druzeyne said: "My dear fellows, if you take me on board your galley, I would be your cook until we come to your land." The sailors said: "Just come on board! For we will not be ashamed of you. What you desire, that you shall have." She climbed aboard the boat with her two lads. (491) They pushed off from land and rowed away.

They came to the galley and climbed aboard. They took the cook to the captain. They wanted to show him the pretty maiden. As soon as he saw her, he said: "Now, may God slap me and strike me down, or that is Druzeyne, whom we are travelling around seeking, of whom her father has quite despaired." (492) He went over to her and gave her his hand, welcomed her cordially, and said: "Are you not named Druzeyne? Your father misses you; he sent me out to look for you. He knows how you went away with Bovo." Druzeyne wept and lamented her troubles to him and told him what had happened to her.

(493) Thus they left that place. It was in the land of Barbary. They travelled so long that they came to where they saw her city, Armonia. They sailed up to the port. Everyone came running to the galley. There they saw at the front in the bow Druzeyne sitting with her two handsome children. (494) Someone ran quite briskly and quickly and made his way by a winding path and gave the king the message: "Your dear daughter has come, and she has two children with her. I heard them screaming and howling." The king at once hopped for joy and mounted a horse and gave it the spurs. (495) On each side of him ran a page. He wanted to welcome his daughter. And as he came to that place, she was coming toward him. He quickly dismounted and gave her a hearty kiss

and put his arms around her. He saw the two children being carried along behind her and said: "You should tell me who they are." (496) Then she again began to weep. She said: "Bovo sired them, and I bore them, but unfortunately it has not gone well for me. I fear that I have lost him. I am not sure what to think. He was ripped to pieces by lions while we were staying in a savage forest. I am convinced that they ripped him to pieces." (497) He said: "Dear daughter, I beg you, you should let all things be in God's hands, and now and ever after have courage, be honorable, and no longer be foolish. Thus you will grow old with honor, and what you have done will be forgotten. There are more young women who have failed to find a husband."

(498) Thereafter she told him absolutely everything and the misfortunes that she had suffered. She also mounted a horse. She rode behind her father, and thereafter the children were brought to her. She said: "They have not yet been circumcised." The king said: "Not to worry. I will arrange a fine circumcision for tomorrow."

(499) The next day followed. He had the boys taken to be circumcised, but he nonetheless asked Druzeyne: "You should tell me what their names are to be." She said: "Before that blessed Bovo left me, he said to me every day: 'I want to name one of them Guidon after my father, and one of them Sinibald after my foster-father.'" (500) The king said: "That is very good," and ordered that those names be given them. He had a banquet, as is still done. They led a splendid life. At first Druzeyne was cheerful. Many servants, male and female, accompanied her.

Now let us leave Druzeyne with her father and write about Bovo for a while. (501) The same day that she went away, he rode back. There he saw a lot of blood on the grass, and a dead lion lay nearby. He was alarmed and thought: "What is this? I will not wait any longer," and rode over to the hut and dismounted quickly. There he found the hind quarters of Pelukan lying on the ground. (502) Thereafter he looked for Druzeyne, the beautiful maiden. He could find her nowhere. He said: "Alas, my great grief! The animals have ripped her and her children apart! Alas, both of my children! Oh, my dear wife with her smooth skin! Alas, another such as she was never born. Alas, how horribly I have lost her. (503) Where should I now turn? What should I do? Alas, what minuscule joy! I thought that I had now left behind all my misfortune. Now my grief is just beginning. Oh, Pelukan, you dear companion! How you have been taken from me! I would not have thought to lose you this way. Thus you have been ripped apart by the evil animals. (504) Oh, now I am the most wretched knave whom God ever placed on earth." Then he—Bovo, that same worthy warrior—cut a trench with his sword and lifted the piece of Pelukan into it and scraped it full of dirt. He said: "Since I can do nothing else for you, I will honor you by burying you." (505) He had quite despaired of Druzeyne. He thought that she was lost. He said: "Cursed be the day that I was born!"

Now he searched on the sea, and no ship was in sight. He thought: "None will come for a long time. I will just ride away from here overland, (506) and I will just leave the sea behind and bid it farewell, in God's keeping, and I will ride long and hard. I will find something that is fitting for me and again attain to great honor, even if I lose my life for it."

And he rode Rondele on his way, his tears flowed down over the horse. (507) He rode and knew neither path nor trail. He encountered many a dragon and rode through many a savage thicket. He found many a beast with savage form. He encountered a great giant on the road; there he defeated him in battle. Before he killed him, he gave him many a blow. I do not want to write about it; I think it is lies.

(508) He never had either rest or repose until he came to a city with fine towers. He rode directly up in front of an inn. The innkeeper stood in the doorway. He said: "Where are you going, my dear guest? Do you not want to lead your horse in here?" Bovo said: "I would gladly do it, but I have not a penny to spend." (509) The innkeeper said: "That is not a problem. Have no care about the money. I can recognize in you the kind of man who need not pay in advance. I am the kind of innkeeper who can wait for payment, even if you stay until the day after tomorrow."

Bovo began to ride into the stable. There it was full of horses on all sides. (510) Bovo asked what that was about and why all the horses were there. He was told: "A man has come. He wants to assemble a lot of soldiers." Bovo thought: "That is good news. He would not be ashamed of me." He led Rondele into an adjacent stall and ordered a portion of oats be given to him. (511) The inn had rooms beyond number. It was built like a fortress. Bovo went up to the great hall. He found it full of guests. It was everywhere full of many people. They were eating and drinking to their heart's desire. He walked into the room. He was well received by the captain. (512) They all looked at him in wonder—how he strode into the room. One said: "I have not seen such a man in a long time. Surely he must be a great rooster in sword-fighting and combat. I would say that those same lords, Ditrikh of Verona or Hildebrant themselves had risen from the dead."

(513) Bovo walked back and forth in the room before the captain. The captain asked him who he was, of what people and faith, and what it was that he wanted, and whether he wanted to be in his pay. "You will have a good life with me. I will put you in command of four hundred men." (514) Bovo said:

"Noble and courageous captain, I will not turn down your pay. For I have come from Poland in order to pursue just that trade. Where do you wish that I go with you? That indeed you must tell me." The captain said: "Fine and noble warrior, you must go with us to Lombardy. (515) There is a castle there named San Simon. There is a fine captain in it, whose name is Sinibald. I am his son. A duke wants to capture the castle; he lives in Antona and is named Dodon. It is some four hundred miles from here. I have enlisted these troops because I wish to come to my father's aid."

(516) Now Bovo heard and knew for certain, that this was all for his sake, and knew that his name was Teyrets, for together they had learned to read and write. But he did not immediately allow himself to be recognized, just as if he were someone else. But he was very happy to hear it. He thought: "That will turn out well for me."

(517) Now Teyrets summoned the innkeeper and ordered the table to be set right away and ordered him to serve good wine and make a meal with many various dishes. There Bovo gulped down great mouthfuls: he ate more than ten of his peers, for he had not eaten much in many days. Teyrets began to say to the others in a leisurely manner: (518) "I think that this one's greatest talent is ever to gorge and stuff himself. He eats about three times as much as I do. I think he is a common clod. I think that he has come from Poland only to beg and because of hunger. I think that he would out-eat ten before he would fight against one." (519) Bovo heard what Teyrets said but did not respond. And now that everyone had eaten, they wandered off to bed. Bovo was in the same bed as Teyrets, and as soon as day stole up on them, Teyrets ordered the trumpet sounded. The soldiers all got out of their beds. (520) Teyrets said: "Now let us go and be on our way."

There were eight hundred or more of them, some on foot, some mounted on war-horses. Bovo was armed to the teeth. He and Teyrets sat their horses well. They divided the soldiers, took command of them, and rode until they had almost reached San Simon. (521) And now that they were almost at San Simon, Sinibald came out to meet them with great fanfare, and with great joy he greeted his son. And he was pleased with the soldiers, and when he now saw the handsome captain, who was the grandest among them all, he said: "Dear son, where have you been so long, and where did you come up with this handsome captain?" (522) Teyrets said: "My dear father, I found him quite by chance, and while he is indeed quite courtly and fine, who knows how he will perform. I think he is one of the greatest gluttons who has ever lived on earth. I have seen no manliness in him except that he can eat ten times more than I can."

(523) Bovo heard this a second time, and the speech aggravated him a great deal. He went up to Teyrets full of rage. He said: "You should moderate your speech. That I can also fight well, I will still demonstrate to you, and if you have courage, then you must promise me that you will have a friendly joust with me. (524) And it should be for one month's pay. And my heart will be loyal to you all the days of my life." Teyrets said: "Gold is the guarantee! That is also alright with me!"

So they immediately went to get ready and rode onto the square together. (525) Their soldiers followed them. They were eager to watch them. Sinibald lay at a high window and wanted to watch from afar. The two rushed at each other; they charged at each other with their lances. Bovo broke Teyrets's shield to pieces with his lance, so that both he and his horse fell on their backs. (526) He fell down there right in the sand, so that he remained stuck there. His men all ran to assist him and, greatly alarmed, help him back to his feet. He again mounted his horse with great shame and rode out of the square and said: "I will revenge myself on that villain. I will stab him to death with my own hands."

(527) When Sinibald had seen all that, he at once sent for both of them and mediated with good words, in order to reconcile them. He said: "Both of you now call it even and live in peace and joy. In that way you two can defeat all comers." He made them swear loyalty to each other. (528) He made them embrace and kiss, and they practiced great kindness toward each other. Teyrets clothed him from head to toe; he had him wear his own livery.

Now, dear sirs, you should know that I forgot to tell you that Bovo had asked to be called Agustin, so that no one might recognize him. (529) So they called him Agustin the Fair.

And after all that had taken place, and that day had passed, Bovo began to say to Teyrets: "Brother Teyrets, if you wish to follow my plan, let us ride out to see what our enemies in Antona are doing, whether we can take some provisions from them." (530) Teyrets said: "I will not pass that up. Let us wait until tomorrow." On the next morning, the trumpets sounded as is customary. Then they made their great preparations. They took along eight hundred soldiers. Teyrets and Bovo rode in the lead; the soldiers followed on horseback or on foot. They bore Guidon's standard on a staff.

(531) They came to Antona early in the morning, just as the shepherd had driven out his flock. There they took many calves and cows and some seven herds of sheep. They drove them away with great difficulty. Not a hoof was left behind. It was known in Antona, for they had seen it from the battlements. (532) They immediately tolled the alarm bells. They raised a hue and cry for

their livestock: one lamented his nanny-goat, another his ram, yet another his cow and sheep. And two thousand men came storming helter-skelter out of the gate. Duke Dodon had heard the uproar. He and his brother Alborigo also wanted to come along. (533) Many mighty men marched with them with their arquebuses and bows and arrows. Alborigo charged after them, and he quickly began to rush ahead of them. Duke Dodon quickly followed him.

Perhaps scarcely from a half mile away, Bovo saw them approaching in their pursuit. He ordered those with the livestock to flee at once. (534) And he and Teyrets remained behind, and they quickly turned to face them. Bovo said: "Who are those two who are rushing this way?" Teyrets said: "I will tell you no more than 'may God protect me from their hands.' The first one is called Alborigo the Mighty. He aids his brother in war. (535) And the other is the rogue who struck my dear lord dead. A falcon is painted on his shield. Do you not see it in the front?" Bovo said: "I am going to give both him and his falcon a good scouring." He ran at him with his lance and said: "Defend yourself, you traitor from Mainz!" (536) Alberigo ran at him, too. He bound his helmet tightly. Bovo stabbed him in the belly with his lance, which came out the middle of his back. He fell down there without even saying "ouch" or "oh." Bovo quickly pulled the lance out of him and quickly also ran at Dodon. Dodon had seen that and was burning with rage. (537) The worthy warriors thrust at each other, so that both of their lances shattered. Thereafter each took his fine sword and hewed and thrust at each other, both wanting to kill the other. A great cloud rose up from their throats. Bovo gave Dodon a knot the size of a pear: he hacked a great wound in his forehead. (538) Thereafter he stabbed him in the side, so that he was at once about to faint. Thereafter he gave him another stroke, so that he at once fell off the horse. He was quite pale in the face. He sank right down to the ground. Bovo wanted to finish him off, when the great army descended on him. (539) They saw their lord thus wounded, which began to disturb them greatly. They all came running at Bovo there with halberds and swords and lances. Indeed they wanted to slay him! They were shooting arrows at him. They had surrounded him on all sides. What a sight it would have been to see him fight there! (540) He made many of their heads quite red. What a sight it would have been to watch the youth! He slew some twenty of them before he forced his way out of the circle. He defended himself; he was in danger. And quickly he bounded away on Rondele. Many of them pursued poor Bovo; the others stayed there and raised Dodon up. (541) Because of the great, hostile blows, he could not stand on his feet, nor could he ride any more. He could not move his hands and feet. They bound two great shields together and laid him lengthwise on them and quickly carried him into the city. Teyrets and Bovo fought with the others.

(542) Bovo had turned back with Teyrets and only now began a difficult fight. Teyrets was also fighting aggressively. How grand it would have been to see that! And woe to him whose fate it was to encounter them! They saw that the battle was turning against them. They were not ashamed to retreat. (543) They rushed into San Simon. They had the fortress firmly closed. The others also did not pursue them too closely. They let the bastard escape. That army marched back to Antona. One could see blood flowing from many of them. In Antona they grieved and lamented, and in San Simon they rejoiced greatly. (544) The square and all the streets were filled with the livestock that they had taken. They did not know what to do with so much. They had to slaughter many of them.

Teyrets now said to his father: "Oh, how well did Agustin perform. He stabbed Alborigo to death, and he well avenged us on Dodon. (545) And I can tell you in truth that he struck him deep wounds. I have never in my life seen a more courageous man. Praise be to God that I have found him! He is as fiercely devoted to the cause—he was thrashing around like a dragon. And even if Bovo himself—and if he had come back, he would have been devoted enough to the cause." (546) Sinibald said: "I am well consoled that he will avenge my dear lord." Thereafter he had a good feast prepared. He ordered many sheep and calves slaughtered; they laid good roasts on the grate, and they began to drink and tipple.

Sinibald's wife also heard about the rejoicing; she also came with her maidens. (547) Sinibald ordered his wife to sit next to him, and Bovo sat diagonally across from her. She did not take her eyes off Bovo during the entire meal. She began to say to herself: "I think that he must certainly be Bovo, for he has the same gray eyes and the same fine mouth with little white teeth. By Almighty God, he is very much like him." (548) When they had eaten, she left and called her husband into an adjacent room and said: "I have looked closely at Agustin. Bovo does not look very different from him. I reckon that he has become such a fine man. That may well be he, on my life!" Sinibald said to that lady: "By Goat, you are indeed a fool. (549) Bovo was executed long ago, and his evil mother keeps it secret. When I remember it, my heart breaks. For that reason I will ever wage war on them. But Agustin looks as much like Bovo as if he had climbed out of his ass." Then they lay down together to sleep. The lady kept thinking about Bovo all night long.

(550) When the next day came, when they again sat down to eat, the lady again came walking in and at once sat down across from Bovo. She again

noticed how much he resembled Bovo. She could by no means stop thinking about it. And as soon as they had left the table, she took her son Teyrets by the hand (551) and led him into a chamber and said: "Either the evil plague must take me, [or] your comrade, the fine captain Agustin, is, according to all my senses, Bovo." Teyrets said: "By Goat, it could well be. What do we do, so that we can find out?" His mother said: "Listen to me closely. I will give you a good tip." (552) Go and lead him into the bathhouse. Thus will I tell you how you will recognize him. He has a mark on the lower part of one calf. I once accidentally burned him. It is round like a wheel. And on his shoulder there are two moles." Teyrets said: "I will soon see about that," and went to Bovo and said to him: (553) "Agustin, my dear comrade, would you like to go to the bathhouse with me? Then we will drink sweet wine, and I have taken along a roasted capon." Bovo said: "Very well, let us do it!"

Thus they went together, the brave warriors. They went inside and undressed. Bovo had a body that looked like pure strained milk. (554) They sat next to one another in the bath. Teyrets began to look at the moles. Thereafter he saw the mark on his calf and began to say to him: "Alas, what a great pity, what happened to your leg?" Bovo said: "I cannot tell you. I have had it all my life."

(555) Teyrets could hardly wait until they left. He bathed only for a short while. He ate a bit and took a break and hurried quickly home and ran to his mother in her house, much more quickly than an arrow from a bowstring, and said: "If I am not greatly mistaken, Agustin has all those marks." (556) The lady said: "On my oath, then I will go and be the first to welcome him."

She ran to him with great joy, stretching both her hands to him and embraced him with both her arms and kissed him on his red cheeks and said: "Are you not Bovo, whom I raised, and you suckled from my breasts?" (557) Bovo said: "May God give you joy. Yes, it is I, you noble lady. But I beg you, make no proclamation of it. Keep it to yourself and tell no one anything, except for your two loved ones, your dear son and my dear foster-father, whom I love as much as if he were my father."

(558) Just then Sinibald walked in, for Teyrets had told him what was going on. Both of them embraced Bovo and welcomed the excellent warrior. He kissed them; they kissed him more and asked him where he had been and led him home with both arms wrapped around him. Bovo told them everything that had happened to him.

(559) Now we will let them stay together and have much enjoyment with each other, and we will again return to Duke Dodon and write about him for a while. He issued a proclamation in his land that all the doctors of wounds

and bodies were to come and heal him, and whoever did not come was to be drawn and quartered. (560) So now all the doctors came from near and far. They also heard of it in San Simon. Bovo said: "I will not delay either. So help me God, I will also go there. I will ride there on a mule and present myself as a doctor, and I will take the villain's life." (561) Teyrets said: "That is a good plan, but it will not happen without me. I will go along with you as your servant; people will look at me as your attendant. And as soon as you have slaughtered Dodon, I will kill ten of his lords. And I will organize the old lords and the loyal comrades down by the gates, (562) so that when they hear a cry, they will immediately blow the horn. Then my father will be waiting in the hay-fields with our excellent warriors, and when they blow the horn once or twice, they will come running to the gates. They will all shout 'Bovo, Bovo.' So everyone will come running in to join us."

(563) Sinibald said: "I would approve, but I fear that Teyrets will be recognized." Bovo right away said: "Then I can burn a powder; then I will make him blacker than coal." He told him what he needed for it, and he made the powder in all respects just as the beggar had taught him. (564) And when he had the powder ready, then he began to smear him with it: all over his hands and face, neck and ears and forehead. And he was dressed just like a Moor, as if he were a man of great wisdom. And he had a suitable jacket, and on his rump he wore a rapier. (565) Bovo had a scarlet coat and a long scarlet cloak made for himself, and a wide belt with golden buckles, and under the coat he equipped himself well: he girded on Pomele. And on his shoulders he had a hooded cape, and had a high-peaked hat. (566) Sinibald presented him with a fine mule, so that he could ride like a doctor, and he gave an old nag to Teyrets so that he could trot along far behind him.

They rode away and were not idle and came to Antona in a short while and lodged with the best innkeeper in Antona: that inn was named The Crown. (567) Teyrets got up immediately and went out and sought out all the lords and gathered them into one house, so that he could tell them the good news. He said: "If you can be quiet as a mouse, then your situation can still turn out well. I want to tell you some very good news. Thus and so has Bovo returned. (568) And I am Sinibald's son. We intend to take Dodon's life. And we intend to do him thus and so. You should therefore pay attention to that and tell no one anything about it and take effective control of the gate, and when you hear that he has been slain, then one of you is to run up on the wall and blow a horn. (569) My father is waiting with a thousand well-armed men not far away from here. As soon as they hear it, they will come in. You should open the gate." These words were welcome to the lords, and they were happy and went away and prepared themselves with great care. Now this was not to take place until tomorrow.

(570) Now it was heard throughout the city, how a fine doctor had come. He knew more than Galen and Hippocrates; he healed the lame and the crippled. Avicenna had never learned as much as this doctor knew, and he was a handsome man in appearance. The wicked Brandonia was also informed about him. (571) She sent one of her servants for him, so that he would come to her tomorrow. She wanted to make an arrangement with him right away. He need not grant her credit even for a penny. If he could restore her husband's strength, he would have no worries for the rest of his life. His servant went and gave him the message. Bovo could hardly wait for dawn.

(572) As soon as the light of day had come, he and Teyrets walked to the palace. Brandonia quickly ran to him and welcomed him tearfully. She said: "I give my dear husband over to you completely. I fear that it is all over for him. Therefore, my dear scholar, if you can heal him, I will share my body and property with you." (573) She tried by force to shake his hand, but he did not wish it to happen. He turned away toward the wall. Because of her villainy, he did not want to look at her. So she led him to where he found the duke. Then Bovo began to say to him: "Gracious my lord, what a shape you are in. Do not worry, I will make you well. (574) Therefore, you need have absolutely no fear. Just let me see your wounds, and strip yourself stark naked. Let me see how you have been hacked. But order everyone to leave. I want neither man nor woman here." Then he drove his men and women out.

Bovo at once went and locked the door. (575) Dodon did not long delay; he quickly took off his bandages. Bovo sat down beside him on the bench, and Dodon showed him his wounds. He said: "My dear scholar, I am so ill! I would like to overcome it." Bovo said: "How did the battle proceed, and how did the enmity begin?" (576) Dodon said: "It is an old conflict. It has endured for many a day. And if fate gives me the victory, I will not put up with it from them. And the one who triumphed over me so that I am lying here now—that one I would like to look in the eyes. He also stole my cows and calves. I think he is the Devil incarnate." (577) Bovo said: "He is perhaps the son of the one whom you murdered. Perhaps he, as an excellent warrior, wants revenge for his father." Dodon said: "Now, you can just stop that! That one is long dead. I need not be concerned with him at all. I had his mother execute him." (578) Bovo said: "Now, have a good look at me. Does it not seem to you that I resemble Bovo. Was it not enough, you treacherous man, that you took my father's life. Does it not seem to you that I can pay you back? I will give you the wages that you deserve." He quickly drew his sword and hacked the villain into tiny pieces.

(579) And when that had now taken place—that Bovo had avenged himself on Dodon—Teyrets learned of it, and he killed about ten of them. Bovo now went to him there; the heads of many were broken. Bovo was seen raging in doublet and hose, and the horn was blown from the wall. (580) No one knew what was going on. They knew nothing of their misfortune. One ran this way, another that way. A vehement weeping and wailing was heard. Meanwhile Sinibald and his troops arrived there; they bore Guidon's standard before them. "Bovo, Bovo," they shouted repeatedly, and they were churning violently through the people from Mainz. (581) They hacked into them as if they were dogs, until they had slain them. The battle lasted ten whole hours until they had overcome them all. Many of Sinibald's troops were also wounded. There was a vehement shouting and roaring. When it seemed to Bovo that they had killed them all, he had a proclamation made and sounded on the trumpet: (582) "Everyone is to lay down his weapons, if he otherwise does not wish to be hanged."

All the townspeople who wished Bovo well came forth rejoicing. Bovo right away went to the palace, accompanied by a long trail of followers. They accompanied him as far as the steps. Everything now became still and quiet. (583) Bovo ordered Dodon to be carried away and buried in the fields, and they were to do the same to the others. He did not want to permit it in any other way. Thereafter his evil mother now came out and thought to receive mercy from him. She fell down on the ground before him and screamed and wept and behaved wildly. (584) "Dear son, I am in your power. You may do with me as seems proper to you. If I have done anything to you that you did not like, I ask that you forgive me. I am after all your mother. Blood is thicker than water. Dear son, grant me my life."

Bovo could not speak a word to her. He said: "Sinibald and Teyrets, I hand this over to the two of you." (585) And he quickly went into another room. And Sinibald began to say to her: "Brandonia, Brandonia, you evil toad! You had your husband slain, and you wanted to have your son delivered up to death. How can that be tolerated from you! You deserve to be beheaded and dragged through the streets by your braids. (586) But because you are his mother, for that reason it will be granted that your life will be spared, but you will be confined to a nunnery." Teyrets said: "That also seems good to me." They ordered their servants to lead her away and locked her in a nunnery. She would have to stay there until Easter in a jubilee year.[21]

(587) Thereafter Sinibald brought his entire household there, and he led a splendid life with Bovo. Both Sinibald and Teyrets were doing quite well. And when a half year had passed and no one had opposed Bovo, once while he was playing chess with Sinibald, someone brought him a letter from Babylon. (588) In the letter was much strange news that Margarete the Fair had written him: how her father, the sultan, had died, and how she was now all alone, and how Sir Pashamont had all but driven her out of her own country and treated her as was hardly to be believed, for he wanted to have her as his wife. (589) And since she had now heard that things had gone so well for him [Bovo], she requested that he reciprocate and help her out of her trouble, for the sake of loyalty to her for her helping him when he was imprisoned in the dungeon, and if it came to pass that he could drive him [Pashamont] out, then she would gladly become his [Bovo's] lawful wife.

(590) As soon as Bovo saw the letter, then he began to be very alarmed. He gave it to Sinibald and said to him: "I do not wish to leave her in the lurch. She also helped me when I was in trouble. I would otherwise have died on the spot." Sinibald said: "If she was so useful to you that you ought to help her, then it can certainly be done." (591) Meanwhile Teyrets joined them. Bovo told him about those matters. He said: "You, too, must come along. I will make you my captain." Teyrets said: "I will not miss it. It is just the thing for me." Bovo said: "Foster-father, you will also have to take on the task of temporarily being in charge of my lands." (592) Sinibald said: "I promise you surely that you need have no worries." Bovo quickly had a proclamation made quite openly on all the squares, and ordered that three thousand men prepare to render service to him, so that they were ready by the next day and came mounted before the palace, and he would take them along with him to Babylon.

(593) And when the next day had come, they all mounted their horses and rode there in front of the palace. One could hardly see the ground among them. And now that they were indeed all there, then the two worthy warriors came riding up. Bovo gave Teyrets fifteen hundred men, and he took the others, and they set out (594) and rode on their way and were not lax. They took along enough provisions. Bovo taught them the way, for he knew all the routes. They rode many a day and many a month before they came to Babylon, and when they saw the city from afar, then Bovo ordered a messenger to ride ahead (595) to tell Margarete the news that Bovo was not far away from there, and that she should be aware of that and order all her men to arm themselves, and when she thought that Bovo had arrived there, then they should open the gates and charge out at the heathens. "Then we will completely shatter and disperse the army."

(596) The messenger ran away and never looked back, just as if the Devil were chasing him. He got through the enemy—I do not know how—and gave Margarete the message. When she heard it, how happy she was. She no longer despaired for her honor and quickly gave orders to her army. Meanwhile night began to fall. (597) They armed themselves to the teeth and began to ride to the palace. There were two thousand of them or more. They waited the whole night for Bovo.

Now let us leave them standing there at the palace and speak of Bovo's struggles, how he had taken his army and had now come right up to the city. (598) And Teyrets took his position with all his mighty warriors. They found very many of the heathens there, having surrounded the city on all sides. There a great slaughter began. They waked them quite un-maternally, and very many of them were slain. Meanwhile day began to break.

(599) Pashamont said: "By Goat's sweat! I want to see who these people are." He quickly moved forward to the vanguard, and at once he seethed with rage. Meanwhile Teyrets at once encountered him. Quickly they began to charge at each other and thrust at each other with their lances so that both their lances shattered. (600) When Pashamont saw that, he began to be alarmed. He said: "Just wait, just wait, you dog! I will be bragging about your death, and I will deprive you of your well-being. I will cripple you with my sword." They began to draw their swords. Neither wished to flee from the other. (601) There one saw the two undaunted men strike each other great blows, but Teyrets could not overcome him; he was no match for Pashamont. He struck him so that he began to stagger. His strength began to leave him. And as they were thus striking each other, then Bovo began to watch it from afar (602) and saw how Teyrets was in trouble, and how he was allowing himself to be overcome. He turned Rondele boldly and quickly and rode swiftly to him. He slashed many a heathen to death along the way—woe to him who let himself be found! He stabbed Pashamont so that his horse staggered and tossed him out of the saddle. (603) He had pierced him through and through so that he lay stretched out on the heath. He called out plaintively to his Muḥammad, but he gave him little joy, and before he had even finished pronouncing the word, he was already quite dead. And the other heathens who saw that—how quickly they fled. (604) They were quite eager to flee from there. Bovo, the brave warrior, followed them.

Margarete's captain also marched out when he heard that Bovo had come. Many a mighty man also followed him. They caught the heathens between them and hacked into them as if they were dogs. They killed as many of them as they found. (605) Bovo gave Rondele free rein, who leapt as if it were flying through the air. Bovo slew many a heathen. None could show his strength. And Teyrets also came charging after him and fought very cleverly. He had taken another lance and had now regained his strength. (606) Margarete's captain quickly followed him with his troops. Bovo struck them [Pashamont's troops] vehemently. Many were pierced by his lance, one after the other. Many of them jumped into the sea, so that they thought to escape from there and screamed bloody murder with high-pitched voices. Water filled their mouths; they learned to swim.

(607) Now that they had completely beaten them, they stopped fighting. Teyrets had now returned to Bovo and rode next to him at his side. Margarete's captain also came there. They rode into the city to the sound of shawms, pipes, and trumpets. Margarete lay above in a tower. (608) When she saw Bovo, how quickly she went down and ran to meet him with her maidens. She embraced and welcomed him with joy and pleasure. She clung to him for a good while and hugged him with both arms. She said: "You have shown me great friendship; because of that, my body and property belong to you. (609) You are an excellent warrior; you are to be praised and not chastised. You have well repaid me for the loyalty that I showed you. And you have given me good payment, such as one very rarely finds. It is not the custom to repay good with good."

Thereafter she led him up to her halls. (610) And when everyone had taken off their armor, she held a banquet with great honor. And when she had eaten and was full, Margarete turned to Bovo. She said: "Do you not remember what I offered you, and you did not wish to follow my advice: you did not wish to convert to my faith. Now I will convert to yours, if you will have me." (611) Bovo said: "If you will do that, then I will take you very gladly and have a splendid wedding now. But it should be delayed for a month. It should be announced even to the ends of the earth. I want to send for princes and lords." Thus she pledged herself to him, as did he to her. Thereafter everyone lay down to sleep.

(612) The next morning Bovo had a festive assembly proclaimed and let foreigner and local, king and prince, duke and count know that they were to show diligence at that time, and the wedding was to take place joyously right away exactly on the first day of the month of Nisan [March–April]. The envoys rode out to every land, and in Babylon there were great preparations made. (613) Neither by day nor by night did anyone have any peace—for great joy and the ringing of bells.

Now let us leave them to their preparations and sing for a while of Druzeyne. She was with her father—you know where—and heard that Bovo had gained honor and that Margarete the Fair had accepted him, (614) and that the wedding was soon to take place, and that a great many people were coming there from afar. Druzeyne was happy and thought to herself: "No waiting here any longer: I will go to him as he came to me, at just the right moment, at the blessing of the wedding guests, but my father is not to know of it; otherwise he will not let me leave here."

(615) Now she had meanwhile learned to play the lyre well, and Bovo had once taught her so that she knew about the powder that one used to make oneself as black as coal. Then she smeared her own face and those of her children with it, and she dressed herself just like a beggar-woman and set out with her two children. (616) She got up an hour before dawn and had her lyre at her side. She tired herself out with walking so that she often had to lie down; she went quickly in a short time, but not as quickly as I can tell it. She caught sight of Babylon from afar. She began to say to her children: "You will find your father in the city."

(617) Thus they went into the city. She went into a large inn. She asked the innkeeper whether he would take her in. The innkeeper asked her whence they had come. She said: "I want to go to the wedding; perhaps I can earn a penny. I will go around with my lyre and sing with my children." (618) The innkeeper said: "You are quite right: you will earn plenty of money." He ordered food brought to her. "She will have to play the lyre for us, too." A servant showed her to a room. There she ate and drank, and thereafter she had to play the lyre all night and play dance music for the wedding guests. (619) In the morning, she took up a position in front of the palace and began playing her lyre and singing a song that she had composed that was all about Bovo and Druzeyne, and how she was living in a forest, and about Makabrun and Pelukan and everything else, and what they had done with each other as they made their way through the land. (620) And when she had finished the song, Bovo was lying at a window nearby and was quiet as a mouse and listened to her closely and said to his servants: "Lead her up here into the house. Give her food and drink. I want to ask her where she is from, and where she learned that tale." (621) Druzeyne quickly ran away. She said: "He need not give me anything."

Bovo sighed deeply and began to think seriously: "Perhaps Druzeyne is still alive and well. I hear that in this tale." He began to chastise and curse his servants; they were to go and look for the beggar-woman. (622) His servants ran from the hall much faster than deer. They asked everywhere about the beggar-woman. They could not find her anywhere. Thereafter they looked in the infirmary among the lame and blind. No one knew anything about her, for she had quickly hidden in the inn. (623) The servants went back, and they told Bovo, their lord, how they had been everywhere and had not been able to find her. That made Bovo very sad. His heart became very heavy. He could not forget those words. They sat down at the table, but he did not want to eat.

(624) Now Druzeyne had returned to the house and took her two boys and dressed them up in doublets and hose that were worked with gold threads. She brushed their hair again: they had no lice; their hair was like spun gold. And she put silk jackets on them. They walked around like two courtly dolls.

(625) She said that they should delay no longer before climbing the stairs to the palace, and they were to go into the hall and have the bridegroom pointed out to them and stand courteously before him and bow to him, and if he were to ask them who they were, they were to say: "We ourselves do not know. (626) We are of the lineage of the wolf. We never saw our father. We do not know if animals ripped him to pieces or what otherwise might have happened to him. Our mother is sitting there at her beer and told us to give you this ring, with the expectation that you remember her."

(627) They took the ring and went on their way. They were directed to the palace from afar. They went to Bovo and greeted him and bowed to the nobleman. Bovo took them by the chin and asked them just who they were. He said: "You are two fine youths. Where did you come from, trotting in here? (628) And who are your father and mother? You should really tell me that." They said: "We have never seen our father. Wild animals ripped him to pieces, and our mother is here now and goes around in rags and tatters and is much blacker than coal and says that you should also accept her greetings. (629) And she told us still more. We are to give you this ring so that you wear it for her sake and so that you remember her."

Bovo the undaunted warrior recognized the ring by its artistic workmanship and said: "On my life, I gave it to Druzeyne as a bodice-clasp, (630) and it is worth an entire country. Should I not immediately recognize it?!" He took the two boys by the hand and said: "Run with me and show me who sent you here. I want to ask her what her name is." The two boys were indeed to be praised. They said: "We will be happy to point her out to you." (631) Bovo followed the boys with many servants and lords. The youths hurried to their mother, and when they came to the inn, Bovo said: "Go ahead and point her out to me." There she stood, far away from him on the other side, and as soon as she saw his fine figure, she could no longer hold herself back, (632) and she ran to him there quite nimbly with great joy and exultation. She said: "I will not be at all ashamed." She kissed him in front of them all. Bovo saw that it was Druzeyne. He almost fell down in a faint. He said: "I thought that you were dead. Here I have regained you, with God's help." (633) Druzeyne began and said to him: "Dear Bovo, you need not be ashamed, for when I was about to marry Makabrun, you also made a place for yourself at my wedding. Now let us call it even between us. You need only take me back. Since God has thus brought it about, I will be content with you." (634) Bovo said: "You dear one, you need not worry: I am your husband; you are my wife. Margarete will have to allow me to take you and to drive her away." Thereafter he took his two fine boys and began to hug and kiss them. He let them know that he was their father. (635) And they went to the palace quickly. He took one in each hand.

Margarete was given the unhappy message that Bovo's first wife had come. She was so shocked that she fell down as if dead and then spoke as much as mute people. Bovo himself had to revive her. He said: "You must have mercy. (636) It is something that is quite obvious; our elders have demanded it; so just put it out of your mind, and let our Lord God rule. But listen to what I say to you. I will maintain you in honor and will enable you to have a good life. I will give my comrade Teyrets to you. (637) He is just as good for you as I am. You need not be ashamed of him." Margarete said: "If only he wants me, how gladly I would take him, for I fear that if I delay longer, troubles will arise." Bovo quickly sent for Teyrets and made him sit next to Margarete. (638) He made them promise loyalty to one another and vow to marry.

Thereafter Bovo had Druzeyne change into new clothes. A splendid wedding was begun. First they built a courtly structure. The wedding was quite praiseworthy. A great many strangers came there: some three prayer quorums[22] of foreigners had come to the wedding. (639) There one lived well and joyously—it lasted around four weeks. There was dancing as at all weddings, as well as leaping, fencing, and jousting. Druzeyne and Margarete were both pleased. Each of them was content with her own [husband]. Teyrets had a body as if turned on a lathe, but Druzeyne would nonetheless not have traded with her.

(640) And now when the wedding had taken place, Bovo helped Teyrets conquer many a city, and when he had completely conquered the land and possessed the entirety of the sultan's land, Bovo went to him and to Margarete and said: "I want to leave here. I beg of you that you grant me leave, for you can live well without me." (641) Teyrets said, and Margarete with him: "If you wish it, then depart; you will not lack our leave. You have our permission." Bovo ordered trumpets blown, as is the custom there. He took his wife and his two boys. Teyrets ordered Margarete to prepare and accompanied them with his entire army. (642) So they rode away from there together, and when they had accompanied them two miles, there they now said farewell, and, weeping, they spoke with each other, and there was much embracing and

kissing. Bovo also took his leave from Margarete, and she said: "I thank you for all your constancy; I do not regret marrying Teyrets."

(643) Thereafter Teyrets turned around with his army; they came back to the city, and Bovo rode on his way. He had a long and arduous journey. He came to Antona with great honor. He was well received by Sinibald, and he asked where he had left Teyrets. Bovo told him all appropriate information, (644) how wife and children had come to him, and how he had given Margarete to Teyrets, and how he was such a great lord, and how he had such a splendid life. Sinibald said: "That is good news. At my age, it is fitting." So he gave his land back to Bovo, and Bovo took up residence in Antona (645) and entertained himself with Druzeyne. He did not know what to do with her.

He conquered a land that was broad and vast; he drove out many a lord. I do not want to write about all these battles and conflicts. He also had to come to the aid of his father-in-law, when Makabrun almost took away his entire country. (646) The conflict lasted for many an eternal day—I cannot tell you about it—before Bovo won and slew him in battle, and he ruled that same land, too, for they brought the key out to him—he also acquired Makabrun's land, and his father-in-law had also died, (647) and that land was also his. He did not have to conquer it very much: without any battle he captured it. He found great wealth in it. Thereafter he marched in. They were very happy to have him there. Now he had peace from all sides, from all wars and from all battles. (648) He was a king, great beyond measure. He was a king who ruled three kingdoms. His two sons were also grown and were two noble warriors, and he gave to each of them property in his land. They had no equals in the world. They had much land under their control. Herewith the book ends.

(649) But I would like to name the one who made and wrote the book. Indeed he is called Elye Bokher. He worked on it for an entire year, and made it that same year that is reckoned as 267 [= (5)267 = 1507 CE]. He began it in Iyar [April–May] and completed it in Nisan. May God grant us protection against all evil, (650) and deliver us from all our suffering, and grant us the grace that we all may be worthy to live in the age of the Messiah. May He lead us into Jerusalem, or into some little village near there, and rebuild the Temple for us. And in truth may it thus be God's will. Amen.

The treatise "Bovo d'Antona" is finished.

Praised be God, who has helped us to print the book, and we two lads—Yousef and Elye—have type-set it; our father is named Honorable Teacher and Rabbi, Itskhok Behem of Rome, and Dame Khane is our mother's name. And the one who made the book is our grandfather, and we have made it as completely pure as a little pearl, with great diligence, so that no error remains in it. And may God, who has granted us the favor to print "Bovo," also help us to print the book "Glucke the Fair" and even other Yiddish books. And may it thus be God's will. Amen.

Now I would like to write the Italian words that are found in a number of passages, and want to define them in Yiddish, kindly and joyfully.

ankar. A ship's iron that one throws into the sea on a line.
almozan. What one gives to poor people.
babiloniya. The city of Bovl [Babylon].
bonatsa. When the sea is windless.
bast. A saddle made of straw.
baron. A lord at the king's court.
brizalikh. Meat roasted on a grate.
gratsia. Thanks.
timun. The shaft at the back of a ship.
tulpan. What the Turks put around their heads.
tavern. A common inn.
tera demore. Land of the Moors.
trizia dperlan. Something from the apothecary.
yustitsiya. Justice.
madona. A fine lady.
munestad[23]. A first course.
matrats. A bed made of wool.
mariner. Sailors.
port. Where the ships are tied up.
patron. The head of the house.
piligrin. A beggar.
pitsentsiya. mercy.
putane. A whore.
pater noster. That with which Gentiles pray.
par Haman. He is like Haman.
fortuna. A sea storm.
far. Type of wheat.
feste. A joyous circumstance.
kontent. Quite satisfied.
kompanyon. Good comrade.
kistigar. Punish.

rigats. A messenger.
rumor. Shouting and confusion.
stoyrn. Coverings made of bast and straw.

Printed in Isny in the year that one reckons as 301 [= (5)B301 = 1541 CE].

The End

8

Pariz and Viene

פאריז אונ׳ וויענה / *Pariz un Viene*

Anonymous, 1556/1594

Until the discovery in 1986 by Anna Maria Babbi of a complete copy of the Verona 1594 edition of the Yiddish text of פאריז אונ׳ וויענה *Pariz un Viene* (Pariz and Viene), published by Francesco dalle Donne—which had been known up to that point only in fragmentary texts—this poem had generally been attributed to Elia Levita (albeit without any specific evidence in support of the attribution). In the complete text, however, which includes a previously unknown preface, "Elye Beher" (Elye Bokher or Elia Levita) is mentioned apparently as the mentor of this book's author, who himself expresses his sadness at Levita's departure from "this land" (his death?). Convoluted reasoning indeed is then required in order to maintain the earlier attribution of the text to Levita.[1] Although there was until recently no available edition of the poem, now there are two editions for scholarly use—a facsimile of the edition of Verona 1594 and the definitive edition by Chone Shmeruk.[2]

Pariz un Viene clearly derives from and participates in the same northern Italian Renaissance cultural milieu that produced Levita's *Bovo of Antona*, and both are in fact adaptations of Italian source texts into Yiddish *ottava rima* stanzas. Whereas *Bovo* was apparently adapted from a Tuscan *ottava rima* version of the romance, *Pariz and Viene* had as its source a prose romance published no earlier than the version that appeared in Venice in 1528 (Sessa). In this case, however—unlike Levita's entertaining but hardly intellectually ambitious *Bovo*—the Yiddish version utterly transforms its source into a veritable masterpiece of Renaissance poetic narrative, carefully crafted in 717 stanzas, organized into ten cantos. The conventional plot of the vassal's son who must prove himself before being granted the princess as bride is transformed from hackneyed cliché into a complexly layered and dramatically progressing, politically serious, and delightfully humorous tour de force. As

Chone Shmeruk claims, *Pariz un Viene* is "not only the most important and enjoyable literary work of the sixteenth century but of all early Yiddish literature."[3] Quite in the tradition, and under the direct influence, of Ariosto's *Orlando furioso*, all cantos but the first begin with an excursus in which the narrator steps back momentarily from the narrative in order to provide some commentary on its significance (generally) in a larger social and moral context:[4] for example, on the insensitivity of relatives (canto 2), on the cruelty of women to their lovers (canto 3), on Odoardo's (and not the author's) responsibility for the upcoming misogynistic diatribe (canto 4), on those individuals who are too proud of their own virtue (canto 5), on greed and its effect on the arrangement of marriages (canto 6), on the absence of Venetian Jewish hospitality (canto 7), on the necessity for the inviolability of vows (canto 8), on how money obstructs recognizing one's true friends (canto 9), and on the necessity to finish the tale (canto 10). As Jean Baumgarten points out, "By means of these satirical stanzas, the author communicates a personal conception, conveys a code of ethical values, and even calls the audience to witness some bitter truths about his time and his contemporaries. These preludes form a sort of mirror of the poet's world, who, by means of laughter and invective, attempts to exorcise certain evils from that world. Various obsessions dominate: above all, the duplicity of human relations."[5] These diatribes then generally provide transitions directly back to the thematically closely related moments in the plot of the particular canto. Thus, both the plot and these moral lessons are tied together, giving them both greater significance and turning the entire romance into a meditation on human ethics, without, however, its ever becoming a didactic tract.

Pariz un Viene is at root about love and the mutual quest of lover and beloved to attain one union. Such a topic, already in the background of Levita's *Bovo d'Antona*, here becomes the driving force of both the depicted lives of the protagonists and the narrative itself. This obsessive focus is new and revolutionary in Yiddish literature and indeed Jewish literature up to this time. That this romantic focus is expressed via a Renaissance love epic is likewise novel and more than slightly risqué in the Jewish cultural tradition. One ought immediately to note, however, that while romantic love is the constant *movens* of the plot, immoral behavior as conceived by sixteenth-century Jewish piety is conscientiously avoided. Thus, when the two (still chaste) lovers run away from Viene's father's court, they are never alone together, and the subsequent (thorough) interrogation of witnesses (including a priest) concerning their behavior convinces both the reader and Viene's very concerned and very skeptical father of the specific details of Viene's scrupulous maintenance of her chastity. Likewise, in such episodes as when Odoardo buys property next to the tower where Viene and Isabele are imprisoned and digs a tunnel to their cell, he does not break down the wall, but rather makes only a small hole in it, scarcely large enough to allow the passage of food and drink through to them. For the original audience then, if nothing else, it is very clear that this vigorous young man is not in the same dark, isolated, and enclosed space with the unmarried and unchaperoned maidens.

The love of Pariz and Viene is thus a pure and transformative love, a quasi-philosophical love, as love necessarily also is, for instance, in the Ariostan conception. The lovers suffer in, from, and for their passion: Viene is condemned to imprisonment in the dungeon of a prison tower *by her own father* for her refusal to marry the suitor chosen by him as proper; Pariz goes into nomadic exile in the Muslim East.[6] But it is also a love that drives the lovers mad, so that Viene binds dead chickens to her armpits and lets them rot there, in order to allow the stench to convince her father and her would-be suitor of the putrefaction of her putatively diseased body. Pariz likewise becomes the conventionally distraught lover who is deprived of his beloved and thus driven into melancholy madness, giving up the aristocratic pursuits of hunting and jousting to mope around the house, prompting his parents to mourn his transformation. The language of Pan-European literary eroticism in a Petrarchan vein thus enters Yiddish literature, with its "inflamed hearts" and "faces gone pale."[7]

Both Pariz and Viene are conventional characters of Christian romance—wealthy, noble, beautiful, virtuous. But in the Jewish context, Viene transcends those conventional markers, for she is an independent *female* subject with a primary speaking role, independence of action, and a will of her own that bends to no one else; she verbally bullies Pariz when he suggests joint suicide as a means to escape capture by her father's henchmen; she refuses her father's marriage arrangement and chooses instead to spend years living on bread and water in an underground dungeon. Above all, she is a strong and independent character who simply refuses to give up hope. Baumgarten calls her "the first great female character of Old Yiddish literature."[8]

At the same time, however, it is necessary to keep this conception of her character in perspective. After all, her highest aspiration in life is to marry a member of her own society *and* class. Thus, she does not differ from her father in positing marriage as the ultimate goal of a princess's life, but rather simply in her definition of who belongs to the set of appropriately marriageable bridegrooms. She does not, for instance—to make an altogether anachronistic and inconceivable suggestion—imagine renouncing her royal status to live unmarried with Pariz, her athletic musician lover, or to strike out on her own to seek her fortune, unencumbered by familial and dynastic concerns—except if she can marry her Pariz by doing so. Her "rebellion" against parental control, such as it is and striking though it may be in the context of sixteenth-century Yiddish literature, is still on the whole rather tame. Both her father and her mother allow her to waste away in the dungeon for years, permitting her to come forth only when she agrees to marry her father's choice of bridegroom (who is now, seemingly quite by chance and unexpectedly, also *her* choice)—in other words, precisely the course of action on which he had insisted from the beginning. *She* then seeks *his* forgiveness, and *he* triumphantly insists on *her* transgression and the punishment by incarceration as deserved (st. 685–88). Hers is thus no protofeminist insurrection such as one finds, for instance, in a broad range of texts penned by Venetian (Christian) women during this same period in which the Yiddish text was written and published.[9]

Interestingly, while early Yiddish literature generally either suppresses positive or neutral references to Christian religion or indeed presents them in an overtly mocking manner (as in the episode of the despoiling of the monastery in Levita's *Bovo*), in this poem a bishop, a priest, and a monk play narratively significant roles, and, though none of them ever takes on more than a flat functionality, the poet neither replaces these characters adopted from the source text by nonclerics nor mocks or satirizes them.

Jean Baumgarten has made an intriguing suggestion that the narrative of *Pariz un Viene* is an allegory of a quest through exile toward redemption and the Messiah, with the character of Viene representing the *shekhinah* (the Divine Presence); her father, Dolfin, as the Divine; and Pariz as the exiled soul seeking the *shekhinah* and redemption.[10] Thus, the whole is construed as a quest for reestablishment of the lost originary unity, the *tikkun*, the return from exile and the redemption in the terms of kabbalah as developed by the sixteenth-century mystic of Safed, Issac Luria. According to Baumgarten's interpretation, as in the traditional Jewish interpretation of the Song of Songs, the rhetoric of erotic passion is a thin veil over an allegory of redemption; the mention of the Messiah at the text's conclusion (st. 716–17) is thus the culmination of the allegory, revealing its hitherto masked purpose. While I find much that is provocative in Baumgarten's suggestion, there do seem to be a number of troubling obstacles: Dolfin is depicted in the poem neither in a positive light nor as a figure of majesty. He is, after all, the vassal of the king of France and is thus summoned and sent as his servant to spy on the sultan's lands in the guise of a pilgrim; he is captured, imprisoned, and must be rescued by Pariz, the object of his overt class bigotry; he is a petty and cruelly tyrannical bigot mocked by the poet himself. It is difficult to conceive of that character as a representative of the Divine. The expressed hope for the coming of the Messiah at the conclusion of the narrative is, on the other hand, not peculiar to this text or its narrative purpose, veiled or not, but instead is in fact quite conventional in the colophons of a broad range of early Yiddish literary texts. Indeed, *Pariz un Viene*'s narrative trajectory of stasis > loss > quest > victory > reestablishment of enhanced stasis is, after all, the defining plot structure of (medieval) romance in general. If the romance plot is universally an allegory of redemption, then its proposal here adds little to our understanding of this particular text.[11] It nonetheless seems to me that Baumgarten's line of inquiry might well be fruitfully pursued further.

Israel Zinberg notes that *Pariz un Viene* is a more mature work than *Bovo* and, lacking giants and sorcerers, is likewise more "realistic," and thus while he considers the characters of *Bovo* "wooden mannequins," the characters in *Pariz and Viene* have "the breath of real life, the forcefulness of temperamental personalities. . . . The dialogues are highly dynamic. The events are portrayed in clear, sharp forms, and the octaves very frequently overwhelm one with their poetic resonance and high level of technical achievement."[12] Baumgarten suggests that, through its creative engagement with Renaissance Italian culture and its consequent problematization of the conflicting nodes of tradition and innovation, and the public and private, *Pariz un Viene* "may be considered the first modern work of Yiddish literature." In its "transformation of taste," "formation of a new sensibility," "mirror[ing] the conflicts which characterized the Jewish consciousness during the Renaissance," and "condens[ing] the essential questions posed by thinkers of the time," he considers the author one of the "great creators of Renaissance literature such as Ariosto and Rabelais, [who] produced modern European culture."[13]

Whereas the earliest extant edition of the text was published in Verona in 1594, the list of privately owned Jewish books (required to be) presented to the Catholic censor in Mantua in 1595 twice lists an edition of the text from Sabbioneta (then in the Duchy of Mantua), once with the publication date of 1556.[14] There is no further reliable evidence for the existence of that edition. The translation is based on the Verona 1594 edition.

Source: Verona, 1594 (Francesco dalle Donne); extant: Verona, Biblioteca del Seminario Vescovile, Fonds Venturi, no. 192.

Edition: Valerio Marchetti, Jean Baumgarten, and Antonella Salomoni, eds., *Elia Bahur Levita, Paris un Viene, Francesco Dalle Donne, Verona 1594* (Bologna: Università degli studi di Bologna, Dipartimento di discipline storiche; Arnaldo

Forni Editore, 1988) (facsimile of Verona 1594); online facsimile of Verona 1594, http://www.hebrewbooks.org/44679; Chone Shmeruk, ed., *Pariz un' Viene: Mahadura biqqortit be-ẓeruf mavo, he'arot ve-nispaḥim* (Jerusalem: Israel Academy of Sciences and Humanities, 1996) (Italian translation of the introduction, "Studi su 'Paris un Viene,'" *Rassegna Mensile di Israel* 62, nos. 1–2 [1996]: 93–124).

Research: Zinberg, *History*, 82–102; Erik, *Geshikhte*, 195–202; Shmeruk, *Prokim*, 97–120, 143–44; Baumgarten, *Introduction*, 186–206; Anna Maria Babbi, "In margine alla fortuna del Paris e Vienna," *Quaderni di Lingue e Letterature* (Verona) 11 (1986): 393–97; Chava Turniansky, "Pariz un' Viene—mi-sifrut yidish be-italyah shel ha-meah ha-16," *Chulyot* 4 (1997): 29–37; Erika Timm and Gustav Adolf Beckmann, *Paris un Wiene: Ein jiddischer Stanzenroman des 16. Jahrhunderts von* (oder aus dem Umkreis von) *Elia Levita* (Tübingen: Niemeyer, 1996); Armin Schulz, *Die Zeichen des Körpers und der Liebe: "Paris und Vienna" in der jiddischen Fassung des Elia Levita* (Hamburg: Kovac, 2000).

The book is called Pariz and Viene, taken from a Christian language and made into the Yiddish language, and it has been printed other times, but never in such a form or in such fine and clear letters, with all its illustrations, as you will well see. May it be thus, in God's name. Amen. *Selah.*

Printed here in the city of Verona by the hand of your servant, Abraham, son of my lord father, the learned master Matisyohu Bas-sheva, may his rock and redeemer protect him.

In the year that is counted 5354 in the month of Shevat in the pericope *bo el par'o.*[15]

In the house of Messer Francesco delle Donne.

Preface:

(1) No man or eagle, ox or lion could stand or move from its place, nor could any leaf move; no thing could have either beginning nor end, except that God—whose Holy Name befits Him—allows it. He so artfully created the world from nothing. Thus there is nothing possible contrary to His Name. (2) Therefore I beseech Him and call on Him that it be His will for me that I be able to finish the book, as it was my intention to do, and that He help me, as He helped the man from whom the entire world still resounds, so that I can rhyme my book and forge and bond the words as he did.

(3) I grieve indeed for this man, as if he were my father or father-in-law. And when he departed from this land, I shed many a tear for him. His name is no disgrace for him: I mean the aged master, Elye Beher. His name lives on

and will never die—that is, the books that he completed. (4) He has already had six or eight published in the holy language. The benefit is great; the honor is high, and no one can take it away from him. Since the worthy man departed from this land, we are like roosters without hens, although many people hold his holy books in high esteem: just as a sow does a necklace or pearls.

(5) I fear that I am speaking too much, for which reason I will drop [the subject of] his holy books and will speak of Yiddish things. But then I must come back to him: who will now put on a Purim play, recite proverbs and sing bride-songs? Who will set in rhyme and write whole books, so that you will pass your time in laughter? (6) No other person surpasses him—he remains unique, although I do indeed know many who have carried on their impropriety, and many years ago they copied his entire book and were not even ashamed to sign their own names to it. (7) They thought to indicate therewith that they had invented it all. But the person is recognized by his writings and by his abilities. If one were to do the same to my book, I would in truth not pay much attention, for I do not intend to deceive anyone or to achieve any profit or honor from it.

(8) For that reason, the book says at this point, my name will not be mentioned anywhere. If it but come into a person's hand, then I think, he will know me. I myself ought not to announce my shame, but I must confess my sin to you. I do it only because of a maiden who lies ever deep in my heart. (9) And she is already quite far from me. So I hope that it will fly to her and will in time prove to her that she is the center of all my thought. Perhaps it could also soften the obduracy of her heart, so that once she might delight me, as do the lovers about whom you will read in this book. (10) When I think of the hard thing, then I must at once sigh and pine. Now I tell you even more, so that you not think that I am being deceitful: I say that the book that I am here making, is found in the Christian language, and many have read it and will know it. It is called, and I also call it: *Pariz and Viene.* (11) The one who wrote it in the Romance language was no fan of verse. Now, I have courage: I want mine to rhyme completely and everywhere. Know well: if I become fatigued, then I will stop it right in the middle, and if my weariness were remedied by rest, then my book will be divided into ten parts. (12) If I begin a part rhyming, and if I were to veer off the path, let it not surprise anyone, man or woman, read on and do not be disturbed, I will indeed come back around and not leave you in the lurch. And the one who will pay close attention to this, will not, I think, scoff at this work. (13) Now I want to get to the point, and do not wish to ramble on at you any longer. Indeed it has now been almost an hour. I hear how you have begun to shout. It seems to me that your mouths are now

saying: "He has enough spittle as three people." Therefore, I will leave off the unnecessary words, and ask you to listen to me attentively.

Herewith concludes the preface. May God soon send us the Messiah. May it take place during our lifetimes. Let us all say "amen" to that.

Canto One

Here I begin; listen to me, great and small.[16]

(14) Once there was a mighty king—as in the stories begun by girls. His peer in virtue was not to be found. He had a land that was stately indeed. He filled his days with love and peace and pleasures. Vienne the Fair was the name of his capital city. One could not make a circuit of it in a month. (15) Indeed he also had a lawful wife; he had bound her into his heart. In this woman, of whom I write, no fault could be found, except that in the course of many years she was unable to bear a child. The good king wished to die of grief because he would have no heir after his death. (16) Every day and quite zealously, the king and queen fasted, and they bore great sorrow for it, and they prayed to God that He be the comforter of their great lament and grant them their prayer this time and grant her a child through grace. (17) The almighty and merciful God Who has never abandoned anyone, man or woman—whoever maintains complete fidelity and prays to Him with a pure heart and with proper form and weeping eyes, He will not leave that heart at a distance. These people prayed before Him from the heart, for which reason they received great mercy from Him.

(18) Great mercy was granted to them in a short time, in brief days, so that their grief was changed into joy. The noble queen became pregnant. The joy was so increased, that it is not possible to tell it all here. All their days were they praising and giving thanks to Almighty God in all their thoughts, (19) although she had a difficult pregnancy: she could eat neither chicken nor doves. She did not value any good food, but only plums and unripe grapes. Her cry day and night was only that unripe fruit be picked out for her. She rewarded well anyone who brought it to her. She did this for nine whole months. (20) And now that the time had come that she should give birth, she had many ladies at her side, the noble and distinguished queen. She screamed so that it was heard from afar: "Alas my body, alas my limbs!" The labor pains came on her with excessive severity, but the child just did not wish to be born. (21) Now there were a great many ladies there, who began to practice their arts. This one asked for a white onion; the other for turnip seeds; this one for a left

shoe; that one for a boot, and three lice buried in an egg; this one wanted to whisper in her ear; that one to write on her navel. Each one of them wanted to poke her own snout into the business.

(22) The queen was in agony and pain; she could have no rest. She said: "If God delivers me from this child, it will indeed be my vow, and I bind it to my life—I know no other remedy—I will lie with my husband no more." She kept this vow, just as all women are accustomed to do. (23) Now that she had sworn the oath, she was immediately delivered of a large, plump and beautiful girl, to whom she there gave birth. Now there was great joy in the castle on the part of everyone who was inside. Many people who did not know of it were quite alarmed by the salvos of the great arquebuses and the ringing of bells. (24) The child was now held up high. It was given to a noble maiden who herself diligently raised the child. She gave it her full attention. And when the child thereafter grew up, she loved her more than her life. The nurse, the noble maiden, was named Isabele. She could not leave the child's side, day or night. (25) The girl also loved the maiden and treated her with the greatest honor. Such joy she had with her, that she was never allowed to leave the castle. Each was always with the other, just like doves in their nest. They were together in modesty and honor, just as if they were actual sisters.

(26) She now taught her quite adroitly to sew well with needles. With her pure, white hands she could copy any design. And when they finished their work, they chatted quietly with each other. Thus did they also entertain each other well. She also taught her to write and read well. (27) She taught her many a noble skill that was suitable for a king's daughter. She let nothing escape her attention; the nurse sought out all whims and desires. She showed her everything; she was also fortunate that she did not need to touch on a thing repeatedly. Truly she had no trouble with her: quite quickly did she take everything to heart. (28) She was so courteous and prudent, that when she turned thirteen, she took the prize in the land. Her praise was resounded on all sides: this one's heart was inflamed; that one's turned to ice, and many became quite ill because of her. Indeed everyone wanted to have the beautiful Viene—such was her name; thus did they call her. (29) There were many dukes and princes there who right away wished to die for her. They came there through broad green swards. For her sake they wished to perish. But not one of them was so bold that he could gain even the tiniest nod. She did not wish even to glance at any of them, for of such things she still knew nothing.

(30) Now, there was a count in this city who was called Sir Yakomo by name. Now, the king was fonder of him than of all the lords who took precedence over him. He never tired of his company. So well did all his deeds

become him; among all his counts there was none greater who had as much wealth, property, and castles. (31) The noble king did nothing without consulting him. He was with him day and night: he was his braise, and he was his broil. Now, the count had an only son who was courtly and well accomplished. He was quite handsome and bold in all his limbs. None finer had ever been seen before or since. (32) That youth was named Pariz. Now, he was some fifteen years old. He was as strong as a giant but was happily without entanglements. His nobility well demonstrated that he had not wasted his time. He had studied reading and writing. He had long since sharpened his mind therein, (33) and also in the playing of all stringed instruments and in such noble things his heart took great delight, he could dance well and also leap, and he had learned much about music from singing solfège. There was no charming or lovely thing that he could not do exceedingly well. (34) Now, he spent many a day with goshawks and hounds. Whenever he knew of a fine hunt of which someone informed him, he wished to explore thoroughly all the forests and great game enclosures. His hounds and his horses ran well at all times, so that few animals ever escaped him. (35) He was also quite courageous and dauntless in all battles and in all tournaments. Indeed he had no fear even of three opponents together, and, I might almost say, even of six. If someone approached, whoever it might be, he would have to break a lance with him, and against such a one did he always triumph, so that everyone was quite astonished by it. (36) Now, many a count was quite fond of him and was glad to know him well. Everyone wanted to have his company. They held him in great esteem.

Now, at that time the youth had chosen one noble knight from all the knights, counts, and lords, with whom he then spent all his time and had all his dealings. (37) He was very fond of him and liked him well, much more than all the others, for earlier they had often gone on outings, and I also remember that they went as far as the land of Flanders. They had sworn brotherhood to each other: each would have given his life for the other. (38) In truth the good and dear companion was named Odoardo. Pariz had not missed the mark with him; he very much enjoyed his companionship.

Now, Odoardo was very fond of a maiden: he had bound her into his heart. He thought of her at all times, mornings and evenings, although she was far from him, in Brabant. (39) But Pariz, that noble lord, knew nothing of courting: he had focused all his pleasures on fencing, sword-play, and jousting, and riding and hunting were all his desires, and otherwise also going out riding. He was always the first in line—therewith did he delight his father. (40) He loved his son deeply, more than was fitting for a father. When he was to ride up to the gates and into the king's castle, how frequently, often, and quickly did he take the youth with him. When he looked at him and could speak with him, it at once seemed to him that he was in Paradise.

(41) The youth also made acquaintances at court, for they found him noble in all his deeds. He passed all tests and all trials with great honor. Now a both lovely and sorrowful thing entered the life of Pariz, the noble count: he often saw Viene sitting with the king. As a result his heart began to be quite inflamed. (42) Sometimes he went up there four times—which he would otherwise have refrained from doing—and had a look and gave a stolen glance. But he did it in such a way that he did not want anyone, not even her, to notice. Indeed he loved her, but he nonetheless thought: "I am a count, and she is a king's daughter. (43) What have I gotten myself into! Now how could I be her peer? I trail behind her, where I cannot and never will be able to catch up with her. Am I a child or a man? How do I wish to deceive myself?" He often spoke such words to himself. But he could not get her out of his heart. (44) She was causing him deep heartache. He knew of no way to help himself. Had the dissimulation lasted longer, he could in truth have died of it. Thus he decided that he would confide everything to Odoardo. In that situation will I leave you for a while. Now let this song suffice for you as this canto.

I beseech you, let yourselves be satisfied, for the first canto does not prove to be any longer.

Canto Two

May God grant me good fortune and health so that I can compose the second canto.

(45) I have heard people say that relatives are of aid in times of need. Yes, well, if one were to find one of them who would at least give counsel to a poor wretch! I view them as worse than dogs; I think they would probably have one killed. Neither acquaintance nor all good will is of any aid, when it is a matter of a few guilders. (46) Some advice from a trusted companion is sometimes—and quite often—better than all the help that one hopes that one's relatives ought to provide. A good companion—waking or sleeping, in darkest night or in the light of day—he makes of his companionship a reward to his friend, although one finds it even now quite rarely.

(47) Pariz, the noble warrior, sees there that he would have been quite lost, if he had not had a counselor to consult—the companion whom he had won for himself. If he had kept that hidden in his heart any longer, I think that he would have died of it. Now he wished to tell him how the matter

had progressed. That would be of future aid and great honor to him. (48) He said: "Odoardo, my dear brother—you are mine indeed—I have none more capable. For that reason do I entrust the matter to you alone, which has almost brought me down to death. I request your counsel and your aid. Do not refuse me. I know my great error in all its dimensions. But I tell you in advance: I cannot renounce it. (49) Therefore, do not oppose me and thereby cause me still more grief." He said: "Viene!" and heaved a sob. "Alas, my heart is broken to pieces, and for as long as I am not altogether confounded, I will ever be her servant. But I do not want her to know of my service, for it is not worthy of such a person. (50) I now want to do service in love of her, but be aware of this, by the way, that I do not want her to become aware of it. Therefore, you must give me your aid." Odoardo did not take time to consider it, but said: "My help, my body, my life are always prepared at every moment to go, to stay, to travel, and to ride for you." (51) Pariz said: "I would not allege that your good deeds be otherwise." Now Odoardo was also quite noble, and he turned to all kinds of pleasures. It is indeed also said that two like things gladly consort together: he could also play stringed instruments well; no better musician was to be found far and wide.

(52) Now they together decided that they would go play together. Whether it was organ, harp, or lute, I cannot tell you. Two hours before day began to break, Pariz and his trusted companion went out with their best weapons beneath the chamber in which Viene slept. (53)[17] And they played so sweetly that they could have healed a sick person. Very often did they greet her; very well did it also please her. She could, however, never recognize who the good musicians were. The king was also delighted to hear the playing, but he did indeed wish to know who they were. (54) The sweet music—whose like has never again been heard on stringed instruments—pleased him well, so that it seemed to him that no other playing was worth two mites. He said to a servant: "I command you to prepare a dance for me and bring me all good musicians." He thought he would recognize them by their playing or singing.

(55) Now, whatever musicians heard of that [the king's dance] unpacked their gear. There were many organs and fiddles there; fiddlers and lyre-players did not miss out. Many lutes, harps, harpsichords, drums, flutes, and sackbuts were there. Many came who could blow horns, and one also came with a six-course cittern. (56) They played their very best. The king paid them fairly, although he thought it not worth a chestnut, for none of it pleased him. He rushed through one after the other and recognized that not a single one of them all was one of those accustomed to play beneath his chamber. He could not get that out of his heart. (57) And he took it more and more to heart

because he saw that his Viene was no longer in high spirits, for she longed to know them. He said: "If I am granted good fortune, then I will in truth find out who they are."

In the meantime, he had his daughter take walks every day, so that she might banish it from her mind. (58) Every day the dancing was begun anew. He also had made her ride and hunt, and often go fishing in the fish weir. And she often rode out in the coach. But none of that helped her to banish it from her heart. There was nothing any more that could lighten her heart, except to hear them playing or singing. (59) And although the maiden was by no means interested in any courtship, nonetheless this (music) well delighted her, and every day on a daily basis, she thought of it and noted well that they—for the sake of her love—quite often came there by night thus to play. For that reason, she would very much have liked to know their names. (60) And she often said to her nurse: "Even a blind man could see this: that they play and pipe every night at this time for my sake." Her father said: "Now wait, now wait. I am going to get them!" And he ordered ten of his mighty warriors: "Pay attention. All of you stand guard tonight and lie in wait in three or four different places. (61) And make sure that you all remain awake and alert to everything. For around midnight it will happen that you will hear string music and singing. When they have finished, then pay attention and leap on them like heroes. And even if they were genuine demons, pay close attention and bring them before me tonight." (62) The vassals said: "We will do it," and took up their best weapons. And when the time had come that everyone had quite gone to sleep, then they quickly ran from there, and they slipped into all their places and were waiting for the musicians in such cold weather that they thought they would freeze stiff.

(63)[18] At the right time it happened that the two companions and a youth, who carried their gear for them, came there and made music—as well as they had ever played and sung. When they had quite finished making music, how quickly did the ten men surrounded them. (64) As if they were not immediately foes, they greeted them amiably. They returned the greeting, so that they would not catch on—and kept their feet moving forward. They said: "Know, brothers, that tonight you must go before the king." Pariz was alarmed and said: "Do not rush us, and I will soon give you an answer."

(65) And he took Odoardo aside and wanted to consider this with him. Indeed they let them speak there, for they could not escape them. Pariz now said few words: "We have been found out, and now we are caught. So our entire scheme will be divulged. (66) The situation does not look good for us, now that this has taken place. Now we must try to save ourselves, and it will

not help to delay for a long time. And we must also save our young servant along with ourselves. All would be lost, if we left him here. Therefore, we must be very zealous with respect to him. (67) Nothing else causes me pain and grief but that you might here be injured and disgraced tonight for my sake. Otherwise, I have already long ago decided that I will here take a stand with my shield and sword and dagger. Let no one say that I was taken alive: I wish either to be free or carried before him dead." (68) Odoardo said to Pariz: "Make sure only that the youth is kept safe. You know that I will never desert you. You need not worry about me, for wherever you die, there will I also die, and there do I wish to be buried. Whatever happens here will happen to us both. Death alone will separate us."

(69) These words accorded well with Pariz's intent. He was delighted to hear that that was what he wanted to do, and he said to the youth: "Get away from here." And he turned to the people and spoke good words to them: "It would be better not to block our way. We are here only for reasons of honor and courtliness. Therefore, let us go where we wish. (70) Both of us are the king's men: we are passionate in our service to him—for good, for honor, for gain, for joy, and whatever else you might add. But we would both be very sorry to be recognized tonight."

He spoke these words to them, as well as other similar ones, and they [Pariz and Odoardo] were constantly moving forward. (71) The others also noticed the trick and paid them very close attention. They said: "Come along without any trouble, and do not think of trying to escape us." With a single word, with a single movement, they all drew their swords. There were no more and no fewer words uttered. They struck one another so that there was a great clattering. (72) I wish that it had not been night, so that one would have been able to see how the two distinguished warriors boldly fought those ten. They were not able to avoid injury; in a short time it came about that they took command of the field with great strokes: six were wounded and four dead. (73) They now went on their way home. Their affair remained quite secret.

The uproar that occurred the next morning was indeed exceedingly great. The deed greatly distressed the king, and he took a very hostile stance on it, because he had thus lost his good men. It caused him pain and grief and great anger. (74) He immediately had some twenty-five mighty men summoned before him. Each of them could have defeated an entire host. They were as tall as fir trees. He said to them: "Kill them dead, so that they do not get away from here. Bring them to me dead or alive. I want to see these people with my own eyes!"

(75) Armed to the teeth, they lay in wait for them many a night. They were aware of it: the net was spread in vain. If they had come back there again, they would have been more the fools. As it is said: "Never was such a fool to be found who ever let himself be caught more than once." (76) Never more did they return there at night. They feared what might happen to them. Pariz now brooded on the fact that he dared never go near that place. He was languishing in such grief that one could hardly even look at him. Day by day his cares grew more bitter. He was no longer seen with hounds and goshawks. (77) His thrusting and parrying had come to an end: he was no longer fencing or fighting, nor did he any longer take delight in fishing, hawking, riding, and hunting. Sometimes he crossed the square as if he had been struck in the head, and he was no longer seen laughing heartily, and no one could tell what was the matter with him.

(78) Now, there was a bishop there in Vienne, an elderly man with wrinkles. Never had a more honorable man been seen. He was considered a saint. All cases of great penance came before him—of rich and poor, young and old, local and foreign; everyone dealt with him. The king was also very fond of him. (79) Pariz began a great acquaintance with that man and showed such friendship that the good bishop did not have food or drink served to himself before the noble youth had come to him. Their acquaintance daily grew stronger, for he was fond of him because of his nobility. (80) Pariz was also with him constantly; he loved him better than his own life. He [the bishop] saw that he [Pariz] was not happy. He thus wished to distract him. He [Pariz] said not a word of Viene; he kept that hidden within himself. But he often spoke of the matter in confidence with his companion Odoardo.

(81) I will now leave Pariz for a while and will sing to you of Viene, how great was her misery there, because she could not find out who they [the musicians] were. It affected her so seriously that her heart was inflamed. The sweet playing had so enkindled her heart that the depth of her great love could not be fathomed. (82) That those four were lying dead because of her—that she could also recognize for certain—and that the musicians did not come back to play anymore—that made her grief still stronger. She lamented to Isabele; otherwise no one knew of this matter. That her heart was suffering, was clearly to be seen by everyone. (83) Her father was full of grief and sorrow. His heart was breaking from the pain. After all, he had no other child and did not know what was wrong with her. The proverb hits the mark: "love is blind." I have often heard it said in my day: the one to whom a matter pertains—the Devil baits and badgers him so that he is the last to know it.

(84) Now, the king had thought to himself that he would amuse his daughter. He organized a noble tournament. He thought therewith to delight her. In diverse lands, wherever he could, he invited everyone,[19] and whoever could fight well with a sword was to come riding to his tournament. (85) A beautiful crystal shield, inlaid with pearls and rubies, was hung up on an iron nail. Believe me, it was praiseworthy! The one who demonstrated great might here was to win that shield, a chaplet, additionally, that was worth many a guilder, and above all else the favor of the beautiful Viene. (86) Viene had made that noble chaplet with her own hands. Although she was in great pain, and no one could assuage her grief, she took a bit of comfort: she steadfastly hoped that it would end. She thought: "Who knows—among the jousters I might recognized the one who has broken my heart." (87) Thus went forth the great proclamation in broad lands both near and far that knights, counts, and all kinds of other people bold in their lives, were to come on the first day of May. That very day was the appointed time.

Now, everyone who heard the proclamation indeed wanted to be there at that time. (88) Many did not have enough patience. They came there by difficult routes. The route might well have brought about their deaths—and all because they wished to win the favor of Viene, for in all lands which people could reach, her good and noble name was illustrious. (89) Many a worthy warrior came there—dukes, counts, and also knights, with noble armor and fine horses, lordly people of bold stature: when they but walked on the ground, they made the entire place quake with their stature, their noble weaponry, and their many noble squires who galloped alongside them. (90) I would also identify the lords by name, one by one, but I know that you have neither seen nor would know any of them. Only this alone will I tell you: how they galloped at once to the tournament. But they will have to wait—I have commanded—until I go and fetch Odoardo and Pariz.

(91) Now, Pariz was deep in thought. He asked Odoardo his advice—whether he, too, ought to take part in the tournament and also test his strength there. Odoardo looked at him and laughed and said to him: "May God strike me down! I would be ashamed for the rest of my life, if we did not also go to the tournament. (92) I will say, in honor of Viene, we do not want to miss this tournament. But I would very much like our arms not to be blue or green or yellow, so that we are not recognized, and so that we conceal the matter well. If we do not ride our own horses, no one will imagine that we are there."

(93) Secretly and with great diligence, they quickly prepared themselves. Their armor and lances, and the caparisons and horses on which they rode,

were all white. With good lances and bold hearts they came there at the appointed time. The jousting had just begun. Many a good knight was to be praised there. (94)[20] More than a few were praised, but many were considered scoundrels. For each one there was recognized by the coat of arms that he had on his helmet: this one a lion, that one an ape, that one a fool, and this one a saint, and that one a cross. These two came in directly and in haste so that everyone was gaping at them. (95) And everyone was attentively looking them over, for they were wildly going at it. Pariz did not shy away from any joust, even if it had cost him his life. In his hands the lance was flying so that not a single person who was standing there had ever seen anything like it, and Viene, too, was astonished. (96) And she said indeed to Isabele: "Whose jousting seems best to you today?" She said: "The one who is riding there in front of us, who has the lion on his helmet." Viene said: "The one dressed in white: no one has any success against him. It seems to me that no one else has dared so much today in order to gain honor for my sake." (97) Her heart told her this, and it was also true that no one jousted with greater might. None of all those who were there defeated him in the battles. He beat many of them black and blue, and no one could imagine who he might be. His name was honored only by his great strength, which he demonstrated from morning until evening.

(98) Now that it had become late, the great combat was to cease. Everyone said: "The one in white has won," and pointed to him. Pariz with his Odoardo quickly bowed before the king. Viene quickly turned to him and gave him the prize with her own hands. (99) As soon as he had taken that in hand, he quickly galloped away. It grieved both locals and foreigners that they could not recognize that one, and that when they returned to their countries they could not identify by name that good knight and noble lord who had won the tournament with such honor. (100) Everyone went home to their cities. They told of the disguised man; they spoke of how well he had conducted himself for Viene's sake. They could not talk their fill of it: how in all their days they had never seen such sword-fighting, thrusting and striking for the sake of a beautiful and noble maiden. (101) "That he was so noble in life, that he twisted and turned like a dragon, indeed that did not seem strange to us, for he had already engaged in a great deal of combat for the sake of such a lady whose peer in beauty is not to be found. Such beauty and nobility are seldom found, and one might say, not at all in the world." (102) They praised her greatly in every way—how her beauty was a miracle.

Many knights and counts were there who went pale with rage and said: "There are more than three to whose beauty Viene's is no equal: the daughter of Sir Hans and of other people besides him, as well, have asses that are prettier than her face." (103) And one said how Lady Kostanze was the most graceful in all her gestures. One said that he would be hanged if the most beautiful women were not in France. They named there a great number that I cannot even remember. They made such an uproar that they deafened me.

Therefore I will them leave them until they have finished their yowling, (104) and will in the meantime speak of King Dolfin[21] and of his dear daughter Viene. Thus was indeed his name, as I have now identified him. For the sake of his daughter was the tournament held in Vienne, and she did not recognize it at all. I will tell you more, but do not rush me. Now I am tired and will rest for a while.

Canto Three

Now help me God and be with me, so that I can compose the third canto.

(105) It is most certainly a wondrous thing that the world should be such that women's hearts are as hard and cold as the stone of hard walls. If a man were to take a naked sword and wish to give himself a wound by his own hand, they would not for that reason soften or grow warmer in order to show mercy to their faithful servant. (106) It is thus: I have given it some attention and know that I am not telling a lie. A poor youth steadfastly ponders how he might accommodate his beloved in some thing. He serves her day and night, and it seems that he can never do enough—I must indeed say—even if everything were done with great effort, as if one were to wash a donkey's head with soap.

(107) May Viene be ever blessed in both this and the next world. I think her unique; and if there are more like her, there are not many of them. Her heart was flesh and not of stone. No ice could have cooled it: so much had the [lover's] service alone—without her knowing the servant—warmed it and made it burn. (108) From the fact that she but knew that someone had played music and sung for her sake, such an affection remained in her heart—no maiden had ever had such affection for a young man, and the behavior that she now displayed, I told earlier with my own tongue. The tournament was organized to comfort her in her sorrow. At first all of that resulted in nothing but the worst. (109) The tournament functioned like straw that made the fire flame up. In truth her soul left her, and she often said to her nurse: "As God is ever in the high heavens, you may be just as certain that those who came there clothed in white and fought so boldly, were the ones who often here so sweetly played on the strings. (110) He has thrust his lance into me so that he has almost split my heart in two. It is now full in all its parts with nothing but hard and sharp

darts. And until I can discover who he is, my wounds will never heal. Because of his great might and very good works, he can only be of noble blood." (111)[22] Now, Isabele wished to comfort her. She said: "He must indeed be a bold warrior, and believe me, I, too, am true to him, and wish him well for your sake." If I were to sing all their words, I would use up the entire day. Therefore, I will leave them there for a while and write a bit about Pariz.

(112) Earlier I said how he galloped away, that noble and so worthy warrior. He was unrecognized by any weapons, armor, or even by his horses. He took the shield and the chaplet at once. There was nothing dearer to him on earth. Therefore, he hid it away and took good care of it. No one could imagine that he had it. (113) It was dear to him, and he had great hopes that it would be of benefit to him and not harm him. Nonetheless, he had neither peace nor rest. He did not know how to drain this tub: Viene was a great burden to him of which he could not unburden himself. He was never seen relaxed and at ease, but only with the bishop and according to his state.

(114) He acted like a man who had completely given up all hope. Whenever his father looked at him, he averted his eyes. He all but contracted a disease from the grief that he suffered as a result. The old man complained day and night that the young man thus allowed himself to grow faint. (115) Once he took him aside with his mother, Diane. He said: "My son, listen to my words! Tell me, why—tell me, wherefore—the local bishop is so close to you that you love him more than all other people? What are his mumbling and his chatter to you? Do you wish to become a monk or a priest? (116) My son, why are you taking that path? What do you lack? What would suit you? Why have you become so listless that you have given up? Oh God, where have the days gone that you were the delight of my life with the playing that you did here, and honors and tournaments that you won? (117) Where are your goshawks? Where are your hounds? Where are your steeds? Where are your palfreys? I thought that your blood would be inflamed, but it becomes colder by the day! Is that the joy that you are announcing that is to comfort me in my old age? This will so weaken my limbs that I will go down to the grave in grief. (118) You are indeed my only child. I no longer expect another. Therefore, have no worries at all; do as a noble son should. I have lived enough years that I am almost becoming feeble-minded. Only now is my life becoming an agony because I see you so miserably grieving. (119) I beg of you, grant my plea. Oh dear heart of mine, my own dear life: defend and attack and seek honor. Dance and jump and laugh and jest. Do it for the sake of your old father. Do it for the sake of your troubled mother." He spoke many a word about such things that could have made a stone crack.

(120) Pariz spoke to his good father in few words: "Dearest beloved, do not be displeased. Have no worries for my sake; do not make yourself weak. Let your life be peaceful and let there be no displeasure. Banish care from your heart. I hope that my affairs will soon turn around." (121) He said and indeed promised him that he would leave him in peace for a while, but Pariz was never happy, because of his great affection and heart-ache.

Now I will leave you here, and will go to separate those people. For since I have been speaking about this topic, they have there all but beaten each other to death. (122) I mean those who were arguing about the beauty of ladies. They came at each other with words as if they wished to start punching each other. When the French king heard it, he also wanted to see the conflict, for if the quarrel got any worse, they would have hacked each other to bits. (123) Dukes, counts, and the nobility were on all three sides that had spoken angry words, so that it came to the wild conflict. It would have grieved the king, had he not acted in time there. Therefore he had all of them together summoned before him. Like obedient subjects they all came at once.

(124) He said to them with good words: "I want you to obey me willingly. There is nothing to gain from the quarrel, and it cannot come to a good end. I have conceived of a plan, by means of which you will all retain your honor, and which will bring about both justice and happiness. You are all to be content with it. (125) I will tell you what it is: there is to be no protest from anyone! On this square here in Paris, I will erect three silken banners. Three banners there are now to be—one for each of the ladies, and I will have golden letters written on them, on each one the name of one of the three ladies. (126) And to the extent that I can and may, I will have a great proclamation made that whoever excels in jousting and combat and whoever is possessed of noble courage, he should come to the tournament on that day for the sake of the beauty of one of the three, and for the sake of the one for whom he wishes to fight, he is to take his place under the banner with her name. (127) There is to be a tournament at the appointed time, and to the one who there demonstrates himself to be the boldest, to that same man and to the lady will I grant the honor and victory in beauty." The knights all shouted with one cry: "This is both just and proper for us, for we all hope that the Almighty will grant His aid to the one most deserving."

(128) The quarrel was now settled for a while. Preparations began to be made. The news spread far as quickly as an arrow from a bow, and also rigorously and at great speed, three envoys quickly rode away. Each took a particular path—to the friends and relations of these three maidens.

(129) The king had thus ordered them that they tell them the entire story, and how he would like to see them and would be delighted that, when the quarrel had been settled, they would all be there. Thus did he prefer to settle it. And they were to bring a gift to present, so that the one who won the honor would remember it. (130) Indeed everyone was very keen for this tournament and battle. Whether early or late, whether day or night, people chattered about nothing else. Now Pariz was, however, very thoughtful about whether he should attend or stay at home. But I think that he decided to take counsel with his comrade. (131) Odoardo said: "If you do not go, I swear by Goat, you will come to regret it. If Viene were not to win the honor, then it would be we who had befouled it. Then you will say: "If I had been there, I would have won her for certain, guaranteed. If a stranger wins her, then go into your chamber and see how Master Death will deal with you."

(132) Odoardo was well acquainted with noble combat, and seldom was a more noble one to be found. Thus had he quite persuaded him that he, too, should go to the celebration that day. And for the one who goes willingly to the dance, it is easy to play. For that reason, they prepared themselves quite secretly, disguised from head to toe.

(133) And now that the time drew near, there was a great crush as many people came from distant lands and far paths, dukes, counts, knights, and youths. Many wished to take part in the combat for the ladies, of whom I have already sung. Each of them wanted to be the one to win the honors for them. Pariz and Odoardo were there among them. (134) The duke brought from England, for the sake of his sister Kostanze, a golden crown, weighing three pounds, encrusted with diamonds. And Floria is also not known; I am not accustomed to naming her. She was the daughter of a worthy noble; she sent a caparison. (135) Our Dolfin also came with the honorable Sir Yakomo and otherwise many other people from Vienne who came as his retinue. Now, they also brought with them a beautiful hat that he took from home. The one who would win the tournament for Viene would well acknowledge his great and sublime high treasure.

(136) The counts and lords were altogether quite cordially welcomed. The silken banners were brought, one by one on a pole. The gift for each fine lady was hung from her banner there. These three banners were raised in three places on the open esplanade. (137) And when the appointed time had come—it was precisely the tenth of September—there were many people there, both locals and foreigners; what an uproar and bluster there was there. Both merchants and nobles were standing at the appointed place, as well as artisans

and shop-owners, and rich and poor with their kith and kin, just as the Jews stood around the golden calf. (138) Each one wanted to be a part of it: it was indeed a pleasure merely to watch. Three people were actually crushed there, but they all nonetheless suffered it gladly. The knights and the noble combatants began to separate from each other. And those who fought for one of the ladies all rode beneath her banner. (139) The book indeed names the knights, but I do not wish to say their names. I said it before and will say it again: you know none of them, nor have you ever seen them. This I will indeed let you know: each lady had some ten of them. Under whose banner the esteemed Pariz rode—we said it before, I will tell you again. (140) Now it began in such a manner that I am not able to express it elegantly: how they there sliced and stabbed and shot, how they were clawing and mauling. If I were to say how they spilled blood there, I would make the ladies shudder. For this reason I will not sully myself further with this topic, so that I not make anyone seethe and boil.

(141) With brief speech and few words I want now to tell you the result. Many mighty knights were there. They were striking each other without restraint. But none was in the same class as Pariz: none more bold had anyone ever seen with his eyes. He was taunting them all and leading them scuttling back and forth until they were exhausted and flailing about. (142) Thereafter he held the entire field—I am in truth not telling you a lie. Although he won the banner, it was quite violent enough. I think that God on his heavenly throne now wanted to arrange it thus. He won the tournament with great honor. Dolfin and the king of France were delighted to see that.

(143)[23] Pariz was now summoned by beckoning, for no one knew him by his name. When he had come before the king, the king took the crown, the caparison, the hat, and the silken banner all of them together in his own hands and gave them to Pariz, and said: "This is yours by right, for you have won it all like a king." (144) He took it all and did not make a fuss: he rode home with Odoardo. No man living knew anything about his having gone to the tournament. He slyly told the bishop and made him aware in good time how he was to be traveling in such and such a place. Now he returned to his earlier activity.

(145) All the knights and guests returned to their lands. Each one again crept into his nest with great injury and great shame. Pariz had been the best, which caused the others pain and grief. The Dolfin wanted to depart with his retinue and also wanted to go home with great joy. (146) He had completely won over the noble and worthy king of France. He demonstrated to him in word and deed the joy that he took from this stroke of fortune. He said: "Your

daughter is altogether noble. Her beauty surpasses all others. Bring her the crown; my wife presents it to her." There were more speeches; I cannot record them all.

(147) With leave and thanks he went on his way and rode until he reached home. Tears of joy flowed from his eyes. Viene came out to meet him. He fell on her neck and took her on his lap and said: "My life! Where is your peer to be found? You are the most beautiful and the noblest. That was proven by the tournament that was held in Paris. (148) A knight in disguise fought heartily for you. Indeed I swear to you on my oath. He defended your honor with great might. It grieves me only—only this did I find deficient in him—that he never let himself be recognized nor identified himself, so that I could have recompensed him in part. (149) He took the banner and the hat, the caparison and also the crown. On the basis of his skill and his fine deeds, he must indeed be of noble blood. If I am not to recompense him well for it, then I pray to God to reward him for it." He spoke many such words. They quite inflamed Viene's heart.

(150) She was thinking about who the noble lord might be who had preserved her honor with such benevolent might. She remained thus silent until night fell. Her suffering was ever increasing. She was bearing it all in her heart, and she thus said to Isabele: (151) "O, my dear and beloved sister! What am I to do? How am I to bear it? Hour-by-hour my pain increases. That is proven by my poor appearance. A flame has entered my heart and never lets it cool. I have often said to you with bitter words how a noble knight loves me in his heart.[24] (152) And I think for certain that the one of whom my father has spoken is none other than the one who played such sweet music with pipe, organ, and trumpet. That one has indeed shackled me with thick and tight iron chains. Unless he soon comes to unbind my heart, he will find me miserably dead. (153) I know that he is true to me. His fine deeds prove it to me. And if I were not to love him, my heart would have to be of iron." Isabele answered right away: "Your words and deeds are praiseworthy. But it should be done with purpose and reason and not in the heat of great passion. (154) You lament and weep and suffer grievously for one whom you have never seen. You know that I have never tried to restrain you, for I have often heard it said that one always desires that which is most difficult to attain. Place your hope in God who may perhaps deliver you, for good always follows the bad." (155) With such sweet words and speech did she revive her a bit. But she could not attenuate her grief. She could not banish him from her mind, and she wanted to know who he was. She wanted to know him; she wanted to see him. Day and night she was ever searching for him, and her heart was flickering in hellfire.

(156) I will leave Viene there. Of Sir Yakomo will I read to you for a while. He had joy with his wife that Viene had been victorious. On the other hand, he grieved that his Pariz was not also there. His heart and all his reason made him think: he might easily have won the tournament. (157) The poor man had no peace. He could not endure the way that Pariz was living. He said to him: "Good lord, what has happened to your noble deeds!?" Pariz had also been stricken with grief so that his father recognized his state. He comforted him and would have tried anything, but his great love would not leave him alone. (158) His father's grief broke his heart, and his love for Viene blinded him. Now when the elderly and aggrieved man saw that he could change nothing with his words, then he also wanted to try something else and sent for Odoardo. He took him into a closed chamber and said: "One service do I wish from you. (159) You have always been like a son to me. I have never lost faith in you. Because of my grief I now want to make a request. You alone may help me in this. Otherwise my hopes are all dashed. I know of your great power with Pariz. Your good companionship has well proven that to me. (160) His aimless inactivity is destroying me: one sees the signs in my appearance. He is quite deaf to my reprimands. I cannot soften him with my pleas. He is going to put me in my grave before my appointed time has come. By Goat, I fear that the cursed bishop has bewitched the poor youth. (161) Therefore, I beseech you earnestly that you manage the affair wisely, that you talk him out of it and see that he leads a life that is more useful." Odoardo said: "My father and my lord, I will do everything that is possible."

And with those words he departed and found Pariz, his esteemed companion. (162) He led him out through the city gate. They took hands. Odoardo said: "Indeed I think that you will believe my words, but I would like to ask you in advance that you not take offense, if I speak to you for your own good and with a pure heart, as a brother and as a trusted comrade. (163) I have heard here on the square, everywhere and in all the streets rumors and chattering how you have involved yourself in bad behavior. It is embarrassing everyone, both great and small, and they hate your indolent life. They say: 'He was noble with weapons and helmet. Alas, what a rogue has come from that!' (164) For that reason your father and mother lament and weep grievously, for they both have indeed only you: from their root are you the seed, and you are giving them very little joy. Your soul will indeed have to make amends for that: he who afflicts his parents—you should know—it may be that he will atone for it later in the next world. (165) Indeed do I advise you that you give up this dance: stop it and pull yourself out of it. Revive your life with sword and lance. Wipe this love right out of your heart. If you cannot unburden yourself of her entirely, then at least add something else to the mix. You love and bear in your heart a person, and she knows nothing whatever of you. (166) And even if she were to know you, she would scarcely ask about you. She would think you worthless. Indeed if I were wrong about this, and if she were to show you love, what would you do? Would you believe her? Would you dare? It is best not to get entangled with the ruling class and best not to count your chickens before they hatch. (167) You love her thus so boldly as if you had her in your clutches. You do not yet know the roguery that lurks behind maidens."

I will leave you therewith for a while, for I am about to start coughing. This affair is beginning to become wearisome. I am tired now and have to rest for a while.

The end of the third canto.

Canto Four

May God be my guide and my shepherd, so that I may also compose the fourth canto.

(168) O fine maidens, o fair missies, o gentle damsels, o noble lassies: let me not lose your love if I here speak too boldly. I cannot now pay court to you. I will babble it all out fittingly, and if I were to say something that does not please you, then I beg you all for your pardon. (169) But be quiet and have some patience, for in times past, too, women suffered. That I not lose your good will because of this, I beseech you with all my heart. You should blame Odoardo alone, for it is not my custom to speak ill. Were I indeed to say something bad, I would, in truth, only be saying what Odoardo said.

(170) This time even he could not speak from the heart. He loved someone as well as I do and begrudged her neither good nor honor. He now said what he would do, as advocates always do: in order to aid their clients or relations, they say what is necessary, whether truth or lies. (171) Thus did Odoardo also, so that he served Sir Yakomo well. Well do you remember how he promised. If you do not remember, then recall it to mind. He said a woman is a stream from which nothing but roguery issued forth, and not one of them is to be believed or trusted. Therefore one should not rely on either her words or gestures. (172) And he continued with these words; he said: "Pariz, my dear brother, do not be eager for a lady's favor. They possess a full cart-load of malice. When you think that you are in a good position, she will set a trap for you, so that you lose both your fortune and your life, so that you wish that you had never been born. (173) You are not yet well acquainted with their deceit: how they will betray a poor youth. They smile at him a time or two or three,

and nod their heads. Then his heart burns like an ember so that it might lie directly before her. She would then let it burn completely to ashes before she would extinguish it with a spoonful of water. (174) They have no other desire than to gad about, one by one. When they have enchained a man, then they leave him in the lurch. They take up with another in the midst of it all, but him, too, they give the brush-off. For they boast of it and in a gaggle laugh about it: "O, how I can drive a man crazy!" (175) We do indeed love them, and we could indeed not be more generous to them—and they are worse than vicious animals, they are wilder than wolves and bears.

"If we give them but a glance, it seems to us that we have an accurate picture. Indeed they are pictures, and that is no secret: for they are tinted and painted like pictures. (176) When a poor man then thinks that he is seeing the courtly form of a maiden, what he actually sees is white lead and sublimate of mercury, mercury and spittle he is seeing; he is looking at brazil-wood and vinegar, lemon, egg, bean blossoms, alum, talcum powder, and sugar-pulp. You cannot imagine it! The cursèd dissimulation! (177) They make their hair yellow like gold with sulfur and oil, which they press into it. One sees indeed how they pluck their foreheads and eyebrows with tweezers. If we think them beautiful and fine, they have cleverly prickled us. All their beauty is like pure white snow under a hot sun. (178) O, I say to you and to all my brothers who think they stand straight, thick and tall as fir trees: let them look and see what is inside their corsets, and their six-inch platform shoes, and three or four petticoats—a whole pile! Then they would perhaps not smile at them so. He who sees them discreetly going to bed sees three quarters of 'them' lying beside the bed. (179) Whoever sees her early in the morning, before she is decked out and spruced up: dry meat in a yellow brew is what one sees.

"I would rather not take the trouble and would rather not give you a fright: otherwise I would make you see with your own eyes that it is four times worse than I say. (180) In truth there are many more points to be made, but I cannot remember them all. Therefore, remember, know, and believe that when they begin to age, then they have rotten teeth and faces full of wrinkles. They stink, complain, and they grunt and screech and take the form of demons from Hell.

(181) "Therefore do not believe in their beauty. I will tell you in advance and warn you: neither Jew nor Christian has found either loyalty or honor; nor has anyone ever found anything fine or good, but rather nothing but pride, roguery and deceit. They make their fraud into a snare. The one who is virtuous escapes it, while the sinner is ensnared by it. (182) A lady has no other virtue than that we men are born of them. They whelp us quickly, but their

rights are therewith at an end. Look, even a fragrant red rose grows from a rough thorn, and lilies come from stinking grass. We are fond of flowers, but root out the weeds."

(183) He let many a word issue forth from his mouth. Whether willingly or not, I will not say at this time, for I treat the honor of maidens with care. I am indeed also in the same alliance that loves and ever desires them, above all one, whom I will not name, although she, too, refuses to acknowledge my favor. (184) Indeed I tell you that he is not right to speak so harshly and even more so: if there are five, six, seven, or eight of the wicked ones, let him reprimand and condemn them, but there are on the other hand perhaps a hundred who are true, honest, and honorable. Indeed I say "perhaps" and do not wish to provide evidence, for if I were to say it for certain, I might be wrong.

(185) Odoardo had said enough to serve Sir Yakomo well. He said: "Pariz, you are wise and know more than four times as much as I. I say to you: look and perceive and pay attention. You can lose both property and honor in this, and it would be worse for you, if you were to see that it happened because of a lady. (186) If you care for dad and mom, you ought indeed not be stiff-necked. The old man is always sitting lost in thought, as if he were about to be beheaded. Your mother weeps; she weeps by night, and her tears are on her cheeks, and she has no comfort to make her forget her grief, unless you were to change your actions. (187) Do otherwise with the counsel that I give you: follow it. I counsel you in your own best interest. Do it for my sake and the sake of mom and dad—whom I should have named first."

He long continued to press this point, setting a firm foundation for it, so that he at this point quite persuaded Pariz. He heaved a sigh from deep in his heart (188) and said: "Odoardo, my esteemed friend, you are right. What am I to say? I cannot refute you. I wish only to lament for my fortune. I will abandon that thought; I heartily wish to see it annihilated. I wish to beat it out of my heart, and, therewith, an end to that thought, so that I cause dad and mom no more pain."

(189) This answer pleased Odoardo well. He left him in peace for a period of two weeks, but the matter did not show any progress. So Odoardo said: "I will try something and will do everything that I can to make him renounce it entirely." And he went to Pariz one day and embraced him with both arms. (190) He said: "Pariz, my dear brother, you know that I have been expected in Brabant for some seven months, and it is my custom often to be on the move. Now I would like to go there, if only I had no worries for your well-being. Because I am concerned for you, I cannot leave you. Therefore, I would like us both to go. (191) Now, I have many friends and relations there, as you have

previously come to know. Therefore, I would very much like to go there, if only you would also come with me. Indeed I swear to you—and may God punish me [if it is not true]—it is something that I intend to do. Let us there spend a good while going for rides, and dancing, leaping, fencing and jousting." (192) Pariz said: "Indeed I swear that your excessive words seem strange to me. Of course I will come and with pleasure, if you wished to go to the ends of the earth. I have had such aid and honor from you that I could never repay you."

Now the good warriors delayed no longer and made all preparations. (193) He and his good comrade took armor and lance and spear and sword. Now they were to mount their horses; they had just fed them. Pariz locked his chamber securely and gave the key to his mother. He asked her not to let anyone go inside. Thus did they mount their horses and ride on their way. (194) They rode away and reached their destination, and there they let nothing be lacking in all the joy that then was to be found there: in dancing, leaping, feasting and drinking. They also took great delight in sword-play, parrying, lance-thrusts, and jousting. Pariz always held his ground with honor. Everyone was fond of him and liked seeing him. (195) Everyone did him great honor and treated him with great courtesy. He was praised often and much, everywhere and at all times.

Nonetheless his heart was still heavy; even all of that could not relieve his grief, although he never wanted his comrade to see it nor himself to reveal it. (196) No one knows who has not tried it, how painful is the love for a woman. Some say that it is good to flee: out of sight, out of mind. Whoever seeks aid—he is jesting about his love. One ever bears true affection in mind and forgets it not whether near or far. (197) Indeed do I see that also in Pariz. Look, that which Odoardo had requested of him—because of the grief that he saw before him that was occupying his mother and father—that move took place so that he might free himself from the burr. Nonetheless love was stronger than everything, although he did not let Odoardo notice it. (198) When Odoardo thought he was sleeping—it struck eight and nine and ten—he cried out "Viene, alas Viene! When will I see you again? If only you were to see the deep wound that I have received for your sake! Just as you have split my heart, so I trust you to heal me."

(199) While he thus passed his time there with Viene ever in his thoughts, his mother wrote him a little letter, how his father was unfortunately ill. When he heard that, it was as if he had been struck dead: his limbs collapsed for horror. He would have risked practically anything for the sake of his father. He thought: "When it rains, it pours." (200)[25] It was indeed true: he had the fever

and had quite red urine. For this reason he was sending for Pariz, as all honorable fathers do. He again had tertian fever; it was, thank God, not dangerous. He could not shit, which was worse than the fever; every day [an enema] had to be blown into his ass.

(201) King Dolfin was fond of him, as you should all indeed already know. He went to visit him two or three times and comforted him with his sweet speech. In addition, he also wanted his daughter to go and convey her greetings to him. She was glad to do so: his request did not fall on deaf ears: as is the case with all maidens, when they are out making their visits. (202) Viene now made the trip there with many of her maidens and Isabele. Lady Diane made a great reception; she gave her a most friendly greeting, such a kiss, such an embrace, and they all took off their headscarves. There were some seven of them standing around the old man. That day his fever had not returned.

(203) Viene began to chatter and make a racket, as all women are wont to do. She asked him how and when and why he was sick with the disease. The old man said: "On my honor, it is all because of my son—from the great ill humor that I have suffered, because he has thus abandoned his good deeds. (204)[26] He told her the entire tale, how he had been thus and so, but it did not affect Viene greatly, for she still knew nothing of that whole matter. She moved closer to the old man and said: "Just try to get well!" She comforted him a great deal with her words and also taught him a great many folk-remedies.

(205) Now that they had conversed well, she took her leave of him. She said: "God be with you, dear father. May our Lord God send you a complete recovery." He thanked her again from the bed: "May God grant you all things good." And he turned his head toward his wife and said that she should show them all the palace. (206) Thus did they all come out. She gave them a tour of the entire palace, unlocking the doors of the chambers, attic, and the great hall. There was fine ornamentation everywhere—more than was suitable. When all that had then been shown, they were led into the chamber of Pariz. (207) She opened the windows wide. He had had them all nailed shut earlier. The elderly Diane showed them much finery, but she did not budge from the spot. A bed stood there in the courtly manner, which made one want to thrash around on it. The remaining furnishings were indeed also quite courtly. It would have been suitable for a king's son. (208)[27] There were two or three rods in the room, on which armor and helmets were hung. In addition there were many courtly things hung there: lances and swords with fine blades. Now they went into a small chamber, which was also full of such things: with banners, caparisons, and knightly surcoats, which he had hung out there to air. (209) There were also many courtly coats of arms hung there, made of gold and silk and pearls. They

all looked at them as marvels. Viene said: "I tell you in truth—this is a noble man. He lives a noble and lordly life. I tell you Isabele, he is praiseworthy. His noble effects demonstrate that clearly to me."

(210) By chance she turned around and saw in a corner there a surcoat and a steed's caparison which were completely white. She turned pale and colder than ice: so stupefied was she by joy. She did not give herself away immediately, without first slowly saying to Isabele: (211) "Alas, my Isabele, am I not to recognize these garments immediately, in which that one won the tournament, who just as quickly galloped away?" She trembled and went pale. The nurse said: "Listen, Viene: one should not so easily jump to conclusions. Is there but one red cow in the world? (212) There are more such clothes, I think, and other people who wear them." Viene said: "Explain it to me; you may not deny me an answer."

And as she was thus standing there, she became very dizzy. I think that she was simply faking it, because she wanted to hurry all the ladies out of there. (213) She feigned that she was ill. She told the ladies all to go away. She said that she had gotten a sudden pain and would like to lie down for a while. A brief nap was her desire, for which reason they were not to wake her. Thus was everyone driven out, and Isabele alone remained with her. (214) Indeed she threw herself onto the bed for a while. But she had not lain on it for longer than it took me to say it before she sprang up and said to Isabele: "I bet that this man jousted for my sake. Now, let us search for better evidence." They again went and sneaked into the chamber. (215) As she looked more closely at the garment, turning it back and forth, she accidentally caught her hand on something, and a small door opened. The door was indeed in the wall. But Pariz, the noble lord, had hung many garments in front of it, so that no one would notice it or go inside. (216) Our Lord God simply granted her the good fortune that it not be kept secret any longer. The door that I just mentioned led far downward, down some stairs. Viene boldly went down, where she found lying on a table—she found and saw lying there with her own eyes—oh, God, I cannot, for my great joy, even say it: (217) she found the shield made of crystal and also found there the noble chaplet and found thereafter all the banners that he had won in France, as well as other things beyond numbering, all of which he had won with his lance: he also had the caparison and the crown there, and the hat that she had sent with her father. (218) When she saw that, she was dumbstruck; she was transformed. Love for him now inflamed her more than ever, so that it burned both inside and out. With her heart, with her mouth, she thus began: "God in the high heavens be praised, who has freed my heart from pain. (219) If I have had a hard life; if his arrows have pierced me; if his naked sword has penetrated me; if he has now spilled my blood: the noble lord is well worth it. Now suddenly it is no distress for me; my misfortune does not grieve me: it was a nobleman who did it to me, not a peasant."

(220) She would have continued with such words, but Isabele interrupted her. She said: "Be fond of your honor and do not be overeager. Do not let him please you too well. He is not as wealthy and noble as you, even if all his deeds were noble. You are courtly, noble, wealthy and quite intelligent. No duke or even king will you lack." (221) Viene said: "Your idea would then be that I not grant my favor and myself to a noble man who has risked his life ten times for my honor? I tell you now, and swear to you: I love him; he is of my own status. And I will love him until the end of my days, and your base words will not change my mind. (222) What are a lot of dukes' sons to me, who grub around day and night in money, and who are not noble and bold enough to go four miles from their doors? Noble honor is always fresh; the essence of virtue can never wither. One can lose money and goods and land; a good man can never perish. (223) On money and goods I—if you will pardon the expression—shit. As far as I am concerned, he is good and honorable and honest. As far as I am concerned, he is courtly and white and ruddy, adroit in all his limbs. For that reason I say to you quite assiduously: speak no further word of opposition to me. And give me aid and counsel with all your diligence, or we will be at loggerheads." (224) Isabele said: "Now do not be too hasty. I told you my idea. I did not thereby cast shame on him. So, do not get so angry. I am prepared with all my might and with all my aid to get to the bottom of the matter."

Now they were in alliance and had decided to take the things that were there. (225) It seemed to them good to leave the shield there and to take those things that were smaller: the crown, chaplet, her hat, and the three courtly silken banners. Viene said: "Now it is my intention that no one notice: let us hide it all underneath our clothing. Then let us leave them all here.

(226) Now, all that took place before anyone could turn around. Viene said that she was no longer in pain, and she took her veil of crêpe-silk. Thus with "farewell" and "many thanks" and "may your visitors come to you in love and joy," did they part from one another and go home. They exchanged still more words, but I do not wish to sing them.

(227) Viene was indeed better than she had been before, when she wandered around in the garden of fools. She nonetheless sighed more times than she had hairs. The time that she waited for him so that she could see dear Pariz—a day seemed to her as long as a year. I well believe that the days were long for her, for I have also suffered from this disease.

(228) Now, several days passed. Sir Yakomo had recovered completely. Pariz was also not lax. He was hurrying home quickly. He thought that his father was still ill in bed. He covered many a mile in a few days. He arrived at home with great joy and delight that he found his father healthy. (229) Everyone welcomed Pariz and Odoardo before they had even quite dismounted from their horses. The bishop embraced him; he showed him his great affection. That same day Pariz also went and did obeisance before the Dolfin, although his visit was made because he wanted to see Viene. (230) His plan went off according to his intent. Thus was she also able to arranged it, that when he took his leave from the Dolfin, then he there saw his beautiful beloved. He saw her well, and she saw him, which revitalized them both. What a comfort it was for the noble maid. Pariz also went home with that same joy.

(231) That all happened on the first day. That very same night, before he went to bed, he inspected everything in the chamber: his lance, his armor, and his weapons. He also wanted to go into the small chamber; there everything was wide open. The door was gaping—opened wide—on its hinges, and all his beloved garments were missing. (232) Terror pierced deeply into his heart: "I am lost," he said to himself, and he was unable to sleep the entire night. When dawn came, he had had no rest. Then he called his dear mother and lamented miserably to her. He said: "You did not guard my chamber!" But he did not say what had happened to him. (233) His mother had perhaps forgotten that people had been everywhere, or she simply wanted to deny it, so that he would not be angry with her. She said: "My son, you are wrong. Your chamber was never opened."

The answer caused him pain and grief. He feared lest he come to great disgrace. (234) He feared lest there had been a thief who had stolen those things from him, and lest it thereby become known what he had concealed for so long. Likewise, he could not complain about it at all: whatever consolation he was to receive he had to supply for himself. Thus did he pass his time miserably.

Now, I want to write about Viene for a while. (235) She was now moderately happy; her suffering was indeed somewhat diminished, for her Pariz was there again and was quite courtly, bold and spirited. But she saw and recognized well that he was morose and sad and that it was all for the sake of her favor and also because he had lost his gear. (236) She said to Isabele one night: "My dear sister, give me some advice: you know that Pariz is my might and main. Without him my heart will perish. Therefore I have conceived of a means of relief for me and hope that I am also successful with it. I want to become acquainted with his bishop. By that means things may improve. (237) Through him I will let him know that my love for him has taken me captive and that I have all his garments, so that he no longer is worried about them." Isabele said: "Let it be done." And when several days had passed, Viene was sitting with her mother and had chatted with her for a good while. (238) She interposed one matter into another and said: "Listen, my dear mamà, you know that I am a great devotee of pleasure. Probably I sin often therein. I know of nothing else good to do that would benefit my soul. I have need of an elderly and honorable man to teach me how to behave. (239) And I have heard that the local bishop is pious and aged and is also honorable. Therefore, dear mother, if I knew how to do it, I would like to receive his admonitions." Her mother said: "Now, he must either come to you, or you go to him. Praised be God who stretched out the heavens and who has awakened your heart to good deeds."

(240)[28] How quickly was he summoned. He came riding there on his mule. He came quite quickly, as one is accustomed to do when one is summoned by a king. Viene bowed deeply to him, as is still the courtly custom there. Then they were allowed to go alone into her chamber. She wished to make confession, so her mother reckoned. (241) That same day she presented herself as if she were altogether pious and honorable, and spoke not a single word of Pariz, but kept her eyes lowered modestly. Indeed did she implore and command him that he come to see her often. He promised her that he would and would do it willingly, for he also took great pleasure in courtly young ladies. (242) But she did it with a spoonful of sugar, so that she could train him to be flexible. In the end he went there simply and directly. No one asked any further about it. Now that she indeed had the time, she thought that she would certainly risk it. So she said: "I have recognized that you are pious. Therefore, I wish to confess a sin to you, father. (243) I want to tell you what there is here. Recently a great deal of courtly clothing with golden trim and a great many fine gemstones has come into my hands. Now, I know that someone took from Pariz all his courtly gear. Therefore, I would ever like to unburden my soul and do not wish that he suffer the loss. (244) I would just like to give it back to him, but I would like to do it with my own hand. Therefore, bring him tomorrow to the place that I will now tell and show you. When both of you are there, then I will speak to him discreetly. But it is better not to mention me at all before you bring him to me there."

(245) The matter did not seem insignificant to the bishop. How quickly did he speak with Pariz and said: "Whoever loses here, he accuses and blames much and thus sins greatly. Now, I have heard the confession of a woman today—whose name I may not reveal to you—but she has garments that were stolen from you; and who she is, you could never imagine. (246) Now everything will be returned to you, and she herself wants to speak with you about

it, and tomorrow morning, when dawn arrives, then both of us will go to see her." It often seemed to Pariz quite bitter, and often it seemed to him that he was in Paradise. He had the sense that he should be delighted, and his heart pounded; he could not believe it.

(247)[29] And when morning came, they quickly went to the place. There they found Viene alone with her nurse, Isabele. Pariz was so alarmed that he could force not a single word out of his mouth. The noble maiden had to greet him first; he offered her a response with his sweet voice. (248) He quite lost his power of speech from his great joy and terror and embarrassment, until she took him by the hand and led him aside into a corner.

I have babbled until my tongue is lame. I cannot go on; I bid you farewell. And if you would like to hear more concerning those four, then be patient: first I have to go wet my whistle.

The fourth canto concludes here.

Canto Five

May God give me wisdom and reason so that I can also compose the fifth canto.

(249) No one should let his spirit become arrogant when he is successful in all his endeavors. If he already has a great deal of money and property, he ought not therefore to oppress other people, for it often happens that whatever one does, his good fortune falls to pieces; and it often comes to a reversal and loss, so that he descends to the depths of Hell. (250) Thus likewise, on the other hand, one should not despair when his fortune turns adverse and calamitous. He should rather lament his sin; let him put his hopes in God and just be honorable; let him bear it with a good will. For in a short while, when God deems it suitable, He will raise him from the mire into Heaven.

(251) Indeed, regard Pariz, the poor fool: had he suffered much misfortune? You know whether she, who had cut out his heart, was stuck in his craw. He had been devastated by the loss of the garments that she had taken from him. Now, in a single day, in a single hour, he found everything together. (252)[30] You well know how she drew him aside there into a corner, so that the bishop could not hear them. Likewise the young man asked no further questions. Now she began with her sweet words, when he dared not, because of his embarrassment. She began to tell him quickly why she had sent for him. (253) She did not immediately explain that he had wounded her heart so severely, only how she had been with his father when he had been ill and how she had taken his gear and how and where she had found it, and how she had just simply carried it

away, that it pleased her well, but now she regretted it. (254) She said: "I will no longer keep it thus—let it not cleave to my soul—I do not have it with me here. Otherwise I would give it to you on the spot." Pariz was quite delighted by her words. It seemed to him that she breathed life into him, and he thanked her with great courtesy for visiting his father during his illness.

(255) He answered her: "Now, the garments, keep them all, with my permission. I was initially quite angry; about that you can certainly believe me! I could have no greater joy than that it fell into your hands. At first the loss was quite bitter for me; recently a foreign knight gave it all to me as a present." (256) When the noble lady heard that—that he would not reveal himself—she put aside her shame and said to him with a sweet voice: "I know that you are also burned by a flame and have now for a long time concealed it. Conceal it no more, my dear beloved, reveal your heart to me, joyfully and clearly. (257) Tell it to me, so that the noble Creator will make you rejoice with your father and mother, so that God will delight you with your beloved. Tell it to me, my beloved, so fine! If you tell me that, with all that goes with it, your life will be ever calmer. Tell me, was it you who all those times so often played me to sleep with sweet string music? (258) Are you the one who won the shield with a white garment, horse and lance and who, with his might, preserved me in great honor in Paris? Your dignity resonates and resounds, even if you prefer to conceal it. Here you are, and if you deny it, then you must repudiate it, for the garment is proof of it all for me."

(259) Whoever has seen a stupefied person when lightning strikes, followed by a great thunderclap, let him come and also have a look at Pariz now—by these words he was thus stupefied. While she was saying all these things to him and was certain of it all, item by item, then his heart began to soften. He said: "There is no longer a reason for me to deny it." (260) He said to her: "My noble beloved, I implore you, have mercy on me. I know well that I have done wrong in not remaining free of you. But love, blind love, has done it to me. I have caused a great misfortune. I am not worthy to wash the soles of your feet. For that reason, too, have I always kept it hidden. (261) No one has yet noticed my love, except for Odoardo, to whom I revealed it. Otherwise it was hidden in my heart which it burned to embers. Since you know everything about it, I will indeed also confess it. It is all true, and much more besides. I beg you: forgive my foolishness, (262) and if you only take me as a servant, I will desire no more from you." Viene said: "It would be proper for you to be my noble lord." She answered him in few and simple words, although she would have liked to say more, but the time and place were dangerous. They also wanted to spare the bishop any trouble from it.

(263) She said to him: "My strength, my might, my blood, my flesh, my body so distinguished, be on your way, my heart, and pay attention that you again come to the place when it is time." They decided on a place for themselves; there was never a better one, before or since: in a deep cellar at a grate, so that neither mother nor father could notice it. (264) Thus did they all go on their ways. How quickly did he find Odoardo and tell him how his deeds and affairs stood. He was then quite delighted, for their lives were bound to each other. Pariz now sharply admonished him that he was to help him with a pure heart. (265) He promised him much and did it, too. His comradery was a great support for him. He had held him dear for a long time, and their amity was renewed every day. And if they had been born from the same hole, they could not have been more loyal to each other. He gave him counsel in every moment of need, and stood by his side at all times with body and soul.

(266) Thus did Viene also do with Isabele, her nurse. Never had one seen such a friendship; they were never apart, and when the maiden said four words, three of them were the name of the young man. If one were but to mention Pariz, it seemed to her that she was up in Paradise.

(267)[31] Meanwhile Pariz came to the place that she had earlier identified for him—so secret and so quiet that no living person knew of it. Now he went there as much as was pleasing to him and as was appropriate for him, and that was all his desire and his comfort—that he could there chat with his beloved, (268) which well pleased them both—they there spoke with each other without any shame or deceit; the ice had now been broken. He told her now that which was then important for him: that he had nobly fought as her champion, and he had suffered much worry and fear that he might be cut to tiny pieces. (269) And she also recounts her part concerning her favor and her longing, and how she had been bound by a cord that had stretched her heart inside her body, and she never imagined that she would again be healthy. Now she praised God who had shown her that her redeemer was the handsome Pariz.

(270) They often came to that same place and chatted with each other. With heart and soul, each single word, with joy, with words, they delighted each other. The desire and delight that was there at that time—what money or what property could equal it in value? The great affection and the love so sweet, hoping to atone for their desires with their rights. (271) The honeyed words, the noble gestures—I do not now want to mention them all to you, for when I think of them, then I must lament my own infelicity: how I give my heart and soul and do not even get a thank-you in return. Therefore I want to write about the mistakes—the wicked ones—for I have to take comfort only in wicked things. (272) I will let the good deeds wait; listen now to

grievous events: for three full months or more, the worthy lovers talked with each other.

Now, one day Pariz heard from a count in all earnest that the king was involved in great negotiations to contract a marriage between Viene and a man. (273) When the noble lad heard that, it was as if he had been stabbed with a dagger. He thought to himself: "Alas, I was afraid of this, and now it has happened." And certainly I believe him, that the words were for him like wounds. He could find neither rest nor repose because of his misery before he told his Viene the story. (274)[32] He told her, that fine warrior, with his head bowed. She said: "My beloved, do not be disheartened. If I were to be unfaithful to you, may God torment me. I know that no marriage will take place—my father will also ask me about it. May I then suffer a violent death, if my body were ever to do that. (275) I will not say 'I do' to anyone except you, you bold warrior."

Pariz was indeed delighted by these words—that he saw her so resolute. Nonetheless he spoke to her thus: "I have always known your good will; all your will, however, will not recompense me, that I see the customs of this world. (276) I am a poor youth; you are the daughter of a noble king, and how can a low threshold be comparable to the high mount? Unfortunately I see clearly and plainly that you will stride off with a king. I implore you only this—neither more nor less—that you take me with you as a servant."

(277) The maiden turned pale at these words. She said: "You have no faith in me. You think this, because it is constantly said that a lady's words are not trustworthy. My body will never be unfaithful to you: I will never repent for what I say to you. If I did not hope that my father would support me in this, I would indeed have tried to bring it about in a different manner." (278) Pariz did not give her an answer to that, because he did not wish to burden her any further. He said: "Until I become completely dumbfounded,[33] I am at your command in love and joy." And with a sigh and a moan they took leave of each other. Viene called after him, that he ought to pay attention to whether anything new came of the matter. (279) And off he went on his way and came to his comrade greatly troubled, and they took counsel about how the matter might now be brought to an honorable conclusion.

Not long thereafter, not more than five or six days, it was publicly proclaimed that the king had espoused his daughter to a noble duke's son from Meissen. (280) It was thus said everywhere, so that it also came to her ears. It was as bitter as gall for her; it caused her pain and grief and anger. Pariz, however, sneaked inside and came to her quite forlorn, until she revived him with her words. She said: "My dearest, do not be alarmed at this. (281) Now

I want to see what you are worth, if you can devise some means of aid." He said: "The affair is too difficult, so that my reason and wits do not suffice. If it were to be settled with the sword, I could not imagine a better way to resolve it. I would win you with my might, or death would deliver me from my pain. (282) Now I know of nothing else to do than to spend all my days in lamentation and to leave you in your honor, as I have long feared." She said: "No, no, my dear beloved, I do not wish thus to be left hanging. Not everything can be won with the sword. For there is counsel for all things, except for death. (283) If you will now do what I tell you—no matter whether it is easy or difficult for you—so I hope and promise you that we will succeed in the affair. I tell you now, and I am certain of it, that my father will grant me with body and soul and good will all things that he could even imagine that I would want. (284) Therefore it is my command and my plea that you not leave it thus, and consider and ponder what one might do in order that one prevent the marriage and consult with my father so that he give me to you in marriage. And your father would be best for that, for he is the most beloved whom he has in the fortress. (285) I know that he loves him well. He will not reproach him for his words. And if that should not succeed, then we will aim for it in another way. Therefore, make an effort now so that we soon get an answer, for in a single moment one can lose what one cannot find in three or even four years."

(286) Pariz then heaved a great sigh. He saw and recognized that it would end badly. Nonetheless he promised her everything, for his great love blinded him. He stifled his misery and now went home boldly and quickly. All that night he sighed and agonized until the next morning arrived. (287)[34] Then he came to his father's bed with great fear and shame in his eyes. He said to him: "My dear father, you have done my will all your life; therefore, I want to make a request of you. Do not deny it to me. Promise me that you will do it; otherwise I will not tell you my request." (288) He gave him a long preamble about how he should forgive him for his improper behavior and otherwise a great deal of folderol, so that he not leave him in the lurch. His father said: "Now, out with it! I promise you indeed by my life, as a father ought to do for his son; thus will I also do whatever I can." (289) Pariz had no patience: it cut him to the heart to say the words. He nonetheless told him all about his love for Viene, what he suffered because of it, and how that was to blame for his renouncing his proper mode of living. He now told all of it to the poor old man, up to the point at which they now stood. (290) And at the conclusion of all his words, he was quite agitated in his desire that he [Yakomo] just speak with the king about whether he would give her to him in marriage.

When the sick, old man heard that, he would have liked to die for grief. He said: "Dear son, as God is my witness, I fear that you have lost your mind. (291) Alas, what has happened to your good sense? Do you not recognize yourself? Do you think that King Dolfin would grant you his daughter Viene? I would not take half of Vienne to make this request on your behalf: if he were to hear such words but once from me, I would never dare go before him for the rest of my days. (292) Therefore, my dear and beloved son, make requests about, and engage in, other things, and I will do it all willingly. But this I cannot accomplish for you." Pariz said: "Now I see indeed that my love means little to you. I did not expect this answer from you, insofar as you hold me for a beloved son. (293) I know it just as well as you, that it is quite bitter for you. But I am forced to do it: I have caned my own ass. If you do not help me, I will have no peace. Hope no more that I will ever again have a good day. Therefore, merciful father, I wish to implore you: do not deny me your aid. (294) Now give me all your good will and your aid and fulfill my request. Your own son whom you love—will you slay him with your own hands?" The misery that had long obsessed him brought the father around: he saw his son in pain, and he thus suffered even more, as a father takes pity on his children. (295) He said: "If indeed you want it to be done, then I will risk life and limb, and if it is not thus settled, then I will indeed have lied." Pariz said: It is not a matter of my having conceived it by myself, and I am doing what my Viene asked of me, and your love and loyalty may thus be recognized."

(296) Deeply aggrieved by such things, one day, when it seemed to him the proper time, he went up to the king and bowed to him from afar. The king welcomed him cordially and wanted to have him sit down beside him. "No," said the poor old man, "I do not wish to sit: first, I would like to expose my folly. (297)[35] But I wish to implore you, with a breaking heart and tear-filled eyes: if I say something that seems improper to you, pardon my transgression. The relationship that I have with my lord reassures me that I can say it to you. I say it and likewise know—may dysentery befall me!—that it is not possible and even less proper. (298) I know that it is not proper, but the love of my son Pariz has forced me to do it—the folly of the poor lad." The old man, the poor fool, sniffled for fear; his tongue would barely move. The king said: "Tell me what you want to have. I will certainly forgive you for it—have no worries." (299) First he constructed an entryway, which I do not wish to describe for you at present. Because of his great fear and because of his great horror, he could scarcely stay on his feet. In the end, the substance of the matter came forth. He said: "I desire your beautiful and capable daughter as the lawful wife of my son Pariz, if it were possible."

(300) He wanted to continue his speech, although his voice was quavering, but the king interrupted him with a monstrous rage and ferocity. Indeed it was no illusion: one saw the fire smoldering in him. He said: "If I had not granted you immunity, I would make you quite regret this speech. (301) You rogue and thief and miscreant, how dare you show yourself before me? You are not good enough, you are not worthy to bow to me. My throne or my crown is after all worth more than all that you possess. Would you now set your son, in possession of a single castle, on a par with my daughter and an entire kingdom?" (302) He gave his head a good scouring without any soap. Indeed he was incensed. And his greatest complaint was that he [Yakomo] was in comparison with himself quite poor.

I do not wish to sing any more of that, for I take pity on him. Therefore, I will close my section here. And if you would like to hear more, then come again.

Here ends the fifth canto.

Canto Six

I beseech you, God, that you awaken my heart, so that I can compose this, the sixth canto.

(303) Cursed be money and property and whoever puts his faith in them. A man can rest neither day nor night because of them—often by the law, often by thievery, and often by the sale of flesh and blood—just to gain a great treasure. The Devil draws them as a match does fire, and as a great wind drives the fog. (304) If someone wishes to give his daughter a husband or give his sons wives, no one asks if he has any talent, or whether he is a scholar or scribe. But rather money is the only thing of interest. And if he were nothing but a donkey driver, a dwarf, a fool, a moron, a nothing—if he has money, he will be snapped up. (305) A lad, a maiden, go on and work it out, but be aware of one thing: his first question, his first desire is: "Does she have a lot of money; is he loaded with ducats." One asks no more about intelligence or wit, or honor or good character. Money conceals every kind of bad trait, even if he were an illegitimate son conceived in menstrual impurity. (306) Now look, if a poor fool is afflicted with a small defect in his own body or in his family, which he inherited from his forebears, everything, alas, weakens him, thereby ruining all his abilities. Neither praise nor anything good can undo it for him. If, on the other hand, a rich man has a defect four spans broad, there is nothing shameful about it, and the money is the main thing. (307) In this world an old man often has what a young man ought to have, and only because he has

money has he been able to subjugate a young maiden for himself. Thereafter he makes her cold by night, and in his arms she dies of hunger. Our sages forbade it long ago, for young with old can never prosper. (308) But that does not stop anyone—money makes one blind, and no one has any shame about it. No one considers how, like the wind, misfortune often takes one's money, and jewels and gold very quickly disappear, and then the gross beast remains there and can never recover from his loss. And then it is of no help—"I had" or "I was." (309) In general people's sights are still set on money and no one wants to think any further.

Thus did the good Dolfin, too. Pariz was destroyed by that. I left him [Dolfin] shouting at the old man; I imagine that he is shouting still. Because of the great sorrow, I would rather not write for you how he drove the poor man away. (310) Now he spoke many an irate word and said to him angrily: "Take care that neither you nor your son ever again come into my sight."

The poor fool went away quite rebuffed, as if he had been beaten on the head. He returned home in great distress and told his son the bad news. (311) Pariz was greatly alarmed by the report, and he soon let Viene know. She could find no rest or repose, since now she could not satisfy her desires. Now she wanted to sound out her father and went to him and greeted him. He was delighted to see her and said: "Listen to what happened to me today. (312) Did Pariz not send his father—I thought I had no more loyal servant—he spoke of a marriage match for the two of you. Just imagine how that enraged me. The answer that I then gave him will sour all the days of his life. Before I would marry you to the poor man, you would have to spend the rest of your life in my own household. (313) But it will not be long before I marry you to a rich man."

Viene now understood the tone and did not wish to reveal her interests. Having taken her leave, she rushed from the room and collapsed, murmuring: "Before I marry anyone else, I would hang myself: Judah and his [sacrificial] cock do not agree [about the sacrifice]." (314)[36] She quickly told everything to her nurse, and in addition said to her: "My father has now decided to marry me to a stranger. And he wants to kill Pariz. Now, pay attention to how stubborn I can be, and I will have him and no other, for he could indeed be king of Holland and Flanders. (315) Therefore, I will take unexpected action: I wish to enter into marriage with Pariz, so that my beloved is my husband, and I his wife. That is to be done, so that no man any longer anticipates obtaining me. My father will not maltreat me for that. When he sees and becomes aware of it, perhaps he will also have to let it take place." (316) "What are you saying?" said Isabele. "Do you wish thus to disgrace your father and, with your own hands, kill me, and yourself, and Pariz, too? Is your brain so weak that your desire has so blinded you? The thing is short, but it has long fringes. No, no; on principle I would not advise you to do it."

(317) When the noble maiden heard that, she said: "Is that your aid? Is that your comfort for my suffering? Alas, do you also wish to break with me? I will draw a dagger from its sheath and will stab myself because of my suffering. If I were to lie dead in your arms, then your commiseration would be of no help." (318) She said many such things, which would have calmed whoever was angry, and she promised her great rewards and that all her days would be prosperous. She persuaded her—for in truth ladies are all certainly fickle—so that she promised her and swore to her that she would aid her in all her desires. (319) And she said still more to her: "Do that and also what your mind tells you. I will always support you, even if I lose my life in doing so."

Now, Pariz was to go to that place one night, around four o'clock. They had chosen that time, because he no longer dared to do it by day. (320)[37] In the meantime, Pariz became aware of the fact that the king was dealing with him perfidiously and that his rage was still great and was becoming more deeply rooted by the day. Pariz thought: "By Goat, he may well one day bring me to a fall. My father was old when he cursed him so vigorously. It is vile to rant beneath the gallows." (321) He consulted every day with his distinguished comrade. In the end it was as he advised him: he ought to remain clear-headed for a while and stay out of his [the king's] way until his rage relented. Although his heart was inflamed, he wanted first to take leave of his beloved. (322) Thus he went there one night, as they had earlier arranged, and he said to her: "My strength, my might, I leave you against my will. I see that your father's rage seethes. For that reason, I must calm it thus. I am going away and leaving my heart with you; if only that you might sometimes remember me. (323) And I would like to ask you in addition that you occasionally write me a word. I do not plan to go far and hope not to have to stay away long." Viene said: "That is too hard. No, no, I do not wish thus to remain here. A radical change would have to come over me before I would wish to let you go away alone. (324) If you really want to go, then I will come along, even if you were to go to the ends of the earth. I ask you only for two favors, and let my request be granted this time: do not leave Isabele behind; you ought always to reward her loyalty. And you are to do nothing that would dishonor me until you have married me somewhere far away. (325) Indeed now I want you and me to take vows to each other in all things, and when we find some repose, let us have a joyous wedding. If you wish to do it, then prepare yourself. In such deeds one must keep a good watch. Thus saddle the horses and make the necessary arrangements. Then let us depart in peace."

(326) Pariz was delighted with her fine reply, although he recognized the great danger and said to her: "My heart, by beloved, how can I ever recompense your good will? That which you have now said—that will I do and will not be dissuaded by either toil or fear." And there they made their vows to each other, and he also promised her to fulfill her other request.

(327) He went and quickly found a servant whom he trusted with life and limb and gave him an entire purse full of money and promised him in addition a great reward. He said: "An enemy has come upon me here, whom I see hanging around. I trust that you will remain loyal to me, for which reason I tell you that I want to stab him to death. (328)[38] When I have given him his wounds, then I want to go away across the sea. Therefore go on ahead and be not lax, and let it cost what it will, and make arrangements at inns and order three or four horses at every stage, and hire a ship and have it ready and waiting, so that when I arrive there I can cross over."

(329) The loyal servant was named Gregol; as soon as he had heard his lord, he went as he had been ordered and took a winding path to the sea. He did it all and did it well. In eight days, he returned and gave a report of all his doings. Now Sir Pariz also began to get ready.

(330) He filled a leather bag with coins, and he prepared his horse and lance. For three whole days, or almost four, he consulted extensively with his comrade, and when it seemed to him that the time was near, then he let Isabele know that the two of them were to expect him that night—he would come through the garden to fetch them. (331) Thus did they wait all that night; they had everything well prepared when the time came. Isabele did not think well of it, but she could do nothing for it, since she had already made a commitment. They waited for a long time and in poor humor. They were beshitting themselves in their great fear. Now, worthy Pariz came at the appointed time with lance and sword and with the horses. (332)[39] He soon came to that place and with great effort and few words helped to let them down from a window; he did it all quite without difficulty. How quickly did he raise them both up and set them on their horses—I mean, of course, Isabele and his Viene. Then they began to gallop away without constraint. (333) His loyal servant was also ready, and a lad stood on the side. When he now came, he said to him that they were to ride ahead, and he with his ladies would ride a short distance behind them.

They rode through the night and yet another day during which they neither rested nor even dismounted. (334) The way was even more burdensome for them: when they had then covered a distance of no more than four miles, it began to rain, and it poured, and the weather became ever worse. It rained as hard as if one were pouring it from tubs. Indeed it did not stop at any time along the way, and often it also began to hail great hailstones. (335) Finally, when it was now quite late, they entered a small village. There was little wine or bread to be found there, except with a gluttonous but honorable priest. He saw them wet and coated with muck. He courteously took them in. They nibbled on whatever food they had and warmed themselves at the fire. (336) They ought to have gone to sleep; it was late. Pariz wanted to have the sleeping arrangements thus: Viene and Isabele in one bed, while he was with the priest in another. The book speaks of how he did that—anyone who believes it is a bastard; I cannot imagine that I would be able to do it, and if he did so, then may he live to regret it.

(337) He slept poorly all night long, and the accursed rain never ceased. In the morning, before the sun had properly risen, the noble warrior was soon up and swiftly mounted one and all. He was determined to go on farther from there. He gave great payment and thanks to the good curate, and they rode until they came to a stream. (338) The water was perhaps not very deep; to get to the other side one had to cross a bridge. But the rain had so flooded that it had washed it away in pieces. Pariz was alarmed when he saw and understood that he could not pass this way. The servant said: "What harm can come of it: I will step into it and see if one can wade across." (339) He gave rein to his horse and spurred forward as it seemed best to him. When he got to the middle, they sank because of the great depth, and the current took control of them, so that he and his horse drowned. I have no power either to say or to write how Pariz lamented for him. (340) Then they no longer knew what to do. They turned back to the priest. Pariz asked him cordially and nicely to buy them wood and nails and find him people to hire for whatever payment they desired for their labor; and they were to rebuild the bridge and spare no expense in the matter.

(341) I will leave them there with their purchase to chop and cut and saw and drill, and will also tell of Dolfin who had now lost Viene. He had her sought through all Vienne; she was nowhere to be found. Now the king realized without any doubt that she had run off and disappeared. (342) In a foul mood and with a sorrowful will he summoned his knights and his heroes and said: "Be quick and quiet and tell no one of this business: ride off and seek in cities, villages, meadows, and forests until you pick up the trail of my daughter. Catch her and bring her here to me. (343) And if anyone opposes you in order to protect her from adversity, strike as if it were the Devil and kill every last one of them." He gave them the orders in a towering rage that turned his face quite red. The knights quickly hurried away: their horses flew as arrows

from a bow. (344) They flew boldly across the earth, and when they were far from the city, the people divided up and rode in all directions and on all sides.

One knight indeed came riding right away to that same village and immediately found the priest with a peasant who was also supposed to come and help build the bridge. (345)[40] The knight soon shouted at the priest: "The king commands you: tell me, have you seen here—or have they ridden through—two ladies and accompanying them a man or two or three? Thus and so are the distinguishing marks; thus and so are their forms, and thus and so their faces. (346) If you can find them at a single stroke, then out with it and do not delay, for to what purpose: before two hours pass, fifty others will give me the information. We are searching for them high and low; we want to capture them all. And if you know their whereabouts and conceal it, you will be hanged by your still warm neck." (347) The priest listened in grim horror. He turned pale from great fear. That it was the ones whom he had in his house—*that* he recognized from the distinguishing marks. He said: "My lord, I will come out with it quickly. I do not wish to betray either you or myself. I will investigate far and wide. Wait here. I will bring you an answer."

(348) And he immediately set out by a winding path until he came to Pariz. He said to him: "Most honorable my lord, I have been quite robbed of my wits." He told him the whole tale that he had heard from the knight: the distinguishing marks, the mission, and the mode, and how he had threatened his life. (349) "I have thus far said nothing about you. I have taken good care of your friendship. He is awaiting an answer on the village green. I dare not scoff at the crown. Therefore, my lord, depart from here, so that I not fall into great danger." Pariz thanked him in his great terror and asked him to wait a while to one side.

(350) And he went quickly to Viene with tears in his eyes, and with a face as pale as ashes he told her all that had happened, and with a sigh and a sob, he thus began to lament: "Alas, my aid and my counsel are all in vain. Cursed be the day that I was born. (351) O God, why must misfortune take aim at me alone? The flood had to wash out the bridge, so that I not escape harm. Alas, I could overcome all my pain, if my blood were not spilled so that you had to return home and suffer pain and do so because of me. (352) Alas, if I had never seen you, you would never have given me your favor. Woe is me that ever I felt the prick, so that now I am in this situation. Alas, alas, unhappy man, for your pain and fear, Pariz. Now all the world will rightly say that you have brought about the death of that noble person. (353) O God, grant me the grace, grant me the consolation, grant me the joy: load onto me the pain, torture and affliction that my Viene is supposed to suffer. And grant me death right now.

How willingly would I now depart this life, if I knew that things would go well for you, beloved, and that you then would have a long and happy life. (354) Since we are so cursed that we cannot indeed change things, it seems to me the best escape to kill ourselves with our own hands and to die here in honor and decency, so that no other person can dishonor us. And as we wished to unite our bodies, thus would our souls be together."

(355) Look how a captain laments when the enemy defeats his people; look how milk now coagulates when it curdles and yields up its whey; look at the red and shining sun when a thick cloud moves before it—thus also did Viene's form change: that could not have been turned any better on a lathe. (356) From white and ruddy it turned to greenish-yellow as she listened to Pariz, and she fainted right away, so that she could not speak, like a mute. He held vinegar under her nose until she recovered. The first word that came out of her mouth was "Pariz, Pariz," and she began to wail. (357) And she said: "O God in the high Heavens, why have you cursed me thus? Misfortune has accompanied me from childhood; it has never let me taste anything good. Even today it pursues and seeks me in every corner. Now that I was thinking to forget all my sorrows, you have again set them all on me. (358) Alas, alas, the joy so small, alas, how quickly has it disappeared. I thought to myself, it ought to go well for me for a while—then sorrow again found me. Now I must again go home alone and die each day with a healthy body. O God, I maintain that two pure hearts do not deserve such great sorrow and pain.

(359) "Therefore, my Pariz, what do you wish to do? Let us not kill ourselves. Depart from me here secretly, and just let your life continue. And I will now go back to my father. I think that he will not hang me for this. He will spare his own flesh and blood and care for his own honor and will also prefer to keep it all hidden. (360) I will let in the messengers who set out in my pursuit. If they find me here alone, then they will ask no more questions. My 'no' will count more than their 'yes.' They must have indeed been lying. I will affirm it there and will say that I was out for the sake of my own entertainment—riding and hunting."

(361) "No," said Pariz, "that would be too hard. I wish to depart from this life." And he quickly reached for his sword with his hand and drew it naked from its sheath. He turned it toward his belly. But Viene, the noble maiden, interrupted him quickly and quite adroitly and said: "Give me the sword. (362) If you slay yourself so lightly, then you lose your life and additionally your soul. Since you wish to lose your life, conduct yourself so that your soul is not lost, and give me your sharp blade, and let me here be the one to give you death." She spoke thus to him and persuaded him until she was able to coax the sword

out of his hand. (363) And she turned it to her own breast and said to him: "You must go away. Promise me now and do it. Otherwise I will thrust the sword into myself here. If you are not captured, then I will still conceal it all. I hope that God will bring it about and in time he will grant us sufficient joy."

(364) Pariz said: "If you so wish it, then I cannot prevent it." Then did they begin to weep and clap their hands together. "Alas, I did not think that our joy and delight would end so soon." Thus did each say to the other, and they lamented it to God in Heaven. (365) Viene at once took a small ring that she always had hanging from her neck and which was set with a diamond. She gave it to her Pariz and asked that he wear it on his hand so that he should always think of his vow. He was to let her know, she again requested, where he went and where he stayed.

(366) The great lamentation that took place there—in truth I cannot describe it all. They would have done more, too, if the priest had only left them alone. The priest realized what had to be done. He poked and prodded—he should have long since responded [to the knight]—so that they not be caught: that was his fear. (367) Whoever were to hear the two lovers there—who had become as one flesh—whoever were to see their lamentation and sorrow and their faces so pale; whoever were now to see their parting, their speech, their gestures, their loss of strength—whoever were to see it and not weep would have a body and heart of stone. (368)[41] The final words, the last gesture—they were holding each other tightly and kissing, so closely and so long, and so tenderly and so sweetly, that they fell right down onto a bench. They could no longer stand on their feet. Their hearts and minds were so full that they could not speak a single word.

(369) Thus mutely did Pariz, the worthy and noble warrior, mount his horse. He galloped to the stream, that youthful and worthy one. He could take no other path. And since one who has set his life on the line is accustomed to sorrows, thus was Pariz not terrified and wished to swim across the water with his horse. (370) The flood had perhaps abated somewhat, or his horse was not overloaded, or God simply thus wished it that the water do him no harm. Indeed he had more luck than rightful claim that he wade across on horseback. He went across and proceeded at a canter until he came to the sea, as he had wished.

(371) He found the ship right there that the servant had earlier hired for him. He went aboard; they shoved off, and he went his way with no problems. Then he again came to a sandy shore, and he made haste with his horse until he reached a city that, according to its distinguishing features, was called Genoa, (372) and he came to a good innkeeper and arranged for a room for

himself. Then he went into the square in his finery; his worthiness shone clearly. Many knights saw him and joined him, because he was noble and even more so because he was, alas, a foreigner and an exile. (373) He was treated with great honor. He was no longer allowed to eat in the inn.

I will write no more of him. I have sat at this canto until I have almost grown stiff; I have sung long and much, and I forgot to stop. Now that I have remembered it, I will stop so that I not go on too long.

Canto Seven

I ask my God, whom I love steadfastly to give me aid with this, the seventh canto.

(374) Many people there are who open their mouths and are always quite garrulous and often babble lies about our brothers in Venice: they say how they are in general untrustworthy and ungracious; they do not like to see any foreigner. Now pay attention to how they grant him neither goods nor aid. (375) If a foreign guest comes into the city, then they immediately act as if he stinks. He will have to fast for a long time before they give him anything to drink. If they were to nod to him, it would seem a great burden to them; it would be too great a hardship for their mouths, if they were to welcome him with a "Peace be with you." (376) That no one speaks a word to him, that no one even notices him—he will probably have to go around for a long time in the ghetto before he finds company there—unless there were someone who did it so that he could get something from him or wanted to prickle him with jests. Then there would be a crowd around him like cocks around the hens. (377) They often think that they have a fool before them and thereby disgrace themselves, and often someone in a sinister cloak who would terrorize them out of Venice. If they make no more than snap and clap, they think that they have won the prizes and are lords of Venice with its buildings, while we are their servants and peasants. (378) Perhaps we are peasants and even cattle, so that if one of them pays us any attention, then we hang on them both early and late; we cannot show them enough honor; no amount of money or effort is too much for us: and it is all for nothing, freely and in truth. As soon as they leave us, it has all disappeared, or they simply suppose that we are obligated. (379) Of such notions I know a great deal more. I do not want to take them all for myself; I want to leave them inside my quill. I fear they would hate me because of it, although I have defended them in every city, square, and street and sharply reprimanded such gossips and said: "If it were thus, then it would be their mode." (380) The mode, however, is not good; let no one oppose me

in that statement. We are all of flesh and blood, and God preserves us all. It is not thus done in Mantua and Ferrara, nor in Udine, Padua, or Verona. Still less has it been attested in Genoa, where now our Pariz had arrived.

(381) He was in truth greatly honored, and he had never before been there. I know that I told you earlier how they treated him. Now he never lost his love; he could not be healed of this disease. He found no amusement in any delights; the fire was still blazing in his heart.

(382) That word has just reminded me where I earlier left Viene. Therefore, I will leave Pariz here and will also write of her for a while. Viene returned with the messenger, as did Isabele, her chamber-maid. She rode in with the servant and the girl as if she had been somewhere for the sake of amusement. (383)[42] She took the priest with her there: he was wanted as a witness. The king asked him what had happened. He was to recount it all to him in detail. He told him the entire tale and swore to him on his soul how they had not besmirched their honor, as if they had been brother and sister. (384) The king said: "Now, tell me—otherwise I will hang you on a high tree—tell me quickly: where is the man who entered your house with them?" The priest swore by St. John: "He fled through a deep stream. I think it almost certain, as it seems to me, that he drowned in it, just as did the squire." (385) He let the priest depart in peace and requested of him that he make note of it: and if anyone in Vienne were to ask him, he was to attest to the chastity and honor [of Viene]. Now, the king had indeed not yet spoken a word with Viene. Indeed he had arranged with his wife for her to speak with Isabele beforehand.

(386)[43] It took place on a Sunday that the queen summoned her and intimidated her so severely that she was afraid even to look at her. But Isabele also defended herself and covered herself as best she could. In the end she told her the whole tale, and she was thorough from beginning to end, (387) and she swore up and down that Viene had retained her honor and was as completely a pure virgin as when she had come out of her belly. The consolation was not small, when the king heard that. He saw that the story corroborated the one that he had heard from the priest. (388) Then the king himself went one day with a full heart to Viene. He gave her head a good scouring without any soap, so that she might acknowledge her error. He said to her: "Indeed do I tell you—by rights I should have you burned, if not that it would be too much of an aggravation for me to spill my own blood. (389) I must have a raw heart, just as you have one of stone. You have caused me such dishonor as I would not have expected from you. Is this the child who was so devoted to me and was weeping every day before God? If only I had never loved and yearned for you, since you so dishonor and disgrace me."

(390) Viene answered quite simply with a bitter heart and sweet words. She saw that he was quite right. She therefore fell quickly at his feet and said: "Burn, and hang, and slaughter! I have sinned; make me atone for it! And that which you wish to do to me, do it quickly! Then my torture will therewith have an end." (391) The king immediately went away and in the same rage he put the father of Pariz—that distinguished one—in prison, and all his property and noble clothing were also to be taken from him. He was shut away in prison, and he had to pay the piper for Pariz, (392)[44] although he did not suffer great hardship: dear Odoardo was caring for him. He left him alone neither early nor late. He spared no expense for him, and otherwise he inquired every day whether he might find out anything about Pariz. His father was more sorrowful and fearful for him than for the fact that he himself was suffering hard imprisonment.

(393) The matter of that poor soul caused Viene pain for her father [-in-law] and was ever in her mind. In time she wanted to liberate him. Pariz was even more in her heart; she had often asked Odoardo to inquire after him to the extent that was proper and quickly let her know any news. (394) Thus passed many days, and meanwhile the crashing of the waves faded away. The king was also asking his wife how he ought to bring the matter to a conclusion. Thus they both came to a decision that they wanted to stop the mouths of the wicked gossips and did not want to execute Viene but to find her another husband. (395) They did not, however, know that she had betrothed herself to Pariz. They thought that she would do it willingly and would praise God at all times.

Thus did it stand at present, and then they began to hold the grandest balls imaginable, in order that no one might believe in Viene's transgressions. (396) At first Viene was always at the dance and entered with radiant splendor in gowns of pure gold with fine gems and noble pearls. In one hand she held the train of her gown, and in the other she had indeed a fine plume of feathers which the noble maiden held under her nose. (397) She went indeed every day and night to all the balls and all the entertainments. But it gave her no pleasure. Although she showed her free will, she went and did it with difficulty because she wanted to mollify her father. She could accomplish that quite well with words and with swaying back and forth, so that he gave no more thought to her guilt.

(398) One day she found him in a good mood. It seemed to her the proper time to set the old man free who had been put in prison without having done any wrong. She knew how to do it so effectively, that fine maiden, and she harangued her father so much that he did in fact set him free, as she wished,

and returned all his property to him. (399)[45] In order that she better gain the good will of her father and mother, Viene now often went to see the bishop. They had heard nothing of him [concerning his mediation between Pariz and Viene]. Thus did she make them think that she was quite pious and honorable. Indeed she was honorable and did this for the sake of honor, but Pariz never left her mind. (400) He never left her mind, neither by day nor by night, neither early nor late. She saw him all night in her dreams. Often she was happy, and often she was lifeless. In the morning she told her nurse. She always had to advise her about whether it meant something good or, on the other hand, suffering. She always had to interpret her dream.

(401) I do not want to write about dreams for you, for I do not put much stock in them. If the Devil himself appeared to me with all his infernal demons and brought before me I know not whom, I would have no fear of that. I think: that which is by day no more than a buzz is a bellow in one's head by night. (402) Often the vapors rise to the head when one has too much in the stomach. I think that vexation does the same thing; otherwise dreams are not good for anything.

Therefore I will leave them and go to Genoa, and will tell you of Pariz who has been there for a long time and has been greatly honored in word and deed. (403) It all meant nothing to him, the noble lord: he could neither sleep nor eat with any pleasure. Everything there seemed too difficult for him. He no longer wished to remain there. He wanted to go far away, so that he could quite forget both her and the country. Even so, Viene still held him prisoner there: he first wanted to know what had happened to her. (404) Beforehand he also wanted to let his father and his comrade know what had happened to him in all details, and what his plans were for the future. He wrote two letters at once and summoned an envoy, whom he paid well and instructed to give the letters to Odoardo. (405) He took the letters and rode away without interruption, quickly and swiftly. In ten days he came to Vienne and took the letters to Odoardo. Have you never experienced it? Did it never happen to you that suddenly something delightful happened to you? Thus was Odoardo also shocked by delight when the envoy revealed the letters to him. (406) Odoardo took the letters from him and took to his heels and ran to take Pariz's father's letter to him. It so touched the old man's heart that he began to weep for joy, for both of them were delighted and each began to read his letter.

(407) I do not want to say, word-for-word, what was in the fine letters; only the meaning will I write: I am too tired to chatter so much. The letter to his father made his eyes wet. Thus did he express his unhappiness to him, and thus did he make his miserable lament to him, (408) and [tell him] how he had

decided still more—he wanted to go so far away that no one would know where he was. For many years and for a long period of time he wanted to cross the length and breadth of the seas; he wanted to ride through the land on horseback. Therefore, he ought indeed no longer to think of him, until God grant him aid. (409) He also wrote: "Father, I am going away. I may well die on the journey. Therefore, I would like to implore you now to let Odoardo have all that is mine; he is ever to be your proper son, and after your death, he is to be your heir. He has likewise ever been my dear brother." He also wrote him a great deal more.

(410) In the letter that Odoardo received, it was said how things had gone for him, and how he had come to the city, and how his fortunes had progressed miserably. The point was that he asked him to write him a letter and send it with the envoy how his Viene had been treated after he left her and began his travels. (411) In addition he was also to say to her that she was not to increase her torture and now ought to do with respect to this matter what would be good for her and useful for her honor, because he recognized that unfortunately nothing good could come of him. "Her sorrow is my death; her joy my life. Therefore, tell her to do what suits her. (412) If she still wants to remain true or if the matter were still secret, then treat her the best in all respects. I commend her to you, brother. Do not consider the fact that I am now away from my home and cannot now see, for if I remain in this world, I will reward you for it with love." (413) Indeed he wrote to him even about the matter that he had written to the old man, how he was to be his son in his place in every way and in proper legal form. He also requested of him that it would please him if he thought of him as a father. In this letter he also wrote about his travels, as you earlier heard in the other letter.

(414) When they had read the letters, the old man turned to Odoardo. He said: "His traveling makes me sad. With all my might I would like to prevent it. That which he said to me earlier, I wish to do with all my heart: I take you as a very distinguished son, for I have always been like a father to you. (415) Therefore, write to Pariz to this effect, as we all request and advise him, that he not make the journey and take to the road; and take these five hundred ducats and send them to him without delay along with a letter by this envoy, so that he can remain there and live without cares until the situation at some point improves." (416) Odoardo said: "I will do it all, and will write to him with the request, and I will otherwise also be your son, so that you always have authority over me. Pariz is now to be the legitimate one; you ought not to bypass him. I hope to God that He will still arrange it, so that we will all still enjoy our company in peace." (417) Odoardo thus went away, now that they had taken counsel, and

went quickly to Viene. She had now asked him so often that if he were to learn anything of Pariz, he was not to delay in telling her. Thus did he go to her at two o'clock in the morning and read his letter to her. (418) Now when Viene had understood the letter, she could hardly give him an answer. She was stunned by great joy that her Pariz was still alive, and it indeed wounded her deeply that he wished to drift ever farther away. She said: "Dear Odoardo, my distinguished friend: go quickly, for God's sake, and write back to him (419) and greet him heartily, my dear beloved, and implore him for my sake to stay in Genoa even longer and give up the journey for the moment. I still dearly wish to be his wife, even at the risk of my life. And now we are already bitterly atoning so that the conclusion will be with joy sweet as honey."

(420) So he went and wrote to Pariz, as Viene has requested of him, her words and gestures were all quite precise, and so also were those of his father. And moreover, he indicated in the letter what they had done and were doing, and Viene had been held to be quite blameworthy, but was now again in her father's good favor, (421) and how his father had been imprisoned and how the king had wanted to torment him, and Viene had persisted so long that she liberated him. He wrote him quite a long letter, four whole pages—a full quire-sheet, everything clearly described that had happened there since he last saw Viene. (422) He put the letter in the hand of the envoy and also the money in a purse. He took it and immediately galloped away, quickly, nimbly and swiftly. The hearts that were inflamed in all of them were now somewhat calmed since they had learned through those letters that Pariz was alive and where he was.

(423) Pariz now eagerly awaited that a reply be sent to him. The envoy rode and galloped and flew until he quickly arrived in Genoa. He drew forth the letters and the money and gave it all over into Pariz's hands. He opened them with some anxiety and read them, and when he had finished reading through them, he was pleased. (424) That consummately noble and good lad had great joy and delight in the fact that his Viene was healthy, and his mother and father, too. He immediately put on new clothes, and his mood improved in all ways. He was often full of hope and often despairing, as is common among those who have such a burden to bear. (425) This was always his mode of living, and thus did he pass his time. He also wanted to comply with their wish and stay there a while longer. And whatever happened in Vienne, they wrote to each other. Thus did he pass an entire season waiting to see if a remedy could be found for the situation.

(426) At this time, during these days that these things took place, Dolfin was not lax, and he was making plans for Viene. By means of his father-in-law he found a way; he [the father-in-law] provided him a marriage match with the

son of the Duke of Burgundy—at the time he was the best match to be found. (427) For a while it hung in the balance between him and that other one from England, but it seemed even to the king of France that this one was of higher honor. It was then fully arranged through him. His [Dolfin's] father-in-law was also pleased that he would take this one and not the other one, for I say, he was the prince of Flanders.[46]

(428) This book in the Italian language is quite long in all respects. I do not want just to copy it any longer; now I will omit many superfluous words; otherwise my little book would become too long, and I would not have enough time. Thus whoever has already read it in Italian should not think that I wish to misrepresent it.

(429) Now that it was concluded, the king had great joy from this marriage match, which I described for you. He would have liked to see his son-in-law. By means of an envoy he invited him along with some ten counts and dukes and beseeched him to come and pay him service and make an excursion to visit him for a while. (430) The noble youth was quite delighted, just as I, too, would have been glad. He had of course already heard of her, that she was beautiful and courtly in many ways. And when the fire once tastes the straw—you know well the course of events: how quickly did the bridegroom prepare himself with a hundred knights who all rode with him. (431) They rode there with great joy, as is, after all, the custom of such people. When they were two days' journey from Vienne, they sent an envoy to the king. When the good Dolfin heard that, he summoned his lords and servants that they arise and prepare abundant food and drink so that they might honor all the people. (432) Up to that day, no one knew anything about it; now the die was cast, and when Viene heard it, she locked herself in her chamber and sat there in a corner. She shed many a tear. Now her father and mother came to her with very great joy and cooing. (433) The king and queen were kissing her for joy, and they let her know everything that was happening and that was still to come. Indeed they wanted to talk her into it with fine talk and sweet words. They said: "You may consider yourself fortunate that you have come to such honor and courtliness. (434) Many friends have helped you to this end, although some wanted to obstruct it. Now you will be quite wealthy, and you will be resplendent in jewels and gold. You will attain such peace, which will be for the well-being of you and your children. In three or four days, he will be here. Therefore, go and prepare and adorn yourself!"

(435) When they had then spoken a great deal, Viene wanted to drop dead from her grief. She saw the preparations that were being made and knew that

nothing could come of it. She said: "Mamà and my dear papà, I would like to accede to you, but I do not want to marry now, even if all the kings and emperors were to come here. (436) Neither do I scorn this good man nor refuse to be the daughter-in-law of such a duke. I do not want him or any other. No man is going to bring me around, even if he were wealthy and high-born—even higher than the tower in Cremona." These words grieved the king, but he thought that she did it out of modesty. (437) He left his wife alone with her, so that she would not disgrace herself in the matter. She implored her with a great deal of weeping and made great speeches to her. Viene said constantly: "No, no, no!" Nothing else came out of her mouth. When the king heard that, it enraged him. He lamented that he had ever been born.

(438) Now, separately, the king took the nurse to task as if she were a toad, and said: "Come here, you accursed whore. You have deceitfully robbed me of my daughter." Isabele trembled and swore—from her great terror she was as if dead—she swore and wanted to conceal it. The king said: "I want none of your rumbling. (439) Tell me now on the spot what this behavior means and what you did with Pariz and what that great business there was all about. If you do not tell me everything directly, you will not survive the torture. I will rip your guts out." For terror Isabele began to chatter (440) and told him the whole story, just as it had begun and how it had ended, and how she had promised herself to him. When the king learned of that, then he began to rant and rage, and swore that he would drown her before he would do that or even consider it. (441)[47] And he returned to Viene and rebuked her fiercely in his rage. He said: "Either you have been dishonored or you have lost your mind. Alas, if only I could boast that you had never been born to me! Cursed be the day and the hour that I found you here in the castle. (442) I also would like to give Pariz his earnings—if he ever comes within my grasp! By means of friendly connections—and dukes and counts from all the lands—did I arrange for the marriage match. I hoped to have new relations and honor. Now I will have hostility and disgrace! And you are doing all this to me with your own hands. If you will only say 'yes,' you can turn it all around."

(443) Viene now saw that she could neither deny it nor refuse to speak. Therefore, she began and spoke as follows: "I will not now debase my loyalty. It is true that I promised him 'yes' and will never abandon him."

I will indeed yet complete this speech, but I do not wish to make this canto any longer.

Thus ends the seventh canto. May God let us enjoy the merit of our ancestors.

Canto Eight

Now I ask God, who is just, that he aid me in this, the eighth canto.

(444) How often does it happen in the world that one promises "eternally and forever," and when it comes down to it, the vow falls to pieces. Look, then, how miserable he is and how he is so distressed by this that he wants to cudgel the young man with words, as if his back were against the wall. (445) Loyalty is certainly worthy of honor to rich and poor, young and old. Here's to the one who is ever honest and whose speech is straight and has no convolutions! If someone promises another something in a forest, he ought to fulfill it, just the same as if it had been done in the presence of a hundred witnesses: that which one has once promised should not be repudiated.

(446) Viene demonstrated a fidelity to Pariz such as has never been seen. You know her father's violent mood, and she may suffer great pain because of it, and the new husband, whom she is supposed to marry, was ten times as wealthy as Pariz, and no one was there when she made her vow, and Pariz, moreover, had also given her his permission [to repudiate the vow]. (447) Nonetheless, she did not for that reason wish to do so, as I previously told you. She told him quite clearly how she had made a vow to Pariz. Therefore, she said: "My beloved father, you can spare yourself the speech. You would not be able to force me to do this, even if you were to kill me right here and now. (448) You might well say that my fortune has gone awry, which even a blind man could see. But when you say that I have been dishonored—such a thing will never be. Kill me now and slaughter me, strike me in the head and flay me. And if you are indeed going to do it, then do it quickly, so that this fire in me will be extinguished!"

(449) The king's rage was immediately ignited, for great pain and great terror. He saw before him the shame and disgrace and knew not how he might conceal it. And while he was standing there in this state, there was heard from all sides cheers, shouts and cries of great joy: "He is coming—the king's son-in-law is coming!" (450) At this rejoicing the old man grew alarmed: a mountain lay on his heart, but he sallied forth properly with his troops and took with him many warriors and servants. He welcomed his son-in-law in bad form, for one cannot hide a broken heart, although he soon found a pretext: he said: "I do not feel well. (451) My ailment is not a matter of my ill-health: I am only concerned for your bride. It has been three or four days that she has been in bed. I have not been lax with doctors, although they all tell me that it is only a chill and with absolute certainly she will quickly recover." (452) Now he showed them honor in all things, with food and drink—a fine cuisine: "So

eat and drink and dance and leap!" That carried on thus for two whole weeks. Meanwhile, they persisted with Viene and tried everything to see if they could still arbitrate this marriage. Now nothing could be attained with her.

(453) When the king then realized that he could no longer become his son-in-law, what more should I tell you about it—did his heart not break from grief! Now he did not know what he ought to do in order to have him depart willingly. He nonetheless pondered it for a long time and gave him many opulent gifts. (454) And he said: "Viene's illness is serious—and for your sake, my esteemed son. She was indeed ill when you arrived, and her condition has worsened appreciably since that time. Therefore, since it has become tedious for you, you might as well go back home, and give my very best regards to your father. When she recovers, I will let you know." (455) The poor fool thought it was all true and did not wish to burden her with grief. There was a great to-do in his leave-taking; then he went home, although not altogether happily. He gave his father a very precise report about how they had been treated with such great honor and that Viene had unfortunately been ill, and that he was to return when she had recovered.

(456) Now that the bridegroom had departed, then the king began to rant about his daughter and the nurse more than ever. "Now, make amends, accursed whores!" he said. In a rage and a passion he had them thrown into a tower that was both high and extended deep into the earth. The worthy ladies had no light. (457) Their bed was a bit of straw. Bread and water was their food and drink. Even someone made of iron could not have held out there. The king it was who did this, in order that he therewith demonstrate their guilt: just as one closes the barn door after the horse has bolted. (458) He thought that she still ought to acquiesce and redeem herself through torture. Now it was all indeed lost, since he had already had her crushed. She had nothing but suffering; she had nothing but pain. That Isabele had to suffer this wickedness! She certainly did not take care of her own condition. Thus did another entire month pass.

(459) The bridegroom who had earlier gone home had now waited many a day. In truth he had received no letter. He decided to go back to Vienne, for one hair of the beloved—understand me well—draws more strongly than do three or four ox-wagons. Now, he took one day to arrange everything and then came riding with perhaps twelve comrades. (460) There he came to a familiar place, as if he were coming to his own family. He was cordially welcomed, although the hearts wished to burst. They showed themselves to be completely loyal, hoping that it would not appear otherwise. Now, he was still aggrieved with respect to Viene and dared not ask about her for shame.

(461) Only he constantly went around in the house and looked through all windows and doors, just as a cat looks for a mouse; thus did he also search for her. The king saw that it was all over and that he could no longer give him the runaround. Therefore, he led him into one of the small chambers and began miserably to tell him the tale. (462) He told him the whole story with his eyes full of tears: how he got involved in the matter, that he had intended to become his father-in-law, and how that chance had now been ruined—since he could now not get any closer to accomplishing it, how all his joy had now been undone when he asked his exasperating daughter about it, (463) and how she had quickly said "no," that she wanted neither to marry nor to have a husband, and concerning that matter she was harder than a stone, and for that reason he ought to believe it. He had therefore had her put deep underground, beneath a tower, and made her suffer much affliction and torture, expecting that she would renounce her idea. (464) "Therefore, know, my dear son," said he, "that it is not my fault that it has failed. And God on his heavenly throne knows how my heart has trembled to tell you what I have just said. I might have long since done so, but I had hope and trust that I could make her rue her stoniness. (465) Therefore, dear son, return home! I do not wish to delay you any longer. I ask you then to be my intercessor with your elderly father. And thus I also now ask you to let God have charge of all things. If I may do anything else, then I am at your command." In addition he chatted with him about many other things.

(466) When the noble youth heard that, he was at once stupefied by the great horror, and right then it broke his heart and lungs, which, after all, does not surprise me. But he began to speak with honeyed-tongue: "I know indeed what is special therein: that which is fitting for the marriage of men and women comes down from Heaven—that is where the Author is. (467) And if it is also fated by God, then no human can change it. It has greatly afflicted me, and God has thus ordained it. Thus your words were quite valuable for me; your justification is now at an end. You have not therewith disgraced me, for that which God wills, I will accept. (468) I ask you but one favor, no more do I desire from you: that you let me see Viene and speak with her in modesty and with honor." The king wished him well and said, he would be glad to do that, and quickly it was announced to Isabele that she was to persuade Viene to let herself be seen.

(469) Now, many fine clothes and adornments were sent to her in prison, and in addition a cloak of heavy brown silk, so that he might see her there as at court. She was also sent hens and capons so that she might reinvigorate herself therewith. All those things were taken into the tower. How quickly did Isabele

go to her. (470) She said: "You have now fasted for a long time; now it is going to become quite severe. Therefore speak and free yourself from the burden! Why do you want to kill yourself?" Viene mocked her words and said: "He should stop clinging to me. Now, I do wish to hear what he wants to say, but I want a period of three days beforehand. (471) And so that everything remains honorable, I want the bishop to come along." Viene now said those words, and when Isabele had heard them, they were also conveyed to the bridegroom. It seemed roses and flowers to him: that he would see her and be able to speak with her seemed to him as if he had immediately entered Paradise.

(472)[48] That it was a union bound by iron chains, you may recognize in this prank: what do you think that the good woman did with the rooster and the hen? She split them on a board—the good Viene—and tied them tightly under her armpits on her naked body and left them there for the three days. (473) And when the time had now come, both of the good young men came. The bridegroom stood there on the side; she called the bishop by his name. The young man thought that they were talking there about holy things. And he liked her very much in his heart. It was also that he saw her by candlelight. (474) And indeed he turned to her and said to her: "Noble maiden, you know that your father desires that I be his legal son-in-law. Why are you so set against me. Why must I cause you so much grief? And if I have indeed done anything that has offended you, I beg your pardon and kneel down here. (475) Dear lady, noble beloved, confirm to me your father's and mother's will and also grant me your mercy and say 'yes,' and do it willingly! If I am not already worthy of you, I promise you now and will swear to you, I will be your servant and will perform service for you, only so that you no longer remain in here."

(476) Viene answered briefly and quickly. She said: "Noble lord and warrior, if my father has made you a promise, he did so without asking me about it. I would rather suffer a thousand deaths and ever be tortured before I would now commit a great sin; and if you indeed wish to hear it, I will tell it to you: (477) I have already long had a lawful husband—and how and when I do not wish to say. I cannot take another. Therefore you ought to temper your speech. Furthermore I do not wish on you the disease that I have on my body. Were you to see me, you would be shocked, and if you came close to me, you would smell it. (478) I say that my body is, alas, diseased. I do not wish to deceive you in any way. I know that I will not live long, I am quite decayed; that is the sign."

When they now smelled the stench, they turned pale with fear. And they both thought it was true; they began to weep in compassion. (479) Both of them now indeed thought that she had holes and wounds in her body: it was the stench of that hen that she had tied to her body. Thus did they both run from there. They went immediately to the king and told him the whole story and what they had seen with their own eyes. (480) Thus the young man took his leave. He rode home quite quickly, and the whole land soon resounded with the reason for the bridegroom's return. To whomever he did not say it with his own lips, he had it reported by messenger. He filled every nook and cranny with news of [Viene's] illness, so that he could cover therewith his own shame. (481) Although her father, Dolfin, did not want to believe the scurrility, he swore: "As long as the city of Vienne stands, she will remain buried beneath the tower! There it is that she will have to go around; there it is that she will have to experience a change; there it is that she will rot and fall to pieces—or take a husband who pleases me."

(482) I will leave her there in rage and venom, and let us sing of Pariz. He had received a long letter from Odoardo, his dear comrade. There everything was reported that had happened to his Viene and Isabele, and what had happened with that bridegroom. He spared him none of the incidents, (483) nor how, alas, Viene lay sorely imprisoned in a tower and how she suffered horribly day and night, and she was hard-pressed by many things, and how she did not have either a pick or a saw, nor a drill, nor a file, much less tongs, with which she could break out of the tower, for her father held her cruelly in order to take his vengeance on her. (484) When good Pariz heard that, see how his heart was beating! No breath did he exhale from his mouth. His speech was quite choked off, and his appearance was a very clear sign: very pale and damp with cold sweat, it caused him pain and was consuming him in flames. Every child can understand that! (485) It pierced him deeply, and he began to lament fiercely; his lamentation lasted a full hour. I cannot tell it to you now. He was then in deep despair; he was despondent in all respects. He had never been more anxious in all his life. He said: "It makes no sense to stay here any longer."

(486) So he found a large ship which he soon caused to depart from the port. And he summoned his servant to go with him. With a favorable wind, they sailed briskly. Now he nonetheless wrote a letter beforehand that he indeed left behind and gave to his friend in Genoa so that he might send it to his comrade, Odoardo. (487) Therein was a report of his journey and how he had just departed and that he was not waiting for any further letter, nor should he [Odoardo] expect another letter either. He also implored his dear brother that he spare no pains, if he might in time be of aid to his Viene and Isabele.

(488)[49] Thus did Pariz go swiftly on his way; he had paid the captain well. He sailed away from there as if he were blind; he took no care concerning the weather, although they had a favorable wind and soon came to Valona [Albania]. Then he went further to Adrianople [Edirne] and to the capital, Constantinople. (489) He lingered in Turkey, as do the souls that are lost there. He did that for some three years until he knew the language of the Moors, and he also knew the Turkish language fluently, as if he had been born in that country. Although he had been in the land for a long time, he had nonetheless never forgotten Viene. (490) He could never leave her behind—in his heart she was ever present. Now he had not traveled far enough: he wanted to ride to Egypt; so he prepared himself for the journey to the extent necessary and in good time and then went there with his servant and other honorable people and trade goods.

(491) I will let him go on his way there quickly; I have said enough of him. I wish now to sing of new events, and certainly it is true and no lie. When God is to bring something about, then he can accomplish it in fine manner. Now listen to me a while concerning these strange things and what occurred there, when something was supposed to happen.

(492) Long since had begun in those times and years a great war with the Suldan. He was constantly at war with the Christians. The man was a strong king and very powerful in all respects and ruled the cities and all the lands that the Turkish emperor nowadays has in hand. (493) The heathen king constantly depended on them; he was constantly at war with one after the other. Winter came on him quickly; all battle then came to a halt. Now the Christians wished to make an alliance and not simply acquiesce in this disgrace. The pope and emperor met together and had a great consultation with each other. (494) This consultation remained secret and tacit: that alliance was not to be broken, and moreover enough was to be done so that vengeance could be taken on the heathen. Thus did it please them all very much to fight, burn, hack, and stab, and each one contracted according to his own wealth: one offered ships, another troops, yet another money. (495) It was decided, and the lot fell to the mighty king of France that he alone lead this dance and be commander-in-chief. He was to lead them all in the war, as it would best please him. Thus did he decide and turn his attention to marching all the way into his [the Suldan's] lands. (496) Now, day and night, and early and late, the king thought steadfastly how he could do it both properly and quickly, and in the end he did indeed decide, and he announced it by letter to our Dolfin, the loyal warrior. The letter said that as soon as he read this letter, he should come to Paris. (497) Although I have often said to you how the Dolfin was wealthy in lands, indeed he was powerful and wore the crown, but I will say to you at this point: he was subordinate to the king of France and was obligated to pay

him tribute. Therefore, when he now summoned him, he came riding quickly and swiftly to him. (498) He came to him, as I tell you: the king welcomed him cordially. He had a great complaint against him: that his bridegroom had been sent home. They passed that day with conversation, so that it seemed tedious to neither of them.

And when dark night had come to them, then he took him into a chamber by himself (499) and said to him: "Listen, Dolfin, you know everything about the alliance and that I am commander-in-chief. The burden is not light for me. Therefore I have thought of a plan, so that I will have better success. I trust that my plan will turn out well for me, but I fear that someone might betray me. (500) I can entrust it to no man as well as to you, if only you would do it willingly. You know that it also pertains to you, and you would have great benefit and honor from it. It is in times of hardship that a man distinguishes himself. You do not need me to tell you this. Therefore I say to you, you must take on the task of making a long journey, a great distance. (501) You must soon set out, fully disguised in foreign clothing, and must enter the Suldan's land and spy out everything of his, and what is the state of his cities, whether they are strong or weak, and what they are doing there and what they are saying, and where it would be best to invade first. (502) While you are traveling here and there, I will get everything ready: arquebuses, armor, and lances, and whatever is pertinent for battle, and also supplies and ships for the sea and troops and horses for riding on land. And when next summer arrives, then let us force great affliction on him."

(503) "That will I do," said the Dolfin, "I will do it without fail. I will go there boldly and hope that I conceal it well. Clothed as a pilgrim, I will disguise myself quite properly and hope to accomplish it all successfully." Thus he went home and was pondering it all. (504) Then he began and said: "I have long since taken a vow on my life to a make journey to the tomb of my ancestors. Therefore, I cannot remain here any longer. Now, my crown and also my royal scepter do I give to my dear wife, and she is to take care of everything, both high and low, until I return, with God's help."

(505) Quickly he did as it is done and took off all his silken garments and put on a broad-brimmed hat and took a staff just like a pilgrim and a shabby cloak, as if he did not have three half-pennies to his name, and entered the ship, and they went on their way until they had, with God's aid, sailed to Cyprus. (506) And there he disembarked onto the sand and took other winding paths until he quite came to his [the Suldan's] land and spied out its features.

I will let him go on, for I am concerned for Odoardo, the loyal warrior. I must also tell you about him for a while; he had received the letter many days earlier. (507) I mean the letter and text that Pariz had earlier left in Genoa. It was gall and venom for Odoardo: because of it he was greatly aggrieved. Now, he would have performed great wonders in order to let Viene know about it, and otherwise he would have gladly given her aid, but found no way that seemed appropriate to him. (508) And now that he knew and saw that the king had gone away, he once said to himself: "Now is the time to risk something defiant. No one will take up the cause with any passion; no one will pay any attention or ask about it. I will look to offer Viene some aid for the sake of Pariz, my dear and trusted comrade." (509) To that end he had come up with a plan, about which he had long pondered: he had a house built from the ground up, by means of which he wished to make her suffering disappear. That house stood quite near to the tower where she was imprisoned. He had an excavation made quite deep into the earth, so that he could reach the tower. (510) He dug so long and so deep until he arrived at the point that he could reach the foundation of the tower or prison. Odoardo raised up his voice and called "Viene." She was so alarmed that she went pale, and she could not imagine what that was. She thought that the Devil had come to get her. (511) Finally they both recognized Odoardo by his speech and language. Now they began to break up and dig deeply into that wall, until they made an opening large enough that one could pass many small things through by hand, and one could understand speech quite easily.

(512) Day-by-day he comforted her and gave her much aid through this opening, and what and how, and to what extent, I yet wish calmly to tell all that. Now I am tired and will leave you here. Do not complain about me because of this: when I have rested, then I will sing some more of the loyalty of this very distinguished young man.

I wish to write no more in the eighth canto; therefore I will now leave it as it is.

Canto Nine

Now I ask God, my dear friend, to give me aid in this ninth canto.

(513) When a person is happy and wealthy, he cannot recognize his true friends, for many of the false ones stand around him just like the loyal ones: this one pats him on the shoulder; that one kneels if he is but mentioned; this one flatters him with words and babbling; and that one picks a feather off his cloak. (514) How many standing around him there want to take a bite out of his heart while honoring him in gesture and words, simply in order to get something out of him. If only the wheel and his fortune turn, and his money

trickles away from him, then he will distinguish by signs the loyal friends from those who deceive him with false flattery. (515) No false friends will look at him anymore, once he has lost his wealth. You will not find any of them going to see him. All friendship is taken from him. Only the true friend stands by him. Money does not blind the honorable. If the friendship is one from the heart, then it cannot dim or go dark.

(516) Odoardo's affection was also like that: good in all ways, without any vice. He did not betray his Pariz; no friendship was bound any more closely. Their love did not depend on an object, as did Amnon's desire for his sister. When he was to do service for him, it was like eating honey; it was like the affection of David and his brother-in-law. (517) He did his duty with Pariz's father, which the book has indeed demonstrated to you. I know that I have sung how Dolfin once humiliated him [Yakomo] and had given his servants everything that he [Yakomo] had owned. Odoardo had then shown him loyalty by long supplying him with food at his own cost.

(518) Was that affection, was that loyalty, with which he was now repaying him! Pariz's journey was indeed not new, and it was not known where he was in the world. Yet he began such a building and such an excavation, which was rare there, at great expense and also risked his life, for his sake alone, in order to give aid to Viene. (519) I know that I left you there when he had made an opening, and I promised to tell you more. Now I will indeed keep that promise and may well say this for certain: those were services that had their value. As I told you, he broke open the hole and in that way did he speak with Viene. (520) He spoke and told her everything about how Pariz had gone away, and no one knew where he was or where he had gone into hiding. When Viene learned that, she was greatly alarmed. Her heart wept blood, her eyes tears, and her appearance was such that it seemed time to perform the ritual purification of the corpse. (521) That pure maiden was lamenting without ceasing, enveloped in sighs and wails. She could indeed have made a stone break off from a thick column. And she said: "My bones, my body, my life itself must rot away. Even if I could, I would not flee, for I know not how to go to my Pariz."

(522) Odoardo heard the great lamentation and revived her with his words. He said: "My sister, do not despair. You see how your grief has been mended. God, who can indeed do all things, will yet also send Pariz to you. And I will spare neither body nor property, if I can ever hear anything about him." (523) His words gave great comfort to them, and his deeds even greater aid. He brought good food to them at that place, which gave strength to their limbs. And if he had not bored that hole, you would all have likely heard of their deaths. For otherwise they ate bread and drank water, for which reason one

dared not stint in helping her. (524) The ladies who were in there truly lacked for nothing. And no time was lost searching intelligently for Pariz. They did that for an entire year, during which not a single word was heard from him. Still she hoped, and if not for hope, I would also have gone astray because of grief.

(525) I will leave them all there for a while, pining away in their own ruin, and will say nothing more of them until I can make them laugh cheerfully. In the meantime, I will follow Dolfin and want to see how things are going with him. I am letting him spy out the Suldan's lands. Alas, how he found harm and disgrace there! (526) The king there—the Suldan—knew a count among the Christians; to him he gave whatever he demanded, and whole chests of money and guilders. That evil traitor performed great immorality with deception, and whatever the Christians did and planned, he always reported to the Suldan. (527) Thus he also reported to him that they were plotting against him, and how and when and where and what they wanted to do with great force. He wrote: "If you want to know more, then keep your eye on King Dolfin. He will approach you in such and such clothes, so that he can spy out all your land." (528) The Suldan was then not lax—it had not been said to a deaf person. He stationed many of his young men on all roads and trails. Not many days passed thus until the Dolfin came cantering along; he came with all his identifying signs. How quickly did the youths capture him.

(529)[50] He was brought before the Suldan. He said to him with rage: "You Christians hold me in contempt. You have sworn to an alliance against me. You supposed and thought that I would not hear of it, and you, traitor, take it into your head to come here in order to find out about my affairs." (530) He told him word for word: where, what, how, and when. When the poor Dolfin heard that, he said: "Why should I let myself be goaded? I would only suffer torture and would have to confess even more." Therefore, he confessed everything with hot tears, even how he had been a spy. (531) The Suldan turned red with rage and wanted to stab him immediately or otherwise give him an evil death, but his wise counselors said: "King, hear our counsel: death is no vengeance on any person. When you have killed him, he will soon grow stiff. It is much worse if he lives to suffer pain and torture." (532) That advice pleased him well. He said: "Now indeed must he suffer." And he ordered his servants to shackle him both hand and foot. And he now let them know everything about how and what was to be done to him.

Thus was he taken to Alexandria where there was a prison for captives. (533) There was a tower there, it seems to me, from which it was impossible to escape. Light from neither the sun nor the moon penetrated there, nor—I might also almost add—even a breath of wind. Otherwise it was horrible and wet and damp, which weakened one's body and life. They put the poor Dolfin inside, so that he might lose his life there. (534) He was given nothing but bread and water that was weighed out by the ounce, and mighty men were also ordered to guard all exits. There he was indeed going to have to die—that he had, alas, also realized, for his noble body was unaccustomed to that. Now pay attention as to whether he could make it.

(535) The sorrowful matter became known to the pope, the king, and the emperor. If it aggrieved the King of France, well did he show it with his great lament: he wailed and wept so bitterly that he began to grow hoarse. There was a great lamentation throughout Italy that such a loss took place there. (536) An embassy went before the Suldan in order to try if they could attain anything good for Dolfin. They requested if he [the Suldan] held him [Dolfin] in high regard, he [the Suldan] should order that to be done which he [Dolfin] desired. They did a great deal for the sake of this man and were pressing the king hard. "No," he said, "no money will ransom him: let him burst there as do the wicked!"

(537) If the lungs and heart of his relations, of his wife, were to burst—one sees it in their appearance—I would lament more for her than for his own life. I am indeed a bit hostile to him; I do not wish to flatter him. By my life, it serves him right for not wanting to marry Viene to Pariz. (538) I leave him there, very weak, in prison, just as he left his daughter and child, and I will also go in search of Pariz before he has completely disappeared from my sight. It is so long since I have seen him, that I almost do not know how to find him. For in the time that all these things have happened here, he has meanwhile traveled through many cities and lands. (539) I let him go, that fine warrior, so that he rode to Egypt. Since that time, he has not rested. He has traveled a long way, through India to Kozhikode and other lands on many sides, and in addition many cities that I do not wish to name, for I know that you will not know them. (540) He had now returned to Damascus and there he also did not hesitate. He soon became exhausted; everything was difficult for him. Nowhere did things go well for him. The journey had cost him a great deal of money. Now he again wanted to set forth. Having struck himself on the head as does a mourner, he decided to go to Cairo. (541)[51] Just as a person who is ill: when the heat or the cold is oppressive, he does not lie on either side very long—first on his stomach, then on his back; then he wants to lie on a crate, then on a bench; he thinks he can evade the illness, but in fact he cannot recover from the pain. Pariz's condition was exactly like that. (542) Quickly did he have his fill of any given place: he was moving here and there; now he went to that city. He also wanted to get a sense of that land. He had

had great misfortune earlier; now perhaps his fortune lay before him. He rode and covered a great distance, until he arrived in the city.

(543) The Suldan had the capital of his kingdom in this city. There were houses built there, recognizable by their distinct markings, which were rented to anyone who arrived from a foreign country. Thus did Pariz also take a room there, as was the custom in that land. (544) He wore clothes according to their custom: he had now become accustomed to the turban; his beard shaved as smoothly as the palm of his hand, and above that he had a long moustache. Now no one who did not know him would think him anything other than a Turk. He knew many languages, and the language of the Moors he knew as fluently as if he had been born in the land. (545) And Pariz spent a great deal of time there with his loyal servant. He never ceased in his affection for Viene. I cannot now chatter any more about that.

Outside this city there was a meadow where he often went for relaxation, for there one found recreation in dancing and playing, and early every morning there was hawking there. (546) On a pole there, the king's falconers generally kept many fine specimens of goshawks—both large and small—that caught birds. Noble Pariz wished to participate, for during his life he had had much experience therewith. Every day he went out very diligently, in order to diminish his heartache. (547) Sometimes when he was standing there with them, he let slip a word—which all the falconers heard—that showed that he, too, understood something thereof. One day they spoke to him and conversed with him a long time, and through those words he soon had made the acquaintance of the falconers. (548) Day-by-day and gradually the friendship grew quite close, so that they liked him very much and always showed him much honor. And they wanted him to go hawking with them. Thus did their acquaintance grow ever stronger, due to his noble and fine deeds.

(549) Once, on a day not long thereafter, while he was thus chatting with them, the chief falconer said to him: "I have put up a falcon, which our king values very highly, in the mews; he esteems it as much as an entire country. Recently it was ill and fell from the sky; since then I have been unable to bring it back to health. (550) I have tried some hundred remedies and have had no success with any of them." Pariz said: "I think that I would be able to identify that illness: if it were now to take its first flight, then it must be clipped beforehand. And if I can but once see it, I will teach you a trick by means of which it can soon be made well." (551) The falconer was very interested. He soon showed him the falcon. Pariz said: "Take such and such an herb and put it in its food. Then you will see whether that plant and that herb are valuable." The falconer believed it, but he also indeed would have liked to test it in advance.

(552) He wanted to trust him about it, so he did not wish to delay and gave the herb to the bird, grated with a knife, until he saw clearly and for certain that it got better day-by-day. In less than a month, it had recovered, healthy and vigorous, more so than ever before. (553) How quickly did he run to the Suldan and brought him the falcon, as a wonder, and said: "Now, take it; see what I can do: as healthy as before, and even healthier." He was rewarded with a rich gift. He [the Suldan] thought that he had a very special expertise and continued to give the falconer such gifts that he would remember them his whole life long. (554) The falconer had also realized that it was because of Pariz that it had all taken place. Therefore he shared the gift with him and said to him: "I am at your command, all the days of your life. Your friendship burns in my heart. I am ever in your service, and I promise you that in a few days I will bring you into the favor of the king." (555) The noble youth thanked him heartily and they swore brotherhood to each other.

Now, Pariz had even more friends with whom he had great entertainment: they were monks whom he knew well, who were of the same faith as he. Pariz unmasked himself to the monks, but he did not reveal everything to them. (556)[52] He said: "I came to this land when I was still a small child. I did not know how to find either my father or my mother again. I know not a word of a Romance language—that causes me grief and pain indeed." Thus, in the language of that city did they often have long conversations together. (557) They often spoke of faraway lands. Then Pariz often sighed and moaned. They often spoke of war and battle. Once one of them said in all sincerity: "I have heard that you [Christians] are powerful—the pope with many a Christian king. Therefore, we are all quite astonished, that the Suldan plunders them so mightily. (558) I see how from day to day he causes great injury to the Christians, and there is no one among them who can take even a thread of his." Pariz said: "I tell you indeed that that tune is about to change. I have certainly heard at one place how quickly and adroitly there will be action taken concerning that."

(559) "Indeed," said the monk, "perhaps you do not know that recently, not too long ago, a man came here as a pilgrim. Alas, it did not turn out well for him. The king holds him in shackles, and he is sorely imprisoned in Alexandria in a deep dungeon [and will stay there] until he gives up his soul entirely. (560) As far as I now can understand it, this person is indeed not shameful and wore the crown in his own country, and the king of France sent him so that he might well spy out the land in general in all places. Thus was it reported to the Suldan who then imprisoned him there in great anger." (561) Pariz was then quite troubled in mind. He said: "Might you know what his name is?"

One of the monks said: "It seems to me, Dolfin, but I cannot swear to it." The other said: "He is from Vienne." Thus was he quite convinced of the truth.

Now Pariz was greatly alarmed. He left the monks and was quickly on his way. (562) He now went home and thought it over seriously with a joy that went deep, and he often considered, back and forth, how he had caused his father to grow weak. Then he objected: "He is indeed my lord. Am I now to take vengeance for evil with evil? Although he did not want to give me Viene, perhaps—if I help him—he will acknowledge it." (563) And while he was pondering this way and that, with his heart quite focused thereon, in the end he quite surrendered to it: he wished to go to Alexandria and to risk everything that he had thereon—whether he could bring about his escape. He wanted to try out his reason, intelligence, and skill. Thus did he again go to seek out the monks at home (564) and asked them once again how that story went and how and when and why it was not resolved by ransom. One of the monks said: "Indeed an embassy did come in order to arbitrate the matter. Then they again went their way in disgrace." In addition they told him everything as was appropriate.

(565) Pariz said to one of the monks: "I would like to speak with the man, and since I do not speak the Romance language, what good would it do, if I were not understood? Therefore, my dear and trusted brother, help me to get to the bottom of it and go with me to see him, and do it willingly. I do not ask you to do it for nothing." (566) The monk said: "I like the idea, although I fear that you will fail miserably. Nonetheless, I give you my word here that I will never leave you." Thus was their accord decided; they wanted to be on their way. Pariz said: "Wait while I take leave of my friends." But he did it for the sake of a great necessity.

(567) He went and found his falconers; they were to provide him with aid, although it seemed to them shameful, and his plea vexed them. But there is a proverb in German lands: "misfortune teaches one to parry." And our sages have moreover said: "necessity often breaks both stone and iron." (568) Thus did he go to see them one day and found them all, indeed great and small, and implored them, as I tell you, and exhorted them all for the sake of their friendship and made first a great lament and began to weep for his love for them. He said: "Now I have to leave you. God knows that it causes me pain in my heart. (569) Now it is necessary; I must do it. God knows that I depart unwillingly. I know no one along this road and have, additionally, little money for provisions. Therefore, I ask you sincerely and properly: grant me a letter from the Suldan that frees me from all tolls and fees; it should be worded as though I were traveling in his service."

(570) All the falconers were alarmed by this journey, for they had grown accustomed to him. The said: "If you were to remain here longer, I believe, the king would reward you." "No," he said, "I must in any case go; I promise you for certain: in six or eight months I will come back for a longer period. Then I will pass all my days with you." (571) They said: "If you really want to go there, then you will have the letter as your own, and if you were to follow our idea, then come and present yourself to the king." Thus did he go with them one day. He bowed to the Suldan. The falconers all spoke and reported good things and praised Pariz. (572) They praised him in all respects as noble and honorable in all things, and how he had healed the falcon that no one could revive. "Such people," they said, "cannot be found at any price," as well as other things that I do not care to sing. Then they spoke of the letter that he wanted, and they all requested that he grant it to him.

(573) The king liked Pariz well and also believed the falconers. He said: "My son, if it were your desire to receive pay from me, I would give you as much as I give to my falcon-boys. Remain here with them," the Suldan said, "I will never again allow you to lack for anything." (574) Pariz thanked the king with great courtliness and great honor, and said: "King, this journey is necessary. I therefore ask you not to forbid my going. I hope to God that I will indeed quickly and soon return to you. In six months or less I will be here; then I will be your servant all my days."

(575) The Suldan now said that he would do it and not fail. He had his scribe quickly summoned and quickly gave him orders for the letter. He did more for him than he himself had requested. He said: "Go and write a letter for the young man, giving him free passage through my land—for him and for all three of his comrades— (576) and also a ship and horses and lodging in all places. Write the letter for him in such a way as if I were sending him in my service." He wrote the letter without delay and gave it to Pariz in his hands and had him newly clothed. Then he departed from there, having expressed his great gratitude.

(577) Pariz was eager to set out. The falconers wanted to hang on him: each one drew something forth and presented it to Pariz. He set out and they called after him that he ought to remember to come back soon. He said: "Yes," and galloped straightaway and found the monk, who was filling his sacks. (578) How quickly did they have everything prepared. They scrimped on nothing and boarded the ship that same night and boldly sailed away. They were all—those who were there—often quite concerned about bad weather. They went their way—I will not say otherwise—until they arrived safely in Alexandria.

(579) Pariz disembarked quickly and nimbly and went to the municipal judge and there showed him his letter, and they chatted together for a while. Pariz was quickly assigned to quarters and provided with everything, and he was told: "If you want to travel or ride farther, then I will make ready the ship or the horses." (580) "No," said Pariz, "I do not want to do so now; when I have need of it, I will say so. The journey, the sea, and the great heat have weakened me a great deal. Now I will stay here and rest for a while. That will not disrupt my journey." He thought: "He is truly noble," and held him to be worthy and honorable in all things.

(581) Thus did a whole week pass. He had everything there that was possible. Now he himself said: "This thing must be carried out properly and cleverly." Now, you all know without my singing it, that he was clever and prudent and capable. Now, he was thus making a great many inquiries, so that he might find out where Dolfin was being held. (582) He was in a high palace in which the prison had been built. Pariz indeed went up there once and was strolling in front of the prison. He saw his lord through a hole and did not identify himself to him. He bowed with great courtliness und honor to two great and mighty Mamluks. (583) The Mamluks were two men who could easily go on a rampage. The Suldan had sent them there to guard the king. He greeted them; they looked at him and also offered him their amicable compliments. They had also indeed heard of his letter and thought that he had come there on the Suldan's business.

(584) Pariz now went to see them often and thus was jesting with them. He often went there with full hands and gave them a number of gifts. He knew them thus well in word, deed, speech, and gesture that he gained a close acquaintance with them, so that they would have died for his company. (585) That affection prospered day-by-day, so successfully was he able to sow it. The person who has such charm—so do I indeed think, according to my conception, and no one can convince me otherwise—he has the best amulet around his neck. He gained their favor in a few days, so that I can say it all without lying.

(586) Now, when it seemed the right time to Pariz, he asked about the king with such cleverness and from such a distance that he deceived them all with it. They concealed not a mite's worth from him: in not a single word did they lie to him about how and when and why he was clanging around inside there, although he knew it as well as they. (587) Then he said: "My dear comrades, does he know our Moorish language?" "No," they said, "He knows only Romance, for he was born in Italy." Pariz then said, casually and subtly: "If I could understand him, I swear in truth, I would often dare to go see and

comfort him, for I would like to chat about that land." (588) The people said: "And what more do you need? There are indeed Turks and heathens here who understand Italian and would explain everything to you." Pariz did not want to act too eager and thus casually departed and said, just as he was going out the door: "I will bring a translator with me."

(589) Now he let it remain so for eight days, because he did not indeed want to act too eager. One day he came with his monk. He first introduced him. He came as he was often accustomed to come, and requested of his comrades that they unlock a small opening there: he wanted to chat with that lord for a while. (590)[53] A servant ran there quickly and did it quickly and did not stint. Pariz immediately recognized Dolfin, and his heart began to yearn mightily, but the king did not recognize him, for previously he had neither a beard nor a moustache. And still less did he ever enter his thoughts since he came with the subterfuge of the translator. (591) He deceived both of them well: the monk, as well as the lord.

Now the monk said: "We are sorry that you have been imprisoned here. Do not think that he is a Turk or a heathen: he is a Christian, I can swear to you, and has brought me with him even from Cairo, only because he wanted to come to see you." (592) It seemed to the king that he would immediately have some peace, just from speaking with the Christian, and before the monk left there, he made his lament to him about everything and sighed deeply. The monk explained every word to Pariz—for he did not know of his trick—about how and when and what he was lamenting, until tears came to the eyes of Pariz. (593) Pariz said: "So, ask him whether he has a wife and whether he has children." The monk did so. Dolfin said: "Yes, I have a wife—I do not mind telling you—and after my death I will have no heir. That grieves me more than anything else. Indeed do I have a daughter, but believe me, she wants to have no husband her whole life long." (594) Now Pariz then had had enough, since he had heard something concerning Viene. He said: "Now tell him to suppress his grief, which will perhaps come to an end." Dolfin, with gratitude and a deep bow, asked him to come often.

Thus did he promise him and departed from there and went to find the guards, those two men, (595) and spoke thusly: "I have come to understand many things about faraway lands. It immediately liberated my spirit to chat about those foreign lands. I will often spend time with him, when at times a yearning comes over me. It seems to me that he is an honorable and honest man. Therefore, I ask you not to make it so difficult on him." (596) Although the Suldan gave all the commands, including that they were to torture him, now for the sake of him of whom I sing, they now left a little door open, and in many things they let him off more lightly. That gave him a bit of hope. Up to that day no man had ever been more indigent; now he had indeed come up one step in the world. (597) Now Pariz went to see him often. The comrades permitted it all, for they liked him very much. They practically invited him to come. He also knew how to arrange it, so that they immediately trusted him. It would never have occurred to them that he intended to help him escape.

(598) Indeed Pariz had no other plan and thought that the time had now come, and said to the monk: "I have decided to help him escape from prison. You know that he is king of Vienne. Are our hearts not to grow tender at the fact that he is lying here among the dogs. And if we do not help him, then we are sinners." (599) The monk replied to Pariz: "Although I recognize the great danger, I nonetheless also want to do what you wish, for to Goat alone is my devotion." "No," said Pariz, "I want to execute the plan properly and want to make things easy on us." And he said to him how he wanted to initiate the action. The monk danced as he piped for him. (600) Now Pariz said: "Tomorrow night—I wish to delay no longer. Tomorrow morning then, have a look and pay attention that we speak and make our plans with him, so that he will also be prepared and awake. Then I will indeed accomplish the matter." "Now let us sleep," they said to each other, "so that we can stay awake better tomorrow night."

(601) This episode reminds me—since they are speaking of sleep—that I am becoming a bit groggy over this poem. I have indeed held out for a long time; you have indeed no cause to complain about me. Let me also lie down, just as they now do. Then I will tell more, if only I can.

The ninth canto will I now leave it as it is; I now wish to write the tenth canto.

Canto Ten

May God, who has made me forget my grief, help me to compose the final canto.

(602) O, if a pile of silver *scudi* were lying here, and if we all dipped our hands into them, no child, no Jewess or Jew would tire of picking them up. Now I would wager that we have all grown tired of this book: you are tired of listening to these stanzas, and I am tired and fed up with reading aloud to you. (603) It has already occurred to me that if I for shame only dared here and now indeed to conclude it and to destroy all the rest—but I do not dare. What am I to do? You still have to listen to me for a while. I see my characters

scattered out in all directions. It would seem to me that I would commit a sin, if I were to leave them in the lurch.

(604) I see Dolfin in great adversity and see Pariz gasping for sorrow, and I see the queen all but dead because of her great grief, and likewise I see the care and fear that Odoardo has with those ladies in the dungeon. I see them in the worst possible situation—now I will look to console them one-by-one. (605) I will help them one-by-one, if you will listen to me diligently. Only this canto remains for me to sing; therewith will I conclude my book. When I began the book, I kept its compass narrow; now it is beginning to annoy me, too. Therefore, I will also abbreviate it and hurry through to the end. Therefore, I entreat you: listen for a little while. (606) I still remember where I stopped. I will not let the matter grow cold anymore. Only one piece of advice will I give you in advance: take it to heart and remember it: everyone does what he likes, rich and poor, young and old, for one says: the mountains never move, but people often come together. (607) Never do what harms people, neither with your deeds nor with your words, for you already have power and wealth, and honor is overcome by poverty. There is nothing that does not have its place, and no one who does not have his time. Take to heart the poor and the children, for often a giant chokes on a fly.

(608) I say to you, it is not right that one repays evil with evil. Pariz did not do it, as you now see. But his kind is rarely found. And he perhaps had his own reasons for doing it, and it was likely worth something to him. But Dolfin did not imagine in any way that he would ever come into the power of Pariz. (609) Now he did indeed fall into his hands, and you have understood how and when. I know that I left you before they turned over in bed. They slept until full daylight had come. Now they again got up. And the first thing that the good comrades did there was to arrange for a good ship and crew. (610) The ship was chartered with the plan that it be prepared in secret. Then they went to the Dolfin and bid him good morning. The monk began to comfort him, saying: "Be cheerful now, and worry no more. My comrade is resolute and focused: today he will take you out of this prison." (611) Dolfin said: "What is the cause of this that you wish to increase my grief today? How would you get up here? Do you want to do it with a rope or with ladders? Therefore, dear brothers, pay attention that you not fail in this endeavor. I would rather spend the rest of my days here than have you suffer for my sake." (612) "No," said the monk, "Give thanks to this man, and do not be surprised by this matter. He will play a trick on the Mamluks, so that he need not break into the prison. He will give them a sleeping potion, and before they wake up, we will unlock this prison and make off in a ship."

(613) The king understood the situation; he immediately broke out in a sweat—for joy and for fear. He said: "O, my dear brothers, carry out this affair with prudence and discretion, and if you bring me to my country so that I can sit on my throne, then the effort, the trouble, and the journey will not be too costly for you: it is no peasant for whom you will have done it. (614) I will thus reward you well: as well as is fitting for you. And your comrade is to be my son. I will give him my possessions and all my lands: only the throne will I keep as long as I still have to live. And when I die, then he is to inherit land and people and also the throne." (615) Thus did they part. They liked what they had heard. Each one was to gain something for himself. The monk sought files and tongs, in order to break open the king's shackles.

Pariz hastened to his comrades and feasted with them on that morning, and briefly said to them: "Indeed, today we ought to drink with each other." (616) "We will not let you down," said the good Mamluks. Pariz said: "By Goat, I also have good things to drink." He parted from them with their permission and said: "I will return to you dry and thirsty." Thus did he go and grind roots to powder that would make them all tumble into sleep. (617) And when it had thus grown late, Pariz went to his benefactors. They had all drawn near there; they were idle profligates. Pariz also brought along pretzels and bread, doves, quail and chickens, and good, strong wine in two jugs, one of which would have sufficed for five or six men. (618) Night came on and there were only three who there sat at the table—the good gluttons—and ate just for their own pleasure: chickens, capons, goats and lambs, with a howl and a cry, with a pounding and a roar, and in the end all their craft and skillful work dribbled away via their tankards. (619) Therein was good wine that was indeed quite certainly a breaker of heads. Pariz had mixed in his powder and served it to them in full mugs. They were waiting for it all: just pour it down—as noble people and as good guzzlers! He made the jug go around so often that they got hot without either fire or summer.

(620) I do not know what Pariz himself did, but his companions all got quite drunk. This one had fallen onto a board; that one had sunk under the table. It seemed to Pariz that it was now late; they were all asleep, as it seemed to him. Thus they went to the king, as was their custom; and if they had awakened, it would have been of no concern. (621) And through the monk, he said to him: "I hope that you will be free even today. Then I hope also to bring you safe and sound to your land. I will desire one thing from you; you ought to show me mercy in this and swear an oath to me here that in time you will grant it to me." (622) The king said: "I will swear here immediately by my soul, body, and life: if you help me get out of this prison today, then order and

command what is proper for yourself, even to the half of my kingdom, and if you were to want it all, then I would give it."

Pariz was well pleased by these words, and ran off to his erstwhile comrades. (623) They were lying there in a mess: this one had vomited; that one had befouled himself with urine. He reached into the pocket of one of them and took the keys to the prison from him and gave them quickly to his monk and said: "Unlock it meticulously and saw off all the king's shackles and keep an eye out and go about it slowly and quietly. (624)[54] I will stand here with my sword and will keep watch in the meantime. You see that they are all sleeping quite deeply. I do not think that they will awake. If it happens that one of them gets up, then it will not be a laughing matter for him. If that one awakes from whom I took the keys, then I will whack off his head along with his gullet."

(625) The monk went and was still frightened and was jiggling the lock for such a long time: the poor fool could not find the keyhole, so greatly did his heart and his hand tremble. In the end, he did indeed get inside. Dolfin still feared that it was the guards, and when he caught sight of the monk, just look how his heart was reinvigorated! (626) He neatly freed him from his shackles and then led him out. Pariz encouraged them all, and quickly were they out the door. They [the guards] were lame; they were deaf; they did not move a hair. I will leave them asleep there on that ground until, by God's will, they become good Jews.[55]

(627)[56] Well can I tell you that none of *these* men was sleeping: they were all quite eager to flee. They made haste directly to the ship: their thoughts were on the ship alone. Each of them took hold of the king; they had difficulty pulling him along. He was unaccustomed to walking and staggered until they could finally toss him into the ship.

(628) Then shove off! Unmoor! And cast off! The sail was then hoisted, and, down from his high Heaven, God sent them a favorable wind. They sailed away quickly. Or rather: they did not sail—I think they flew, just as a ball flies from an arquebus. I never saw anyone sail so swiftly here in Muggia.[57] (629) Finally they came to Beirut and took on good food supplies there. Everything was going according to their plan. All of them together indeed praised God. Now the good warriors continued on until they also came to Cyprus. There they were supplied with all things, for it was bordering on his lands.[58] (630) There he took many purses of money and supplies and ships of his country. But Pariz was the cause of all the joy that he now had, and the fact that he did not understand his language caused the king pain and sorrow, and he was often saddened because he could not show him his favor.

(631) They traveled on, a while by ship and a while on horseback. I do not want to write any more about them, this journey, or the danger. Now they arrived safely in Vienne, the good warrior and worthy king. His wife was informed, and everyone in general—whoever had two legs—came running. (632) Such a firing of great arquebuses and such a tolling of bells! Nothing could be heard but bang-bang and clang-clang. Anyone who did not know what was going on would have been alarmed. There was a great press of both great and small, including even women with their distaffs. Everyone was welcoming the good king; everyone wanted to accompany him home. (633) The whole land had great joy that their beloved king had been delivered. It was now already known throughout France and into Lombardy. The noble maidens, who were still waiting in prison, were also happy. Since her father had done them the harm of putting them there, her mother had not wished to set them free.

(634) When many days had then been spent at his court in joy and cheering, then townspeople, knights and counts were summoned in the king's name to a hall, and the king recounted in front of them all everything that had happened to him, from beginning to end, from that day on when he was so severely imprisoned, and both before that and since. (635) He said: "You dear and noble people, look at that most stalwart man," and he pointed at Pariz and said: "He has returned me to you, and if not for him, you would not see me today standing before you on my own two feet. If that man had not offered me his help, then my limbs, just as my body and life, would be rotting. (636) Therefore it also seemed fitting to me that I reward such a thing. Therefore I ask you all, and this time may my request be granted: when I lay my body down so that I depart from this world, you are to accept this man willingly as your king and supreme lord."

(637) All the counts and the entire council—they were standing around and beside him there—they all said and quickly shouted: "Long live our lord, the king! And in a hundred years, when you are dead, he is fitting for us in your place." Thus were they embracing and kissing Pariz. The monk explained it to him and made him understand what was happening.

(638) He had of course understood everything himself and was in very good spirits. Now when he saw that it was going well for him, then he said to his good monk: "Now it is time that I press my advantage. Therefore courteously request of the king that he give me his daughter in marriage, whom in his rage he has forced into prison, (639) and that he forgive her for everything that she has done to displease him." The monk did not hesitate for a moment but knelt quite quickly before the king and said: "King, if it so please you, I

would now like to make a request for my comrade." "Say," said Dolfin, "what he would like; if it is at all possible, then everything will be granted him." (640) The monk now said: "His desire is that—if only it is fitting for you—that you forgive your daughter, who is sorely imprisoned there, all her guilt and misdeeds and in all courtesy and honor give her to him in marriage, so that she be the queen and his lawful wife, since he is to be the king of this land." (641) The king was delighted by those words, *and* they broke his heart, for he knew what lay packed away and waiting, and that his power had little effect. He said: "I have promised him 'yes.' Insofar as I can, I will keep my promise. I will indeed pardon her for all her faults and will again take her into my favor. (642) And it is also my will—I wish to God, that it had already taken place—if it is her will. I will not coerce her: I have indeed already affirmed this thing. I will certainly bring it about that she is asked. That which I will do, you will witness." Thus was her bishop summoned so that he go and move her by his pleas.

(643) The king said to Pariz, that he should go with the bishop. Thus did he go, as did the monk. How quickly was the prison unlocked. Pariz was inflamed when he saw her and did not want to identify himself. Thus did the bishop begin to preach her a sermon. He said: "Viene, today I will set you free, (644) and you are to be loved as never before and better cared for. Only—take this person whom you see here as your husband, and let God's will prevail. Do it indeed, and say 'yes' quickly. And you should not think it a disgrace for yourself: this is the one who helped your father out from behind many hard stone walls and close-set prison bars. (645) He helped him out of all adversity and brought him here, from death to life. For that reason your father also has given him the kingdom after his death."

Viene listened to his very long speech—and more in addition—very attentively. Then she said: "Dear people, I do not wish to be defiant: such things cannot be done on the spur of the moment. (646) It is not suddenly to be administered like medicine: a person who is to be hanged is given an interval of time. I, too, wish to have an interval of three days, and I will indeed reflect on this. Then I will give you an answer. Now you will hear no more, neither words nor gestures." Thus did they go and give the answer to Dolfin and waited until the three days had passed.

(647) What did Viene do in the meantime so that she might banish the pain? She again killed a large hen and did with it what she thought fitting. Now that the third day had come, Pariz could hardly wait to see her again. Thus did all three of them again go there and ask her to what her reflections had led her in the meantime. (648) And the bishop again began with his babble

and with his gestures and sung the man's praises to her: how noble, honorable and worthy he was. Viene said: "I do not grant it to him nor to any other person on this earth to take me to wife, for I have such a disease on my body. (649) For a long time I did not want to say anything about it. But I must indeed reveal my own disgrace. I am, alas, quite rotten and diseased. You must also be able to smell it yourselves." Now, Pariz already knew the trick. He thought: "That will not scare me away." And he said to the monk: "Tell her as follows: I will not give her up because of the illness." (650) Viene heard that and was immediately stunned that it did not work for her. She then went on the attack and said: "You must have hung either muskrat musk or some other good scent around your neck that prevents your sensing the stench. And if you are a noble and lordly man, then indeed you ought not to increase my torture. (651) You see the illness that I have which is destroying my skin and hair, and what I need is to be revitalized, and you come and increase my torture. Now I will suffer from it to my grave. Let me but endure it; I suffer it all willingly. I vowed to God that I would thus live. Therefore, I can give no other answer. (652) And if you are noble—as you are—do not demand that I break my vow. Have mercy on my suffering that burns and pricks me at all times."

The maiden spoke many such words, and the good monk was her translator. Pariz said to the monk: "Speak to her thus: if she did not even have flesh, or bones, or internal organs, (653) I would still be well-disposed toward her and am more loyal to her than to my own life, and have in my life attempted by many arts and skills and deeds to bring this about and have never wished for anything else than to have her as my wife, although—and I would swear and affirm that—I have never in my life seen her."

(654) At first Viene was quite stupefied; it seemed to her that he had cut right to her heart, and she raised her eyes and said: "Lord God, give me patience and help me according to your custom." And she quickly said to the monk: "I ask this of you, that you also ask him: if he is noble and distinguished, that, for God's sake, he leave me in peace. (655) If indeed I had a thousand lives, they would all be subject to him in this world. The loyalty that he showed my father is so great that it is rarely found. Therefore my constant prayer to God is that he recompense and reward him. But he ought not to cause me any more suffering—that I become his wife, that is no viable plan. (656) He can indeed not now insist on it. Therefore, may he just leave me in peace. And if I must also say more to him: I have sworn an oath to that end. And if you would like to understand it fully, then do not let it make you angry. I wish to suffer bad things and worse, until God sends me my liberator. (657) I am ever waiting on a person to whom I have given my heart and my troth. My body is to be ready

for him, as long as life remains in it. I hope to be filled with joy by him, if it so pleases God at some point. And if he does not come, I decided long ago that I would pass my life in this prison."

(658) Pariz once again went on his way, when he saw her so resolute. The tears flowed freely from his eyes, although he controlled himself in every way. He saw her loyalty and the great torment, all of which she had suffered for his sake. Now he did not want to reveal himself at that moment, although he held her in his heart. (659) And he again went to Dolfin and told him the whole story—how and what, and that it had not been possible to make any arrangement with her at all. The king took it and pondered it deeply and did not know what he ought to say to him. He said: "Is that now to continue forever?" And he was very troubled by that.

(660) Now Viene had been left alone. All her limbs were aflame, and she had been reminded of her Pariz, the unblemished one, so that she began to weep so fiercely that her tears immediately flowed, and she raised up her eyes to Heaven and once again spoke in this way. (661) She heaved many a sigh and did much else besides; then she said, with a great cry: "O, Pariz, Pariz, beloved of my heart. Woe is me that you thus left me. Woe is me that I have been left behind without you. If I only knew where you were and under what conditions. My eyes and my mouth cannot show how my heart is oppressed and debased. (662) My torment would be light for me, if I could see you and greet you but once, if only I knew how things are with you, or that you know of my state—how I am in prison, how I am breaking to pieces, and how I am suffering for your sake. And my heart breaks when I think of your appearance and your noble speech and gestures. (663) O, Lord of all the worlds, do not now suppress your mercy, and keep my Pariz hale and hearty, and if I might dare to ask for more, then hasten, Lord God, for once the hour that I might hear something from him. Let me have the benefit of seeing him again. Thereafter I would be quite happy to die." (664) The lamentation was quite long and grievous, and Isabele also wailed. They counted up how long they had been in that prison. They wailed and heaved deep sighs. "We would have long since turned up our toes, if Odoardo had not fed us for so long. Even so, our lives cannot endure long."

(665) They spoke many such words—you should not imagine that I will write them all here—if a dog had heard them, it would have had to weep along with them. But they comforted each other steadfastly—those dear people, those pure ladies—and hoped to God with their whole hearts, that he would help them out of their suffering and pain.

(666) Thus did it continue for eight more days. Pariz could no longer dissemble. Viene was dear to his heart, and he also grieved for his companion whom he saw with his own eyes and dared not reveal himself. Then he said: "It is over! Even if I am to be burned at the stake, I will identify myself to Viene." (667) Thus did he not let it continue any longer. He took his leave of the Dolfin. He said: "Let me go one more time. I also want to have the bishop with me. And if she does not cease her stalling, then I will accept my misfortune." The king said: "Go! May God grant that that person might change her mind for once." (668) Thus did they go, the three of them. The doors were quickly unlocked. Viene sat there in the middle. They winced in shock. Pariz was delighted; she, however, was not. His heart laughed, while she was grumbling. He had the question posed to her and desired to know whether she had reconsidered and decided in the positive.

(669) Viene said: "What do you want? You will not change my nature. Now speak! I will allow you to speak, but you are speaking to a wall: that which I have steadfastly said—that will I do, whether it is sweet or sour for me." Now Pariz well recognized in her deeds that his Viene was holding tightly to her principles. (670)[59] He said to the bishop and the monk that they were to wait for him outside; he also wanted to speak to her with gestures for a while. How quickly did they make room for him, and when Isabele saw that, indeed she also withdrew to one side. Her heart gave her the hint that he did not wish to speak in front of those people. (671) Pariz began in Italian and said: "O, dear lady Viene, you do not want me as a husband; you do not want to recognize my love. Well, I cannot do more than I can do." And with those words he untied and took out, wrapped in a little thing, a noble little diamond, a golden ring (672) and said: "Now indeed, take this from me. A Tatar gave it to me. Now I give it to you, and if you will wear it, therewith will my favor be remembered."

Viene drew back quickly, but she took it and thanked him. She thought: "This comes from Tatary. How might I now best rid myself of him?" (673) As soon as she had it in her hand, she immediately grew pale as a result. She well recognized the noble little ring—there were many identifying characteristics on it—and she turned to Isabele. She wanted to hide the fact that she was afraid. When she had shown it to her, Isabele said: "That is the little ring that you gave Pariz, (674) and I say and would even dare to swear that that one who is now standing there is he." "It seems to me," said Viene, "that he has his gestures and his speech." Viene looked at him again, and they both turned to him. Then she saw a mark on his forehead. "It is he, by God, certainly," said the dear maiden. (675)[60] Now, the youth, Pariz, noticed it all and smiled and turned and spoke many a word with his sweet tongue. Viene did not let him finish and leapt to him in a single bound and clasped him with both her hands and embraced him with both arms and could not speak a word for joy.

(676) Because of her joy nothing came out of her mouth, but only tears from her eyes. That lasted almost a quarter hour. Her heart was just pounding and beating. Pariz was also inflamed with joy and wept hot tears and indeed said: "I am Pariz, your husband, whom misfortune pursued and rode down at every step. (677) Misfortune has everywhere pursued me even up to this point. Now I hope to the Lord God that evil has all departed." He spoke much and wept a great deal. Isabele was also there and welcomed Pariz anew and also embraced him heartily (678) and said: "Pariz, O lordly brother, what pains we have suffered since our journey was interrupted in that village, so that you parted from us there." Now Viene pressed him closely with both her arms. She could not be sated or satisfied by the hugging and embracing and kissing (679) and said: "O God, is this a joy that ought nevermore to be hindered. This is a delight without measure and without limit; one cannot indeed reckon the worth of this joy. Now I have everything that I want. Suddenly God gave me joy. Now may His Holy Name ever be praised, Who has indeed brought us together again."

(680) Then she began: "I am all but dead." And she wished to reckon up her misfortune. Pariz said: "Be silent, now, for God's sake. In time we will yet speak much. Now, let us do what is necessary, so that those who are outside wait no longer. Now, I wish to ask a favor of you." Viene said: "Just say it, I will do it gladly." (681) He said: "I have had my fill of this matter, and every day more so: your father and the entire city now think that I am a Turk or a Tatar. Therefore, now I would like for us both simply to go and see your father. But look that you do not speak a word or even whisper before I give you a sign or clear my throat."

(682) Thus did they all three come running out quite cheerfully. When they stepped forth thus boldly, the two clerics were immediately stupefied. One thought that it was immoral; the other merely gaped in astonishment. The monk crossed himself a hundred times. Pariz said: "Calm down! (683) I do not know what kind of people you are. You have missed out on a great deal of talking, and I only made gestures to her, and I have been able to persuade her by means of pleading. Now, you will all see it today. Just come along with me to see her father." Thus did all of them together follow him until they came before King Dolfin. (684)[61] When the king saw his daughter, his eyes filled with tears. Pariz said to his monk that he should tell the dear king that he, too,

ought to ask her himself, so that she might no longer refuse him. Thus did the monk quickly and adroitly do.

Dolfin turned toward his daughter (685) and said: "Listen, O my daughter, hear my words, dear Viene. You have suffered great pain. You deserved it and may acknowledge it. Now I am willing to call it even and will neither admonish nor even mention it. But listen to me now—I will not stretch it out—see the man who there stands with the moustache— (686) that good and noble lord? He has shown me such loyalty, much more than if I were his father and than if my wife had suckled him. He drew me out of a grievous prison, where I was death's own. He brought me back here and into the world. For that reason do I wish to reciprocate with loyalty to him. (687) Now I request a favor of you: you are not to oppose me. Take him as your lawful husband. He is quite worthy of it, this most distinguished man. Say 'yes!' I ask you as earnestly as I can, and if it would help me, I would kneel down. Know that after my death he will inherit my throne, my crown, and my kingdom." (688) Viene said: "O dear father, I have obviously broken faith with you. I know that I did wrong. For that reason I do not wish to disgrace you anymore, and will do everything that you here say, and it is to be as you said, and for your sake I will marry this man. And if I were not to do it, it would shame me. (689) Therefore I kneel before you, dear beloved [father], and I ask your pardon, and of all the sins that I have committed, now absolve and pardon me." The king said: "My beautiful daughter, now you have quite delighted me. May God forgive you and grant you long life. I have absolved you of all your guilt."

(690) Now, Pariz heard all of that, and his heart pounded without ceasing. Now, he fell to his knees. He put his life on the line: he put a noose around his neck and a dagger to his heart and thus began to speak in Italian: "Know, my lord, that I no longer wish to dissimulate. (691) Now, you should know who that one is, who is here to become your son-in-law. Although I have always passed myself off as a Turk or a heathen, now I say to you that I am your servant, Pariz, and will explain it to you even more clearly: I am Count Yakomo's son, who with great suffering has ever borne Viene in his heart, (692) and I have done everything that I have done in order to win her. God knows whether I have suffered many an evil day and very bitter night. Now I hope to have my reward, and if it is just that I die, then so be it. I stand here ready to do so. If you want your revenge, then hang me quickly or stab me to death."

(693) When King Dolfin heard that, he turned stiff as a stave from shock. Thus were all the people stunned who were present there—every single one of them. The king could not speak a word for his stunned gaping and great astonishment. Finally, he stood up, that worthy king, and himself raised Pariz from

the ground, (694) and he embraced him and said: "Is it you, my son Pariz? If you are the nimble hero who showed me so much loyalty, then everything is now to be forgiven you, from the beginning up until now." Thus did Dolfin say with many a tear: "You are to be my son-in-law and I your father-in-law, (695) and I am very glad that you are Pariz, the noble lad, and that I know that I marry her to a count who also believes in my religion. I see that God has inscribed this, and God wants it to be so. Since he has thus granted it, then I will also do so and do it gladly. (696) The king wanted to carry it out altogether and quickly right there at that assembly and sent to have a golden ring fetched and quickly had "good fortune" etched into it, and he had Pariz and Viene married immediately without the conventional braiding of the bride's hair, without bride songs, no chattering of rabbis or women was heard there, without harp, lute, or six-course cittern. (697) And he immediately ordered his trumpeters to make the proclamation everywhere that he had given his daughter in marriage, and how and to whom—the whole story, and for the sake of the joy and the happy news, he invited all the locals and foreigners. The court was to be open for a full month for eating, drinking, entertainments, and dancing.

(698) In half a quarter hour the whole city was buzzing; everyone was talking about how Pariz had returned with the king. Everyone knew how things stood and how he had married Viene. How quickly did his father and mother, and also Odoardo, his good comrade, find out about it. (699) They rushed there as if in flight, until they came to the lad. They saw him, and it did not seem possible to them to experience this joy, for whoever always tastes only evil can scarcely believe good news. The clothes and that moustache were also to blame for his not resembling himself even the tiniest bit. (700) His elderly mother recognized him indeed and threw her arms around his neck. His elderly father, the poor man, also embraced him as one should do. Odoardo kissed him a hundred times and shed many a hot tear; they flowed from him for joy, and his heart was quite full. (701) His father wept abundantly, and then he said: "Oh Pariz, my son, I never thought to see your face again, and now God has even let me see your wife. Praise be to God, who has brought you here that I might see you on this day. Now I can die content, since I have now lived to see your face."

(702) Never had such crowds been seen in this palace and at this court: of townspeople, knights, and counts. Everyone wanted to welcome Pariz. There seemed no end to greetings and congratulations. I am not capable of saying or writing of all the activities and the joy that was had there.

(703) The book speaks of how the lad, Pariz, called Odoardo, his comrade, and gave Isabele, the noble lady, to him in marriage, and all his father's land

and property and whatever God had granted him—he gave all of that to these two loyal people, and God also blessed them in all their deeds.

(704) I am so tired of writing that I almost forgot the best part: now I have to write another couple of pages about the bride Viene and her bridegroom. Now that she had married Pariz, in the night, after they had eaten, they were quickly shown to a place to sleep. They did not wish to go there slowly, but instead ran. (705) Good Lord, was that a joy for them! How that chamber was a treasure-house for them! The noble maiden had no need of a guard. As luck would have it, she was ritually pure.[62] They both lay down, and if I were tell it to you straight, in the bed where they lay, they thus carried out very many of the acts that lovers perform. (706) They carried on with that for many an hour and many a year, so that their love never grew cold; they never lost their affection. In the end, all the elders died, and all the promises that they had made to them previously were now kept: the land was given over to them and they possessed it, and they had well earned it all.

(707) Now I do not wish to write any more for you about the deeds of individuals by name—how they ruled their lands with great honor and how many children they produced. It is enough that I have brought the two of them together here. Now I will conclude my book; I do not wish to stretch it out any further. I will just say to you that they were both crowned. (708) Viene earned another crown for the sake of her great loyalty, and for that reason God gave them their reward, so that she passed her days in joy. Who is the lady who would now do it? Who is the maiden who would maintain such favor or such loyalty to her manservant? I say: half of them, a quarter, or even fewer. (709) Who is the lady, who the maiden, who the girl or lass who refuses to endure any pain!? I cannot understand that. Tell me, which one would pass up a dress? Which one would want to miss out on a dance? Which one would want to wait or lie ill for a single year, a month, or even two weeks?

(710) Nowadays one finds those who summon a lover for themselves, and he sits beside her in the city, and she sees her companion every day, until she inflames his heart; there she is behaving amiably. And then quite suddenly she throws the poor fool over and loves another there before his very eyes. (711) The first foreign lad who comes by and gives her so much as a smile—if he has a fine silk cloak, a fine jacket and hose, even if he were a cursed fool and incapable in all things—she likes him very well, thinks him suitable, and acts as if she would raise him up to the heavens. (712) And if a third then came with a fine gold chain, I tell you, she would take him and would also drop the earlier one. She would give all her love to that one; I would bet my life on it. They are as constant as leaves on a tree in the wind and rain. (713) I am not saying

that all of them are evil. It is said that there are also many honorable ones to be found. I do not think that they are the norm, so I have not set them apart. I do not, however, find a great many of them; I do not know where they have all gone. I say, therefore: good for the lad and youth who has never given up his freedom for the sake of desire for a woman. (714) And good for the lad and also for the maiden as long as they have not yet been married. They do not know what joy they have there and how good a life they have. How often do many regret it that they tie themselves down too early and too young. And if I wanted to write all the whys and wherefores, then I would be at it for ten more days.

(715) I have ever had the idea in my head—you can see it in me and believe me, however much one might say to me: "Plug up your mouth or go talk to the deaf. It is a matter of your being a poor fool and knowing no one who will have you." Now, formulate the sermon however you wish: God be praised, I am still single and free. (716) If I were then also to be tied down, then it would be the proper time for me, although I would hope that a great tumult would appear here from afar. The tumult and my hope it is that one will come riding on a gray ram with long ears, and he will blow on a terrifying horn. (717) And he will bring us into the city that God chose long ago, so that all our bodies and souls will be laid to rest there. There we will speak as much as we desire and tell of God's help, and not of Pariz, Viene and Isabele. Let this be so, in God's name. Amen. *Selah.*

Printed in the house of messir Francesco dalle Donne by the hand of your servant of all good friends, both male and female. Believe me without my writing it out explicitly, for I have done it so that you should not be idle, and I have had it printed in this size, neither too small nor too large, although it will be difficult for some. But they will understand it quickly, once they get into it. You have now understood me well up to the point to which I have come. Therewith do I wish to conclude. Those who have bought it need not be distressed, for you will certainly be able to say in truth that you have not seen its like in all your life, through the hand of your servant, as I began by saying. And so now let us ask God that he let the anointed one come forward, the Messiah ben David, may His name be exalted. And may He lead us into the Holy Land. There we will have peace. To that let us all say amen. Amen. *Selah.* The end.

The book was just published here in the city of Verona which has three bridges over the Adige, that swift river that comes flowing so swiftly and mightily, and two fine strong castles on the mountain. When one stands below, he seems to be a dwarf. And one castle also next to the swift stream. When one sees the fine city, the heart rejoices. On the first of Nisan in the year that is numbered 5354 [March 22, 1594] under the honorable rule of Venice, may her splendor be preserved.

By the hand and in the name of your servant Abraham, son of my lord, my father, the scholar, may his name be honored, Matisyohu from the tribe of Bas-Sheva, may his rock defend him.

In Verona, by Francesco dalle Donne. MDXCIIII.

Appendix A

The Book of Kings

Appendix B

Briyo and Zimro

Notes

Bibliography

APPENDIX A

The Book of Kings

ספר מלכים [מלכים-בוך] / *Seyfer Melokhim (Excerpts)*

Anonymous, composed fifteenth century, earliest ms. 1515–25

While the ספר מלכים *Seyfer Melokhim* (Book of Kings) (often called the מלכים-בוך *Melokhim-bukh* [Kings-book]) was first published in Augsburg in 1543, the watermarks of a fragmentary paper manuscript from the Jewish National and University Library in Jerusalem (heb. 8° 6992) can be dated to the years 1515–25, indicating that the poem is at least that old, and it seems likely that the poem was composed in the fifteenth century. As is demonstrated in the poetic style and form of the poem, it is clear that the author was well versed in the broad-ranging textual traditions of Jewish culture, including the Bible, Talmud, commentary traditions, and midrash, in addition to having extensive knowledge of non-Jewish secular epic literature. The *Seyfer Melokhim* exhibits the same stanzaic structure as the *Seyfer Shmuel* (on which see the headnote to that text), and with its 2,262 stanzas the *Seyfer Melokhim* is the longest poem in Old Yiddish literature.

The poem's author is unidentified in the text itself, and no plausible author has been proposed by scholars, although most scholars agree that the poem was not composed by the same author as the *Seyfer Shmuel*, generally owing to stylistic and aesthetic differences in the two poems, one of the most obvious being that the *Seyfer Melokhim* devotes far less attention to battle scenes than ethical and didactic topics and moralizing. That distinction in focus must, however, at least in part have to do with the differing content of the two biblical source texts.

It has long been the lore of early Yiddish literary studies that the *Seyfer Shmuel* and *Seyfer Melokhim* are the matched set of biblical/midrashic masterpieces. The reader might then legitimately wonder why, in a volume in which all other epics included are complete, only two brief excerpts from the *Seyfer Melokhim* are found. There are two primary reasons. First, the genre of midrashic epic is here already quite well represented, in both its short form (in the texts from the Cairo *geniza* and *Akeydas Yitskhok*) and its long form (in the *Seyfer Shmuel*), and, in the chronological range of those texts, thus also in both its early and its later forms. Second, as some previous scholars have noted, the *Seyfer Melokhim* is, in terms of both narrative interest and aesthetic quality, not on nearly as high a level as the other texts included here. Many episodes of the poem are well narrated, but the narrative is quite inconsistent, perhaps in part because the biblical source has so many disparate themes and characters and is not focused on a central figure or small group of thematically connected central figures (such as Samuel, Saul, and David in *Seyfer Shmuel*). Felix Falk notes in his facsimile edition of *Seyfer Shmuel* that although the *Seyfer Melokhim* is one of the best of later imitations of the *Seyfer Shmuel*, it was in many ways far less successful.[1] Unlike the biblical material of the book of Samuel, the book of Kings does not so easily lend itself to epic adaptation: there are, for instance, many more folk proverbs and fewer battle scenes, while elaborate descriptions of the fine details of the temple's construction are essential components.[2] Additionally, the author of *Seyfer Melokhim* is less free in his adaptational strategies than was Moses Esrim Vearba in the *Seyfer Shmuel*, which, according to Falk, makes much of the *Seyfer Melokhim*'s narrative *eintönig und ermüdend* (monotonous and tedious).[3] Fuks also notes that particularly in the middle sections of the narrative, where the source material consists primarily of the recording of a rapid succession of kings, the narrative becomes *trocken und einförmig* (dry and monotonous).[4] As transmitted in the Augsburg edition, rhyme and verse and stanzaic structure are, according to Fuks, often imprecise,[5] whether inexpertly composed or corrupted by a previous scribe or the typesetter. Falk notes finally that the *Seyfer Melokhim* did not have the audience success enjoyed by the *Seyfer Shmuel*, for it is scarcely mentioned by later authors.[6]

Indeed, the deficiencies of the *Seyfer Melokhim* would often make it difficult to present the text in the same way as the other texts—as a connected narrative—since its narrative logic and even syntactic coherence break down so very often. One might opine that this text is in fact "too midrashic" (almost in the sense evoked by Barbara Könnecker) to be narrative,[7] that is, it functions as quasi complementary to the midrashic tradition as commentary on commentary. Such supercommentaries are, of course, common in a variety of religious textual traditions (including Judaism, Christianity, and Islam), but precisely that density of the fundamental intertextuality can function to obstruct narrative per se. While this characteristic may not make the text any less "epic" (in its own peculiar sense), it certainly does set it apart from the general mode of epic—even early Yiddish midrashic epic—where narrative (that is, telling a compelling story) as the hallmark of epic poetry is everywhere of primary significance. It often seems that the poet of the *Seyfer Melokhim* is almost diverted from that task as an epic poet. Thus, the specific character of the *Seyfer Melokhim* may perhaps best be studied and appreciated by those individuals engaged in the study of the texts in the original language. It would nonetheless be inappropriate to exclude this text altogether from an anthology of early Yiddish epic, for which reason two brief excerpts have been chosen for inclusion here in order to illustrate the recurring brilliance of narrative episodes, for indeed just as there are troubled passages in this epic, there are also splendid narrative and poetic passages.

Because the only extant version of the text not derived from the Augsburg 1543 edition is itself a fragment (the Jerusalem manuscript noted above), the text of the Augsburg edition is translated here. The two excerpts included here are the title page, encomium to God, and the opening episode of the epic concerning David and Abishag (st. 1–26) and Solomon and Ashmodai (st. 255–348).

Source: Augsburg, 1543 (? Paulus Aemilius or Chaim b. David Schwartz [Shaḥor]).
Edition: L. Fuks, ed., *Das altjiddische Epos Melok̲îm-Bûk̲*, 2 vols. (Assen: Van Gorcum, 1965) (facsimile of Augsburg 1543); online facsimile of Augsburg 1543, http://books.google.com/books?id=R4g6AAAAcAAJ&pg=PP4#v=onepage&q&f=false.
Research: Zinberg, 115–16; Erik, *Geshikhte*, 121–22; Ginzberg, *Legends*, IV, 123–91, and VI, 277–315; Shmeruk, *Prokim*, 114–16, 192–99; Baumgarten, *Introduction*, 140–42, 151–55; Georg Salzberger, *Die Salomo Sage in der semitischen Literatur: ein Beitrag zur vergleichenden Sagenkunde* (Berlin: Max Harrwitz, 1907); Felix Falk, "Di talmudishe agade fun Shloyme hameylekh mitn Ashmeday un dem shamir in tsvey alt-yidishe nuskhoes," *YIVO-bleter* 13 (1938): 246–74; Gertrud Zandt, "Zum Melochimbuch, einem Epos in jüdisch-deutscher Sprache," in *Amsterdamer Beiträge zur älteren Germanistik* 43–44 (1995): 589–600.

The Book of Kings [translated] finely and properly into the Yiddish language, also quite entertaining to read.

Printed in the imperial city of Augsburg, in the year designated 303 [= (5)303 = 1543 CE] according to the small count.

(1) I praise You, God, from my heart. You are indeed worthy of praise. With Your might You created Heaven and the earth, and in addition many wonders and signs (which no one can number), tame and also wild, woman and also man. (2) Thus it is better to keep silent—after all, one cannot ever complete the telling, for You are so mighty that You can control all things. Thus should one fear You; that is right and proper. You can make all crooked things straight. (3) Quite often have You given signs to the children of Israel, for which reason they owe their allegiance to You as Lord and ought to fear Your Name. That is good and useful for them. The person who transgresses against Your name is a simpleton. (4) When the children of Israel were in the land of Egypt, You showed them many signs by Your mighty hand and led them out of exile into the savage wilderness and gave them the Torah on Mount Sinai. (5) You fed them for forty years with heavenly bread, until Moses our Teacher, alas, had to die. Thereafter, Your servant Joshua led them into the Holy Land. He subjugated them by force through Your mighty hand. (6) They possessed it for a long time; no one else dared to speak out.

Israel desired a king, indeed just as other peoples, who should rule them and fight for them, so that they can remain at home, safe at all times. (7) Then God, blessed be He, set a king over them from the land of the Jews. Saul, son of Kish, was the hero's name. No man of Israel was his peer in splendor and courage. And in the matter of Amalek he kindled God's wrath. (8) God said to Saul: "Kill the people of Amalek. Leave none alive from one border to the other. Make sure that none survives, whether large or small. Amalek must make restitution to me: so it is written." (9) Saul marched with his troops into the land of Amalek. He left nothing alive that he found there. But Saul took pity on the fattest sheep. He thought he would be judged well by God, blessed be He.

(10) The king sinned there in that same matter, so that, alas, he could not survive against the Philistines. He wished firmly to take vengeance, but, alas, he lay dead because of the same sins—that he broke God's commandment. (11) Israel made great lament for the dear king. They had to let him go at that time. But it did not take long: David, son of Jesse, of the tribe of Judah became king there. (12) He was the most noble king among the Jews. His like had never arisen and is rarely born. He surrendered himself fully into God's service. He did that for all the days of his life, as long as he lived.

(13) And when King David was old and had come into his days, he began to be very cold, as the book tells us here. They took many garments and wanted to cover him—no featherbed and no mantel sufficed for him. (14) For indeed he had sinned—that most noble king—for he had cut off a large piece of his father-in-law Saul's fine silk robe and garment. For that reason he often had to be cold—that took precedence.

(15) He was also quite alarmed when he saw the angel of death with a hand outstretched and a sword, wanting also to slay Israel. His heart then went cold, and he began to be freezing cold from fear. He had no desire to dance or for any courtly amusements. (16) When his servants perceived and saw that, they went to the king and said to him thus: "Dear king, listen to our traditional remedy: a courtly young maiden is better than an old and indecent one. (17) Lord King, she who is young in years will also seek out her desire. When you begin to get cold, she will warm you, both front and back. She will then arouse you, and you will thus become warm: lay her down one time behind [you], and one time lay her in your arms." (18) Then throughout all Israel the most beautiful maiden was sought for the king; she was to be prepared for him. The maiden's name was Abishag, the Shunammite. Her peer was not to be found in all Israel. (19) She was brought to the king in his chamber. He embraced her quite pleasantly and amiably let her enter with him. She served him properly and warmed him well, and when he was cold, she quickly took him in her arms.

(20) Once Abishag lay atop the king's body. She said: "Gracious king, take me as your wife. I will serve you better than I do now when you are cold and I move over here to you." (21) "No," said the king, "you distinguished maiden. God has spoken and forbidden me; I would certainly be sorry for it. I may not have more than eighteen wives during my life. How gladly I would take you, if God would permit me." (22) She said: "Gracious king of noble birth. Let what I say to you arouse no anger

against me. You are acting like the thieves who find nothing to steal. They want to act polite while hiding their works. (23) And they boast to the people: 'I would sooner die than steal and ruin someone.' Thus do you do as well, king, since you no longer have any strength. You are much too old and your loins have gone lame." (24) King David said: "You must understand that I do it for the sake of moral reasons for God, my Lord."

He had Bathsheba, his lawful wife, summoned. She had to nestle against him very close to his body. (25) He had Bathsheba summoned and sent in to him in his chamber, so that he made a proper "arrangement" with Bathsheba, like a young householder who has just been married. "By the true God, I had sworn it off!" (26) Beautiful Abishag thus said: "You are an honorable man. I would not have expected such unusual behavior of you. Forgive me for it, dear king. I am sorry for what I said." The king let her stay with him as a pure maiden.

Solomon and Ashmodai:

(255) The house[8] was built using only fine stonework: no hammer or iron struck the stone inside there. Then the king considered: "What am I to do now? I cannot cut stone without using iron."

(256) Then King Solomon said: "Who will explain it to me? I may not work the stone with any iron tool." He had the scholars summoned so that they would advise him. He was not permitted to use any iron tool: God had forbidden it. (257) "Indeed I will not hew them out with my fingernails. I have to have your very good counsel." The scholars then said: "King, you must do it thusly: there is a worm that is called Shamir; you must have it. (258) When wise and prudent Moses our Teacher, when he excavated the [stones of the] breastplate that the high priest wore, then he took this worm that is called Shamir." "How do I bring it about? Tell me!" (259) The scholars then said: "King, you must defeat the demons. As you sing for them, so must they indeed dance, so that they tell you where it [Shamir] is. Such a thing is not hidden from them. They certainly know it."

(260) The king defeated the demons from Hell. They all had to come along with their companions. When they now came, how frightened they were. They were very agitated and they listened very closely. (261) They all fell down before the stately king. They said: "King Solomon, tell us now why you summoned us so quickly." The king said to them in a very loud voice: (262) "Where is the worm that is called Shamir? And do not do otherwise, and tell me right away. If you hide it from me and do not tell me, I will have you all slain on this very day." (263) Together they said: "We have no knowledge of it, but the chief demon is zealously in charge of it. He knows such things and is unrestricted in his skills. He is the master of all demons and is named Ashmodai. (264) If you could defeat him, the game is won." Then the king said: "I would like to ask you: tell me where he has his dwelling. He cannot conceal himself.

I will have him fetched here." (265) They said to the king: "There on that mountain, where no giant or dwarf has ever come. On that same mountain he has dug himself a pit, which he fills to the top with water and which he must have every day. (266) He covers it with a stone and puts a seal on it. He greatly fears lest someone uncover it, for each day he goes to Heaven. He studies in Heaven and does not stint. (267) When he has finished, he descends again. He runs to his pit [to check] that no one has defiled it. He checks whether his seal has been broken and whether the stone has been moved. (268) He does not allow anyone to drink from it. That we can tell you. He is very zealous about it—that we can tell you—and is very shy."

Thus did the king grant all the demons leave to depart. They went away together with a monstrous roar. (269) The king immediately had the noble Duke Benaiah summoned. The servants said to him: "Go quickly to the king." And when Duke Benaiah came to the king, he bowed down as was fitting for him to do. (270) Then the king said: "Duke, I must bother you: you must get ready; you have to take a look at this matter. I must have Ashmodai. Bring him to me here. Be diligent in this, I beseech you. (271) Take with you the iron chains and the ring on which there is written a character so fine. A very great name [of God] is too mighty for Ashmodai. I need not instruct you; your instinct will instruct you. (272) A keg and a wad of new wool and a keg of wine you could well prepare for where he may be." "Gladly," said Duke Benaiah. "I will do what I can." He took the equipment like a bold man.

(273) He came into the mountains where he found the pit. Benaiah said: "Let us see what the demonic scoundrel wants." Downslope from the pit, he there dug another pit, and upslope from the pit, yet another like it. (274) At the downslope end of the pit he made a tiny hole, so that [the water] flowed from the [chief demon's] pit into the other pit. He took the new wool and stopped the hole, so that no one would notice it. He closed it up very well. (275) And out of the topmost pit there was a very small hole, so that the wine flowed in [to the chief demon's pit]. And again he stopped it up so that no one could notice it, and then at once backfilled the pits [that he had dug].

(276) Then Duke Benaiah went and took a seat in a tree. As soon as Ashmodai came from Heaven, he was quite thirsty. He immediately looked at the seal. "It is in order," he said to himself: (277) He moved the stone away and began to be alarmed, when he saw the wine and began to smell it. "I will not drink you. Indeed it is written that you have mocked many and have practiced deceit on them." (278) He was grieved in spirit; his thirst conquered him. He could not refrain from it. How powerfully did he drink. After he had drunk, how drunk he was! He fell down asleep on the green grass. (279) When he had fallen asleep, Benaiah crept over there. He took the iron chains—he tread very quietly—he put them around Ashmodai's neck. The very noble warrior locked them quite well.

(280) When Ashmodai awoke, he began to become very alarmed. He struggled mightily with all his strength. He fiercely bewailed the iron chain. "Now, what are

you doing, Ashmodai! You will not escape me. (281) The name of your Lord has taken possession of you." Ashmodai said with a wail: "I was distracted." Benaiah led him away like a bear. He had to amble along behind him, much as he was displeased by it. (282) They came before a huge tree, which he knocked down. Benaiah boldly yanked him around back on track. They came before a small hut. Ashmodai began to rub himself on it. A widow dwelt there. He [Ashmodai] began to wail. (283) The poor widow came out and pled with him: "Do not break my little house, dear my lord." Since she pled so earnestly with him and he wanted to lean away from it, he broke one of his legs. (284) Then Ashmodai said: "A proverb that people are accustomed to say just happened to me: 'A tongue breaks a leg with gentle words.'" Benaiah led him away even though he was thus limping.

(285) While they were thus going along, Ashmodai could not budge. A poor blind man was coming toward them. He—the poor man—went off the path and lost his way. Ashmodai said: "I must help you." (286) He led him directly to the road. They also encountered a drunkard from whom wine spewed forth. He also lost his way. Ashmodai led him right back down so that he came walking directly back to the path. (287) They came to a place where a splendid wedding was being celebrated. They were enjoying themselves very much with dancing and leaping. Ashmodai began to weep. If someone had from afar seen him walking along there, he must indeed have become sad. (288) They came to a shop, in which a cobbler dwelt. A man stood before the shop and requested: "My dear and trusted craftsman, I would pay you well, if you would make me a pair of shoes to my liking: (289) with good, thick soles, sturdy and strong, so that I do not have to run to the market all the time, so that I can wear them for seven years without their wearing out." The craftsman said: "I would be very pleased to make them." (290) When Ashmodai heard it, he began to laugh heartily, so that his whole body made cracking sounds. Thereafter they went further and saw someone sitting there who was performing a great deal of magic and offered up his insights about it. (291) When Ashmodai saw that, he again began to laugh.

And when they came to Jerusalem, everyone said: "What will happen now?" Benaiah took Ashmodai to court. They did not want to let him in. They left Ashmodai standing before the gate of the palace for three days. (292) When Ashmodai saw that they would not let him in: "What does that matter? In there I will only have vexation." Thus did Ashmodai speak. "What does this mean?" The king had it said to him that he had drunk too much wine. (293) Many bricks lay in front of the palace. Ashmodai stacked them, one on top of the other. They went to the king and told him what Ashmodai had done: how he had stacked one brick on top of the other. (294) The wise king then said: "By that he means: 'I have drunk too much. Here I ought to drink more: when one drinks a lot, he can remain sober while drinking.'" Ashmodai began once again: (295) "Is it not yet time that I am to be let inside?" When the king heard it, he laughed excessively. He let it be said to him that he had eaten too much. It was said to Ashmodai while he was sitting outside. (296) When he heard that, he again took the bricks and laid them down on the ground. The king was told what he had done. The king then said: "If you do not understand that—(297) Ashmodai means: 'if one eats too much, then he must refrain from eating, if he wishes to become healthy.'"

After the three days, he was let in. He took an ell[9] measure with him and went in. (298) The demon came walking in to the king. He was led on an iron chain. Listen to what else he did. He took this ell measure and measured off four ells right in front of the king, where he was sitting. (299) Ashmodai said to the king: "And are you still not satisfied? The entire world has been subject to you, but you still do not have enough, so you subdued me, too. No more than four ells in length belongs to you. (300) What can you amass here in this world? Nothing beside gold and money. You must indeed die. That you will certainly have, and will have to leave the world before you wish it."

(301) The king then said: "I had to have you, because I may neither hew nor engrave; I may not raise against them [building stones] either copper or iron. I need the Shamir; reveal it to me." (302) Ashmodai then answered him: "I certainly do not have it. The angel in control of the sea has it, in truth. He trusts it to no one but the wood grouse, in the oath of which he puts his trust, and otherwise no man, (303) so that it [the wood grouse] takes it [Shamir] to the top of the highest crag that it can find and has heard of and lays the worm on the hard stone and lets it split small clefts, (304) into which it [the wood grouse] threw seeds so that it might bear fruit, on which it and its young feed for many a day."

The king had a search made where there was a wood grouse on its nest and provided his servants a very clear glass. (305) The servants took that glass and searched there for a nest. They found one on a mountain; they were quite pleased. The wood grouse was not on its nest. In that nest there were many wood grouse chicks. (306) They took the clear glass and plunged it over them and hid themselves so that they could not be seen. The wood grouse came flying over its nest. Because of the glass, it could not get to it. (307) It lamented mightily, as did its young. It hopped to and fro, for it could see them clearly. It arose and flew away again, and the good wood grouse brought the Shamir back with it. (308) It [the wood grouse] laid it [Shamir] on the glass; the servants shouted at it. It flew away, for it feared the danger. It left the Shamir lying there. They took it away with them, and the wood grouse did not know what to do. (309) It had sworn to the angel to bring it back and return it. It died from its very great sorrow and strangled itself because of its great grief, and they carried the Shamir with them; they began to depart from there.

(310) They brought it to the king. How delighted he was, when the magnificent worm was laid down in a place there. Now, Duke Benaiah said to the demon Ashmodai: "Let me ask you a few things: (311) What was your intent, when you were coming with me—when the blind man lost his way, and you led him back and showed him the way, and you also helped the drunkard out of the mire?" (312) "I will explain that to you, why I led him back—the blind man—so that he did not lose his way, for I

had heard said in Heaven concerning him that he has been an utterly pious man all the days of his life, (313) and whoever is an honorable man and does good works here, it will be reckoned to his credit in the world to come. And I also immediately helped the drunkard, for in Heaven it is shouted at him every day (314) how he has been a villain all the days of his life, expecting that he may have no merit of the world to come." Then Benaiah again said: "But why did you weep so profusely there at that wedding? What did you mean by that?" (315) Ashmodai again replied: "I will tell you that. The bridegroom will die in thirty days. He has a small younger brother who is still lying in the cradle. Meanwhile the bride must always sleep alone. (316) She is in the meantime not allowed to marry any man. She must perform the ceremony of *ḥalitzah*: she will have to wait thirteen years for the little lad. On my honor, it is indeed to be pitied that she must sleep alone: she is so afraid, poor thing." (317) "I must ask you more: why did you laugh, when the man was standing with the cobbler who makes the shoes for him that are to last for seven whole years? Is that not to happen? Tell me the real truth." (318) Then Ashmodai said: "It could well be. But how can he know if he will live seven days. He may die tomorrow and be carried away. What good will then be the soles and the leather?" (319) "Now I wish to ask you yet another thing. Explain to me so that I also understand it: why did you laugh while that one was performing magic?" "Am I not supposed to laugh, when he did nothing? (320) The simpleton thought he was performing powerful magic concerning whether there might be a great buried treasure—while he was actually sitting atop a royal treasure that no one could buy. He set his sights elsewhere where he might find one! (321) If he does not himself know for certain what is there [where he is], he can also not know what there is elsewhere." Thus did Duke Benaiah go his way. He left the huge demon Ashmodai lying there.

(322) Ashmodai thus had to stay there with the king for a long time: until he had built the Temple, stately and fine. Once the king was alone with Ashmodai. They were talking together about a variety of things. (323) The king then said to the demon Ashmodai: "Let me ask you, be it as it may: it is written how the angels have great might and also that the demons have power. (324) The possession of great power astonishes me indeed. That angels have great power I knew already. But what power can a false demon have? That has astonished me all the days of my life." (325) "Well, first of all, you know nothing," said Ashmodai to the king. "If you wish, I will show you something grand, so that you may experience many an adventure that you have never seen, either last year or this year. (326) Take the iron chains off my neck. I will show you what you want—what I have learned. And give me your ring from your hand. I will show you some fine tricks that you do not know."

(327) King Solomon did as he had requested and took the iron chain off his neck. As soon as the iron chain came off his neck, he snatched King Solomon; how quickly did he take him away. (328) He made himself huge and gobbled Solomon up. He put one wing on the earth and the other in Heaven and soon again spit him out an

exceedingly great distance, some four hundred miles. (329) And this demon set himself in Solomon's place. No one else knew but that it was the king. He acted like a king properly should. He lay with all his [Solomon's] wives with whom he wished to lie.

(330) Now when King Solomon saw himself so poor, he said to himself: "Am I dreaming? Am I King Solomon, or am I not?" It happened to him as to the baker of Vurkham who had lost his horse. (331) When he had long pondered and now realized that he had been king, [he said:] "Most beloved, Almighty God, how poor am I! Where are all my servants? May God have mercy! (332) Now where is my wealth? Where is my property? How naked am I in my great poverty! Once I was a king. Now I am a beggar." He went around with a walking stick.

(333) While King Solomon now saw himself in great poverty: "God, is it Your will that has taken place here?" Thus spoke the poor Solomon: "That which a human being attains—how quickly it betrays him! (334) No one should rely on his property and on his wealth. I ruled the entire world. I would be very happy if someone were to give me a scrap of bread, so that I not fall dead of great hunger." (335) He ran to all doors and knocked: "For God's sake, give me something. I am a poor man. If you would recognize me, I am King Solomon. On my soul, you can believe it; it is true." (336) When the people heard it, they began to laugh: "Look, dear people, what is supposed to be happening here: there is a fool here who claims to be king. He has perhaps only a penny or two of his own."

(337) When they mocked the poor king, then he again went further on his way, as it is written, and said to the people: "Do you not recognize me? I was a king; King Solomon is my name. (338) Indeed I was king of Jerusalem. You may certainly believe it; it is true, on my oath." When the finer people heard that he was still saying such things: "What is the meaning of this? Something is not right here. (339) If a person is a fool, he does not speak so consistently, and this one ever claims that he was a mighty king." The [members of the] Sanhedrin had Duke Benaiah summoned: "My dear man, tell us truly and explain it to us. (340) You are the one who rides next to the king. Tell us about how you were recently with the king." Benaiah then said: "I may say, I cannot remember how many days it has been (341) that I have not been with the king." The [members of the] Sanhedrin then said: "What sense does that make? What is going on? Something is not right here. It is difficult to comprehend such strange happenings." (342) They sent to the queen: "Does the king also lie with you?" She replied to them sincerely: "He does indeed lie with me." They replied to her: "Pay close attention to his legs: what is their form when you are alone with him?" (343) For the scholars well knew that if he were not a human or a man, then he was a demon and would have feet like a chicken. The queen then replied to them: "I cannot know: he wears socks and is very meticulous about it. (344) Moreover, he forces himself on me—it astonishes me—when my period comes so that I am impure. I cannot understand this bizarre thing. He also makes demands—thus and so—of his mother, Bathsheba."

(345) The [members of the] Sanhedrin said: "That cannot be Solomon." They summoned the poor beggar: "Come inside to us. Tell us what happened to you such that you are always saying that you are King Solomon, and you are not. (346) Tell us everything." He gave them all the clear indicators [of his identity]. They were well able to recognize that there was nothing false therein. King Solomon then said: "I myself did something foolish. If a prudent person does something foolish, it is not a small folly." (347) The [members of the] Sanhedrin then took an iron chain and a ring, on which was engraved a fine and sacred name, with which the poor Solomon departed, wishing to imprison Ashmodai. As soon as the demon saw him, he flew very far away. (348) When he had now fled, Solomon was again king, and so very splendidly did he sit upon his throne. But King Solomon was not free of anxiety, for he was constantly in fear of the demon Ashmodai.

APPENDIX B

Briyo and Zimro

בְּרִיעָה וזִימְרָה / *Briyo ve-Zimro*

Anonymous, 1585

The inclusion of the heroic prose tale בְּרִיעָה וזִימְרָה *Briyo ve-Zimro* (Briyo and Zimro) in the appendix to a collection of epic poems has been justified above in the introduction: the narrative is, one might suggest, precisely the kind of material on which chapbook epics (*Volksbücher*) of the period were based; it is itself a typical late-sixteenth-century epic in all respects except that it is not in poetic form. According to my own definition, however, that is precisely the deciding factor, and thus despite its otherwise "epic" content, it is here included in the appendix as an illustration of that transition between verse epic and its functional cultural replacement in the coming decades by the development of the adventure novel.

This remarkable story combines numerous traditional and folkloric motifs, such as the sword in the stone, parental prohibitions that block the union of star-crossed lovers, a verdict that demonstrates a young jurist's sense of justice, the hero's journey to the Otherworld on the back of a magical horse (while there attempting to retrieve his beloved), a prohibition on eating (or even touching) anything in the Otherworld, a divinely sanctioned wedding in the afterlife, and a riddling hero who saves his life by means of the intellectual conquest of his nemesis while in his power, among others.

The tale thus resonates for the modern reader with Solomon's judgment of the two mothers, the stories of Orpheus, Persephone, Gawain and/or Perceval, Romeo and Juliet, the Norse warrior poet Egil, and King Arthur—quite a roll call of analogues.[1] In early Yiddish literature, the narrative also presents a love story without peer. It is, incidentally, almost exactly contemporary with Shakespeare's great dramatic love stories, and also with the greatest of the early Yiddish "secular" epics, *Pariz un Viene*, although it is still more emotionally intense. As is also the case in *Pariz un Viene*, this narrative offers a significant instance of an important female character who takes a full participatory role in the narrative. While the tale combines a number of motifs from a broad range of Pan-European narrative traditions (not unusual in Ashkenazic literature of the period), it nonetheless remains quintessentially Jewish in content. In fact, even despite its quasi-secular identity (insofar as it has no biblical source), it participates to a surprising degree in the mode of midrashic epic and actually draws on midrashic sources.[2] There is a profound syncretism in the interplay between fantasy and history in the combination of plot motifs: the narrative is set in a period in which Jewish kings rule, with a king named *Hurk*(e)*nis* (Hyrcanus II, thus logically during the late Maccabean period), and there are high priests in Jerusalem (thus logically prior to the destruction of the Second Temple), *and* a pope in Rome, although the functional primacy of the bishop of Rome was not recognized until at least the early fourth but more generally the sixth century CE, and the conflation of the office of pope with that of quasi-imperial temporal ruler belongs altogether to the realm of fantasy. Although such obvious anachronisms are striking, they are no more so than others commonly found in sixteenth-century European tales set in a fantasized antiquity. The motif of the prideful father's refusal to allow his daughter to marry a suitor whom he deems of lower status is conventional in post-chivalric European literature of the period, linked as it was with the quasi-feudal conceptions of power relations that draw more on medieval than ancient epic traditions. Obviously, this motif dovetails rather closely with the similar issue as it appears in the Jewish tradition—the *yikhes* motif—as becomes clear through its frequent recurrence in the tales included in the present volume.

There are three primary strands of the text tradition that are distinct enough from each other that no critical edition is possible. The earliest text witness, Munich, Bayerische Staatsbibliothek, Cod. hebr. 100 of 1585, is the base text translated here. That manuscript garbles the introduction of the primary characters, however, such that Hurknis seems to be the unnamed king's second in command, while Zimro is first identified as the son of Tovas[3] and then immediately thereafter (in the judgment episode) as the brother of Tovas and both as the sons of the king. The Prague edition of the text almost certainly preserves the correct conception of the relationships of the characters and is thus taken here as the source of the translation in the few sentences of the opening passage in which the character-name relationships are established.

Source: Munich, Bayerische Staatsbibliothek, Cod. hebr. 100, folios 67r–73v; online facsimile, http://daten.digitale-sammlungen.de/~db/0003/bsb00036332/images/index.html?id=00036332&fip=fsdryztsxdsydensdaseayaenweayayztsyzts&no=1&seite=1; Prague 1620–60 (extant: Oxford, Bodleian Library, Opp. 8° 1100).

Edition: Erik, *Roman*, 147–78; *EYT*, 67.

Translation: Joachim Neugröschel, *The Dybbuk and the Yiddish Imagination: A Haunted Reader* (Syracuse, NY: Syracuse Univ. Press, 2000), 81–94.

Research: Max Erik, "Vegn 'Mayse Briyo veZimro,'" *Shriftn fun yidishn visnshaftlekhn institut* [*filologishe serye*] 1 (Vilne 1926) = *Landoy-bukh: Dr. Alfred Landoy tsu zayn 75stn geboyrnstog dem 25stn november 1925* (Vilne: Kletskin, 1926), col. 153–62; Israel Zinberg [Yisroel Tsinberg], "Oys der alt-yidisher literatur," *Shriftn fun yidishn visnshaftlekhn institut* [*filologishe serye*] 3 (Vilne: Kletskin, 1929), col. 173–84; Yitskhok Shiper, "A yidishe libe-roman fun mitlelter, tsushtayern tsu der geshikhte vegn dem ufkum fun mayse Briyo veZimro," *YIVO-bleter* 13 (1938): 132–45; Erika Timm, "Beria und Simra: Eine jiddische Erzählung des 16. Jahrhunderts," *Literaturwissenschaftliches Jahrbuch*, n.s. 14 (1973): 1–94 [Germanized Roman-alphabet transcription], reprinted in Erika Timm, *Graphische und phonische Struktur des Westjiddischen unter besonderer Berücksichtigung der Zeit um 1600* (Tübingen: Niemeyer, 1987), appx. 4, 521–53.

A tale took place: one was named Briyo, and the other was named Zimro. It was in the days of Hurknis. There was a lord who was second only to the king and was held in honor among the Jews, a leader among the people, and his name was Zimro; and Zimro had a son whose name was Tovas. And Tovas had a son who was noble and wise and a Torah scholar. And the king loved him more than all his servants and put him in charge of his kingdom. And he named him Zimro after his grandfather. And the king made him judge over all the people of Israel, to teach them Torah. And the king gave him a house next to his castle in Jerusalem and next to the houses of the priests, for he was a judge over all of Israel the three times a year when they went up [to Jerusalem] during the year to the festival, and every day they came to offer the sacrifices.

And on one Rosh Hashone[4] the king sat on his throne, and his servants stood before him. There came before him a woman with two of her sons, and they had a quarrel about an inheritance that their father had left them. One of them had two heads and spoke with two mouths and wanted two shares, for the claim was that he was two people. So the king said to Zimro and to his son: "Make your judgment! I want to see how you will render the verdict." Then they answered: "My lord, father and king, we are happy to do so."

Then the one with two heads came before them, and Tovas was not sure how to render a verdict, and Zimro commanded that hot water be given to him in a jug, which was done. The hot water was poured over one of his heads. Then the other head screamed. Then Zimro said: "Why are you screaming? Indeed I have done nothing to you. Thus I also see that you are one body. You should also receive a single share." The king and all his people then laughed because of Zimro's verdict.

After these things had come to pass, modest Zimro saw the beautiful Briyo, the daughter of Feygin, and she was very humble and quite honorable, and he liked her very much. And the maiden also liked him a great deal, for she heard that he was a learned and honorable man. And she desired him in her heart.

One day Feygin had a banquet and invited Tovas and Zimro. Then Zimro rejoiced. When it was time to dine, he said: "Now I will reveal my heart to the maiden." Now when they entered the house of the high priest, a very magnificent banquet had been prepared, and the table was set with many noble dishes, such as they had never before seen at any person's house. And the people were very astonished by that. Then he said: "Those are not noble dishes. I have a much more beautiful thing," and led them—the king and Tovas and Zimro—with him into a room where he showed them his beautiful daughter. She was the most essentially beautiful person that anyone had ever seen. Her beauty is indescribable; so I must give up trying. And Zimro looked directly at her and could not be sated in looking at her, and was stricken by love, so that he turned pale, and people clearly noticed it in him and laughed at him. But they kept silent about it. Thus they left her and went back into the other room and went to sleep—so drunk were they. But Zimro did not sleep and thought how he wanted to go to the beautiful daughter, even if it were to cost him his life; and thus he went cheerfully to her in the room where she was. As he opened the door, and she saw him coming, she got up and faced him and welcomed him quite cordially and well, and he in turn thanked her courteously, and she led him by the hand, and they sat down beside each other. Then he began to speak: "In the meantime I would like to say something to you in all propriety and honor and would also at the same time like to ask that you not take it amiss." Then she said: "Dear Zimro, say what you wish, I will not take it amiss." Then he said: "From the moment that I first looked at you, I have been captivated by such love that I have no peace and beg you to promise me that you will marry me. Then I will arrange with my father that he speaks with your father, so that he gives his permission. I will do it so that it comes about quite honorably." Then she said: "Dear my lord Zimro, you do not like me nearly as much as I love you. I cannot tell you the love that I have for you. If it is the will of God, blessed be He, then we will bring this thing about."

Thus they parted from each other in good spirits, and Zimro returned to the people and behaved as though he had not stirred the waters but had slept because of drunkenness. Thus the guests again took their leave, and each went home in peace. When Zimro came home, he became ill and did not want to eat, drink, or sleep and was quite sad. Then his father said: "My dear son, tell me, why are you so sad? Tell me, what is the matter?" Then he said: "Dear father, sir, I must tell you: since I saw the high priest's daughter, I am so captivated by love for her, that if I cannot obtain her, then I must die from my great love. For that reason, dear father, sir, speak with the high priest so that he gives her to me as a bride." Then his father, Tovas, said: "My dear son, be silent and do not disgrace yourself or me. If I am not mistaken, I am not of the necessary status to become his in-law. For that reason, obey me and give up this plan." Then Zimro said: "In that case, dear father, I would like to share a secret with you, and thus you will hear that I am not going to bring disgrace on myself by what has happened. When we were guests of the high priest, and other people were sleeping, I went secretly to her with all propriety and honor. There we both made and accepted vows to marry each other."

Thus Tovas heard just where the matter stood and said: "Now, dear son, so be it. I will try my luck." So Tovas left his son Zimro and went to four men, the most prominent in the city, and told them his son's concern and wish and asked them to speak with the high priest so that he would give his permission and promise them a good match. Then the four men said: "You and your son can be confident; we will certainly bring this about; we have no doubts. Go on and prepare for the wedding." Then Tovas said: "It is too early to prepare for the wedding. I have plenty of time. Ask him first."

The four community officials went to the high priest and presented him with the request of Tovas and Zimro that if he were to become his in-law, then he would give his son great wealth. Then Feygin, the high priest, laughed and said: "Dear officials, my good friends, I well know that Zimro is the most handsome and noble lad in the land and kingdom. But to give him my daughter's hand—that will never under any circumstances happen. I would rather drown her. Now you have my decision. Go, and long life and peace to you."

Thus the four officials returned to Tovas and told him the decision. Then Tovas said: "That is just what I predicted! You want me to buy the bucket before the milk-cow! Now it is a disgrace for me that I began this." The news came to Zimro: to whom could it have caused more pain than to him? His heart wished to shatter into pieces from grief. Then his father said: "Be silent, my dear son. I will certainly find another bride for you, and twenty thousand gold coins, in addition." But Zimro could not be comforted and said: "If I do not get the beautiful daughter, then I must die of grief."

When Zimro saw that he could accomplish nothing through his father and the four officials, he went to the king and told him his concern, for he was dear to the king, and he asked him to speak to the high priest, so that he would give him his daughter in marriage. Then he said: "I would be happy to do it," and sent for the high priest and said to him: "I would like to make a request of you; you will not refuse to do it for me: give your daughter Briyo to Zimro in marriage." Then the high priest took fright and said: "Dear my lord king, would you advise me to join myself to a lineage lower than my own? All Jews will ridicule me. It is not in my nature, and I will, moreover, not do it. May your royal highness do as he wishes." Then the king said: "I will not force you." Thus he departed. And Tovas and Zimro came to the king and wanted to get good news from him, but it was not what they wished for. Then the king told them what answer the high priest had given him. "Therefore, my dear Zimro, give up your desire. Try what you will, it will not happen."

Then Zimro waited until they went to the synagogue; then he went into the high priest's house. As soon as she saw him, she let him in and welcomed him, and he began to weep. She then said: "Why are you weeping?" He then said: "Because your father will not give you to me in marriage." Then she also began to weep and said: "May God have mercy!" Then Zimro said: "My dear beloved, I would like to make a request of you, if you would grant it to me." Then she said: "Ask whatever you wish; it will be granted to you. I know that you will not expect anything sinful or shameful." Then he said: "Then I ask that you take no husband besides me, and

I will promise you that I will take no other wife besides you." Then she said: "I will gladly do that." Thus they vowed to each other. Zimro sighed deeply and looked at her. Then she said: "O why are you doing that?" Then he said: "I would like to make one more request of you: if you would not refuse me, I would like to kiss you." Then she said: "You would be permitted." Then he kissed her a thousand times, and she kissed him also.

Then it was almost time for people to leave the synagogue. There they stood, weeping with each other. And she said: "Dear Zimro, when you ride with the prince, ride first before my house. Then I will stand at a window, so that I can see you, but you cannot see me if I do not open the window. But every morning when the morning prayer begins, I open the window and listen to the opening of the prayer. Then you can see me. And when you see a towel hanging at the window, then come to me."

At this he departed with a cheerful spirit, and every morning he passed beneath her window, and they looked at one another. Once the prince came riding and said to Zimro: "Should we go for a ride outside the city?" Then Zimro replied: "Yes." So they rode out together. Zimro heaved sighs and was gloomy. So the prince said: "What is the matter with you, Zimro, that you are so gloomy? In times past you made leaps with your horse, and now you are riding as if asleep. You really must tell me, what the matter is or what troubles you." So Zimro said: "The high priest has a daughter, and if I cannot have her, I will die of grief." Then the prince said: "Do not let it bother you. Be silent. She will certainly be yours. I will tell my father; he will have to send for him and speak with him, so that he gives her to you in marriage. He will not refuse my father."

Thus they rode with each other up to the castle. There the king said: "What is the matter with you, that you look so serious? I do not think that you are feeling well." So the prince said: "I will tell you." Then he told him that he should ask the high priest to give his daughter to Zimro in marriage. So the king said: "I have already asked him once. He rejected my request." So the prince said: "I would ask him and arrange it so that if he were to refuse you again, it would cost him his life."

He again sent for the high priest and said to him: "I already insisted of you once before that you give your daughter to Zimro in marriage, and you refused me. Now I am asking you, and do not rebel against me." Then the high priest said: "I am certain that if I do not do it, you will kill me, for whoever refuses to do what the king says has lost his life. But still I will not do it, no matter what happens to me because of it. Although Zimro is a handsome, well-educated and wise lad, I would rather drown my daughter than let her marry him." The king was angry and said: "I will have you killed because of your contempt for me. So keep your daughter. I will give Zimro another bride, leaving your daughter out of it." The king said to Zimro: "Seek throughout my kingdom for another bride for yourself. I will give you in addition great wealth." But it did not please Zimro. He had only the beautiful Briyo in his heart. So he thanked the king and departed sorrowfully.

After these things had come to pass, there was a pope in Rome who was a great villain. He forbade women to go to the ritual bath, boys to be circumcised, and Jews to come into his presence. If one were to do so, he was to be killed. And the Jews were informed by letter, and the high priest was asked to pray that such evil decrees be rescinded.

The high priest thought: "Now I will get rid of Zimro. I will tell him, if he will go to the pope and plead for the Jews, so that he rescinds the decree, then I will give him my daughter's hand. Thus will the pope kill him, and thus I will be rid of him." His daughter heard this and thought: "I will warn him." And when people went to the synagogue, she again hung out the towel. Then Zimro saw it and went to see her, and she welcomed him very warmly and told him everything that her father had planned. "Therefore do not let yourself be persuaded, so that you do not lose your life, or I will not keep the promise that I made to you." Then Zimro said: "If your father gives you to me in marriage, then I will risk my life for your sake." Then she wept piteously. He said: "Farewell! God, blessed be He, will grant me good fortune, so that nothing happens to me." He then took his leave from her with moist eyes, and she said: "Go forth, and may God grant you good luck and good fortune!"

Now when people had left the synagogue, the high priest took Zimro aside and laid the proposal before him. Then Zimro answered: "If you would follow through on what you propose, then I would risk my life." He took an oath to him before witnesses. Thus Zimro went forth and told the beautiful Briyo nothing more about it. The high priest then said: "We are rid of Zimro! He will not come back alive!" When his daughter heard that, she shrieked and wept and lamented bitterly for as long as he was away; and every week that he was away she fasted three days and three nights.

Zimro traveled as long as it took him to come to the pope in Rome. He asked the Jews how he could get to the pope. They told him that if he came before him, he would be killed. He then held his peace and went to the money exchange and changed ten guilders into nothing but groats. He then went into the castle and dropped a lot of groats on the ground. The gatekeepers let him enter while they were gathering up the coins. When he entered even into the courtyard, Gentile aristocrats and counts came toward him and wanted to ask who his lord was, so he again dropped money on the ground. Once again, they gathered it up and let him pass. Thus did he come inside into the presence of the pope. The pope asked him who his lord was. He then said: "I am a Jew." The pope was then shocked that he had entered in this way and that nothing had happened to him. And the guards wanted to kill him. He [the pope] then ordered that he be allowed to live, but he [the pope] wanted to have all the gatekeepers killed.

The pope then said: "Now, tell me, my dear Jew, what do you want? For I will at least listen to it, since God has granted you the good fortune to come before me unharmed." Zimro then said: "Most worthy and lauded Sir, I would like to ask your honorable grace for two things, and may your grace not take offense but grant me the requests." So he said: "Ask whatever you want, just nothing concerning the Jews!" He then said: "I want to ask you a question concerning the Jews, which will be of service to you." The pope then said: "Then go ahead and ask!" Zimro then said: "My dear sir, if you were to have enemies, would you prefer them to be weak or strong?" The pope laughed and said: "That is a very clever question. If I were to have enemies, would I not prefer that they be weak rather than strong? Now, dear fellow, tell me what your point is and why are you asking such a perverse question!" Zimro then said: "If you will give me a moment, I will tell you, for I have come to you for your own sake. And you are right, but your counselors are not giving you good advice in good faith, for the Jews are your enemies, and there is no weaker or more feeble nation on earth than the Jews, for they are circumcised at the age of eight days so that they bleed, which makes them weak. But if they are not circumcised, then one Jew can defeat ten Christians. And you forbid the Jews to practice circumcision anymore. In ten years all your land will be full of Jews."

The pope then said: "That's true! What is then your other question?" Zimro then said: "My dear sir, if you were to have enemies, would you prefer that there were many of them or few?" He then laughed again and said: "I would prefer that there were few rather than many. Tell me what your point is!" Then he said: "I will tell you. You have forbidden Jewish women to go to the ritual bath. Where earlier one Jew was born, now four will be born, for the Jewish women are shocked by the cold water and do not soon become pregnant again. They are also not permitted to lie with their husbands. But if they are not allowed to go into the cold water, they will lie with their husbands sooner and passionately, so there will be as many of them as the sands of the sea—(So may they multiply!)—and they will wage war against you and will kill you."

Then the pope said: "Jew, you have spoken the truth. I have never heard many Jews more clever than you. Therefore, I will give you many presents and allow you to return home in peace." And he gave him a great deal of money and jewels and a fine document which rescinded the evil decree. Then the pope had all the gatekeepers killed, who had let him enter (So may they perish!).

And Zimro took his leave from the pope and returned to his lodgings with the Jews. Then he told them how he had had the evil decree rescinded and showed them the money and the document that the pope had given him. Then the Jews also wanted to give him a great deal of money, but he did not want to take anything, because he had already received enough. He said farewell and rode back home to his country. There everyone was pleased, especially his most beloved Briyo. But the high priest was so shocked that he almost gave up the ghost. He had indeed thought that they would have killed him. Good Zimro showed the document, and everyone was happy that the evil decree had been rescinded. Then Zimro said: "Now give me what you promised me." The high priest refused him and once again did not want to give him his daughter's hand. "Even if I were to lose my life because of it." Zimro then said: "May God, blessed be He, have mercy." And he said: "For what purpose then were the great hardships and treachery that I have endured? And now it is again for nothing." And he was quite miserable, indeed beyond description.

The good but miserable Zimro waited until people went into the synagogue, and then he again went to his beloved Briyo. She welcomed him most beautifully and lovingly with many joyous words, and he told her how her father had reneged on his promise to him. Then they both wept and lamented a great deal, and she embraced him and kissed him and said: "My dear Zimro, may God hear our lament! I well know that I must die of grief." Then Zimro said: "May God forbid it," and he kissed her, and she kissed him, and there such kissing that if she had not already been beautiful, she would now have become beautiful. And he left her thus.

As soon as he had left her, she died of grief. For that reason, no one should kiss another person when leaving. But Zimro did not know that she had died. There was great lamenting and wailing, and she was honorably buried.

One day Zimro went before both the king and the prince and was well received by them. When he left the castle, he was met by his father, who said: "My dear son, I would like to ask you something, if only you will not be overwhelmed by it." He then said: "No, I will not be overwhelmed." Then he said: "You were miserable because the high priest refused to give you his daughter in marriage. Now you will be even more miserable, for she has died of grief. Do not let it overwhelm you." Then he said: "Why should I be overwhelmed: that which God, blessed be He, does is well done." But what was in his heart, everyone can well imagine. When he got home and went to his room, he lamented and tore out his hair because of his grief. Such lamentation cannot be described. After such lamentation he again left his room and wiped his eyes, so that no one would see it. This he did perhaps for eight days in a row.

When the king had become old, he summoned his counselors and lords, for he wanted to have his son crowned king while he was still alive. That took place, and he had a great banquet. Zimro was close to the young king, and the young king said to Zimro: "My father has given over the possession of the kingdom to me after his death. Come with me to my lord father, the king, and, with his counselors as witnesses, I will transfer it to you after my death, so that you will possess it. For that reason, wait for a little while, and then you must ride with me to the castle." Zimro agreed and got himself ready with beautiful clothes and all other necessary things. He waited for a little while, but it was taking too long for him, so he went ahead at a leisurely pace, thinking: "He will overtake me riding." But as he went up the hill, he began to get tired—for it was a very high hill—and he stopped and stood still for a while. There he saw a most beautiful horse running before him, quite well caparisoned with harness more beautiful than he had ever seen in his life. And the horse acted as if it wanted to ride down the hill. He then thought: "If I could catch it, I would ride up the hill." He went toward it, and it stood there still. As soon as he mounted the horse, it galloped away helter-skelter, as if it were the Devil himself, and it galloped into a great forest with him, where a multitude of herbs were growing. Thereafter he came to a meadow on which grew a multitude of roots. There the horse stopped. He was happy and climbed down from the saddle onto the meadow and wanted to enjoy himself for a while. Then the horse galloped away and disappeared before his very eyes so that he did not know where it had gone. Then he did not know where he was. He shrieked and was so miserable that it cannot be described. He yelled again and again: "Grief on top of grief! Misfortune, how you do grip me! I do not know which way to turn and am so far from my father and friends, and see and hear neither person nor house nor city. Where am I, or what has happened to me?"

In addition to such discomfort, he was very hungry. He found nothing to eat except for the roots and herbs, and he drank water, and walked for a long time on the meadow or moor and thought that he would get home. But the longer he walked, the more lost he became. Finally he came to a beautiful stream. He stepped into it, for it was not deep. There he found many jewels, of which he took many and put them inside his shirt. The stream was full of jewels and flowed out of Paradise. He undressed and walked through the water, whose current was fast and strong. He got across and came to a fine road. There he saw before him a large stone in which a sword had been cast [by a smith]. There was also a wheel on the stone so that it rotated and struck at every path and passage, so that he could not go on, for it was so constructed to guard the entrance to Paradise. Then he said a prayer, and the wheel stopped and let him pass by. He went further and came to a meadow which was full of shearing blades with their sharp edges turned upward. There he again said a prayer, and the shearing blades parted, and he passed through. Then he came to a field where a small house stood before him. He was very happy and went inside. There were many people sitting inside eating who looked at him and greeted him with "Peace [be with you]."[5] He thanked them and was happy to hear that they were Jews. He went and wanted to wash his hands and eat, too. They shouted at him: "Do not wash your hands, and beware lest you touch anything!" Then he said: "Why?" They then said: "We are all dead and are neither joyful nor miserable, and we must stay here a whole year, each of us according to our sins. Dear Zimro, pray for us! We well know what you are doing here. Yesterday we heard that you would be summoned."

He asked them much, but they did not want to tell him anything. So he again left them. Then he looked around more carefully and saw his beautiful and loving Briyo sitting under the stairs. He was startled and said: "Alas, what are you doing here, dear Briyo?" Then she said: "My dear and most distinguished Zimro, I have to sit here for eight more days, but if you pray for me, I will get out soon. Dear Zimro, I committed no sin on earth, except that I allowed you to kiss me." He went to her and wanted to kiss her again. She then said: "Beware for your life, and do not touch me, or you will have to die!" Then he said: "I do not know where I am or what has happened to me or where I should go. I want to kiss you, so that I will die and stay here with you." Then she said: "No, on your life! Get away from me—across the meadow—thus will you get home again."

Full of grief and weeping and wailing, he then left her. Then on the meadow he met an old, gray man with a long beard. Then the old man said: "Now that is a peculiar man in these parts!" Then Zimro said: "That is true indeed: I do not know where I am or where I am to go. My dear rabbi, show me how to get home, and tell me what I have done that such a tale has happened to me." Then he said: "You have committed no sin, except that Briyo died because of you.[6] Now you should go back home." Then Zimro said: "My dear rabbi, tell me who you are!" Then he said: "I am the prophet Elijah." Then he said: "My dear rabbi, bless me!" Then he said: "I do not wish to bless you now. I well know that you must return home."

He had forgotten that he had not prayed for Briyo. When he now returned, he went into the house to his Briyo. It seemed to him that someone was with her with both her breasts in his hands. Then he said: "My dear Briyo, who is embracing you?" Then she said: "My dear Zimro, do not be alarmed! Satan wants to tempt you." And he went to his Briyo, and she said: "Beware! Do not touch me until I have finished speaking!" Then he said: "So, say what you want to say!" Then she said: "So, my dear Zimro, do you want to share a throne with me, or would you rather wait longer?" Then he said: "I do not want to wait longer." Then she said: "Then go back home and tell your father and my father! Whether they like it or not, you will indeed have me. He did not want to give me to you while I was alive. So, he will have to endure it—without silver and gold—that you have me in the afterlife. And go to the ritual bath and purify yourself and say farewell to your friends! On the third day you will certainly be dead. I tell you truly: on the third day you will certainly die, if you touch me." He said: "I want to touch you, even if it were to cost me my life a second time." And he embraced and kissed her and thereafter went away.

Then the old, gray man again came to him and said: "Come here, my dear Zimro! I will lead you home and will meanwhile prepare for your wedding." Then he blessed him. Then he prayed for his dear Briyo to be released from beneath the stairs and from the cottage. That was done, and she entered the luminous Paradise. Whoever does not believe it is nonetheless still a Jew.

Then Zimro returned home. The king was angry that he had been away so long. Then he told him everything that had happened to him and how he was to die, and the king was quite miserable about Zimro's death. Thus it was that Zimro came to his father and Briyo's father and said what Briyo had commanded: that he would have to die on the third day. All of his friends were quite miserable about Zimro's death. He said that when he was dead, they were not to bury him; they were to lay him on top of his grave and leave him there and go back home.

Thus he went to the ritual bath and purified himself and said farewell to everyone. There was a great wailing and weeping that was heard throughout the city. The same was true of the high priest, who now sorely regretted thus losing his daughter.

The conclusion is: on the third day, the good and honorable Zimro died, may God have mercy on him. His friends did as he had commanded them. They mourned greatly for him, more than one can describe. Then, after long wailing and weeping, everyone went home and left him thus unburied in the cemetery. Then the angels Michael and Gabriel came and took him and carried him—as was proper, for he had never committed a sin—and brought him to Paradise to his most beloved Briyo and had a noble wedding for them. The Holy One, blessed be He, gave the blessing, and the angels were the jesters; Moses and Aaron led the bride and groom under the wedding canopy. Then there was eating and drinking and dancing, and King Solomon recited the seven blessings.

It was such a splendid wedding, as there has never before been in any Jewish community. Now, you dear people, you have indeed read in the little book what great love brings, for which reason, let each individual well consider in advance what might be the conclusions to be drawn therefrom: there are still many noble and honorable people in the world who could belong to him, if he otherwise has fortune and good luck. With that I would like to end. May God, blessed be He, send the old, gray man to us, too, and with him indeed bring the Messiah. Amen. May it happen in this year.

Written in the year 345 [= (5)345 = 1585], I—the writer/scribe Yitskhok b. Judah (may his memory be for a blessing) of Reutlingen—pray for that.

Notes

Introduction

1. The codex had been studied long before Fuks's edition by Ernest-Henri Lévy, who was in the process of preparing an edition when he was murdered by the Nazis; his unpublished edition was lost. See Jean Fourquet, "Ernest-H. Lévy et le Dukus Horant." The codex is now cataloged as Cambridge University Library T.-S. 10K22. The editions of the entire codex are L. [Leo] Fuks, ed., *The Oldest Known Literary Documents of Yiddish Literature (c. 1382)*; Eli Katz, ed., "Six Germano-Judaic Poems from the Cairo Genizah"; and Heikki J. Hakkarainen, ed., *Studien zum Cambridger Codex T.-S. 10. K. 22*; 1: *Text.* Katz's edition, based on ultraviolet photographs of the manuscript made under optimal conditions before the more recent conservationist damage to the manuscript, still remains the only reliable edition of the entire manuscript. Further codicological information may be found in Jerold C. Frakes, ed., *Early Yiddish Texts, 1100–1750, with Introduction and Commentary*, texts 5–9, pp. 8–11. In general on the hundreds of thousands of documents from the Cairo *geniza*, see the popular recounting of the rediscovery and early scholarly work in Adina Hoffman and Peter Cole, *Sacred Trash: The Lost and Found World of the Cairo Geniza*, near the conclusion of which the authors remark: "As it happens, very little in the Geniza glittered; but almost all, in its way, was gold" (223); on the Yiddish texts in the *geniza*, see the brief section on pages 235–36 and note on page 283. The classic and thus far most exhaustive study of the documents and their cultural significance is S. D. Goitein, *A Mediterranean Society: The Jewish Communities of the Arab World as Portrayed in the Documents of the Cairo Geniza.*

2. Throughout the present volume, ancient, medieval, and modern book titles in non-Roman alphabets are generally transcribed into the Roman alphabet according to the scholarly transcription standard for that language; terms and text citations are generally translated into English without citation of the original text; when the original language is pertinent, however, that text is also transcribed. In the case of Old and Middle Yiddish, however, for which no adequate and standardized system of transcription exists, terms, titles, and citations are—at their initial usage—cited in the Hebrew alphabet, provided with both a transcription that represents one of multiple *possible* phonetic renderings and an English translation; subsequent use of titles is in transcribed or translated form only. Thus, in the present case—original Hebrew-alphabet title, Roman transcription, and translation: פאריז אונ׳ וויענה *Pariz un Viene* (Pariz and Viene), with subsequent references to *Pariz un Viene.*

3. Now cataloged as Verona, Biblioteca del Seminario Vescovile, Fonds Venturi, no. 192; facsimile edition: Valerio Marchetti, Jean Baumgarten, and Antonella Salomoni, eds., *Elia*

Bahur Levita, "Paris un Viene," Francesco Dalle Donne, Verona, 1594; critical edition: Chone Shmeruk, ed., *"Pariz un' Viene": Mahadura biqqortit be-ẓeruf mavo, heʿarot ve-nispaḥim.*

4. The director of the archaeological project in Cologne, Dr. Sven Schütte, did not respond to repeated requests for current information concerning the excavation. The information here provided concerning the excavation as a whole derives from the preliminary report by Elisabeth Hollender, "Die Schriftfunde"; preliminary information concerning the epic text of interest here was graciously provided by Professor Erika Timm (Trier) in a private communication (September 23, 2012), supplemented by her article including an edition of the text (with both the Hebrew-alphabet Yiddish text and a Germanized Roman-alphabet transcription), "Ein neuentdeckter literarischer Text in hebräischen Lettern aus der Zeit vor 1349."

5. Hollender, "Die Schriftfunde," 143. While the date of the fire obviously sets the end limit to the inscription of the tablets (*terminus ante quem*), Hollender provides no evidence for her speculation on how long, before the fire, the tablets are to be dated.

6. Ibid., 149–51. Helpful as Hollender's preliminary description is, it in general seems quite rushed, imprecise, and often contradictory. She never actually indicates how the texts were inscribed: whether, for instance, by incision *into* the stone's surface or written *on* the stone's surface with chalk or charcoal or some other substance. She mentions a stylus (*Schreibgriffel*), which would imply incision into the surface, but also notes that a previously inscribed text was washed off (*abgewaschen*), which would imply that the writing was only on the surface (149). She assumes that the most of the slate tablets were manufactured as roof slates but were never used as such, while the larger ones were purchased for the purpose of writing on them, but offers no evidence for either assumption. She also quizzically comments, "Die Kritzeleien sind alle mit dem gleichen Griffeln gemalt" (The doodles are all painted with the same stylus) (149). But since a stylus (*Griffel*) is a (generally metal or metal-tipped) tool designed and used to incise into wax tablets or other surfaces, it is neither designed nor generally used as a means to apply paint. In another context, a contradiction arises within a single sentence when she notes that in the fourteenth century, slate was being used by Jews as a writing surface in classrooms, but then claims that slate was not used in schools until *after* the end of the Middle Ages (149). Timm specifies that the text was incised with a metal instrument ("Ein neuentdeckter literarischer Text in hebräischen Lettern aus der Zeit vor 1349," 422–43).

7. Hollender, "Die Schriftfunde," 151–52; Timm, "Ein neuentdeckter literarischer Text in hebräischen Lettern aus der Zeit vor 1349," 420. Now cataloged as Köln, Archäologische Zone, Jüdisches Museum, Tafel, 596–10; photographic plates of both sides of the slate in Hollender, "Die Schriftfunde," 145–46, pl. 213–14; and Timm, "Ein neuentdeckter literarischer Text in hebräischen Lettern aus der Zeit vor 1349," between pp. 432–33; the resolution of the photographs is inadequate for the purposes of reading the text.

8. See below in this introduction for a discussion of the specific usage of this term with reference to a subgenre of early Yiddish epic.

9. He acknowledges the aid of H. Beem and M. Klein in the preparation of the German version: *Documents*, 2:3n.

10. Moyshe Knaphays, *Elye Bokher, "Bovo-bukh."*

11. "Elia Levita's *Bovo-Bukh*: A Yiddish Romance of the Early 16th Century" (PhD diss., Cornell Univ., 1968), later published as Elia Levita Bachur, *Elia Levita Bachur's "Bovo-Buch,"*

translated by Jerry C. Smith, xxvi. Claudia Rosenzweig characterizes the work as a "free rewriting" ("The Jewish Knight, the Jewish Princess, and the Sceptical Reader," n. 12).

12. Joachim Neugröschel, *The Dybbuk and the Yiddish Imagination: A Haunted Reader*, 81–94.

13. Here as elsewhere in transcriptions of early Yiddish in the present volume, [ou], as here in *Yousef*, is to be pronounced as a diphthong, almost as if two vowels, long *o* followed by *u*; the phoneme developed into modern Yiddish [oy].

14. Joachim Neugröschel, *No Star Too Beautiful: Yiddish Stories from 1382 to the Present*, 6–8.

15. The text additionally lacks any introduction or apparatus: Heidi Graw, *Dukus Haurant*, 7.

16. Armin Schulz, *Die Zeichen des Körpers und der Liebe: "Paris und Vienna" in der jiddischen Fassung des Elia Levita.*

17. J. R. R. Tolkien, "*Beowulf*: The Monsters and the Critics," 52. Perhaps one should note here that while Tolkien is now most famous as the author of *The Lord of the Rings*, popularized in recent years by the films of Peter Jackson, he was also the Rawlinson and Bosworth Professor of Anglo-Saxon at Oxford University (1925–45) and Merton Professor of English Language and Literature (1945–59) and in his day one of the preeminent scholars of the language and literature of Anglo-Saxon England.

18. Some attention is given to the range of historical causes (especially in the twentieth century) for the gaps in the research on early Yiddish literature in my *Early Yiddish Texts*, xliii–liii.

19. Judah A. Joffe et al., eds., *Groyser verterbukh fun der yidisher shprakh*; Alexander Harkavy, *Yiddish-English-Hebrew Dictionary*; Uriel Weinreich, *Modern English-Yiddish, Yiddish-English Dictionary*; Yitskhok Niborski [Bernard Vaisbrot], *Dictionnaire Yiddish-Français* and English translation *Arumnemik yidish-english verterbukh / Comprehensive Yiddish-English Dictionary.* Two further indispensable lexica in the present project have been M. A. Shapiro, I. G. Spivak, and M. Y. Shulman, eds., *Russko-yevreiskiĭ (idish) slovar' / Rusisher-yidisher verterbukh*; and Marcus Jastrow, *Dictionary of Talmud Babli, Yerushalmi, Midrashic Literature and Targumim.*

20. J. A. Simpson and E. S. C. Weiner, eds., *Oxford English Dictionary*; Jacob Grimm and Wilhelm Grimm, eds., *Deutsches Wörterbuch.*

21. Matthias Lexer, *Mittelhochdeutsches Handwörterbuch*; Alfred Götze, *Frühneuhochdeutsches Glossar.*

22. The *prosimetrum* or *chantfable* form known in later European tradition (for example, the Old French *Aucassin et Nicolette*) should, however, be acknowledged here, for it is indeed the primary form of the broad and deep oral epic traditions in, for instance, both Arabic and Turkic languages, among others. There the narrative is expressed by lengthier prose passages recurringly interrupted by briefer, reflective (and rarely narrative) poetic interludes. This form is, however, a specifically literary form devised precisely for *epic* narrative, unlike, for instance, the prose of heroic biblical and medieval Hebrew narratives. A general orientation in this vast genre of Arabic epic is offered by M[alcolm] C[ameron] Lyons, *The Arabian Epic: Heroic and Oral Story-Telling.* The Turkic tradition is treated by Karl Reichl, *Edige: A Karakalpak Heroic Epic*, esp. 17–18, 116–41; and V. M. Zhirmunskiĭ, *Narodnyĭ geroicheskiĭ epos*, chap. 3.

23. See especially Frank Moore Cross, *Canaanite Myth and Hebrew Epic: Essays in the History of the Religion of Israel* and *From Epic to Canon: History and Literature in Ancient Israel.* In the latter book, he seems aware that he is on methodologically shaky ground, when he suggests that "Hebrew epic continued in the tradition of the older Canaanite epic singers, that is, that much was orally composed in poetry," while only a few lines later seeming to contradict that claim: "There can be no question of early Israel eschewing poetry as somehow inappropriate as a vehicle for recounting the mighty acts of Yahweh or Israel's early times" (32). The contradictions mount when he attempts to illustrate the "exquisite poetry in epic style" in ancient Hebrew in Exodus 19:3–6, but in order thus to function the text must first be editorially "stripped of . . . prose particles" (33), that is, turned into poetry by what amounts to editorial recomposition.

24. Among those scholars who have objected to his appropriation of the term "epic": Charles Conroy, "Hebrew Epic: Historical Notes and Critical Reflections"; S. Talmon, "The 'Comparative Method' in Biblical Interpretation—Principles and Problems"; and Robert Alter, "Sacred History and Prose Fiction."

25. Susan Niditch has, for instance, pointed out that Judges is "a collection of tales about various rambunctious warrior heroes" and that "the judges are frequently regarded as epic heroes," in "Epic and History in the Hebrew Bible: Definitions, 'Ethnic Genres,' and the Challenges of Cultural Identity in the Biblical Book of Judges," 86. She also notes that James A. Kugel has pointed out that "the line between 'poetry' and 'prose' is often blurry in Israelite literature" (*The Idea of Biblical Poetry: Parallelism and Its History*, 76–95), such that "large portions of the narratives of Judges, which modern readers might consider prose, are also presented in highly stylized language" (92).

26. Ben Zion Wacholder, "Theodotus."

27. The first fragment may deal with the binding of Isaac, the second with the fountains of Jerusalem, and the third with Joseph's rule in Egypt. See Ben Zion Wacholder, "Philo."

28. It should be noted that Leo Landau's summary listing of Jewish versions of originally non-Jewish romances and epics includes no actual verse epics in Hebrew, but rather simply prose paraphrases, fables, legends, and tales, some of which Landau merely conjectures, that is, they do not actually exist. Leo Landau, *Arthurian Legends; or, The Hebrew-German Rhymed Version of the Legend of King Arthur*, xiii–xxi.

29. Israel J. Kazis, ed., *Immanuel ben Jacob Bonfils, Sefer Toldot Alesandrus ha-Makdoni*; Wout Jac. van Bekkum, ed., *A Hebrew Alexander Romance according to Ms Héb. 671.5 Paris, Bibliotheque Nationale*; Wout Jac. van Bekkum, ed. and trans., *A Hebrew Alexander Romance according to MS London, Jews' College no. 145.*

30. See Landau, *Arthurian Legends*, xiv.

31. Curt Leviant, ed. and trans., *Sefer ha-šamad ha-tabla ha-agula* [*Kinig Artus*]), *King Artus: A Hebrew Arthurian Romance of 1279*; Moses Gaster, "The History of the Destruction of the Round Table, as Told in Hebrew in the Year 1279."

32. Leviant, *King Artus*, 51.

33. Extant in Parma, ms. de Rossi 1394/2.

34. Yonah David, "Moses ben Isaac da Rieti."

35. Efraim Gottlieb, "Mordecai ben Judah Dato"; Giulio Busi, *La istoria de Purim io ve racconto. Il libro di Ester secondo un rabbino emiliano del Cinquecento.*

36. Kenneth R. Scholberg, "Miguel de Silveyra."

37. See especially Vera Basch Moreen's analytical introduction and translation of excerpts from ten representative texts: *In Queen Esther's Garden: An Anthology of Judeo Persian Literature*, 26–175. Among earlier important studies of this tradition, see also Wilhelm Bacher, *Zwei jüdisch-persische Dichter Schahin und Imrani.*

38. Moreen, *In Queen Esther's Garden*, 11–12.

39. Amnon Netzer, "Shāhin." See also Moreen, *In Queen Esther's Garden*, 26–31, and a sampling of Shāhīn's epics there, 31–119.

40. David Yeroushalmi, ed., *The Judeo-Persian Poet ʿEmrānī and His Book of Treasure.* See also Amnon Netzer, "Emrāni"; and Gilbert Lazard et al., "Judeo-Persian."

41. There were nonetheless Judeo-Persian historical poems on events in contemporaneous Jewish history and, most interestingly, Hebrew-alphabet transcriptions of classical Persian epics, such as Niẓāmī's *Haft Paikar* (The Seven Beauties) and *Khosrow o Shirin* (Khosrow and Shirin).

42. Jean Baumgarten, *Introduction à la littérature yiddish ancienne*, edited and translated by Jerold C. Frakes, *Introduction to Old Yiddish Literature*, 128, 131. See also Nokhem Shtif, "Ditrikh fun bern: Yidishkayt un veltlekhkayt in der alt-yidisher literatur."

43. See especially A. M. Astakhova, *Byliny: Itogi i problemy izucheniia*; and Vladimir Propp, *Russkiĭ geroicheskiĭ epos.*

44. In both the *bugarštica* and *deseterci* traditions, see especially the extensive representative collections Borislav Đuriđ, ed., *Antologiya narodnikh epskikh pesama*; and John S. Miletich, ed., *The "Bugarštica": A Bilingual Anthology of the Earliest Extant South Slavic Folk Narrative Song.*

45. The Old English poems are edited in Elliott van Kirk Dobbie, ed., *The Anglo-Saxon Poetic Records: The Battle of Brunanburh*, 16–20; *The Battle of Maldon*, 7–16; *Waldere*, 4–6; the *Hildebrandslied*: Wilhelm Braune, ed., *Althochdeutsches Lesebuch*, 84–85; the Eddic lays: Hans Kuhn, ed., *Edda: Die Lieder des Codex Regius nebst verwandten Denkmälern: Sigurðarqviða in scamma*, 207–18; *Atlaqviða in grœnlenzca*, 240–47; that edition of the latter poem is now superseded by Ursula Dronke, *The Poetic Edda*, 77–141.

46. A third, minor, category, the chapbook, will be briefly treated below.

47. On the epic poems based on biblical books, see Shmeruk, *Prokim* (1988), 179–85; and Wulf-Otto Dreeßen and Hermann-Josef Müller, eds., *Doniel: Das altjiddische Danielbuch nach dem Basler Druck von 1557.*

48. See Chava Turniansky, "Shtei shirot epiot be-yidish al Sefer Yehoshua."

49. Wulf-Otto Dreeßen, ed., *Doniel*, 1:1–11; and "Midraschepik und Bibelepik: Biblische Stoffe in der volkssprachlichen Literatur der Juden und Christen des Mittelalters im deutschen Sprachgebiet."

50. Dreeßen, "Midrashepik," 83–89.

51. Barbara Könneker, "Zum literarischen Charakter und der literarischen Intention des altjiddischen Schmuelbuchs."

52. Galit Hasan-Rokem, "An Almost Invisible Presence: Multilingual Puns in Rabbinic Literature," 225.

53. Steven D. Fraade, "Rabbinic *Midrash* and Ancient Jewish Biblical Interpretation," 106.

54. And it seems a direct description of the early Yiddish midrashic biblical paraphrase, the צאינה וראינה *Tsenerene* (Hanau [Basel] 1622); see *EYT*, no. 98; a reprinting from 1663 is available in facsimile online, http://books.google.com/books?id=taJEAAAAcAAJ&pg=PT4#v=onepage&q&f=false.

55. A text that conventionally is dated to late antiquity, although its first textual witnesses are much later (see here *ad* Gen, cap. 39); see also the parallel traditions in *Sefer hayyashar* (Warsaw, 1889), 66 (the composition of which may well postdate the composition of *Joseph the Righteous*).

56. Robert Alter, *The Art of Biblical Narrative*. See also the slightly differing exploration of this complex of techniques in Meir Sternberg, *The Poetics of Biblical Narrative: Ideological Literature and the Drama of Reading*.

57. Felix Falk and L. Fuks have provided extensive notes on the specific midrashic texts relevant for the *Seyfer Shmuel* and *Seyfer Melokhim*, as have Percy Matenko and Samuel Sloan on the *Akeydas Yitskhok*: "The Aqedath Jishaq: A Sixteenth Century Epic, with Introduction and Notes." On the midrashic context of the midrashic epics in the Cairo *geniza* codex, see Dov Sadan, "The Midrashic Background of 'The Paradise': Its Implications for the Evaluation of the Cambridge Yiddish Codex (1382)."

58. Note well the use of this term enclosed by quotation marks in the present volume to indicate the qualified character of the genre's secularity.

59. Christopher Sanders, ed., *Bevers Saga, with the Text of the Anglo-Norman Boeve de Haumtone*.

60. See especially Baumgarten, *Introduction*, 155–57.

61. Hebr. גַלָח *galaḥ* (tonsured/Christian priest/monk) = Christian in language, origin, or even alphabet.

62. In the manuscript collection of Eisik Wallich is found a brief poem, "Hildebrant lid" (Oxford, Bodleian Library, Ms. Opp. add. 4° 136), which is *distantly* related to the body of legend underpinning the Old High German heroic lay, the *Hildebrandslied*. See Felix Rosenberg, "Über eine Sammlung deutscher Volks- und Gesellschaftslieder in hebräischen Lettern."

63. See Shtif, "Ditrikh fun bern"; and John A. Howard, ed., *Dietrich von Bern* (1597), a facsimile edition with accompanying Germanized Roman-alphabet transcription.

64. Published in Hamburg, 1730. See Max Erik, *Vegn altyidshn roman un novele: Fertsnter-zekhtsnter yorhundert*, 198. A manuscript version is also extant, copied by the scribe Isaac b. Judah Reutlingen (Munich, Bayerische Staatsbibliothek, cod. hebr. 100, fol. 1–66, from 1580). See the edition by Theresia Friderichs-Müller, ed., *Die "Historie von dem Kaiser Octaviano"* and *Die "Historie von dem Kaiser Octaviano": Überlieferungsgeschichtliche Studien zu den Druckausgaben eines Prosaromans des 16. Jahrhunderts und seiner jiddischen Bearbeitungen aus dem Jahre 1580*.

65. In addition to the version in Munich, Bayerische Staatsbibliothek, cod. hebr. 100 (fol. 90–132), printed versions also exist: Basel, 1602; Berlin, 1707; Offenbach, 1717; Amsterdam, 1663, 1674, 1676. A portion of the text was also printed once without place and date, under the title *Di maase fun Ludvig un Aleksandr*. See Arnold Paucker, "Das Volksbuch von den Sieben Weisen Meistern in der jiddischen Literatur"; and Erik, *Geshikhte*, 215.

66. See Munich, Bayerische Staatsbibliothek, cod. hebr. 100 (fol. 143–91). There are also two printed versions (Hamburg, 1737; Frankfurt am Main, n.d.).

67. Published in Amsterdam, 1700, 1717, and one edition without date; Offenbach, 1777, Fürth, 1798. See Arnold Paucker, "Di yidishe nuskhoes fun *shildburger bukh.*"

68. Published in Offenbach in 1717 and Amsterdam between 1700 and 1730.

69. Published in Frankfurt am Main in 1699; facsimile edition by John A. Howard, ed., *Fortunatus: Die Bearbeitung und Umschrift eines spätmittelalterlichen deutschen Prosaromans für jüdisches Publikum.*

70. Published in Fürth in 1698 and 1791, Prague in 1705–11, and Offenbach in 1714.

71. See Landau, *Arthurian Legends*, especially xxiv-xxvii, 43–45, 84; Israel Zinberg [Yisroel Tsinberg], *Altyidishe literatur fun di eltste tsaytn biz der Haskole-tkufe*, 61–102, English translation, *Old Yiddish Literature*, 49–86. Erik divided Yiddish literature into three periods, the second of which (fourteenth–sixteenth centuries) is designated "the minstrel period of Yiddish literature"). See Erik, *Geshikhte*, 68–69; and Erik, *Vegn altyidishn roman un novele*, 13–29. See Dreeßen's remarks on the strange fact that the concept of the *Spielmann*, borrowed whole cloth from German studies into Yiddish studies, continued to live on in the latter field long after having been abandoned by the former. Dreeßen, "Midraschepik und Bibelepik," 79.

72. By contrast, the very real performative function of such verbal gestures in actual oral epic, such as Jumabay Bazarov's Karakalpak *Edige* (from central Asia), recorded in September 1993, transcribed and translated by Karl Reichl, is obvious: "Bul gäp tura bersin büyerde, endigi gäpti Nuradinnen eshitiñ . . . / Now let us stop here with this; let us now hear news from Nuradin . . ." (*Edige*, 231, 357). While such gestures here, too, are obviously both traditional and conventional, they are in such performances also functional and not merely rhetorical, as they are in written texts divorced from a tradition of improvised public performance.

73. One should note, in general, that medieval European epics were performed as song or chant with a specific melody, and the practice of early Yiddish epic conforms in this way, too, to ambient conventions. The melody of *Seyfer Shmuel*, for instance, became quite famous and was then used for many other poems, such as the *Seyfer Yehoushua* (Kraków, 1594).

74. See Chone Shmeruk's systematic and magisterial refutation of the *shpilman* theory in Yiddish literature, in "Tsi ken der keymbridzher manuskript shtitsn di shpilman-teorye in der yidisher literatur?"

75. Walter Johannes Schröder, *Spielmannsepik* (1967), and Schröder, ed., *Spielmannsepik* (1977); Michael Curschmann, *Spielmannsepik*. See even the early essay by Hans Naumann, "Versuch einer Einschränkung des romantischen Begriffs Spielmannsdichtung."

76. Shmeruk, "Can the Cambridge Manuscript," 17. See also the insightful opposition to the idea of a "midrashic *shpilman*" by Felix Falk, *Das Schemuelbuch des Mosche Esrim Wearba: Ein biblisches Epos aus dem 15. Jahrhundert*, 1:6.

77. Shmeruk, "Can the Cambridge Manuscript," 23; Erik, *Geshikhte*, chap. 5, "Der letster shpilman," 177–202. While Erik's attempt to moderate the adulation heaped on Levita's *Bovo* by other scholars is in part justifiable, his purpose in that move is ultimately to trivialize the life and work of Levita, in order to downgrade his reputation as august scholar and man of letters to the role of vagabond minstrel, which is not reasonable.

78. Shmeruk, "Can the Cambridge Manuscript," 15–16.

79. As indicated by Erika Timm, between 1474 and 1602 there was a "goldenes Zeitalter" (golden age) of Yiddish literature in northern Italy; between 1545 and 1602 there were at least thirty-two Yiddish books published there. See Timm, "Wie Elia Levita sein *Bovobuch*

für den Druck überarbeitete: Ein Kapitel aus der italo-jiddischen Literatur der Renaissancezeit," 61.

80. See especially the various types of evidence collected by L. Fuks for the connection of the *Seyfer Melokhim* to Italy. Fuks, *Das altjiddische Epos Melokim-Bûk*, 26–36.

81. See Shmeruk, "Difusei yidish be-italyah"; and Chava Turniansky and Erika Timm, eds., *Yiddish in Italia: Yiddish Manuscripts and Printed Books from the 15th to the 17th Century / Manoscritti e libri a stampa in yiddish dei secoli XV-XVII.*

82. See Baumgarten's especially clear and concise explication, *Introduction*, 163–65; Cecil Roth, *The History of the Jews in Italy*; Moses Avigdor Shulvass, "Ashkenazic Jewry in Italy," "Dos ashkenazishe yidntum in italye," and *Ḥayye ha-yehudim be-italyah bi-tkufat ha-renesans.*

83. Baumgarten, *Introduction*, 164. See also Yosef Hayim Yerushalmi, *Haggadah and History*; and Turniansky and Timm, *Yiddish in Italia*, no. 24, pp. 46–47.

84. Baumgarten, *Introduction*, 163.

85. On the severe limitations on Christian knowledge of Hebrew during the period, even among scholars, see the introduction to my *The Cultural Study of Yiddish in Early Modern Europe*, 1–81.

86. One might here recall the case of the Venetian Jewish poet Sarra Copia Sullam, who endured incessant badgering to convert by her correspondent the Genoese monk Ansaldo Cebà for at least four years without, apparently, ever even considering the possibility of conversion. See Dan Harrán, ed. and trans., *Jewish Poet and Intellectual in Seventeenth-Century Venice: Sarra Copia Sulam.*

87. Victor Brombert, "The Idea of the Hero," 21, 12.

88. C. M. Bowra, *Heroic Poetry*, 23.

89. Thomas M. Greene, "The Norms of Epic," in *The Descent from Heaven*, 55–56, 59.

90. Morton W. Bloomfield, "The Problem of the Hero in the Later Medieval Period," 41.

91. Norman T. Burns and Christopher J. Reagan, preface to *Concepts of the Hero in the Middle Ages and the Renaissance*, vii.

92. While the differing syntax of Yiddish verse and English prose occasionally complicates line division in the translation, the line markers generally indicate successive ten-line segments.

93. The most complete manuscript of *Vidvilt* is now missing many entire pages (hidden beneath page reinforcements); rather than simply omitting such large blocks of the narrative, I have compromised through the use of parallel and near-contemporary supplemental manuscripts of the same recension of the poem, in order to present a coherent narrative; see the details in the headnote to that text.

94. "Diese Sprache besteht hauptsächlich in der Widerholung gewisser Redeformen, im Gebrauch bedeutungsloser Füllworte oder nichtssagender Zusätze zur Herstellung eines Reims, in der Aufführung ständiger Beiwörter für bestimmte Gestalten und Sachen, in der Anwendung immer wiederkehrender Wahrheitsbeteuerungen, mit denen der Dichter zum Hörer oder Leser in Beziehung tritt" (*Schemuelbuch*, 2:114).

95. Construing the word ענטוורן as "answer" (already a common Middle Yiddish denotation of the word) and thus "today God, blessed be He, has answered you . . ." only seems the simpler and thus preferable choice, since the following phrase is then without logical and syntactic connection.

96. Baumgarten, *Introduction*, 182. Baumgarten astutely also refers to Mikhail Bakhtin, *Rabelais and His World*, 368ff.

97. One might nonetheless note that this usage resembles the time-honored epic trope of *hysteron proteron*, as, for instance, famously in Virgil's *moriamur et in media arma ruamus* (let us die and rush into the midst of arms) (*Aeneid* 2.353). The trope seems, however, not otherwise to have been part of the Yiddish epic tradition.

98. The Yiddish equivalent of this phrase actually occurs and is so translated earlier in that episode (st. 592).

99. On this general issue in literary translation, see, for instance, Gerald N. Sanday's comment in the introduction to his English translation of the late-antique Latin adventure romance *Apollonius of Tyre*: "It has also been hard to resist the temptation to correct deficiencies such as repetition, parataxis, and the failure to subordinate one idea or event to another, or even to differentiate between distinct periods of time." Gerald N. Sanday, *Collected Ancient Greek Novels*, edited by B. P. Reardon, 737–38.

100. Not necessarily anything shameful, as Horace notes of Homer: "bonus dormitat Homerus" ([even] good Homer dozes) (*Ars poetica*, 359).

101. The cited translation is from Smith, *Elia Levita Bachur's "Bovo-Buch,"* 5. In addition to the misconceptions already noted, in this case Smith also misunderstands and mistranslates the phrase in question, which is a conventional phrase used at the beginning of an undertaking, meaning "in a propitious hour," that is, more or less "may it go well."

102. In the case of a few technical terms, such as, for instance, the three types of signals sounded on the ritual ram's horn, those terms are added in a footnote.

103. Compare John Mandeville's differentiation of the two locations: "that Babyloyne [. . .] where that the soudan duelleth, is not that gret babyloyne where the dyuersitee of languages was made." M. C. Seymour, ed., *The Bodley Version of Mandeville's Travels*, 28.

104. *Paris and Viena. Inamoramento de li nobeli amanti Paris & Viena: historiato: & nouamente corretto* (Venice: Melchio Sessa, 1528), extant: Harvard, Houghton Library, Typ. 525 25.750; HOLLIS number [006444826], here sig.Hvi.r.

105. Rather than, for instance, from Mesopotamian Babylon down the Euphrates to the Persian Gulf, around the Arabian Peninsula, and then (during a period subsequent to the silting of ancient Suez canals and still centuries before the modern Suez Canal enabled boat passage to the Mediterranean) around the whole of Africa and across the full breadth of the Mediterranean to Alexandria (albeit a century after Vasco de Gama's circum-African voyage): such a lengthy voyage would probably have merited mention in the narrative.

106. See also the note by Meir Wolf, "Mekom ḥiburo shel ha-Melokhim bukh," 132; his unproblematized assumption of the equivalence of גויץ (idol) and בוק (ram/[euphemism for God]) is troubled.

1. *Abraham Our Father / Avrom ovinu*

1. Or perhaps: "how could my feet hurt me any more [than this]?"

2. *Joseph the Righteous / Yousef ha-tsadik*

1. See the analogue (not source) traditions in the *Midrash Tanhuma* (on Gen, cap. 39) and the *Sefer hayyashar* (Warsaw, 1889), 66.

2. בּור מעשן may also mean "foolishly."

3. *Book of Samuel / Seyfer Shmuel*

1. See also the suggestions in Turniansky and Timm, *Yiddish in Italia*, 12.

2. The stanzaic form, deemed by Max Weinreich the "Hildebrand-stanza," is generally based on the form characteristic of the Middle High German *Nibelungenlied*, which differs only in that its final half line has four accents. Weinreich, *Bilder fun der yidisher literatur-geshikhte*, 99.

3. Wulf-Otto Dreeßen, "Midraschepik und Bibelepik: Biblische Stoffe in der volkssprachlichen Literatur der Juden und Christen des Mittelalters im deutschen Sprachgebiet," 88–89.

4. Falk, "Einleitung," *Das Schemuelbuch*, 1:4–7; Shmeruk, "Can the Cambridge Manuscript," 19–20. Shmeruk thus maintains that the author of the *Seyfer Shmuel* was an educated member of the learned elite and by no means uneducated or a wandering minstrel.

5. Zinberg, *History*, 117.

6. The sixteenth-century Yiddish poet, who lived in the age of steel weaponry, seems poorly informed about metallurgy: he consistently uses the term קופֿפֿר *kupfer* (copper) to designate the metal used for biblical helmets (st. 329), shields (331, 1153), and bows (507, 1721), while biblical swords and mail coats were שטעהליין *shtelin* (of steel) (for example, st. 75, 79). Each designation is anachronistic, for weapons in the late Bronze Age Palestine depicted in the biblical book were indeed made of bronze (a copper-tin alloy), which was far superior to the hopelessly pliable pure copper of the earlier Chalcolithic epoch and far inferior to the steel technology of the later epoch of steel production. Some ambiguity should be acknowledged, however, on both counts: his terminological imprecision in conflating copper and bronze is, for instance, not particularly unusual (see also, for instance, the ambiguity in Latin *aes* [bronze, copper]), and in late Bronze Age Palestine, *iron*-working had already begun (though not the much later steel technology), so perhaps the poet is again somewhat imprecise in his distinction between iron and steel.

7. Baumgarten, *Introduction*, 147.

8. See Otto Behaghel, ed., *Heliand und Genesis*.

9. See Johann Christoph Wolf, *Bibliotheca Hebraea*, 4:201; Franz Delitzsch, *Zur Geschichte der jüdischen Poesie vom Abschluß der heiligen Schriften Alten Bundes bis auf die neueste Zeit*, 81; and Nathan Süsskind, "Shmuel-bukh-problemen," 67. Zinberg also calls the *Seyfer Shmuel* a "true national-hero poem" (*History*, 111) and a "secular-national epic" (115). See also Baumgarten, *Introduction*, 145.

10. Fuks's extensive lexicographical notes, especially his citation of presumed Middle High German cognate forms as relevant or explanatory of the Middle Yiddish words, are, however, often inaccurate and should be consulted only with great caution.

11. This Hebrew exhortation (Prov. 4:5, 7) appears above the book's title, as part of the elaborately illustrated border.

12. The biblical incident of the unnamed messenger bearing news of the defeat and capture of the ark to Shiloh (1 Sam. 4:12) is here transformed into a narrative intrusion introducing the heroic character of Saul who here rescues the tablets and takes them to Shiloh, despite the fact that the narrative thereafter reverts to the situation in which the ark/tablets still remain in Philistine hands. See *Midrash Shmuel* 11,1 and *Midrash Tehillim* 7.63 and *Seder Olam Rabba*, xiii.

13. Saul's words?

14. Cf. A'driel (1 Sam. 18:19).

15. Fuks's suggestion (*Schemuelbuch*, 2:156) of a connection between the noun used here, שפוט (mockery, disgrace), and Middle High German *spuot* (haste) is not pertinent, since the former is grammatically masculine while the latter is feminine and thus grammatically impossible in the structure of the Yiddish phrase here.

16. Hebrew נבל *naval* (villain, scoundrel, godless).

17. Cf. Hachilah (1 Sam. 23:19).

18. The two stanzas 793 and 796 are all but identical; st. 793 seems logically out of place in the narrative.

19. Cf. Eshtemoa (1 Sam. 30:28).

20. Cf. Hormah and Bor-ashan (1 Sam. 30:30).

21. Cf. "the pool of Gibeon" (2 Sam. 2:13).

22. Cf. Eglah (2 Sam. 3:5); cf. also *Yalkut Shimeoni*, ad loc.

23. In the passage that follows, several names differ in the Yiddish and biblical texts: Adohite/Ahohite, Arbi/Ribai, Tirathite/Pirathon, Hirai/Hiddai, from Arhot/Arbathite, Armaveth from Parhayim/Azmaveth of Bahurim, Arudite/Hararite, Ahiram the Ardite/Ahiam son of Sharar the Hararite (2 Sam. 23:28–33, *Seyfer Shmuel*, st. 1011–14).

24. רום *Rom* or *Rum* (*Seyfer Shmuel*, Augsburg ed., 1020,1); manuscripts: רמה *Ramah* or *Roma*; צֹר Tyre (2 Sam 5:11).

25. Some of the names in the Yiddish text again differ from the names of the biblical tradition: Elisha/Elishua, Nephesh/Nepheg, Japhnia/Japhia (2 Sam. 5:15–16; *Seyfer Shmuel*, st. 1023).

26. Cf. Hadadezer (2 Sam 8:3).

27. נון בין איך דוך כֵן יוד (*Seyfer Shmuel* 1316,2). The sentence is ambiguous: the Semitic word כֵן (thus, so, yes) (unusual in Yiddish) is a homonym of Yiddish קיין (no, not), which makes it possible to understand the *spoken* sentence as "Now, I am indeed a Jew" or "Now, I am indeed no Jew." Thus, Joab manages *aurally* to deny his ethnicity to the non-Jewish enemy while, as the *written* text indicates, avoiding an outright lie and denial of his identity. Two sentences later Joab again cleverly implies that he is not Jewish while not explicitly denying it: "I, a Jew!?"

28. Cf. Baal-hazor (2 Sam. 13:23).

29. A gesture less widely known in some parts of the Anglophone world: see Grimm and Grimm, *Deutsches Wörterbuch*, 3:1444, *feige* 2: a defiant and obscene gesture known already in medieval Italy, "made with the fingers to imitate the shape of a vulva," nowadays (as then?) generally a fist with tip of the thumb inserted between the index and middle fingers and indicating a broad range of obscene insults having to do with sexual intercourse.

30. Falk/Fuks, ad loc, note that the verbal expression of this widespread obscene gesture stems ultimately from Italian, *far la fica*.

31. Cf. Adoram (2 Sam. 20:24).

32. Cf. Sheva (2 Sam. 20:25).

33. Cf. Armoni (2 Sam. 21:18).

34. As is common with the genre, David's biblical prayer of praise (2 Sam. 22ff) is quite abstract and at times opaque in meaning. While the *Seyfer Shmuel* rarely follows the biblical

text very closely, in this passage the connection is quite tenuous and characterized by syntactic and semantic ambiguity, especially toward the end of the prayer.

35. אוֹפַנִים cf. Ezek. 1:15.

36. וואַרט *vort* (word) and אורט *ort* (quarter guilder).

37. This couplet (ll. 21–22) thus does not rhyme גיבט *gipt* (gives) and ליגט *likt* (matters).

4. *The Binding of Isaac / Akeydas Yitskhok*

1. See Zinberg, *Geshikhte*, 121–23.

2. Baumgarten, *Introduction*, 137.

3. This proposal is based on the state of the language. See Erik, *Geshikhte*, 125.

4. The three sounds traditionally blown on the ritual ram's horn (*shofar*) are here named: *teqiah* (a bass note with an abrupt termination), *teruah* (a bass-treble-bass trill), and *shevarim* (a legato triplet).

5. *Duke Horant / Dukus Horant*

1. Fuks, *Documents*, 1959.

2. See the analysis and further bibliography in Jerold C. Frakes, *The Politics of Interpretation: Alterity and Ideology in Old Yiddish Studies.*

3. The Middle High German *Kudrun* survives in a single sixteenth-century manuscript, the so-called Ambraser Heldenbuch, which in general comprises a collection of other medieval German epics that are themselves extant in earlier, generally twelfth- and thirteenth-century, manuscripts. It is this aspect of the manuscript's contents that constitutes the only, rather unstable, grounds for the common scholarly dating of *Kudrun* to that same earlier period, which also then accounts for the aberrant scholarly practice in editions of the text of *Rückübersetzung* "retranslation" by its scholarly editors from its actual sixteenth-century linguistic form in the Ambraser manuscript into a quasi-thirteenth-century Middle High German. See, for instance, Karl Bartsch, ed., *Kudrun.* Those readers interested in the actual text of the *Kudrun* would do better to consult the edition of the manuscript itself: Franz H. Bäuml, ed., *Kudrun: Die Handschrift.* On the bridal quest of *Kudrun* and the gender politics of that narrative, see Jerold C. Frakes, *Brides and Doom: Gender, Property, and Power in Medieval German Women's Epic*, 182–265.

4. See Erik Nylén and Jan Peder Lamm, *Bildsteine auf Gotland*; and Victor Millet, *Germanische Heldendichtung im Mittelalter: Eine Einführung*, 245 (photograph).

5. "Widsið," ll. 21–22, in *The Exeter Book*, edited by George Philip Krapp and Elliott van Kirk Dobbie, 150; and "Deor," ll. 39–40, ibid., 179.

6. Finnur Jónsson, *Edda Snorra Sturlusonar, Skáldskaparmál*, c. 50.

7. Ibid. See also Millet, *Germanische Heldendichtung im Mittelalter*, 243.

8. J. Olrik and H. Ræder, eds., *Saxonis Gesta Danorum*, vol. 1, c. 5.

9. See especially Donald Ward and Franz Bäuml, "Zur Kudrun-Problematik: Ballade und Epos"; and Donald Ward, "Nochmals Kudrun: Ballade und Epos. Eine Erwiderung."

10. See, for instance, "Die sagen- und literaturgeschichtlichen Probleme," a subchapter of the introduction to Peter Ganz, Frederick Norman, and Werner Schwarz, eds., *Dukus Horant*, 75–131.

11. The repositionings of the philological project have been taking place in waves over the course of the past few decades. Interesting moments of stock taking may be found in, among others, Stephen G. Nichols, "Philology and Its Discontents"; Michelle R. Warren, "Post-Philology"; and Bruce W. Holsinger, "Medieval Studies, Postcolonial Studies, and the Genealogies of Critique" and his more recent book *The Premodern Condition: Medievalism and the Making of Theory*.

12. The illegible gaps in the manuscript, marked here by [. . .], not only produce gaps in the translation but also compromise the interpretation even of the words that are legible in such passages, many of which become a patchwork of seemingly random phrases separated by longer and shorter gaps (the reader should keep in mind that it is often difficult to know how much text is lost in such gaps—whether a single word or several, and sometimes even an entire line or more is lost). The phrases here supplied in the translation are indeed translations of those words and phrases that appear in the manuscript, but lacking the full text and context, they are ultimately simply fragmentary attempts to suggest meaning where none can be constructed: a legible but isolated דר *der* could, for instance, mean "the" (nominative masculine singular ["*the* man is . . ."] or dative feminine singular ["with *the* lady . . ."]), or it could have demonstrative force "that," or could be a verbal prefix. Thus, even the paltry "the" printed here in such cases offers much less than it might seem to promise.

13. בש זינגשטא *bas sinigste*; if the phrase were, however, construed as something like (the rather less likely) *bas singeste*, it might perhaps already be a reference to Horant's reputation as the "best singing" man, although neither morphology nor context here recommends that interpretation.

14. The medieval West was unacquainted with Homer's *Iliad* and knew the tale of the Trojan War by means of Latin versions such as the ones by Publius Baebius Italicus, and especially Dares Phrygius and Dictys Cretensis, which tell versions quite distinct from Homer's and on which were based most of the many adaptations during the medieval western European tradition. In the context of this complex tradition of adaptation, in which not just individual names but indeed most major plot components were subject to revision and change, it is not surprising that the Yiddish poet has, for instance, conflated the name of Helena and one of the bynames of the city of Troy, Ilion, and attributed Menelaus's death to Paris.

15. In several of this episode's "pledges" to carry out one of two alternatives, the syntax and semantics are sometimes more, sometimes less troubled; the two alternatives are often not mutually exclusive, or they do not seem to be opposing alternatives at all. The general sense is, however, clear.

16. These last two clauses are quoted from a famous Middle High German Crusader song, the ironic wit of which usage here would not have been lost on the Jewish audience.

17. Both here (st. 126,4 = fol. 31r, l. 9) and below (st. 154,1 = fol. 33r, l. 10), the word has generally been transcribed by scholars as תִּיפְלָה/תִּפְלָה = תיפלה *tiflah/tifle* (frivolity, impropriety, indecency), a conventional (denigrating) Jewish designation of the period for a Christian church, although it is only in the word's second occurrence that the manuscript unequivocally reads תיפלה, while the earlier occurrence could well be תפלה and thus perhaps = תְּפִלָּה/תְּפִילָה *tefilah/tfile* (prayer). Multiple plausible interpretive possibilities thus present themselves: both uses are to be understood as denigrating designators of a Christian church, or both as designators of prayer, or the former as "church," the latter as "prayer," or perhaps there is wordplay involved such that in one instance Christian prayer is denigrated, and in the

other it is designated with a Hebrew-component Yiddish word conventionally used to specify Jewish (*not* Christian) prayer. The denigration of Christian religious practice through slight verbal deformation is also known from Bosnian epic, for instance, in the use of *zvornik* instead of *zvonik* for church steeple in *Sila Osmanbeg i Pavišić Luka* 463 (as performed by Murat Žunić; text ed., http://enargea.org/cave/BosKrajina/pages/1971p.html). As David E. Bynum comments, "It was customary in this tradition deliberately to distort the pronunciation of nouns relating to Christian holy places as a way of ridiculing them." David E. Bynum, trans., *Serbo-Croatian Heroic Poems: Epics from Bihać, Cazin, and Kulen Vakuf*, "Mighty Osmanbey and Luke Paulson," 320n20.

18. An oriental brocade of silk and gold thread.

19. The number of stanzas here is only an estimate: the lower halves of folios 39v and 40r are so poorly legible that stanzas cannot be reconstructed.

20. Only a short, narrow strip of the upper part of the manuscript's final folio is preserved, at the right margin of the recto and left margin of the verso, yielding a few words on each side; at that point the poem breaks off, lacking a conclusion.

6. *Vidvilt / Vidvilt*

1. *Wigalois* is a heterogeneous narrative based indirectly on several Old French narratives, perhaps known to Wirnt primarily through the oral tradition, as he claims in the text's epilogue (11,686ff), although one portion of the narrative follows the twelfth-century *Le Bel Inconnu* of Renaut de Beaujeu rather closely.

2. Such is the hero's name in the Middle High German text, while early scholarship on the poem arbitrarily assigned it the title *Wigalois*.

3. Irving Linn, "Widwilt, Son of Gawain," lxxxiv.

4. In the first such instance, it is the hostile maiden who directs Vidvilt to exercise mercy (st. 1570).

5. Cambridge, Trinity College, F.12.44; Hamburg, Staats- und Universitätsbibliothek, Cod. hebr. 255 and Cod. hebr. 289.

6. Landau, *Arthurian Legends*, xxxii-xxxiii; Linn, "Widwilt, Son of Gawain," xxxiv.

7. These reinforcements were already in place when Linn edited the text.

8. I have translated ורײטאג in its conventional sense of a "free day," that is, a holiday, and שולן as a reflection of the Italo-Yiddish *sollazzo / solacium* (relief, relaxation), as found in the Hamburg manuscripts. But the specific word choice here could conceivably suggest a Jewish context or subtext: sabbath eve/Friday (ורײטאג) in the synagogue (שולן); the latter word might also simply mean a "school," which he and his twelve-year-old peers attend.

9. This sentence is truncated and garbled in the Cambridge manuscript, here supplemented from the Hamburg manuscripts.

10. Hamburg mss. *Lorign*. Although it may well be the case that a distorted form of *Lothringen* (Lorraine) is at issue here, it may just as easily be a distorted form of *Logres* (*Logris/Loegria*), the name generally assigned to King Arthur's realm in Arthurian romance, deriving from Middle Welsh *Lloegyr* (England).

11. At least a part of one line is missing.

12. This last clause is garbled; the translation is conjectural.

13. That is, the gatekeeper's lord.

14. Text is lost at this point in the manuscript. In Landau 121a, 42–122a,4 (that is, Wagenseil's edition): "The maiden who had brought him from King Arthur's court / how very heartily she requested of him / and said: 'You really ought to have spoken with me, if I had only wished it. I think that you now would like to make good for that.' Then Sir Vidvilt began to laugh. The maiden fell at his feet and again began to plead in a friendly manner that he speak with them both."

7. *Bovo of Antona / Bovo d'Antona*

1. English translation in Jerold C. Frakes, "Cultural Revolution in Ashkenaz: The Emergence of Early Yiddish Literature" (forthcoming); Italian translation by Claudia Rosenzweig, *Elye Bokher: Due canti yiddish, rime di un poeta ashkenazita nella Venezia del cinquecento.*

2. Without evidence or further comment, Judah A. Joffe identifies as "dem eyntsikn miglekhn original vos Levita hot genitst" (the only possible original that Levita used) for his Yiddish version of *Bovo* the 1497 Tuscan text by Guidone Palladino: *Buouo di Antona di Guidone Palladino. Regunto et reuisto* (Bologna: Caligula di Bazalieri, 1497), extant: London, British Library IA 28994 (fragmentary). See Judah A. Joffe, ed., *Elye Bokher, poetishe shafungen in yidish, ershter band: Bovo d'Antona*, 25. Claudia Rosenzweig concurs: "Gli esempi testuali a conferma di questa ipotesi non lasciano dubbi in proposito" (The textual examples to confirm this hypothesis leave no doubt in the matter). Claudia Rosenzweig, "La letteratura yiddish in Italia: L'esempio del *Bovo de-Antona* di Elye Bocher," 166. Erika Timm, however, seems to have been the only scholar actually to compare passages of Palladino and Levita. Timm, "Wie Elia Levita sein *Bovobuch* für den Druck überarbeitete." While she seems convinced by that comparison, there is in fact little resemblance between the texts compared beyond a sporadic and *very* general similarity of content. Levita's text is certainly not a translation—in any sense of the term—nor indeed even a paraphrase of Palladino. It is a retelling of the Buovo tale that more or less follows the first half of the tale as told by Palladino. It has likewise sometimes been claimed that Levita effectively and artistically condensed the 1,400 stanzas of Palladino's narrative to 650 stanzas in the Yiddish adaptation. In fact, Levita's narrative covers only the events of the first two dozen folios of Palladino's text, omitting all treatment of the final thirty folios, and thus—if he used Palladino at all—reducing his narrative by more than half with a single pruning cut. Otherwise, the vast differences between that text and Levita's Yiddish text—which become clearly apparent in a parallel reading of the two texts—make clear that Palladino's text was not Levita's source in any but the most general sense that Levita might have gained a general idea of the plot and character names from Palladino and then retold the tale essentially on his own and without further reference to Palladino. Or perhaps Levita used a different text altogether as his source.

3. Sanders, *Bevers Saga, with the Text of the Anglo-Norman Boeve de Haumtone.*

4. The epilogue specifies that text was completed in Nisan (5)267 (= March 1507 CE). One of the manuscripts (a fragment) preserves stanzas 238–590 (Paris, Bibliothéque Nationale, MS hébr. 750, fos. 123–57); a second manuscript (Jewish National and University Library, Jerusalem, Heb. 28° 7565, formerly Schocken Library 816) is almost complete.

5. Smith, *Elia Levita Bachur's "Bovo-Buch,"* xix.

6. In attempting to translate the text in a form appropriate to the original, I am reminded of the comment by the eminent Persianist A. J. Arberry: "As every translator is aware, there is no more baffling labour than to endeavour to do justice to the mediocre; the result is bound to be mediocre at best, and at worst it may be intolerable." Arberry, trans., *The Ring of the Dove by Ibn Hazm*, 14.

7. See, for instance, Zinberg, who claims that there is a more pronounced mocking tone of "the foreign world of chivalry with its behavior" in *Bovo* than in its Tuscan source (*Geshikhte*, 75). See also Smith's similar claim (*Elia Levita Bachur's "Bovo-Buch,"* xix). I find no such distinction in tone between Levita's text and his supposed source (Palladino).

8. See especially Erich Köhler, *Ideal und Wirklichkeit in der höfischen Epik: Studien zur Form der frühen Artus- und Graldichtung*.

9. Timm, *Paris un Wiene*, cxxvii–cxxviii.

10. By means of the conventional alphanumerical use of the Hebrew alphabet, the sum of the numerical value of the letters of the phrase אֵלִיָּה הַמְחַבֵּר "Elye the author" equals 302 and thus here in fact designates the year in the "small count," that is, without notating the thousands: 302 = 5302 = 1541–42 CE, in this case 1541.

11. Or simply: *in Hebrew*.

12. A peculiar turn of phrase; perhaps: " . . . foils of horn."

13. Literally, "take a mile for a suit of armor," also a contemporaneous early New High German proverb, according to Grimm and Grimm, *Deutsches Wörterbuch*, 6:1909.

14. Madeira, earlier often designated Malmsey and here named *Malvasia*, designates a range of Mediterranean wine varietals.

15. Perhaps "hose" or "shoes."

16. There is a pun here on the word שווערן that means both "noble/worthy" and "annoying/troublesome."

17. This statement is the first hint that in the Yiddish text Bovo, and later Druzeyne, is not unambiguously conceived as Christian.

18. Grammatically, the horse's name is neuter, owing to the diminutive suffix (and subsequent pronoun referents are also neuter), thus providing no indicator of the horse's sex. Despite the fact that the horse is named and otherwise also depicted with more than a modicum of personality in the narrative, it will nonetheless here be designated with a neuter pronoun.

19. Interestingly, the word used here is קהל *kool*, which conventionally designates only a Jewish community.

20. That is, like a Spanish pilgrim; probably the reference is to pilgrims en route to the famed pilgrimage destination of Santiago de Compostela in Galicia.

21. According to Jewish tradition, a jubilee year occurs only once every fifty years, and thus her confinement would likely last for the remainder of her life. On the other hand, viewed from a strictly Jewish perspective, because a Christian Easter will *never* occur as part of the Jewish annual festival calendar, the combination here humorously suggests that she would never emerge from the nunnery, no matter how long she lived.

22. According to Meier Schüler, a now lost manuscript of the text (which he had seen) read נ = 50 at this point, which in some manuscript hands could easily have been misinterpreted by the typesetters as ג = 3, thus resulting—in the 1541 printed text—in the rather surprisingly modest number of wedding guests. See Schüler, "Das Bovo-Buch," 93.

23. Probably a printer's error for *munestar*.

8. *Pariz and Viene / Pariz un Viene*

1. As, for instance, Erika Timm and Gustav Adolf Beckmann, *"Paris un Wiene": Ein jiddischer Stanzenroman des 16. Jahrhunderts von (oder aus dem Umkreis von) Elia Levita*, cxxxvi–cxlv.

2. The student edition for German readers (with Germanized transcription) by Erika Timm and Adolf Beckmann (*Paris un Wiene*) offers copious notes and glosses. As the translation here frequently illustrates, however, I quite often disagree with those glosses and explanatory notes, which seem almost obsessed with finding the most circuitous path possible toward defining rather straightforward terms. Let one example suffice: in a context where a terrified monk is trying to unlock a lock but cannot get the key into the keyhole "and was *jiggling* the lock for such a long time" (625,2), I understand the Middle Yiddish word גרויטילן to be cognate with early modern German ([*ge*]*rütteln*). Timm and Beckmann instead attempt to connect this verb with the noun *Gruttel*, whose definition they adduce from the Grimms' *Deutsches Wörterbuch* as *Aufregung/Unruhe* (excitement, disquiet), which may well describe the monk's state, but not what he was doing with the lock. Thus, they construct their own understanding of the word as "herumhantieren" (mess around with), which is not a bad guess, based on context, but not actually what the text says, which is in this case perfectly straightforward.

3. Shmeruk, *Pariz un' Viene*, 12.

4. See also Baumgarten, *Introduction*, 193–94.

5. Ibid., 194.

6. Which, incidentally, signifies rather differently for the Christian audience of the Italian romance than for the Jewish audience of the Yiddish romance, since the Ottoman Empire at the time was home to large numbers of Jews, especially Sefardim exiled from Iberia, some of whom had returned West to settle in Venice. The quality of life for Jews was at the time generally better in Ottoman territory than anywhere in Europe, except perhaps in Venice and Amsterdam.

7. Much as in the earliest extant love song in Yiddish, "Whither Shall I Go?" (*EYT*, no. 14)

8. Baumgarten, *Introduction*, 198–99.

9. Such as Moderata Fonte, *Il merito delle donne* (1600); Veronica Franco, *Rime* (1575); and Arcangela Tarabotti, *Tirannia paterna* (1654).

10. Baumgarten, *Introduction*, 202–3.

11. The New Critical construction of romance would seem the most appropriate avenue of theoretical analysis for Baumgarten's line of inquiry; its canonical codification is Northrop Frye, *The Secular Scripture: A Study of the Structure of Romance.*

12. Zinberg, *Geshikhte*, 91, 94, 97; English translation, 75, 78, 81.

13. Baumgarten, *Introduction*, 205–6.

14. Sh. Simonson, "Sefarim ve-sifriyyot shel yehudei Mantovah, 1595"; Shmeruk, *Pariz un' Viene*, 29–38; Timm and Beckmann, *"Paris un Wiene,"* xiv.

15. Ex. 10:1; January 23–28, 1594.

16. Caption to the woodcut preceding st. 14: "I imagine that that is Dolfin with his wife, Lady Diane."

17. Caption to the woodcut between st. 52–53: "Pariz came with his harp; Viene and Isabele heard it."

18. Caption to the woodcut between st. 62–63: "That is Pariz with his comrade; they took up a position beneath Viene's window."

19. The expression here, כל ישראל (all Israel), commonly means "everyone" in the context of a closed Jewish community in which "everyone" is constituted by an exclusively Jewish population. In this particular context, however, the expression is obviously generalized to mean "everyone," without reference to ethnic or cultural identity.

20. Caption to the woodcut between st. 93–94: "Pariz came riding there with his lance at his side."

21. Until 1350, *le Dauphine* was the title of the Count of Vienne; from 1350 to 1791, the title transferred and became a designation for the heir to the throne of France. In this narrative, Viene's father, as king of Vienne, is thus called Dolfin, and often indeed "the Dolfin," as in French usage of *le Dauphine*. This usage, sometimes with and sometime without the definite article, is preserved in the translation.

22. Caption to the woodcut between st. 110–11: "There Viene sat quite courteously and fine, telling Isabele how her heart was inflamed."

23. Caption to the woodcut between st. 142–43: "Then Pariz again came riding; he again proved his great might."

24. Or "in my heart."

25. Caption to the woodcut between st. 199–200: "The king again pays a call on Sir Yakomo. He tells his daughter that she should go to see him, if he desires anything."

26. Caption to the woodcut between st. 203–4: "Viene took her leave from Sir Yakomo and went with Isabele into Pariz's chamber."

27. Caption to the woodcut between st. 207–8: "There Viene searched diligently in the chamber and found Pariz's white clothing."

28. Caption to the woodcut between st. 239–40: "Then the bishop sat down there and wished to hear Viene's long speech."

29. Caption to the woodcut between st. 246–47: "Pariz came there with the bishop, to find out about his stolen gear, as he had heard."

30. Caption to the woodcut between st. 251–52: "The bishop and Pariz came there, and Viene took Pariz aside."

31. Caption to the woodcut between st. 266–67: "Pariz's heart burns like coals, for which reason he had come to Viene in the secret place."

32. Caption to the woodcut between st. 273–74: "Pariz heard how one wished to give Viene a husband; he therefore went to see Viene in a very melancholy mood."

33. Or "until I turn into carrion," that is, "until my dying day."

34. Caption to the woodcut between st. 286–87: "Pariz then came and wanted to speak with the father of the groom, as Viene had implored him."

35. Caption to the woodcut between st. 296–97: "There Sir Yakomo knelt down before King Dolfin. He did all that for the sake of his esteemed son, Pariz."

36. Caption to the woodcut between st. 313–14: "Viene pours out her heart to Isabele. All jesting aside, she wanted no one but Pariz."

37. Caption to the woodcut between st. 319–20: "Pariz came there with a despairing heart; he wanted to tell Viene that he wanted to leave the city."

38. Caption to the woodcut between st. 327–28: "Pariz and his servant then consulted secretly: he was to make arrangements for a ship and for horses at all points for him."

39. Caption to the woodcut between st. 331–32: "Then Pariz came—you ought to believe me—he wanted to hurry away with his Viene."

40. Caption to the woodcut between st. 344–45: "The knight then came and summoned the priest. He was the same one who there pursued Viene, seeking her."

41. Caption to the woodcut between st. 367–68: "As Pariz was to part from Viene, he had great sorrow in his heart."

42. Caption to the woodcut between st. 382–83: "Here Viene has taken the priest along, so that he might say how she has kept her honor."

43. Caption to the woodcut between st. 385–86: "Dolfin cordially arranged with his wife that she try to discover the truth from Isabele."

44. Caption to the woodcut between st. 391–92: "Dolfin was enraged at Sir Yakomo; therefore he had him put in prison."

45. Caption to the woodcut between st. 398–99: "How Viene was affecting piety; there-with she wished to deceive her mother and father."

46. In the Italian source, it is Dolfin's father-in-law who is the prince of Flanders; here it is unclear, although in fact all others here mentioned have been identified by other geographical determinants.

47. Caption to the woodcut between st. 440–41: "Dolfin's rage burned fiercely in him; he attacked Isabele with angry words."

48. Caption to the woodcut between st. 471–72: "The bridegroom wanted to see Viene. She did not want to let it occur without the bishop."

49. Caption to the woodcut between st. 487–88: "Pariz did not wish to remain any lon-ger in Genoa; now he wanted to board a ship."

50. Caption to the woodcut between st. 528–29: "There Dolfin knelt before the Suldan; I think that all his limbs were trembling."

51. Caption to the woodcut between st. 540–41: "Pariz now went away just as does a mourner; he had now arrived in the beautiful city of Cairo."

52. Caption to the woodcut between st. 555–56: "Pariz circulated on the square in Cairo, and two monks welcome him cordially."

53. Caption to the woodcut between st. 589–90: "Pariz has now made a close acquain-tance; he contrived it all in order to see Dolfin."

54. Caption to the woodcut between st. 623–24: "Pariz was standing there with his drawn sword, in order to kill the Mamluks if they did not continue to sleep."

55. The text reads "until they become *bar mitsvo*," the designation of a full male member of the Jewish religious community and the celebratory ritual by means of which entrance into that membership takes place, for which one would, in this case, presumably wait forever.

56. Caption to the woodcut between st. 626–27: "Pariz and the monk carried poor Dol-fin, for he could not walk by himself unless he had a crutch."

57. A town on the Bay of Muggia in Venetian territory south of Trieste.

58. Cyprus was in Norman or Lusignan hands until 1473, then under Venetian control until 1571.

59. Caption to the woodcut between st. 669–70: "Pariz said to the monk and bishop that they are to wait for him outside; he also wanted to see if he could arrange anything with them by means of gestures."

60. Caption to the woodcut between st. 674–75: "There Viene and Isabele recognized Pariz; and she took him tightly into her arms."

61. Caption to the woodcut between st. 683–84: "The bishop and the monk, together with Pariz and Viene and Isabele, all came before King Dolfin."

62. Customarily, the date of a traditional Jewish wedding is set such that the bride is not made ritually impure by the rules governing the menstrual cycle. In this case, by chance, Viene's ritual purity is not compromised by Dolfin's insistence on an immediate wedding.

Appendix A. *The Book of Kings / Seyfer Melokhim* (Excerpts)

1. Falk, *Das Schemuelbuch*, 1:12.

2. It seems that the poet frequently did not understand the Hebrew text or did not know how to express such specialized vocabulary in Yiddish, or perhaps simply did not have access to as accurate a biblical text as is now generally available.

3. Falk, *Das Schemuelbuch*, 1:13.

4. Fuks, *Das altjiddische Epos Meloḵîm-Bûḵ*, 1:25.

5. Ibid., 22–23.

6. Ibid., 25. One must nonetheless be wary of this last type of evidence as an indicator of general aesthetic value or cultural importance: the same may, for instance, be said of the lack of popularity of the *Pariz un Viene* in comparison to the *Bovo* epic, even though *Pariz un Viene* is so vastly superior aesthetically.

7. Barbara Könneker, "Zum literarischen Charakter." See also the introduction to this volume.

8. That is, the Temple in Jerusalem.

9. One ell equals eighteen inches or forty-six centimeters.

Appendix B. *Briyo and Zimro / Briyo ve-Zimro*

1. In a move typical of the Germanistic drive to deny any and all originality to early Yiddish literature, and apparently based on little more knowledge of the complex tradition of the originally Arabic tale of Layla and Majnun and its virtual ubiquity in the Pan-Islamic world than can be gathered from a modern German translation of Niẓāmi Ganjavi's (definitive) medieval Persian version of the tale, *Layli o Majnun* (Layla and Majnun), Erika Timm implausibly proposes Niẓāmi's epic as the source of *Briyo ve-Zimro.* The two narratives nonetheless differ in all essential aspects: after the rejection of his marriage suit, Zimro does not withdraw from society and go live in the desert, as does Qays (Majnun); Zimro is not a poet, as is Qays (the activity that defines his entire life and even his love for Layla); Zimro undertakes no military action to win his beloved, as does Qays with the aid of Nawfal. On the other hand, Qays is not a scholar, diplomat, or trickster, as is Zimro, nor does he undertake an international quest, as does Zimro in his mission to the archenemy's capital city of Rome. Unlike Layla, Briyo is never married to another man. In fact, the two narratives—like scores of others nearer in time, place, and modes of cultural access—share nothing except that they are tales of unhappy lovers who are united only in the afterlife. Timm conveniently interprets the few similarities in plot as evidence of direct borrowing, while the myriad differences as evidence

of the Jewish author's deliberate revision. See Erika Timm, "Zwischen Orient und Okzident: Zur Vorgeschichte von 'Beria und Simra.'"

2. See Erika Timm, "Beria und Simra: Eine jiddische Erzählung des 16. Jahrhunderts," 45–93.

3. The spelling of the name of Zimro's father is inconsistent in the manuscripts: sometimes טֹובַת, טָבת, טובת, and טוּבַת, the first three of which are consistent with the pronunciation Tovas, while the last must be Tuvas.

4. The first day of the seventh month of the Jewish calendar (*Tishri* = September/October), which marks the beginning of the civil year in the Jewish calendar and is the first of the Jewish High Holidays.

5. The traditional greeting, *sholem*!

6. Just as, a few lines earlier, Briyo had indicated that her only sin in life was to kiss Zimro, here his only sin is that by kissing her and thus causing her to sin, he has himself caused her death. Here Joachim Neugröschel misconstrues the common early Yiddish idiom דען דש (except that) in the passage and mistranslates as: "You've committed no sin that cost Béria her life," thus not only obscuring the interesting phraseological parallel in the two passages but in fact undermining the tale's fundamental moral lesson. See Neugröschel, *The Dybbuk and the Yiddish Imagination*, 92. See also Jeremy Dauber, *In the Demon's Bedroom: Yiddish Literature and the Early Modern*, 249, who seems to have been led astray by Neugröschel, which compromises his own interpretation. Both Neugröschel and Dauber thus eliminate the interesting contradiction in the tale's later maintaining that Zimro is without sin (see below, the end of the tale).

Bibliography

Alter, Robert. *The Art of Biblical Narrative.* New York: Basic Books, 1981.

———. "Sacred History and Prose Fiction." In *The Creation of Sacred Literature: Composition and Redaction of the Biblical Text,* edited by Richard E. Friedman, 7–24. Berkeley: Univ. of California Press, 1981.

Arberry, A. J., trans. *The Ring of the Dove by Ibn Hazm.* London: Luza, 1953.

Astakhova, A. M. *Byliny: Itogi i problemy izucheniia.* Moscow: Nauka, 1966.

Babbi, Anna Maria. "In margine alla fortuna del Paris e Vienna." *Quaderni di Lingue e Letterature* (Verona) 11 (1986): 393–97.

Bacher, Wilhelm. *Zwei jüdisch-persische Dichter Schahin und Imrani.* Strasbourg: Trübner, 1907–8.

Bakhtin, Mikhail. *Rabelais and His World.* Translated by Hélène Iswolsky. 1968. Reprint, Bloomington: Indiana Univ. Press, 1984.

Bartsch, Karl, ed. *Kudrun.* Rev. 5th ed. by Karl Stackmann. Wiesbaden: Brockhaus, 1980.

Baumgarten, Jean. "Une chanson de geste en yidich ancien: Le *Shmuel bukh.*" *Revue de la Bibliothèque Nationale* 13 (1984): 24–38.

———. *Introduction à la littérature yiddish ancienne.* Paris: Cerf, 1993. English translation by Jerold C. Frakes, *Introduction to Old Yiddish Literature.* Oxford: Oxford Univ. Press, 2005.

Bäuml, Franz H., ed. *Kudrun: Die Handschrift.* Berlin: Walter de Gruyter, 1969.

Behaghel, Otto, ed. *Heliand und Genesis.* Altdeutsche Textbibliothek 4. 9th ed. by Burkhart Taeger. Tübingen: Niemeyer, 1984.

Berenbaum, Michael, and Fred Skolnik, eds. 2nd ed. *Encyclopaedia Judaica.* 22 vols. New York: Macmillan, 2006.

Bloomfield, Morton W. "The Problem of the Hero in the Later Medieval Period." In *Concepts of the Hero in the Middle Ages and the Renaissance,* edited by Norman T. Burns and Christopher J. Reagan, 27–48. Albany: SUNY Press, 1975.

Bowra, C. M. *Heroic Poetry.* New York: St. Martin's, 1961.

Braune, Wilhelm. *Althochdeutsches Lesebuch.* 15th ed. Tübingen: Max Niemeyer, 1969.

Brombert, Victor. "The Idea of the Hero." In *The Hero in Literature,* edited by Victor Brombert, 11–21. Greenwich, CT: Fawcett, 1969.

Burns, Norman T., and Christopher J. Reagan, eds. *Concepts of the Hero in the Middle Ages and the Renaissance.* Albany: SUNY Press, 1975.

Busi, Giulio. *La istoria de Purim io ve racconto: Il libro di Ester secondo un rabbino emiliano del Cinquecento.* Rimini: Luisè, 1987.

Bynum, David E., trans. *Serbo-Croatian Heroic Poems: Epics from Bihać, Cazin, and Kulen Vakuf.* New York: Garland, 1993.

Caliebe, Manfred. *Dukus Horant: Studien zu seiner literarischen Tradition.* Berlin: Schmidt, 1973.

Conroy, Charles. "Hebrew Epic: Historical Notes and Critical Reflections." *Biblica* 61 (1980): 1–30.

Cormeau, Christoph. "Die jiddische Tradition von Wirnts *Wigalois.*" *Zeitschrift für Literaturwissenschaft und Linguistik* 8, no. 32 (1978): 28–44.

Cross, Frank Moore. *Canaanite Myth and Hebrew Epic: Essays in the History of the Religion of Israel.* Cambridge, MA: Harvard Univ. Press, 1973.

———. *From Epic to Canon: History and Literature in Ancient Israel.* Baltimore: Johns Hopkins Univ. Press, 1998.

Curschmann, Michael. *Spielmannsepik.* Stuttgart: Metzler, 1968.

Dauber, Jeremy. *In the Demon's Bedroom: Yiddish Literature and the Early Modern.* New Haven, CT: Yale Univ. Press, 2010.

David, Yonah. "Moses ben Isaac da Rieti." In *Encyclopaedia Judaica*, edited by Michael Berenbaum and Fred Skolnik, 17:297–98. 2nd ed. New York: Macmillan, 2006.

Delitzsch, Franz. *Zur Geschichte der jüdischen Poesie vom Abschluß der heiligen Schriften Alten Bundes bis auf die neueste Zeit.* Leipzig: Tauchnitz, 1836.

Dobbie, Elliott Van Kirk. *The Anglo-Saxon Poetic Records.* Vol. 6, *The Anglo-Saxon Minor Poems.* New York: Columbia Univ. Press, 1942.

Dreeßen, Wulf-Otto. *Akêdass Jizḥak; Ein altjiddisches Gedicht über die Opferung Isaaks; mit Einleitung und Kommentar kritisch herausgegeben.* Hamburg: Leibniz, 1971.

———. "Goliaths Schwestern und Brüder." In *Röllwagenbüchlein: Festschrift für Walter Röll zum 65. Geburtstag*, edited by Jürgen Jaehrling, Uwe Meves, and Erika Timm, 369–89. Tübingen: Niemeyer, 2002.

———. "Horant als *Schadchen?*" *Jiddistik-Mitteilungen*, no. 23 (Apr. 2000): 1–9.

———. "Lilith und der Artusritter." *Jiddistik Mitteilungen* 29 (Apr. 2003): 1–9.

———. "Midraschepik und Bibelepik: Biblische Stoffe in der volkssprachlichen Literatur der Juden und Christen des Mittelalters im deutschen Sprachgebiet." *Zeitschrift für deutsche Philologie* 100 (Sonderheft *Jiddisch*, 1981): 78–97.

———. "Widuwilt." In *Verfasserlexikon: Die deutsche Literatur des Mittelalter*, edited by Kurt Ruh et al., col. 1006–8. 2nd ed. Berlin: de Gruyter, 1978.

———. "Wigalois—Widuwilt. Wandlungen des Artusromans im Jiddischen." In *Westjiddisch: Mündlichkeit und Schriftlichkeit/Le Yiddish occidental: Actes du Colloque de Mulhouse*, edited by Astrid Starck, 84–98. Aarau: Sauerländer, 1994.

———. "Zur Rezeption deutscher epischer Literatur im altjiddischen: Das Beispiel 'Wigalois'-Artushof." In *Deutsche Literatur des späten Mittelalters: Hamburger Colloquium, 1973*, edited by W. Harms and L. P. Johnson, 116–28. Berlin: Erich Schmidt, 1973.

Dreeßen, Wulf-Otto, and Hermann-Josef Müller, eds. *Doniel: Das altjiddische Danielbuch nach dem Basler Druck von 1557 Litterae 59*. 2 vols. Göppingen: Kümmerle, 1978.

Dronke, Ursula, ed. *The Poetic Edda*. Vol. 1, *Heroic Poems*. Oxford: Clarendon Press, 1969.

Đurið, Borislav, ed. *Antologiya narodnikh epskikh pesama*. 2 vols. Belgrade: Novi Sad, 1969.

Erik, Max. *Di geshikhte fun der yidisher literatur, fun di eltste tsaytn biz der Haskole-tkufe, fertsnter-akhtsnter yorhundert, mit bilder un melodyes*. 1928. Reprint, New York: Alveltlekher yidisher kultur-kongres, 1979. Online facsimile, http://sammlungen.ub.uni-frankfurt.de/jd/content/titleinfo/1806399.

———. *Vegn altyidishn roman un novele: Fertsnter-zekhtsnter yorhundert*. Warsaw: Der veg tsum visn, 1926. Online facsimile, http://archive.org/details/nybc203961.

———. "Vegn 'Mayse Briyo veZimro.'" In *Shriftn fun yidishn visnshaftlekhn institut* [*filologishe serye*] 1 (Vilne 1926) = *Landoy-bukh: Dr. Alfred Landoy tsu zayn 75stn geboyrnstog dem 25stn november 1925*, col. 153–62. Vilne: Kletskin, 1926.

Falk, Felix. "Die Bücher Samuelis in deutschen Nibelungenstrophen des XV. Jahrhunderts." *Mitteilungen zur jüdischen Volkskunde* 11, (1908): 79–85, 97–116, 129–50. French translation, *Mélanges bibliographiques sur les livres de Samuel en strophes de Nibelungen, précédés d'un exposé général sur la littérature judéo-allemande*. Leipzig: Kaufmann, 1909.

———, ed. *Das Schemuelbuch des Mosche Esrim Wearba: Ein biblisches Epos aus dem 15. Jahrhundert*. Einleitung und textkritischer Apparat von Felix Falk, aus dem Nachlaß herausgegeben von L. Fuks. 2 vols. Assen: Van Gorcum, 1961.

———. "Di talmudishe agade fun Shloyme hameylekh mitn Ashmeday un dem shamir in tsvey alt-yidishe nuskhoes." *YIVO-bleter* 13 (1938): 246–74.

Faverty, Frederic Everett. "The Story of Joseph and Potiphar's Wife in Mediaeval Literature." *Harvard Studies and Notes in Philology and Literature* 13 (1931): 81–127.

Fonte, Moderata. *Il merito delle donne* (1600). Edited by Adriana Chemello. Venice: Eidos, 1988. Edited and translated by Virginia Cox as *The Worth of Women: Wherein Is Clearly Revealed Their Nobility and Their Superiority to Men*. Chicago: Univ. of Chicago Press, 1997.

Fourquet, Jean. "Ernest-H. Lévy et le Dukus Horant." *Études Germaniques* 14 (1959): 50–56.

Fraade, Steven D. "Rabbinic *Midrash* and Ancient Jewish Biblical Interpretation." In *The Cambridge Companion to the Talmud and Rabbinic Literature*, edited by

Charlotte Elisheva Fonrobert and Martin S. Jaffee, 99–120. Cambridge: Cambridge Univ. Press, 2007.

Frakes, Jerold C. *Brides and Doom: Gender, Property, and Power in Medieval German Women's Epic.* Middle Ages Series. Philadelphia: Univ. of Pennsylvania Press, 1994.

———. *The Cultural Study of Yiddish in Early Modern Europe.* New York: Palgrave, 2007.

———, ed. *Early Yiddish Texts, 1100–1750, with Introduction and Commentary.* Oxford: Oxford Univ. Press, 2004.

———. *The Politics of Interpretation: Alterity and Ideology in Old Yiddish Studies.* Albany: SUNY Press, 1989.

Franco, Veronica. *Rime* (1575). Edited by Stefano Bianchi. Milan: Mursia, 1995. Edited and translated by Ann Rosalind Jones and Margaret F. Rosenthal, *Poems and Selected Letters.* Chicago: Univ. of Chicago Press, 1998.

Friderichs-Müller, Theresia, ed. *Die "Historie von dem Kaiser Octaviano."* 2 vols. Jidische schtudies 1–2. Hamburg: Buske, 1981.

———. *Die "Historie von dem Kaiser Octaviano": Überlieferungsgeschichtliche Studien zu den Druckausgaben eines Prosaromans des 16. Jahrhunderts und seiner jidischen Bearbeitungen aus dem Jahre 1580.* Jidische schtudies 3. Hamburg: Buske, 1990.

Frye, Northrop. *The Secular Scripture: A Study of the Structure of Romance.* Cambridge, MA: Harvard Univ. Press, 1978.

Fuks, Lajb [Leo], ed. *Das altjiddische Epos Melok̲îm-Bûk̲.* 2 vols. Assen: Van Gorcum, 1965.

———, ed. *The Oldest Known Literary Documents of Yiddish Literature (c. 1382).* 2 vols. Leiden: Brill, 1957.

Ganz, Peter, Frederick Norman, and Werner Schwarz, eds. *Dukus Horant.* Altdeutsche Textbibliothek, Ergänzungsreihe 2. Tübingen: Niemeyer, 1964.

———. "Zu dem Cambridger Josef." *Zeitschrift für deutsche Philologie* 82 (1963): 86–90.

Gaster, Moses. "The History of the Destruction of the Round Table, as Told in Hebrew in the Year 1279." *Folklore* 20 (1909): 272–94.

Ginzberg, Louis. *Legends of the Jews.* 7 vols. Philadelphia: Jewish Publication Society, 1938–61.

Goitein, S. D. *A Mediterranean Society: The Jewish Communities of the Arab World as Portrayed in the Documents of the Cairo Geniza.* 6 vols. Berkeley: Univ. of California Press, 1967–93.

Goldman, Shalom. *The Wiles of Women/The Wiles of Men: Joseph and Potiphar's Wife in Ancient Near Eastern, Jewish, and Islamic Folklore.* Albany: SUNY Press, 1995.

Gottlieb, Efraim. "Mordecai ben Judah Dato." In *Encyclopaedia Judaica*, edited by Michael Berenbaum and Fred Skolnik, 5:440–41. 2nd ed. New York: Macmillan, 2006.

Götze, Alfred. *Frühneuhochdeutsches Glossar.* 7th ed. Berlin: de Gruyter, 1967.

Graw, Heidi. *Dukus Haurant.* N.p.: Lulu Press, 2009.

Greene, Thomas M. *The Descent from Heaven.* New Haven, CT: Yale Univ. Press, 1963.

Grimm, Jacob, and Wilhelm Grimm, eds. *Deutsches Wörterbuch.* 2nd ed. Leipzig: Hirzel, 1854–1971. Reprint, Hildesheim: Olms, 2003–; http://germazope.uni-trier.de/Projects/DWB.

Hakkarainen, Heikki J. *Studien zum Cambridger Codex T.-S. 10. K. 22*; 1: *Text.* Turun Yliopiston Julkaisuja/Acta Universitatis Turkuensis, ser. B, vol. 104. Turku, 1967; 2: *Graphemik und Phonemik.* Acta, ser. B, vol. 174. Turku, 1971; 3: *Lexikon.* Acta, ser. B., vol. 182. Turku, 1973.

Harkavy, Alexander. *Yiddish-English-Hebrew Dictionary.* 1928. Reprint, New York: Schocken/YIVO, 1988.

Harrán, Dan, ed. and trans. *Jewish Poet and Intellectual in Seventeenth-Century Venice: Sarra Copia Sulam.* Chicago: Univ. of Chicago Press, 2009.

Hasan-Rokem, Galit. "An Almost Invisible Presence: Multilingual Puns in Rabbinic Literature." In *The Cambridge Companion to the Talmud and Rabbinic Literature*, edited by Charlotte Elisheva Fonrobert and Martin S. Jaffee, 222–39. Cambridge: Cambridge Univ. Press, 2007.

Hoffman, Adina, and Peter Cole. *Sacred Trash: The Lost and Found World of the Cairo Geniza.* New York: Nextbook/Schocken, 2011.

Hollender, Elisabeth. "Die Schriftfunde." In *Von der Ausgrabung zum Museum: Kölner Archäologie zwischen Rathaus und Praetorium: Ergebnisse und Materialien 2006–2012*, edited by Sven Schütte and Marianne Gechter, 144–52, sec. 3.4.3.4.2. Bramsche: Rasch, 2012.

Holsinger, Bruce W. "Medieval Studies, Postcolonial Studies, and the Genealogies of Critique." *Speculum* 77 (2002): 1195–1227.

———. *The Premodern Condition: Medievalism and the Making of Theory.* Chicago: Univ. of Chicago Press, 2005.

Howard, John A., ed. *Dietrich von Bern* (1597). Würzburg: Königshausen und Neumann, 1986.

———, ed. *Fortunatus: Die Bearbeitung und Umschrift eines spätmittelalterlichen deutschen Prosaromans für jüdisches Publikum.* Würzburg: Königshausen und Neumann, 1991.

Hrushovski (Harshav), Benjamin. "The Creation of Accentual Iambs in European Poetry and Their First Employment in a Yiddish Romance in Italy (1508–09)." In *For Max Weinreich on His Seventieth Birthday*, 108–46. The Hague: Mouton, 1964.

Jaeger, Achim. *Ein jüdischer Artusritter.* Tübingen: Niemeyer, 2000.

Jastrow, Marcus. *Dictionary of Talmud Babli, Yerushalmi, Midrashic Literature, and Targumim.* 2 vols. 1903. Reprint, Peabody, MA: Hendrickson, 2005.

Joffe, Judah A., ed. *Elye Bokher, poetishe shafungen in yidish, ershter band: Bovo d'Antona.* New York: Judah A. Joffe, 1949.

Joffe, Judah A., et al., eds. *Groyser verterbukh fun der yidisher shprakh.* 4 vols. New York: Yiddish Dictionary Committee, 1961–.

Jónsson, Finnur, ed. *Edda Snorra Sturlusonar.* Copenhagen: Gyldendal, 1931.

Katz, Eli, ed. "Six Germano-Judaic Poems from the Cairo Genizah." PhD diss., Univ. of California at Los Angeles, 1963.

Kazis, Israel J., ed. *Immanuel ben Jacob Bonfils, Sefer Toldot Alesandrus ha-Makdoni.* Cambridge: Mediaeval Academy of America, 1962.

Knaphays, Moyshe, trans. *Elye Bokher, "Bovo-bukh."* Buenos Aires: Yoysef Lifshits Fond baym Kultur-Kongres, 1962.

Köhler, Erich. *Ideal und Wirklichkeit in der höfischen Epik: Studien zur Form der frühen Artus- und Graldichtung.* Tübingen: Max Niemeyer, 1956.

Könneker, Barbara. "Zum literarischen Charakter und der literarischen Intention des altjiddischen Schmuelbuchs." In *Kontroversen, alte und neue: Akten des VII. Internationalen Germanisten-Kongresses Göttingen 1985*, edited by Albrecht Schöne, 3–12. Vol. 5, *Auseinandersetzungen um jiddische Sprache und Literatur, Jüdische Komponenten in der deutschen Literatur—die Assimilationskontroverse*, edited by Walter Röll and Hans-Peter Bayerdorfer. Tübingen: Niemeyer, 1986.

Krapp, George Philip, and Elliott van Kirk Dobbie, eds. *The Exeter Book.* Vol. 3 of *The Anglo-Saxon Poetic Records.* New York: Columbia Univ. Press, 1936.

Kugel, James L. *The Idea of Biblical Poetry: Parallelism and Its History.* New Haven, CT: Yale Univ. Press, 1981.

———. *In Potiphar's House: The Interpretive Life in Biblical Texts.* Cambridge, MA: Harvard Univ. Press, 1994

Kuhn, Hans, ed. *Edda: Die Lieder des Codex Regius nebst verwandten Denkmälern.* 4th ed. Heidelberg: Carl Winter, 1962.

Landau, Leo. *Arthurian Legends; or, The Hebrew-German Rhymed Version of the Legend of King Arthur.* Pt. 1 of *Hebrew-German Romances and Tales and Their Relation to the Romantic Literature of the Middle Ages.* Teutonia, 21. Leipzig: Avenarius, 1912.

Lazard, Gilbert, Walter Joseph Fischel, Herbert H. Paper, and Shaul Shaked. "Judeo-Persian." In *Encyclopaedia Judaica*, edited by Michael Berenbaum and Fred Skolnik, 11:548–59. 2nd ed. New York: Macmillan, 2006.

Leviant, Curt, ed. and trans. *King Artus: A Hebrew Arthurian Romance of 1279.* 1969. Reprint, Syracuse, NY: Syracuse Univ. Press, 2003.

Lexer, Matthias. *Mittelhochdeutsches Handwörterbuch.* 3 vols. Stuttgart: Hirzel, 1872–78, 1992. Online, http://woerterbuchnetz.de/Lexer/?lemid=LA00001.

Linn, Irving. "Widwilt, Son of Gawain." PhD diss., New York Univ., 1942.

Lyons, M[alcolm] C[ameron]. *The Arabian Epic: Heroic and Oral Story-Telling.* 3 vols. Cambridge: Cambridge Univ. Press, 2005.

Marchand, James W., and Frederic Tubach. "Der Keusche Joseph. Ein mitteldeutsches Gedicht aus dem 13.–14. Jh.: Ein Beitrag zur Erforschung der hebräisch-deutschen Literatur." *Zeitschrift für deutsche Philologie* 81 (1962): 30–52.

Marchetti, Valerio, Jean Baumgarten, and Antonella Salomoni, eds. *Elia Bahur Levita, "Paris un Viene," Francesco Dalle Donne, Verona, 1594*. Bologna: Università degli studi di Bologna, Dipartimento di discipline storiche, Arnaldo Forni Editore, 1988.

Matenko, Percy, and Samuel Sloan. "The Aqedath Jishaq: A Sixteenth Century Epic, with Introduction and Notes." In *Two Studies in Yiddish Culture*, edited by Percy Matenko and Samuel Sloan, 1-70. Leiden: Brill, 1968.

Miletich, John S. *The "Bugarštica": A Bilingual Anthology of the Earliest Extant South Slavic Folk Narrative Song*. Illinois Medieval Monographs III. Urbana: Univ. of Illinois Press, 1990.

Millet, Victor. *Germanische Heldendichtung im Mittelalter: Eine Einführung*. Berlin: Walter de Gruyter, 2008.

Minkoff, N. B. *Elye Bokher un zayn Bovo-bukh*. New York: Vakser, 1950.

Moreen, Vera Basch. *In Queen Esther's Garden: An Anthology of Judeo Persian Literature*. New Haven, CT: Yale Univ. Press, 2000.

Naumann, Hans. "Versuch einer Einschränkung des romantischen Begriffs Spielmannsdichtung." *Deutsche Vierteljahrsschrift für Literaturwissenschaft und Geistesgeschichte* 2 (1924): 777–94.

Netzer, Amnon. "Emrāni." In *Encyclopaedia Judaica*, edited by Michael Berenbaum and Fred Skolnik, 6:398. 2nd ed. New York: Macmillan, 2006.

———. "Shāhin." In *Encyclopaedia Judaica*, edited by Michael Berenbaum and Fred Skolnik, 18:365. 2nd ed. New York: Macmillan, 2006.

Neugröschel, Joachim. *The Dybbuk and the Yiddish Imagination: A Haunted Reader*. Syracuse, NY: Syracuse Univ. Press, 2000.

———. *No Star Too Beautiful: Yiddish Stories from 1382 to the Present*. New York: W. W. Norton, 2002.

Neumann, Hans. "Sprache und Reim in den judendeutschen Gedichten der Cambridger Codex T.S.10.K.22." In *Indogermanica, Festschrift Wolfgang Krause*, 145–65. Heidelberg: Winter, 1960.

Niborski, Yitskhok [Bernard Vaisbrot]. *Dictionnaire Yiddish-Français*. Paris: Medem, 2002. English translation, *Arumnemik yidish-english verterbukh / Comprehensive Yiddish-English Dictionary*, edited by Solon Beinfeld and Harry Bochner. Bloomington: Indiana Univ. Press, 2013.

Nichols, Stephen G. "Philology and Its Discontents." In *The Future of the Middle Ages*, edited by William D. Paden, 113–41. Gainesville: Univ. Press of Florida, 1994.

Niditch, Susan. "Epic and History in the Hebrew Bible: Definitions, 'Ethnic Genres,' and the Challenges of Cultural Identity in the Biblical Book of Judges." In *Epic and History*, edited by David Konstan and Kurt A. Raaflaub, 86–102. Chichester: Wiley-Blackwell, 2010.

Nylén, Erik, and Jan Peder Lamm. *Bildsteine auf Gotland.* 2nd ed. Neumünster: Wachholtz, 1991.

Olrik, J., and H. Ræder, eds. *Saxonis Gesta Danorum.* 2 vols. Copenhagen: Levin og Munksgaard, 1931, 1935.

Paucker, Arnold. "Das Volksbuch von den Sieben Weisen Meistern in der jiddischen Literatur." *Zeitschrift für Volkskunde* 57 (1961): 177–94.

———. "Di yidishe nuskhoes fun *shildburger bukh.*" *Yivo-bleter* 44 (1973): 59–77.

Priebatsch, Hans. *Die Josefsgeschichte in der Weltliteratur: eine legendengeschichtliche Studie.* Breslau: M. & H. Marcus, 1937.

Propp, Vladimir. *Russkiĭ geroicheskiĭ epos.* Moscow: Khudozhestvennaia literatura, 1958.

Reardon, B. P., ed. *Collected Ancient Greek Novels.* Berkeley: Univ. of California Press, 1989.

Reichl, Karl. *Edige: A Karakalpak Heroic Epic.* Folklore Fellows Communications 293. Helsinki: Suomalainen Tiedeakatemia, 2007.

Röll, Walter. "Awroham owinu ('Unser Vater Abraham')." In vol. 1 of *Verfasserlexikon: Die deutsche Literatur des Mittelalter*, edited by Kurt Ruh et al., col. 573–74. 2nd ed. Berlin: de Gruyter, 1978.

———. "Zu den ersten drei Texten der Cambridger Handschrift von 1382/1383." *Zeitschrift für deutsches Altertum* 104 (1975): 54–68.

Rosenberg, Felix. "Über eine Sammlung deutscher Volks- und Gesellschaftslieder in hebräischen Lettern." Pts. 1–2. *Zeitschrift für die Geschichte der Juden in Deutschland* 2 (1888): 232–96; 3 (1889): 14–28.

Rosenzweig, Claudia. *Elye Bokher: Due canti yiddish, rime di un poeta ashkenazita nella Venezia del cinquecento.* Siena: Bibliotheca Aretina, 2010.

———. "The Jewish Knight, the Jewish Princess, and the Sceptical Reader." In *Early Modern Yiddish Poetry*, edited by Shlomo Berger, 7–25. Amsterdam: Menasseh be Israel Institute, n.d.

———. "La letteratura yiddish in Italia: L'esempio del *Bovo de-Antona* di Elye Bocher." *Acme: Annali della Facoltà di Lettere e Filosofia dell'Università degli Studi di Milano* 50, no. 3 (1997): 159–89.

———. "Il poema yiddish in versi 'Bovo d'Antona' in una versione manoscritta del XVI secolo." *Medievo Romanzo* 26, no. 1 (ser. 3, no. 7) (2002): 49–68.

Roth, Cecil. *The History of the Jews in Italy.* Philadelphia: Jewish Publication Society, 1946.

Ruh, Kurt, et al., eds. *Verfasserlexikon: Die deutsche Literatur des Mittelalter.* 10 vols. 2nd ed. Berlin: de Gruyter, 1978.

Sadan, Dov. "The Midrashic Background of 'The Paradise': Its Implications for the Evaluation of the Cambridge Yiddish Codex (1382)." In *The Field of Yiddish:*

Studies in Yiddish Language, Folklore, and Literature, edited by Uriel Weinreich, 86–102. 2nd collection. The Hague: Mouton, 1965.

Salzberger, Georg. *Die Salomo Sage in der semitischen Literatur: Ein Beitrag zur vergleichenden Sagenkunde.* Berlin: Max Harrwitz, 1907.

Sanders, Christopher, ed. *Bevers Saga, with the Text of the Anglo-Norman Boeve de Haumtone.* Stofnun Árna Magnússonar á Íslandi, Rit, 51. Reykjavík: Stofnun Árna Magnússonar á Íslandi, 2001.

Scholberg, Kenneth R. "Miguel de Silveyra." In *Encyclopaedia Judaica*, edited by Michael Berenbaum and Fred Skolnik, 18:589. New York: Macmillan, 2006.

Schröder, Walter Johannes. *Spielmannsepik.* 2nd ed. Stuttgart: Metzler, 1967.

———, ed. *Spielmannsepik.* Darmstadt: Wissenschaftliche Buchgesellschaft, 1977.

Schüler, Meier. "Das Bovo-Buch." *Zeitschrift für hebräische Bibliographie* 29 (1917): 83–94.

Schulz, Armin. *Die Zeichen des Körpers und der Liebe: "Paris und Vienna" in der jiddischen Fassung des Elia Levita.* Hamburg: Kovac, 2000.

Seymour, M. C., ed. *The Bodley Version of Mandeville's Travels.* Early English Text Society 253. London: Oxford Univ. Press, 1963.

Shapiro, M. A., I. G. Spivak, and M. Y. Shulman. *Russko-yevreiskiĭ (idish) slovar' / Rusisher-yidisher verterbukh.* 2nd ed. Moscow: Russkiĭ yazik, 1989.

Shiper, Yitskhok. "A yidishe libe-roman fun mitlelter, tsushtayern tsu der geshikhte vegn dem ufkum fun mayse Briyo veZimro." *YIVO-bleter* 13 (1938): 132–45.

Shmeruk, Chone. "Difusei yidish be-italyah." *Italia/Italyah* 3 (1982): 112–75.

———. "The Hebrew Acrostic in the *Yosef Hatsadik Poem* of the Cambridge Yiddish Codex." *Michigan Germanic Studies* 3 (1977): 67–81.

———, ed. *Pariz un' Viene: Mahadura biqqortit be-ẓeruf mavo, he'arot ve-nispaḥim.* Jerusalem: Israel Academy of Sciences and Humanities, 1996. Italian translation of the introduction, "Studi su 'Paris un Viene.'" *Rassegna Mensile di Israel* 62, nos. 1–2 (1996): 93–124.

———. *Sifrut yidish: Perakim letoldoteah.* Tel Aviv: Porter Institute, 1978. Revised Yiddish translation, *Prokim fun der yidisher literatur-geshikhte.* Tel Aviv: Peretz, 1988.

———. "Tsi ken der keymbridzher manuskript shtitsn di shpilman-teorye in der yidisher literatur?" *Di goldene keyt* 100 (1979): 251–71. Reprinted in *Prokim fun der yidisher literatur-geshikhte*, 97–120. Tel Aviv: I. L. Peretz, 1988. Online facsimile, https://www.box.com/s/c19lcz826653vpk91efp. English translation, "Can the Cambridge Manuscript Support the *Spielmann* Theory in Yiddish Literature?" In *Studies in Yiddish Literature and Folklore*, 1–36. Research Projects of the Institute of Jewish Studies. Monograph Series 7. Jerusalem: Hebrew Univ., 1986.

Shtif, Nokhem. "Ditrikh fun bern: Yidishkayt un veltlekhkayt in der alter yidisher literatur." *Yidishe filologye* 1 (1924): 1–11, 112–22.

Shulvass, Moses Avigdor. "Ashkenazic Jewry in Italy." *YIVO Annual of Jewish Social Sciences* 7 (1952): 110–31.

———. "Dos ashkenazishe yidntum in italye." *Yivo-bleter* 34 (1950): 157–81.

———. *Ḥayye ha-yehudim be-italyah bi-tkufat ha-renesans.* New York: Hotsa'at Ogen al yad ha-histadrut ha-ivrit be-amerikah, 1955. English translation by Elvin I. Kose, *The Jews in the World of the Renaissance.* Leiden: Brill, 1973.

Simonson, Sh. "Sefarim ve-sifriyyot shel yehudei Mantovah, 1595." *Kiryat sefer* 37 (1962): 103–22.

Simpson, J. A., and E. S. C. Weiner, eds. *Oxford English Dictionary.* Oxford: Oxford Univ. Press, 1992. Online, http://www.oed.com/.

Smith, Jerry C., trans. *Elia Levita Bachur's "Bovo-Buch."* Tucson: Fenestra Books, 2003.

Sternberg, Meir. *The Poetics of Biblical Narrative: Ideological Literature and the Drama of Reading.* Bloomington: Indiana Univ. Press, 1985.

Strauch, Gabriele. *Dukus Horant: Wanderer zwischen zwei Welten.* Amsterdam: Rodopi, 1990.

Süsskind, Nathan. "Shmuel-bukh-problemen." In *Max Vaynraykh tsu zayn zibetsikstn geboyrn-tog: Shtudyes vegn shprakhn bay yidn, vegn yidisher literatur un gezelshaft,* 64–82. The Hague: Mouton, 1964.

———. "Das Šmuel Buch. Eine jüdisch-deutsche Umdichtung der zwei Bücher Samuelis im Stile der mittelhochdeutschen Heldendichtung. Teil I: Untersuchung der Sprache, der Quellen und der Liedtechnik nebst Teilherausgabe des Textes der Pariser Handschrift (Hebreu 92) mit Kommentar, die ersten 350 Strophen umfassend." Ph.D. diss., New York Univ., 1942.

Talmon, S. "The 'Comparative Method' in Biblical Interpretation: Principles and Problems." In *Supplement to Vetus Testamentum* 29:352–56. Leiden: Brill, 1978.

Tarabotti, Arcangela. *Tirannia paterna.* Published as Galerana Bartotti. *La semplicità ingannata.* Leiden: G. Sambix [Elzevier], 1654. Edited and translated by Letizia Panizza, *Paternal Tyranny.* Chicago: Univ. of Chicago Press, 2004.

Timm, Erika. "Beria und Simra: Eine jiddische Erzählung des 16. Jahrhunderts." *Literaturwissenschaftliches Jahrbuch,* n.s. 14 (1973), 1–94. Reprinted in *Graphische und phonische Struktur des Westjiddischen unter besonderer Berücksichtigung der Zeit um 1600,* by Erika Timm, appendix 4, 521–53. Tübingen: Niemeyer, 1987.

———. "Ein neuentdeckter literarischer Text in hebräischen Lettern aus der Zeit vor 1349." *Zeitschrift für deutsches Altertum* 142 (2013): 417–43.

———. "Wie Elia Levita sein Bovobuch für den Druck überarbeitete: Ein Kapitel aus der italo-jiddischen Literatur der Renaissancezeit." *Germanisch-Romanische Monatsschrift,* n.s. 41 (1991): 61–81.

———. "Zwischen Orient und Okzident: Zur Vorgeschichte von 'Beria und Simra.'" *Literaturwissenschaftliches Jahrbuch,* n.s. 27 (1986): 297–307.

Timm, Erika, and Gustav Adolf Beckmann. *"Paris un Wiene": Ein jiddischer Stanzenroman des 16. Jahrhunderts von (oder aus dem Umkreis von) Elia Levita*. Tübingen: Niemeyer, 1996.

Tolkien, J. R. R. "*Beowulf*: The Monsters and the Critics." *Proceedings of the British Academy* 22 (1936): 245–95. Reprinted in *An Anthology of Beowulf Criticism*, edited by Lewis E. Nicholson, 51–103. Notre Dame, IN: Univ. of Notre Dame Press.

Trost, Pavel. "Noch einmal zur Josefslegende des Cambridger Kodex." *Philologica Pragensis* 5 (1962): 3–5.

———. "Zwei Stücke des Cambridger Kodex T-S 10, K. 22." *Philologica Pragensis* 4 (1961): 17–24.

Turniansky, Chava. "Einav ke-khokhavim, se'aro ke-zahav: *Yosef ha-tsadik* be-shir kadum be-yidish." *Tarbiz* 76 (2007): 471–500.

———. "Pariz un' Viene—mi-sifrut yidish be-italyah shel ha-meah ha-16." *Chulyot* 4 (1997): 29–37.

———. "Shtei shirot epiot be-yidish al Sefer Yehoshua." *Tarbiz* 51 (1982): 589–632.

Turniansky, Chava, and Erika Timm, eds. *Yiddish in Italia: Yiddish Manuscripts and Printed Books from the 15th to the 17th Century / Manoscritt e libri a stampa in yiddish dei secoli XV–XVII*. Milan: Associazione Italiana Amici dell'Università di Gerusalemme, 2003.

van Bekkum, Wout Jac., ed. *A Hebrew Alexander Romance according to Ms Héb. 671.5 Paris, Bibliotheque Nationale*. Leiden: Brill, 1994.

———, ed. and trans. *A Hebrew Alexander Romance according to MS London, Jews' College no. 145*. Leuven: Peeters, 1992.

Vos, H. D. "Elia Levita's *Bovo d'Antona*, Commentary." Typescript, 2012 (82 pages).

Wacholder, Ben Zion. "Philo." In *Encyclopaedia Judaica*, edited by Michael Berenbaum and Fred Skolnik, 16:58. 2nd ed. New York: Macmillan, 2006.

———. "Theodotus." In *Encyclopaedia Judaica*, edited by Michael Berenbaum and Fred Skolnik, 19:693–94. 2nd ed. New York: Macmillan, 2006.

Wagenseil, Johann Christoph. *Belehrung der Jüdisch-Teutschen Red- und Schreibart*. Königsberg, 1699.

Ward, Donald. "Nochmals Kudrun: Ballade und Epos. Eine Erwiderung." *Jahrbuch für Volksliedforschung* 17 (1992): 70–86.

Ward, Donald, and Franz Bäuml. "Zur Kudrun-Problematik: Ballade und Epos." *Zeitschrift für deutsche Philologie* 88 (1969): 19–27.

Warnock, Robert G. "The Arthurian Tradition in Hebrew and Yiddish." In *King Arthur through the Ages*, edited by Valerie M. Lagorio and Mildred Leake Day, 1:189–208. New York: Garland, 1990.

———. "Frühneuzeitliche Fassungen des altjiddischen 'Artushofs.'" In *Kontroversen, alte und neue: Akten des VII, Internationalen Germanisten-Kongresses Göttingen 1985*, edited by Albrecht Schöne, 13–19. Vol. 5, *Auseinandersetzungen um jiddische Sprache und Literatur, Jüdische Komponenten in der deutschen Literatur—die Assimilationskontroverse*, edited by Walter Röll and Hans-Peter Bayerdorfer. Tübingen: Niemeyer, 1986.

———. "Widwilt." In *The New Arthurian Encyclopedia*, edited by Norris J. Lacy et al., 512–13. Chicago and London: St. James Press, 1991.

———. "Wirkungsabsicht und Bearbeitungstechnik im altjiddischen 'Artushof.'" *Zeitschrift für deutsche Philologie* (Sonderheft *Jiddisch*, 1981): 98–109.

Warren, Michelle R. "Post-Philology." In *Post-colonial Moves: Medieval through Modern*, edited by Patricia Clare Ingham and Michelle R. Warren, 19–45. New York: Palgrave Macmillan, 2003.

Weil, G. E. *Elia Lévita, humaniste et massorète, 1469–1549*. Leiden: E. J. Brill, 1963.

Weinreich, Max. *Bilder fun der yidisher literatur-geshikhte*. Vilne: Tomor, 1928.

———. "Old Yiddish Poetry in Linguistic-Literary Research." *Word* 16 (1960): 100–118.

Weinreich, Uriel. *Modern English-Yiddish, Yiddish-English Dictionary*. New York: YIVO, 1968.

Wolf, Johann Christoph. *Bibliotheca Hebraea*. 4 vols. Hamburg and Leipzig: Christian Liebezeit, 1715–33. Reprint, Bologna: Forni, 1967.

Wolf, Meir. "Mekom ḥiburo shel ha-Melokhim bukh." *Tarbiz* 51 (1981): 131–34.

Yeroushalmi, David, ed. *The Judeo-Persian Poet 'Emrānī and His Book of Treasure*. Leiden: Brill, 1995.

Yerushalmi, Yosef Hayim. *Haggadah and History*. 1975. Reprint, Philadelphia: Jewish Publication Society, 1997.

Zandt, Gertrud. "Zum Melochimbuch, einem Epos in jüdisch-deutscher Sprache." *Amsterdamer Beiträge zur älteren Germanistik* 43–44 (1995): 589–600.

Zhirmunskiĭ, V. M. *Narodnyĭ geroicheskiĭ epos*. Moscow: 1962.

Zinberg, Israel [Yisroel Tsinberg]. *Altyidishe literatur fun di eltste tsaytn biz der Haskole-tkufe*. Vol. 6 of *Di geshikhte fun der literatur bay yidn*. 2nd ed. 1933. Reprint, New York: Shklorsky, 1943. English translation by Bernard Martin, *Old Yiddish Literature from Its Origins to the Haskalah Period*. Vol. 7 of *A History of Jewish Literature*. Cincinnati: Hebrew Union College Press, 1975. Online facsimile, http://archive.org/stream/nybc200256#page/n0/mode/2up.

———. "Oys der alt-yidisher literatur." In *Shriftn fun yidishn visnshaftlekhn institut* [*filologishe serye*] 3, col. 173–84. Vilne: Kletskin, 1929.

Jerold C. Frakes teaches medieval literature at the University at Buffalo (SUNY). He is the author of *The Politics of Interpretation: Alterity and Ideology in Old Yiddish Studies* and editor of *Early Yiddish Texts, 1100–1750* and *The Cultural Study of Yiddish in Early Modern Europe.*